*Since the nineteenth century, dynamism
and creation have been the hallmarks
of Cartier. We wish to combine our efforts
actively with all those who protect and
develop artistic expression in our country.*

*This is why, this evening the Fondation
Cartier pour l'art contemporain has
been created.*

*I would like to thank all those who, by their
presence, their encouragement, and their
actions have helped in its birth.*

*Alain Dominique Perrin
Jouy-en-Josas, October 20, 1984*

VOIR
VENIR

VENIR
VOIR

VOIR VENIR

Fondation *Cartier*
pour l'art contemporain

VENIR VOIR

THE REAL STORY

Alain Dominique Perrin
President of the Fondation Cartier
pour l'art contemporain

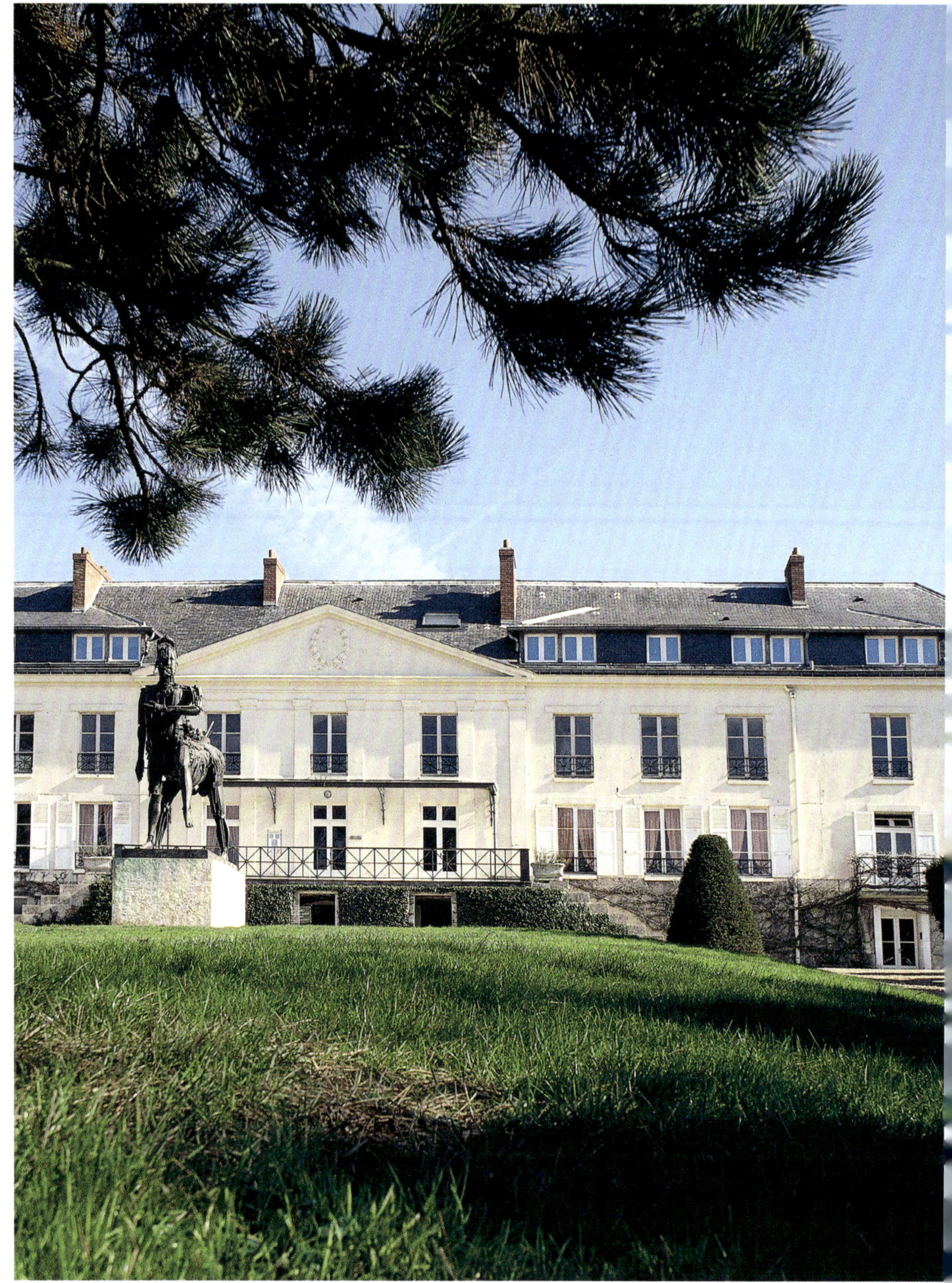

The Fondation Cartier pour l'art contemporain in the Domaine du Montcel,
Jouy-en-Josas, 1984

The idea of a foundation

Forty years after its creation, at a time when the French cultural landscape—especially in terms of the private sector—has grown considerably, it is important for me to tell the real story of the Fondation Cartier pour l'art contemporain. It all began between 1981 and 1983. I had the idea of creating a foundation that would protect French artists all around the world, with the help of two or three lawyers, hired to undertake effective legal action. The idea was simple: I wanted to provide artists with the financial and legal means to protect their name and their work, at no cost to them. At the time, artists complained about being copied all over the place. César, with whom I was very close, had notably been a victim of plagiarism, as had Arman. As President of Cartier, I had also been confronted with the very real problem of counterfeiting; there were shared concerns between jewelry and watchmaking houses creating unique pieces and artists whose talents had been plagiarized. So I began to imagine a foundation, to outline its mission statement and specifications, and to talk about all this with Sylvie Hannequin, a trained lawyer and legal director of Cartier's industrial property department.

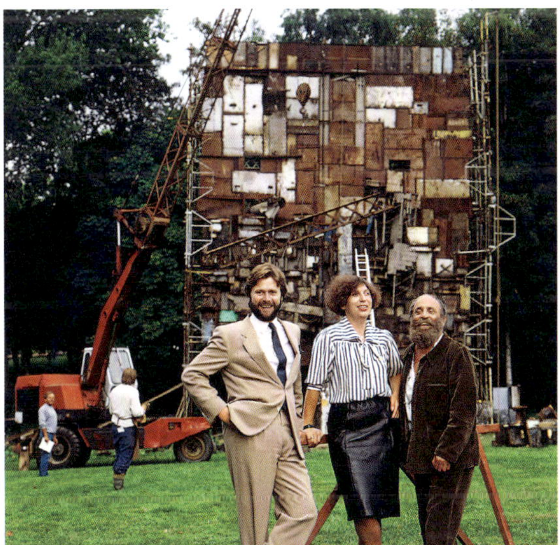

Alain Dominique Perrin, Marie-Claude Beaud, and César in front of *Hommage à Eiffel* during its construction, Jouy-en-Josas, 1984

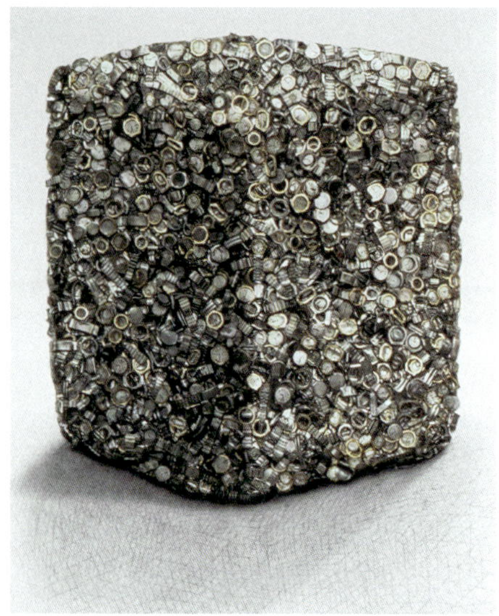

César, *Portrait de compression*, 1983

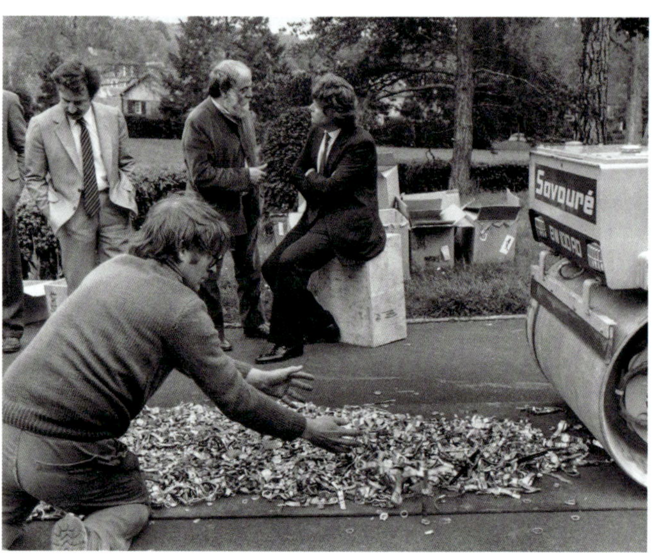

Jean Hamon, César, and Alain Dominique Perrin, 1983

The fight against counterfeiting

In the 1980s, like many luxury houses and brands, Cartier was
hit hard by counterfeiting, particularly in Mexico. I remember
a seminal event in our history. In 1981, American customs
seized four thousand counterfeit Cartier watches in Tijuanao
and repatriated them to the United States. Jim Bykoff, a talented
American lawyer specializing in intellectual property, came up
with the completely crazy albeit amusing suggestion that we
crush these watches with a steamroller, in a parking lot in
San Diego, California. I accepted. I was to sit next to the driver
of the steamroller. When I arrived at the parking lot, I was greeted
by a dense crowd of cameras belonging to some two hundred
and forty American, Japanese, and European television channels.
We set to work crushing the watches, with fragments of them
flying off. We repeated the operation in 1983, at the Domaine
du Montcel, in Jouy-en-Josas, in the presence of Jean Hamon,
owner of the estate. César went on to make "compressions"
from the resulting debris.

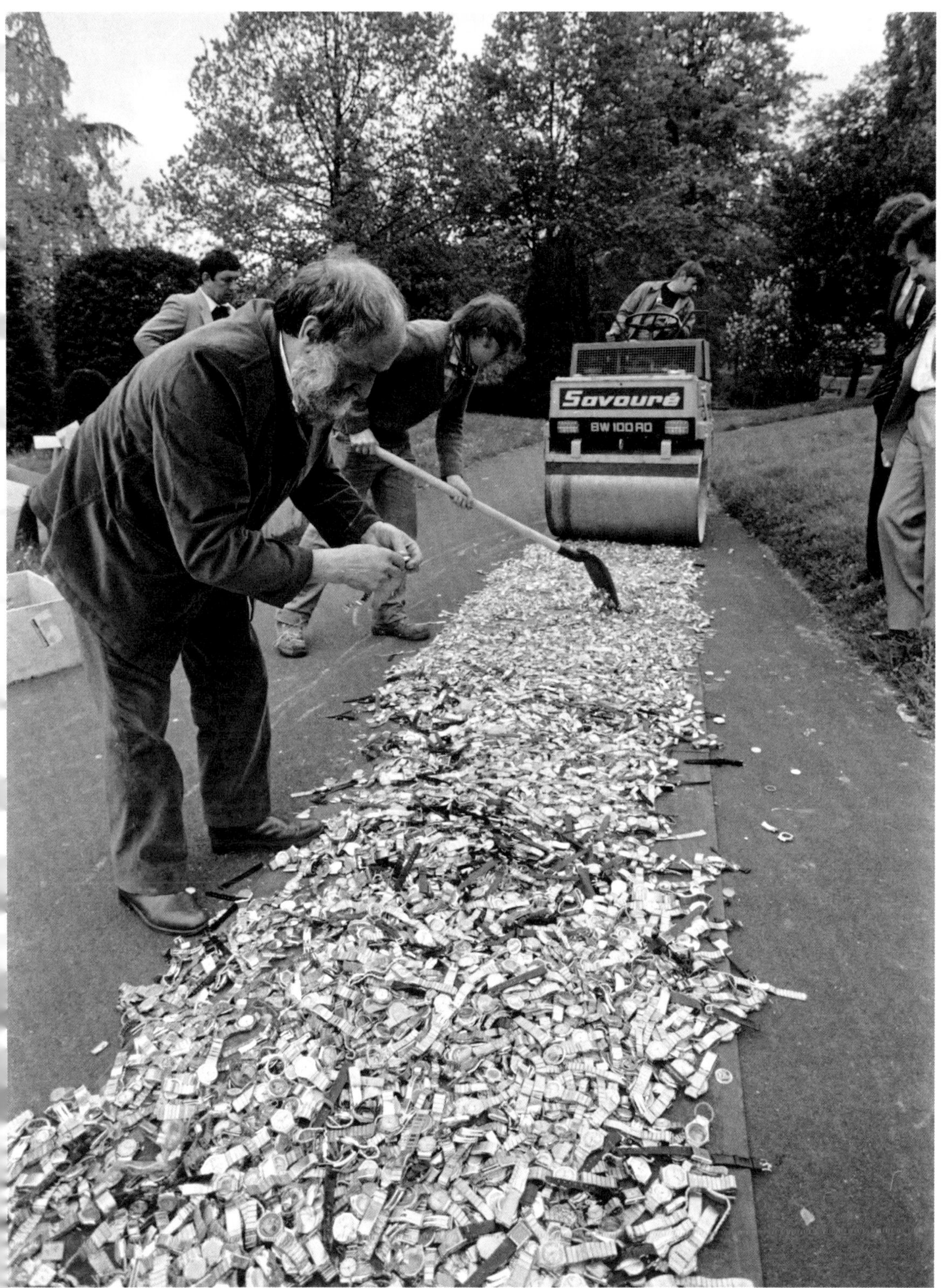

On May 9,1983, in the park of the Fondation Cartier, César drove a steamroller
over 6,000 fake Cartier watches in order to create a work of art.

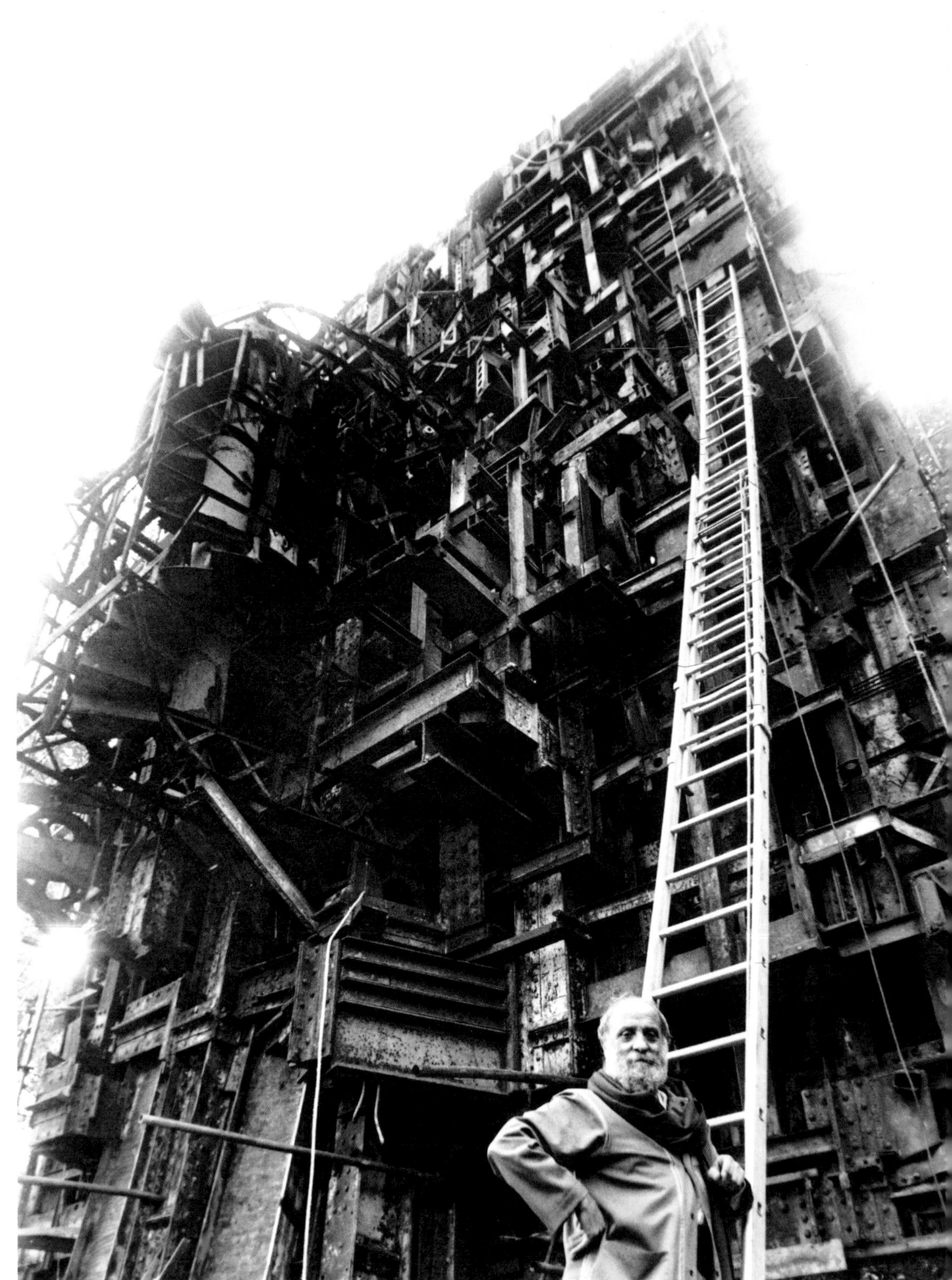

César working on *Hommage à Eiffel*, 1984. It was inaugurated in 1989.

The Real Story

It is thanks to César that the Fondation Cartier, as we know it today, exists. Some time after introducing me to the Domaine du Montcel on the occasion of the crushing operation of the fake Cartier watches, we had dinner together, and with his legendary frankness, he confided in me that the most important thing for him, and artists in general, was not to be protected or defended by lawyers, but to find the money to create and places to exhibit. According to him, getting exhibitions in public institutions took too long; he wanted it to go faster. He believed that we, as entrepreneurs and influential leaders, had the power and funds to act quickly. He mentioned the Domaine du Montcel once again, saying, "That's where you should do something. The estate is up for rent. You could make it into a fantastic exhibition space: the park could host monumental sculptures, the rooms could be converted." I started to think about it very seriously. It was true that the estate was immense: the main building had potential and the park was impressive. Moreover, it already housed some artworks, such as *Long Term Parking* by Arman (1982), *Déjeuner sous l'herbe* by Daniel Spoerri (1983)—the buried remnants of a luncheon party that had been recently held—and *Hommage à Eiffel* (1983–1989) by César himself, which was in the process of being finished.

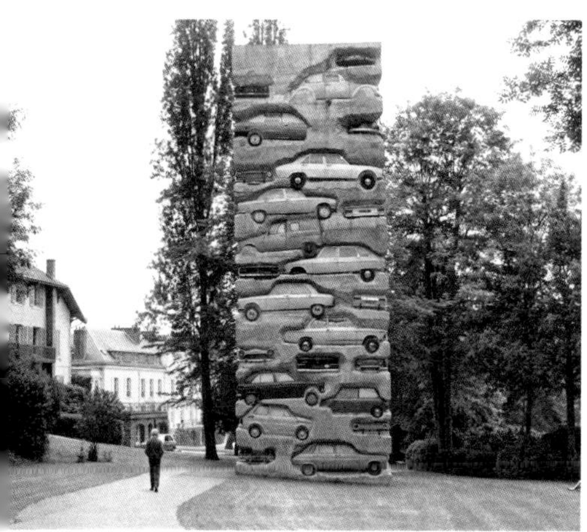

Arman's *Long Term Parking* (1982), Fondation Cartier park, 1984

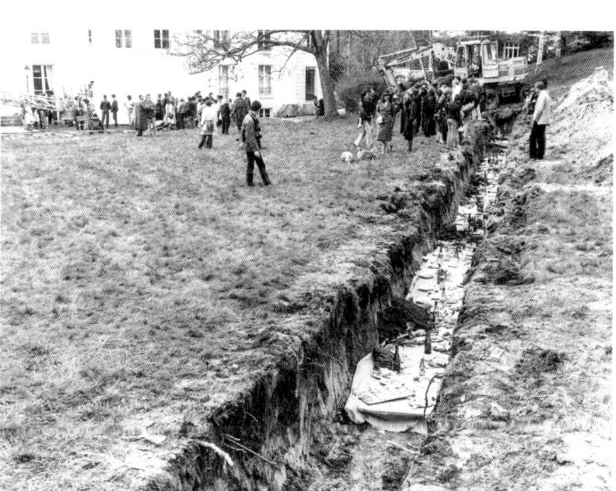

Déjeuner sous l'herbe, a performance by Daniel Spoerri in the park on April 23, 1983

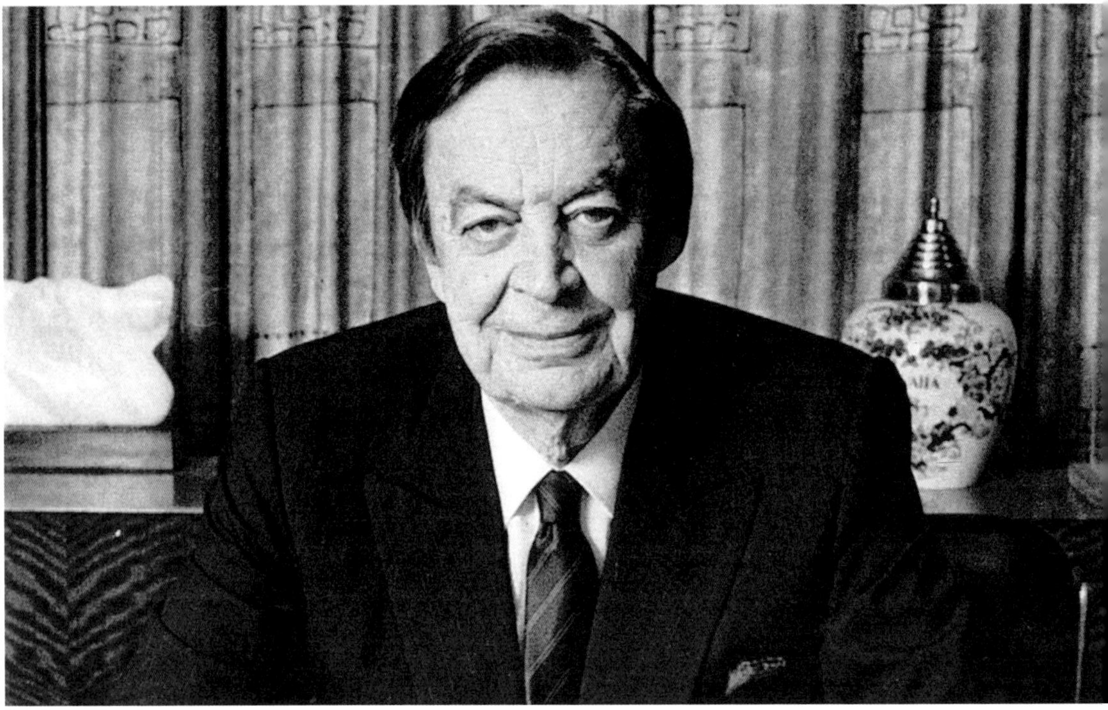

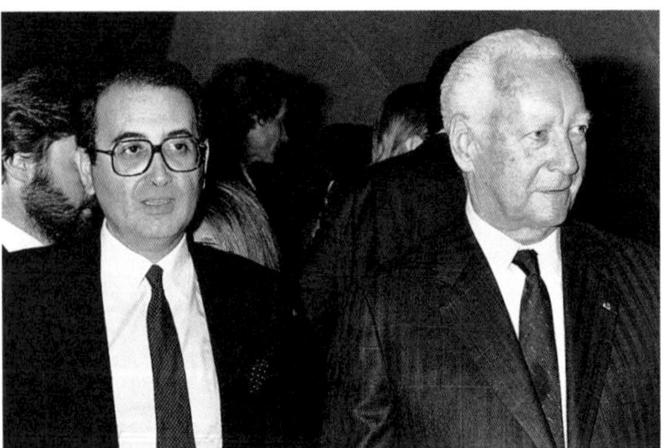

Dr. Anton Rupert

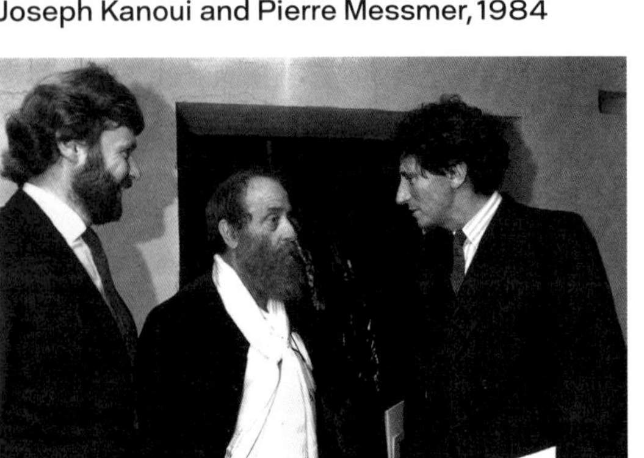

Joseph Kanoui and Pierre Messmer, 1984

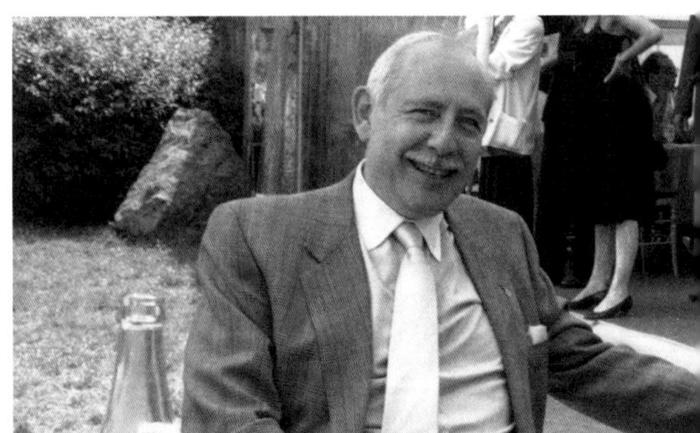

Franco Cologni, 1986

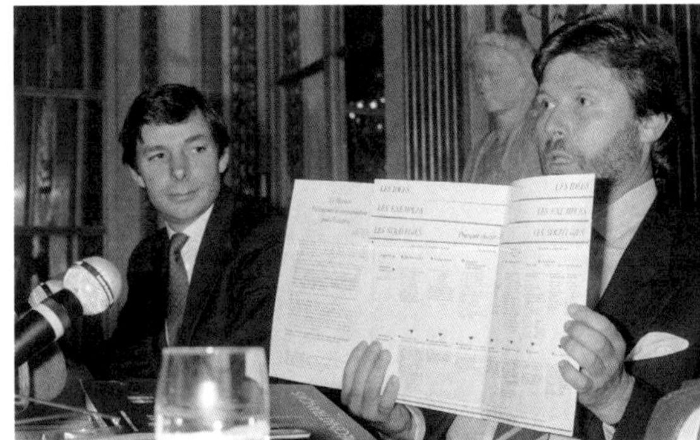

Alain Dominique Perrin, César,
and Jack Lang, 1984

Richard Lepeu and Alain Dominique Perrin, 1987

After this conversation with César, I commissioned a study to find out about the preferred leisure activities of young people in five European countries: France, Germany, Great Britain, Italy, and Spain. The survey allowed us to discover that young people between twenty-five and thirty-five had all kinds of interests, including a keen affinity for art, especially contemporary art. Young people were beginning to return to museums. The year was 1983, and Jack Lang, at the head of a pioneering Ministry of Culture, inspired by the public programs of cultural institutions in northern Europe and the United States, began to open museums focused on contemporary art. And so I decided to create a contemporary art foundation.

That is when I spoke about my project with Franco Cologni, Managing Director of Cartier International, and Richard Lepeu, its Chief Financial Officer. Both were extremely supportive and helpful. We worked on a business plan, and together with the lawyer Jean-Pierre Diehl, we determined the statutes of the Fondation. Chartered accountant Paul Grabli was in charge of tax issues. It is worth recalling that at the time, corporate sponsorship laws did not exist and putting everything in place proved very complex. Once we had come up with a clear and perfectly viable project, I presented it to the President of the Cartier group, Joseph Kanoui. He needed to be convinced. Three days later, I flew to South Africa to meet Dr. Anton Rupert, at the time Cartier's main shareholder. We were very close and I wanted his opinion, as he was a great collector and patron. He had already created a foundation supporting South African artists and owned an incredible number of artworks, including pieces by Rodin and Bourdelle that I had the opportunity to visit with him. I vividly remember our meeting in the offices of Rothmans International in Johannesburg, and particularly the advice he gave me: "Dear Alain, make sure that it will not become a bottomless pit." I gave him my word and returned to Europe with his blessing.

A pioneering spirit

Now that I had the agreement of Cartier and Dr. Rupert, everything was ready to officially create a place of art and culture to support and exhibit living artists. It was now time to recruit the right people to accompany me on this pioneering adventure in France. I had heard about Marie-Claude Beaud and her acquisitions for the Musée d'Art de Toulon. At that time, she was a curator striving to establish a contemporary art fund. Marie-Claude Beaud was hired as Director in May 1984, and I set her the objective of conceiving the program for September. I wanted to open in October. She suggested that Christine Borgoltz, with whom she had already worked, should join us to oversee communications and press relations. Shortly afterwards, Christine was brought onboard by headhunter Didier Vuchot. Everything then happened very quickly. The Fondation Cartier pour l'art contemporain was officially launched and although the months that followed were intense, Marie-Claude, to whom I had given carte blanche, was able, with Christine's help, to create the Fondation's programming and development, following the guiding principles we had established.

The first, and most important principle: it was out of the question that an artist encouraged and supported by the Fondation Cartier be asked to participate in the development and/or promotion of Maison Cartier products. There was to be no confusion between pure and generous artistic action and commercial activity. This was, and remains, the very cornerstone of the Fondation's credibility. For a number of years, other, more recent foundations have been doing the exact opposite of what has always seemed fundamental to us, but that is their business. Next, it was important to me to simultaneously welcome an artist already known to the general public, one already in the media eye, and two young artists who could take advantage of the former's reputation to showcase their work. Based on this principle, the inaugural exhibition dedicated to César (*Les Fers de César*) was accompanied by two other exhibitions, presenting

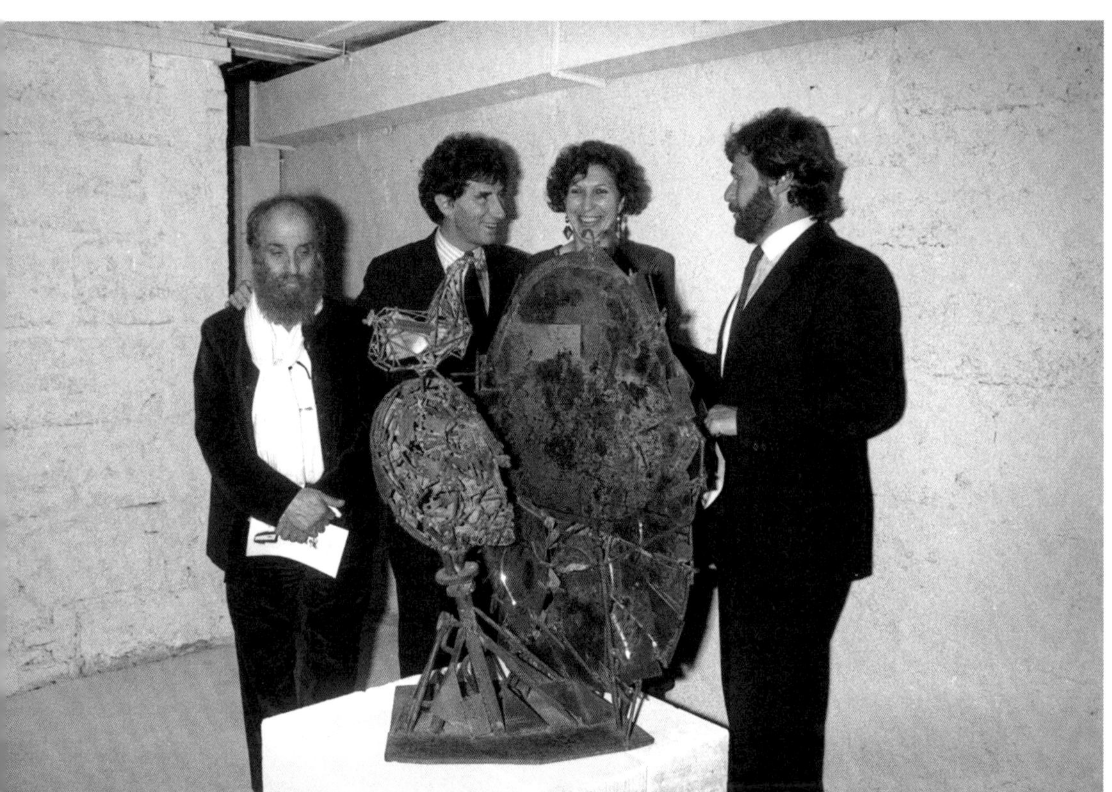

César, Jack Lang, Marie-Claude Beaud, and Alain Dominique Perrin
at the opening of the exhibition *Les Fers de César*, 1984

the work of Lisa Milroy and Julian Opie. We also wanted to create
a space dedicated to all forms of creation: painting, photography,
architecture, design, fashion, and so on. We wanted genuine
interdisciplinarity! This is why I asked Marie-Claude to organize
a major thematic exhibition each year, during the summer.

Built on these main principles, we inaugurated the Fondation
Cartier pour l'art contemporain on October 20, 1984, in Jouy-en-Josas,
in the presence of César, Jack Lang, the Minister of Culture, and
his Representative for Visual Arts, along with a host of artists.
The concept of a private and free space where artists could create
and exhibit was finally a reality.

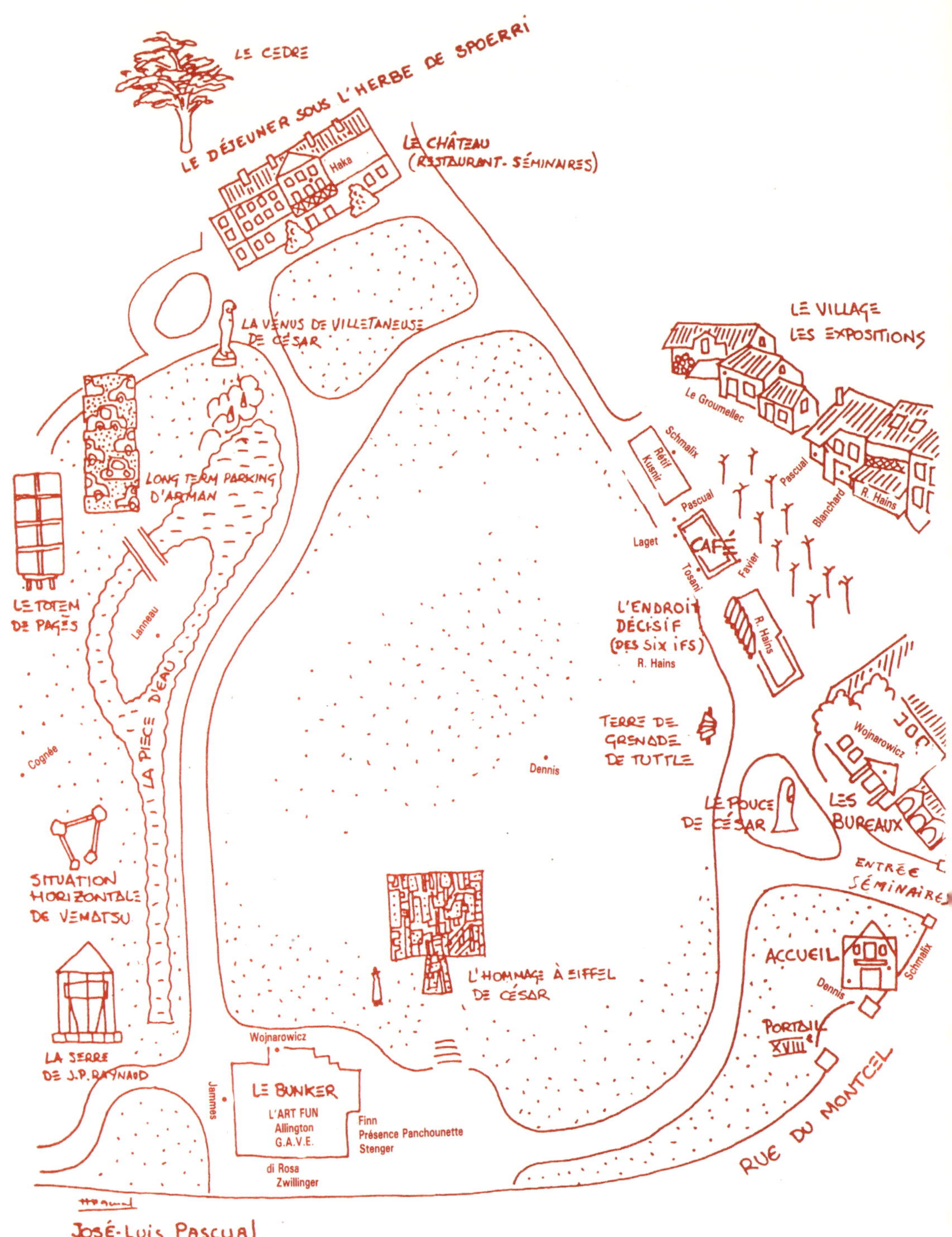

Map of the Fondation Cartier in Jouy-en-Josas, drawn by José-Luis Pascual, 1986

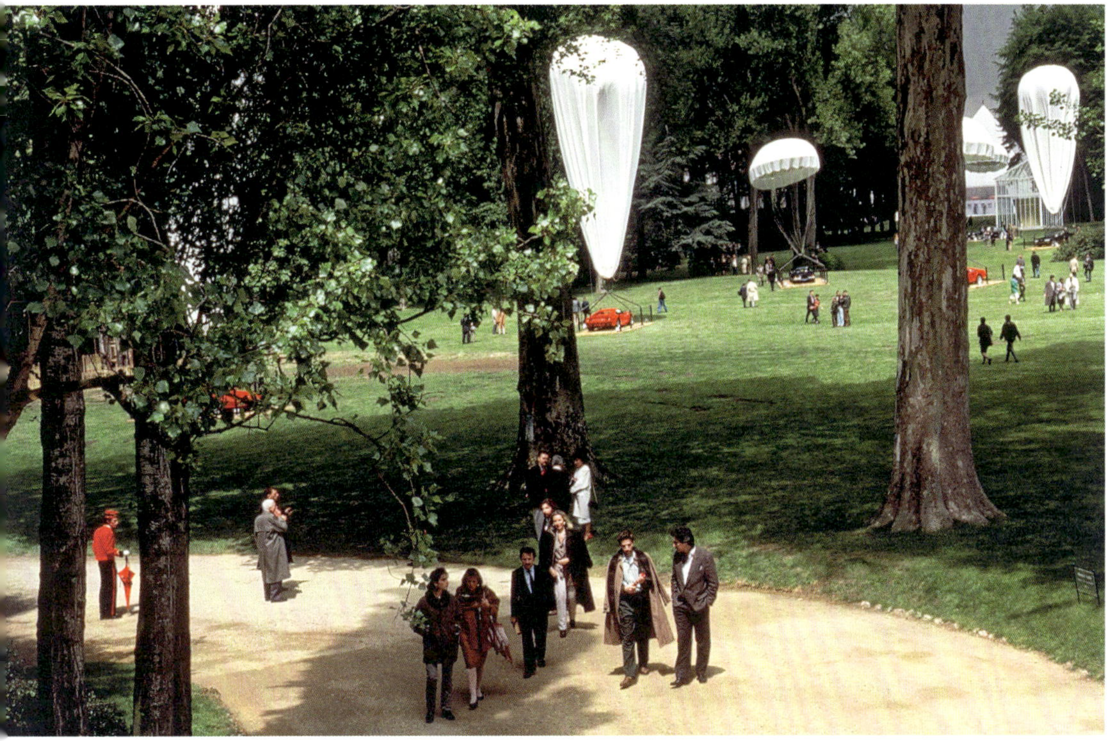

View of the exhibition *Hommage à Ferrari*, 1987

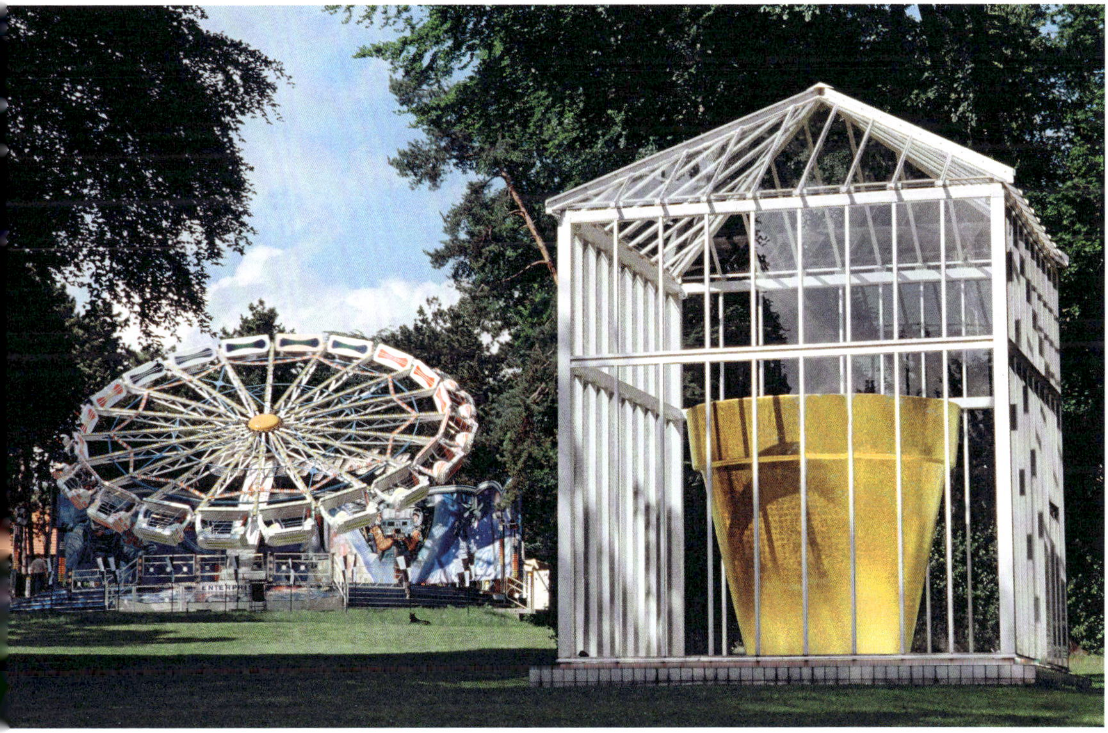

View of the exhibition *La Vitesse*. On the right, *La Serre* and *Le Pot doré*
by Jean Pierre Raynaud (1985)

A place of life and creation

Very early in our history, we wanted to make the Fondation Cartier
a place of life and creation. Marie-Claude Beaud lived on-site and
she wanted to invite artists and offer workshops. The Domaine
du Montcel was ideal for this. In 1985, we welcomed the first
artists on a residency in what was known as "the village," close
to the Fondation's entrance. Up until we left Jouy-en-Josas,
the Fondation lived to the rhythm of the exhibitions presented
there and the artists who created in absolute freedom, with zero
constraints, without imposed themes or even the obligation
to exhibit. I am thinking in particular of Cai Guo-Qiang, Ling Fei,
Huang Yong Ping, Chéri Samba, Marc Couturier, Absalon,
Fabrice Hyber, Jean-Michel Othoniel, and so many others, who
we invited and who were not as well known then as they are today.
At the initiative of Jean de Loisy, curator of the Fondation Cartier
between 1990 and 1993, we also welcomed young critics such
as Hans Ulrich Obrist.

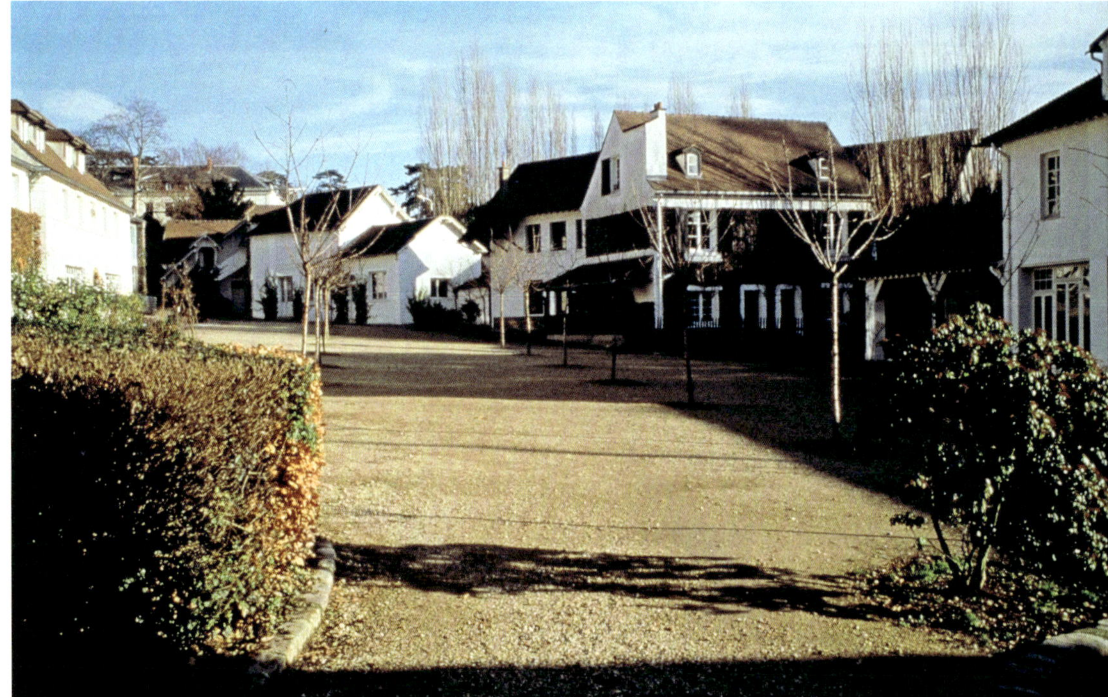

The "village" of the Fondation Cartier, which hosted artists in residence
between 1985 and 1993.

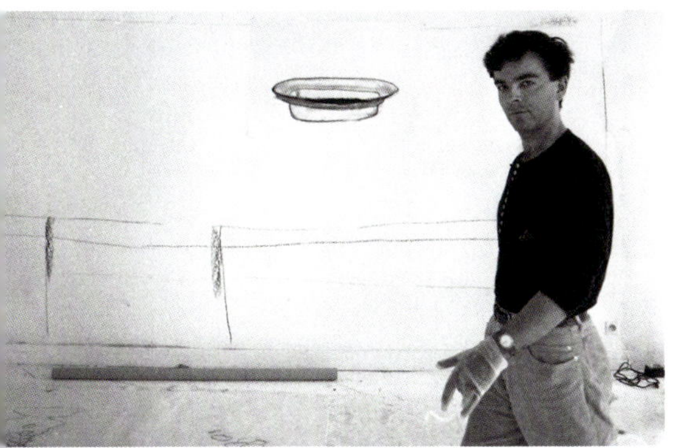
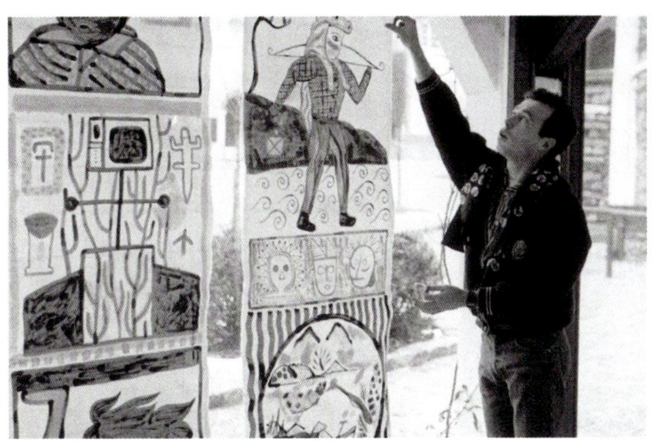
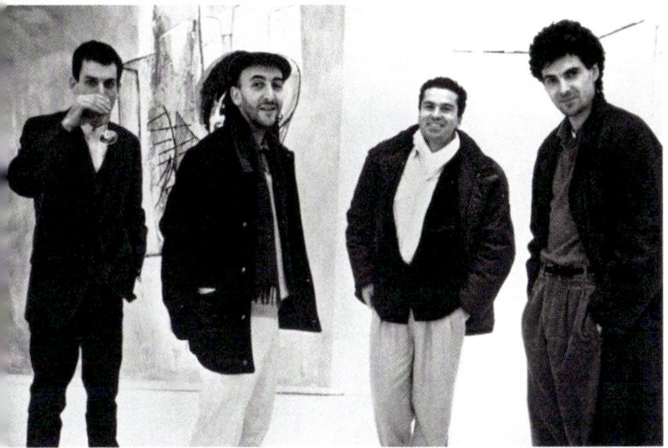
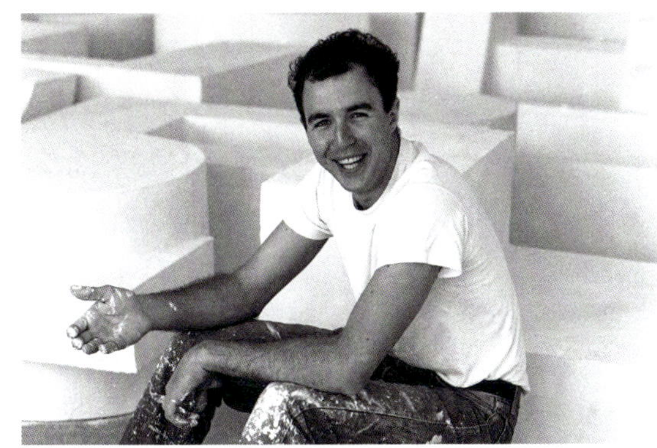
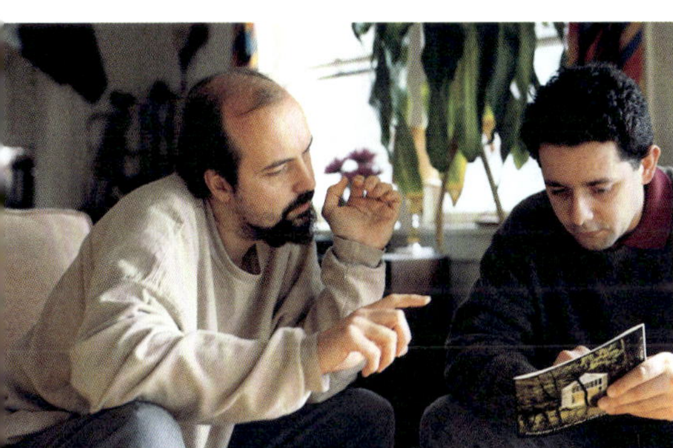
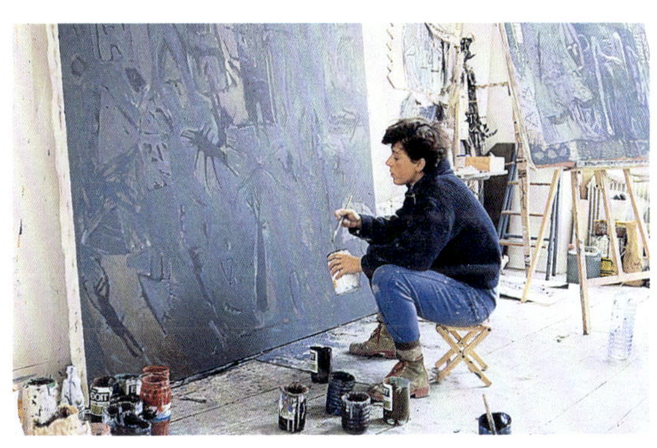
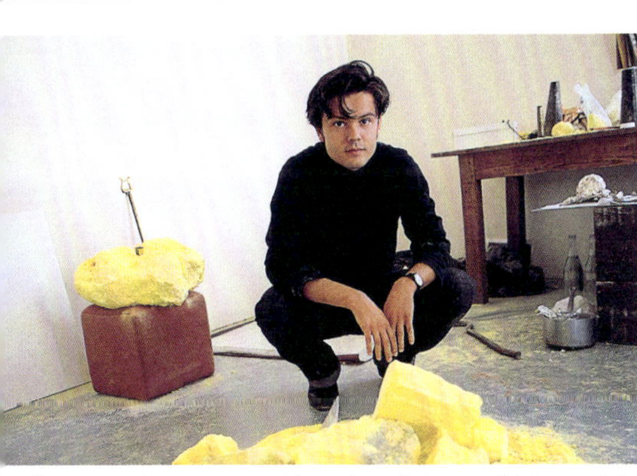
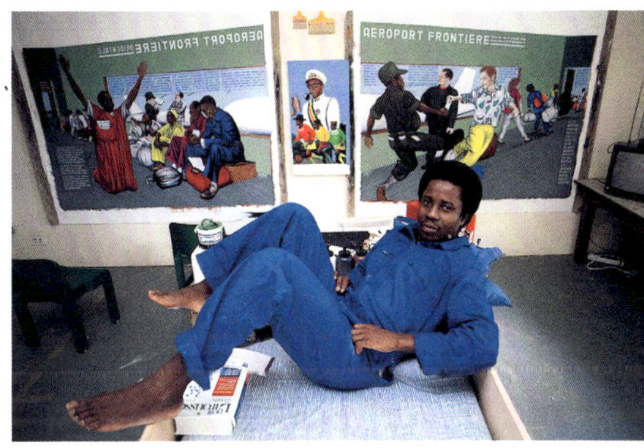

Fabrice Hyber; Rémi Blanchard; Patrick Tosani, Jean-Philippe Aubanel, Dominique Gauthier, and François Boisrond; Absalon; Bill Viola and Jean de Loisy; Hélène Delprat; Jean-Michel Othoniel; Chéri Samba. Residencies at the Fondation Cartier, 1985–1990

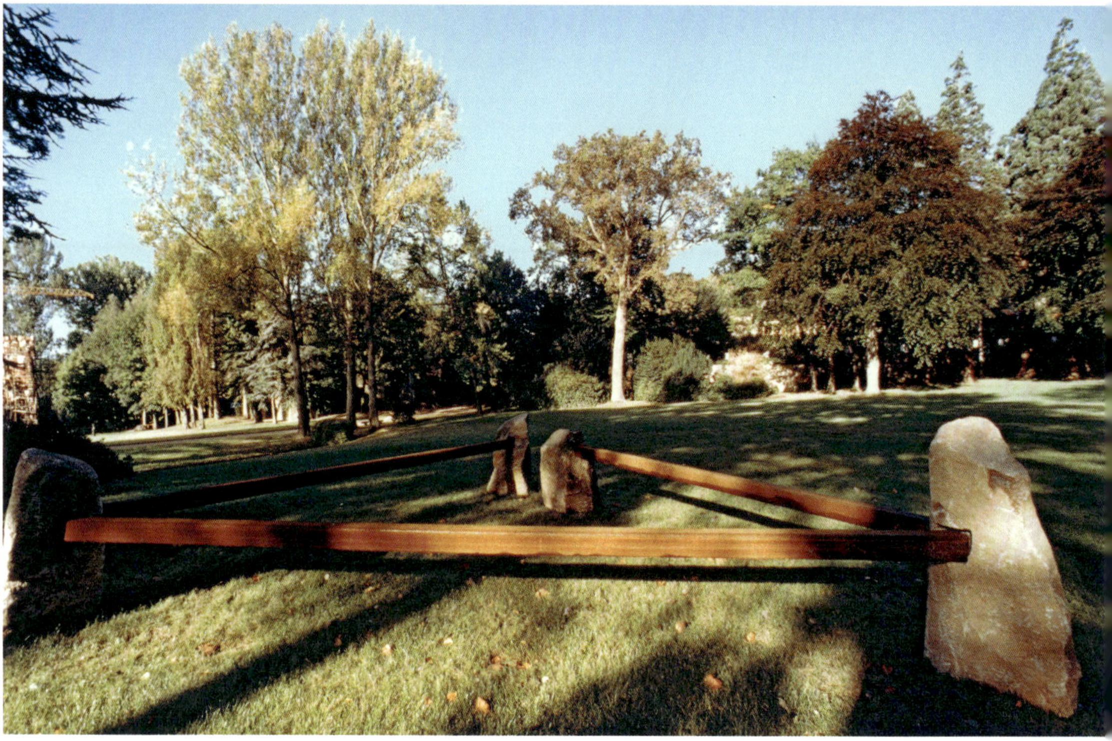

Keiji Uematsu, *Situation horizontale*, 1985

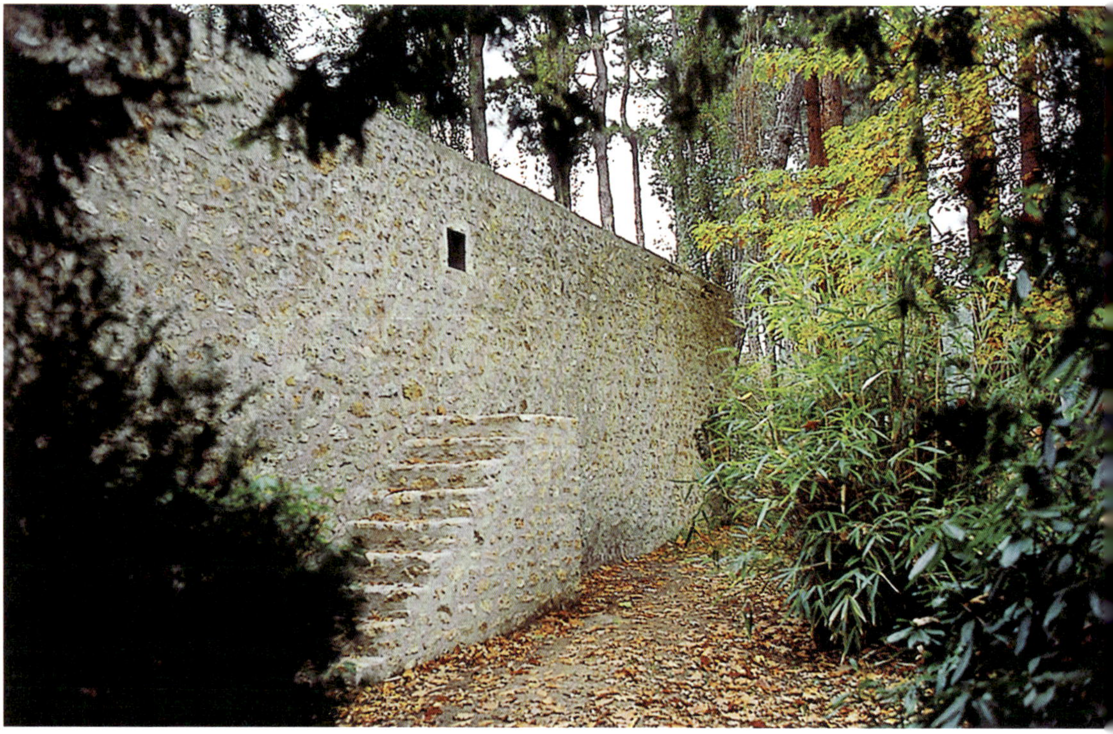

François Morellet, *Le Tombeau de Duchamp ou Étant donné*, 1989

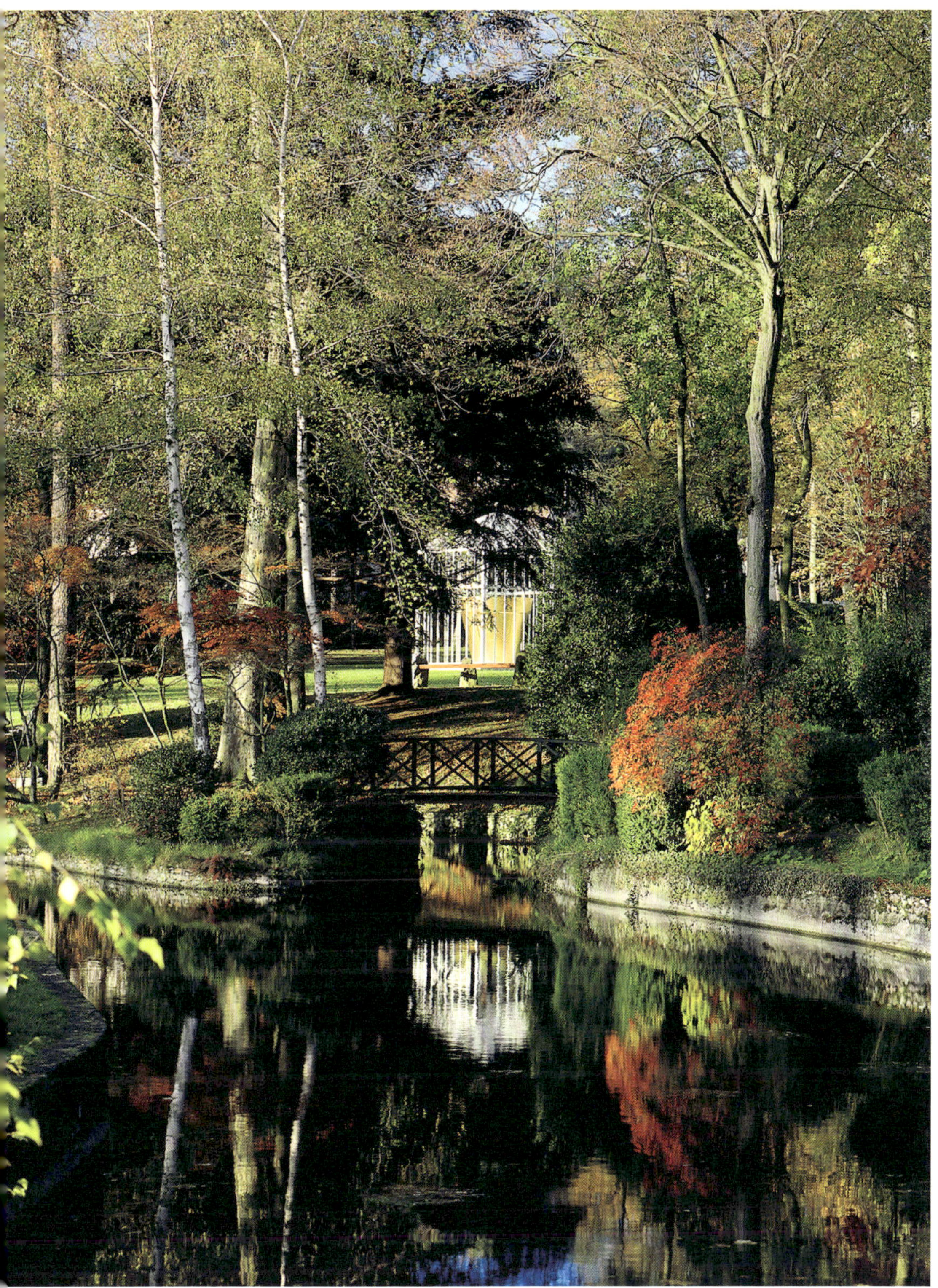

Jean Pierre Raynaud, *La Serre* and *Le Pot doré*,1985

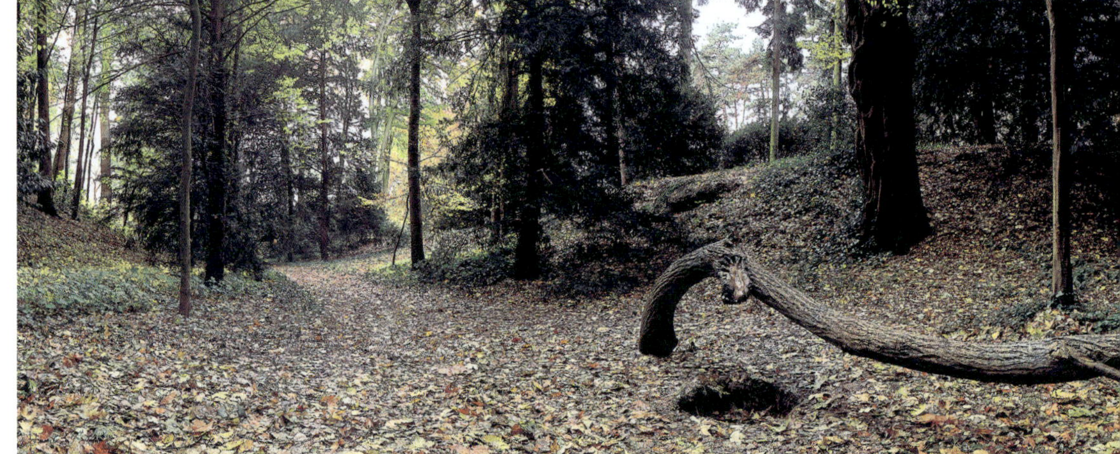

Giuseppe Penone, *Biforcazione*, 1987–1992 (installation in the park of the Fondation Cartier in 1992). FC Collections (1989)

A space of freedom: Fondation Cartier commissions

Since the Fondation Cartier's inception, I have always advocated for a private space with complete freedom, where decisions are made quickly, and where artists exhibit without constraints. In the founding charter, in addition to the main principles I have just outlined, there is another rule that allows for this: for each exhibition, we commission artists, and we buy the works created for the occasion. In addition, as soon as the statutes were drafted, I also insisted on the right to be able to resell the works in our possession. The Fondation de France, under whose aegis the Fondation Cartier is placed, did not immediately accept this. But we convinced them by providing the guarantee that all profits from the sale of works would be used to buy new ones. This is how we began to build our Collections. The works that are part of these Collections retrace our history, and our rich, multidisciplinary program. Today, they can be said to bear witness to the relationships we have forged with over five hundred artists from all around the world, and to our desire to remain open to the world and contemporary society.

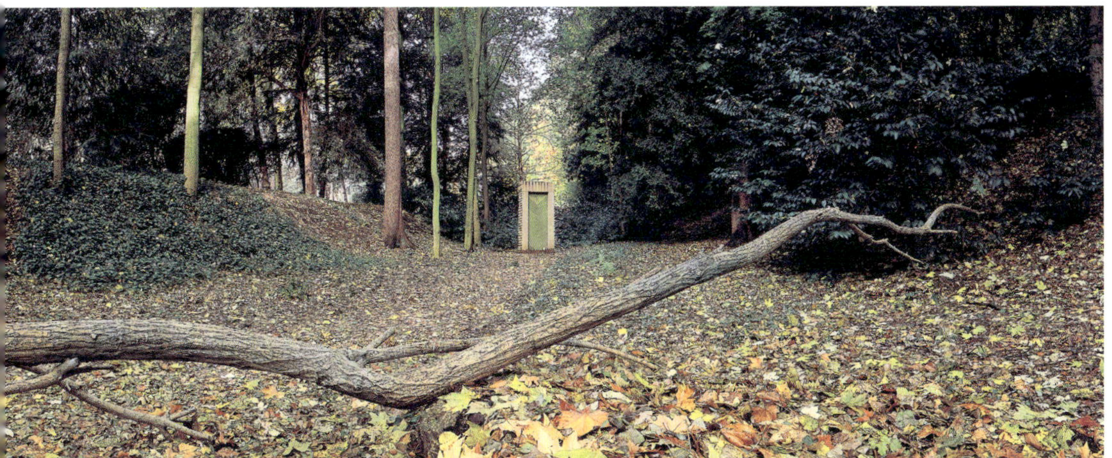

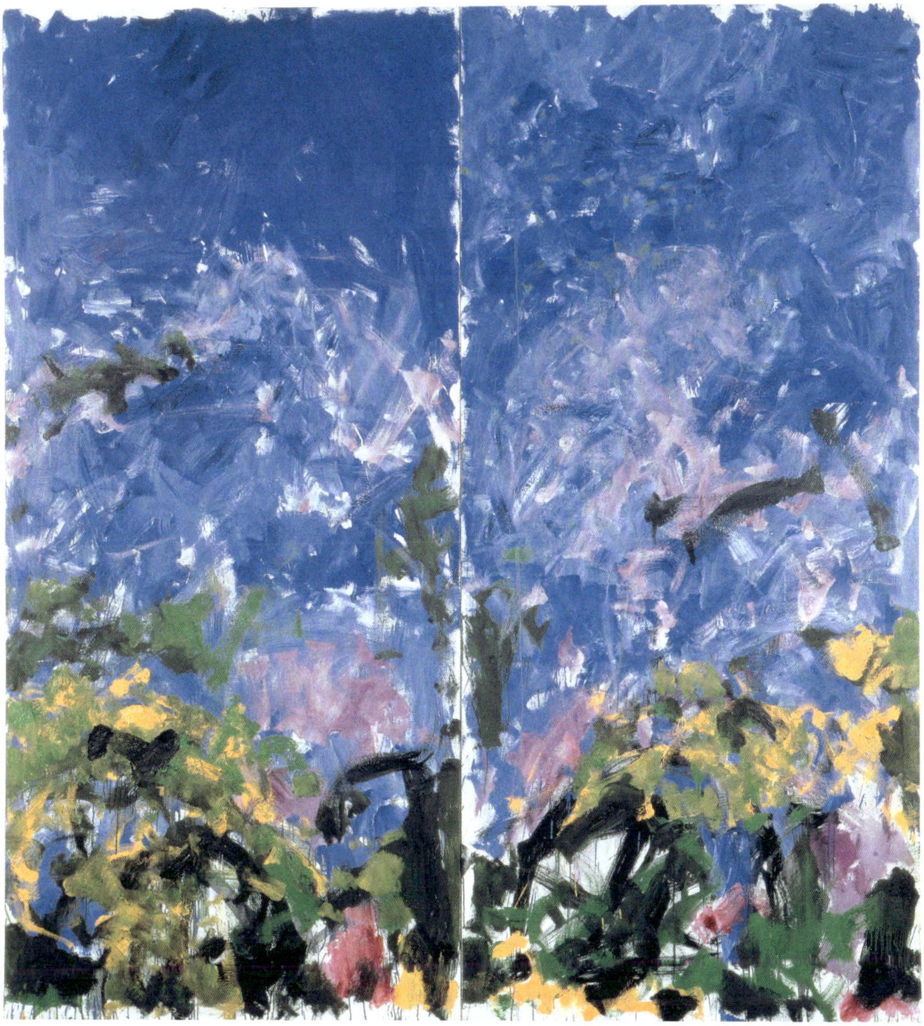

Joan Mitchell, *Grande Vallée VI*, 1984. FC Collections (1985)

The Fondation Cartier was created thanks to an artist, for artists, but it was essential that the employees of Cartier embodied the spirit of the Fondation and familiarized themselves with contemporary art. They were asked to come and see the exhibitions and participate in the seminars, training courses, conferences, and working meetings that we organized, in particular with Édith Krotoff, Secretary General of the Fondation, held in the château of the Domaine du Montcel. Apart from Cartier staff, we also invited suppliers, resellers, retailers, and clients to come to Jouy-en-Josas to attend sales meetings, working lunches, and dinners. In addition to the meeting rooms, we also had reception rooms, as well as the Petit Café, which was a convivial meeting space for everyone: Cartier staff, artists, and visitors alike. Marie-Claude Beaud initiated competitive commissions for artists and designers to create the furniture, lighting, and tableware for these different recreational and professional spaces. Pascal Mourgue for the Petit Café and Nestor Perkal for the château won over the jury that we had put together, even though designers like Philippe Starck, Élisabeth Garouste, and François Bauchet had also presented some very beautiful objects. Shortly after the competition had closed, we presented all these young French designers in the exhibition *Vivre en couleur* (1985), the title of which came to me while listening to RFM radio!

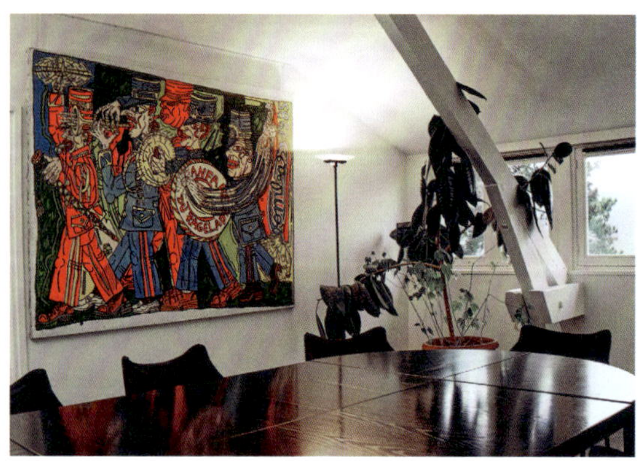

Robert Combas, *La Fanfare du Ragelade*, 1985
FC Collections (1986)

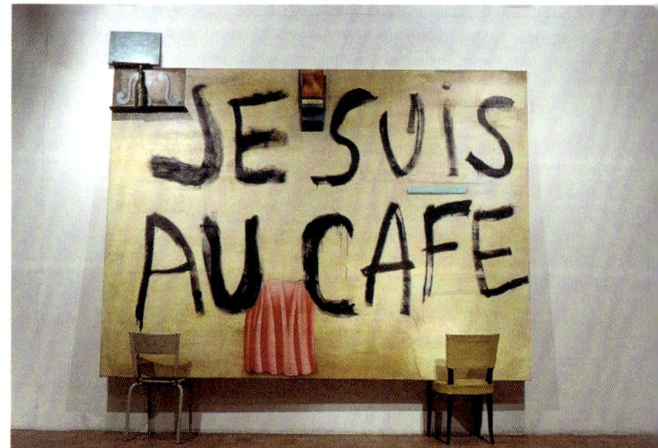

Carlos Kusnir, *Je suis au café*, 1986
FC Collections (1988)

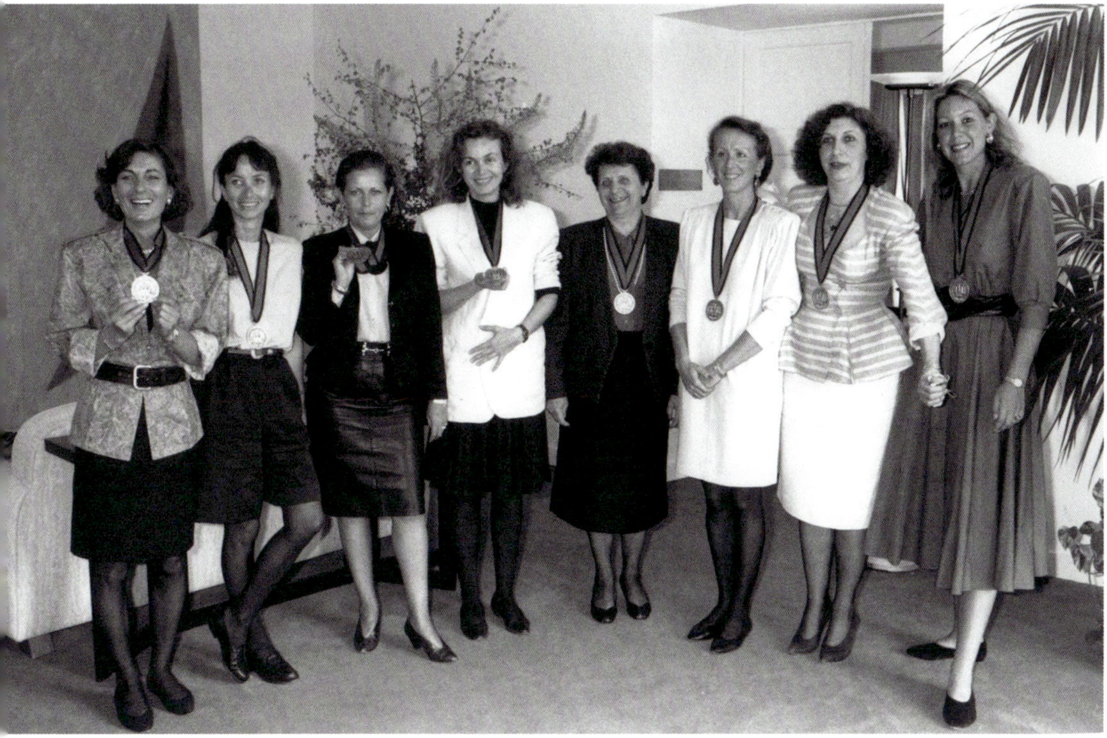

Induction of Édith Krotoff, Marie-Thérèse Perrin, Marie-Ange Lebec, Sylvie Guilloteau, Monique Le Saint (mayor of Jouy-en-Josas), Béatrice Beucher-Renard, Marie-Claude Beaud, and Christine Borgoltz at the Confrérie du Vin de Cahors, Fondation Cartier, Jouy-en-Josas, 1989

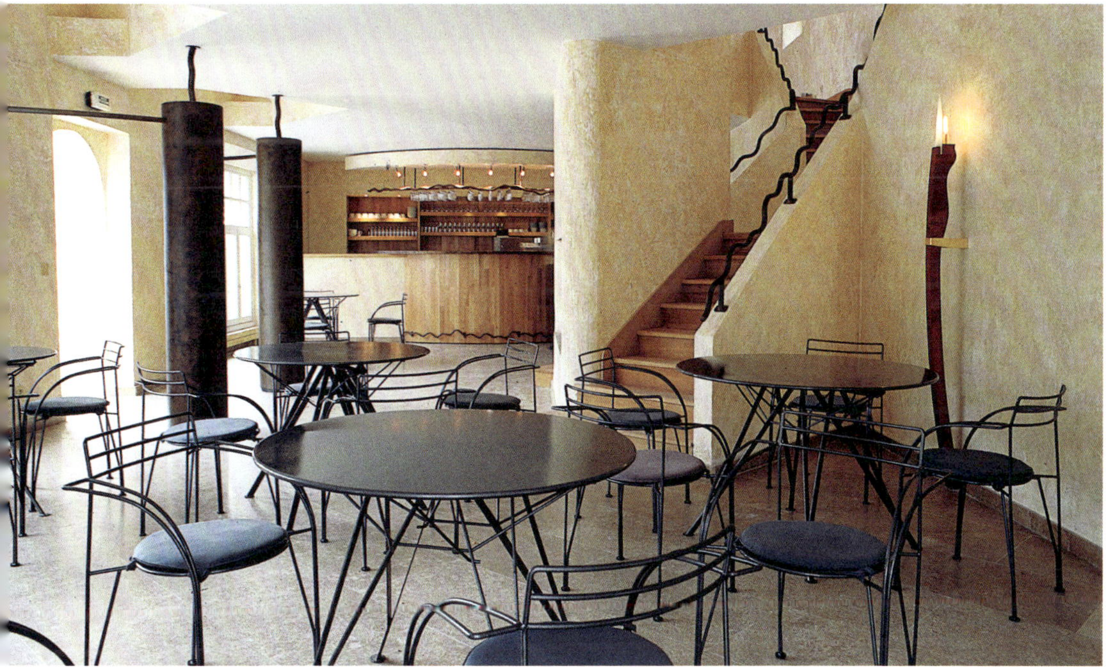

The Petit Café of the Fondation Cartier, Jouy-en-Josas, 1985
Interior design: Agnès Comar; furniture: Pascal Mourgue; lighting and signage: Éric Jourdan

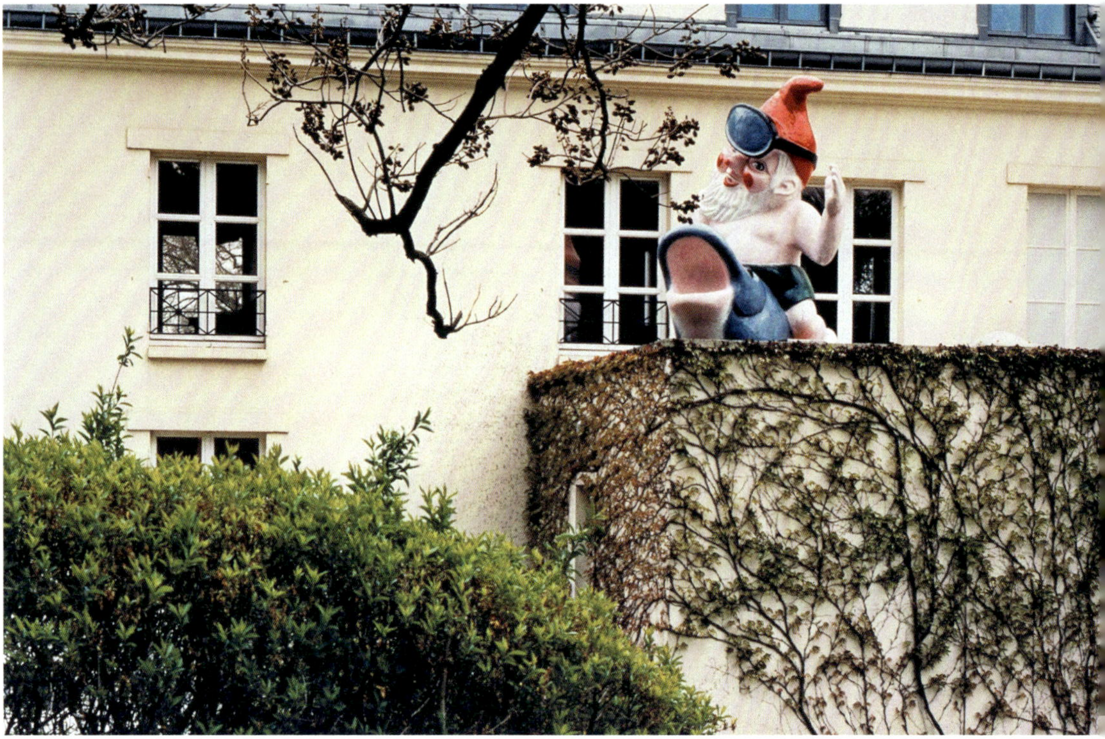

Présence Panchounette, *Dwarf! Dwarf! III*, 1990. FC Collections (1990)

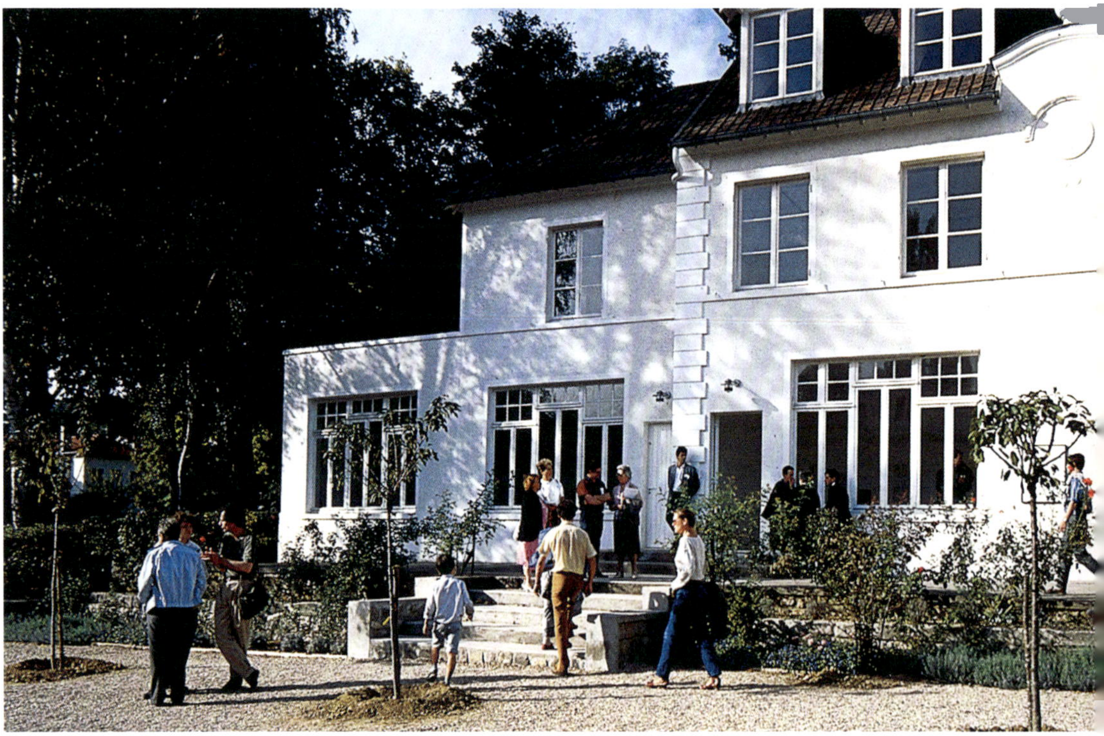

The Petit Café

It was in these vibrant spaces that we guided our suppliers who wanted to become involved with the Fondation Cartier and artists, so that they too could become important players in our philanthropic actions. Many of them became donors who remained by our side for many years. I am thinking of American Express, the communications agency ABC, which later became Mazarine, Givaudan, and several large printing houses with whom Cartier worked. I regret that we can no longer work with them as we did at that time. In any case, Cartier's employees, customers, and suppliers were so receptive to what we were doing at the Fondation that some of them even began collecting contemporary art, even though in the beginning their knowledge was limited!

Richard Lepeu, Michel Guten, Franco Cologni, and their teams organized all of these early events. I was constantly traveling around the world for Cartier, and the three of them worked together with a fierce determination. They shared a strong bond and a love for the project. It's funny, because it was by investing in the life of the Fondation Cartier that they too started collecting art.

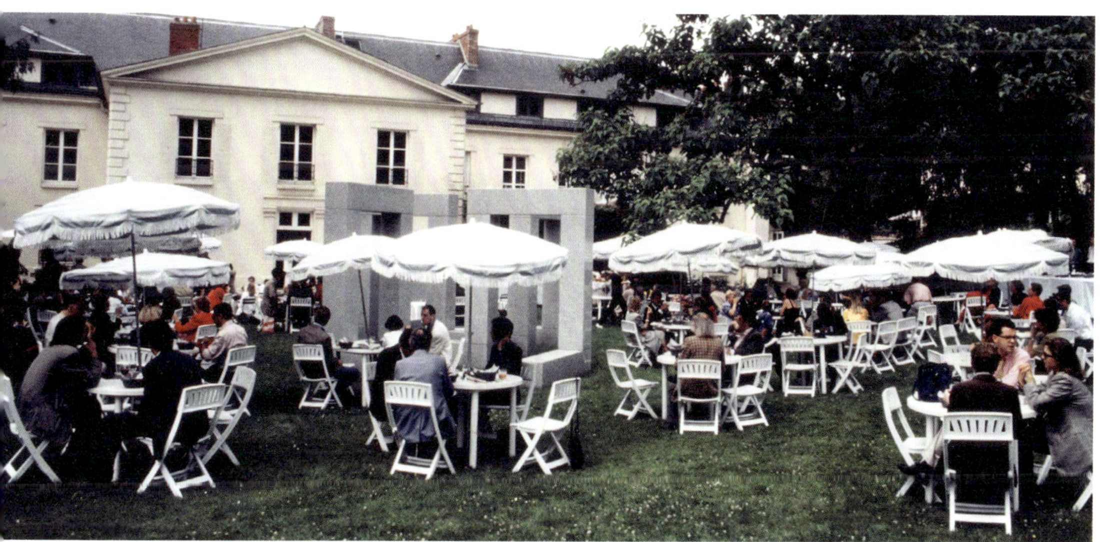

Reception in the park around Max Bill's work *Pavillon*, 1989

Philanthropy passes into law

When I had the idea for the Fondation Cartier in 1981, I had lunch with Jacques Toubon, who would later become Minister of Culture. I told him about my project, explaining that I would deduct the costs from Maison Cartier's communication budget. I wanted to participate in the development of art in France, so I was ready to fight and take legal action should I encounter the slightest problem or obstacle.

In 1984, I opened the Fondation Cartier on this operating basis, and in May 1986, François Léotard offered me the opportunity to regularize the Fondation's status on a silver platter. He had just been appointed Minister of Culture and I had invited him to inaugurate that summer's themed exhibition, *Les Années 60*. And there, in the middle of his official speech, he announced in front of a crowd of guests, including Ringo Starr, Françoise Hardy, and André Courrèges, that he was entrusting me the mission of drafting a report on corporate philanthropy. I was sitting right in front of the podium where François Léotard was standing and I was stunned. I looked at him, failing to comprehend his words. I didn't have the time to dwell on it, but once the surprise wore off, I decided to commit to it completely. At the end of the inauguration, I proudly informed him that Cartier would not only finance the report but that the Maison Cartier would also be the very first French corporate sponsor.

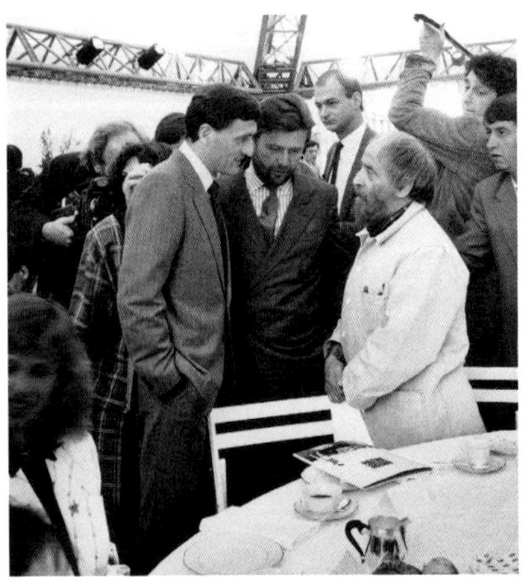

François Léotard, Alain Dominique Perrin, and César at the opening of the exhibition *Les Années 60*, 1986

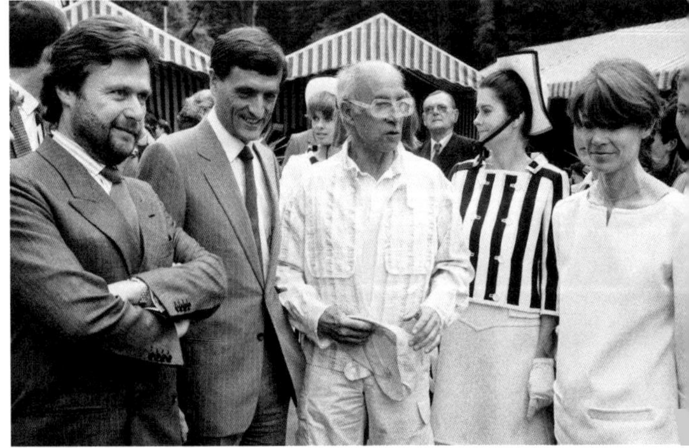

Alain Dominique Perrin, François Léotard, André Courrèges, and Françoise Hardy at the opening of the exhibition *Les Années 60*, 1986

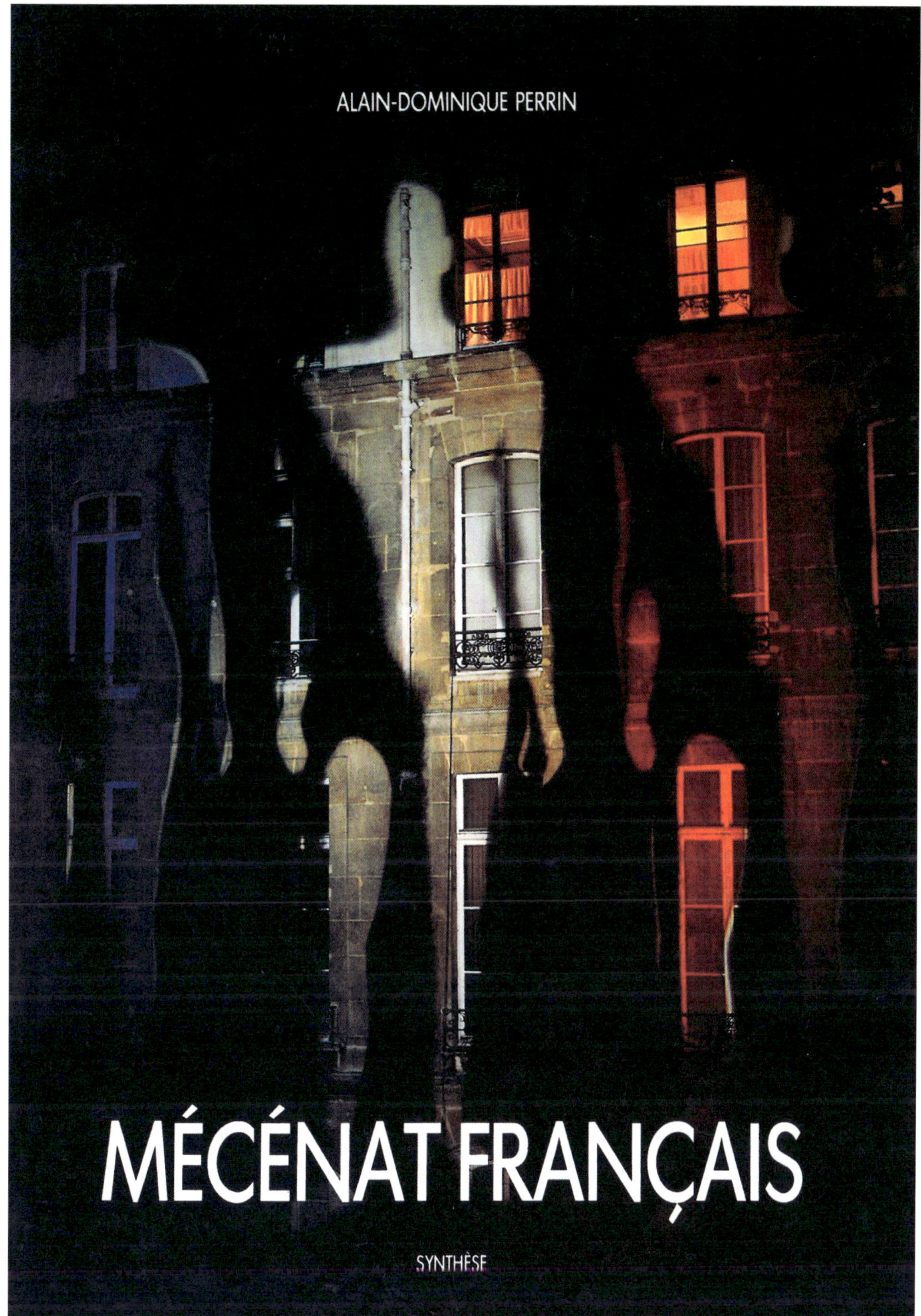

The report on philanthropy, written at the request of François Léotard, 1986

My next step was to tour prestigious business and management schools, including HEC, and universities. I hired forty-four people to study how corporate sponsorship worked in Germany, Great Britain, Italy, Spain, Brazil, Japan, and of course, the United States. Sylvie Dumas, the Fondation's Financial Director, Isabelle Guichot, Deputy Secretary General of Cartier, and a very young Nicolas Bos, now Chief Executive Officer of Richemont, worked closely with these recruits.

The idea was to offer a French style of corporate sponsorship. The only document I was able to find at the start of the mission, and on which we relied, was a memorandum written by Pierre Bérégovoy when he was Minister of the Economy, Finance, and Budget, dating from 1985. We quoted it in the final report in 1986: "The instruction of April 12, 1985 authorizes the deduction of cultural expenses incurred directly. They are considered here as advertising expenses. When carried out on a centrally managed basis, sponsorship expenditure constitutes an act of management. It is an operating expense. Sponsorship then becomes self-serving."

In September 1986, I submitted a lengthy report to François Léotard on how corporate art sponsorship could be developed in France. In early 1987, Édouard Balladur, Minister of the Economy, Finance, and Privatization, took the subject seriously and appointed a commission, led by Georges Pébereau, responsible for making the fiscal aspect of my proposals viable. We collaborated to give birth to the definitive corporate philanthropy project, and in July 1987, the "Léotard Law" on sponsorship was adopted in Parliament by a very strong majority.

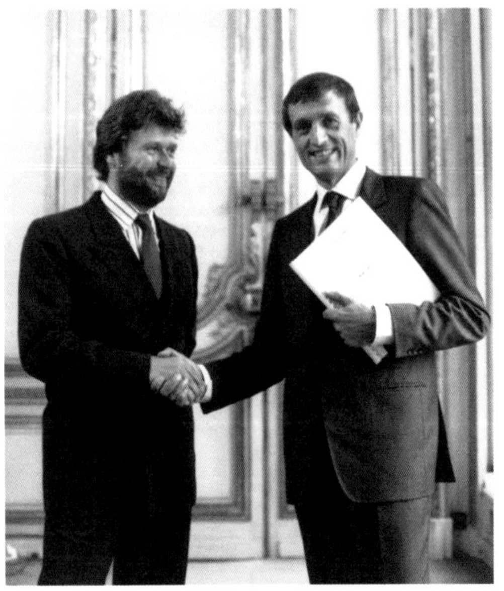

Alain Dominique Perrin and François Léotard during the official presentation of the report on philanthropy, September 1986

la synthèse de cette mission.

L'ambition, c'est de mettre au service de la culture et des créateurs, le dynamisme de l'Entreprise.

La Stratégie consiste à associer la culture à l'Entreprise, pour son bénéfice et celui du public.

La promesse, c'est l'engagement de l'Entreprise au rayonnement de la culture française et de ses libertés.

L'écriture de ce rapport est celle de l'Entreprise. Son langage résolument concret vise à l'efficacité.

Veuillez agréer, Monsieur le Ministre l'assurance de ma haute considération.

Paris. Septembre 1986.

Letter from Alain Dominique Perrin to François Léotard, 1986

The exhibitions that we hosted in Jouy-en-Josas soon found their audience, from the very beginning of the Fondation's existence. Everything was going well and I was very satisfied. Rapidly enough however, I also wanted to promote artists abroad, and I asked Marie-Claude Beaud to develop an international program in collaboration with prestigious local arts institutions. The first exhibition we organized was in Germany, in 1988 — that of artist Jochen Gerz — but things really took off with *Too French* in 1991, at the Hong Kong Museum of Art. It was a major event: this exhibition allowed us to send works that had recently entered our Collections overseas. This was made possible by the Cartier subsidiary in Hong Kong, which really pulled out all the stops. Not surprisingly, we showed works by César, but also by Raymond Hains, Jean-Michel Othoniel, and Bernard Piffaretti. It was after this exhibition that we gave César's work *The Flying Frenchman* (1992) to the city of Hong Kong. This immense bronze sculpture reminds me of a work by Christian Boltanski, *La Réserve des Suisses morts* (1990), which was given to the Tate Modern in London in 1993.

Our international program was supported by the network of Cartier subsidiaries. Thanks to each subsidiary, we were able to forge links with major international museums, the local art scene, and the press. In 1992, *Too French* was presented at the Hara Museum of Contemporary Art in Tokyo. Subsequently, other exhibitions followed, in Korea, Taiwan, the United States, Brazil, Lebanon, and all around the world.

Europe was not overlooked: the Fondation Cartier also collaborated with local institutions offering unique exhibitions and tours of countries including Spain, Portugal, Italy, and Germany. In 1991, in Milan and Munich, we showed the extraordinary exhibition *Vraiment faux*, initially presented in Jouy-en-Josas in 1988. I will always remember Marie-Claude Beaud coming to me, a few months earlier, to tell me that she had found *Mona Lisa* copies at a museum in Buffalo in the United States, and in other

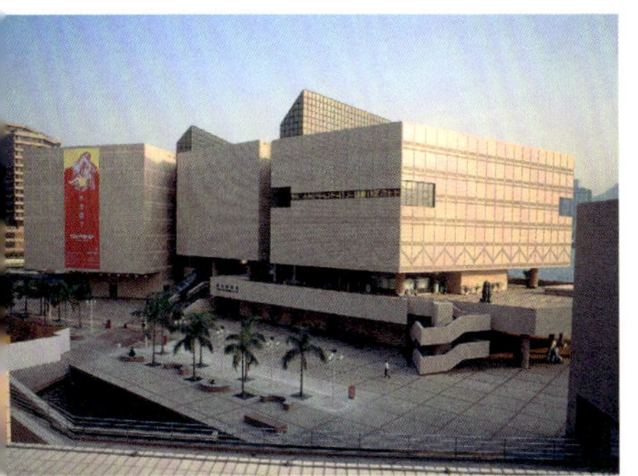

Hong Kong Museum of Art

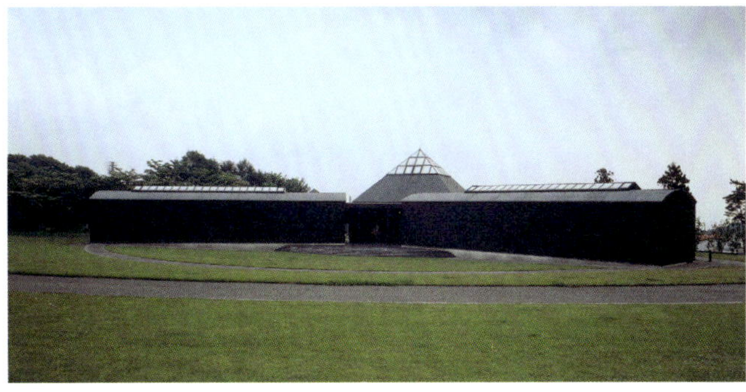

Hara Museum of Contemporary Art, Tokyo

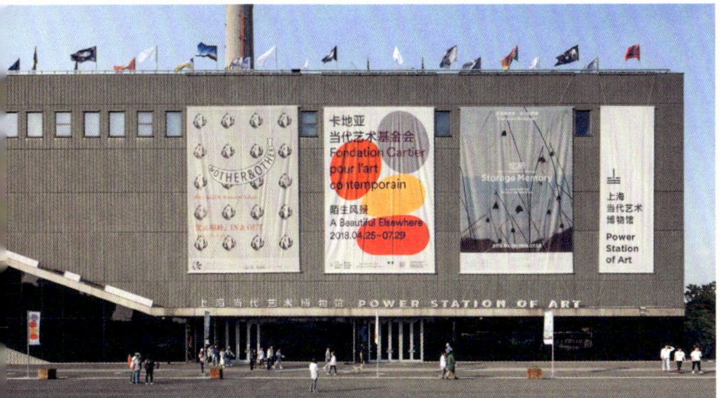

Power Station of Art, Shanghai

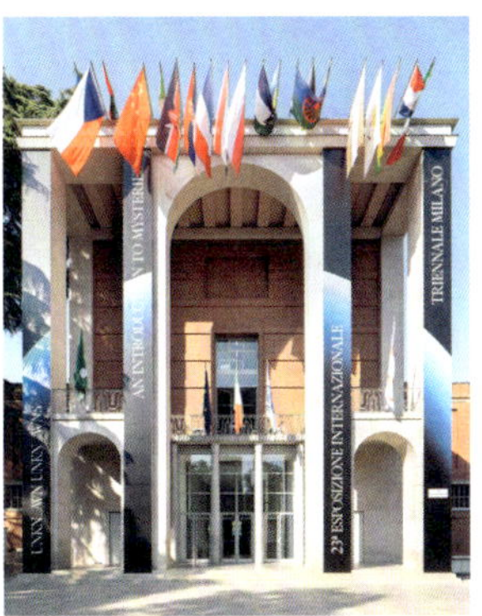

Triennale Milano, Milan

museums around the world! There were at least eighty of these paintings, which we had shipped to be exhibited along with similar artworks and objects. Everything was fake in this exhibition, right down to the catalog's cover, which was made from artificial grass!

In 2008, we began developing close ties with Italy and in particular with Triennale Milano. That year, David Lynch's exhibition *The Air is on Fire* was presented there, which we had shown to French audiences the year before, on Boulevard Raspail. This collaboration continues today. Triennale Milano hosts our exhibitions, and together, we also create exhibitions, such as *Io sono un drago. La vera storia di Alessandro Mendini*, which opened in April 2024.

Although the Domaine du Montcel is vast and comprises several
buildings for which we had undertaken major renovations,
we soon ran out of space. I also believed that it was essential
to anchor the Fondation Cartier in the landscape of Jouy-en-Josas
with a strong architectural project. In 1986, I met Jean Nouvel
through Marie-Claude Beaud and we commissioned him to
design a new building. He imagined a glass and steel building
on a hillside near the site of the Fondation Cartier, but at a distance
of three or four hundred meters from the château. Although
it was conceived to blend into the landscape, this ambitious
project was never actually built, as the region's administration
and public authorities, which were not very open to contemporary
architecture, rejected the project. I was very upset by their
decision. I ended my speech at the meeting with all the elected
officials in attendance by declaring: "The Fondation no longer
exists here."

That was in 1988. It coincided with a letter I received from the
owner of the estate, Jean Hamon, who told me that he was planning
to double the rent. It was too much. I told everyone at Cartier
and the Fondation not to respond and not to move, and I visited
various real estate agencies in an attempt to find a new location,
but this time in Paris. One evening, by chance, I met Maurice
Gozlan, who along with Gan (Groupe des Assurances Nationales),
had just taken over the former American Center located on
Boulevard Raspail. We had a lengthy discussion: he explained
that he was planning to develop the property, which consisted of
demolishing the existing building, and in its place, he was looking
to build a cultural venue, as the planning permission did not
allow for only office space on the site. Putting the Fondation Cartier
there was a godsend for both of us. He had already discussed plans
with architects, but the only person I wanted to entrust the project
to was Jean Nouvel. When Jean Nouvel asked me what I expected
from him, I told him: "A new Parisian monument." He created one.

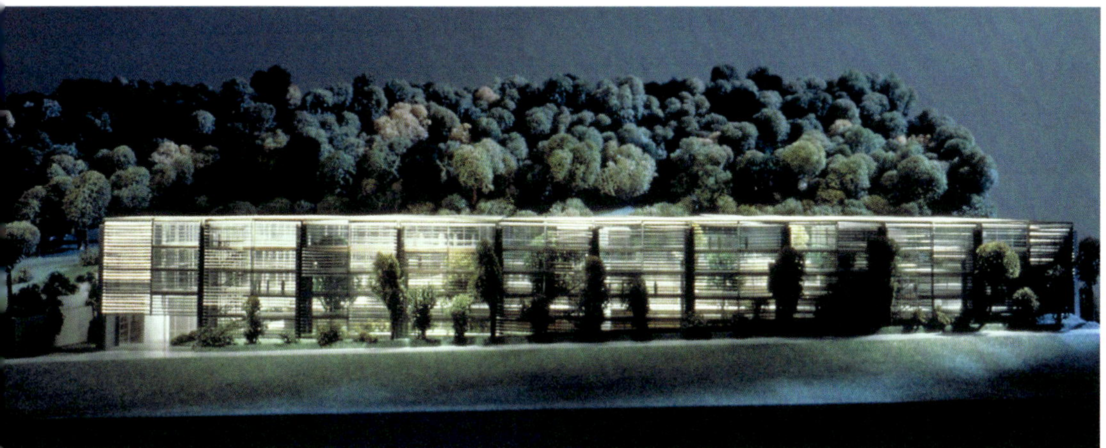

Jean Nouvel, unrealized project for the Fondation Cartier in Jouy-en-Josas, 1987

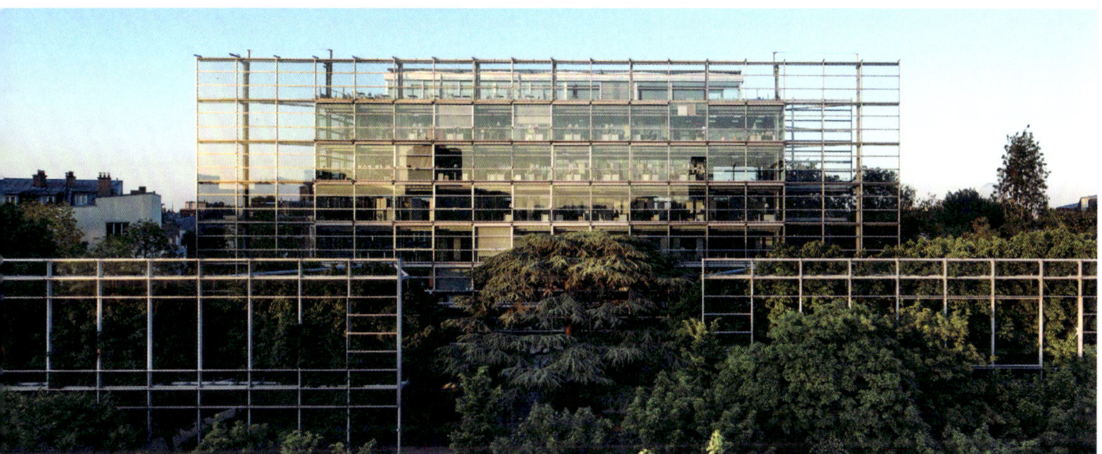

The Fondation Cartier building located on Boulevard Raspail in Paris, designed by Jean Nouvel and inaugurated in 1994

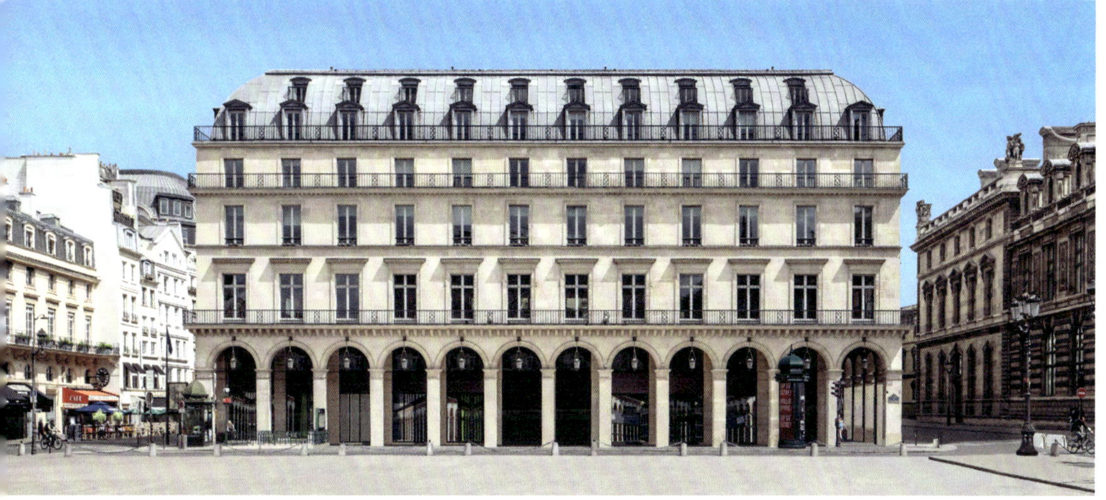

The building that will be home to the Fondation Cartier from 2025, at Place du Palais-Royal in Paris, with the interior architecture designed by Jean Nouvel

It is true that when Jean Nouvel initially presented his plans to Marie-Claude Beaud and me, we were taken aback. There were glass walls and no picture rails: a heresy in terms of presenting exhibitions and displaying works. But according to him, this was precisely the building's ingenuity: the ability to reinvent itself each time, offering completely different scenographic possibilities from one exhibition to the next. Jean was right; he is a true visionary after all. It is for his unique approach to architecture and the city that we have once again entrusted him with designing the interior architecture of what will be our new building that will house the Fondation Cartier on Place du Palais-Royal in the heart of Paris, set to open in 2025. Here admittedly, the challenge is different: it involves integrating an art venue into a building that already has a history. However, the project is worthy of both the man and the Fondation Cartier.

Moving to Boulevard Raspail in 1994, the Fondation Cartier continued its journey under a new impetus: that of Hervé Chandès, who took over from Marie-Claude Beaud. In this new glass setting, he brilliantly decompartmentalized genres and brought together a host of disciplines, arts, and artists: David Lynch and mathematicians, including Misha Gromov, Raymond Depardon, and Yanomami artists, amongst many other wonderful examples.

I created the Fondation Cartier pour l'art contemporain in 1984 in Jouy-en-Josas for all the reasons previously mentioned, but also because it was only natural for a maison like Cartier, which makes its living from its jewelry and watchmaking creations, to share part of its profit with artists. We have pursued this philosophy in our premises on Boulevard Raspail, and we will continue to do so at Place du Palais-Royal, opposite the Louvre.

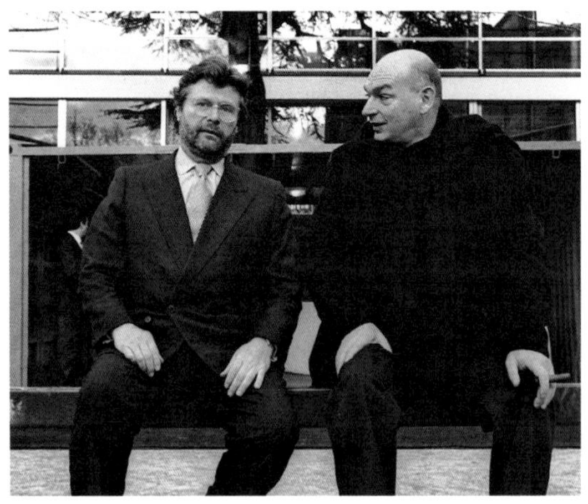

Alain Dominique Perrin and Jean Nouvel, 1994

César

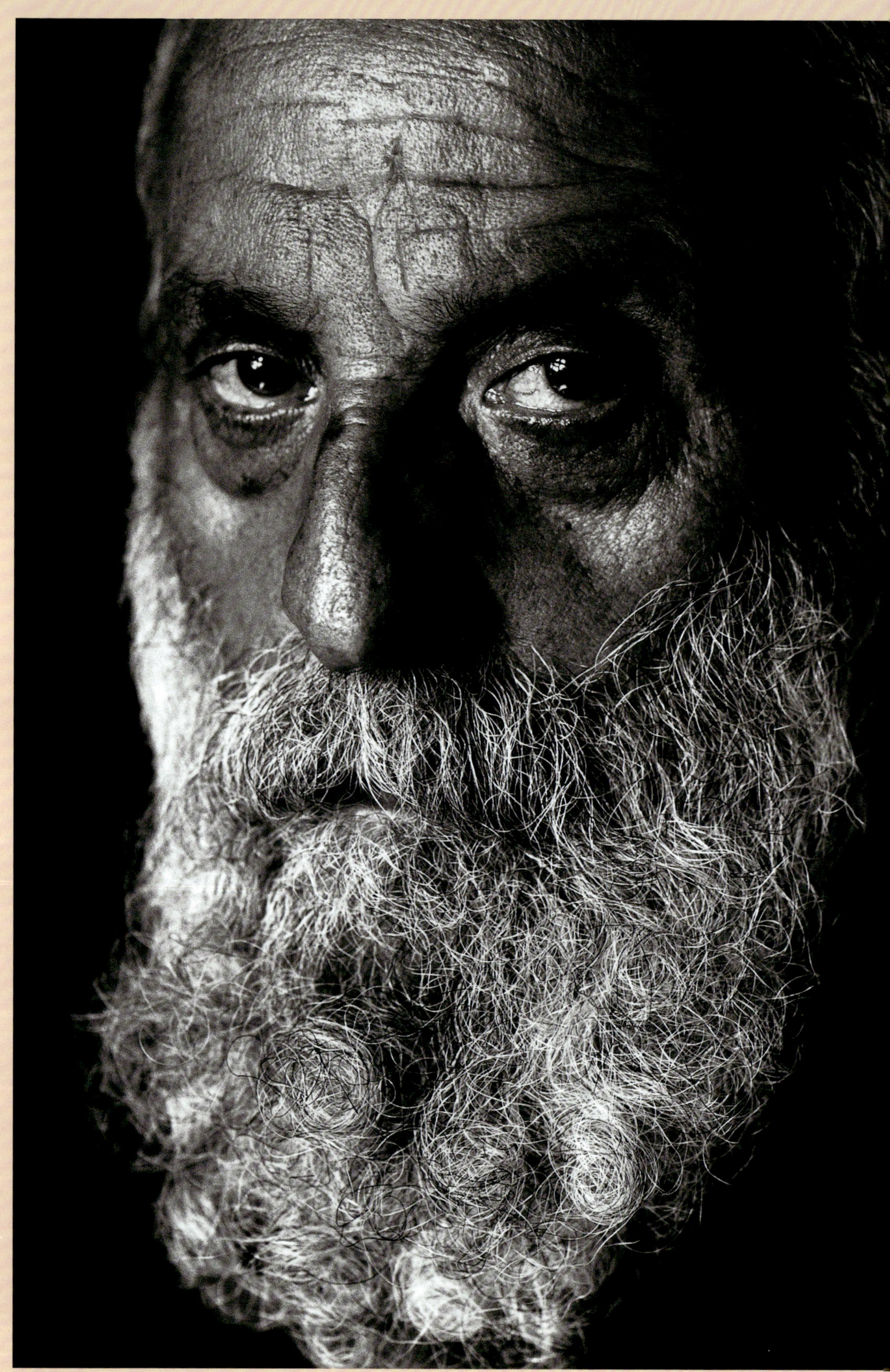

César photographed by Herb Ritts, Cahors, 1993

César

"The things I have made were not premeditated, they were lived." These were the words César spoke when reflecting on his artistic practice and relationship with salvaged materials, while working at the Bocquel art foundry in Normandy, finalizing a bronze sculpture, 5 meters high and 8 meters wide, commissioned by the Fondation Cartier. The year was 1992, and the monumental *Flying Frenchman* on which he was working would soon be offered to the city of Hong Kong by the Fondation Cartier.

César Baldaccini, born to Italian parents in 1921, in the working-class Belle de Mai district of Marseille, is one of the greatest contemporary sculptors. His unique work was evolved during the 1930s and 1940s while he was studying fine arts in Marseille, then in Paris. In the 1950s, the artist found his favorite material—scrap metal—which made him known throughout the world. Over the following three decades, he developed an interest in all types of materials, as long as they allowed him to give free rein to his inventiveness. Whether scrap metal, rubber, or plastic, César searched, welded, assembled, crushed, deformed, reduced, and enlarged. The irons, compressions, human imprints, and expansions he produced—sometimes criticized by institutional academicism, and yet often honored—were exhibited both in France and abroad.

In the early 1980s, Alain Dominique Perrin, President of Cartier and a close friend of César, wanted to establish a foundation aimed at protecting the rights of artists, who, like Cartier, were subject to the scourge of plagiarism and counterfeiting. He confided in César, who encouraged him to imagine a place allowing artists to create and exhibit, rather than purely focusing on the legal aspect. The artist introduced him to the Domaine du Montcel and its castle, located in Jouy-en-Josas, whose park was already home to a number of sculptures, including Arman's impressive *Long Term Parking* (1982). On October 20, 1984, following César's suggestion, Alain Dominique Perrin created the Fondation Cartier pour l'art contemporain on this vast estate, offering both exhibition spaces and artists' residencies. The inaugural exhibition, *Les Fers de César*, was devoted to the sculptor and was accompanied by two other exhibitions presenting the work of young visual artists, Lisa Milroy and Julian Opie.

From that point onward, thanks to the support of the Fondation Cartier, César was free to create. In 1983, he began the construction of his *Hommage à Eiffel* in the park: this monumental plaque, 18-meters-high and weighing 500 tons, and which would take six years to complete, was created from beams removed from the Eiffel Tower to light it. Between 1983 and 1985, he worked on an imposing hybrid being, the *Centaure ou Hommage à Picasso*, which was first installed in front of the Fondation Cartier in Jouy-en-Josas, then in 1988, in the 6th arrondissement of Paris, at the Carrefour de la Croix-Rouge, now Place Michel-Debré.

Exchanges between the Fondation Cartier and the artist continued, and in 1986, a new exhibition titled *Les Championnes de César* showcased his compressions of rally cars, produced the previous year at the suggestion of Jean Todt, then Director of Peugeot Talbot Sport. In 1989, he participated in the *Solex-nostalgie* exhibition, with his remarkable *Compression Solex* (1988) and in 1991, in *Too French*, presented first in Hong Kong and then in Tokyo.

In 1994, the Fondation Cartier left Jouy-en-Josas for Jean Nouvel's glass building on Boulevard Raspail in Paris. In 2008, ten years after César's death, it was the site of a major tribute exhibition, conceived and designed by Jean Nouvel. It brought together some one hundred pieces, featuring his iron bestiary, compressions, and imprints, including his emblematic *Pouce* (*Thumb*), in a range of sizes and materials. The exhibition, titled *César, Anthologie par Jean Nouvel*, reflected a life entirely dedicated to creation, and in the words of Alain Dominique Perrin, this was "an exhibition filled with emotion, love, friendship, and of course, tremendous respect" for this immense artist, a traveling companion of the Fondation Cartier for fifteen years.

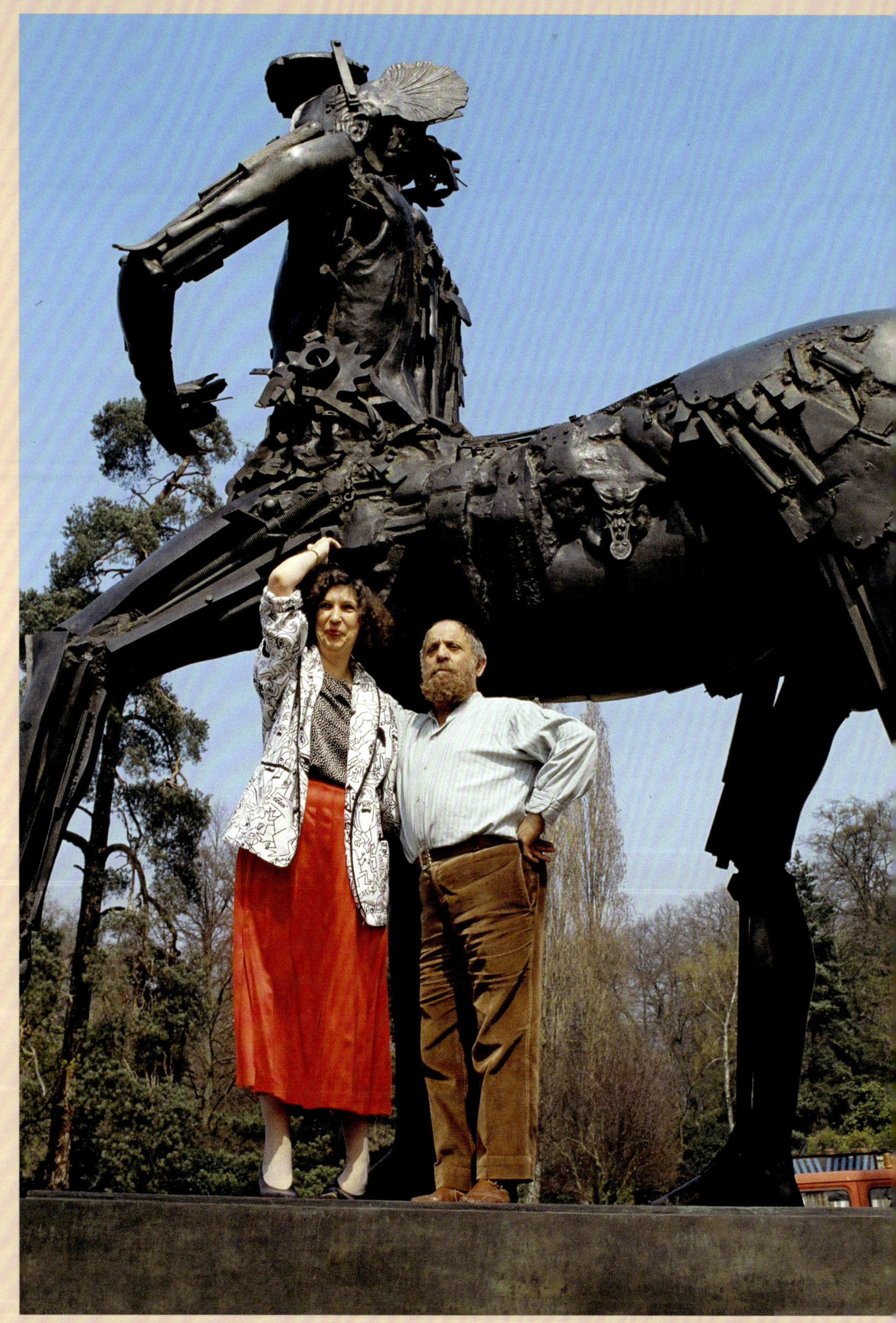

1987   April 16, the *Centaure ou Hommage à Picasso* by César (1983–1985)
was installed in the park of the Fondation Cartier at Jouy-en-Josas, in the presence
of Marie-Claude Beaud and the artist.

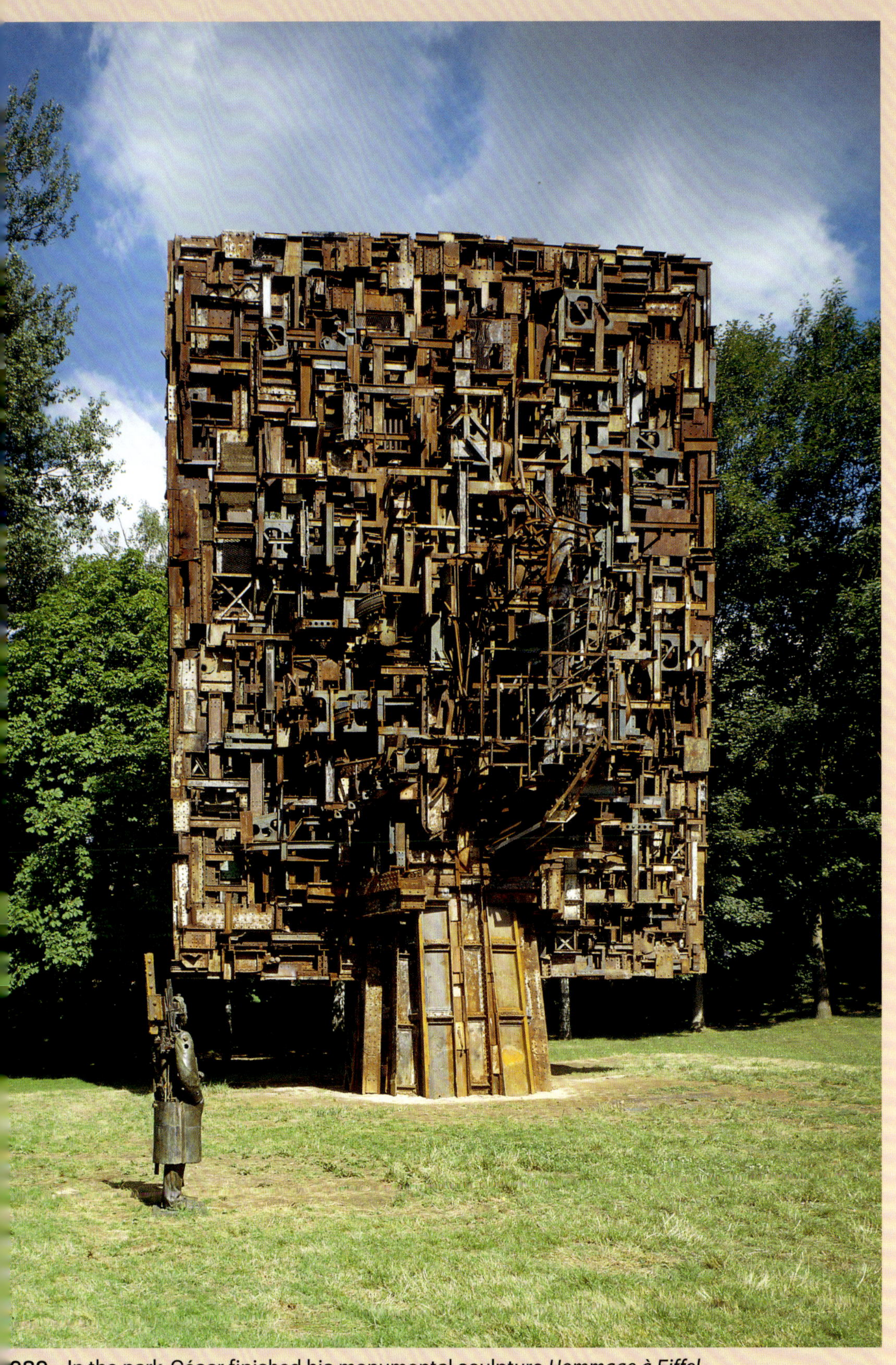

989   In the park, César finished his monumental sculpture *Hommage à Eiffel*, begun six years earlier, and made from fragments of the Eiffel Tower.

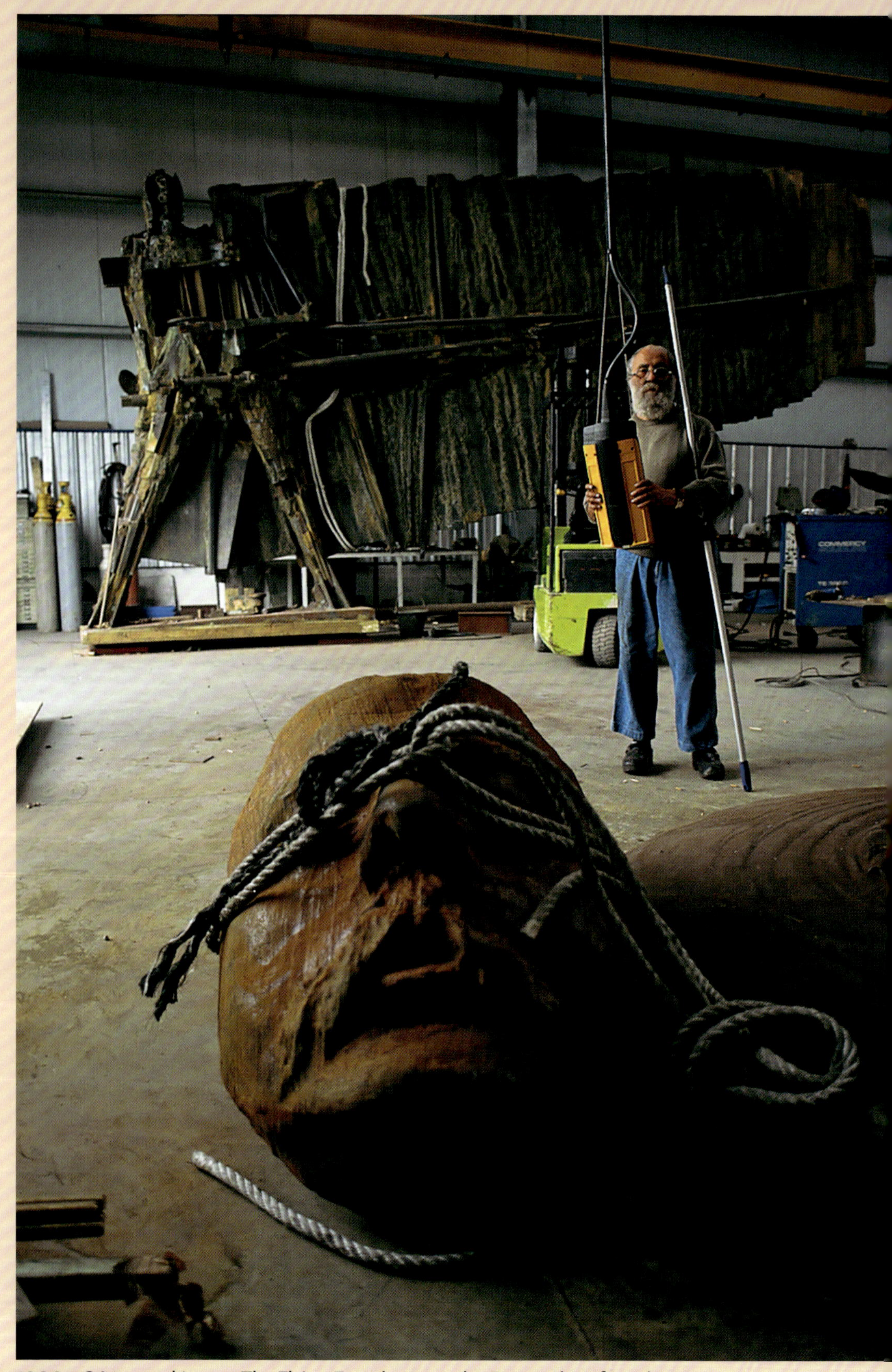

1990 César working on *The Flying Frenchman* at the Bocquel art foundry.

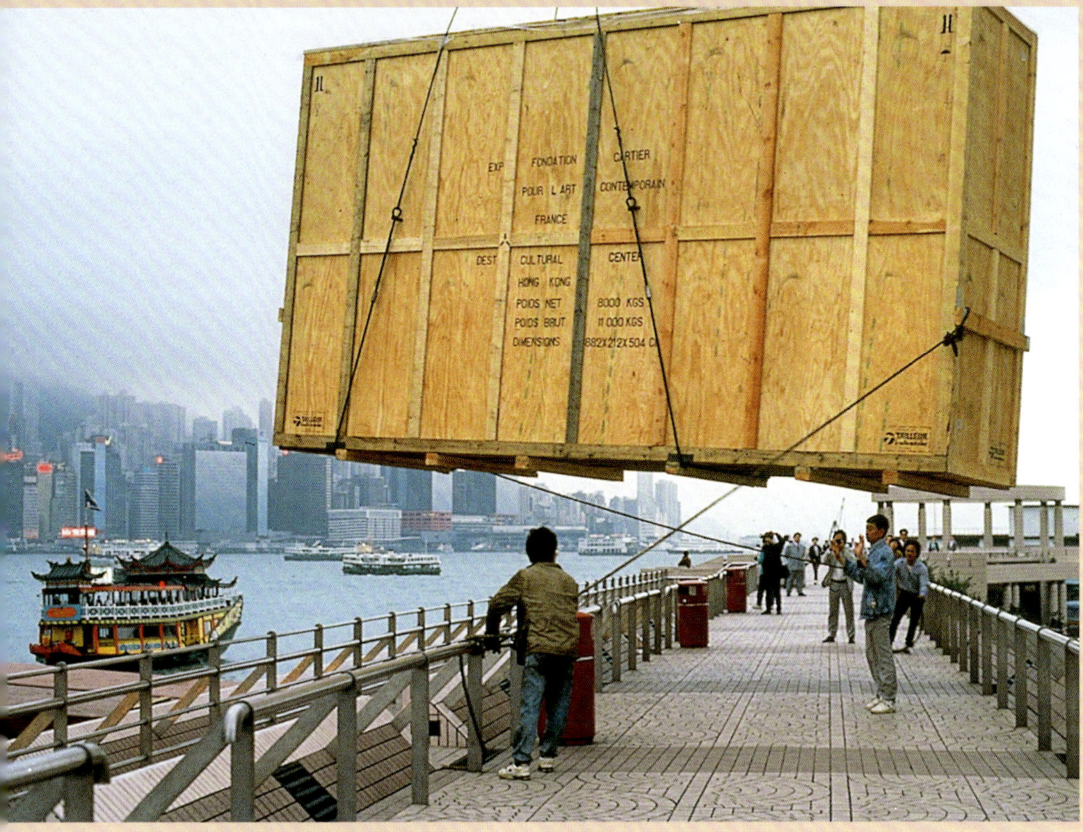

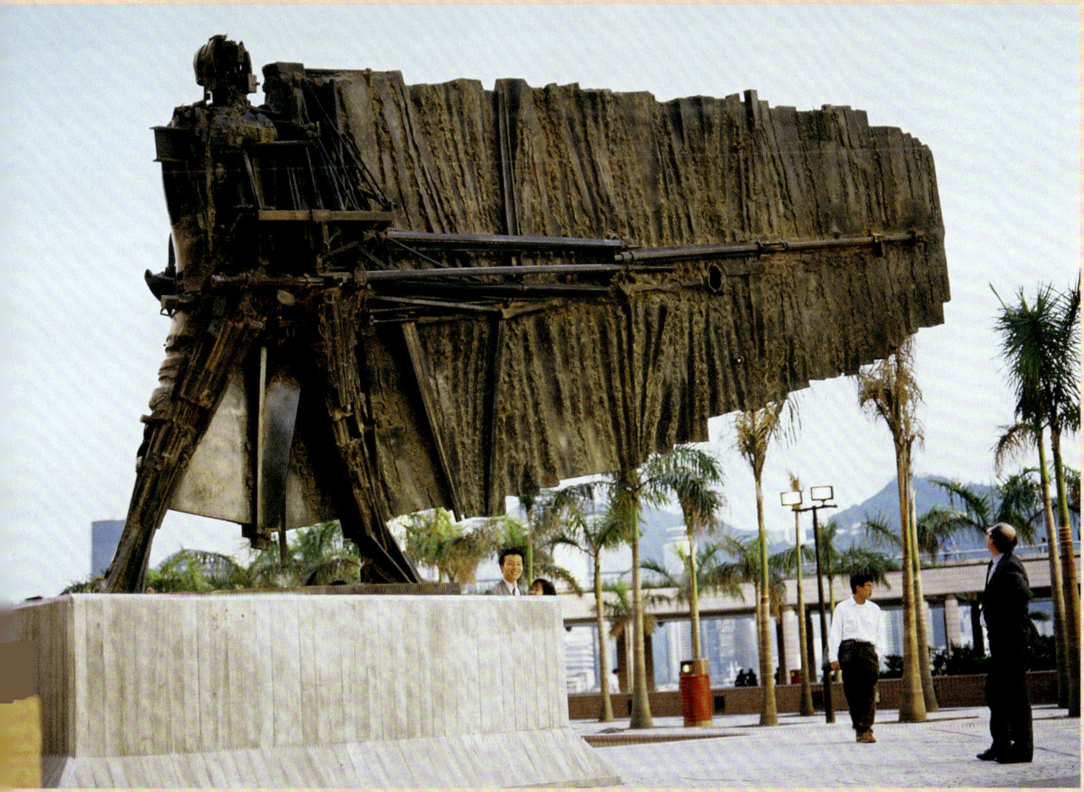

992 After being presented at the Petit Palais in Paris, the Fondation Cartier lifted the work to the city of Hong Kong.

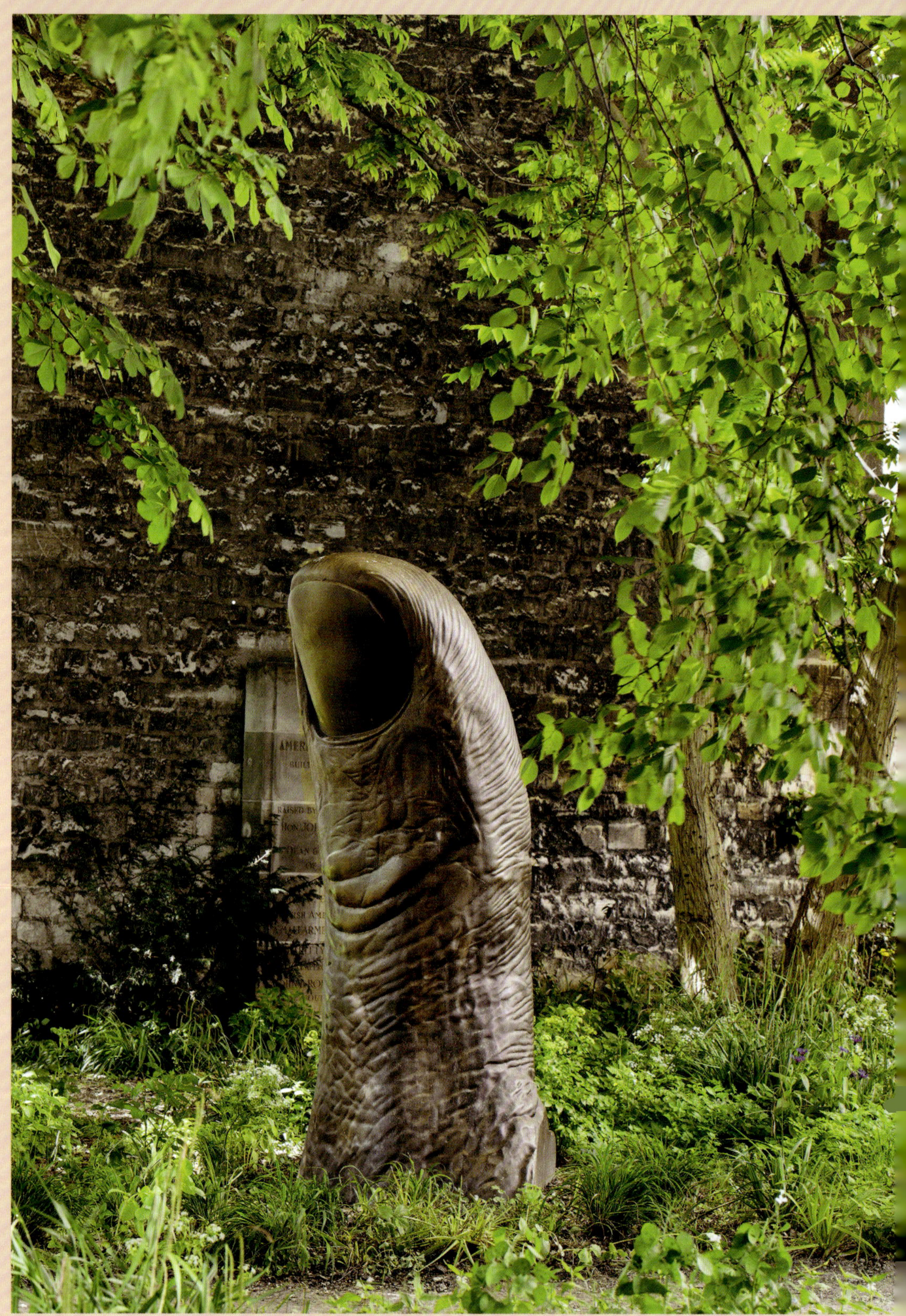

2008   Jean Nouvel was invited to select an ensemble of César's works and showcase them in an exhibition paying tribute to the artist, with whom the Fondation Cartier had collaborated for fifteen years. For the occasion, the *Pouce* (1964–1966), which had been shown in the park at Jouy-en-Josas, was installed in the Fondation Cartier's garden.

VOIR VENIR

Emanuele Coccia
Philosopher

EXPOSE/EXPLODE

Exposing the accident

In the winter of 2002, visitors entering the Fondation Cartier pour l'art contemporain were treated to an unexpected sight: nine hundred filiform aluminum tubes protruding from metal grids which spread across the floor following unpredictable trajectories, as if a major accident had just occurred in the exhibition spaces. As if the glass and steel building designed by Jean Nouvel had suddenly collapsed, and the ceiling had crashed to the floor. But the feeling of being confronted by an unforeseen event was quickly dispelled. This was *The Fall* (2002) by Lebbeus Woods, the centerpiece of the *Unknown Quantity* exhibition, conceived by Hervé Chandès, the Director of the Fondation Cartier, and designed by philosopher and urban planner Paul Virilio.[1] Far from being accidental, it was a planned and deliberate collapse. "The building's spatial system—a rectilinear 3-D grid—descends," reads the exhibition catalogue. "Let us say, for the purposes of understanding the hypothesis, that the exhibition space suddenly collapses, as the ceiling falls down toward the floor."[2]

[1] The exhibition *Unknown Quantity*, which opened in November 2002 in the building of the Fondation Cartier on Boulevard Raspail in Paris, was conceived by Paul Virilio to launch a rational reflection on accidents, their genesis, and their accumulation, in the face of the blindness brought about by the speed of technical progress.
[2] Lebbeus Woods, "The Fall," in *Unknown Quantity* (Paris: Fondation Cartier pour l'art contemporain, 2002), pp. 153–154.

Emanuele Coccia

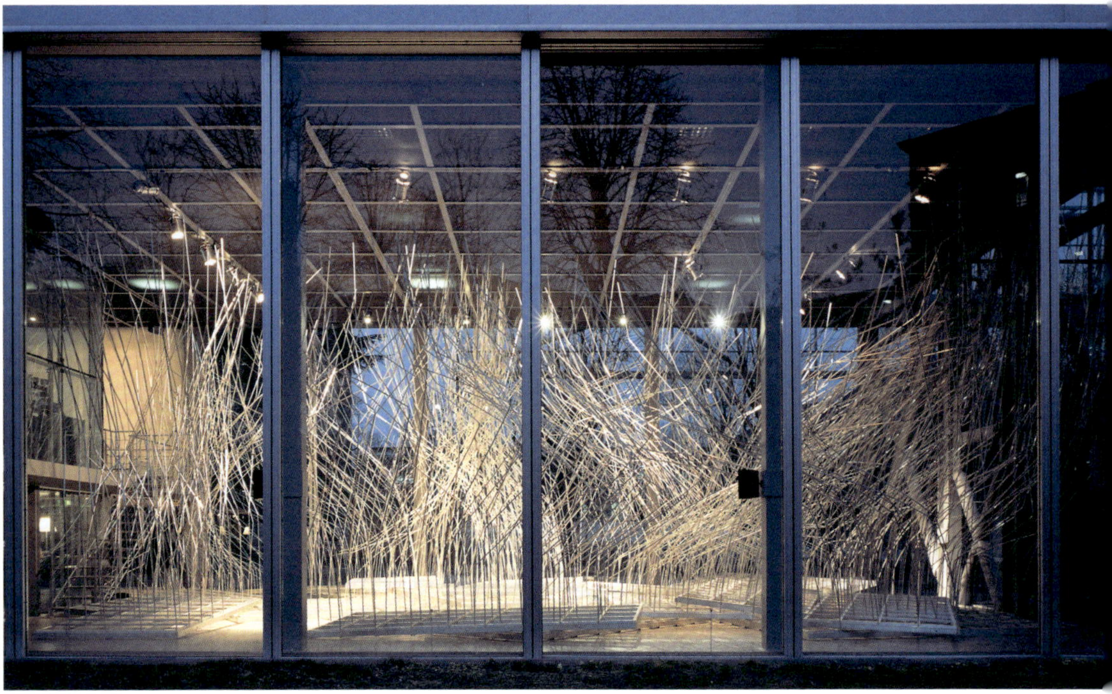

Lebbeus Woods, *The Fall*, 2002. View of the exhibition *Unknown Quantity*, 2002

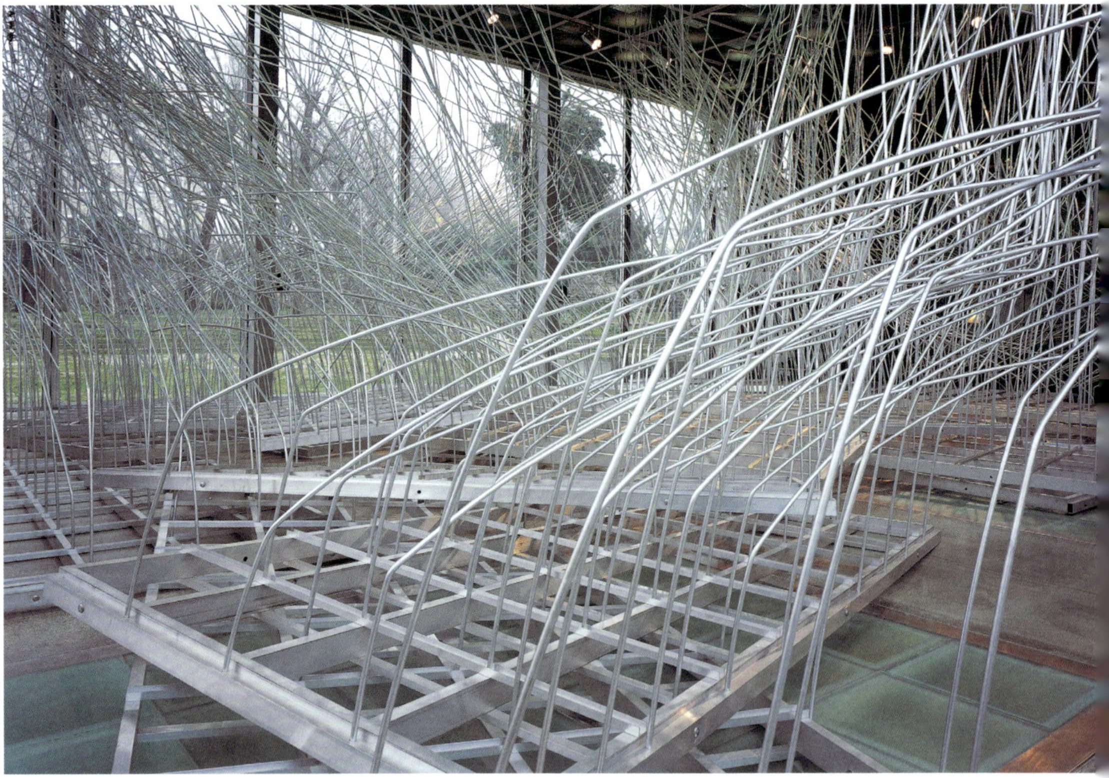

Lebbeus Woods, *The Fall* (detail), 2002

This was the hypothesis of Lebbeus Woods, the renowned American architect and heterodox artist who, a decade earlier, had declared war on everyone and everything in a pamphlet that caused quite a stir. "I am at war with my time, with history, with all authority that resides in fixed and frightened forms."[3] The ruins of the Foundation, exploded into forms that dissolve in the air—"in their descent, the downward trajectories of the grid have become idiosyncratic"[4]—seem to illustrate his most radical thesis: "Architecture and war are not incompatible. Architecture is war. War is architecture."[5] Yet the motive for this conflict and its real target were immediately clear. Why had the war against architecture turned into a war against the museum and the very idea of exhibition space? Admittedly, the Fondation Cartier, a pioneering institution of private patronage in Europe, founded in 1984 by Alain Dominique Perrin, is no ordinary target in this respect: it has always considered architecture to be one of the primary expressions of contemporary art, positioning architectural commissions as one of the main vectors for thinking about exhibitions. But why should fighting architecture mean attacking it when it becomes an exhibition space?

While the intentions may not have been clear, nothing was left to chance: the trajectories of the tubes were carefully calculated, the collapse having been hypothesized as a simple acceleration of the ordinary state, allowing Lebbeus Woods to know that "the collapse of the exhibition space takes less than two seconds. Too fast to see, no doubt, but not at all too fast to conceptualize."[6] In short, the very process of the fall could neither be perceived nor thought about. It could only be imagined: "This is the time-space of the fall—too brief to inhabit—except in imagination."[7]

3 Lebbeus Woods, "War and Architecture," *Pamphlet Architecture 15* (1993): p. 1.
4 Woods, "The Fall," p. 154.
5 Woods, "War and Architecture," p. 1.
6 "Gravity is nothing more nor less than acceleration, induced by the attraction of masses. In this case, the attraction is manifest at 32 feet per second [9.8 meters]. In the first second, the ceiling of the exhibition space falls 16 feet [4.9 meters] towards the floor. After the next second, it would be some 25 feet [7.6 meters] below the floor, well into the building's many basements. The ceiling structures of the basements slow down the building's fall, as the upper floors meet the resistance of the subterranean structure." Woods, "The Fall," pp. 153–154.
7 Ibid.

There is something extremely paradoxical about wanting to subject audiences to the obligation of imagining the destruction of the museum space through visual suggestion. It has often been said that by the beginning of the twentieth century, with El Lissitzky's *Cabinet of Abstraction* (1926–1928) and Ludwig Mies van der Rohe and Lilly Reich's Barcelona Pavilion (1929), the exhibition space had itself become an exhibition object.[8] Lebbeus Woods seemed to want to bring this period to a close by inverting it: the museum space must now exhibit its own ruins, stage its own end. It would be naïve to see this as a lazy attempt to transform the museum's end into a work of art. Rather, what visitors saw before them was a kind of visual demonstration of a new museographic principle: the *more geometrico* affirmation of the exhibition's superiority over its container, evidence of the disparity of forces between an exhibition and its site, between the art on display and the institution housing it. The Fondation Cartier seemed to be offering the spectacle of museums' manifest powerlessness in the face of what was possible within them as a response to the extensive debate about the museum as a disciplinary institution.[9] If the glass and steel shell is unable to withstand what is shown, it is because the imbalance is not simply architectural but metaphysical: the exhibition questions the very substance of its location and its institution. It is, after all, the enunciation of an unprecedented poetics of the museum: a true exhibition requires the art to explode that which exhibits and contains it. Adhering to this poetics, as the Fondation Cartier has done since its inception, means being compelled to reconstruct constantly, exhibition after exhibition, event after event. What is an institution that accepts it cannot survive the exhibitions it hosts and is thus forced to perpetually rethink and reimagine itself, including from an architectural point of view?

8 See for example Beatriz Colomina, "The Museum After Art," in *Now-Tomorrow-Flux: An Anthology on the Museum of Contemporary Art* (Zurich: JRP Ringier, 2017) and *Manifesto Architecture: The Ghost of Mies* (London: Sternberg Press, 2014).

9 See for example Tony Bennett, *The Birth of the Museum: History, Theory, Politics* (London: Routledge, 1995); Tony Bennett, "The Exhibitionary Complex," in *Thinking about Exhibitions* (London: Routledge, 1996); Douglas Crimp, *On The Museum's Ruins* (Cambridge, IL: MIT Press, 1995).

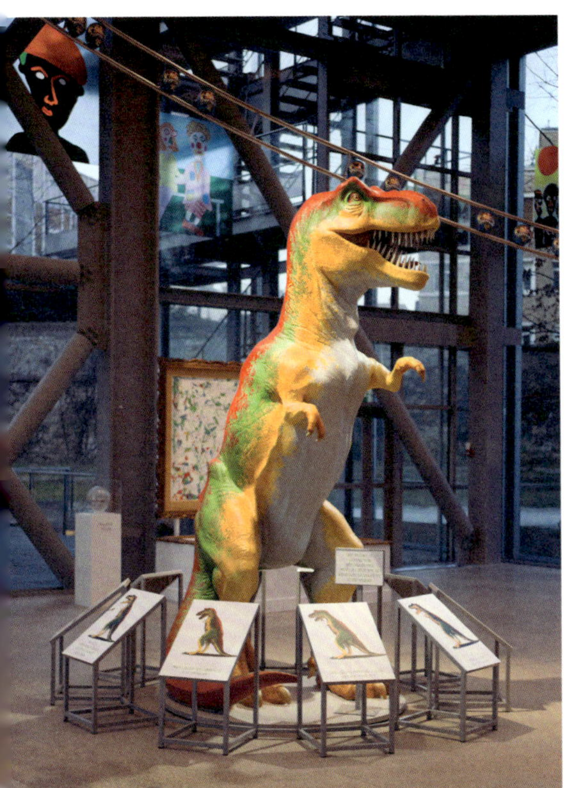

The T-Rex in the exhibition *Beat Takeshi Kitano, Gosse de peintre*, 2010

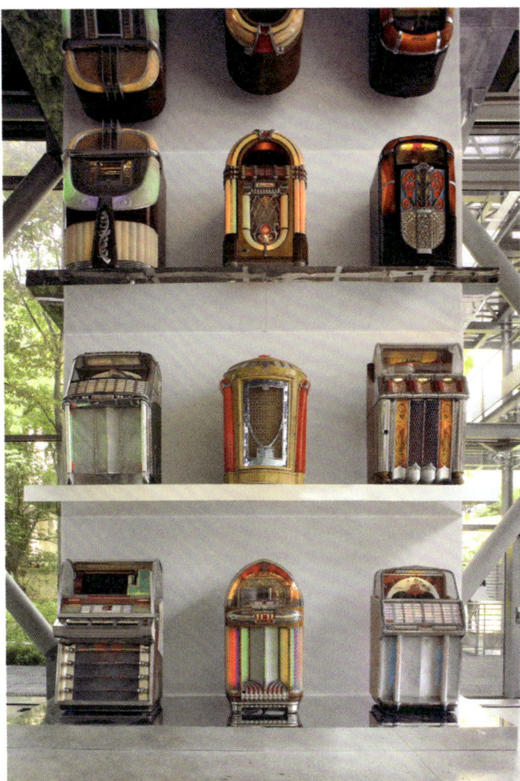

Jukeboxes in the exhibition *Rock'n'Roll 39–59*, 2007

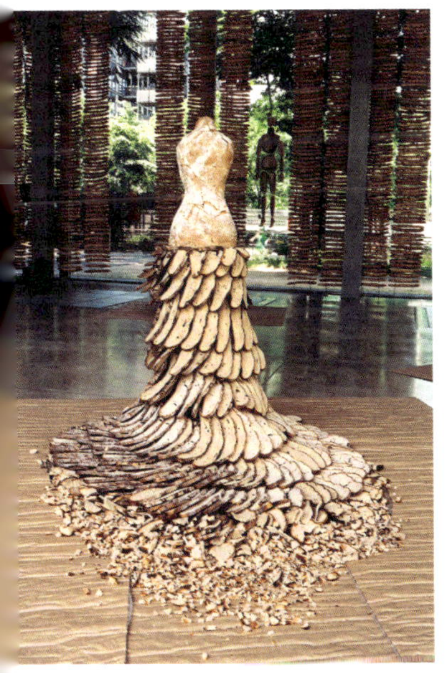

Bread dresses in *Pain Couture* by Jean Paul Gaultier, 2004

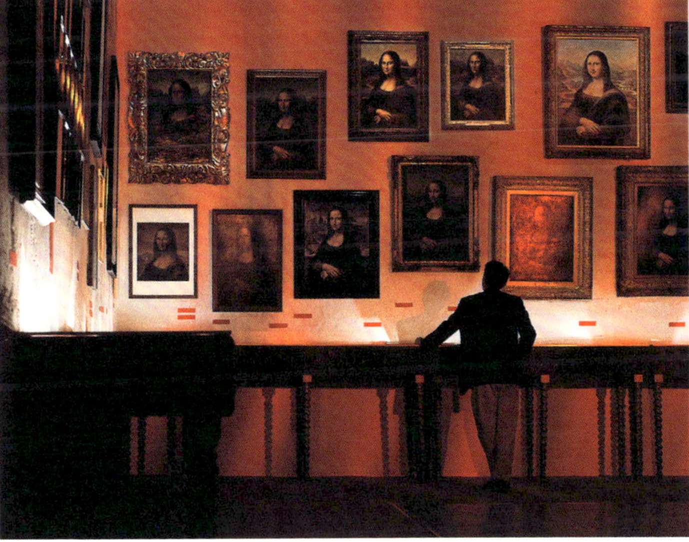

Fake *Mona Lisas* in the exhibition *Vraiment faux*, 1988

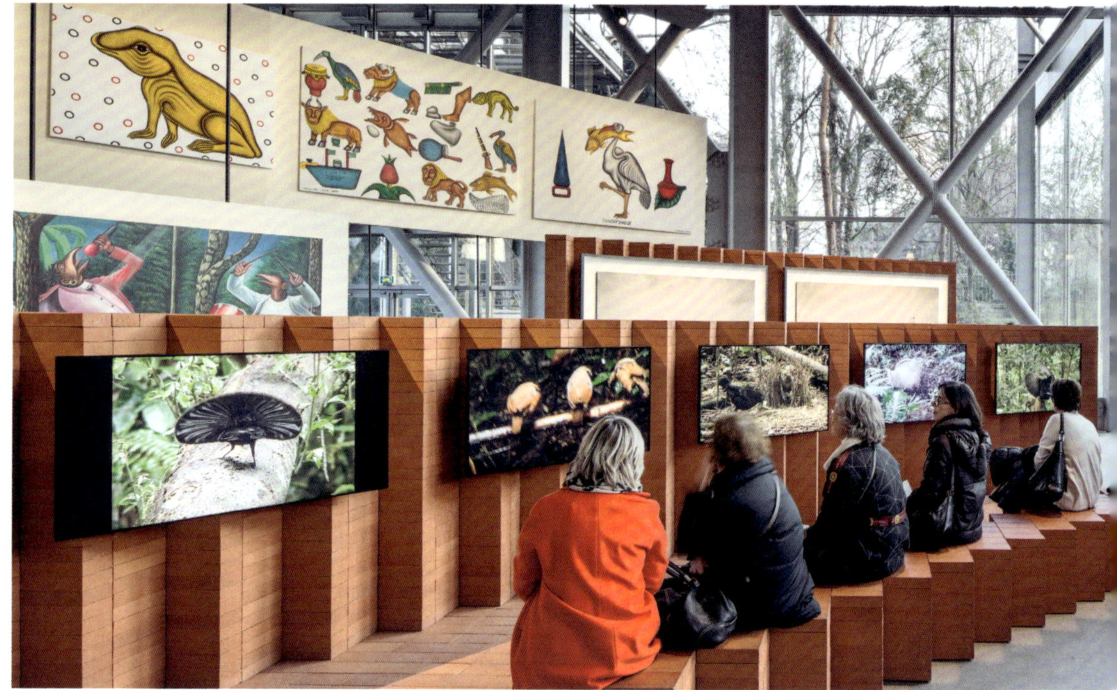

View of the exhibition *The Great Animal Orchestra*, 2016

Firstly, in its relationship with its architectural identity, the Fondation Cartier, as we shall see, seems to be trying to embody several ambitions: to become an institution whose objective is the very explosion of the idea of the museum, of tradition, of the collection. Subjects of its exhibitions include cars (*Hommage à Ferrari*[10]), jukeboxes (*Rock'n'Roll 39–59*[11]), bread sculptures (*Pain Couture by Jean Paul Gaultier*[12]), and fake paintings (*Vraiment faux*[13]). Sometimes it's not even objects that are exhibited, but animal

10 In 1987, the Fondation Cartier, then located at the Domaine du Montcel in Jouy-en-Josas, presented an exhibition paying tribute to Enzo Ferrari. Andrée Putman displayed fifty Ferrari cars in the Fondation's exhibition spaces and its grounds.

11 *Rock'n'Roll 39–59*, presented in 2007, was devoted to the genesis and early years of rock'n'roll in the United States. Presenting objects related to the era's musical culture—radios, microphones, pickup trucks, jukeboxes, and of course the Cadillac, the symbol of social success so prized by rockers—the exhibition showcased the design of the Golden Fifties.

12 In 2004, the Fondation Cartier invited Jean Paul Gaultier to transform its exhibition spaces: in collaboration with several bakers, winners of the Meilleurs Ouvriers de France, awarded to the best craftspeople, the designer created and exhibited dresses made from bread and opened a real bakery in the Fondation's basement, where baguettes were produced each day and sold on site.

13 From forgery to counterfeiting, copying, and republishing, *Vraiment faux* (1988) presented typical examples of forgeries. This wide selection was brought together with the help of official institutions, companies, and rights-holders who had been victims of counterfeiting.

Voir venir

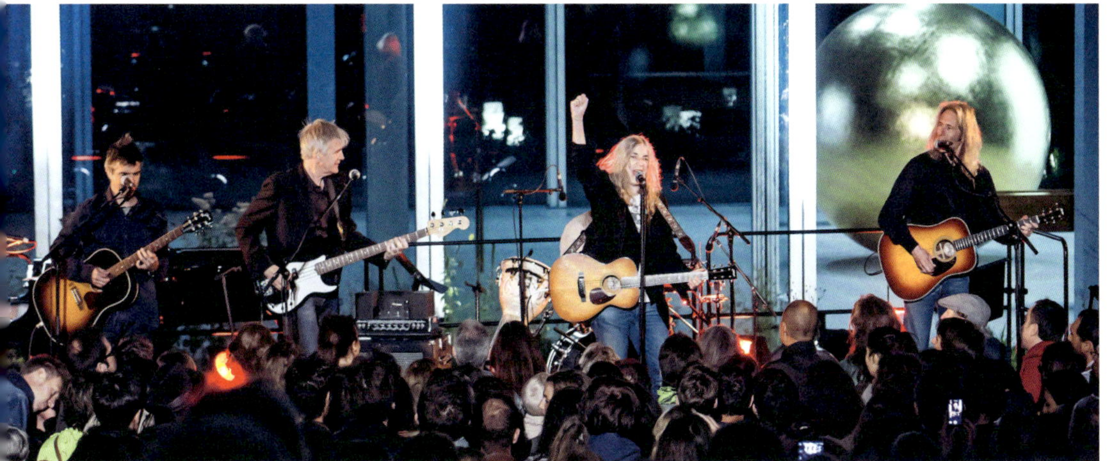

Concert by Patti Smith, *Six Vowels, Green*, September 10, 2014

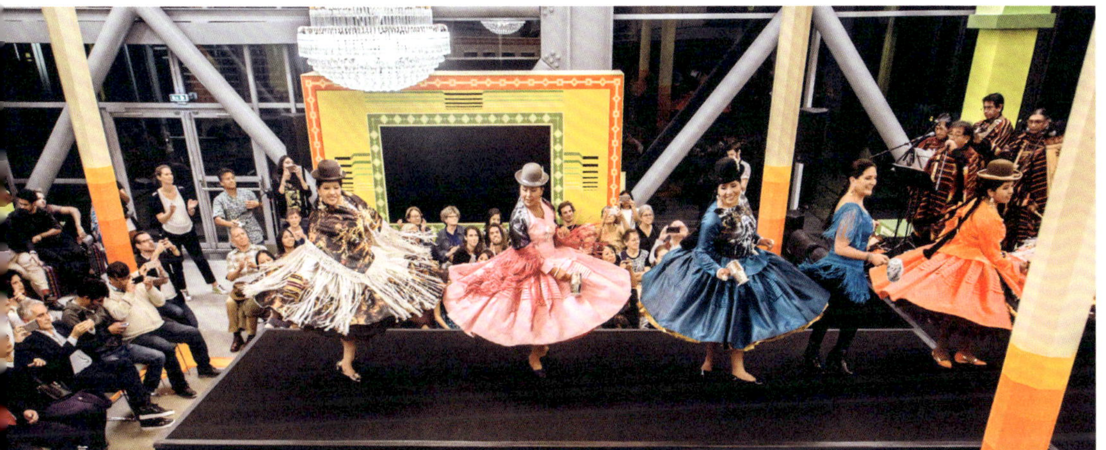

Nomadic Night with Freddy Mamani, Ana Palza, and La Chola Paceña, *Andean Festival*, October 15, 2018

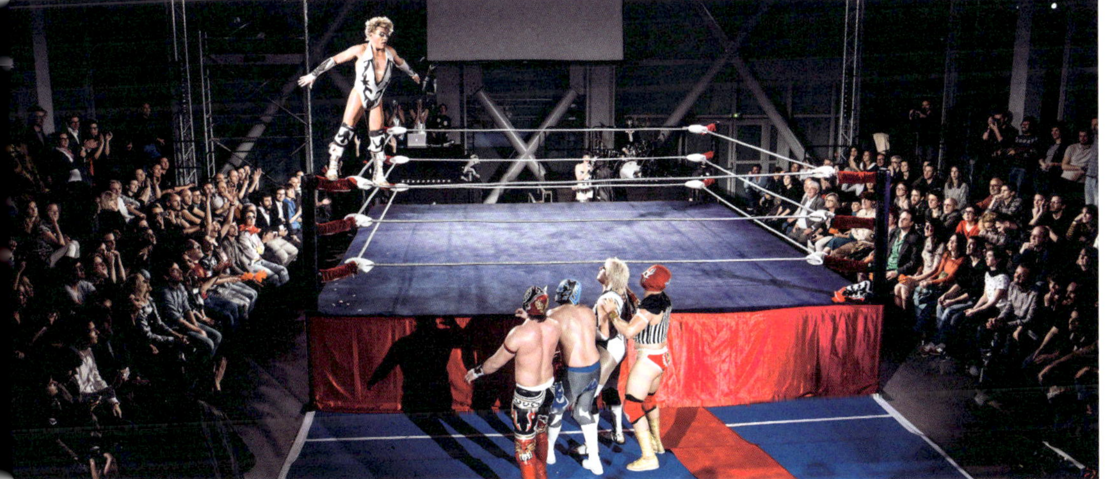

Nomadic Night with Cassandro, El Exotico, a proposal from Marie Losier, November 3, 2014

songs (*The Great Animal Orchestra*[14]), folk choirs, or performances.
The museum must be ready to find art where people least expect it.
And each time, these encounters transform the nature of the place,
transforming its meaning entirely. For example, during the Jean
Paul Gaultier exhibition in 2004, the Fondation was transformed
into a bakery; in 2016, *The Great Animal Orchestra* exhibition was
a kind of intangible zoo. In 2002, *Unknown Quantity* formulated
a principle, in abstract terms and as a "discourse on method"
that the Fondation Cartier has practiced over its forty-year history:
to make the exhibition the apparatus that enables the liberation
of art, that emancipates it from any principle of confinement to an
ideal or a place. This principle implies a curious form of physical
and architectural precariousness of the exhibition space.

The chameleon museum

In 1994, shortly after the inauguration of the building designed
by Jean Nouvel, Raymond Hains exhibited a series of emblematic
photographs documenting the end of the renovation and restoration
work on the Grand Louvre a few months earlier.[15] There was
an obvious irony in showing the oldest and most ambitious
encyclopedic museum in the West as an open-air building site.
Far from being the embodiment of an eternal ideal, or a supposed
monument to the global history of art, the museum seemed
to be admitting its partial, incomplete, artificial nature, forced
to constantly reconstruct itself by changing its face or its skin.
Open to the accidents of history, the museum tends to become
a work in itself, no more singular, eternal, or immense than those
it houses, and therefore incapable of protecting them or making
them accessible to others. But this is the architectural expression
of a much deeper metaphysical instability. Surrendering to the power

14 *The Great Animal Orchestra* (2016) centered on the work of American musician and bioacoustician Bernie
Krause, who has captured the sounds of over 15,000 animal species in their natural habitats. Bringing together
artists from all over the world, the exhibition invited visitors to immerse themselves in an aesthetic meditation,
both sonic and visual, on an animal world that is increasingly under threat.
15 In May 1994, the Fondation Cartier opened on Boulevard Raspail. The exhibition *Raymond Hains, Les 3 Cartier.
Du Grand Louvre aux 3 Cartier* was held from September of that same year.

of what you exhibit ultimately means being prepared to give up your own name, your own identity, your own substance: a museum that has no more power than the objects it exhibits is forced to beg them for these attributes.

Some Raymond Hains's photographs of this series were shown in *Les 3 Cartier. Du Grand Louvre aux 3 Cartier* exhibition. With this title, the exhibition produced a cognitive confusion: through an interplay of homophonies and analogies, visitors were invited to find the name of the exhibition venue — the Fondation Cartier — in objects that were far removed from each other in their nature, medium, or geographical and historical origin, referring to different and incompatible identities: "The 3 Cartier refers to Jacques Cartier, the man who reached Canada, in 1534, the Saga of the Cartiers, Jacques Cartier, in whose London office General de Gaulle wrote his famous rallying speech of June 18, 1940, and the Parisian store Aux 3 Quartiers ['quartier,' meaning neighborhood, is pronounced the same as 'Cartier'], whose name comes from a stage comedy."[16]

The semantic drift that destroys the arbitrary yet immutable link between a signifier and a signified was a common practice in twentieth-century art, from the Dada movement to Marcel Broodthaers. But whereas Broodthaers applied it to the very idea of a work of art, Hains's goal seems to have been the revealing of the impossibility of fixing the place and name of the institution hosting his exhibition once and for all, not only spatially but also, and above all, cognitively and epistemologically. It was not a matter of questioning the museum's identity, in the manner of institutional criticism,[17] but of multiplying it indefinitely, to the point of rendering it coextensive with the world as a whole. Rather than making the museum unrecognizable, Raymond Hains preferred to identify it with each of the objects it houses, and then to make each of them the homophonic equivalent of a thousand others:

16 Hervé Chandès, "Extra-Muros," in *Les 3 Cartier. Du Grand Louvre aux 3 Cartier* (Paris: Fondation Cartier pour l'art contemporain, 1994), p. 7.
17 See the famous anthology edited by Alexander Alberro and Blake Stimson, *Institutional Critique: An Anthology of Artists' Writings* (Cambridge: MIT Press, 2011).

it is no longer just the architecture of the museum that is exploded, but the very concept of it. Indeed, it is as if the museum allows the artist to manipulate it so as to become inextricably linked to one or other of his conceptual works, to become clay in the hands of a creator. Here again, the exhibition seems to embody a poetic principle: in contrast to the impermeability of the white cube,[18] which seems to absorb nothing of what is exhibited, here the site is drawn to the object on display to the point of taking on its name. Unlike the Duchampian readymade, it is not the museum that decrees the artistic status of the exhibited object, but rather the object itself that renames its host.

The things that are exhibited literally give meaning to the institution's name, which is why this meaning changes regularly. It is the reason the institution is forced to migrate from object to object in order to give meaning to its name, the consequence of which is that after each exhibition, the institution completely loses its memory. There is no history of the meanings its name has carried, as if it had no age; it is as if the museum were being successively baptized for the first time.

Having no name other than that conferred by what is exhibited means forcing oneself, in order to survive, to look for synonyms for the infinite number of things that have transformed this space into a museum. This is not just a logical reversal that overwrites the container over the content, or the whole over its parts. It is also, and above all, an aesthetic prohibition. If it is only by seeking meaning in what it houses that the signifier "Fondation Cartier" becomes synonymous with museum, then it becomes impossible to claim to know what art is before encountering it within oneself, within the unstable and fragile perimeter of one's own space. Everything depends on the contingency of these encounters. No definition is possible outside of them. One might say that the history of the Fondation Cartier has been a long, tireless search

18 The term "white cube" refers to a windowless, white-walled space, which has become the archetypal exhibition space for contemporary art since the 1970s.

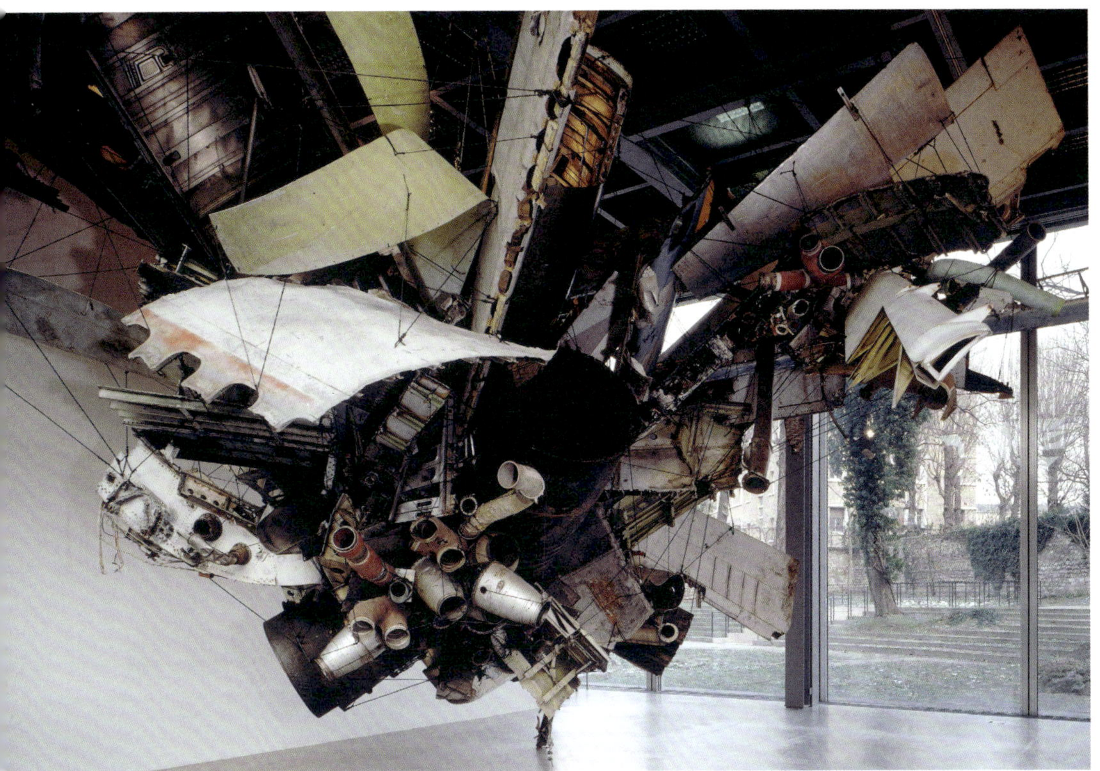

ancy Rubins, *MoMA & Airplane Parts*, 1995. View of the exhibition *Unknown Quantity*, 2002

for forms of homophony and synonymy for the very idea of art: an endless quest to find aesthetic meaning in progressively different and incomparable objects, an absolute and total openness toward objects, formats, performances, and events in which the meaning of art might once again resonate, without ever being capable of stating the idea of a preestablished ideal, without ever knowing what will happen in the next exhibition. And more than anything else, without ever being able to transform the past into a criterion of choice: the Fondation Cartier is a chameleon that systematically identifies with what it exhibits; no previous experience can be equated with any future identification.

Overexposing the city

Making the exhibition the site of a physical and conceptual
destruction of the museum apparatus is not without consequences.
The operation means striking at the heart of the experience of the
contemporary city. Reflections on urban planning, from Walter
Benjamin to Rem Koolhaas, Friedrich Kittler, and Giuliana Bruno,
have often emphasized the way in which European cities became
modern with the instigation of the exhibition (initially embodied
in shop windows and the Universal Expositions) as their structuring
principle. More than technical, formal, or material innovations,
it was the possibility of accelerating and intensifying sensory
life that freed the urban space from any attachment to the past.
Every exhibition is simply a means to multiply sensory life.
Transforming itself into a kind of open-air museum of reality,
the modern city has made its inhabitants receivers of an absolutely
unprecedented quantity of stimuli, who, as Charles Baudelaire
remarked, are to be able "to see the world, to be at the centre of the
world, and yet to remain hidden from the world," just like "the lover
of pictures who lives in a magical society of dreams painted on
canvas." In this way, the "lover of universal life" enters the city
"as though it were an immense reservoir of electrical energy."[19]
Later, Georg Simmel revisited Baudelaire's insight, seeing the
coincidence between the city and the museum as "creating in the
sensory foundations of mental life, and in the degree of awareness
necessitated by our organization as creatures dependent on
differences, a deep contrast with the slower, more habitual,
more smoothly flowing rhythm of the sensory-mental phase of
small town and rural existence." This "intensification of nervous
stimulation which results from the swift and uninterrupted change
of our outer and inner stimuli"[20] is not the result of demographic,
objective, and spatial multiplication. It is first and foremost

19 Charles Baudelaire, "The Painter of Modern Life," in *The Painter of Modern Life and Other Essays*,
trans. Jonathan Mayne (London: Phaidon Press Ltd., 1964), p. 9.
20 Georg Simmel, "The Metropolis and Mental Life," in *The Sociology of Georg Simmel*, trans. Kurt H. Wolff
(Glencoe, IL: The Free Press, 1950), p. 410.

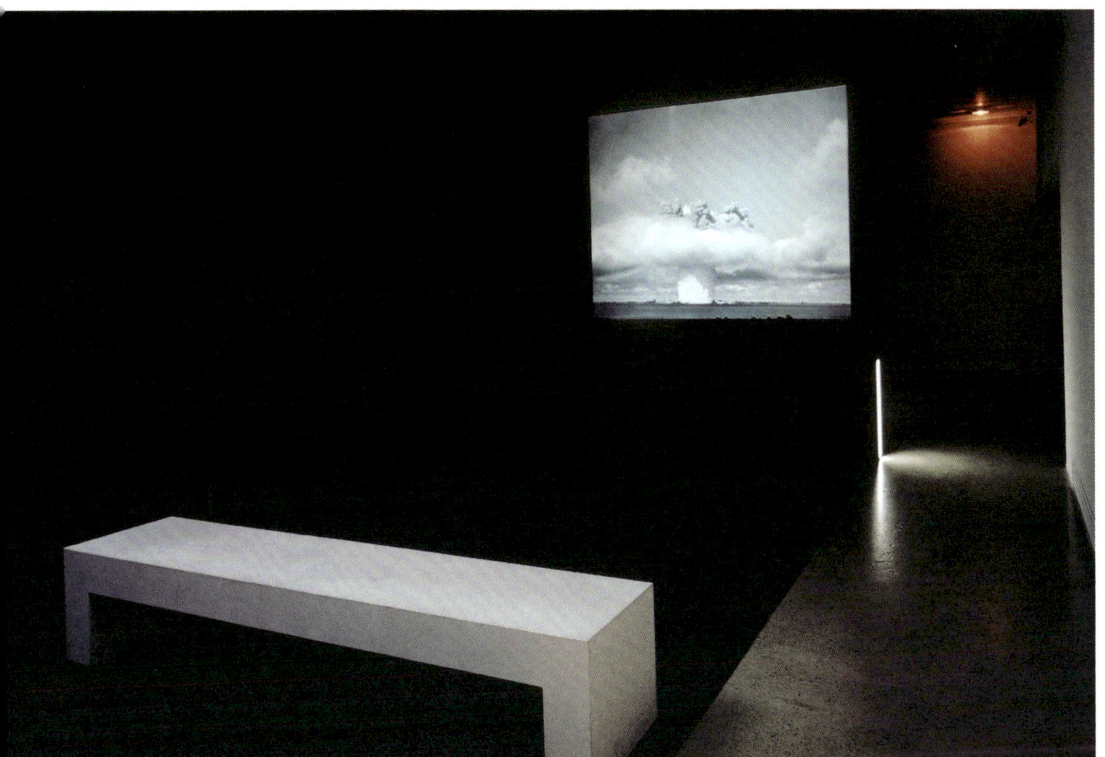

ruce Conner, *A Movie*, 1958. View of the exhibition *Unknown Quantity*, 2002

a torsion by which everything in the city is a permanent object of sensory perception. In the city, everything is shown, heard, smelled, and tasted—this is the hallmark of modern metropolitan existence.

From this point of view, the destruction staged in *Unknown Quantity* in 2002 at the Fondation Cartier was a kind of radicalization of this urban logic: collapsing the museum in order to liberate sensory life. In the rooms adjacent to the Lebbeus Woods installation were the remains of crumpled planes by Nancy Rubins;[21] on the floor below, several video works seemed to extend the destruction to the whole of the urban space: Dominic Angerame filmed the demolition of San Francisco's Embarcadero Freeway in 1991,[22] Peter Hutton captured the destructive force of fire and the life of a city exposed to the most violent weather,[23] while the 1967

21 Nancy Rubins, *MoMA & Airplane Parts* (1995).
22 Dominic Angerame, *In the Course of Human Events* (1997).
23 Peter Hutton, *New York Portrait: Chapter Two* (1980–1981).

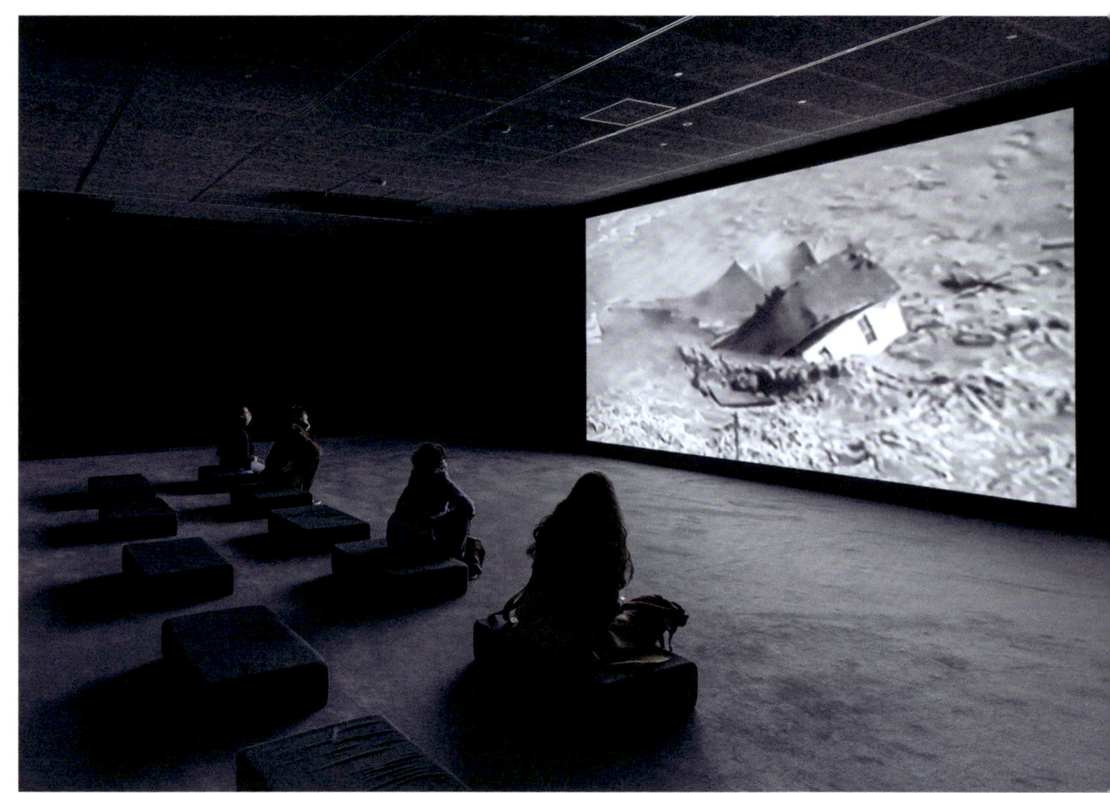

Artavazd Pelechian, *La Nature*, 2020

documentary *Et maintenant Agadir* explores the destruction wrought by the earthquake that struck the Moroccan town in 1960. In other instances, destruction was staged in a more allegorical way: the thousands of pieces of paper littering the streets of Manhattan after a military parade in *Little Flags* by Jem Cohen (2000) or the lost gaze of traders experiencing a stock market crash in *Middlemen* by Aernout Mik (2001). In Bruce Conner's famous *A Movie* (1958), destruction takes on both comic and cosmic forms. Other installations, such as those by Wolfgang Staehle, Moira Tierney, Jonas Mekas, and Tony Oursler, focused on destruction at its most radical: the attack on the Twin Towers in New York on September 11, 2001.

The city and the entire world are burning, and art is the cause, manifestation, and witness. Art must now free the city from its shell and distill it into its purest form: the inferno of events, the explosion of current affairs. It is as if the museum, or the exhibition space, had to accompany and radicalize a tropism specific to the city, something Paul Virilio had begun to reflect on as early as the 1980s: "The figure of the city has faded, dissipated … to the point where it is little more than a memory, a reminder of the neighborhood unit that has continued to suffer the repercussions of the mutation of mass media."[24] With the development of digital technologies, the city is gradually freeing itself from geographical and mineral space, and "the urban form is no longer designated by a dividing line between here and elsewhere."[25] It is as if extension were accompanied by another immaterial dimension in which sensory life unfolds, "a thickness without thickness, a volume without volume, an imperceptible quantity."[26] The urban landscape multiplies and thickens, but "deprived of objective boundaries, the architectonic element begins to drift and float, in an electronic ether, devoid of spatial dimensions but inscribed in the singular temporality of an instantaneous diffusion."[27] Increasingly, the city is a transformation of reality's metaphysical framework, replacing space with time, the tendency toward proximity with a tropism in the direction of absolute simultaneity. Communication is less a figure of space than an intensity of time. The speed of communication cancels out distance and history. As Virilio writes, it allows us "to close the gap between physics and metaphysics":[28] more than a quantitative measure of the capacity to move in space (and therefore to cancel out its reality and reach), it becomes the threshold at which space becomes a pure modality of time. The contemporary city is no more than a perennial observatory of the disappearance of geometric space. It is no longer about living next to one another, but about being able to communicate with one another, in other words, to think each other through each other's thoughts in a relationship of simultaneity. This is the transformation

24 Paul Virilio, "L'Espace critique" in *La fin du monde est un concept sans avenir : œuvres, 1957–2010* (Paris: Éditions du Seuil, 2023), p. 206.
25 Paul Virilio, *The Lost Dimension*, trans. Daniel Moshenberg (New York: Semiotext[e], 1991), p. 14.
26 Ibid., p. 17.
27 Ibid., p. 13.
28 Ibid., p. 63.

that Virilio describes as the metaphysical reversal that transforms the accident into something "absolute and necessary" and defines substance "as relative and contingent."[29] But in a world of accidents, the catastrophe is no longer a "substantial deformation but … an unexpected accidental formation."[30] The conflagration or the catastrophe of the city is, after all, precisely the visual translation of the substance of space, which is entirely consumed in the accident of its occurrence.

A new museology

With *Unknown Quantity*, the Fondation Cartier's main goal appears to have been to sketch out the features of the museum of the future, linked to this urban metamorphosis. If exhibition brought modernity to the city, it was in exhibition spaces that the urban reality was able to articulate its new relationship to time and history. Once again, it was the exhibition, even before the emergence of digital technologies and social networks (which are just an extension of it), that made it possible to articulate this thickness "without volume," where everything exists insofar as it can be communicated. The digital world is nothing more than an exhibition that has become the structure of time: computers and cell phones are portable museums that have moved museums beyond their walls.

A new museum like this can no longer be defined by its position in space. A museum is no more here than it is elsewhere,[31] or to put it another way, it must now be the here that coincides with the beginning of the elsewhere: it is less a portion of space than a whirlpool that transforms space into a time of circulation. More than a repository, the exhibition becomes the original trope of circulation. Objects, ideas, and forms now enter the museum not to be preserved there but to begin circulating in society.

29 Ibid., p. 48.
30 Ibid.
31 Paul Virilio's phrase "Ailleurs commence ici" (Elsewhere begins here) was the French subtitle of the exhibition *Native Land, Stop Eject*, presented in 2008 at the Fondation Cartier, which brought together Raymond Depardon and Paul Virilio to reflect on the relationship between rootedness and uprootedness in the face of the unprecedented flow of human migration in the contemporary world.

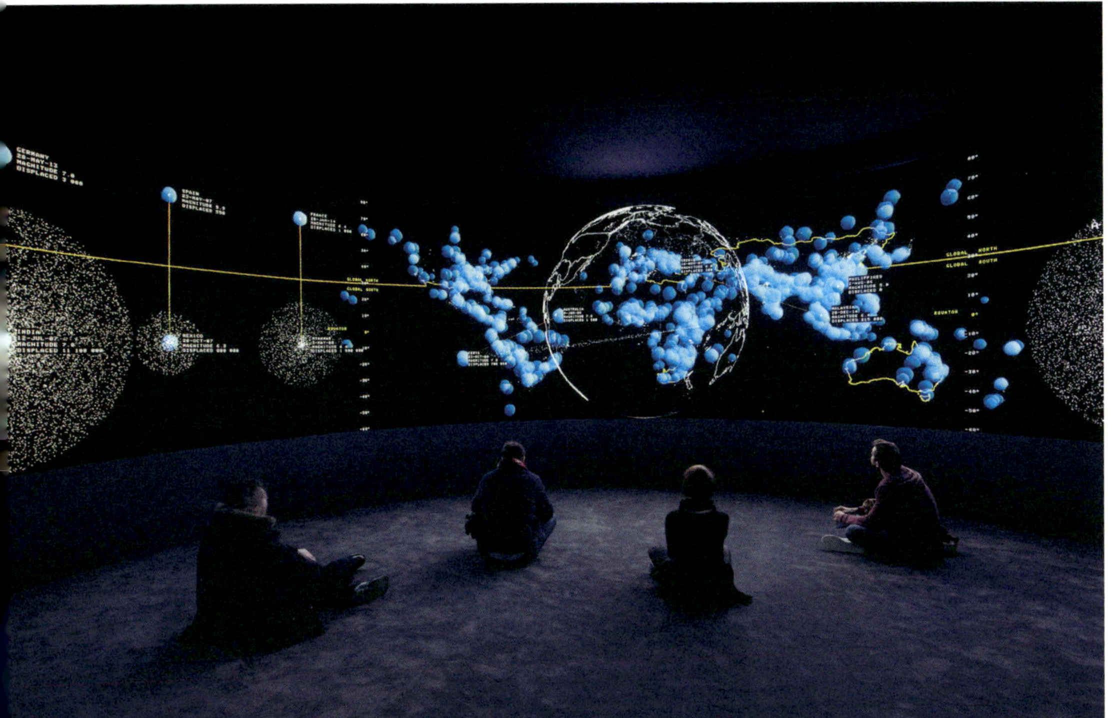

Paul Virilio and Diller Scofidio + Renfro, Mark Hansen, Laura Kurgan and Ben Rubin, in collaboration with Robert Gerard Pietrusko and Stewart Smith, *EXIT*, 2008–2015

They must become "what happens" [the meaning of the French title of *Unknown Quantity*, *Ce qui arrive*], embodying the time that replaces space, the topicality that lets everything that preceded it burn. Conversely, the museum ceases to be a place devoted to preserving the past, and becomes the shaper of the future: it conceives what the city never stops communicating, thereby giving shape to a new ethereal urbanism made up of forms that ceaselessly penetrate our bodies and consciences.

In the final analysis, this is a kind of acceleration and inversion of Le Corbusier's old dream. He invited us to imagine "a true museum, one that contained everything, one that could present a complete picture after the passage of time, after the destruction by time,"[32] and it is precisely the conflagration of reality that has become the content of the museum. The museum reflects everything that is

32 Le Corbusier, *The Decorative Art of Today*, trans. James I. Dunnett (London: The Architectural Press, 1987), p. 16.

happening; it is also the place where it happens: open to accidents, it becomes more like an immense magazine in which urban reality is inscribed at the very moment of its occurrence. "What happens" can never become form, structure, or substance. For Paul Virilio, the exhibition organized by the Fondation Cartier in 2002 was a way "to establish a new kind of museology or museography: one which consists in exposing or exhibiting the accident, all the accidents, from the most banal to the most tragic, from natural disasters to industrial and scientific disasters, without avoiding the all-too-often neglected category of the happy accident, the stroke of luck, love at first sight, the *coup de foudre* or even the *coup de grâce*!"[33]

The museum of accidents is the opposite of the patrimonial or historical-encyclopedic museum.[34] It cannot be seen as an accumulation of history, tradition, or heritage. In a way, it is a kind of three-dimensional projection of a magazine or newspaper. Rather than accumulating there, art history consumes itself.

The art of the explosion

Among the works included in this exhibition, this manifesto of the new museography, were two works by the Chinese artist Cai Guo-Qiang titled *Tonight So Lovely* (2001–2002). These are two videos showing fireworks exploding over the Bund, the Huangpu River, and the Oriental Pearl Television Tower in Shanghai, on October 21, 2001, during the Asia-Pacific Economic Cooperation (APEC) meeting. It is hard to imagine a more radical staging of what art becomes in the museum of accidents.

Born in Quanzhou in 1957, Cai Guo-Qiang is among the artists who have been associated with the Fondation Cartier for the longest period in its forty-year history: this shared commitment embodies the loyalty that the institution shows toward the artists it exhibits. In 1993, the Fondation Cartier invited Cai Guo-Qiang to take up a residency at Jouy-en-Josas,[35] during which time

33 Paul Virilio, *The Original Accident*, trans. Julie Rose (Cambridge: Polity Press, 2007), p. 4.
34 See *Le Musée de l'accident*, *Dromologie* 2, Cahiers Paul Virilio (2022).
35 Between 1985 and 1993, the Fondation Cartier, then based in Jouy-en-Josas, invited a number of artists in residence, including Chéri Samba, Fabrice Hyber, Marc Couturier, and Huang Yong Ping, as well as young art critics and curators such as Hans Ulrich Obrist, Fei Dawei, and Hou Hanru.

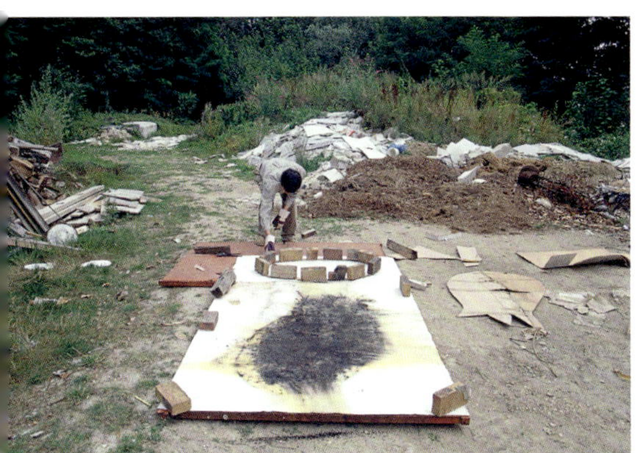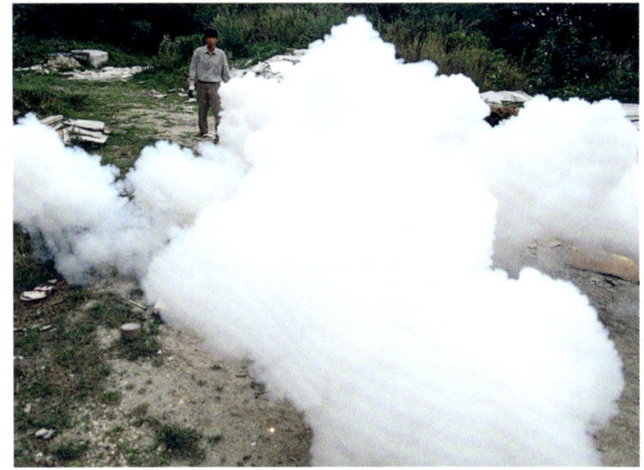

Cai Guo-Qiang creating the explosion for his work *Normandy's Halo: Project for Extraterrestrials No. 19* in the Fondation Cartier's park in Jouy-en-Josas, 1993

he created several works using gunpowder and drew up a "Book of Ideas" containing many of the artistic projects he went on to realize over the course of his career. Five years later, for the Issey Miyake exhibition at the Fondation Cartier,[36] he set off a large explosion on garments from the Pleats Please collection. In 2000, the Fondation Cartier devoted a major solo exhibition to him,[37] and Cai Guo-Qiang's work was shown twice more in the spaces of the building designed by Jean Nouvel, in 2004 and 2016.[38]

Explosions are the common thread running through all Cai Guo-Qiang's works. The artist adopted this technique at an early age, taking inspiration in part from his hometown—which has numerous firecracker and firework factories—and from the memory of his father, who made miniature ink drawings on matchboxes. More than anything else, it was a means that enabled the artist to free himself from tradition and all forms of academicism, be they Chinese or Western: "I started to use dynamite to avoid painting like a 'literati' and to oppose my spatio-temporal environment—to destroy it. Explosions make you feel something intense at the very core of your being because, while you can arrange explosives as you please, you cannot control the explosion itself. And this fills you with a great feeling of freedom."[39]

36 The exhibition *Issey Miyake Making Things* opened in October 1998 at the Fondation Cartier.
37 The exhibition *Cai Guo-Qiang* opened in April 2000 at the Fondation Cartier.
38 In 2004, Cai Guo-Qiang presented a large-scale light installation in the garden for the Fondation Cartier's twentieth anniversary. For the exhibition *The Great Animal Orchestra* in 2016, he created the work *White Tone*.
39 "To Dare to Accomplish Nothing: Fei Dawei Interviews Cai Guo-Qiang," in *Cai Guo-Qiang* (Paris: Fondation Cartier pour l'art contemporain, 2000), p. 132.

The explosion appears as an aesthetic realization of
the metaphysical inversion between substance and accident, as
theorized by Paul Virilio: creation is not the taking of form from
substance but its catastrophe, the accident that literally pulverizes
it. And more than the object or the form, the work of art is the
irruption of the accident into the substance of the world, a torsion
of space-time that opens up a black hole in the continuum of reality.
Which is why there is no longer any difference between creation
and destruction in Cai Guo-Qiang's work: "The canvas, torn and
scorched by the gunpowder, also strongly induces observers to muse
upon the contrast between creation and destruction, the twin
offsprings of violence."[40]

But above all, because the artist uses the properties of the earth
and the soil, it is not just an object that explodes, but reality itself:
"I borrow power from nature by using the 'skin' of the earth (soil)
and other natural materials that are alive as we are alive, and
I use this power to create effects that seem to me wondrous."[41]
It is precisely because someone acts that creation becomes
uncontrollable: "For me, the allure of gunpowder lies in its
uncontrollability and spontaneity; as with destiny itself, much
of the creation entails pure luck. Therefore, behind the artwork,
another artist or force seems to be at work. … The moment of
explosion feels like a direct dialogue with a source of invisible
energy."[42] If the Earth is the true artist, then "every place is
a museum,"[43] and the museum acquires a cosmic force: it is an
invisible energy that extends reality, that "circulate[s] between
the real and the virtual, like the breathing of the universe." Every
exhibition space becomes a gateway to that ulterior, non-mineral
thickness of which Paul Virilio speaks, where "what happens"
produces space and not the other way round. For Cai Guo-Qiang,

40 Cai Guo-Qiang and You Jindong, "Painting with Gunpowder," *Leonardo* 21 no. 3 (July 1988): p. 253.
41 Ibid., p. 252.
42 Philipp Kaiser, "The Land, the Earth, and the Universe: A Conversation with Cai Guo-Qiang," in *Cai Guo-Qiang: Ladder to the Sky* (Munich: Prestel, 2012), p. 79.
43 "To Dare to Accomplish Nothing," p. 135.

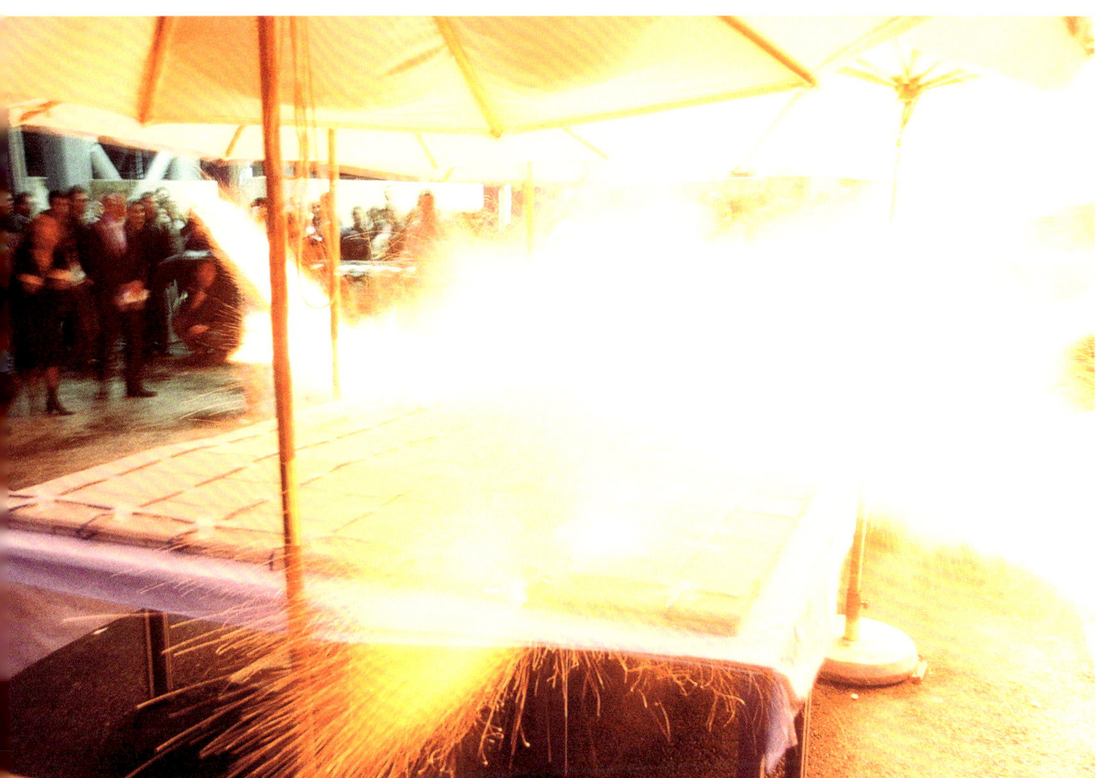

erformance by Cai Guo-Qiang, creating gunpowder drawings on copies of the catalog
f his exhibition at the Fondation Cartier, April 20, 2000

"this is similar to what happens when we go on the Net,"
where it is as if "we could surpass the speed of light" and "see
the past again": "We are the inheritors of the origin of the universe
and we therefore continue to carry within ourselves the signals
emitted at that time."[44]

What the Fondation Cartier was able to draw from Cai Guo-
Qiang's work is the desire to transform the museum space into
a time accelerator that will enable the entire city to exceed the speed
of light and thus "to break down this distance between human
beings and the cosmos, to break down the barriers between cultures
and the borders between countries … to break through the limits
of time, [to] establish an immediate connection to primordial
chaos."[45] Like the city of the future, the museum of tomorrow

44 "Cai Guo-Qiang and Andrei Ujică: A Conversation," in *Cai Guo-Qiang*, pp. 81-82.
45 Ibid., p. 83.

that the Fondation Cartier has always strived to embody since its inception is less a topological order that concentrates the best of the city in a single point of space than a temporal retreat enabling the emergence of a new time. Even in contemporary physics, the explosion is synonymous with a universal beginning, the absolute origin of time. As a cosmic explosion, each exhibition forces the world to begin again. To begin anew.

Paul Virilio

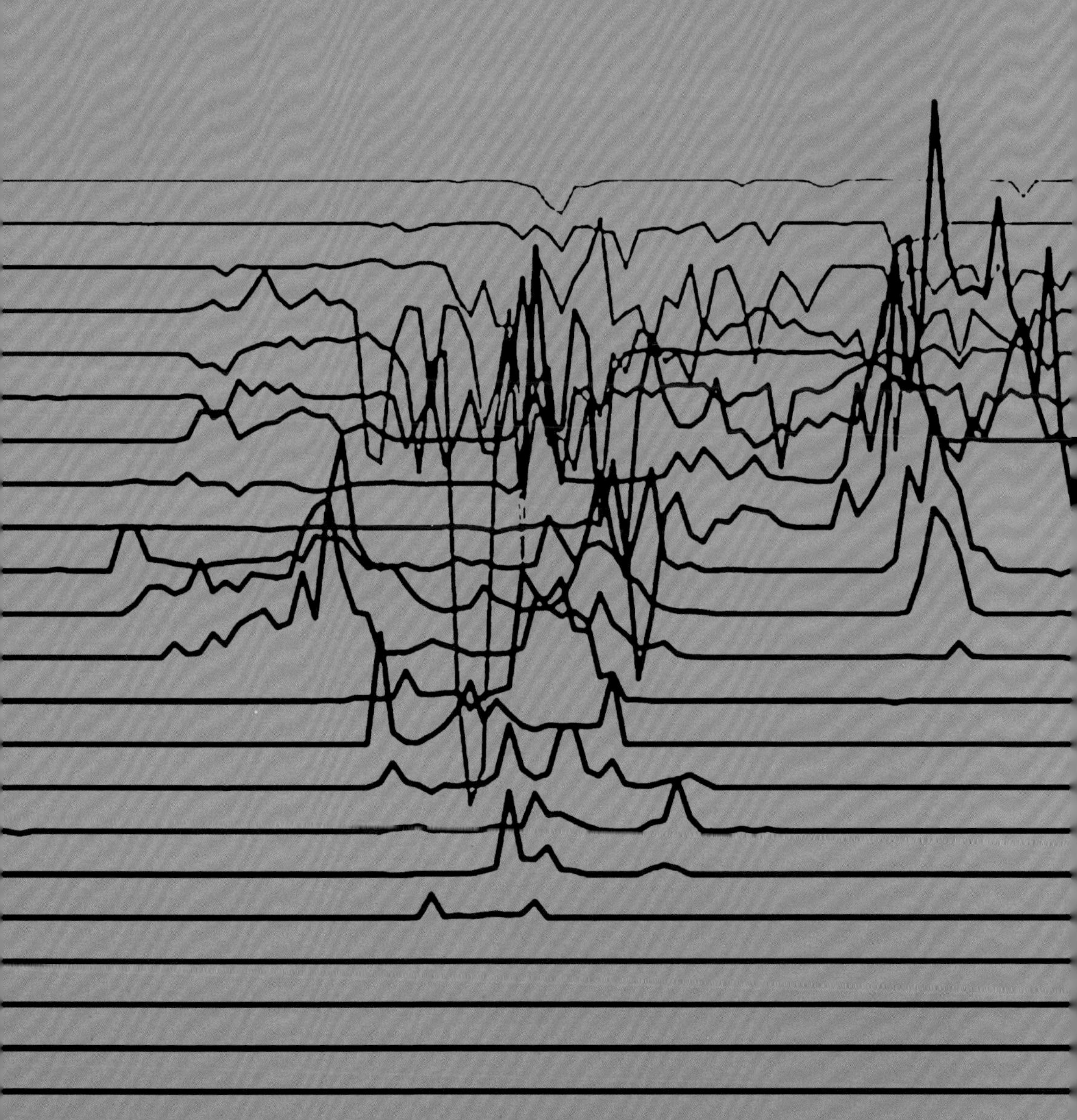

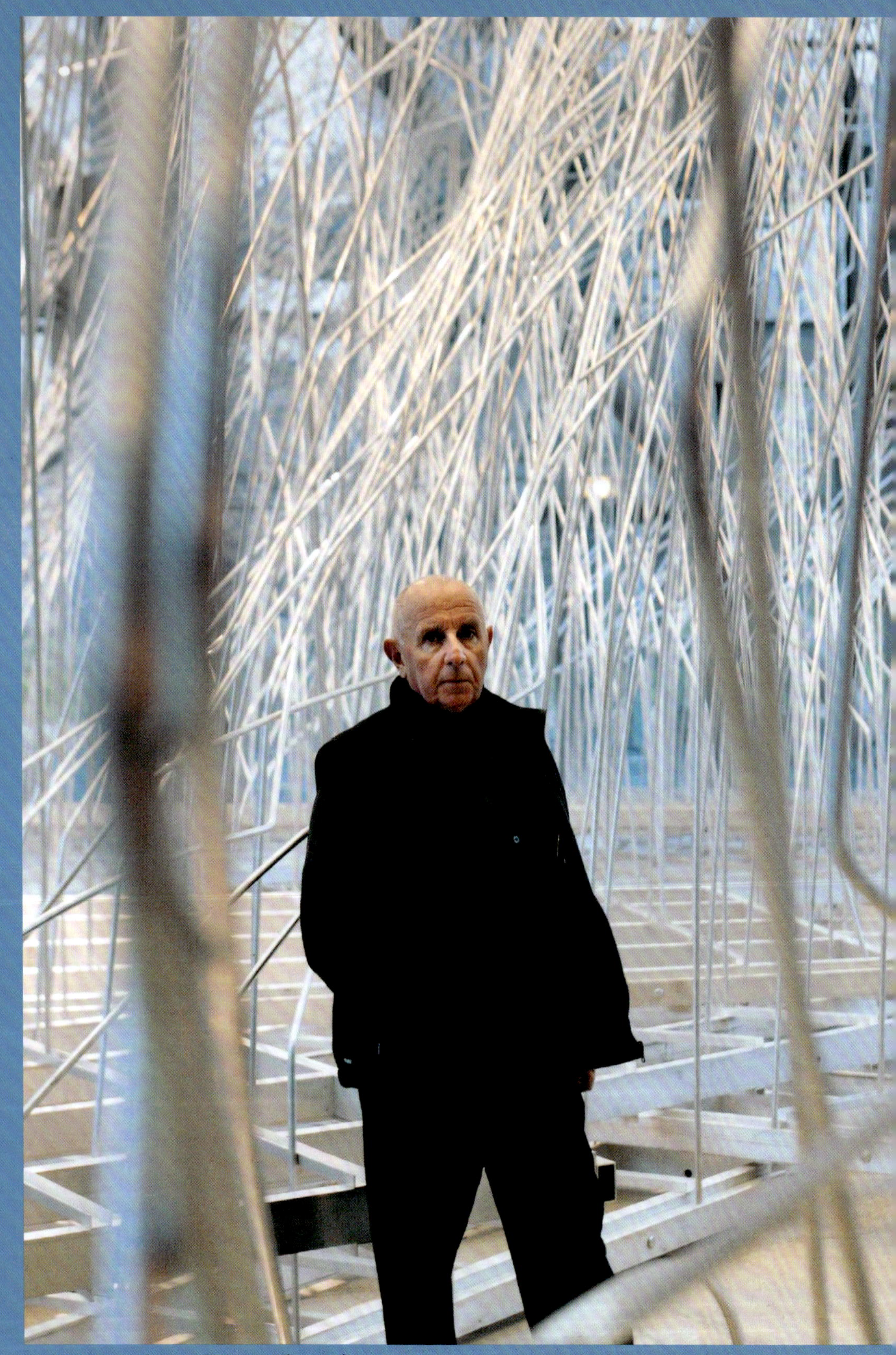

Paul Virilio in front of *The Fall* (2002) by Lebbeus Woods, in the exhibition
Unknown Quantity, 2002

In October 2023, the Fondation Cartier celebrated # Paul Virilio a great thinker and a friend with whom it developed a close relationship over thirty years: architect, urban planner, and philosopher Paul Virilio (1932–2018). To coincide with Éditions du Seuil's publication of an anthology of his texts, *La fin du monde est un concept sans avenir*, the Fondation Cartier and his daughter Sophie Virilio organized a Night of Uncertainty. "The end of the world is a concept without a future" brought together artists, scientists, philosophers, architects, and historians to honor his ideas and allow his words to resonate, five years after his death.

Paul Virilio's visionary thinking and profoundly intelligent writings have accompanied the Fondation Cartier, its exhibitions, and publications since 1988. That year, he wrote a first essay, for the catalog of the exhibition *Vraiment faux*. In 1991, he was asked to write another essay, for the exhibition *La Vitesse*: known for his work on technology and speed, connected through the concept of "dromology," Paul Virilio acted as both an adviser to the exhibition and as an invaluable contributor to the catalog. His text for the *Azur* exhibition in 1993 centered on the horizon, space, time, and matter. Other contributions for the Fondation Cartier followed: in 1999, his conversation with the artist Mœbius and filmmaker Andrei Ujică was featured in the catalog published on the occasion of the exhibition *Un monde réel*; in 2000, he penned a very beautiful text titled "The Twilight of the Grounds" for the book *The Desert*; and in 2004, he developed a passion for *Kelvin 40*, a prototype jet plane created by Australian designer Marc Newson for the Fondation Cartier.

Invited to make his thinking visible in the form of exhibitions for Jean Nouvel's glass building by Hervé Chandès, Director of the Fondation Cartier, Paul Virilio conceived *Unknown Quantity* in 2002, and *Native Land, Stop Eject* in 2008, a project imagined in collaboration with photographer and filmmaker Raymond Depardon. For *Unknown Quantity*, Paul Virilio explored the theme of the accident—one of his favorite subjects— and raised the question of the unexpected

and incredible through the works of the invited artists and writers, including Svetlana Alexievitch, Cai Guo-Qiang, Tony Oursler, Artavazd Pelechian, Nancy Rubins, and Andrei Ujică. With Svetlana Alexievitch— who would receive the Nobel Prize for Literature in 2015—he had a long discussion on the Chernobyl nuclear disaster for Andrei Ujică's film, *Unknown Quantity*. Six years later, *Native Land, Stop Eject* offered a reflection on the notions of rootedness and uprooting, and related questions of identity. Whereas Raymond Depardon gave voice to those wishing to live on their land but are threatened with exile, Paul Virilio instead questioned the very notion of sedentariness in the face of the unprecedented migratory flux the contemporary world is experiencing. "If this exhibition is strong, it's because it isn't about one man versus another, but about town versus country. [...] Raymond Depardon and I are both concerned with the same question: what is left of the world, of native lands, of the history of the only habitable planet today?" explained Paul Virilio. For this exhibition, the philosopher sought to put his ideas on political, economic, and climatic migratory flux all around the world into images. Responding to Paul Virilio's thinking, architects and artists Elizabeth Diller and Ricardo Scofidio created an immersive installation of animated maps generated by data collected from around one hundred international organizations. First presented in 2008, the work *EXIT* entered the Collections of the Fondation Cartier in 2012. Such was its impact that it has been shown at United Nations Climate Change conferences: COP15 in Copenhagen, and then updated for COP21 held in Paris. The latest version has been presented in Korea, Spain, China, and Australia.

"For Paul Virilio, the exhibition is a visible thought experiment, a revelatory art," wrote Hervé Chandès in 2012 in the foreword to *La Pensée exposée*, a work gathering together all the philosopher's collaborations with the Fondation Cartier.

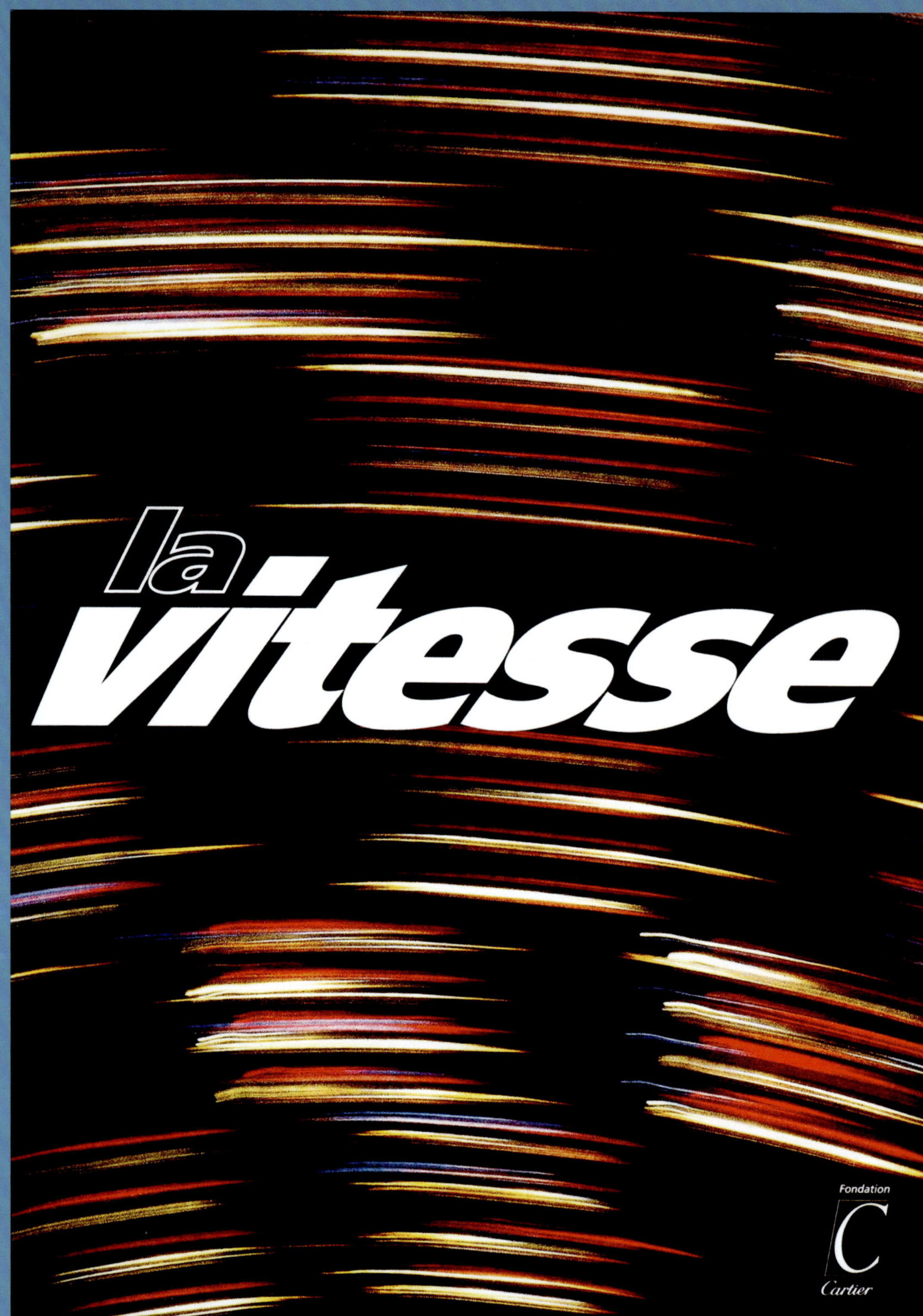

1991 For the exhibition *La Vitesse* at Jouy-en-Josas, the Fondation Cartier invited Paul Virilio to advise on the exhibition; he also contributed to the catalog with an interview with Jean de Loisy and an essay titled "La Vitesse d'exposition."

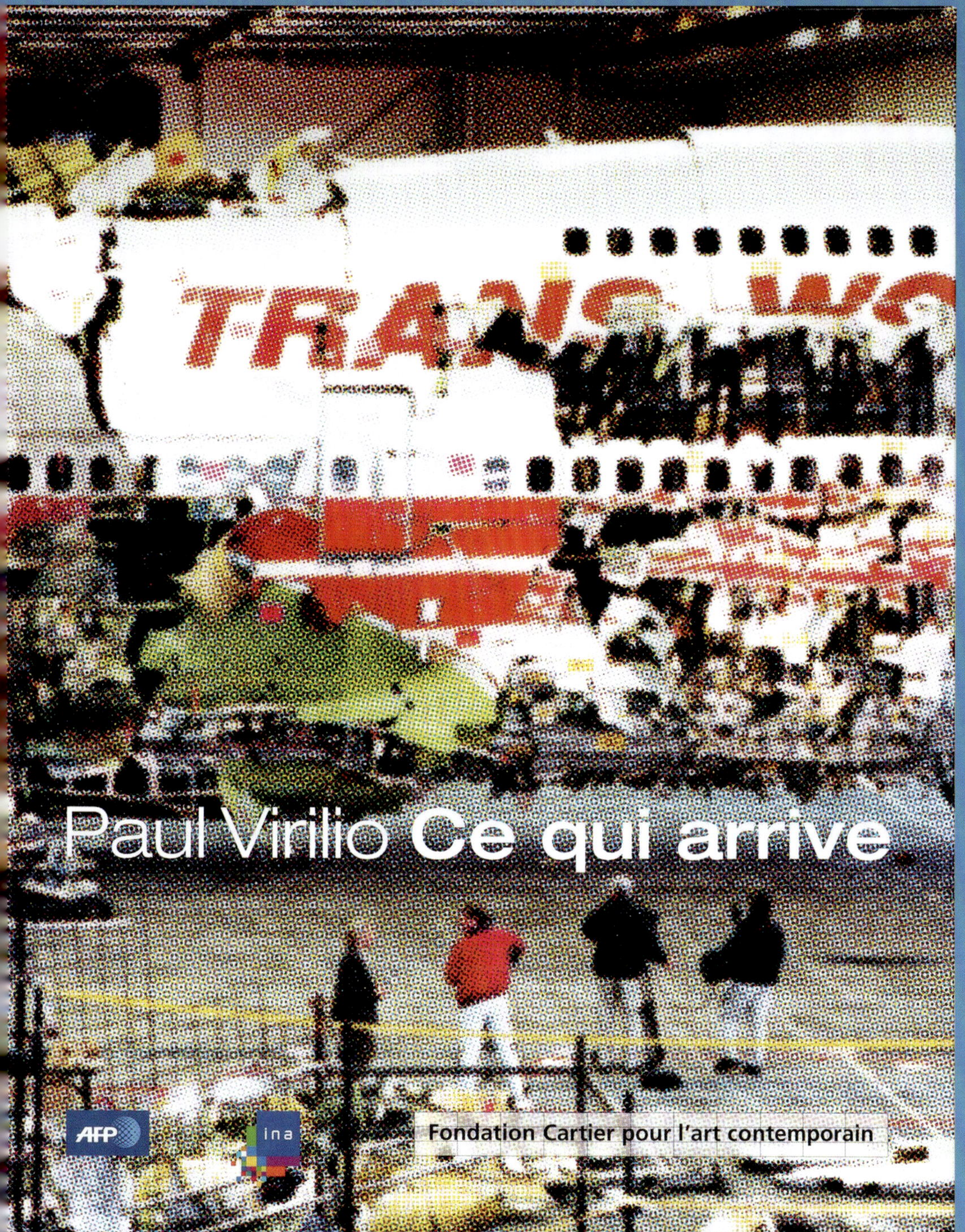

2002   Paul Virilio conceived the exhibition *Unknown Quantity*, and edited its catalog, a philosophical reflection on the theme of the accident, its genesis, and accumulation.

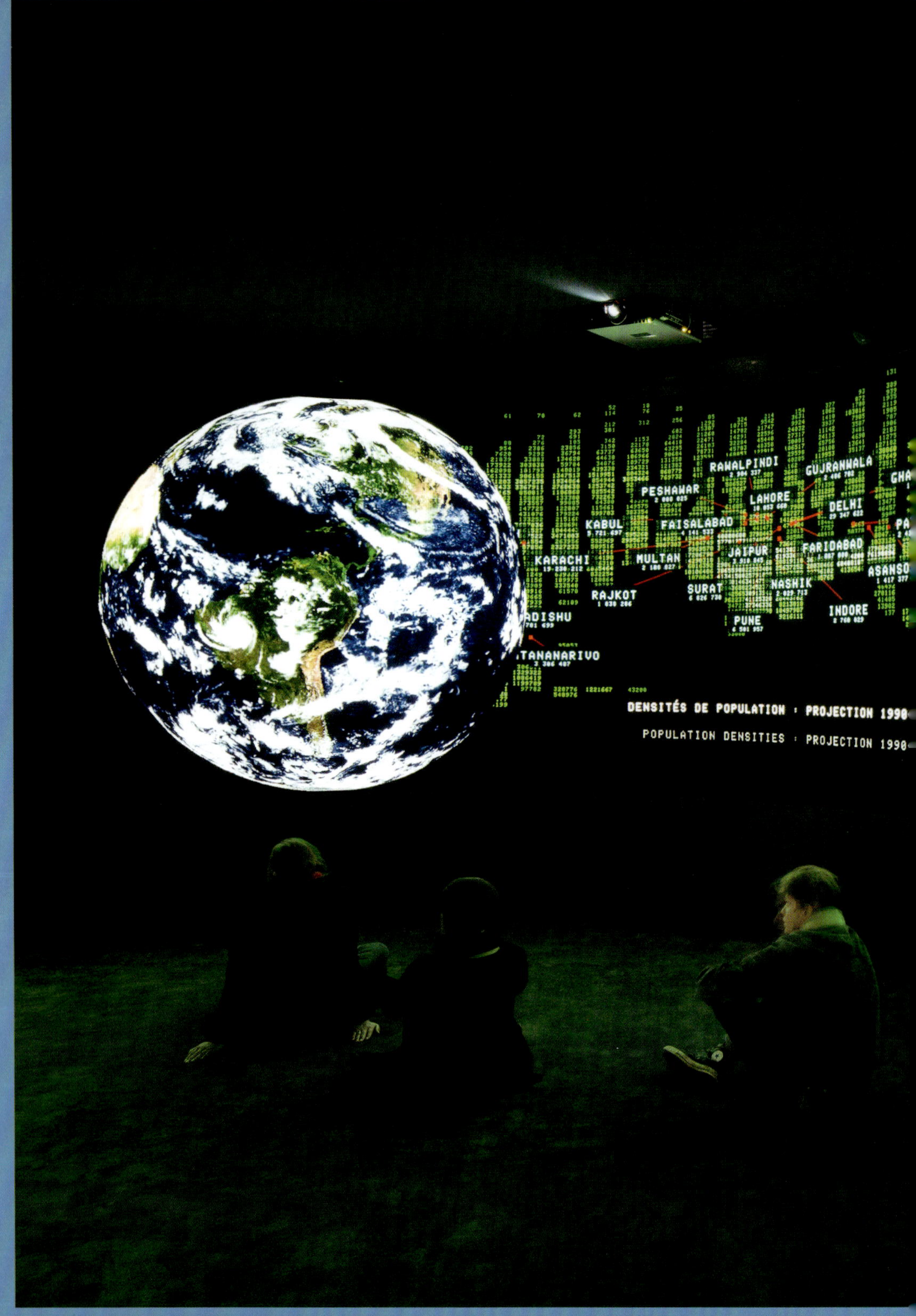

2008   Based on an idea from Paul Virilio and created by architects and artists Diller Scofidio + Renfro for the exhibition *Native Land, Stop Eject*, *EXIT* is an installation showing human migratory flows, as well as the deforestation of tropical zones, and the languages threatened with extinction all over the world.

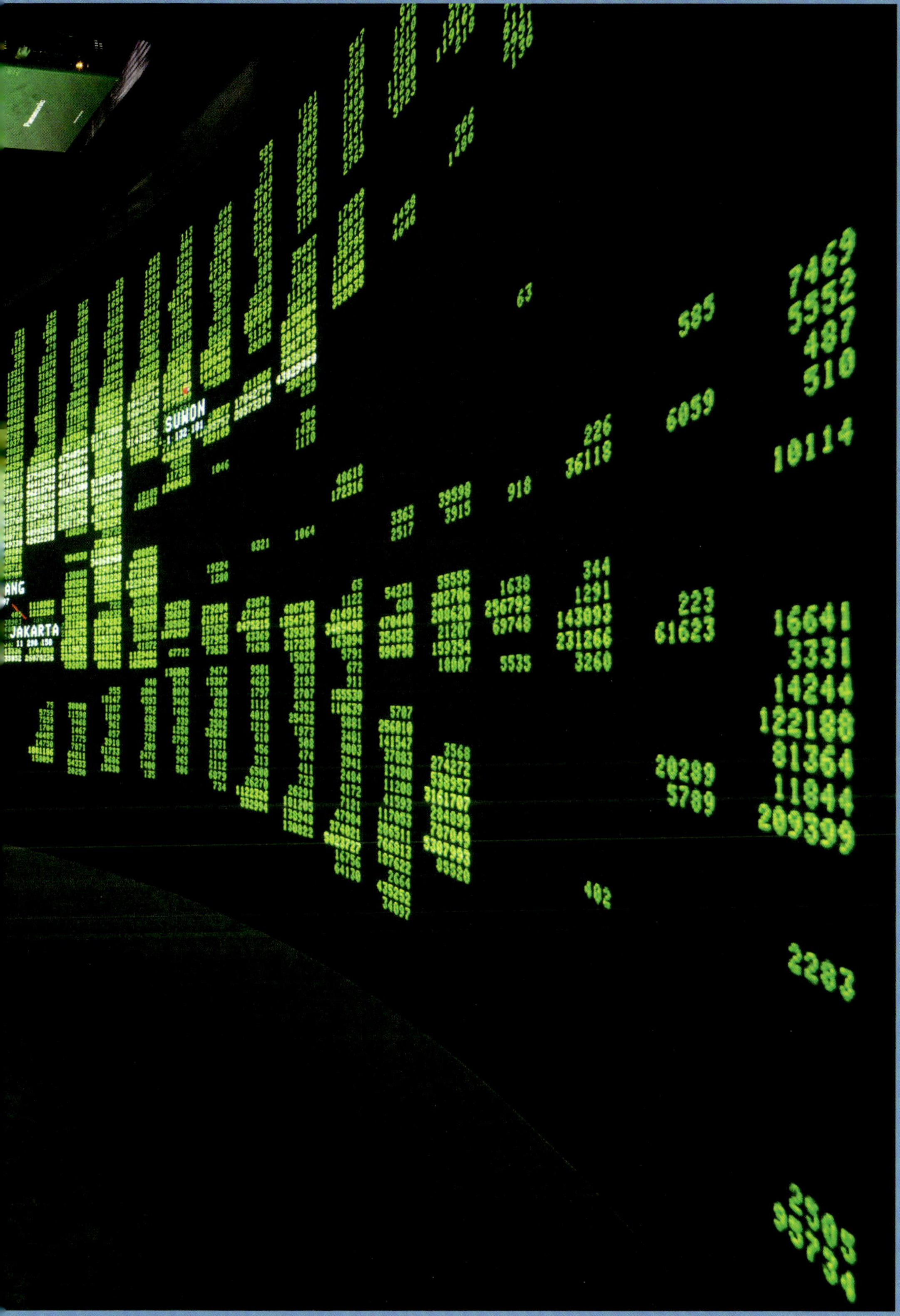

SUWON

ANG

JAKARTA

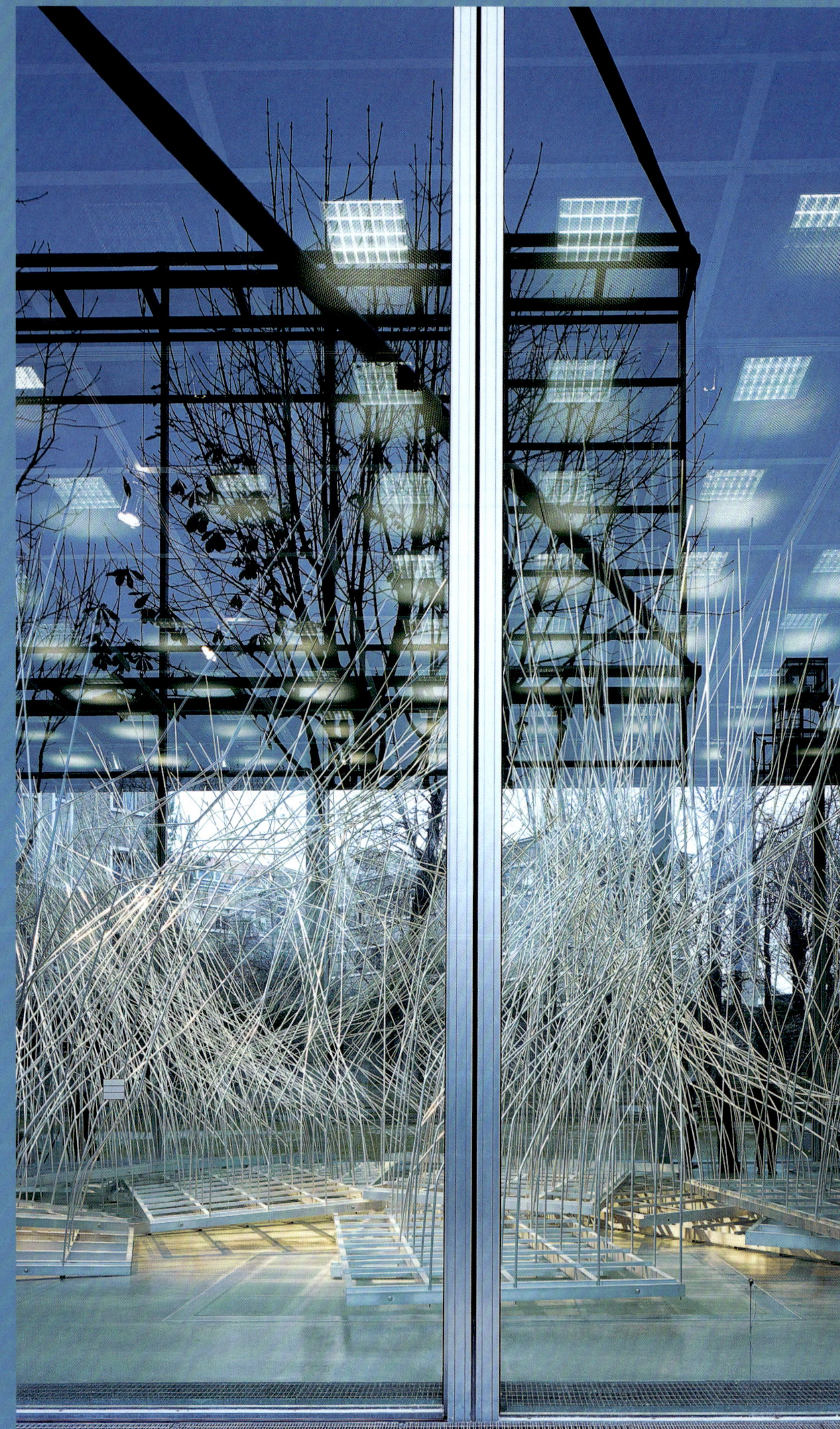

2002 Lebbeus Woods, *The Fall*, 2002. View of the exhibition *Unknown Quantity*

ÊTRE NATURE

The poetics of transparency

From a distance, the building at 261 Boulevard Raspail looks like
a display case without a roof. An immense wall of glass rises up
above the sidewalk, seemingly transforming everything behind it
into an object for contemplation. It is as if the architectural gesture,
which has defined the exhibition itself, from the display case
to the museum, has been isolated here in its purest, most
fundamental form. As you approach, you realize that the first glass
panel is concealing others; it is as if you were facing a kind
of geological stratification of "making visible." The paradox that
the Fondation Cartier building seems to embody is twofold.
On the one hand, anyone can enter the display case, transforming
themselves into something that has the same status as a work of
art: the audience and the work become equivalent in a way, and
seem to swap roles. Things become spectators, and visitors become
objects on display, as if to say that the exhibition is where subject
and object become indistinguishable.

On the other hand, the initial glass panel, which heralds those
that follow, appears to perform a more complex operation: making
an exhibition space into an exhibition object means freeing it
from all typological clichés. The building that Jean Nouvel built for
the Fondation Cartier is a kind of experiment in meta-museographic

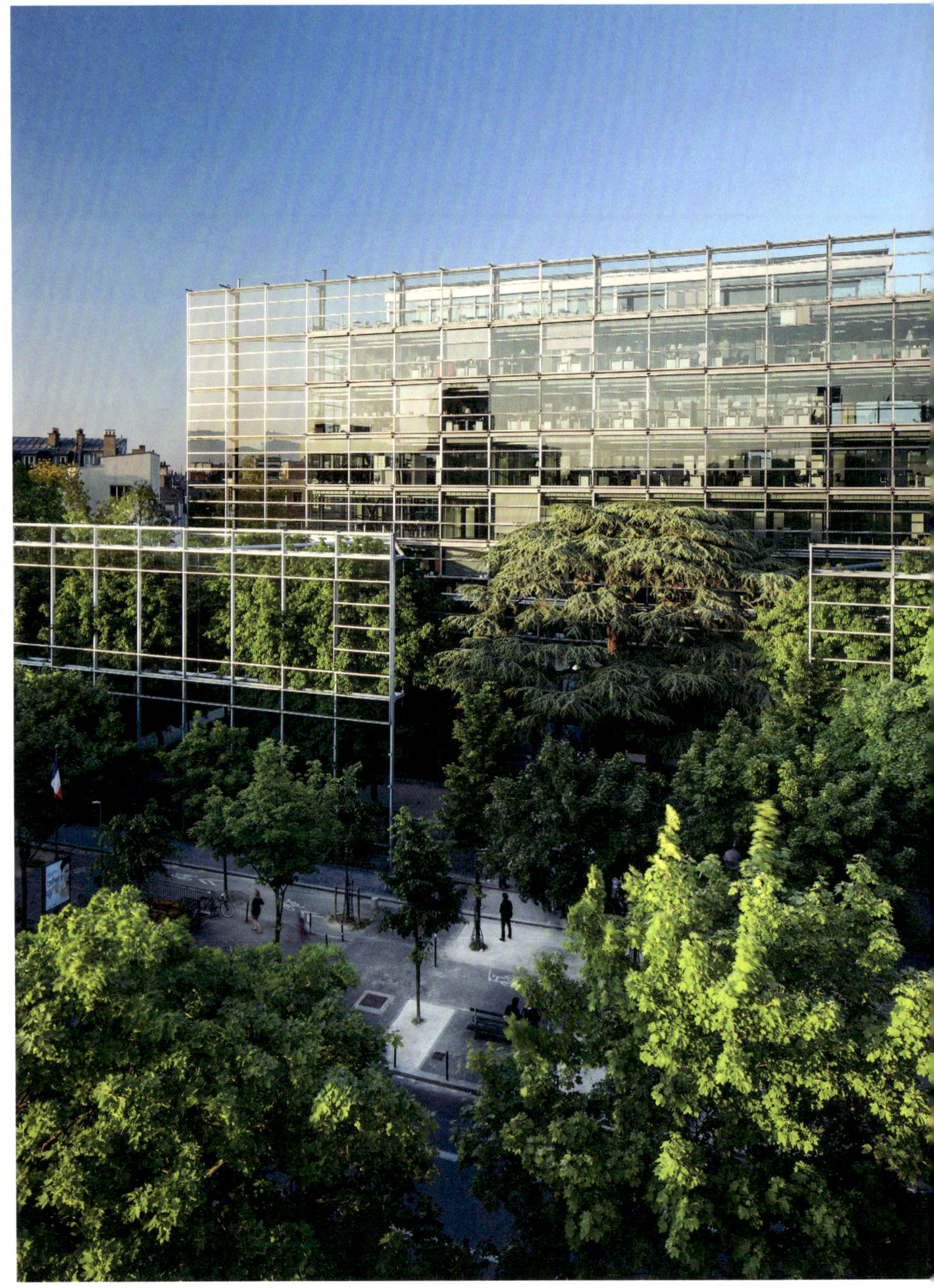

The Fondation Cartier building, 261 Boulevard Raspail, Paris

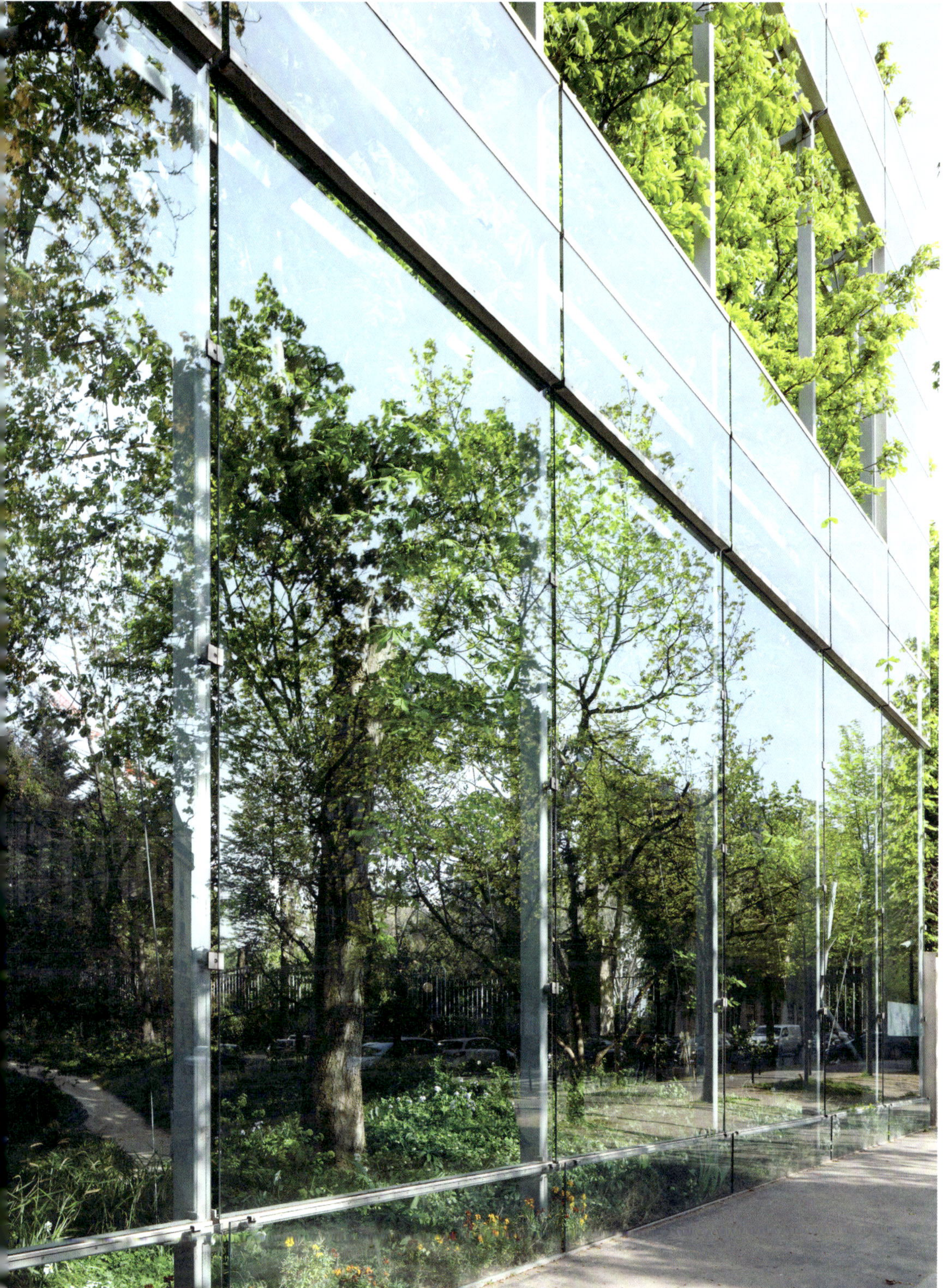

The glass facade of Jean Nouvel's building, seen from the street

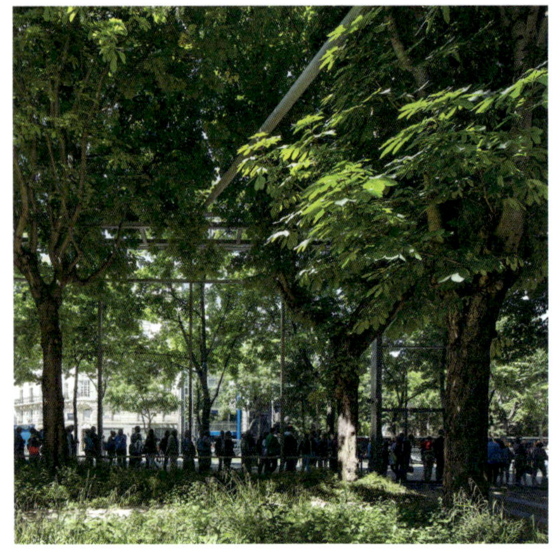

Inside the enclosure of the building

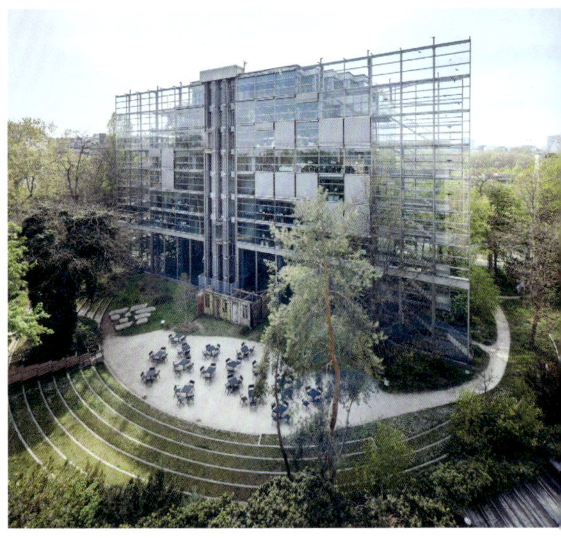

Theatrum Botanicum by Lothar Baumgarten

thinking: it is not a museum but a treatise on museum architecture, a kind of museum squared.

You don't even have to enter the building in order to see art. It is as if art has colonized and laid siege to the building. To achieve this, to exist outside the exhibition space itself, the site appears to have adopted an unprecedented strategy: that of transforming itself into a kind of tiny urban forest, a collection of trees, shrubs, grasses, and stones assembled in an orderly fashion around the glass and steel structure. It would be wrong to think that this is merely a garden. Though it takes the form of a quite traditional manifestation of landscape architecture, this is for more subtle reasons. This small "forest" is the work of German artist Lothar Baumgarten, who studied with the legendary Joseph Beuys in Düsseldorf.[1] The work's title comes from the first great botanical treatise of English modernity, *Theatrum Botanicum*, a monumental 1,755-page folio published in 1640 by John Parkinson, apothecary to James I and royal botanist to Charles I. In this paper theater, he represented the state of the art in systematic botany, covering an extensive period, bringing together more than three thousand eight hundred species divided into seventeen "tribes" according

1 *Theatrum Botanicum*, the garden that surrounds Jean Nouvel's building, was created in 1994 by Lothar Baumgarten, commissioned by the Fondation Cartier pour l'art contemporain.

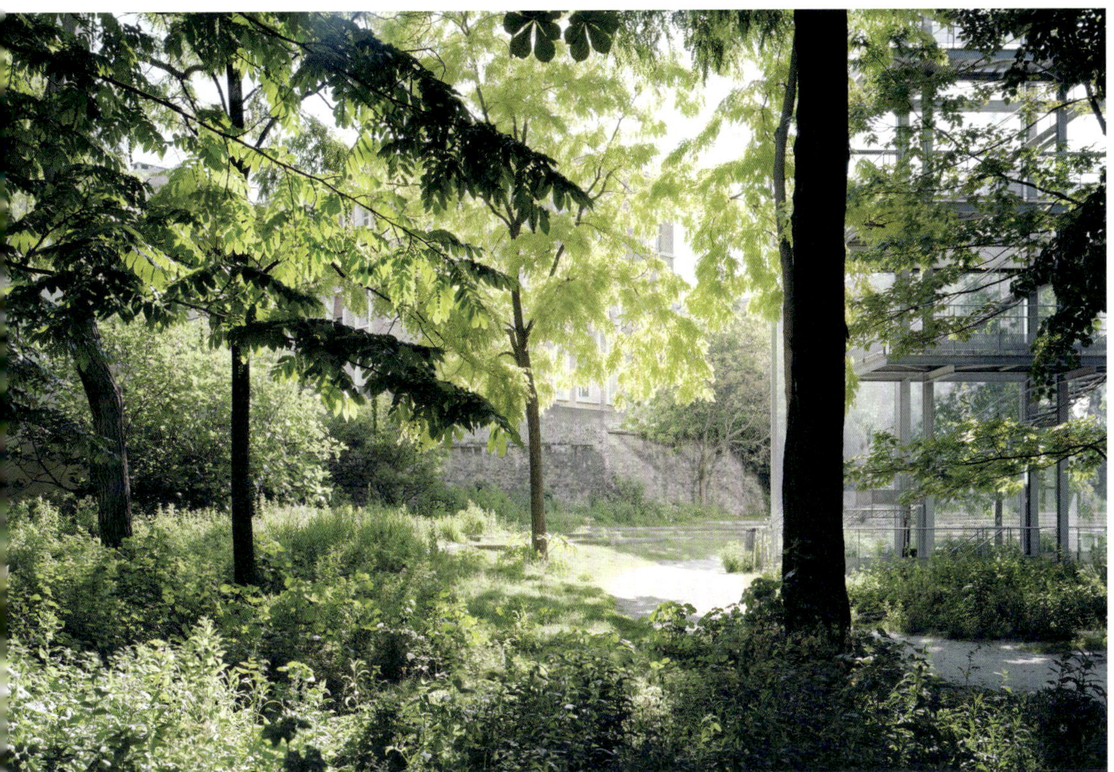

"The world in a crystal, the garden as a metaphor of the universe." Lothar Baumgarten

to their therapeutic capacities and habitat. Thirteen native British species were described for the first time. In the opening pages, John Parkinson makes play on words referring to his debut publication of 1629, recounting how, like Adam, he fell from a "paradise of pleasant flowers" into a "world of profitable herbs and plants."[2] As was common at the time, his first book *Paradisi in sole. Paradisus terrestris*, made all botanical knowledge and practice a form of restitution of the primordial happiness that Adam and Eve experienced in the first space inhabited by humankind. According to the myths crystallized in the Hebrew and Christian bibles, "that Adam might exercise this knowledge, God planted a Garden for him to live in, (wherein even in his innocency he was to labour and spend his time)," writes John Parkinson, "which he stored with the best and choysest Herbes and Fruits the earth could produce,

2   John Parkinson, *Theatrum Botanicum* (London: Thomas Cotes, 1640), p. 1.

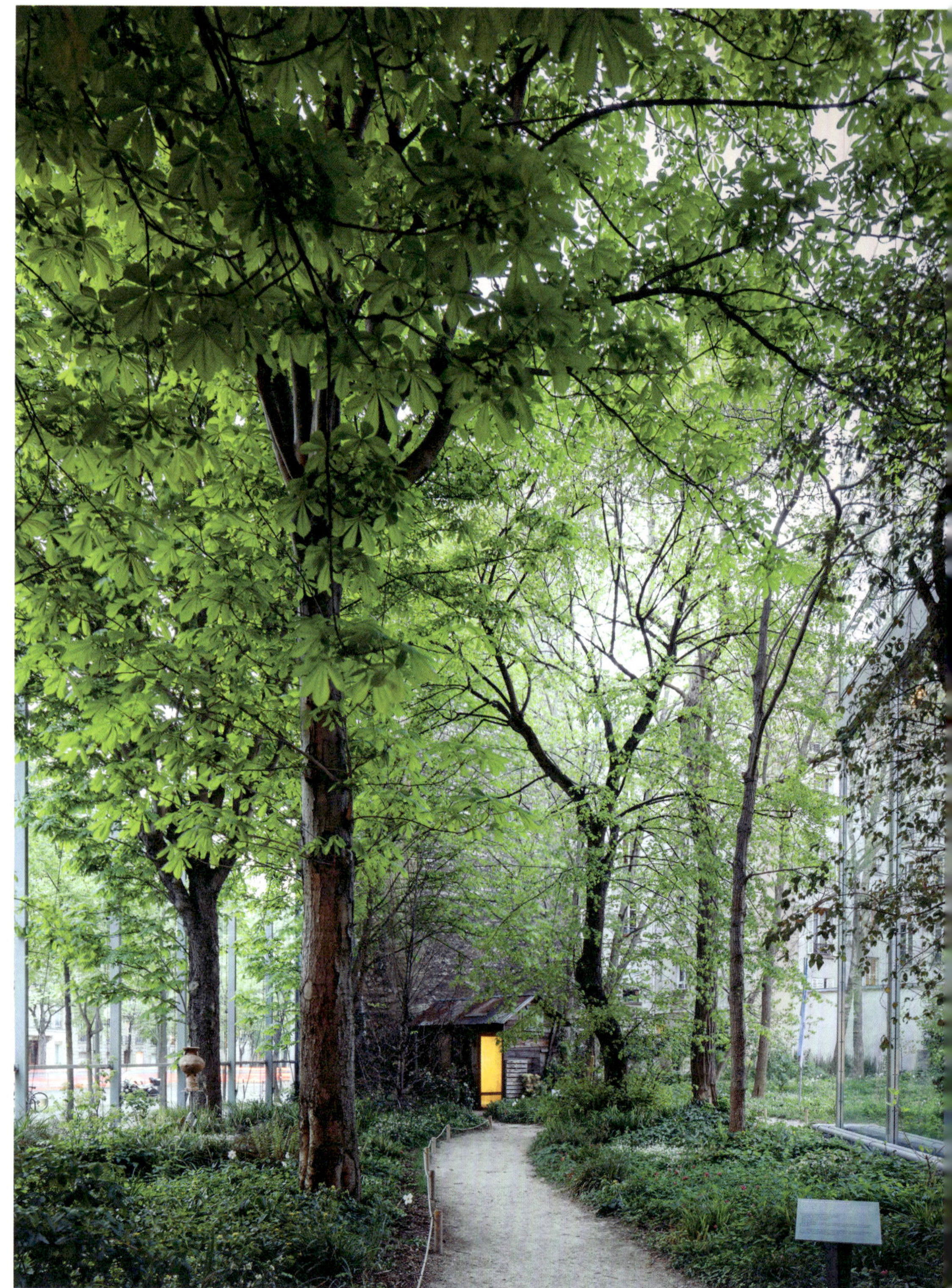

Agnès Varda, *La Cabane du chat*, 2016
FC Collections (2016)

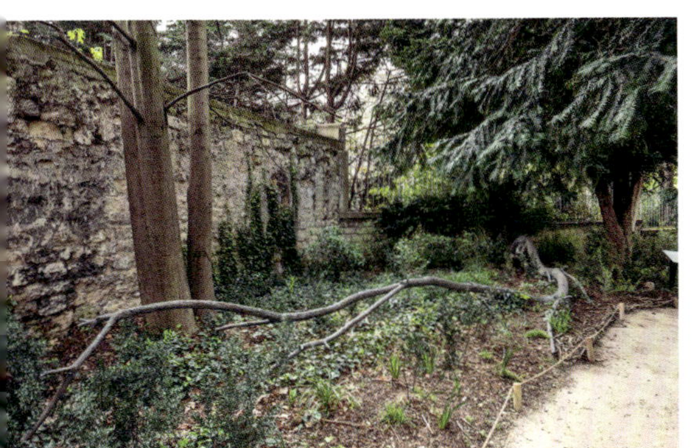

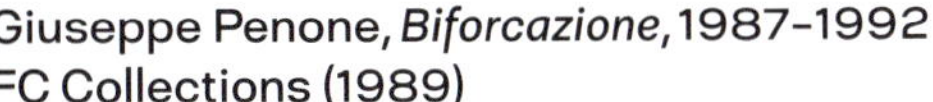

Giuseppe Penone, *Biforcazione*, 1987–1992
FC Collections (1989)

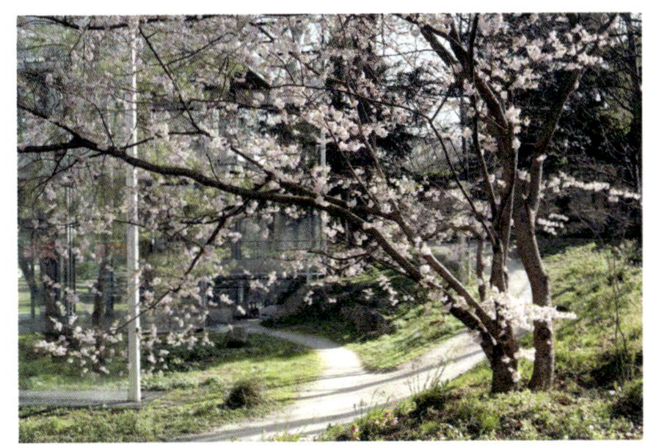

Japanese cherry tree (*Prunus serrulata*)

that he might have not onely for necessitie whereon to feede,
but for pleasure also."[3] It was interaction with other species that
produced a good and enjoyable life. "And although Adam lost the
place for his transgression, yet he lost not the naturall knowledge,
nor use of them."[4] Each and every garden strives to recreate this
original form, of pleasure and attentiveness: it is the theatre of this
happiness that is both lost and recoverable through a nurturing
relationship, paradise reincarnated in the form of a museum.
Lothar Baumgarten's work draws on that of Parkinson and
premodern European botany to reinterpret the concurrence of the
garden and the theater. While the relationship with other species
takes on a museum-like character as a result of the historical
fracture that is original sin, for Lothar Baumgarten the museum
must foremost enable us to rediscover this connection and restore
this lost pleasure.

After eighteen months living with the Yanomami peoples
in the forests of Venezuela and Brazil in the late 1970s, equipped
only with cameras, film, and art materials, filming, photographing,
and drawing these isolated populations, Lothar Baumgarten
spent decades reflecting on and criticizing the destructive force of
modernity. In 1993, for his exhibition *America Invention* in New York,
he transformed the Guggenheim (a "pumpkin with no right angles,"

3 John Parkinson, "To the Courteous Reader," *Paradisi in sole. Paradisus terrestris* (London: Humfrey Lownes
and Robert Young, 1629), n. p.
4 Ibid.

Emanuele Coccia

in his words) into an inverted globe that denounced Western colonial attitudes and articulated an alternative relationship between culture, astronomy, and geography. In *Theatrum Botanicum*, the perspective is reversed: a treatise replaces the denunciation of Western modernity, something between alchemy and architecture, transforming the museum space into a "crystal" that attempts to rebuild a different relationship with nonhuman species.

It is not by chance that the work establishes a close dialogue with Jean Nouvel's building, designed and built around the intertwining of the Parisian sky and a tree. "It was Chateaubriand, in 1823, who planted the famous cedar of Lebanon at 261 Boulevard Raspail," Jean Nouvel said of the site; for him, this tree is "the real monument here."[5] Transforming a tree-monument into an exhibition and museum space was something completely new and almost unimaginable. The Fondation Cartier building was born out of an attempt to answer a question: how to make human and botanical memory coincide, how to build history and culture together, both human and nonhuman.

To weave this dialectic, Jean Nouvel pushed his poetics of transparency to the extreme. All his work is based on the intuition that the evolution of materials used in architecture leads to a fusion between fullness and emptiness, between architectural space and its container. Transparency is the hallmark of this fusion. At the same time, it is a way of resolving the opposition between the modernist assertion of space as the sole element of architectural practice and the postmodern tendency to reduce the building to a screen or surface on which disparate signs can accumulate. Architecture thus becomes a place of reconciliation between the physical and the semiotic, between meaning and matter. According to Jean Nouvel, this is partly due to a necessity linked to the technical evolution of construction materials: there is a kind of Darwinism in architecture that pushes towards immateriality and means that

5 "Jean Nouvel and Hans Ulrich Obrist in conversation," in *Fondation Cartier pour l'art contemporain, 30 Years for Contemporary Art* (Paris: Fondation Cartier pour l'art contemporain, 2014), p. 103.

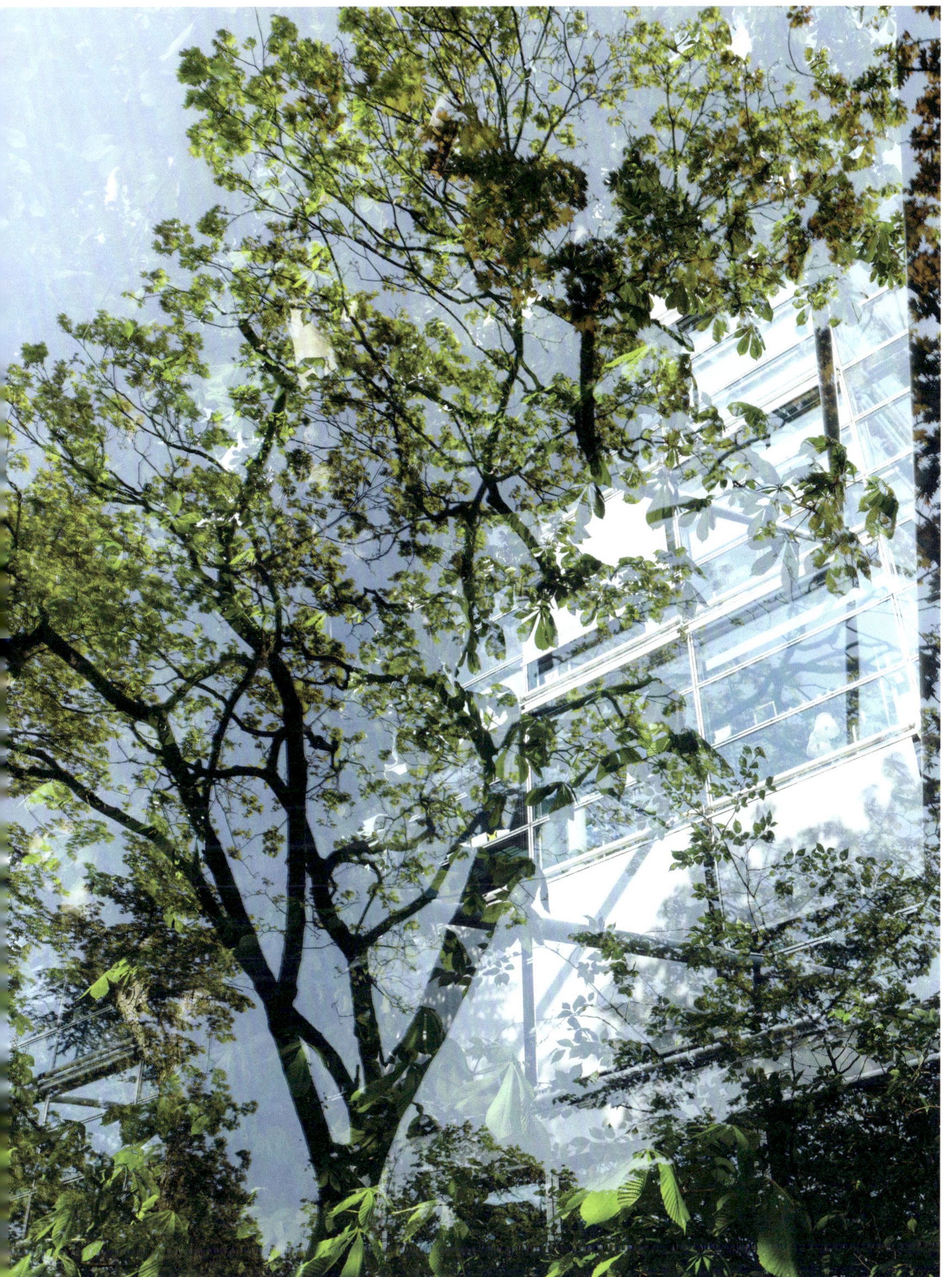

Single trees appear multiplied. Everything is in motion, mirrored in the play of horizontal and vertical rhythms, as well as seasonal changes." Lothar Baumgarten

Emanuele Coccia

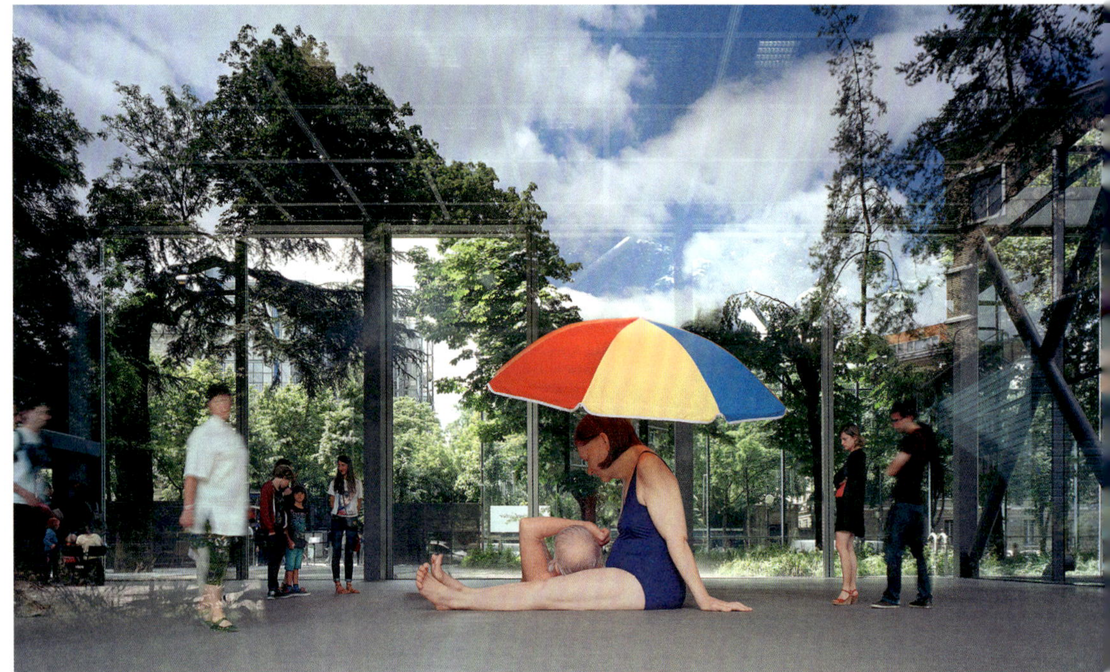

View of the exhibition *Ron Mueck*, 2013

less and less material is needed to accomplish a given task.[6] From this point of view, glass is the immaterial material par excellence, the one that allows us to conceive of space as being capable of giving form to itself and vice versa, form being the consequence of light passing through space.

At the same time, light itself is both space and an instrument for structuring space. Jean Nouvel seems to be harking back to the ancient metaphysical tradition that made light "the first corporeal form," understood as the movement of space, in order to open up to experience.[7] If we suspend our knowledge of physics for a moment, it is easy to see that light is perceived as the impossibility

6 "There is a kind of architectural 'Darwinism' at work, which is an evolutionary process through which man attempts to cover the maximum amount of space, the largest surface, insulate the most but with the least amount of material, without looking like he did anything. There's been a tremendous push forward that still isn't over and never will be. We can summarize it as follows: how can we resolve the most material problems with the greatest amount of elegance? It involves the domination of matter. For example, the progress made in glass technology during the century has been astonishing." In Jean Baudrillard and Jean Nouvel, *The Singular Objects of Architecture*, trans. Robert Bononno (Minneapolis: University of Minnesota Press, 2002), pp. 63–64.
7 "The first corporeal form which some call corporeity is in my opinion light. For light of its very nature diffuses itself in every direction in such a way that a point of light will produce instantaneously a sphere of light of any size whatsoever, unless some opaque object stands in the way." Robert Grosseteste, *On Light / De Luce*, trans. Clare C. Riedl (Milwaukee, WI: Marquette University Press, [c. 1235] 1942), p. 10.

of separating form and space, extension (and therefore emptiness) and the presence of colors, lines, and textures. Jean Nouvel acknowledges that it was the decision to make light the actual object of construction that revolutionized his practice: "Traditional architecture was based on the differentiation between the solid and the void. This approach overlooked the potential of light and its variability. For me, light is a basic material. Once you understand how light changes, and transforms our perception, your architectural vocabulary immediately expands in directions that traditional architecture would never have thought of. An architecture of the ephemeral becomes possible—not in the sense of temporary structures, but of mutable structures that change through light and with light. Not only through changes in daylight, but also by modifying the lighting inside the building, playing with different opacities and transparencies. The effective use of light is a basic principle of my architecture." This intuition took on a more radical form in the concept of the Fondation Cartier building because of its typology. Light is also the medium that makes the world visible, the medium of the exhibition itself: more than anything else, a museum is a particular form of light manipulation and an attempt to give another form to the relationship between light and time. Arguably, this is also why Jean Nouvel's architecture has so often converged with the typology of the museum. As a building that attempts to construct space with light, the Fondation Cartier has become his treatise on museography, a meta-building that is also, and above all, a reflection on the nature of the museum and its relationship to space.

The object and its reflection

The Fondation Cartier site on Boulevard Raspail enabled Jean Nouvel to understand that to make architecture a practice of sculpting with light was to make it a cosmic force rather than a purely urban one. To achieve this, the space in question could no longer be that of the building, but had to be open to the rest of the world, to the nonhuman world. The inclusion of the Chateaubriand cedar became the pretext for this limitless extension of the architect's material (as the horizon was for the unrealized "Tête Défense" project in 1983). In order to use light to interweave the natural and human worlds, the tree and the museum space, Jean Nouvel articulated a new architectural logic of reflection: reflection is effectively the destiny of all forms once they have been touched by light and allowed themselves to be transported by it. The theory behind the Fondation Cartier building, explained Jean Nouvel, "is a simple principle that consists in superimposing the object and its reflection." This is why the structure was designed so that "this building is all about impressions and reflections."[8]

Reflection is form that becomes architecture through light. To transform the cedar into architecture and therefore into reflection, Jean Nouvel surrounded it with two large glass screens: one is the building's facade, the other a 16-meter wall that replaced the wall that already existed along Boulevard Raspail. The resulting corridor, which has no roof, means that the complex has no clear separation between inside and outside, between exhibition space and garden. And the fact that the sky cannot but help being reflected in this surface turns the whole museum into a machine that brings the sky down to earth and transforms it into a moving blackboard for all the world's forms.

But these two walls, and the play of light they generate, produce another paradox, which Jean Nouvel calls trans-appearance[9]: the reflection of one wall is reflected in that of the other, producing

8 Jean Nouvel quoted in the exhibition catalog *Trees* (Paris: Fondation Cartier pour l'art contemporain, 2019), p. 190.
9 Paul Virilio introduced the expression in *Polar Inertia*, trans. Patrick Camiller (London: Sage Publications, [1990] 2000).

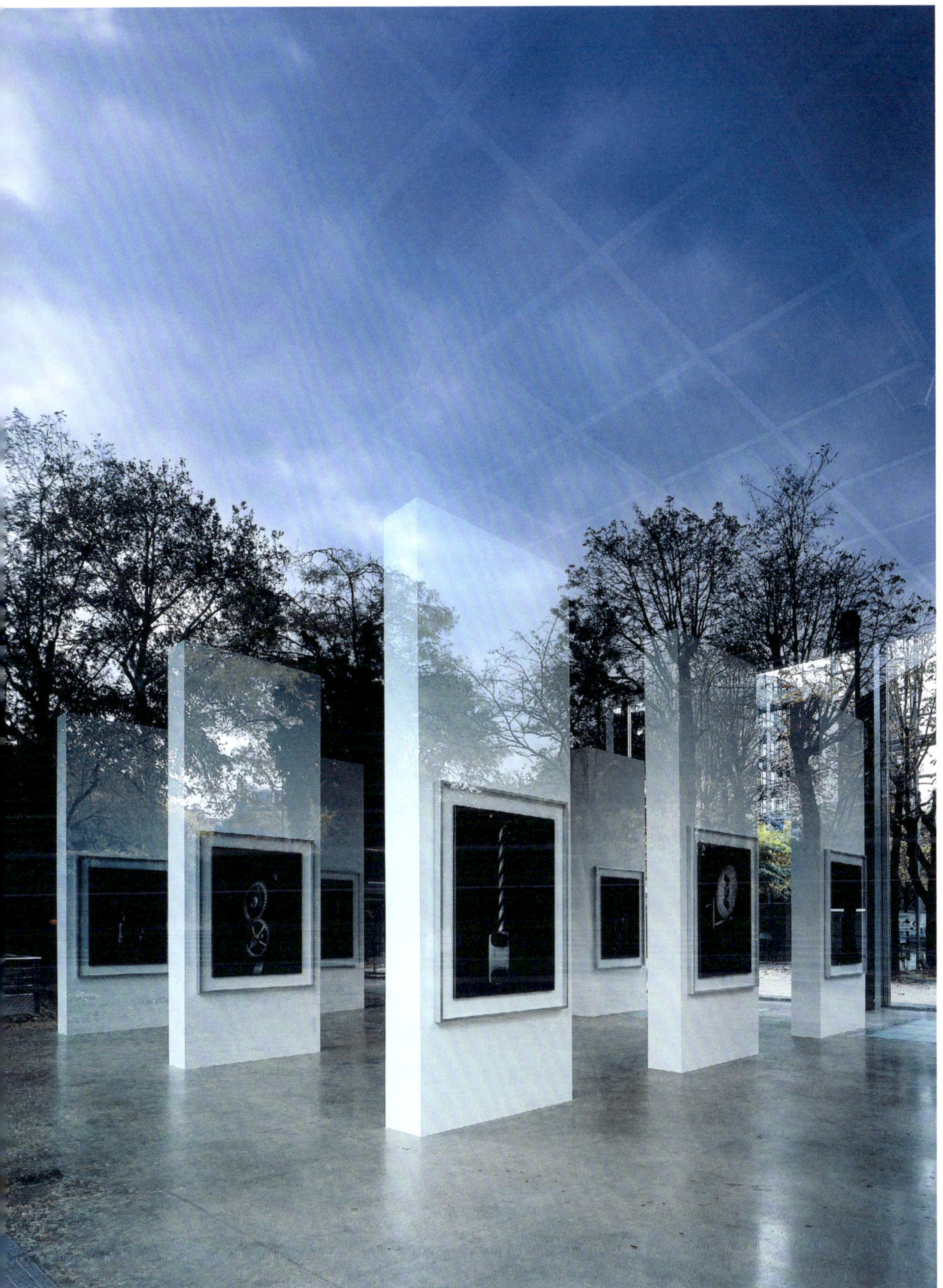

View of the exhibition of Hiroshi Sugimoto, *Étant donné : Le Grand Verre*, 2004,
photographed by Hiroshi Sugimoto

Emanuele Coccia

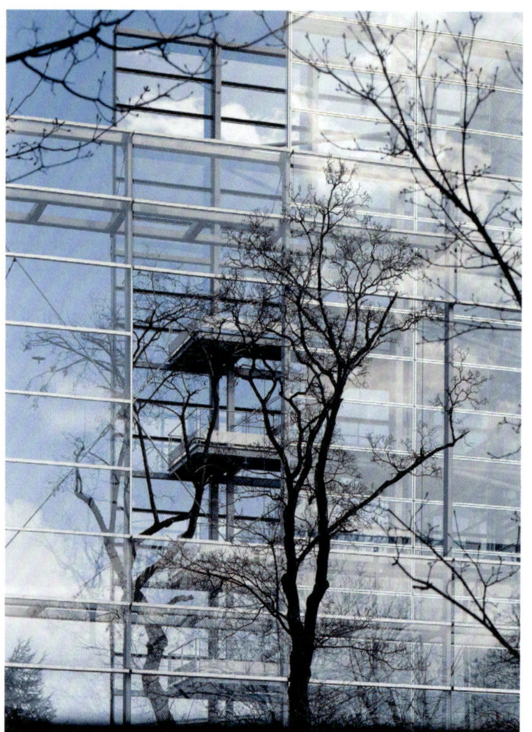

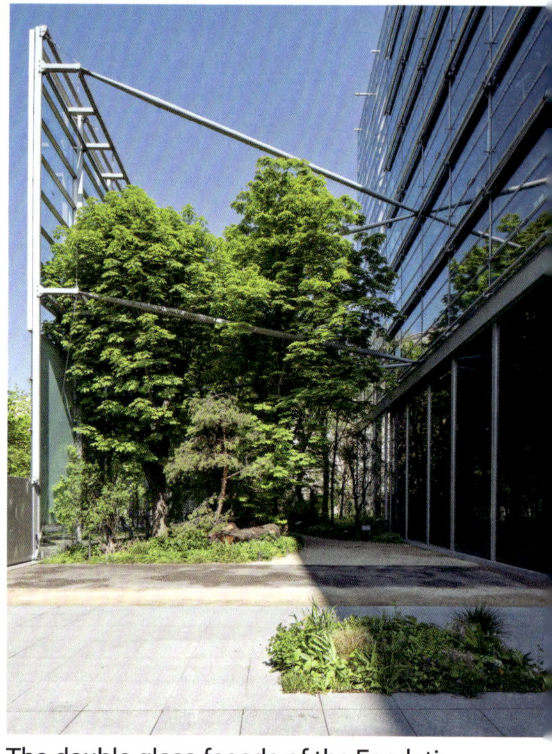

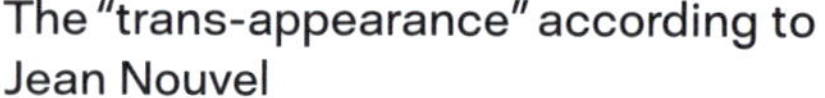

The "trans-appearance" according to
Jean Nouvel

The double glass facade of the Fondation
Cartier building

a kind of squared reflection, the emblematic figure of a reflection reflecting on itself. As Jean Nouvel explained: "And after lengthy observation, I realized that this superposition of the thing observed, and its reflection, created an uncertainty. In other words, if you reflect a cloud in a cloud, if you create the reflection of a tree on a tree, by 'trans-appearance,' something happens that has to do with emotion, something 'unsettling' in every sense of the term. I therefore decided to play on these parameters so that these two walls would reflect the trees standing in front, on the sidewalk, and that this reflection would be imprinted on the trees behind it."[10]

This vertiginous multiplication of reflections is enhanced by the forms that emerge from the garden behind the main building: in this way, the building itself becomes a kind of screen onto which the entire botanical world is reflected. By transforming into an image, it not only becomes a spectacle, an exhibition object,

10 "Jean Nouvel and Hans Ulrich Obrist in conversation," p. 104.

but as a trans-apparition, a reflection on a reflection, it becomes
a kind of museum, a theater of itself. The figure of the reflected
reflection—or trans-appearance—could actually be interpreted as
the visual archetype of all museums. A museum is a space that
transforms the world into trans-appearance: objects are not merely
shown, they don't just become images, they are images *placed on
other images*, so that what becomes visible through them is pure
time, past or future history.

From this point of view, the Fondation Cartier building resembles
a trap that captures the sky and nature in the museum space. It is
no coincidence that two of the first exhibitions that were held in
this building were about birds and nature (*Comme un oiseau* in 1996
and *Être nature* in 1998).

Lothar Baumgarten's garden-theater seems to radicalize this
movement. "There is no defined separation between building and
garden; the ground and its vegetation is part of the whole. There is no
beginning nor end. Single trees appear multiplied. Everything is
in motion, mirrored in the play of horizontal and vertical rhythms,
as well as seasonal changes. Fragments of the garden are captured
within the three parallel glass sections of the architectural grid.
Refracted through kaleidoscopic prisms, light transforms the building
into a crystal. The visitor's position is continuously questioned.
Space becomes mirrored surface."[11] In a gesture of Platonic descent,
Lothar Baumgarten uses every geometric form to reverse the order
between the building and the garden. You only have to look at the
blueprints to understand this: Jean Nouvel's rectangle becomes
a stage whose *cavea* is the garden.

The museum—and with it human and Western art—is now
staged before a nonhuman audience. Not only is it no longer a
place for celebrating, remembering, and reflecting on national
and modern history, but as *theatrum* has for centuries been
the word for thinking in terms of totality and the encyclopedia,

11 Lothar Baumgarten, excerpt from a text addressed to Marie-Claude Beaud and published in *Theatrum Botanicum* (Paris: Fondation Cartier pour l'art contemporain, 1994), n.p.

Lothar Baumgarten's garden transforms the Foundation into
an encyclopedia so vast that it encompasses every living being
on Earth. The museum is not only interethnic and transcultural,
it is also, and above all, the ultimate trans-species site.

Over the years, it is this organization that has compelled
the Fondation Cartier to invite nature into the museum. This is not
simply a question of following fashion or of ecological activism.
For architectural and museographic reasons, nature has been
invited to be both subject and exhibition object, curator, artwork,
and audience.

Whereas the building is defined by what is reflected in it, the
object changes status as soon as it touches the walls. When reflected
on the museum's walls, living beings seem to take on a different
form: they aquire the same status as the artworks. What does
it mean to make the museum a space in which the relationship
with other species must be rethought? How does art rethink this
relationship with species? And most importantly, what happens
to a living species once it has entered a museum?

It is not easy to imagine what plants and animals would do
if they were to take over a museum. Yet this has been the question
that the Fondation Cartier has asked itself most often throughout
its forty years of existence. The syllogism it has articulated over
several decades has established a new relationship between
art and nature.

Jean Nouvel

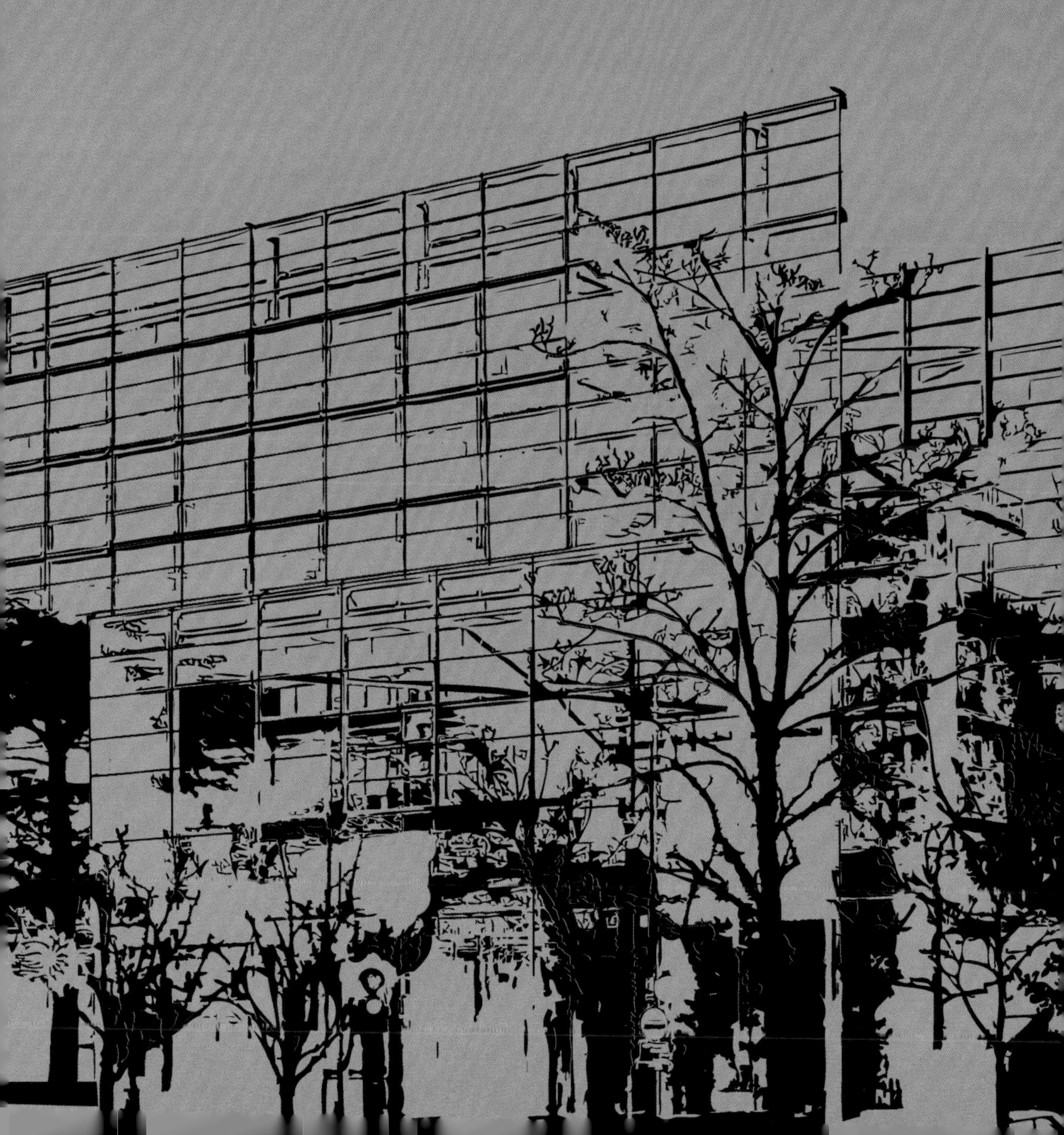

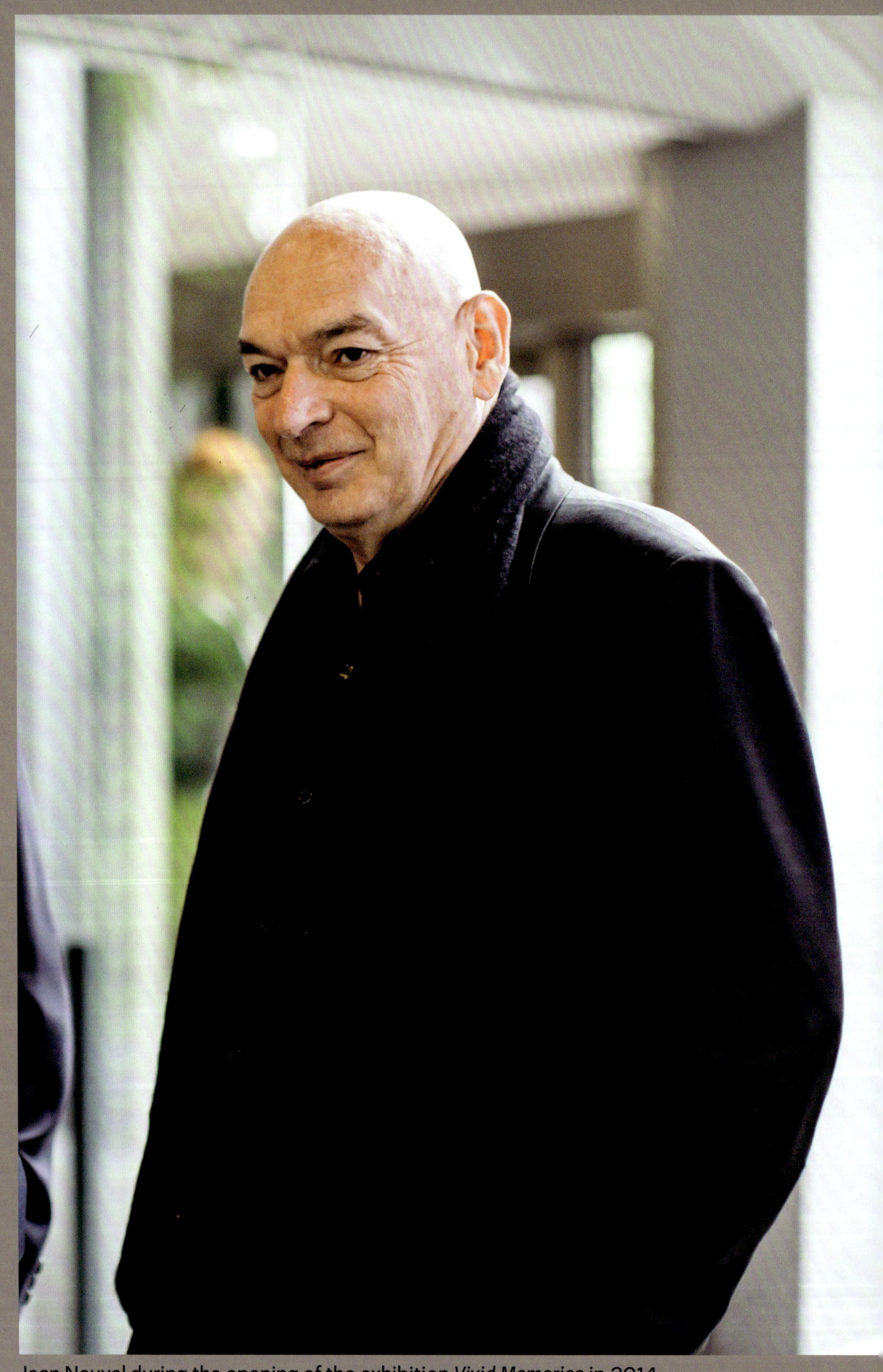

Jean Nouvel during the opening of the exhibition *Vivid Memories* in 2014

Jean Nouvel

In the 14th arrondissement of Paris, on Boulevard Raspail, stands a transparent glass building, filled with light. Like its creator, this structure stands out on the Parisian landscape. This is the Fondation Cartier, designed by Jean Nouvel in 1992, at the invitation of the Fondation Cartier's President, Alain Dominique Perrin, and opened in 1994. Inspired by the history of the site and its surroundings, Jean Nouvel imagined a trompe l'oeil glass architecture, without interior walls, where the reflections of the trees and the sky are pervasive, and the limits between interior and exterior blur. "The Fondation Cartier is a permanent play on layers of light, both material and immaterial. They proliferate, interfere with each other, pick up reflections or drops of water for refraction, disappear because something intervenes, are printed onto the background …. Paradoxically, this play on dematerialization probably makes the Fondation Cartier the building most permeated by its site that I have managed to create," confided Jean Nouvel in 2014.

What binds Jean Nouvel to Alain Dominique Perrin and the Fondation Cartier is much more than a relationship between architect and client; it is a deep friendship that has evolved over time. When construction began in 1992, the two men had already known each other for six years. Marie-Claude Beaud, the Fondation Cartier's first Director, had introduced Jean Nouvel to Alain Dominique Perrin in 1986. The latter wanted to expand the exhibition and administrative spaces of the Fondation, which had been based in Jouy-en-Josas since 1984, and commissioned a strong architectural project that could fit into the landscape. On a hill of the Domaine du Montcel, the architect imagined a glass and steel square, measuring approximately eighty meters long, but the project was not approved by the regional administration and public authorities. No matter. This unrealized project sealed the relationship between the architect and Alain Dominique Perrin. When the founder of the Fondation Cartier identified a new location on the site of the former American Center, he naturally called on Jean Nouvel to design the building. In Alain Dominique Perrin's words, the structure created by Jean Nouvel became "a Parisian monument."

Jean Nouvel—the recipient of numerous awards both in France and abroad, including the Golden Lion at the 7th Venice Biennale of Architecture in 2000 and the Pritzker Architecture Prize in 2008—was invited to design the scenography for two exhibitions in the building on Boulevard Raspail. In 1999, he created the interior spaces for the show devoted to the paintings and sculptures of Gottfried Honegger. In 2008, he acted as curator and scenographer of an exhibition dedicated to his great friend César, choosing to present some one hundred works, among the most important of the sculptor's career: his iron bestiary, compressions, human imprints (including the artist's famous thumb), and expansions. All inhabited the spaces of the glass and steel structure.

In 2009, the Fondation Cartier and Jean Nouvel joined forces once again as part of the urban development project for the Île Seguin, to the west of Paris. The architect designed a 5,000-square-meter concrete and glass structure on the large industrial wasteland of the former Renault factories, intended to accommodate the Fondation Cartier. However, the project never came to fruition. In 2018, Jean Nouvel worked on the extension to the Fondation on Boulevard Raspail on the neighboring site of the Saint Vincent de Paul hospital, which had been abandoned for several years. Once again, this extension had to be abandoned. The project that will finally see the light of day is the rehabilitation of the Louvre des Antiquaires in the heart of Paris, opposite the Louvre. In 2025, after several years of extensive work, the Fondation Cartier will move into this historic building, completely redesigned by the architect. Light, at the center of his architectural vocabulary, will once again be used to reveal the diversity of the 6,000 square meters of exhibition spaces, as well as five large mobile platforms, that will be able to change position as needed. Without doubt, Jean Nouvel continues to write the architectural history of the Fondation Cartier with exceptional virtuosity.

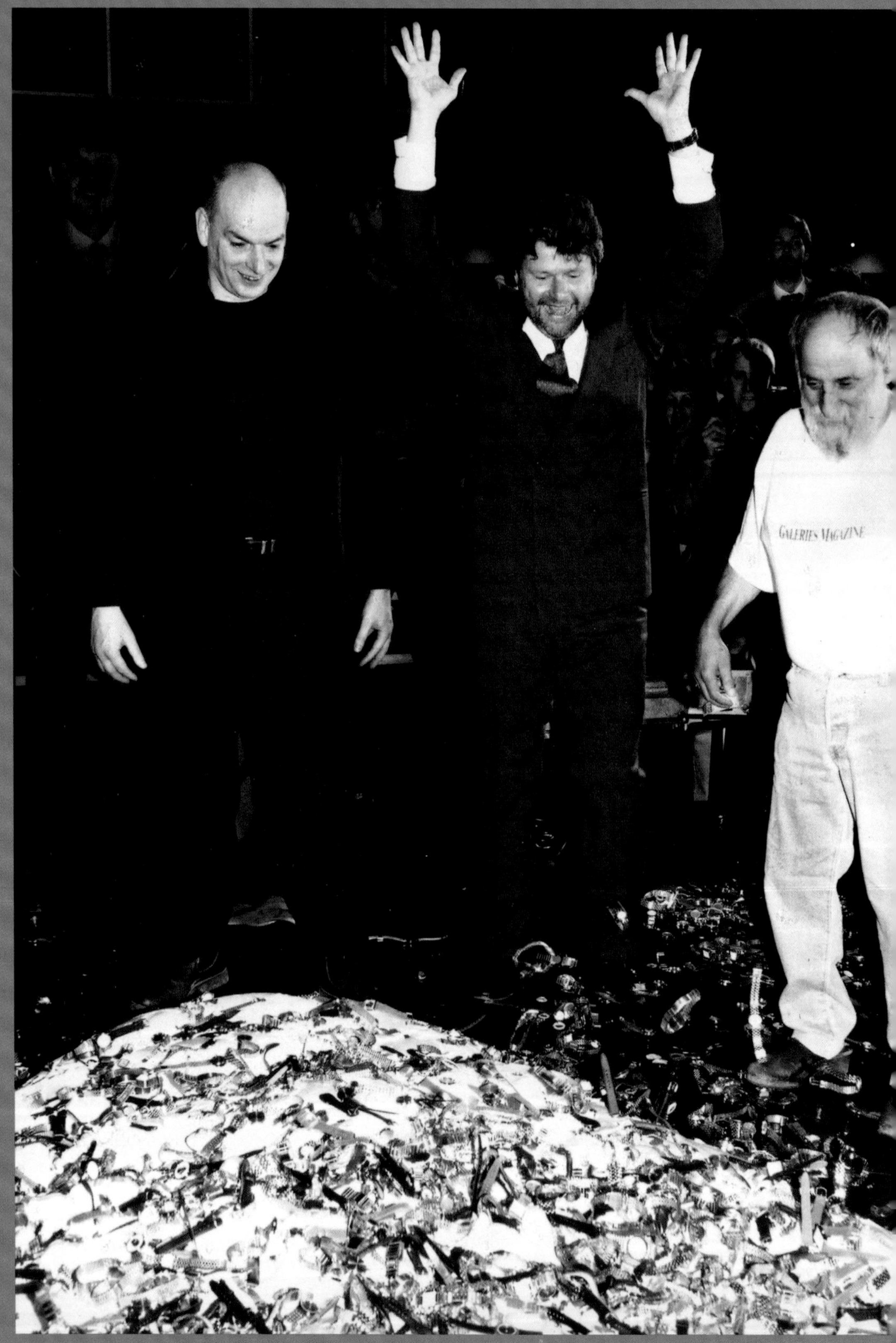

1992 César created an *Expansion* from fake Cartier watches, in the presence of Jean Nouvel and Alain Dominique Perrin during the inauguration of the Cartier-CTL factory in Saint-Imier, Switzerland.

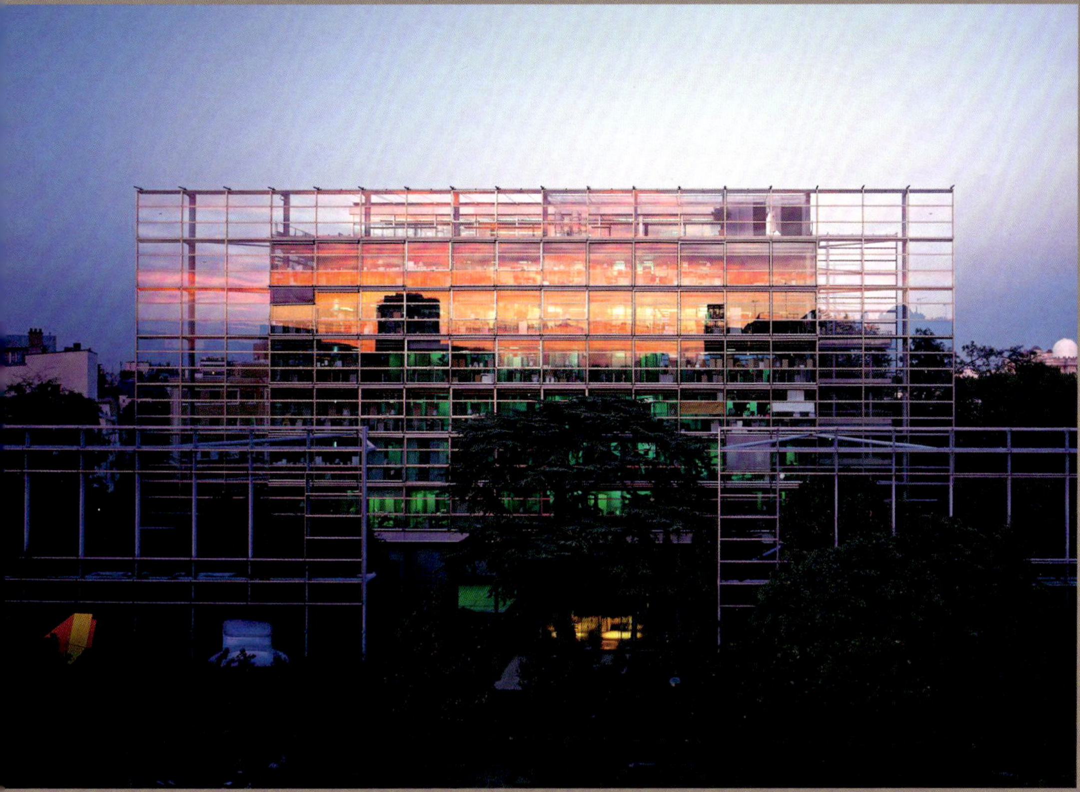

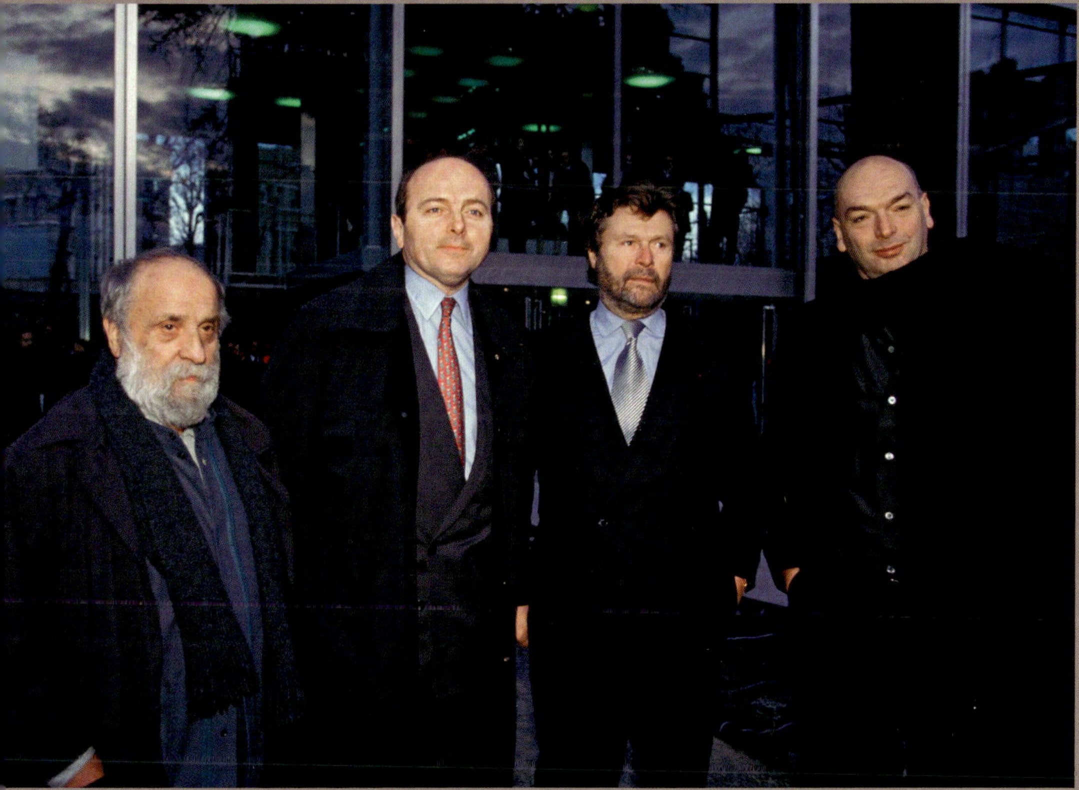

994   On May 10, the Fondation Cartier inaugurated its new building, designed by Jean Nouvel
nd located at 261 Boulevard Raspail in Paris in the presence of César, Minister of Culture
acques Toubon, Alain Dominique Perrin, and Jean Nouvel.

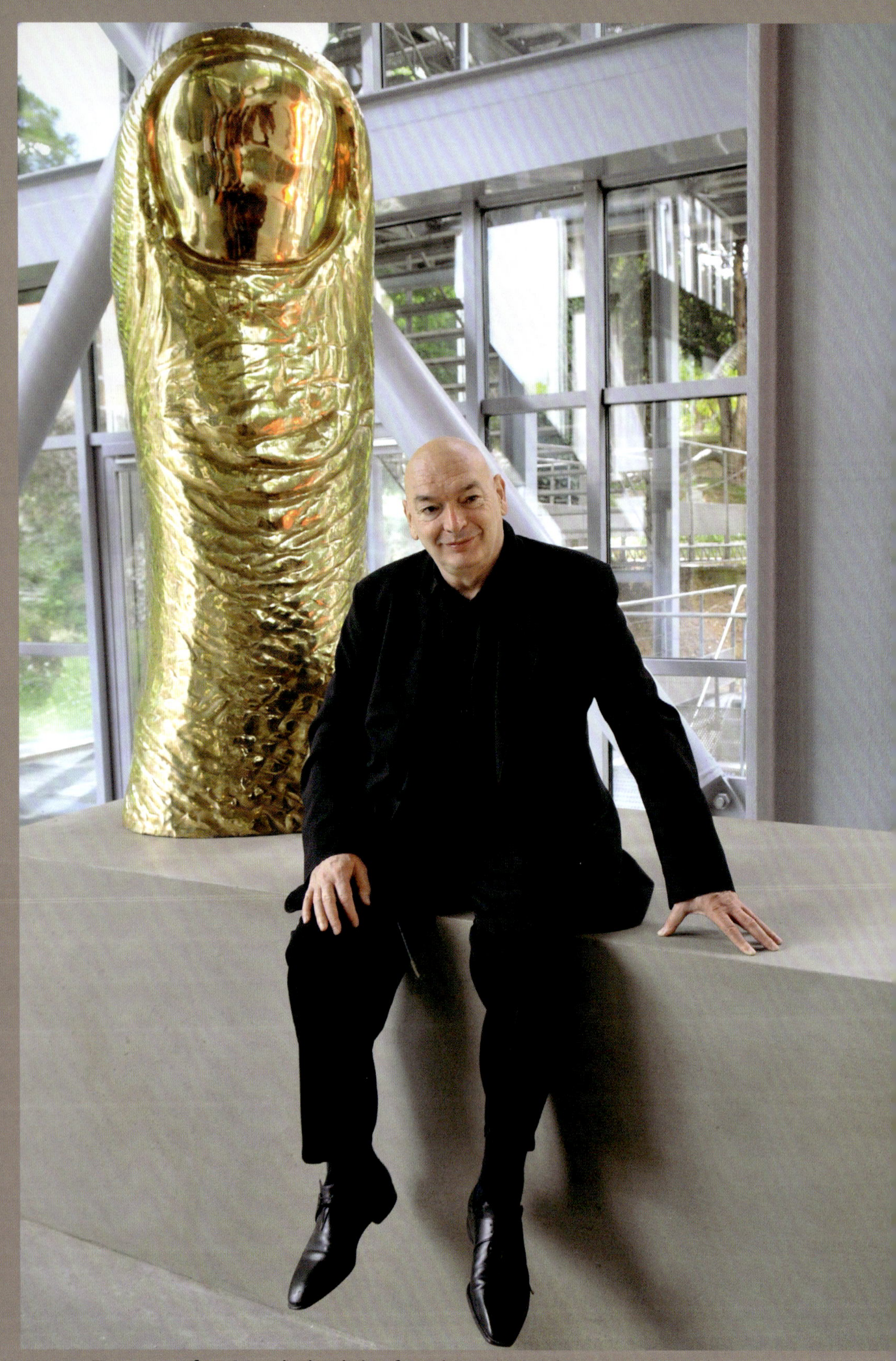

2008 Ten years after César's death, his friend Jean Nouvel was invited to choose and showcase a selection of his works in a tribute exhibition titled *César, Anthologie par Jean Nouvel.*

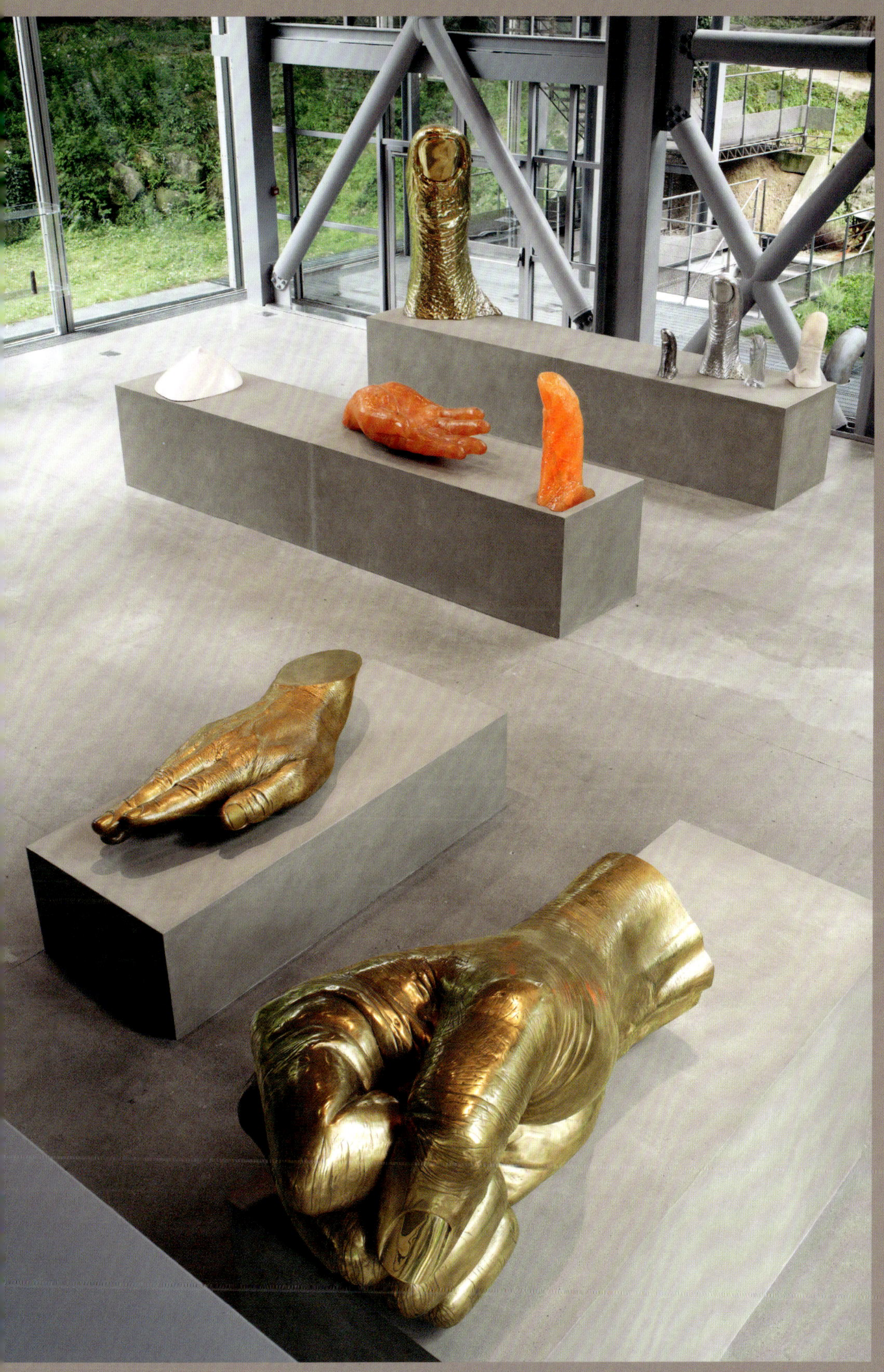

   View of the exhibition *César, Anthologie par Jean Nouvel*

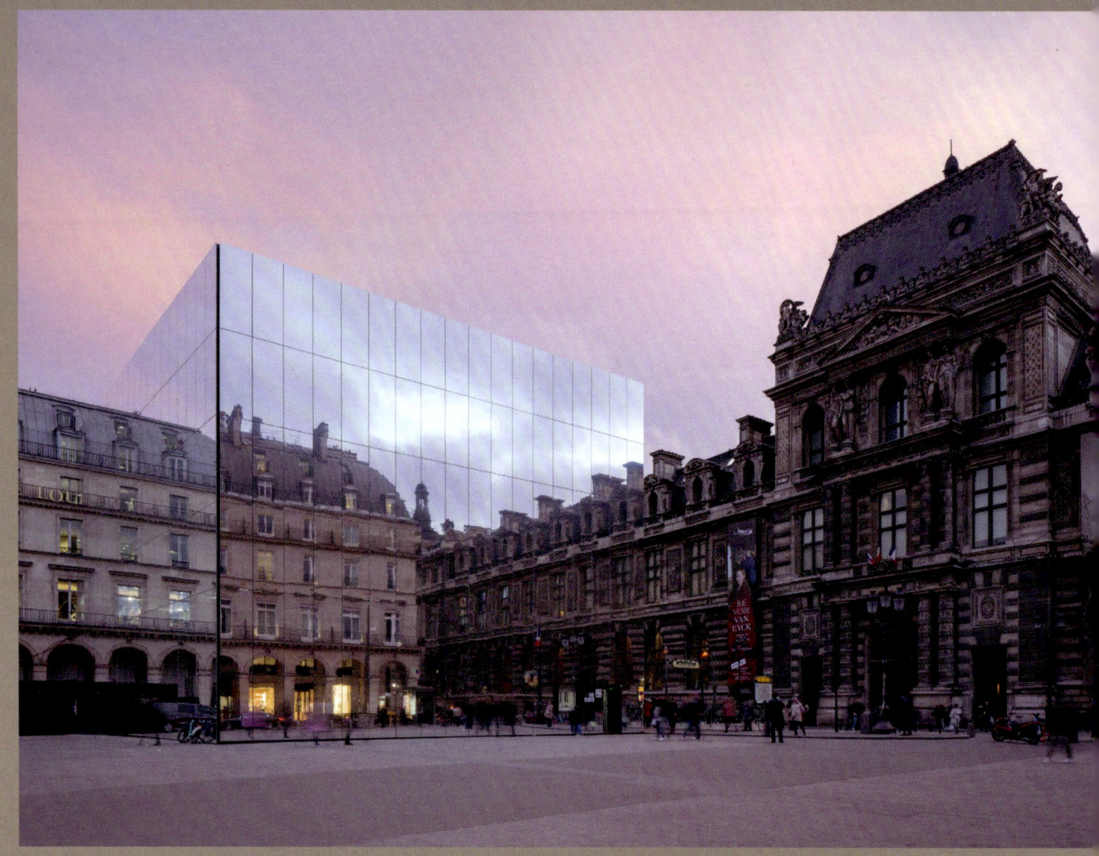

2024   In an historic building on Place du Palais-Royal in Paris, Jean Nouvel works on the future spaces of the Fondation Cartier. Above: Place du Palais-Royal during the work

It is not by accident that we need museums in order to understand what it means to "be nature."[12] In practice, we need architecture to establish a relationship with other species. This is first and foremost a physical need: we cannot have a stable, objective, and public relationship with a fir tree, a cow, a dog, or a mushroom, without the mediation of a house, a road, or a path. We cannot live with those who possess forms other than our own without transforming this relationship into a spatial reality. When these relationships do not become architectural structures, they remain ghosts or individual whims.

And the opposite is also true: every time we decide to inhabit a place, every time we try to give shape to a space, we are obliged to enter into a relationship with nonhuman life. This is also why architecture, in exploring its origins, has often recognized that its first material, its first object, is not stone, but life itself. It doesn't matter whether it's trees or animals: our first real home is the life of other species. There is a reason why the name we give to the relationship that links us permanently to another species is "domestication": making the lives of others our home, making ourselves the home of others, is the first act through which we inhabit space and the planet.[13]

The need to link ourselves architecturally to other living beings therefore has a deeper, more radical meaning: as if it were only through architecture that they could appear to us as subjects, as beings with a voice, a capacity for action, a personality. As well as providing space, architecture enables beings to live as subjects. And the museum is precisely the specific architectural typology that allows objects to appear as subjects. In its spaces, the most

12 *Être nature* was the name of an exhibition presented at the Fondation Cartier pour l'art contemporain in 1998, which brought together art and the living world with contemporary artists from all over the world. Questioning the reciprocal relationship between the work of art and nature, this exhibition created a sense of vertigo in the face of what is born of the artist's hand or what appears to be a "natural readymade," resulting in reflections on what constitutes a work of art.
13 On domestication, see especially Peter J. Wilson, *The Domestication of the Human Species* (New Haven, NJ: Yale University Press, 1988) and Marcelo R. Sánchez-Villagra, *The Process of Animal Domestication* (Princeton, NJ: Princeton University Press, 2022).

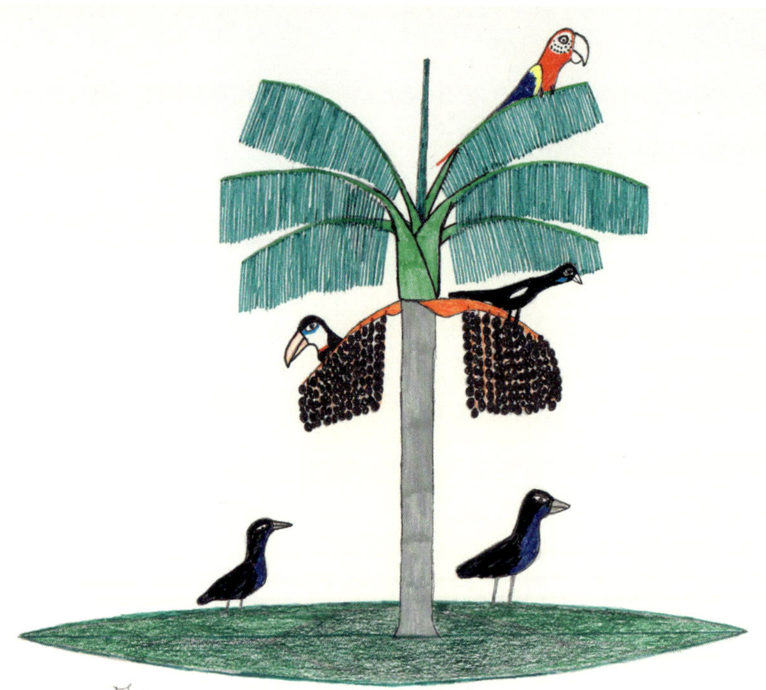

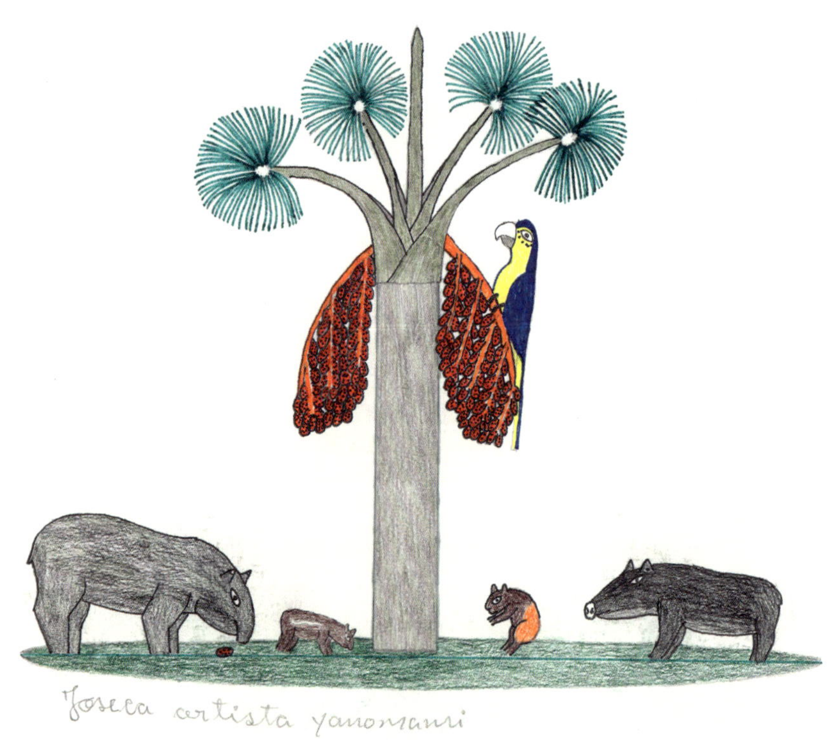

Joseca Mokahesi (Yanomami artist), *Maima si* and *Rio Kosi*, 2018. FC Collections (2019)

insignificant part of matter acquires the same form of existence as a subject and demands to be read as the presence of a soul. It doesn't matter whether it's steel, cotton, pigment, marble, wood, voices, or smells: everything takes on the presence of a Rubens or a Leonardo da Vinci. Nothing in the museum reflects a purely material, objective existence. The form is of little consequence: these objects are essentially the material embodiment of opinions, ideas, feelings, or a vision of the world, of a spirit that does not need organs to exist.

In a museum, everything exists and acts as a subject. Such is the idea behind the posthumous book by Alfred Gell, one of the most eminent anthropologists of the twentieth century.[14] What the anthropology of the previous century, beginning with Edward Burnett Tylor, had called animism, the propensity shown by many non-European cultures to recognize a subjective principle in inanimate matter, is in fact a much more common trait than we can imagine: it is the very idea of art. In the West, art is the name given to the sphere in which every artefact bears witness not to a material nature but to a psychological, emotional, and mental intensity, independent of the nonanatomical nature of the matter of which it is composed. In other words, art is a singular protocol that compels us to interact with an object via an attitude similar to that which connects us to another subject.

Perhaps this is why the Fondation Cartier has been inviting nature into the museum since its inception: it is only within the Fondation that nature can speak, can say "I." Indeed, there is a common thread running through the many exhibitions that the Fondation Cartier has devoted to nonhuman cultures, from *Comme un oiseau* (1996) to *The Great Animal Orchestra* (2016), *Trees* (2019), and *Siamo Foresta* (2023): in the museum, plants and animals speak in the first person. They say "we." And conversely, art becomes less of an exercise in mimesis and representation than an effort at

14 Alfred Gell, *Art and Agency: An Anthropological Theory* (Oxford: Clarendon Press, 1998).

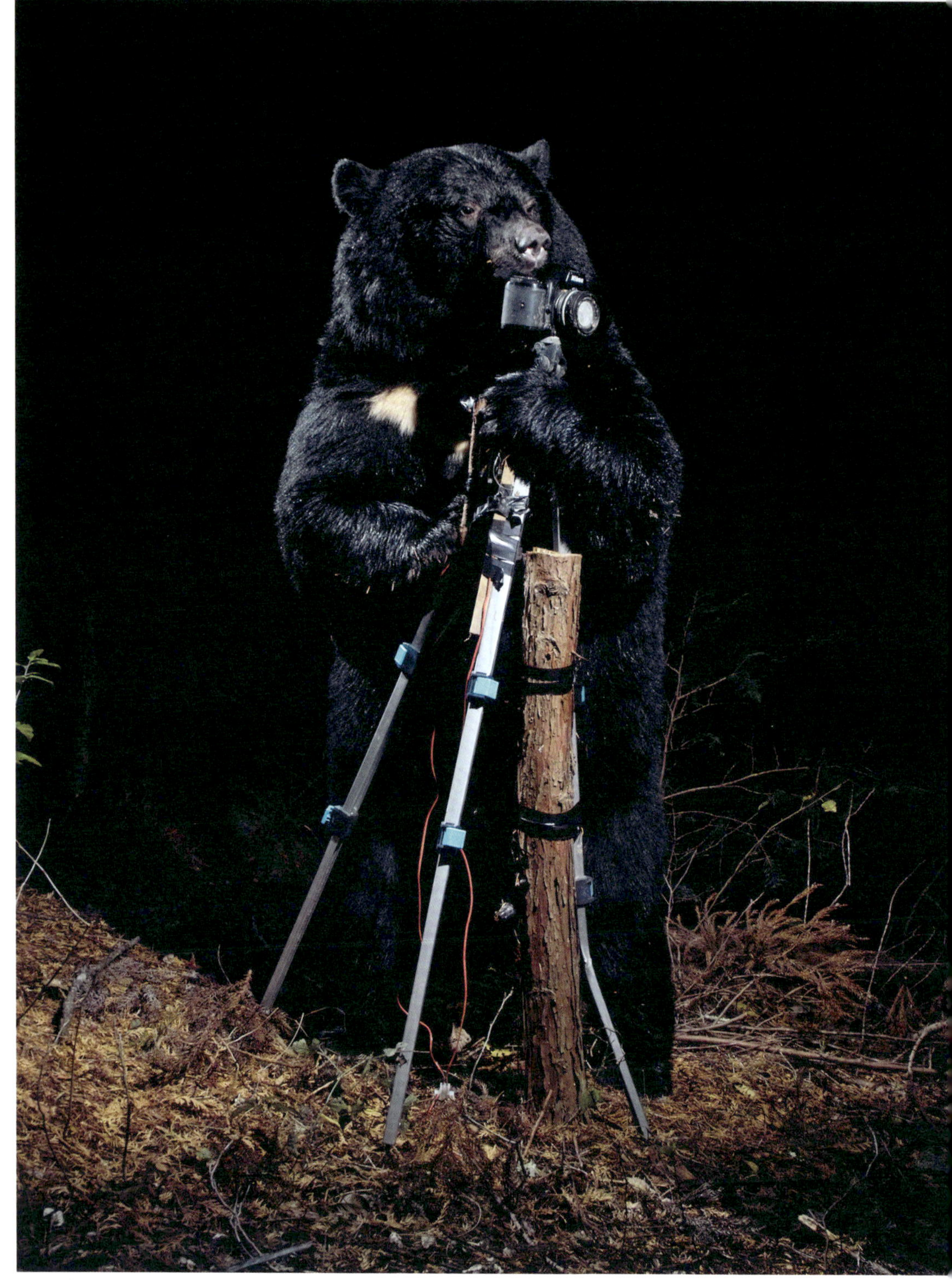

Manabu Miyazaki, *A Black Bear Plays with a Camera*, 2006. Photograph shown in the exhibition *The Great Animal Orchestra*, 2016

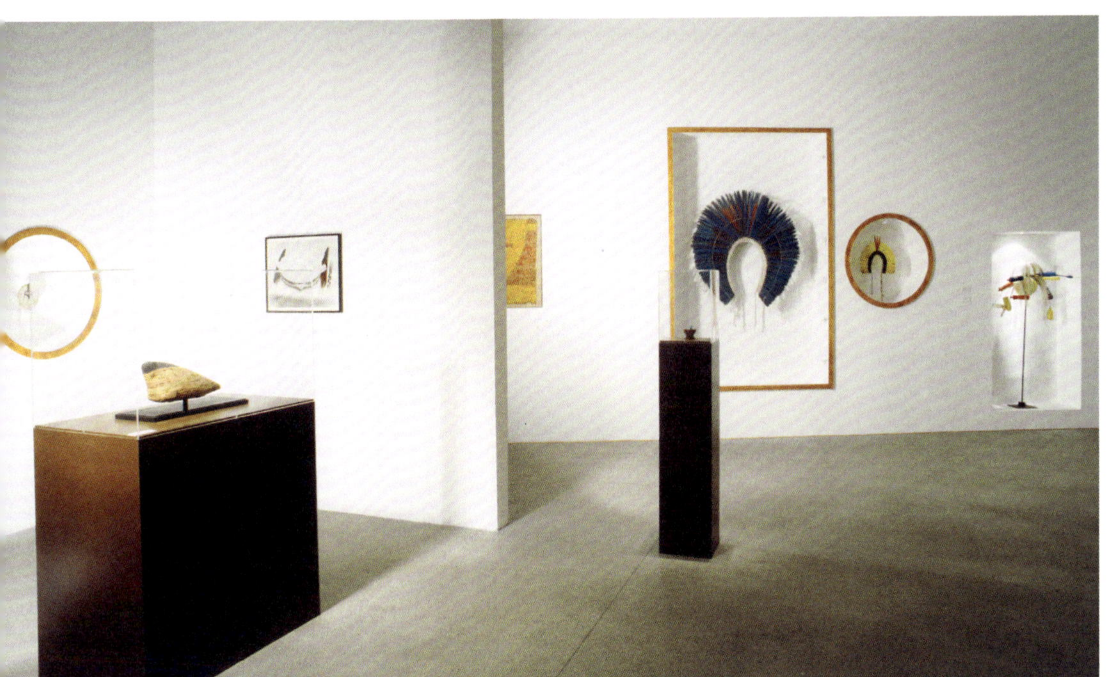

View of the exhibition *Comme un oiseau*, 1996

attentiveness, identification, and ventriloquism. At last, nonhuman species are appropriating human language to speak for themselves.

This new approach was first put into practice in 1996, with the exhibition *Comme un oiseau*.[15] Through paintings, ritual masks, tiaras, dresses, taxidermy, and sculptures, birds were invited into the museum space not only as representatives of a biological taxon distinct from ours. Instead, it was a strange metaphysical space in which life coincided with the ability to create forms and, above all, to take on forms other than our own. The bird becomes a kind of commutative function that transforms every body into an artistic object, and more importantly, every artistic artefact into a form of life or a new species, a form that life has taken and must take over the course of the planet's history. Revisiting and radicalizing Surrealist reflections—of which Roger Caillois was one of the

15 Presented in 1996 at the Fondation Cartier pour l'art contemporain, *Comme un oiseau* focused on humankind's fascination with birds, tracing the unique relationship that civilizations, cultures, and artists have had with the world of birds, from traditional arts to contemporary art, including Western artworks since the seventeenth century.

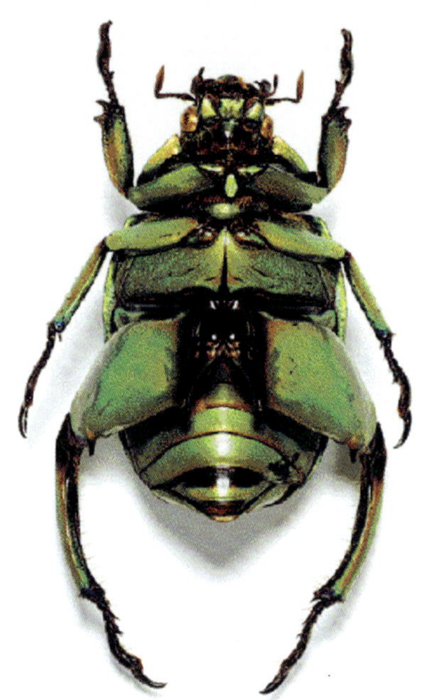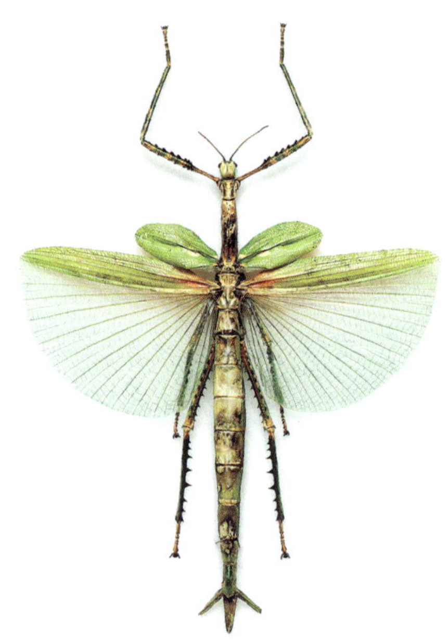

The Hand of Nature, Anne and Jacques Kerchache's collection of insects, presented in the exhibition *Être nature,* 1998

most refined theorists[16] — the exhibition extended artistic practice into a kind of generalized mimetic practice. In place of mimesis — the representation of similarities in the reality of things — the birds seemed to be substituting the notion that similarities are what bind all species together: all living beings resemble each other, represent each other, and make this resemblance their very skin and face. Mimesis is an ontological condition, not just an artistic practice. What's more, entering into mimesis always means entering into the skin of another species: art allows us to live, to feel, to think, and to do so from the perspective of other forms. This resonates with Saint Anthony's vision, as described by Gustave Flaubert: "And now the vegetables are no longer distinguishable from the animals. ... One shrub is bedecked with insects that look like petals of roses ... . And then the plants become

16 See Roger Caillois, "Mimétisme et psychasthénie légendaire," *Minotaure,* no. 7 (1935): pp. 5–10, and Roger Caillois, *Le Mythe et l'Homme* (Paris: Gallimard, [1935] 1938).

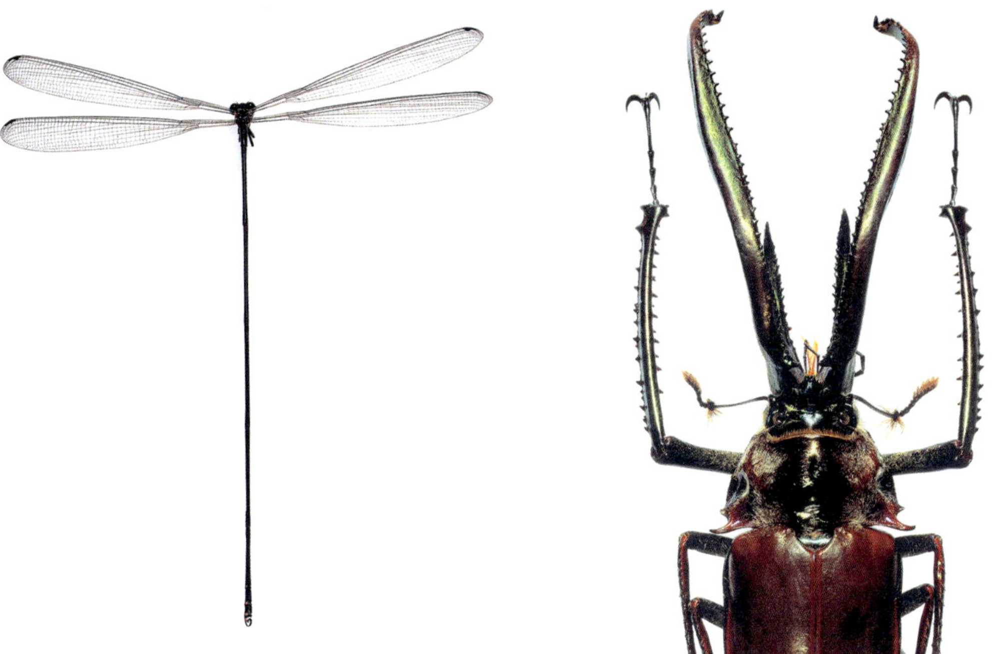

confounded with the stones. Flints assume the likeness of brains; stalactites of breasts; the flower of iron resembles a figured tapestry."[17]

In his comments on the saint's vision, and Flaubert's description, Caillois regarded art as a pantheistic "descent into hell" where "the three kingdoms of nature enter into each other."[18] This is why the bird is also a symbol of the impossibility of distinguishing between nature and culture, and proof that there is nothing purely human about our culture. And so museums must welcome nonhumans into their spaces. Conversely, every living domain must announce itself as culture: as an artificial reality with a history, never identical to itself in time and space. Two revolutionary exhibitions, *The Great Animal Orchestra* and *Trees*, were conceived to do just that.

17 Gustave Flaubert, *The Temptation of Saint Anthony*, trans. Lafcadio Hearn (New York: The Alice Harriman Company, [1874] 1910), p. 259.
18 Caillois, *Le Mythe et l'Homme*, p. 75.

Giving a voice to living things

Inspired by Bernie Krause's book of the same name,[19] the exhibition
The Great Animal Orchestra (2016) featured an installation by
Bernie Krause and United Visual Artists that filled the large room
in the basement of the Fondation Cartier's building.[20] A pioneer
in the use of synthesizers in electronic music, a collaborator
of the Rolling Stones and directors such as Francis Ford Coppola,
Bernie Krause soon became the world's archivist of animal voices
from every latitude. He decided to follow and radicalize Raymond
Murray Schafer's intuition to consider the entire "soundscape"
of a place as a space of melodic and sonic conversation that must
be grasped in its entirety.[21] "Over the past half century, while
recording in the wild," Krause wrote, "I have come to believe that
soundscapes, especially natural or wild ones, hold secrets that
might help us solve many of life's mysteries, if only we had a way
to decipher the code." They are, in fact, "organized expressions,
not unlike some of the Occidental and Oriental musical forms."[22]
The exhibition presented these "concerts" through an immersive
structure whose walls were covered with screens that translated
the soundscapes of different parts of the planet through abstract
linear animations (sonograms) in different colors. Certain
recordings were made in the same place but several years apart,
highlighting changes linked, in part, to the anthropization of
environments and in part to internal historical transformations.
The sonograms were reflected in a basin of black water on the
floor, with surface waves produced thanks to the loudspeakers,
making the reflection another form of the sonogram's existence.

19 Bernie Krause, *The Great Animal Orchestra: Finding the Origins of Music in the World's Wild Places*
(Boston, MA: Little, Brown and Co., 2012).
20 Bernie Krause and United Visual Artists, *The Great Animal Orchestra*, 2016, commissioned
by the Fondation Cartier for the exhibition *The Great Animal Orchestra*.
21 See Raymond Murray Schafer, *The Soundscape: Our Sonic Environment and the Tuning of the World*
(Rochester, VT: Destiny Books, 1994).
22 Bernie Krause, "The Great Animal Orchestra: Voices from the Wild," in *Le Grand Orchestre des Animaux*
(Paris: Fondation Cartier pour l'art contemporain, 2016), pp. 305–306.

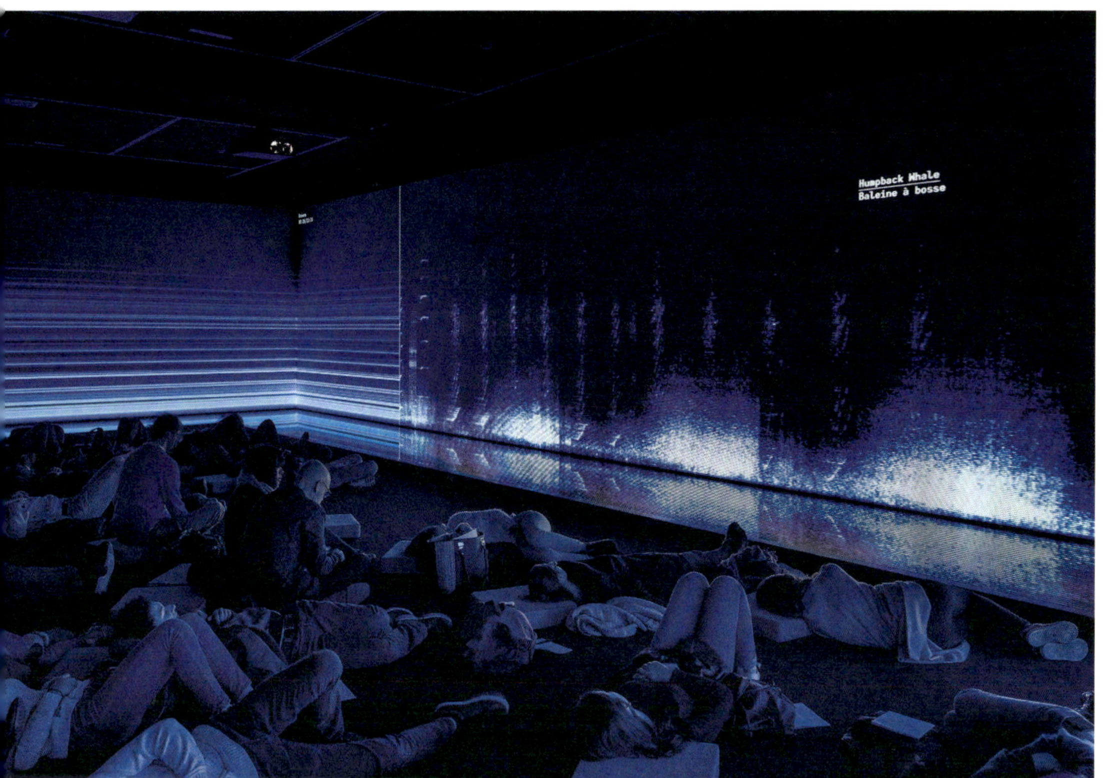

Bernie Krause and United Visual Artists, *The Great Animal Orchestra*, 2016. FC Collections (2017)

In this case, the substitution of the soundscape for the visual landscape enables a double conceptual shift.[23] It is no longer a question of radicalizing mimesis to make art the site where nature's kingdoms merge. Life-forms no longer enter the museum as objects or subjects of representation. Rather, they are subjects of enunciation: they speak, they sing, they say "I." On the other hand, and this is the extraordinary insight that Bernie Krause's work allows us to formulate axiomatically, it is precisely by saying "I" that animals are artists. "Animals are hooting, bleating, growling, chirping, warbling, cooing. They are tweeting, clucking, humming, clicking, moaning, howling, screaming, peeping, sighing, whistling, mewing, croaking, gurgling, panting, barking, purring, squawking ... belching, cackling, singing melodies, stomping feet, leaping in and through

23 "What would change if, instead of the privilege accorded to the visual, we substituted a relation to the world of sound?" Vinciane Despret, "Figures of Re-Composition," in ibid., p. 317.

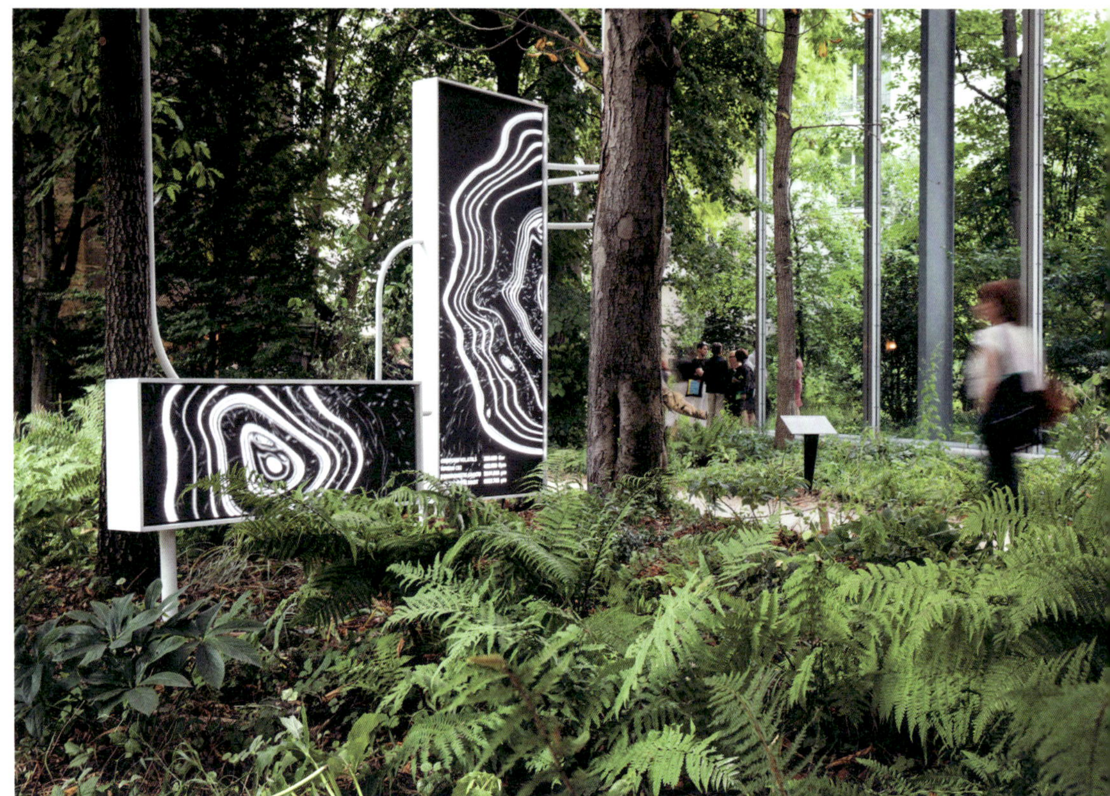

Thijs Biersteker and Stefano Mancuso, *Symbiosia*, 2019. View of the exhibition *Trees*, 2019

the air, and beating wings."[24] In other words, before acting, even
before tracing shapes in space, each species produces a kind
of sound sculpture through its own voice, through its own self.
As Bernie Krause explains, echoing the celebrated American
naturalist and eco-philosopher Paul Shepard, it is plants
and animals that "granted us the fundamental building blocks
of culture, long before the first drawings appeared on the cave
walls of Lascaux, they set into motion our initial ideas of music
and even language—the first structured expressions of our
existence at the dawn of history."[25]

Animals are not the only ones to find a voice in the museum,
though. In the enchanted space of the Fondation Cartier, even species
that have not been heard for centuries are beginning to speak.

24 Krause, *The Great Animal Orchestra*, p. 10.
25 Krause, "The Great Animal Orchestra: Voices from the Wild," p. 305.

The French title of the *Trees* exhibition (2019), *Nous les Arbres* (We the trees) is certainly no metaphor: trees speak in the city. Internationally renowned botanist Stefano Mancuso was one of the exhibition's scientific and artistic advisers; he, along with others (including Anthony Trewavas, Frantisek Baluska, and Richard Karban), conclusively demonstrated that plants and trees are perfectly aware of what is going on around and inside them, and that while they have no need for a nervous system or a brain, they are endowed with a memory and intelligence that are no less acute than those of animals.[26]

They think, they remember, they communicate: through this exhibition, trees started to speak for themselves. To make their voices audible, it was necessary to overturn the system by which plants have been given a name for centuries, at least in the West: the herbarium. It is curious that knowledge of plants should have been acquired through presentations that involved the physical presence of the object under study and not a graphical reproduction of it, unlike in the case of animals, since taxidermy has never had a classificatory function. Herbariums, allegedly invented by the Italian botanist Luca Ghini in the first half of the sixteenth century, are devices that turn each living individual into a kind of museum of itself and its species. Montaigne described Felix Platter's herbarium (1558) as follows: "Among other things, he is preparing a book of simples, which is already well advanced; and whereas the others have the herbs painted according to their colors, he has discovered the art of pasting them in their natural state on the paper so perfectly that the tiniest leaves and fibers appear there just as in nature, and he turns the leaves of his book without anything dropping out; and he showed some simples that had been pasted there for more than twenty

26 See, for example, Stefano Mancuso, *The Revolutionary Genius of Plants: A New Understanding of Plant Intelligence and Behavior* (New York: Atria Books, 2016), pp. 1–16; Anthony Trewavas, "Aspects of Plant Intelligence," *Annals of Botany* 92 (2003): 1–20; Anthony Trewavas "Green Plants as Intelligent Organisms," *Trends in Plant Science* 10, no. 9 (2005): pp. 413–419.

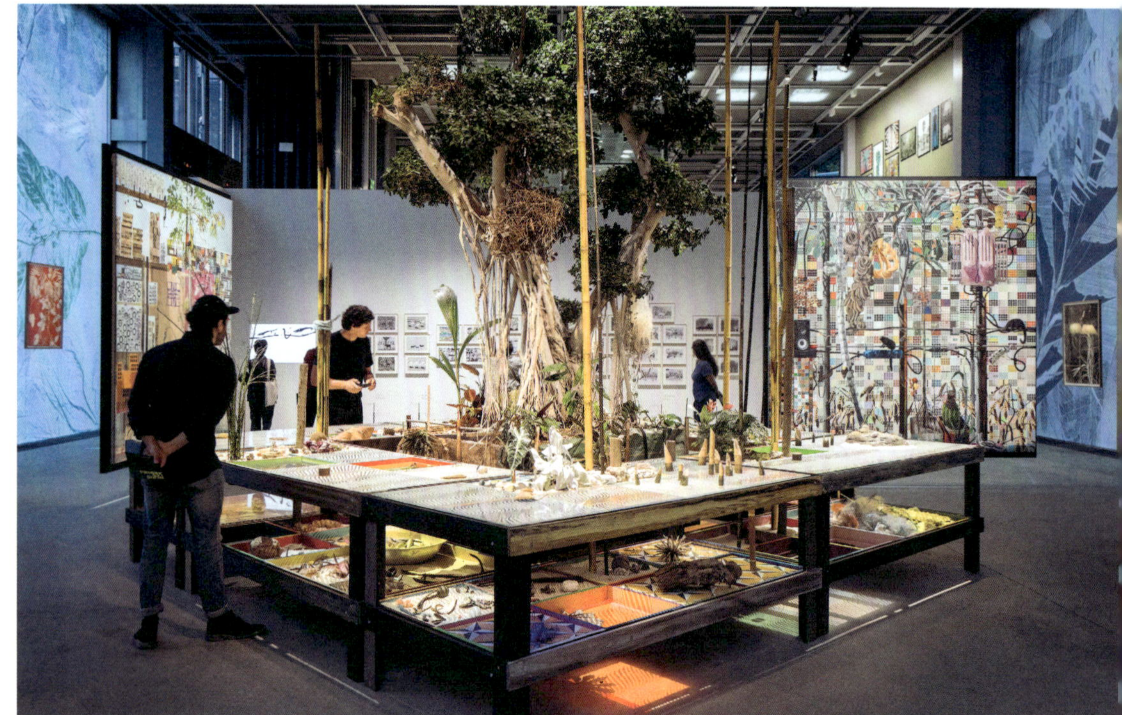

Luiz Zerbini, *Natureza Espiritual da Realidade*, 2019. FC Collections (2019)
View of the exhibition *Trees*, 2019

years."[27] The Belgian botanist Adriaan van den Spieghel, for his part, uses an extremely dense metaphor, calling them "dry gardens" or "winter gardens."

The paradox, both logical and metaphysical, is that an object must die in order to coincide with the knowability of its own form. Just as the ancient Egyptians developed a burial technique to render a body immortal, botany needed to render the body immortal in order to exhume a universal logical form that would be communicable and recognizable in sites other than in the same body that bears and embodies it. In opposition to this system, and in addition to his paintings, Luiz Zerbini set up a monumental anti-herbarium in one of the rooms of the *Trees* exhibition, in which a tree transforms its own form into a celebration of its own existence.[28]

27 Michel de Montaigne, "Switzerland, September 29–October 7, 1580," in *The Complete Works of Montaigne: Essays, Travel Journal, Letters*, trans. Donald M. Frame (Stanford: Stanford University Press, 1943), p. 878.
28 Luiz Zerbini, *Natureza Espiritual da Realidade*, 2019, installation created for the *Trees* exhibition.

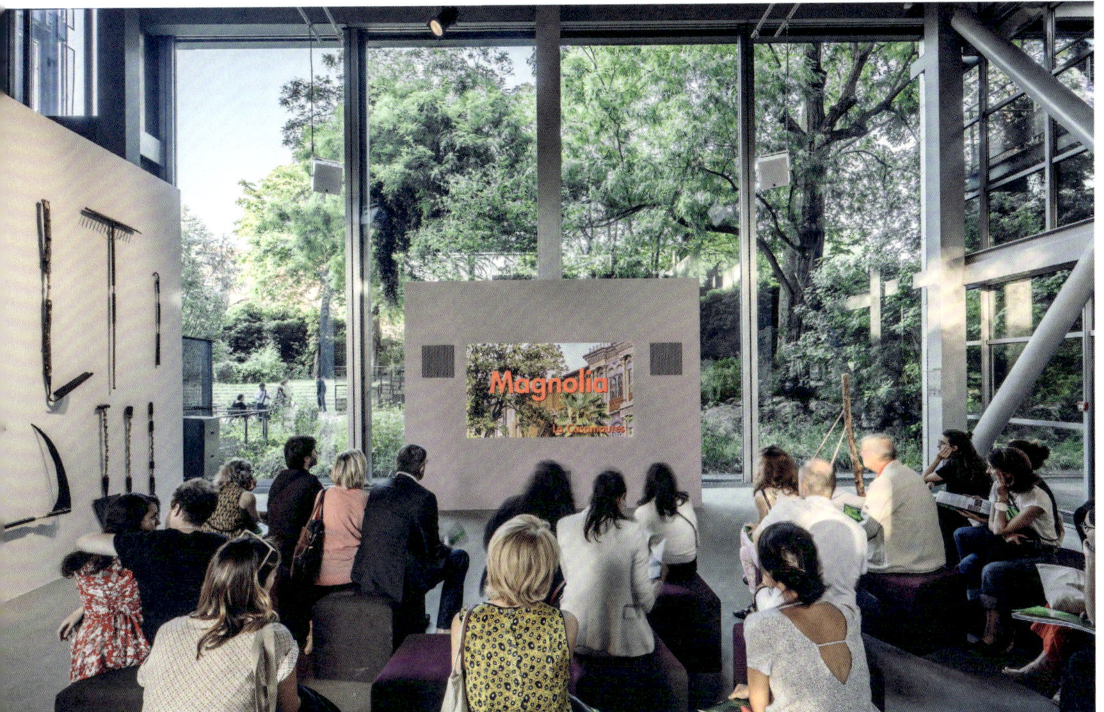

Afonso Tostes, *Trabalho*, 2019, FC Collections (2019), and Raymond Depardon and Claudine Nougaret, *Mon arbre*, 2019. View of the exhibition *Trees*, 2019

Thanks to the exhibition, trees in the city had the chance to express themselves and much more. Through Claudine Nougaret and Raymond Depardon's film, a collection of testimonials about how trees can affect urban life, they seem to claim to be at the origin of urban space itself.[29] For at least a century, anthropology has shown that urban life only came into being when certain communities of human hunter-gatherers linked their dietary and physical destiny to a garden: a group of shrubs and trees placed in a specific part of the territory. It is only through botanical mediation that a community becomes connected to the land: trees do not interrupt the city, they create it. Some of the most important works on display in the rooms in the basement included photos, drawings, and models by Cesare Leonardi and Franca Stagi, the Italian architects

29 *Mon Arbre*, 2019, a film written and directed by Raymond Depardon and Claudine Nougaret, commissioned by the Fondation Cartier for the *Trees* exhibition. "For our film *Mon Arbre*, we have chosen very beautiful and simple trees, in order to give a voice to the men and women who are surrounded by them, cherish them, observe them, defend them, care for them, admire them, and who are also a little tired of living with them." Raymond Depardon and Claudine Nougaret, in *Trees*, p. 352.

who, among many other projects, designed Modena's Amendola Park, and who published a landmark monograph on the structure of trees in 1982.[30] They assert the presence of "another city," beyond the built city, "its parallel and mirror image, its sister, antagonist, and ally at the same time," which not only "produces cool moisture from trees that breathe silently and create oxygen," that alone being a "condition for survival," but also makes it possible to "perceive the passage of time and the changing seasons. It gives us the opportunity to see not just the colors of the city that fade in the sun and the walls of the city that crumble over time but also colors that are renewed and transformed in an endless cycle—beings that are not worn away by time but instead continue to grow and develop."[31]

But that is not all: if trees speak and should speak in the city, it is because we owe them our very existence. We are accustomed to measuring our technical capabilities and progress by the yardstick of our relationship with stone and metal. Even today, when we are asked what the most advanced technological object is, we generally think of the telephone or the computer. It all began when scholar John Lubbock proposed measuring technical progress in terms of its relationship with stone, distinguishing between a Paleolithic and a Neolithic age.[32] This was a kind of historical parallax error: the fact that prehistoric civilization's oldest vestiges to have stood the test of time were made of stone does not mean that they were the first artefacts. The most recent historical analysis has shown that the very first technical tools that humans produced were

30 Between 1963 and 1983, the architects and designers Cesare Leonardi and Franca Stagi ran a studio in Modena, Italy. Over a period of more than twenty years, they carried out a major study of trees, compiling a collection of more than 550 drawings of 212 tree species drawn at a scale of 1:100, with and without foliage, as well as diagrams of shadow projections and plates of seasonal chromatic variations. This study was first published in 1982 in Italian, and for the first time in French in 2019, under the title *L'Architecture des arbres* (Paris: Fondation Cartier pour l'art contemporain). It was also published in English that same year, as *The Architecture of Trees* by Princeton Architectural Press.
31 Franca Stagi, "The City, Green Space, and the Architecture of Trees," in *The Architecture of Trees* (New York: Princeton Architectural Press, 2019), p. 16.
32 See John Lubbock, *Pre-Historic Times, as Illustrated by Ancient Remains, and the Manners and Customs of Modern Savages* (Edinburgh: William and Norgate, 1865).

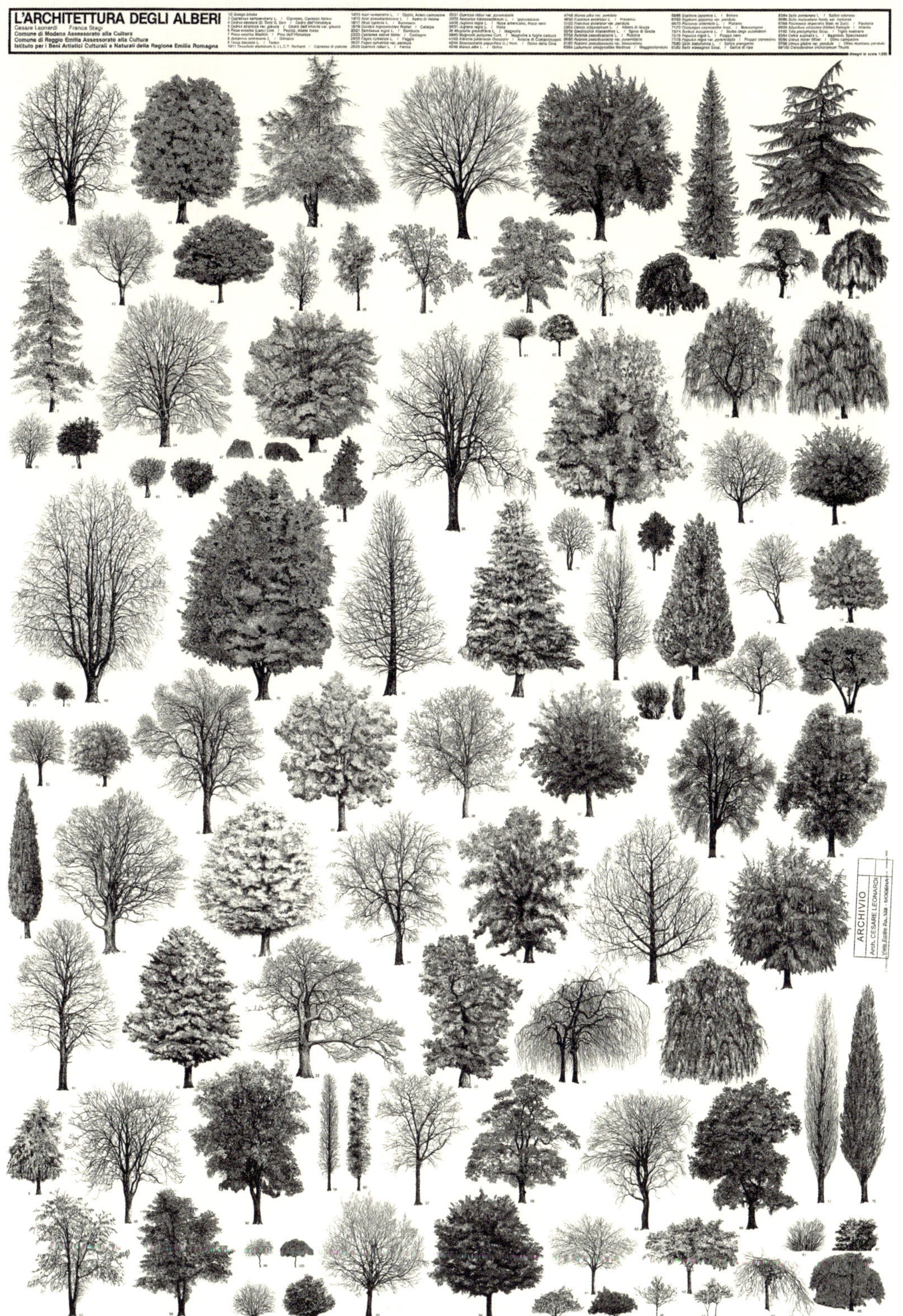

Cesare Leonardi and Franca Stagi, *L'Architettura degli alberi*, 1982.
Poster presented in the exhibition *Trees*, 2019

Emanuele Coccia

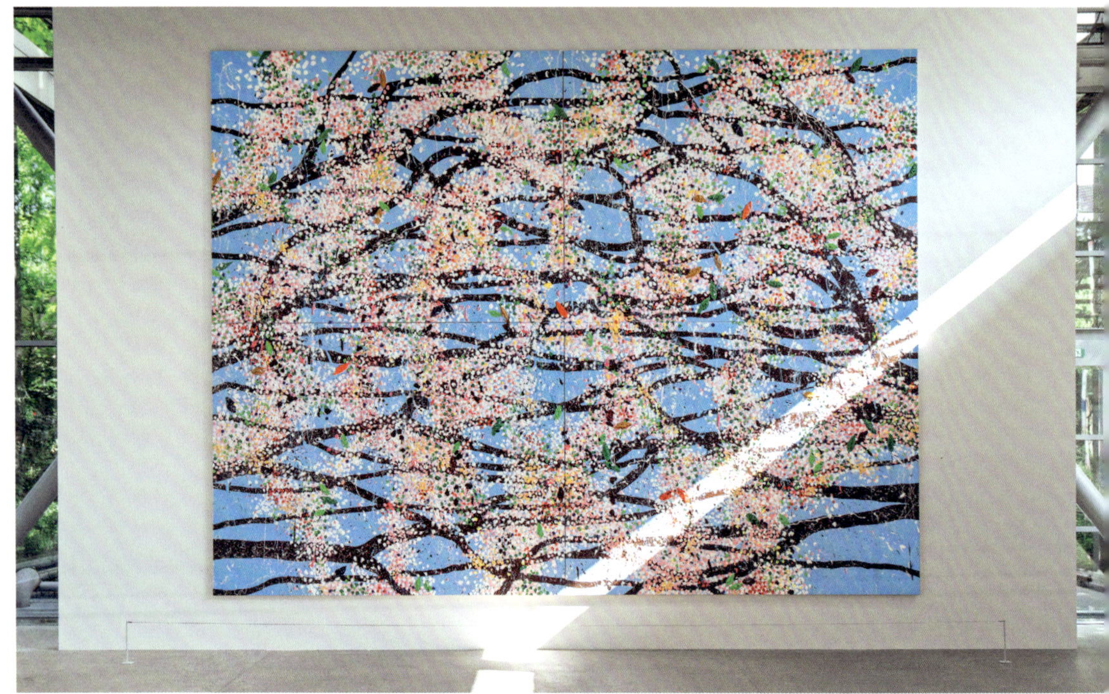

Damien Hirst, *Greater Love Has No-One Than This Blossom*, 2019
View of the exhibition Damien Hirst, *Cherry Blossoms*, 2021

not of stone, but of plant origin:[33] there are no traces because the organic material has not withstood the passage of time. And it was also beneath the cover of trees—for millennia the setting for the development of the hominids that were our forebears—that we learned to use the thumb of our hand. Thus, in a way, it was trees that triggered the liberation of the hand, to which we owe almost all of our technical life. Afonso Tostes's installation for the *Trees* exhibition harks back to this fact, with a series of tools sculpted in such a way as to reveal subjective images in the botanical flesh that evoke the bones of the human body.[34] Once again, the exhibition space allowed the interpenetration of the kingdoms of nature.

33 See Elizabeth Wayland Barber, *Women's Work: The First 20,000 Years. Women, Cloth, and Society in Early Times* (New York: W. W. Norton & Co., 1994); Linda Hurcombe, *Archaeological Artefacts as Material Culture* (London: Routledge, 2007), and *Perishable Material Culture in Prehistory: Investigating the Missing Majority* (London: Routledge, 2014).
34 Afonso Tostes, *Trabalho*, 2019, installation created for the *Trees* exhibition during a residency at the Domaine de Boisbuchet, Charente: "Each tool is unique and carries the marks of its existence. The handles of the tools I sculpt are like the bones of the human body, articulating like the branches of tree, the tree to which this wood once belonged. This is how I become closer to the people who made and used these things in the past." Afonso Tostes in the web series produced for the *Trees* exhibition, 2019, episode 3.

The reciprocal exhibition of species

Plants and animals talking for themselves can be found in the literary and mythological traditions of many different human cultures. Very often, however, the words embody the self-consciousness of the human society that told these stories, rather than that of the depicted species. As the anthropology of the last century has shown, animal and plant life in these myths is a symbol and a means of access to social life: what Claude Lévi-Strauss described as totemism "postulates a logical equivalence between a society of natural species and a world of social groups," with the result that "natural and social groupings are homologous … and the selection of a grouping in one order involves the adoption of the corresponding grouping in the other."[35]

In Europe, fables play a similar role. As one of the greatest theorists of fables, Gotthold Ephraim Lessing noted, the animal fable is one in which animal life is taken hostage in order to dramatize a moral truth: "When we are desirous of illustrating a general moral precept by a particular instance, and in order to bestow upon that particular instance a real existence, we invent a story in which the general moral is intuitively perceptible—such invention is called a fable."[36] To invent a fable is to bring a universal moral principle back to a singular case by giving it reality, and by creating from it a story in which we can recognize a universal principle. Indeed, "in fable we are not to look for the illustration of various truths, but only for a *general moral*; and for the latter not *under the allegory of action*, but in a particular case, constructed so as not merely to exhibit a similarity with the moral, or to conceal or disguise it, but to render it at once apparent and obvious."[37] Animal figures are used because of the moral constancy of their character.

Creating exhibitions based on ecological themes carries the same risk as constructing fables: sermons about humanity in which the natural world is cast as the theater of our guilty conscience.

35 Claude Lévi-Strauss, *The Savage Mind* (London: Weidenfeld and Nicolson, Ltd., 1966), p. 104.
36 Gotthold Ephraim Lessing, *Fables and Epigrams* (London: John and H. L Hunt, 1825), p. 101.
37 Ibid., p. 93.

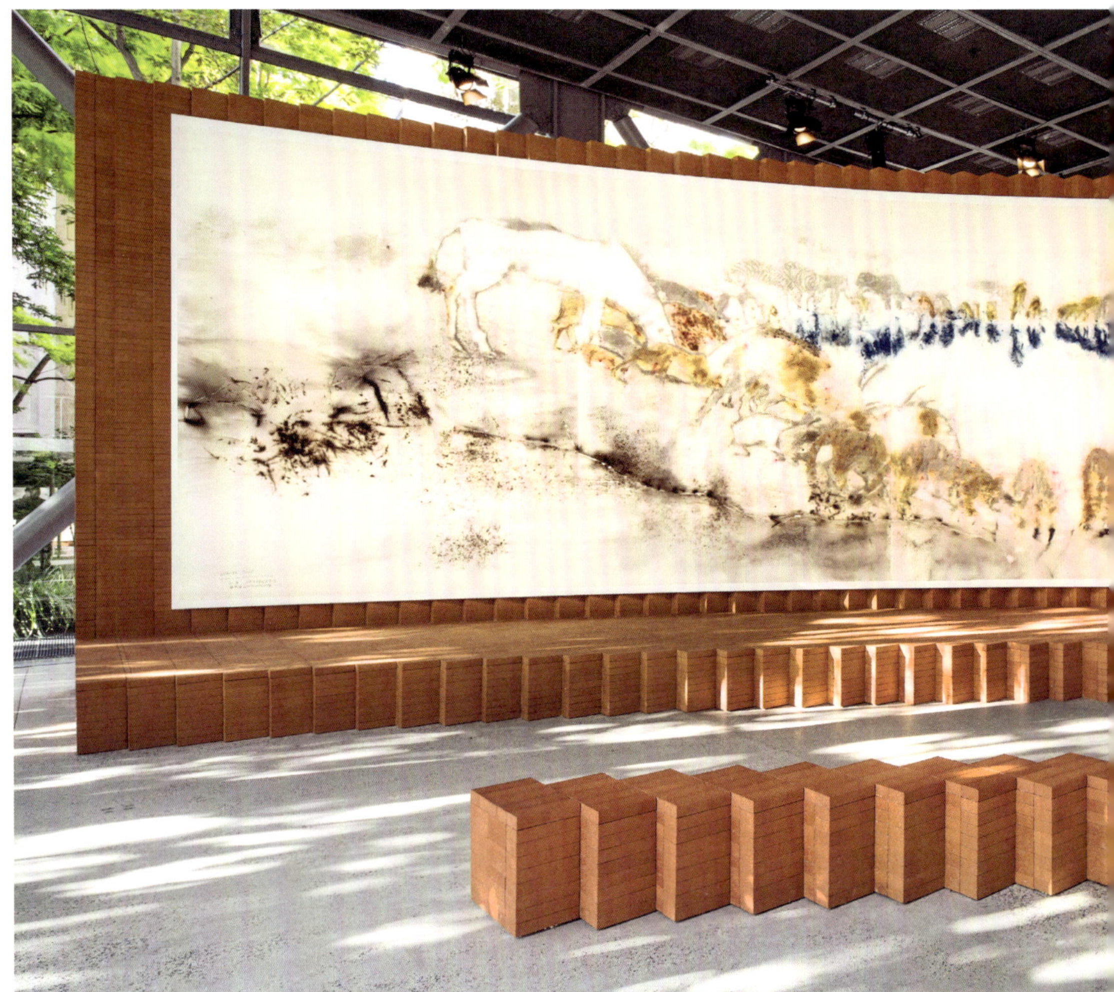

Cai Guo-Qiang, *White Tone*, 2016. FC Collections (2017)
View of the exhibition *The Great Animal Orchestra*, 2016

In *The Great Animal Orchestra*, Cai Guo-Qiang presented a work, *White Tone* (2016), that can be seen as an exorcism against this risk:[38] "I imagined this place being the sole remaining vestige of nature on Earth, the last heritage left for animals. So they no longer fight against each other but they are modestly bending down to drink the last sip of water. Like in a fairytale world, the depicted scene is a beautiful and moving vision but at the same time, it conceals a dark emotion. The pond is still and quiet: it is a void, a white hole swallowing all its surroundings. And it therefore creates a sound void, an image in which all sound has disappeared or is about to."[39]

38 Cai Guo-Qiang, *White Tone* (2016), commission for the exhibition *The Great Animal Orchestra*.
39 Cai Guo-Qiang, in *Le Grand Orchestre des Animaux*, p. 352.

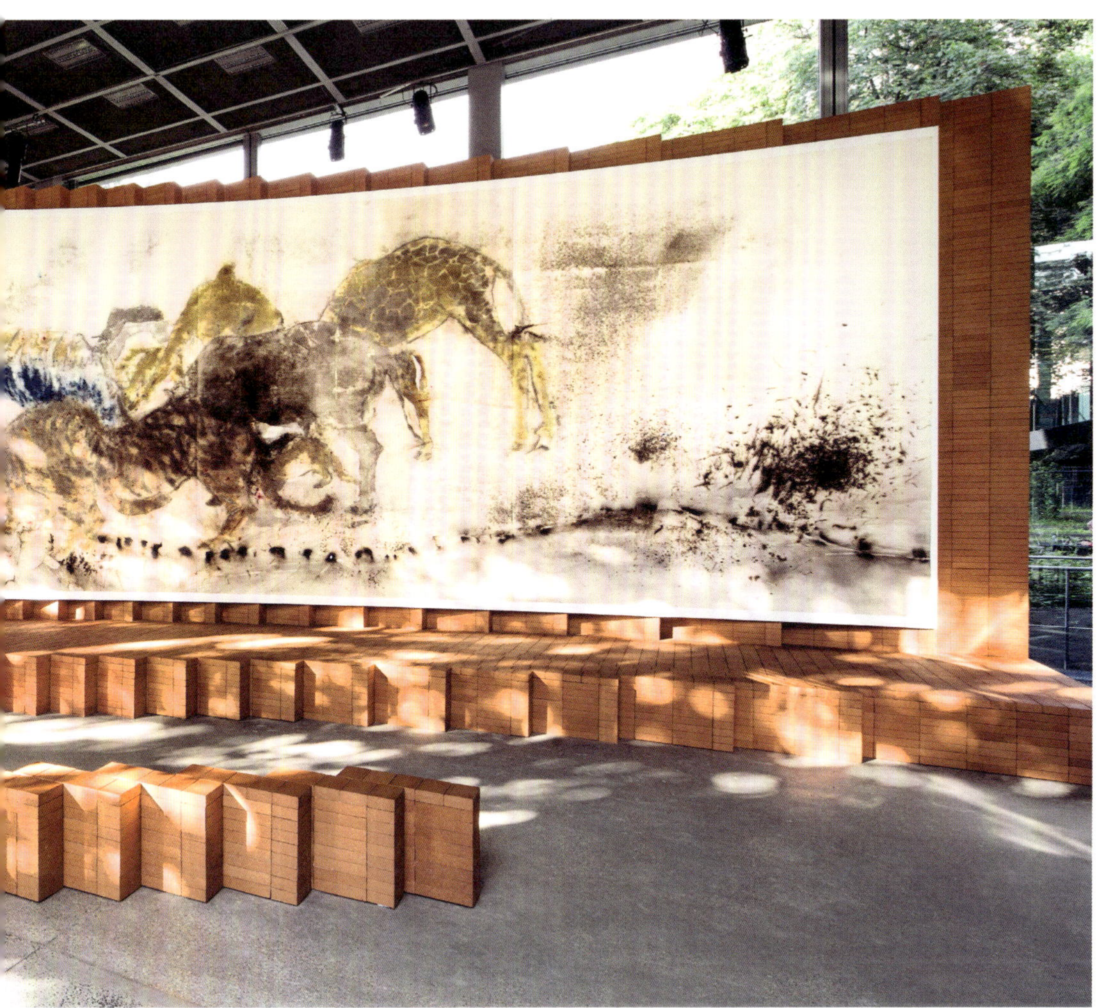

If the Fondation Cartier has been able to avoid such a risk, it is also because in many exhibitions, its Director Hervé Chandès has been accompanied by one of the most profound and revolutionary anthropologists of Amerindian cultures, Bruce Albert.[40] The truth is that human cultures have not passed on any real knowledge of other species as subjects. In a famous passage from his interviews

40 The French anthropologist Bruce Albert is the Honorary Director of Research at the Institut de recherche pour le développement (IRD, Marseille) and a fervent defender of the cause of the Yanomami people of Brazil, whom he has been visiting since 1975. He is the author of numerous books, including *The Falling Sky: Words of a Yanomami Shaman*, written with the Yanomami shaman and spokesman Davi Kopenawa (Harvard: Belknap Press, 2010). For the Fondation Cartier, Bruce Albert curated the exhibitions *Yanomami, Spirit of the Forest* (2003), *Trees* (2019), *Living Worlds* (2022), and *Siamo Foresta* (2023). He has also collaborated on a number of exhibitions, including *Native Land, Stop Eject* (2008) and *The Great Animal Orchestra* (2016). Published in 2022, the book by Bruce Albert and Davi Kopenawa *Yanomami, L'esprit de la forêt* retraces this long history and the intellectual and aesthetic exchanges between the authors and artists presented at the Fondation Cartier since 2003 (Paris: Fondation Cartier pour l'art contemporain / Arles: Actes Sud, 2022).

with Didier Eribon, Claude Lévi-Strauss stated that if you asked an Amerindian about the definition of myth, "there would be a good chance that he would reply: a story from a time when humans and animals were not yet distinct." "This definition," he added, "seems to me to be very profound. For despite the clouds of ink thrown up by the Judeo-Christian tradition to conceal it, no situation seems more tragic, more offensive to the heart and mind than that of humanity coexisting with other living species on an Earth whose enjoyment it shares and with whom it cannot communicate."[41]
It is as if, in reality, the whole of culture were nothing more than an immense work of mourning to console ourselves in light of the impossibility of dialogue with the nonhuman world. The history of the Fondation Cartier's exhibitions over the last forty years can be seen as an attempt to break through this grief and to transform this wall of silence into a first conversation, or rather the reciprocal exhibition of species through art. The museum then becomes the place in which all forms of life show and exhibit themselves to one other.

41 Claude Lévi-Strauss and Didier Eribon, *De près et de loin* (Paris: Odile Jacob, 1988), p. 193.

Trees

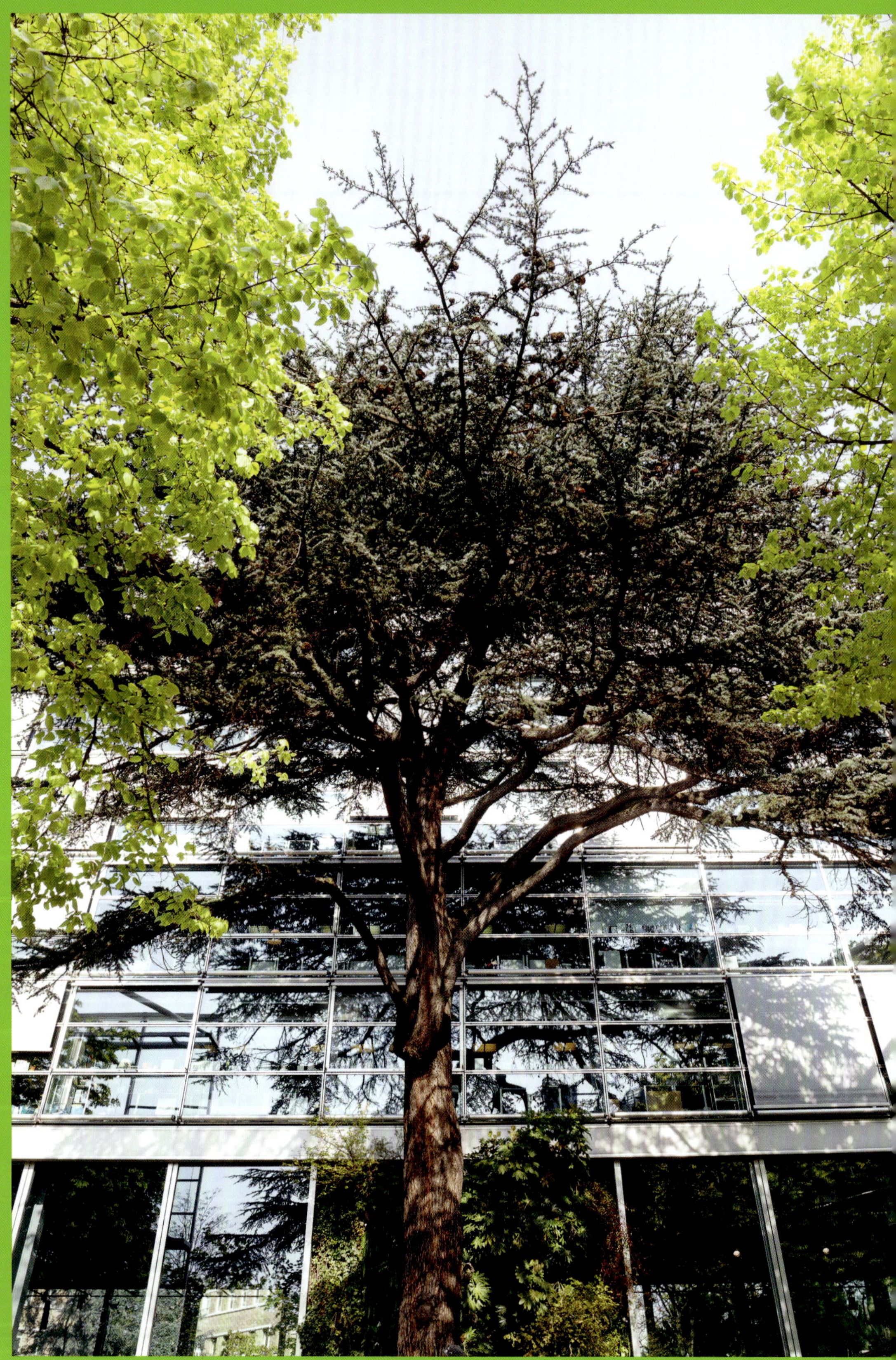

Until 2020, the Lebanese cedar planted by Chateaubriand in 1823 welcomed visitors as soon as they entered the Fondation Cartier's grounds.

Trees

Fig, hazel, chestnut, oak, cherry, Amur maple, Canadian juneberry, Japanese sophora, Japanese tree of heaven, Lebanese cedar, Indian horse chestnut …The garden of the Fondation Cartier on Boulevard Raspail is home to many trees. They stand, leafy in summer and bare in winter, above the visitors who venture into the *Theatrum Botanicum*, designed in 1992 by German artist Lothar Baumgarten at the request of the Fondation Cartier, the future tenant of the premises. "More trees and shrubs will come. Finally, it will be a matter of patience and passion to observe the transformation of an idea into an organic space," the artist explained at the time. He was right. Over the seasons, and over the past thirty years, the Fondation Cartier's garden in the heart of Paris has changed: some trees have disappeared, replaced by younger ones determined to grow tall amongst their elders. What would this garden and these new trees be without those of yesteryear, planted in an immense verdant island, a part of which was owned by the writer François-René de Chateaubriand? This garden is also known for being home, until 2020, to one of the oldest and most remarkable trees in Paris: the tall Lebanese cedar Chateaubriand planted in 1823 when he was living in the house of the old Marie-Thérèse Infirmary, then located in the grounds. Chateaubriand's cedar seemed to watch over its young neighbors, as well as Jean Nouvel's glass building.

The last exhibition to which it was witness offered a curious public, eager for knowledge, a homage to its own kind. Thanks to the artists, botanists, biologists, anthropologists, philosophers, architects, and mathematicians invited by the Fondation Cartier, the exhibition *Trees* (2019) gave a voice to plants, to these "great tutelary ancestors and primary protagonists of terrestrial life," as described by anthropologist Bruce Albert in the exhibition catalog's foreword. *Trees* brought together people from all over the world, and from all cultures, to speak with one voice about the influence trees have on aesthetics and metaphysics. Among the important thinkers and artists who participated in this exhibition, Francis Hallé, a botanist specializing in the ecology of tropical forests, testified to the strong, intimate bond he has forged with trees for over sixty years. His wonderful drawings were shown alongside a large number of works, already existing or specially commissioned for the exhibition, by artists such as Raymond Depardon, Fabrice Hyber, Luiz Zerbini, and Afonso Tostes. Alongside the major catalog, in both French and English editions, the Fondation Cartier also published the first French translation of the vast botanical and aesthetic study—featuring 550 drawings of 212 species of trees, drawn at a scale of 1:100—carried out by Italian architects Cesare Leonardi and Franca Stagi, *L'Architettura degli Alberi*, first released in Italian in 1982, but unavailable for many years. (That same year it was published in English as *The Architecture of Trees*). The exhibition *Trees* also highlighted a work that had been visible in the Fondation Cartier's garden for more than thirty years: *Biforcazione* (1987–1992) by Giuseppe Penone. It was also the opportunity to present the bronze sculpture *Nini sur son arbre*, realized by Agnès Varda just a few weeks before her death.

The Fondation Cartier's interest in the living world had already been demonstrated through exhibitions such as *Comme un oiseau* in 1996, *Être nature* in 1998, and *The Great Animal Orchestra* in 2016. *Trees* was thus the extension of a program that gives the richness of biology an important place within this cultural institution. Presented in an expanded version in 2021 at the Power Station of Art in Shanghai, *Trees* has also given rise to other exhibitions: *Living Worlds* at the Tripostal in Lille in 2022, *Fabrice Hyber, The Valley* at the Fondation Cartier in 2022, and *Siamo Foresta* at Triennale Milano in 2023.

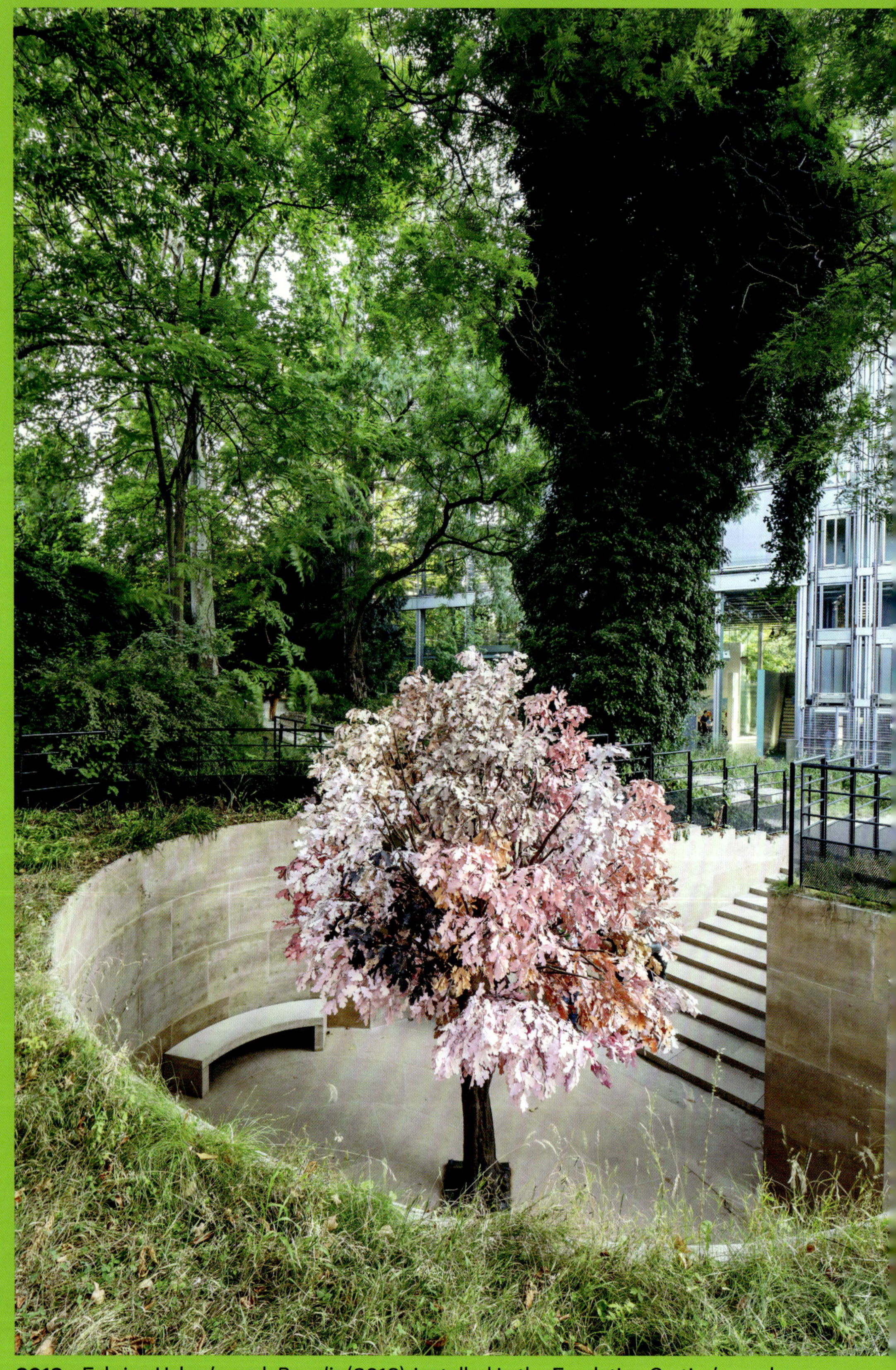

2019 Fabrice Hyber's work *Paradis* (2013), installed in the Fondation Cartier's garden for the exhibition *Trees*.

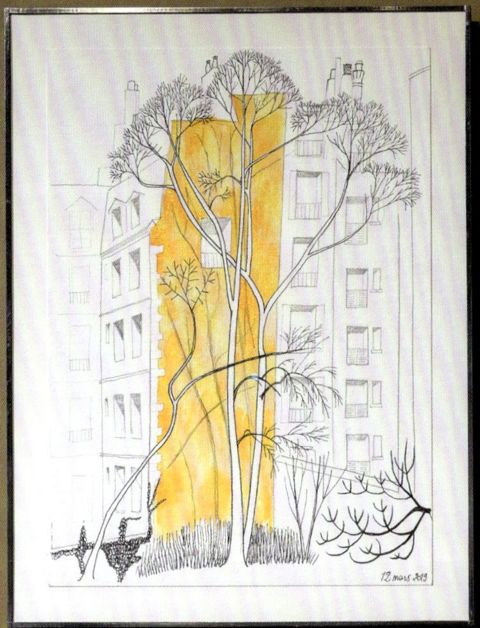

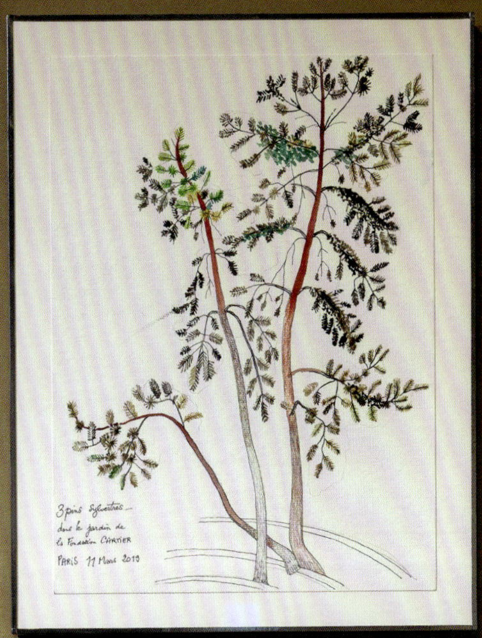

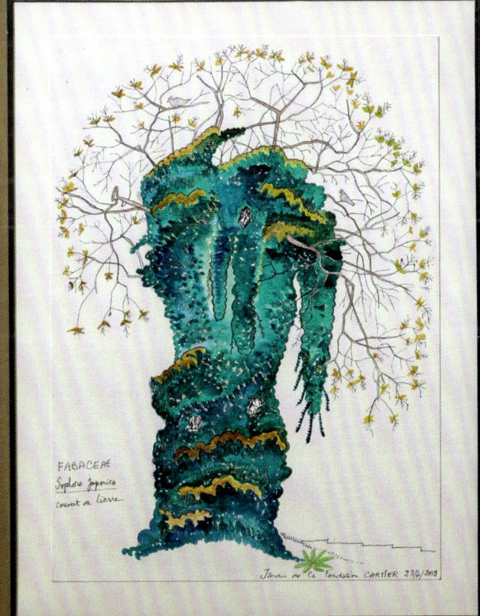

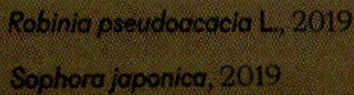

Robinia pseudoacacia L., 2019

Sophora japonica, 2019

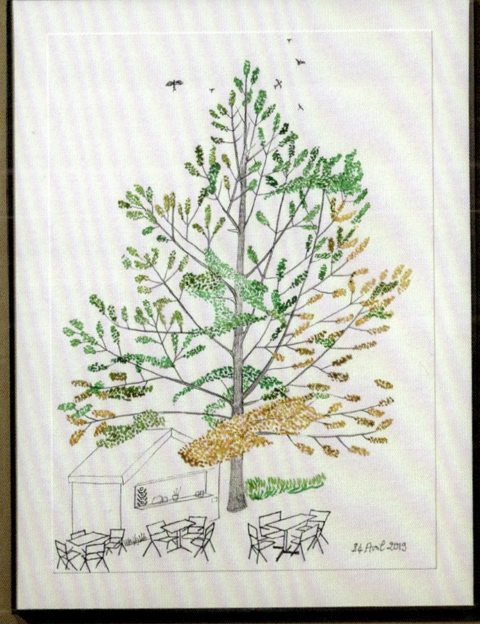

Pinus sylvestris L., 2019

Quercus robur, 2019

2019   For the exhibition, Francis Hallé drew some of the many tree species growing in the Fondation Cartier's garden.

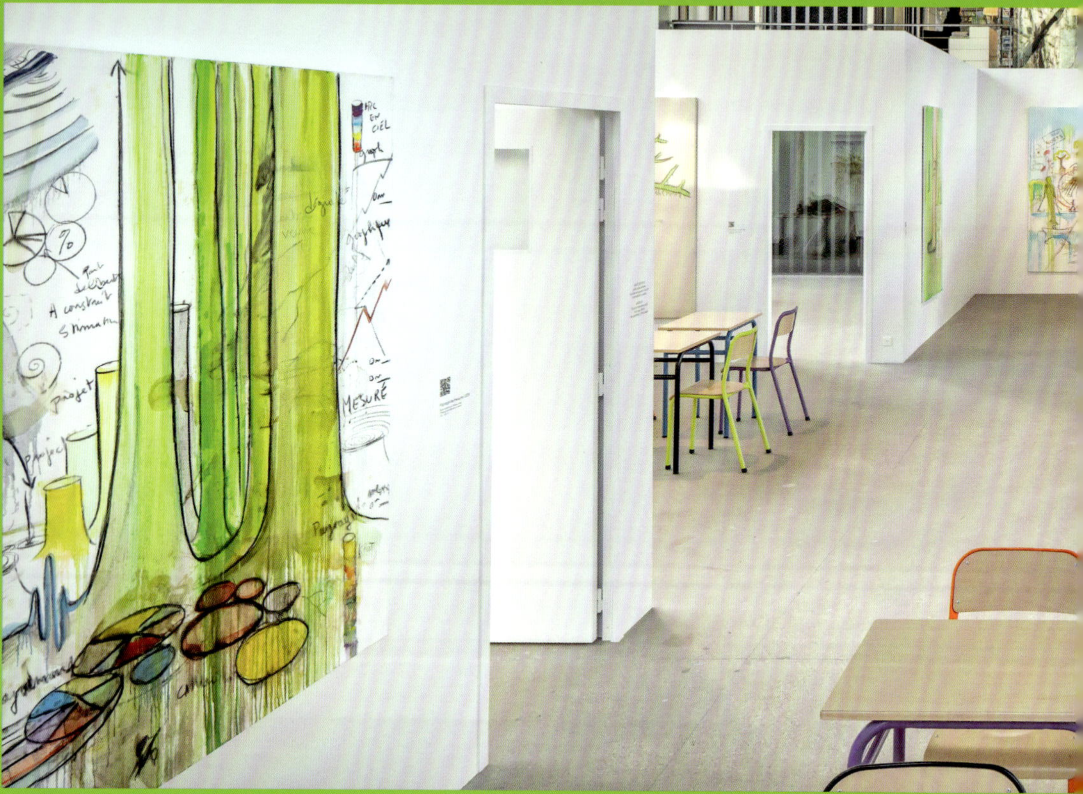

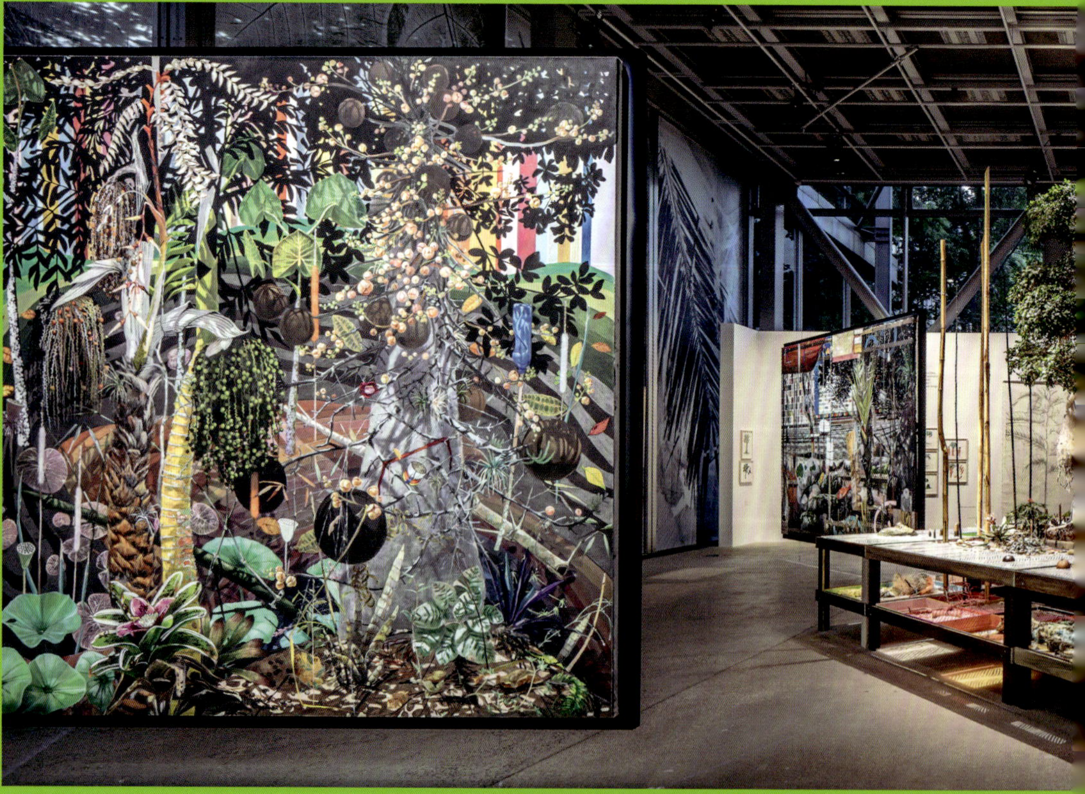

2022 The classrooms in Fabrice Hyber's exhibition *The Valley*
2019 Luiz Zerbini's installation *Natureza Espiritual da Realidade* (2019)
surrounded by his paintings in the exhibition *Trees*

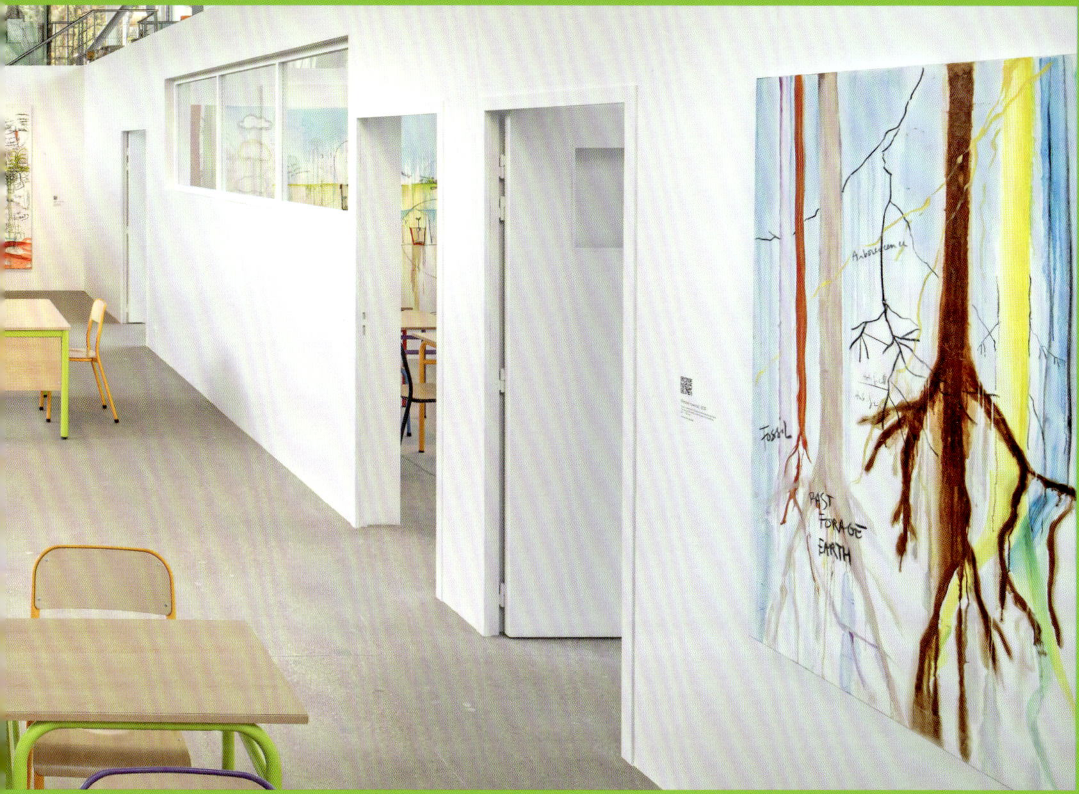

PAST
FORAGE
EARTH

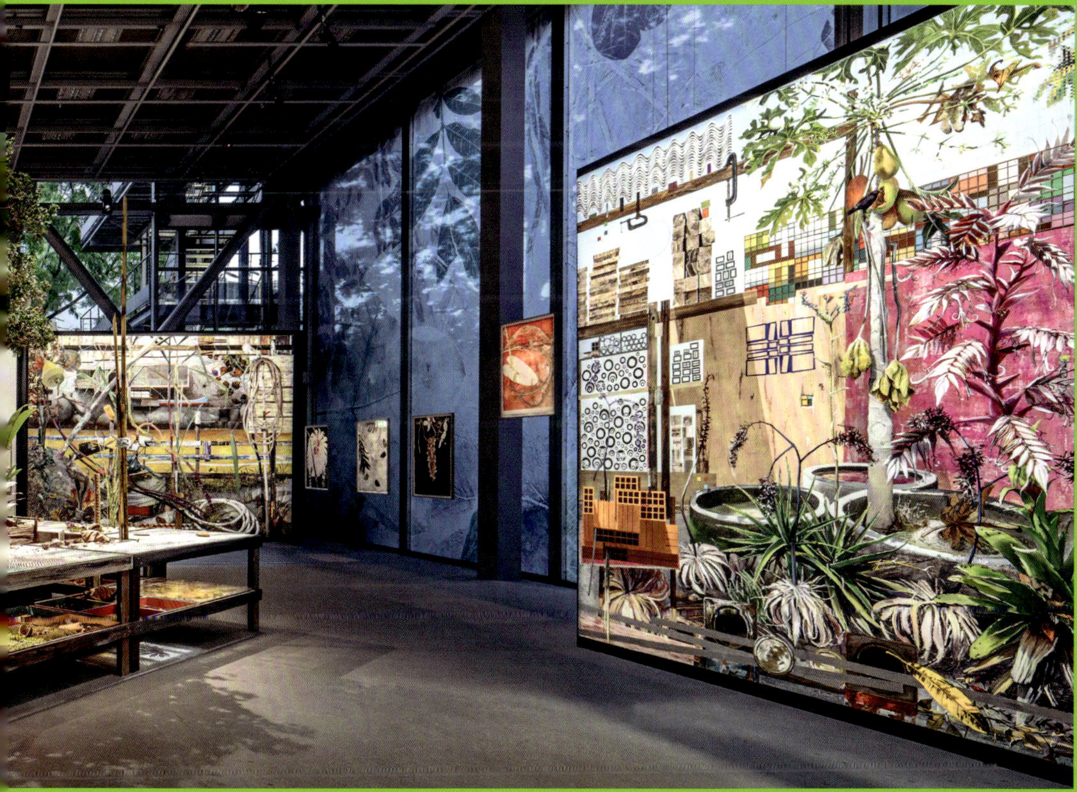

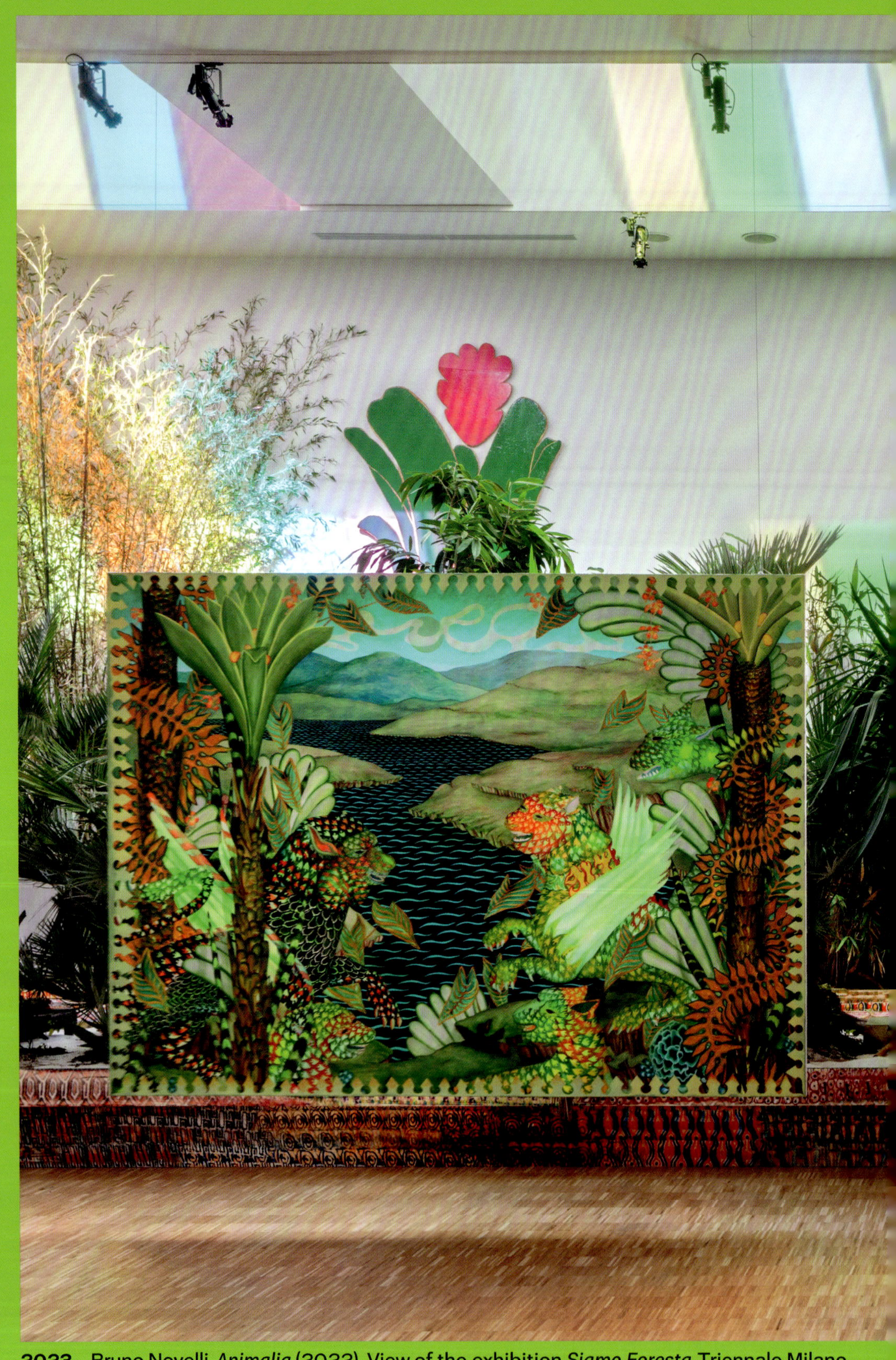

2023 Bruno Novelli, *Animalia* (2022). View of the exhibition *Siamo Foresta*, Triennale Milano, designed by Luiz Zerbini

COLLECTING

The infinite collection

One of the first exhibitions to showcase the Fondation Cartier Collections was titled *Lignes de mire*.[1] It brought together works by artists such as Jean-Michel Alberola, Fischli & Weiss, and Jeff Wall, with each room devoted to an artist. On the wall of one, Allan McCollum placed a group of 240 monochrome paintings of varying sizes. It was only when visitors approached the wall that the nature of the works became clear: they are plaster casts painted black, depicting paintings that are absent or present only through their cast. It is hard to know whether you are looking at a reproduction of an artwork or a model of a painting. The original is rejected, not only to another place but also to an uncertain temporality, between past and future.

Taking up a motif that Stefan Zweig had already highlighted in one of his best-known stories, *The Invisible Collection*,[2] Allan McCollum appears to be reflecting on the paradoxical nature of all collecting. Whereas in Zweig's book, it is the collector's blindness that makes him indifferent to the presence of copies or the simple sheets

1 The Fondation Cartier pour l'art contemporain began collecting the works it exhibited in 1984, the year it was founded in Jouy-en-Josas. The exhibitions *Lignes de mire – 1* and *Lignes de mire – 2*, presented in 1990 and 1991 respectively, showcased recently acquired works by Absalon, Jean-Michel Alberola, Richard Baquié, James Coleman, Fischli & Weiss, Toni Grand, Markus Raetz, Thomas Ruff, Alain Séchas, Hiroshi Sugimoto, Beat Streuli, Patrick Tosani, James Turrell, and Jeff Wall, among others.
2 Stefan Zweig, *The Invisible Collection: Tales of Obsession and Desire* (London: Pushkin Press, [1925] 2015).

Emanuele Coccia

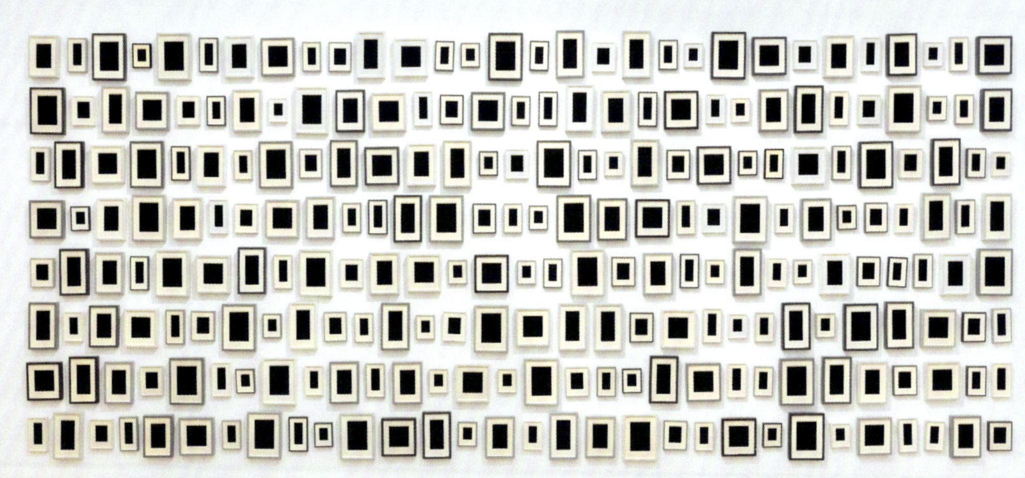

Allan McCollum, *Collection of Two Hundred and Forty Plaster Surrogates*, 1982–1983
FC Collections (1991)

of blank paper that have replaced the original prints and etchings
he had previously acquired, here, it is the very idea of collection
and collecting that makes the works indistinguishable from a
substitute and almost identical to hundreds of others: as Hal Foster
suggested, art is reduced to a pure sign, abstracted from itself.[3]

It is hard to imagine a more vivid mise en abyme for the
paradoxical condition that each artwork seems to assume within
a collection. In a collection, it is as if works have been carbonized,
or returned to an earlier geological state, thereby definitively
losing their status. And it is as if there were a curious dialectic,
a friction between the exhibition and the collection that is
inscribed in the very flesh of the works.

In its forty-year history, the Fondation Cartier has rarely
held exhibitions of its own Collections in its premises on

3 Hal Foster, *Recodings: Art, Spectacle, Cultural Politics* (Seattle, WA: Bay Press, 1985), p. 106.

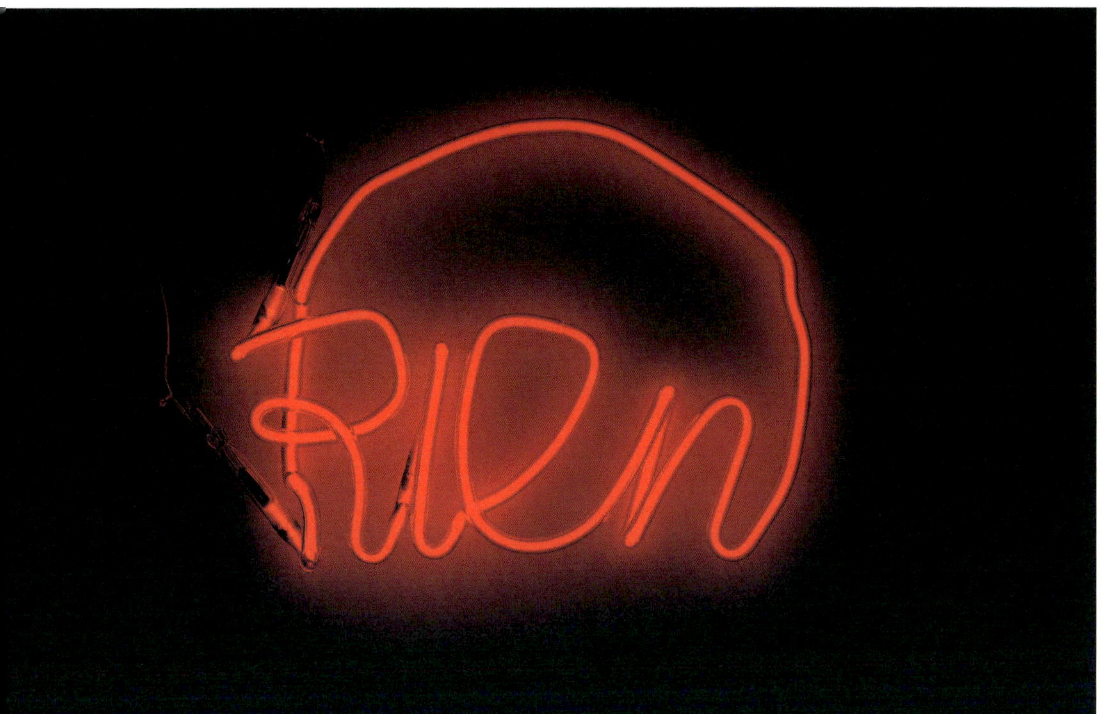

ean-Michel Alberola, *Crâne,* 1995
C Collections (1995)

Boulevard Raspail.[4] This is not a question of modesty or reserve, and it would be a mistake to reduce this choice to the simple decision to give priority to works belonging to others. Rather, it is the reflection of an institutional singularity that is difficult to name, and which makes the Fondation Cartier a new kind of third space, positioned, in terms of typology, midway between a Kunsthalle (which exhibits without collecting) and a museum (which exhibits only its own collections).

The Fondation Cartier has invented a form of institution that can only collect what it exhibits, whether these are preexisting works or works that it commissions from artists. We must not be misled by the simplicity of this approach. In reality, it conceals a two-fold speculative enigma. The first aspect is historical in nature:

4 The Fondation Cartier Collections now comprise almost 2,000 works created by more than 500 artists of 50 different nationalities, and are the result of the Fondation Cartier's own programming and commissions. They were presented in 1997 and 2014 in Jean Nouvel's building, and more regularly internationally. The works in the Collections are also loaned to museums and institutions in France and abroad.

it concerns the list of names, histories, and categories to which
we have become accustomed when designating and discussing
the places where art is visible in the city and where its presence is
deployed with such intensity that it radically alters the urban space
itself. In contrast to the now extensive historiography that reduces
museum spaces to mere effects of heritage policies—be they public
or private—the Fondation Cartier seems to be demonstrating that
exhibition spaces have plural, distinct, and rarely acknowledged
genealogies and forms that shatter any patrimonial reductionism.
Certainly, it is not just the accumulation of value or the desire
to display power and domination that drives humanity to collect
objects and allow them to become an open discourse. We can
and have collected for reasons that are difficult to name, much less
utilitarian and much more complicated to link to the construction
of a form of ownership. From world's fairs to department stores,
from Wunderkammers to the stately homes and aristocratic
palaces of the Renaissance and the modern period, it would
be difficult to reduce the taste for collecting to a single matrix.[5]

But the originality of the Fondation Cartier model is by no means
purely historiographical. The second aspect of the enigma has
more to do with a question that is both poetic and normative.
Understanding what it is to have collections made up of exhibitions
effectively means conceiving of an unprecedented, intimate
relationship between artistic production and the construction
of the canon.

In art, each collection fulfils the same function as the Last
Judgment in Judeo-Christian myths: both aim to redeem the past,
an action that can only be conceived in the form of a judgment.
The primary aim of any judgment is to sever the links between
truth and the Whole: there is only judgment because (and insofar
as) it is not the Whole that is true. If it were, no judgment would be
necessary: it would be enough to name what is, or what has been,

5 On this alternative genealogy of the museum, now much neglected, see Patricia Falguières's preface, "La Société des objets," in Julius von Schlosser, *Cabinets d'art et de merveilles de la Renaissance tardive*, trans. Lucie Marignac (Paris: Macula, 2012).

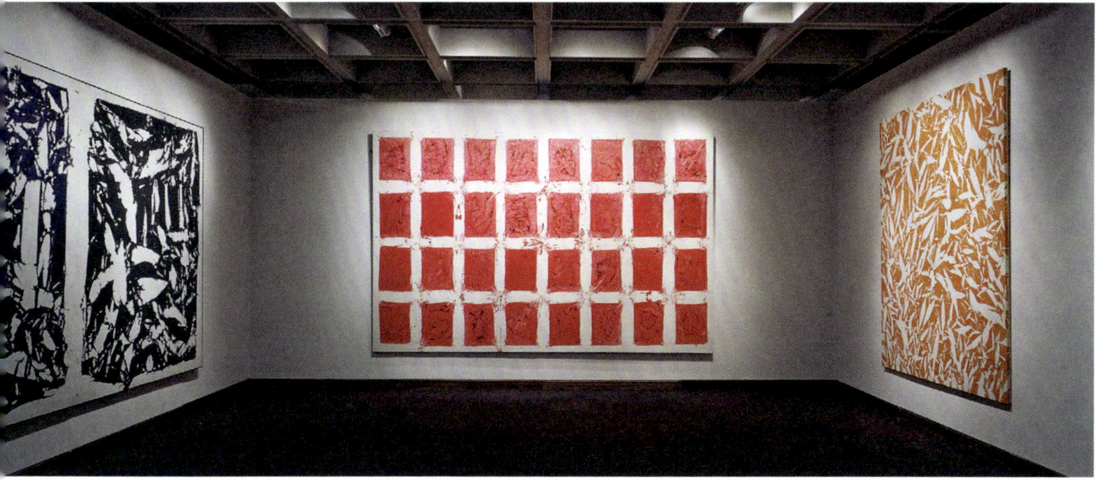

iew of the exhibition *Too French*, Hong Kong Museum of Art, 1991. Works by Simon Hantaï

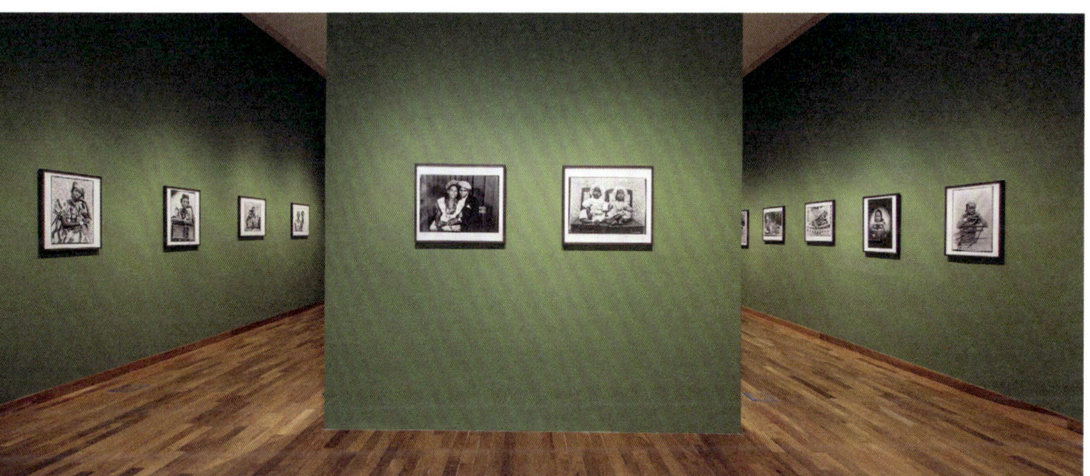

iew of the exhibition *Les Visitants. Guillermo Kuitca Reflects on the Fondation Cartier pour l'art contemporain Collection*, CCK, Buenos Aires, 2017. Works by Seydou Keita

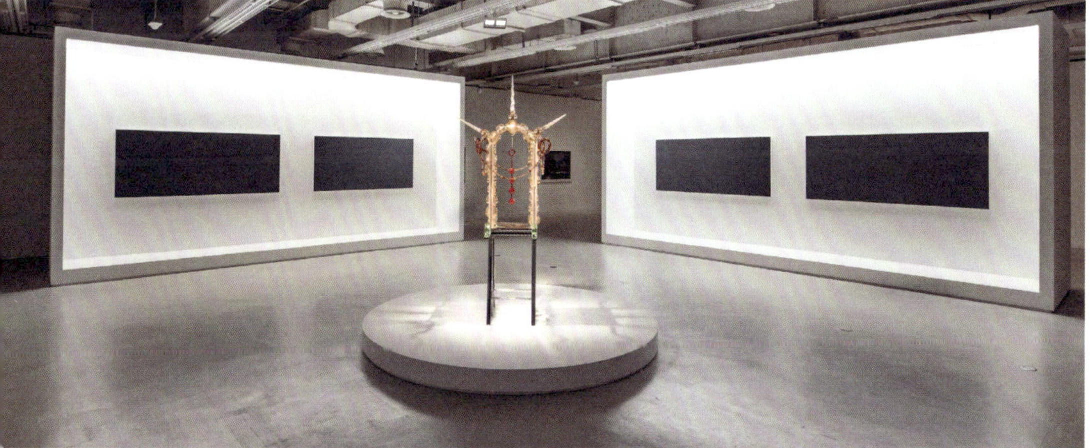

iew of the exhibition *Fondation Cartier pour l'art contemporain, A Beautiful Elsewhere*, ower Station of Art, Shanghai, 2018. Works by Hu Liu and Jean-Michel Othoniel

Emanuele Coccia

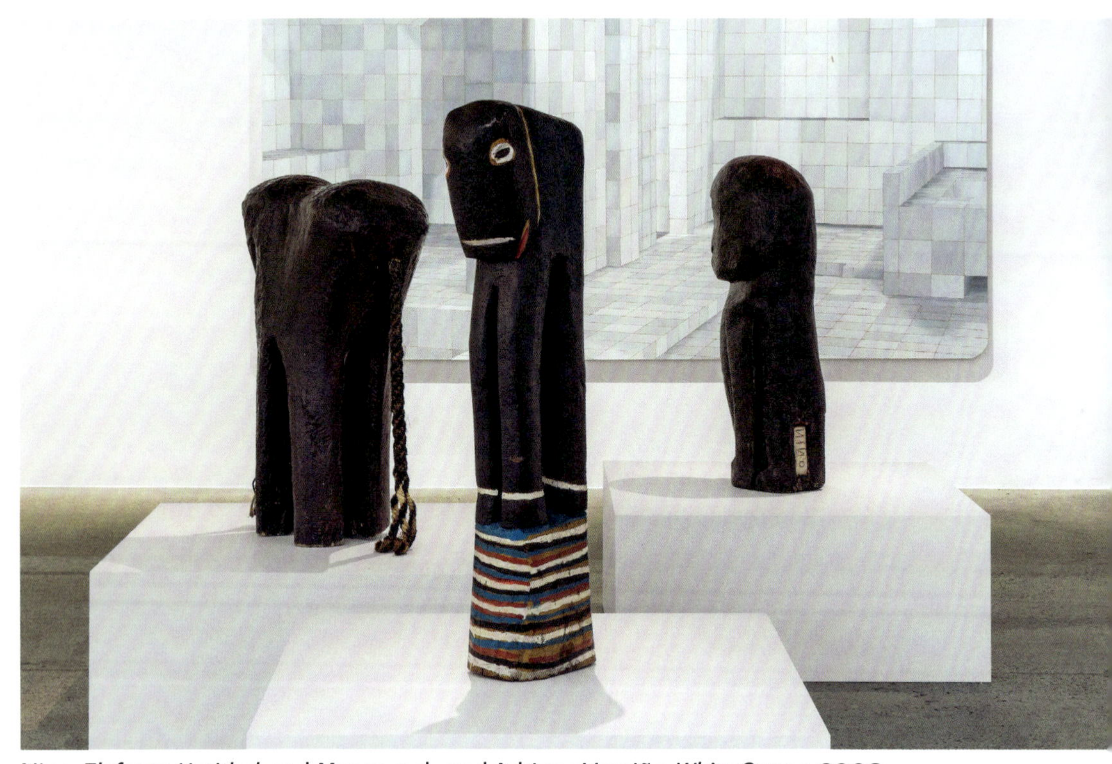

Nino, *Elefante*, *Untitled*, and *Macao*, n.d., and Adriana Varejão, *White Sauna*, 2003
FC Collections (2012 and 2003)

to allow the totality of reality to reach salvation. The canon, on the other hand, is the impossibility of making art and the world, or art and history, converge. In the canon, reality can only become art by loosening its ties to the Whole.

If redemption formulated as judgment is always a necessary condemnation, then the collection is the blissful, unconscious paradise of the saved, corresponding, in the filigree of the now-lost tradition, to the mute hell of the submerged. The museum pronounces universal judgment on human artefacts; the collection is the result of this judgment: not everything in the world is art, and the collection separates art from the world.

It is perhaps possible to extend to the museum the paradoxical movement that philologists have often observed in the transformation of sacred texts into canon. Even in art, the collection — the genesis of the canon — while saving art, nevertheless relegates it to an irremediable, incomprehensible past.

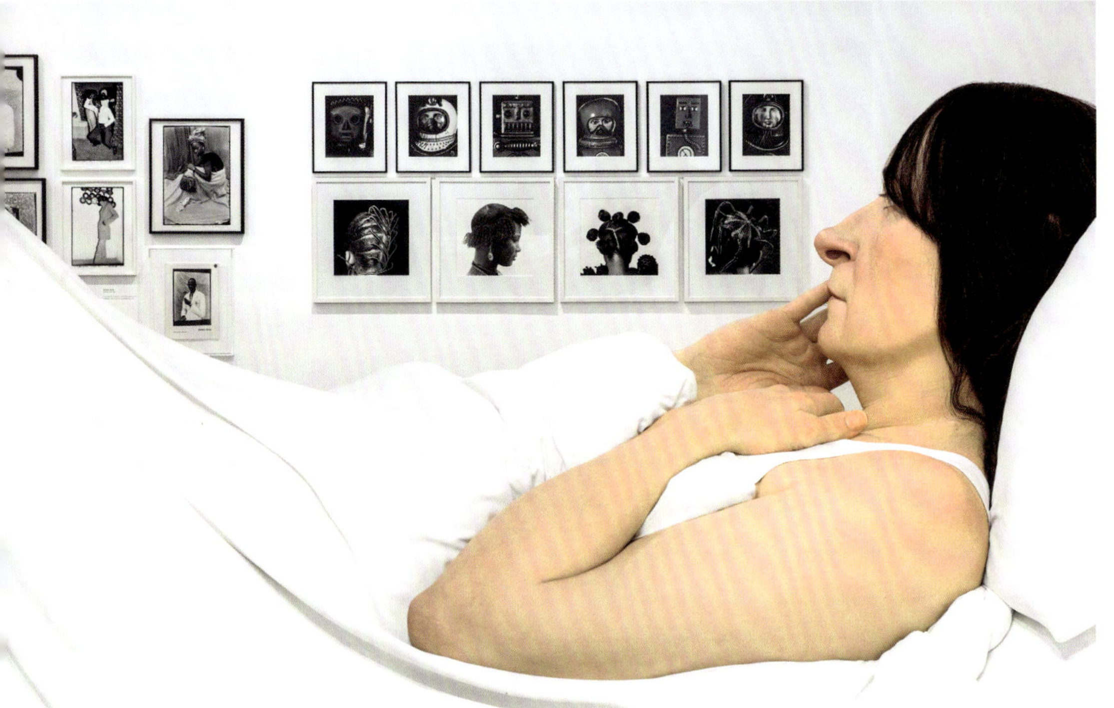

Ron Mueck, *In Bed*, 2005, in front of photographs by Seydou Keita, Valérie Belin, and J.D. 'Okhai Ojeikere. FC Collections (1995–2006)

Franz Overbeck wrote: "In the essence of any canon, there is the capacity to render its objects incomprehensible."[6] In the same way, we could say of any critical edition what can be said of the New Testament writings as a whole, namely that they ceased to be comprehensible the moment they were constituted as a canon. The moment when the revelation of a truth comes to an end in the canon is also the moment when that truth becomes inaccessible: the truth can no longer be written, only copied. And the person who wants to understand it—and give it new life—can no longer be its author. For every work, this moment when a text can only be received and not created, read and not understood, or understood only outside the poetic act, is nothing more than the purgatorial wait for its day of redemption.

To avoid this separation, we need to rethink and reverse the ordinary relationship between exhibition and collection, which is

6 Franz Overbeck, *Zur Geschichte des Kanons: Zwei Abhandlungen* (Chemnitz: Ernst Schmeitzner, 1880), p. 1.

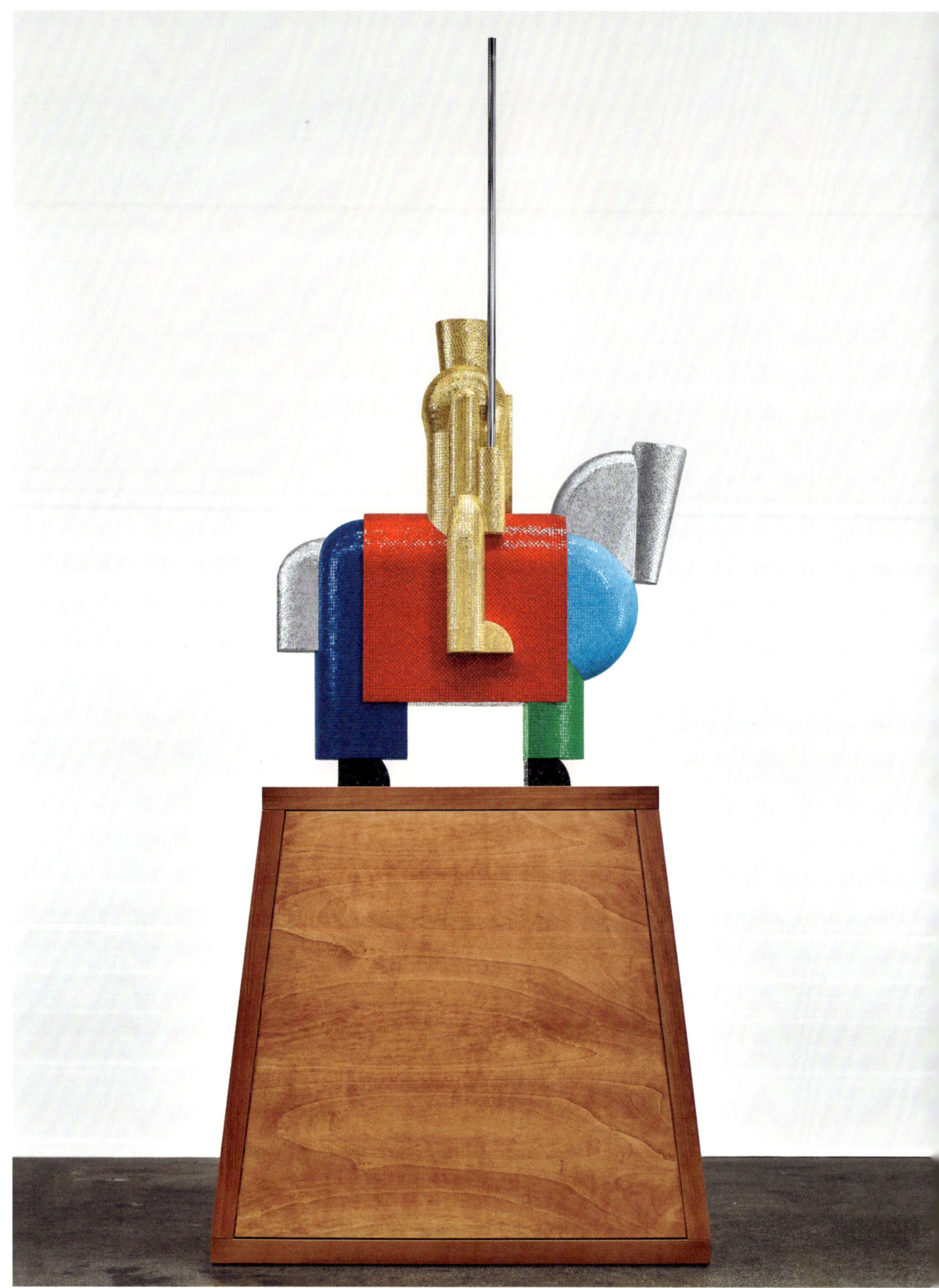

Alessandro Mendini, *Il cavaliere di Dürer*, 2019
FC Collections (2019)

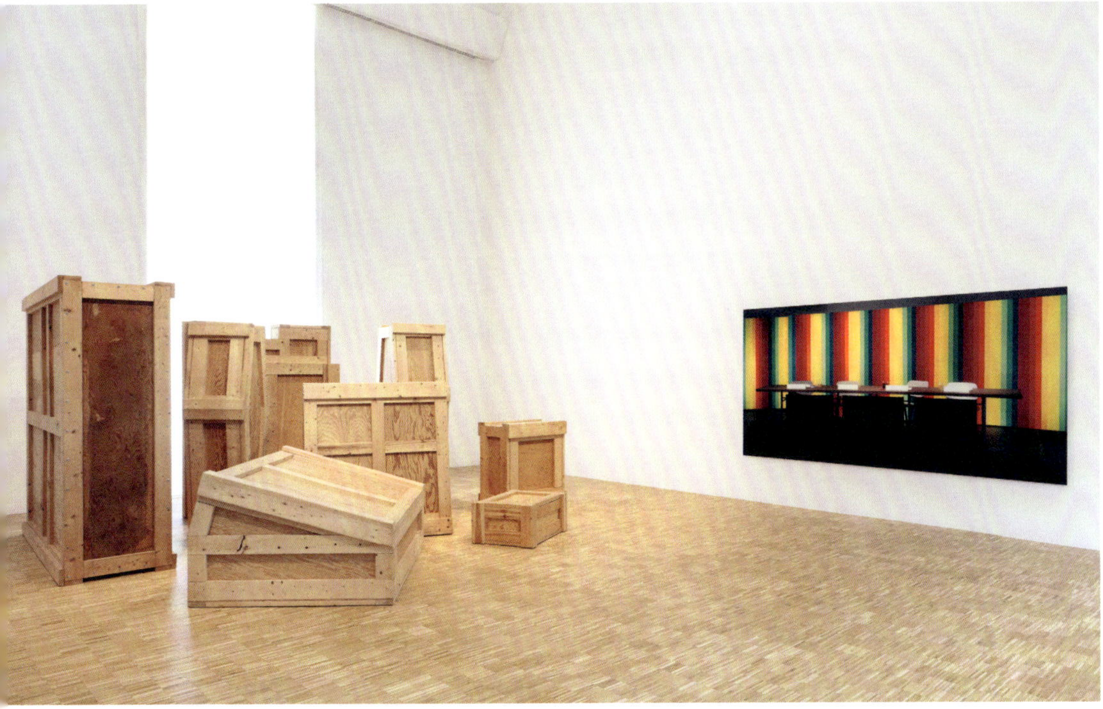

Richard Artschwager, *Archipelago, 8 Crates*, 1994, and Thomas Demand, *Studio*, 1997
FC Collections (1994 and 1998)

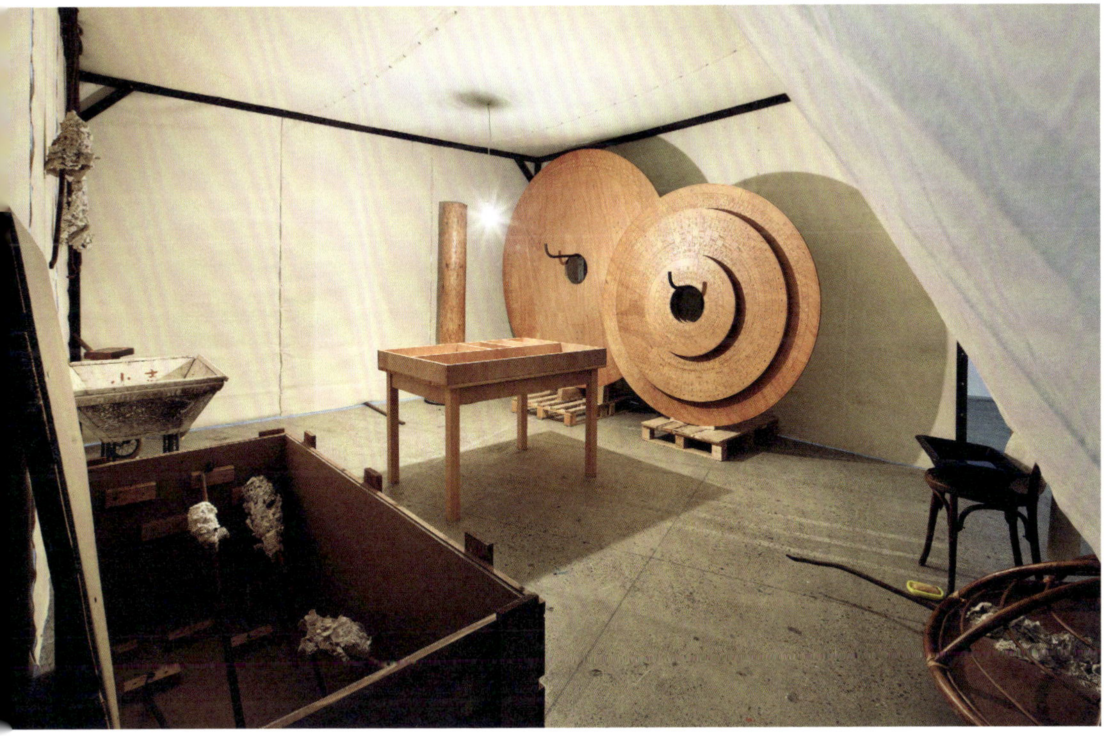

Huang Yong Ping, *La Maison d'augures*, 1989–1992
FC Collections (1992)

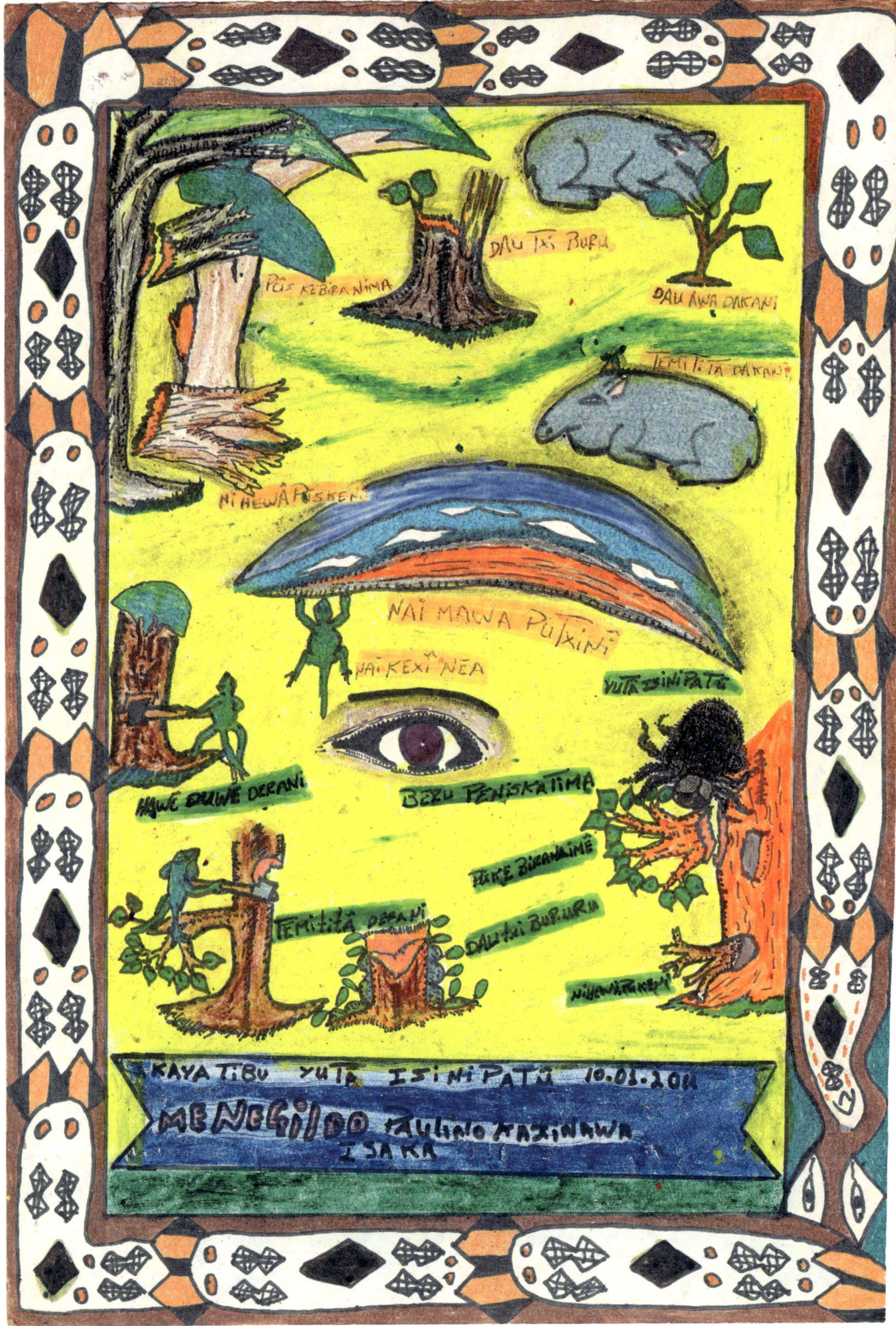

Isaka (Huni Kuin artist), *Untitled*, 2011
FC Collections (2012)

why the Fondation Cartier has invented an entirely new institutional
form. In a collection that is no more than the consequence of an
exhibition, canonization seems inseparable from its creative
possibilities: the transmission of art coincides with its creation,
and tradition recovers its poetic faculties. The collection is never built
in the past: it always waits for a (future) exhibition in order to grow.
This particular inversion can be compared to the change of aspect
which the "vav" operates on the verb that serves as its basis in the
Hebrew language: it passes from the designation of a completed
act (*perfectum*) to that of an unfinished fact, one that has not
yet taken place, and vice versa. Like a writer who likes to add a "vav
conversivum" to each text, each exhibition distorts the state and
appearance of a work, and transforms what is written into something
that remains to be said, to be formulated, transforming tradition
into the highest poetry of memory. The collection becomes infinite
and constantly returns to itself. And conversely, to return to itself,
it must exhibit what does not yet belong to it: betray itself,
deny itself, radically change its face and identity.

This structure of permanent betrayal has been strengthened
and institutionalized within the Fondation Cartier, with its
determination not to make art, its exhibitions and consequently its
Collections coincide with a single medium or a specific geographical
area. Thus, an installation by Huang Yong Ping such as *La Maison
d'augures* (1989–1992) can coexist with Simon Hantaï's acrylics on
canvas; the sculpture *The Mask* (1997) by David Hammons can be
shown alongside photographs by Nan Goldin or Claudia Andujar;
design works by Alessandro Mendini, Andrea Branzi, or Marc
Newson can rub shoulders with paintings by Chéri Samba; Sarah
Sze's installations can cohabit with drawings by Joseca Mokahesi.
This coexistence is not just a spatial juxtaposition of works:
it is a mutual interpenetration of mediums, worlds, techniques,
and practices. The purpose of any exhibition is to render impossible
any formal distinction between the works, as well as between
them and the exhibition space. For example, a small-scale drawing

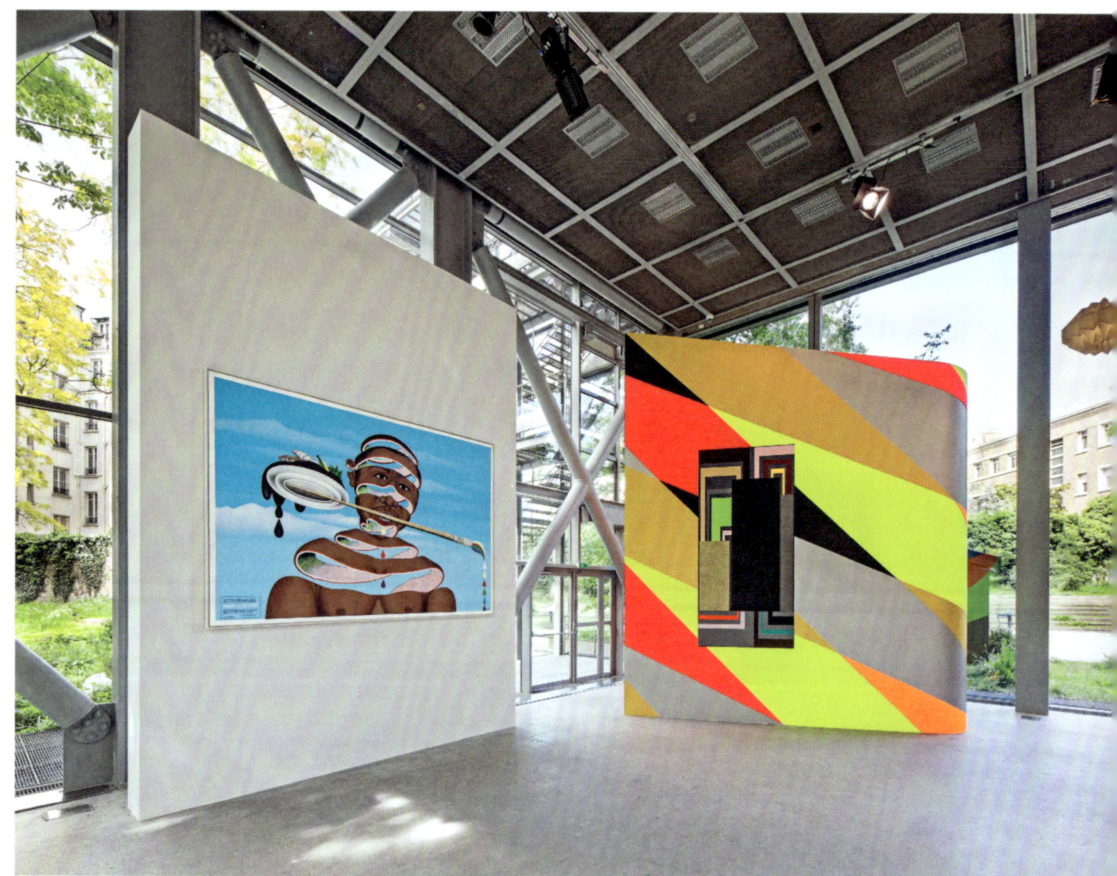

Chéri Samba, *J'aime la couleur*, 2010. FC Collections (2011)
Alessandro Mendini and Peter Halley, *OMG!*, 2014

by David Lynch became the backdrop for one of the rooms in his solo exhibition *The Air is on Fire* in 2007. Guillermo Kuitca then reinterpreted it for the exhibitions *Les Habitants* at the Fondation Cartier in 2014, *Les Visitants* at the CCK in Buenos Aires in 2017, and *Les Citoyens* at Triennale Milano in 2021, all three of which created dialogues between works from the Fondation Cartier Collections. A collection, then, is a fixed image of the alliance that the works establish between themselves, in the space of an instant, in order to become visible.

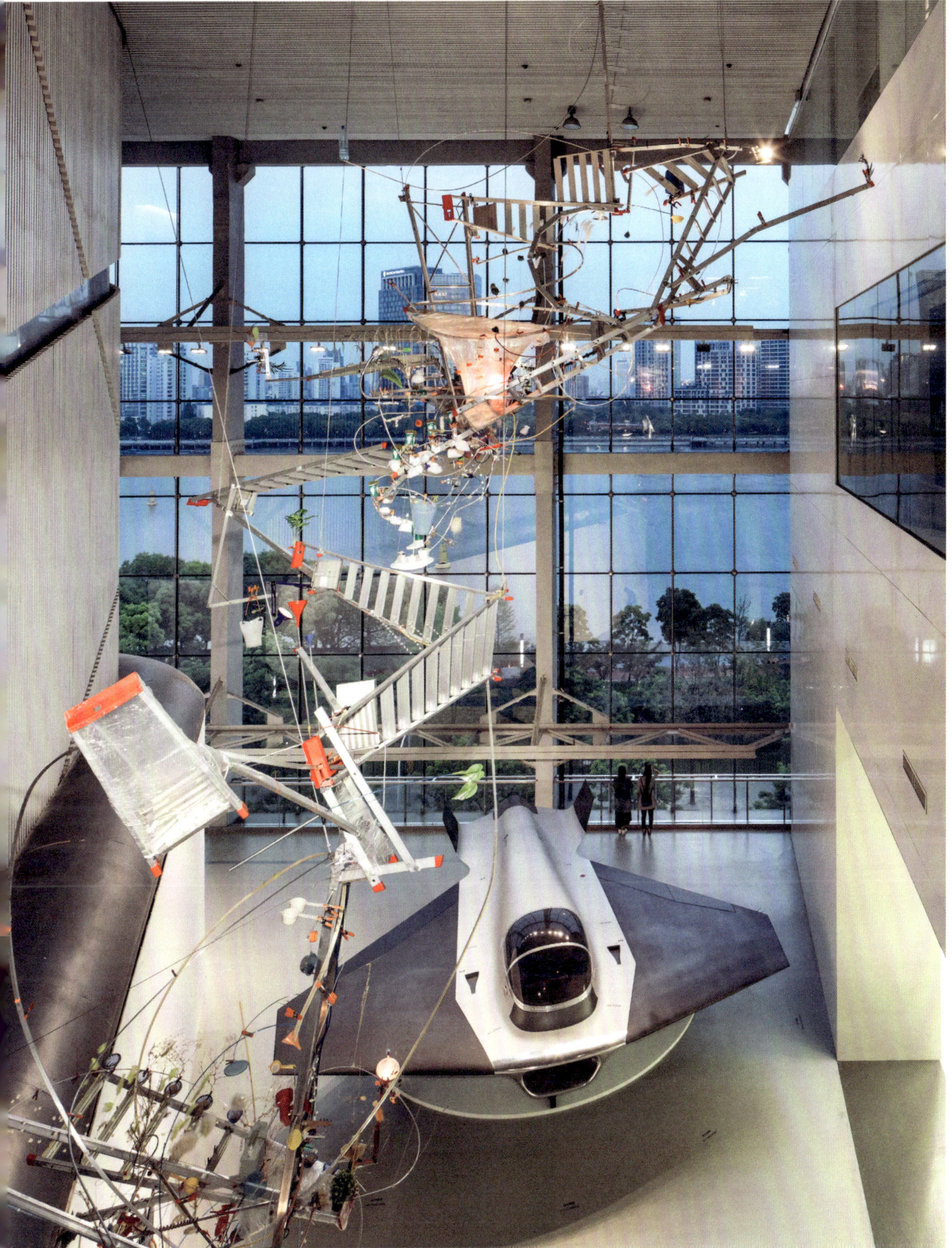

Sarah Sze, *Everything That Rises Must Converge*, 1999, and Marc Newson, *Kelvin 40*, 2003
C Collections (2000 and 2004). View of the exhibition *Fondation Cartier pour l'art contemporain,
Beautiful Elsewhere*, Power Station of Art, Shanghai, 2018

Emanuele Coccia

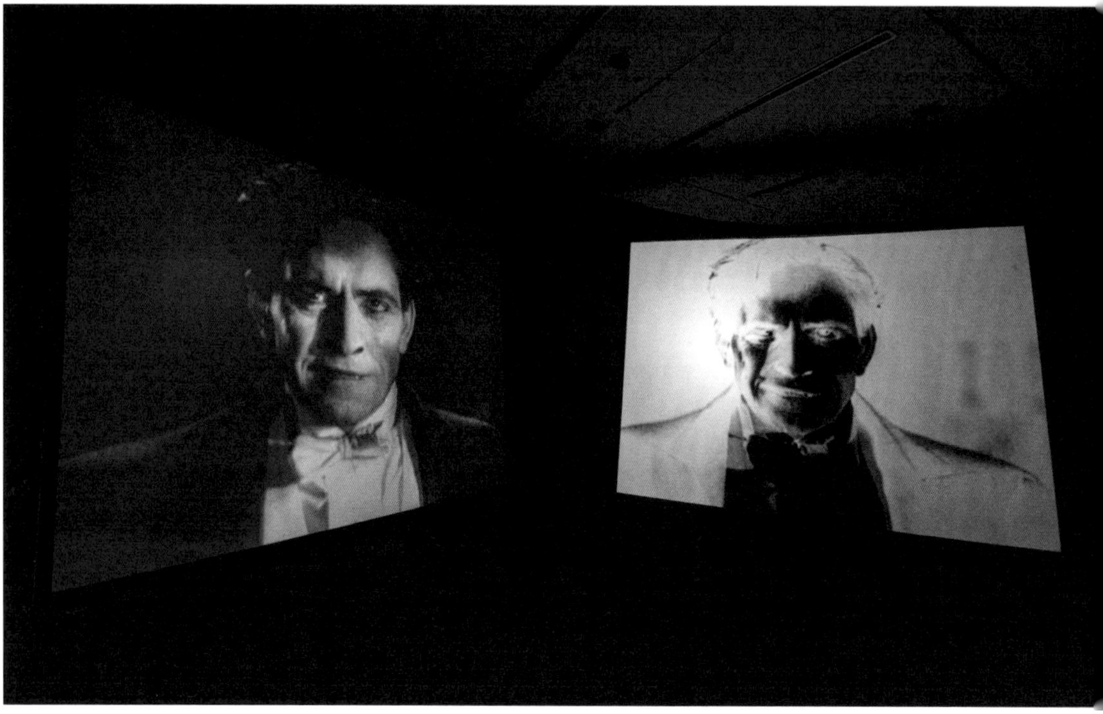

Douglas Gordon, *Confessions of a Justified Sinner*, 1996. FC Collections (1996)

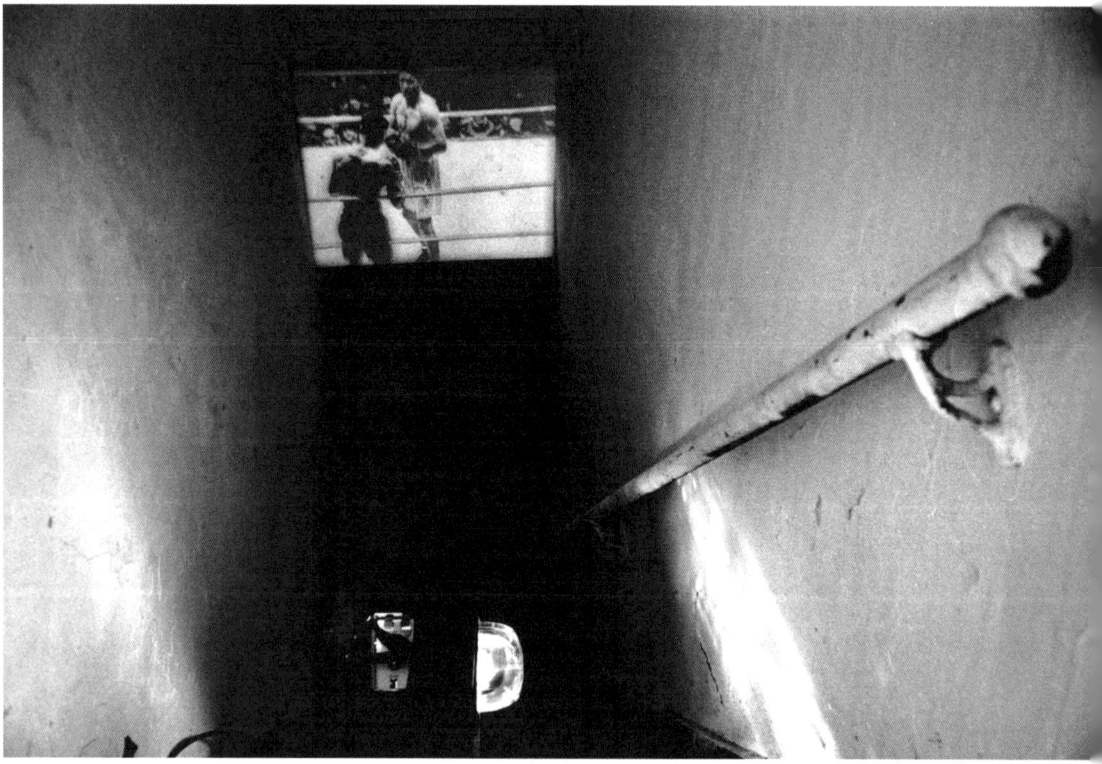

James Coleman, *Box (ahhareturnabout)*, 1977. FC Collections (1990)

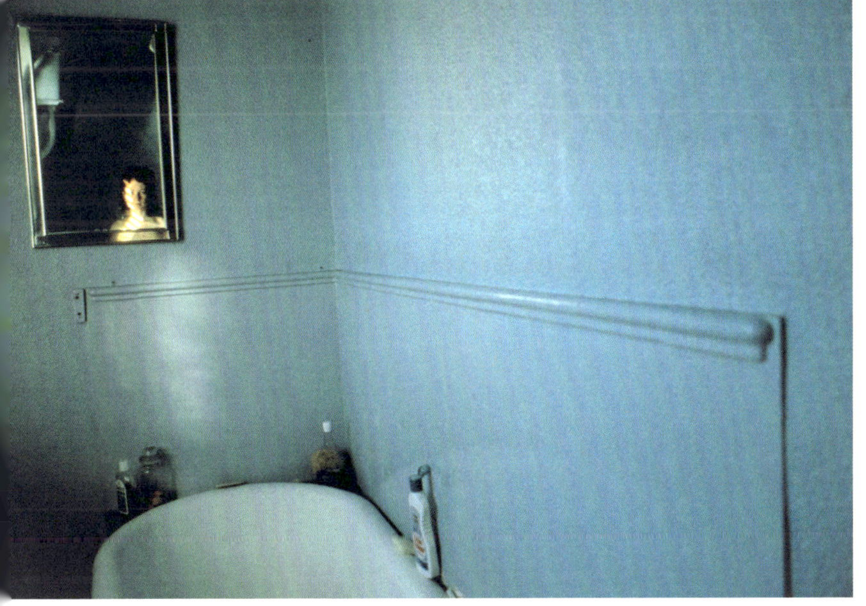

eff Wall, *An Octopus*, 1990. FC Collections (1991)

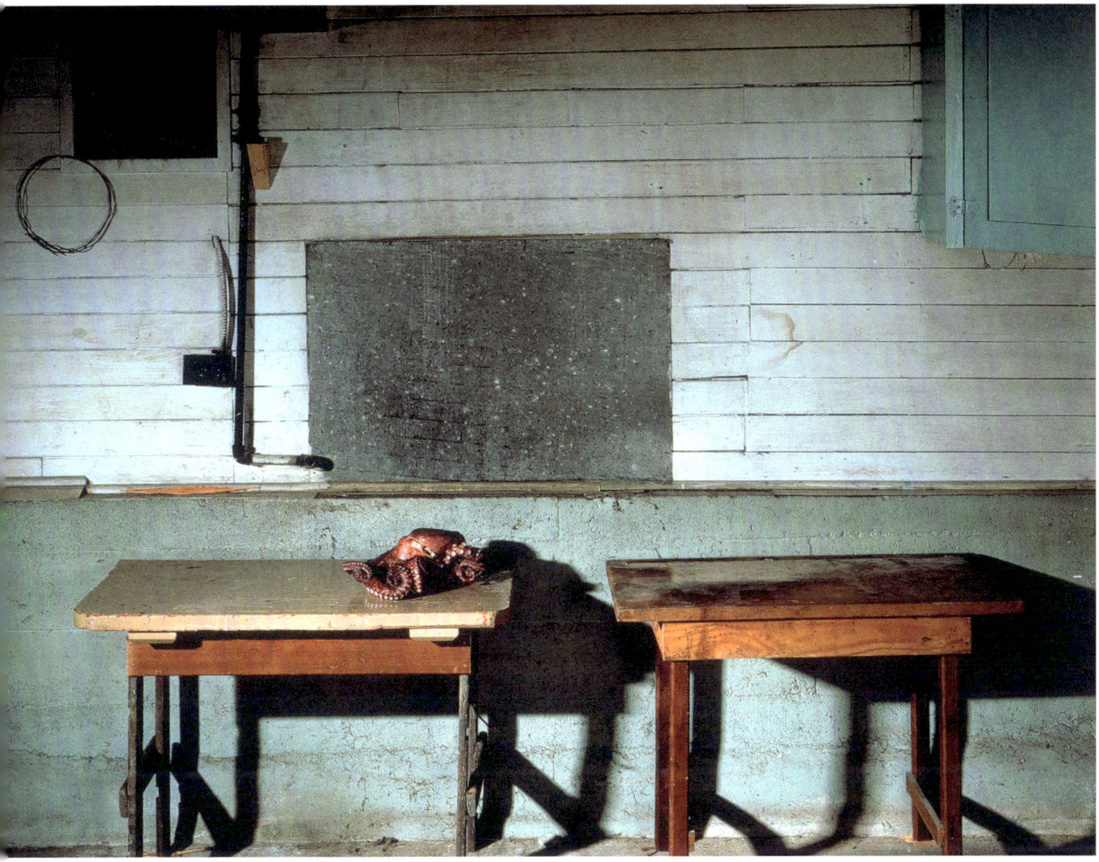

Ian Goldin, *The Ballad of Sexual Dependency*, 1979–1995. FC Collections (1996)

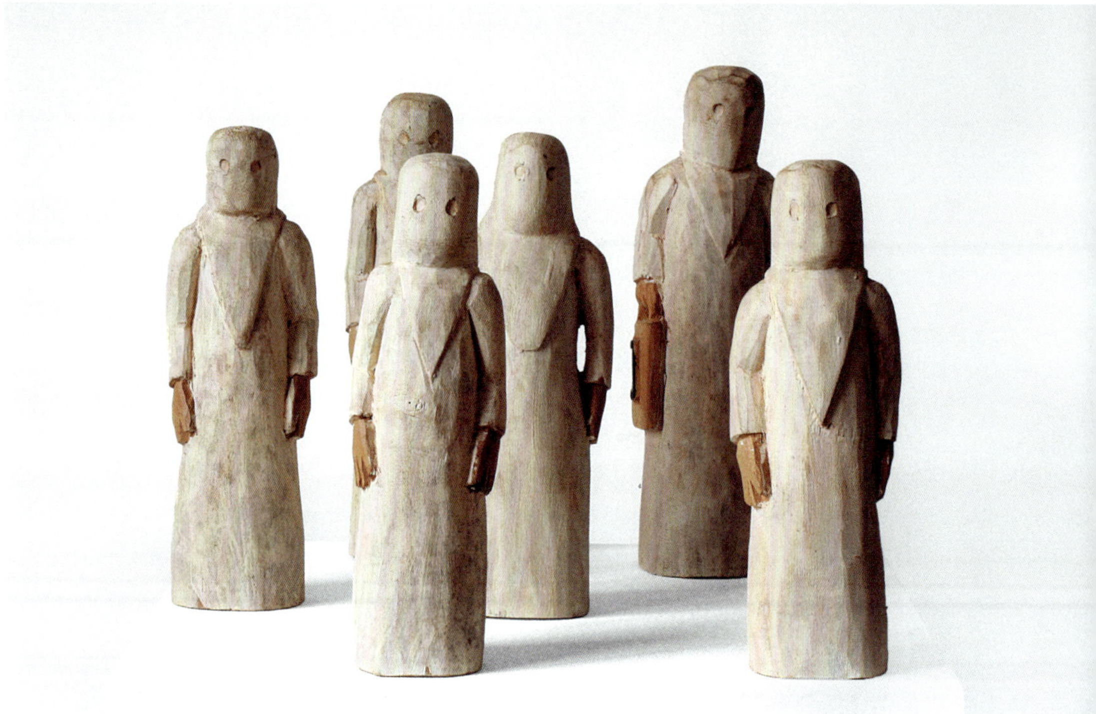

Véio, *Grupo de penitentes*, 1989. FC Collections (2012)

What comes and happens

This necessity never to allow a work to carbonize in the collection, this refusal to establish a definitive canon, has considerable consequences that are not only aesthetic, but also profoundly moral. After all, museums and exhibition spaces are public and paradoxical forms of confession: they are where the city shows its actions, attempts to preserve them and reason about them. However, there are different ways of conserving and confessing the past. There is the ostentation, imbued with pride, of what has been done, displayed like a trophy in pursuit of recognition and privileges. To ensure what has been done is recognized, the ego would like to be perceived in terms of what it has accomplished; it must be anchored and almost denied its freedom to act. There is also the painful admission of the past as a source of guilt, an action or an object that we would like to erase and undo, as if to liberate the power of doing, to rethink it pristine and untouched. The acting subject therefore wants to see themselves as pure, absolute, absolved of their actions.

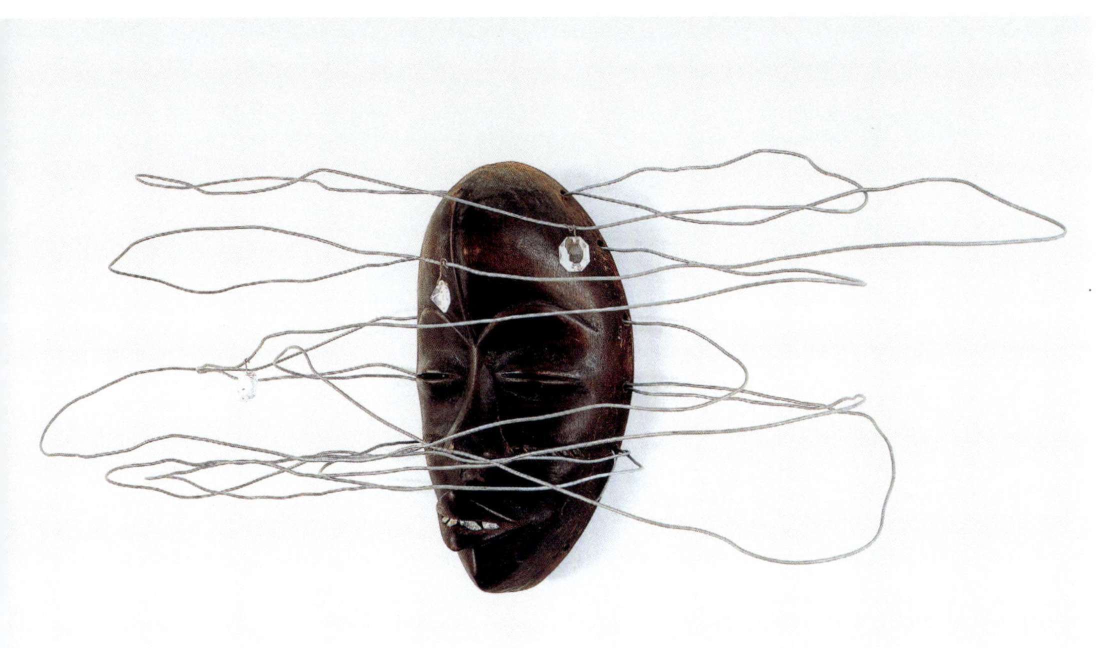

In both cases, the doing and the already-done, the act and the power, the past and the future, seem mired in an unhealthy dynamic, unable to find a true metabolism. This is why confession—be it in pride or in shame—always seems to coincide with a moment of crisis and aporia. And any museum institution or exhibition space that oscillates between pride and shame—or to put it in more contemporary language, between aesthetic militancy and social criticism—risks producing nothing but the impossibility of imagining a different future. Which is why we need to find another balance between doing and acting, between exhibiting and collecting in art. Confession should be a gesture that enables us to change the status of what we have done in the past.

Indeed, our past life never dies in the moment that it took place; there is something that remains, a life that survives the moment in which it was formed, like the thunder we await when lightning has lit up the sky. All the actions of the past seem to condemn life not to die, to haunt us in the form of an echo that wants move our bodies

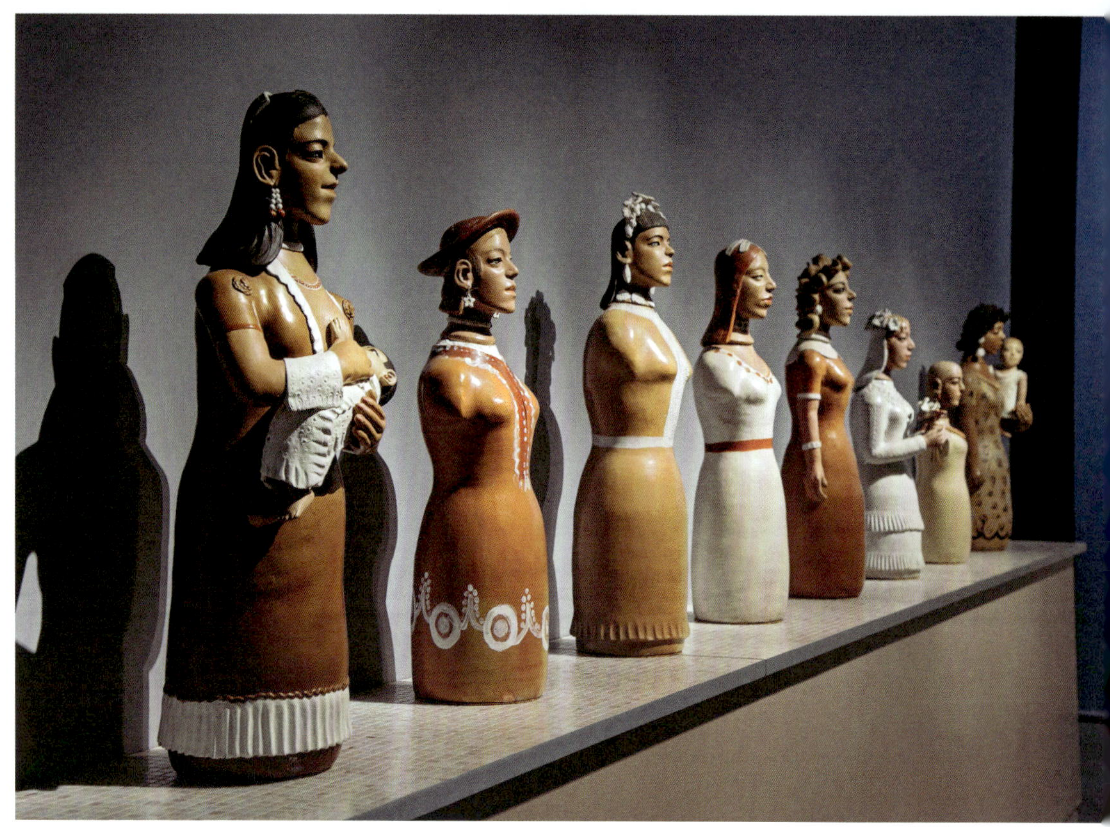

Isabel Mendes da Cunha, *Untitled*, c. 1970–1999. FC Collections (2012)

at least a second time. All that we have done—all that humanity has done—has not been done to the full, or not enough: there is still something to do that these actions have not exhausted. Confession is both a symptom of and the opportunity for this second-degree power (a doing with our doing, an acting on what we have done).

Contrary to what we often imagine, the well-being of our world depends not on the future but on the past. Justice and the happiness of all depend on our ability to do something with this past that cannot really disappear, to invent rituals with these undigested and nonconsumable fragments of existence. Rather than producing guilt or pride, we need to be able to change the status of our past.

And this is the enigma that every institution of "artistic confession" (be it a museum or a Kunsthalle) must resolve: not to set out to offer a prideful exhibition or a critique of what has been

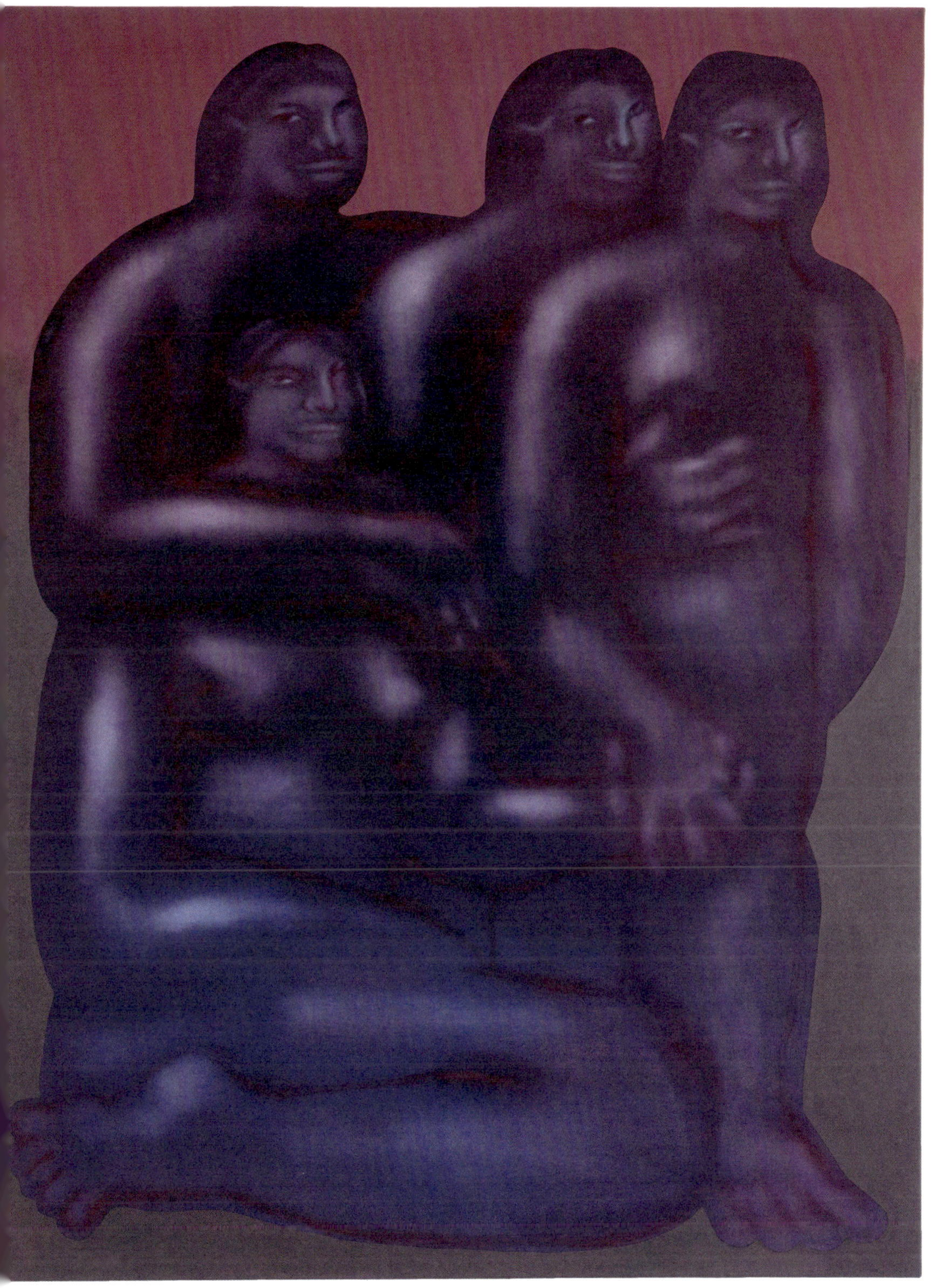

eorge Rouy, *One Mass Set on Red*, 2019. FC Collections (2019)

Emanuele Coccia

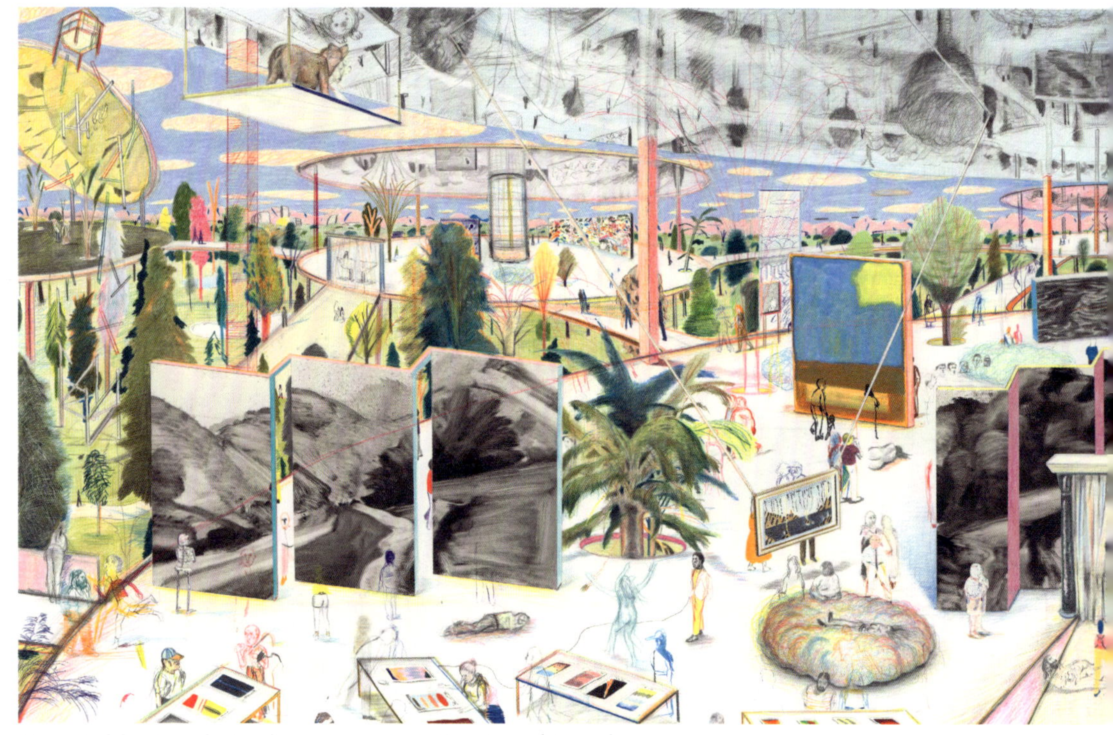

Yann Kebbi, *Mondo Reale*, 2022. FC Collections (2023)

done, but rather to reappropriate this residue of life and action, to sublimate criticism in the evidence that every action and every work of art can be extended into something else. It is precisely in order to bring about this inversion of the aspect of art and its temporality that the Fondation Cartier has established itself as a third space, between the model of the museum and that of the Kunsthalle. The exhibition and the Collections become two parallel moments in an infinite confession of art. Art, in turn, becomes the technical space for the confession of humanity as a whole. To go and see an exhibition is no longer to contemplate the past, but to brood over the desire for a future that can never be definitive.

In one of his preparatory notes for the *Native Land, Stop Eject* catalog (2008), Paul Virilio chose to title one of his texts "Voir Venir," in reference to *EXIT*,[7] the work created for the exhibition that was

7 Based on an idea by Paul Virilio, *EXIT* (2008) was designed by architects and artists Diller Scofidio + Renfro, architect Laura Kurgan, statistician Mark Hansen, and designer Ben Rubin, in collaboration with researchers from a range of disciplines, including Bruce Albert, François Gemenne, and François-Michel Le Tourneau. It is an immersive installation presenting human migration, tropical deforestation, and endangered languages around the world.

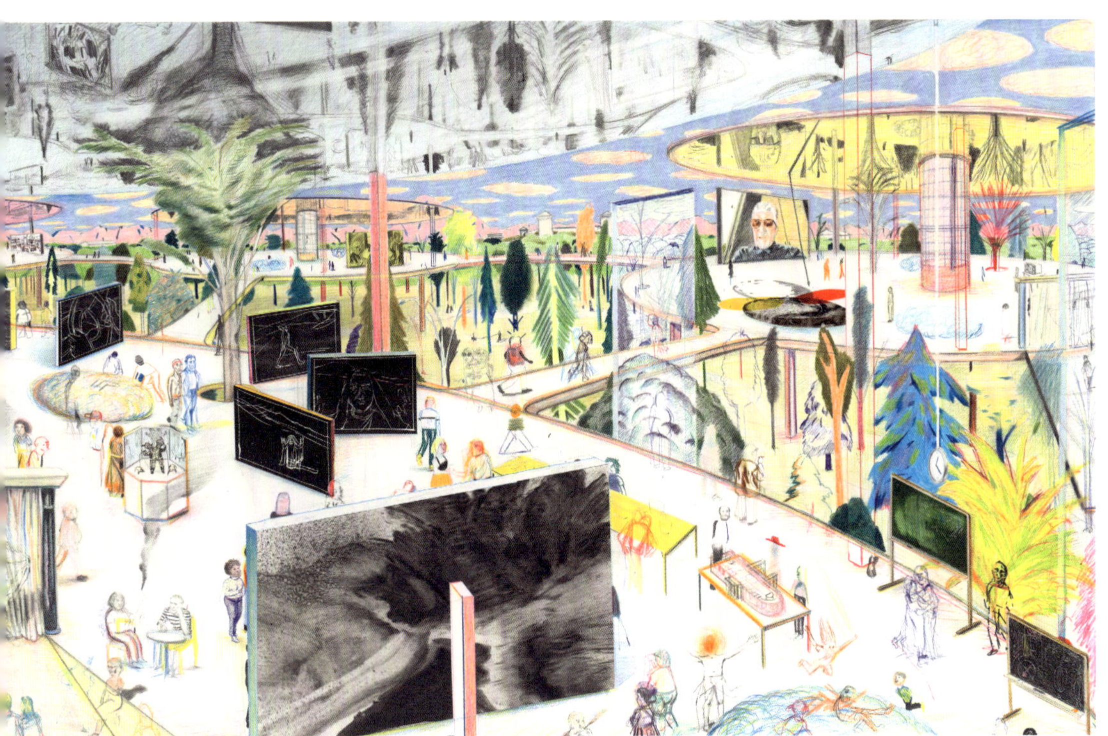

subsequently included in the Collections of the Fondation Cartier in 2012. This immersive installation maps a world "disrupted by the crisis of location,"[8] visualizing population movements linked to climatic, economic, and political factors. It is a paradoxical cartography, closer to a tarot card than an actual map, because it allows us to glimpse and guess at the future rather than representing the present or the past. Each exhibition at the Fondation Cartier seems to be a map of this kind, showing not what has been done, but what can be done with what has been done. The exhibition becomes the movement that transforms the future into a shared canon. And a collection is nothing more than a catalog of those futures that will never stop coming to pass.

8 Excerpt from the film accompanying the work EXIT in 2008. To explore the work based on Paul Virilio's thinking, visit the website www.atelierpaulvirilio.com.

VENIR VOIR
1984–2024

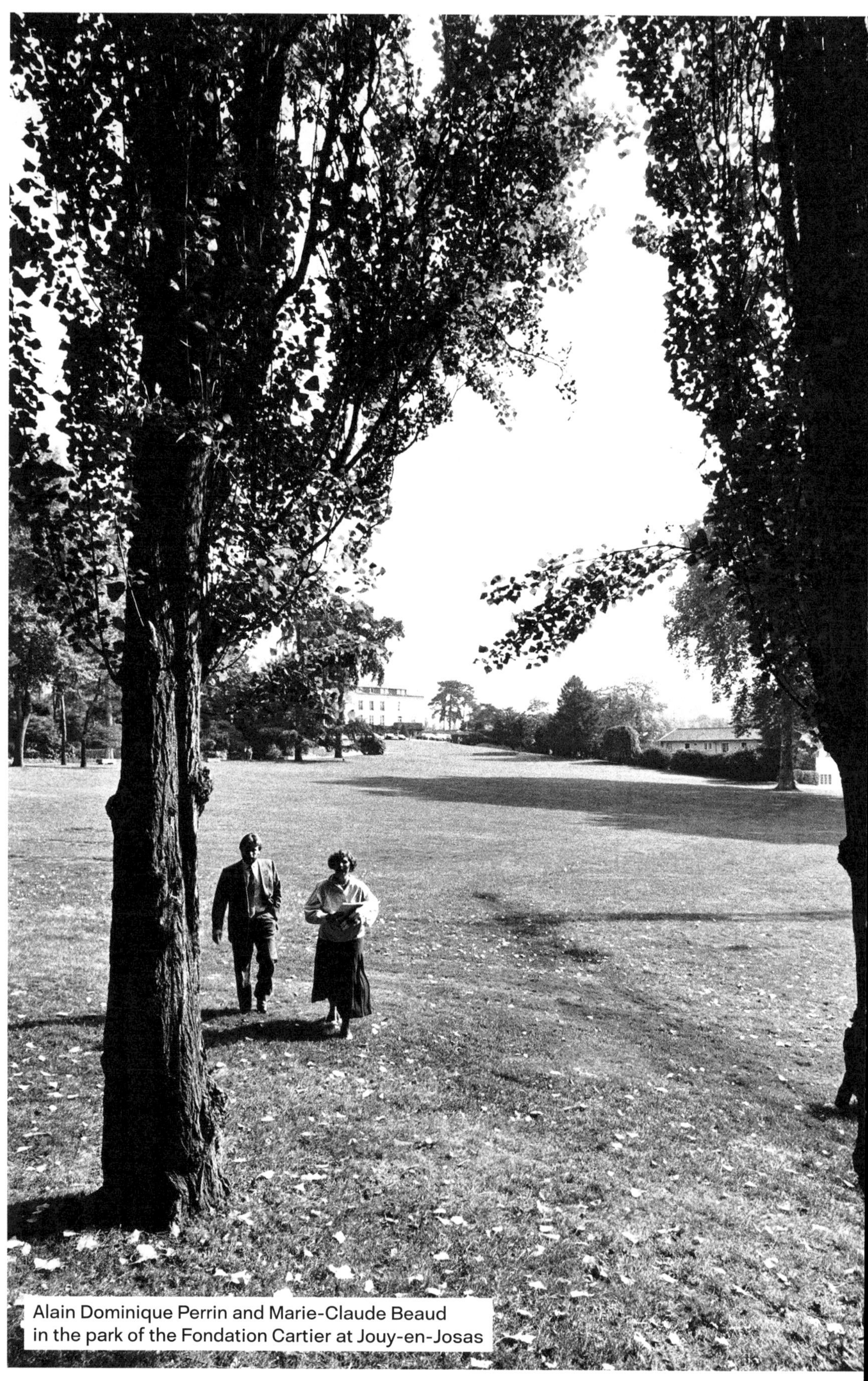

Alain Dominique Perrin and Marie-Claude Beaud
in the park of the Fondation Cartier at Jouy-en-Josas

1984-1993

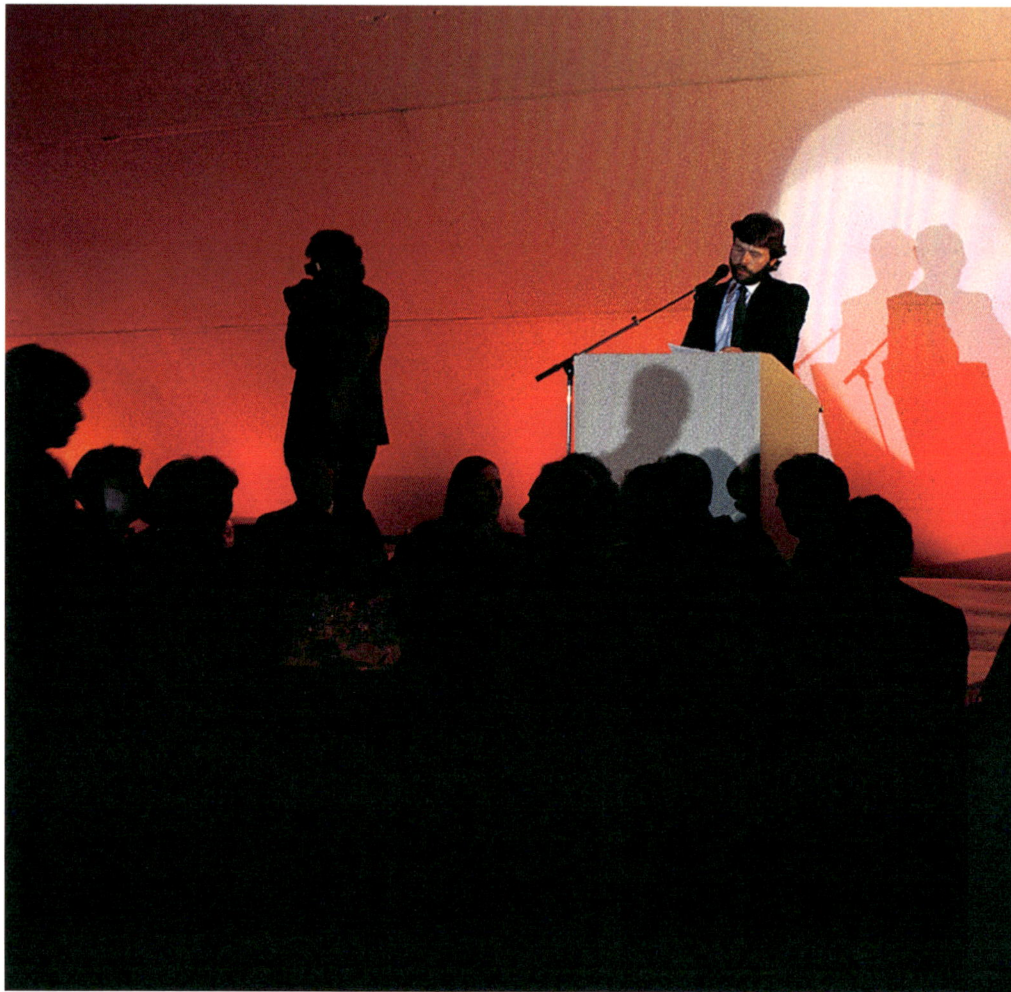

On October 20, 1984, Alain Dominique Perrin, then President of Cartier,
inaugurated the Fondation Cartier pour l'art contemporain
at the Domaine du Montcel, in Jouy-en-Josas.

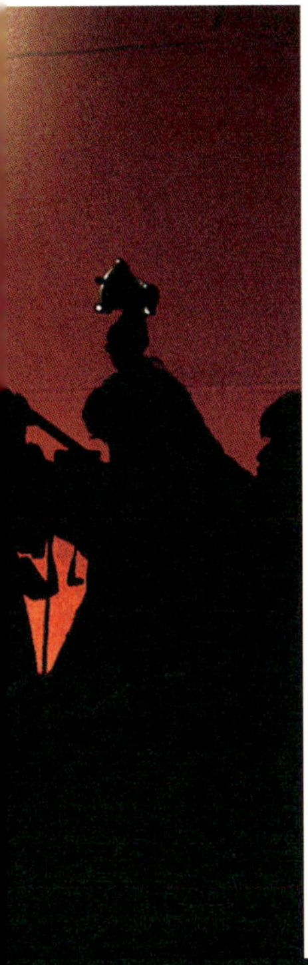

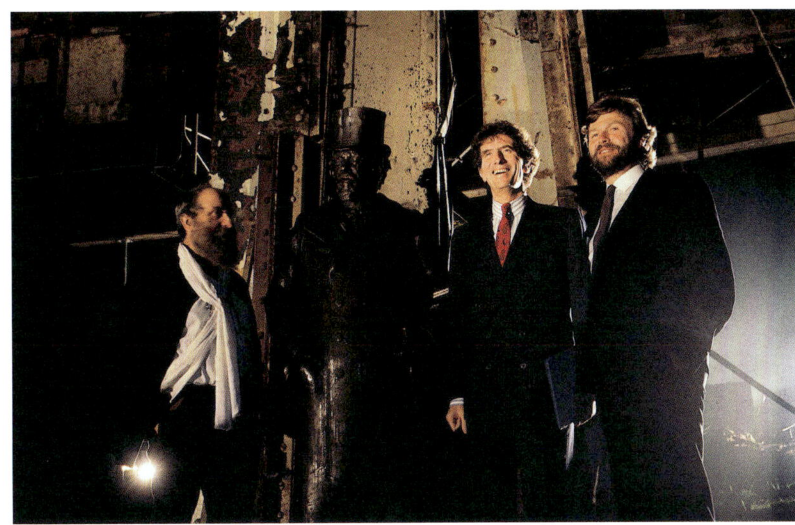

César, Jack Lang (then Deputy Minister for Culture), and Alain Dominique Perrin during the Fondation Cartier's inauguration evening

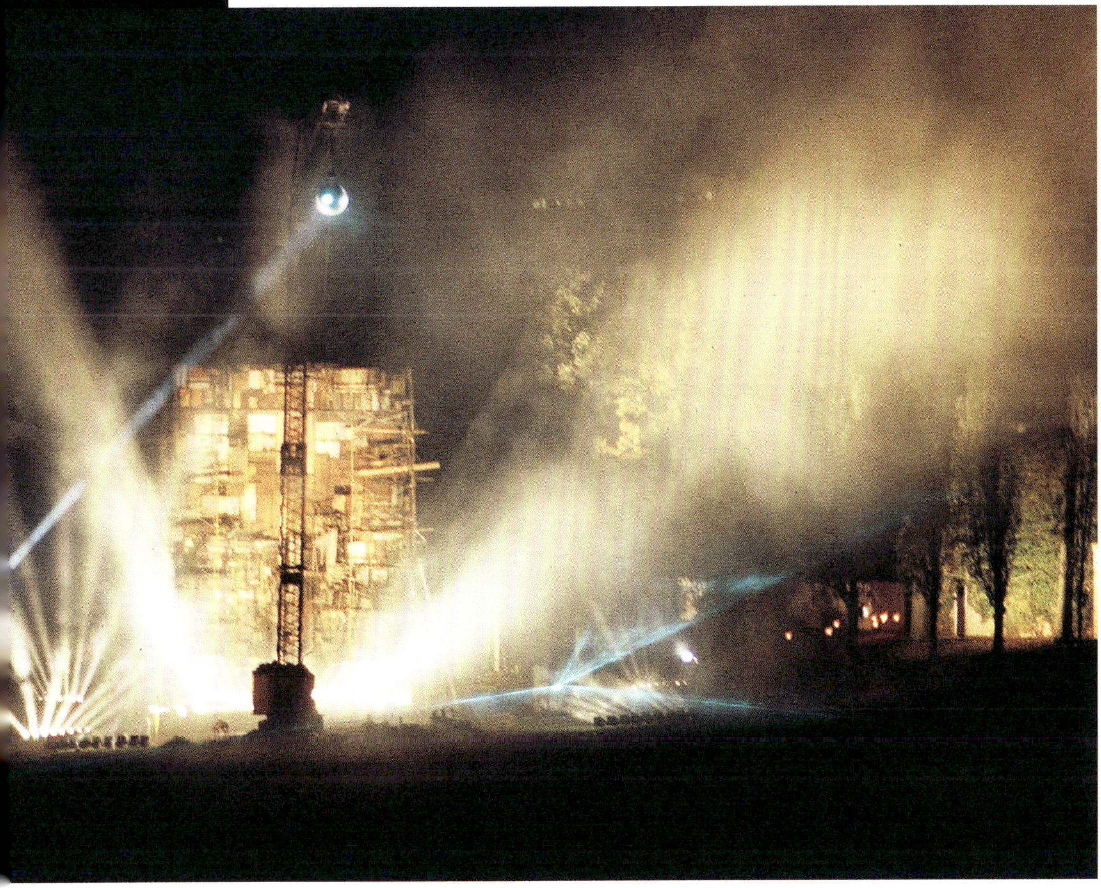

César's *Hommage à Eiffel*, created in the park of the Domaine du Montcel, was illuminated for the evening. The work was still in the process of being made.

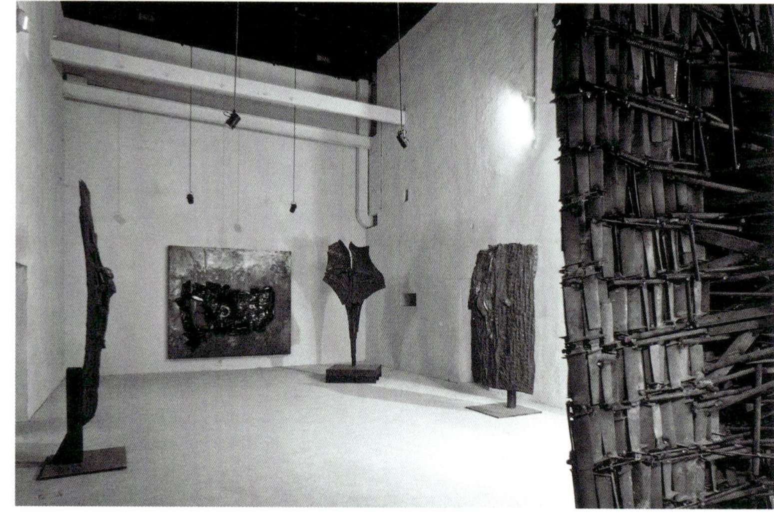

The inaugural exhibition *Les Fers de César* was the first devoted to the artist, showcasing an important group of his welded iron works, created between 1955 and 1963.

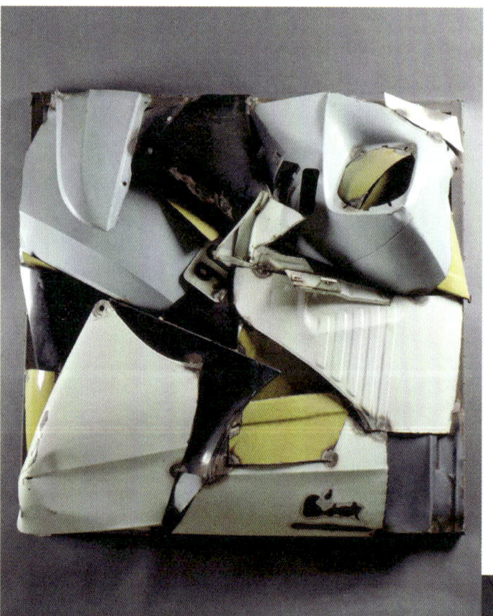

César, *Relief tôle*, 1961

César, Jack Lang, Marie-Claude Beaud, then Director of the Fondation Cartier, and Alain Dominique Perrin during the opening

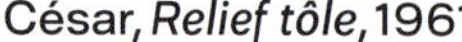

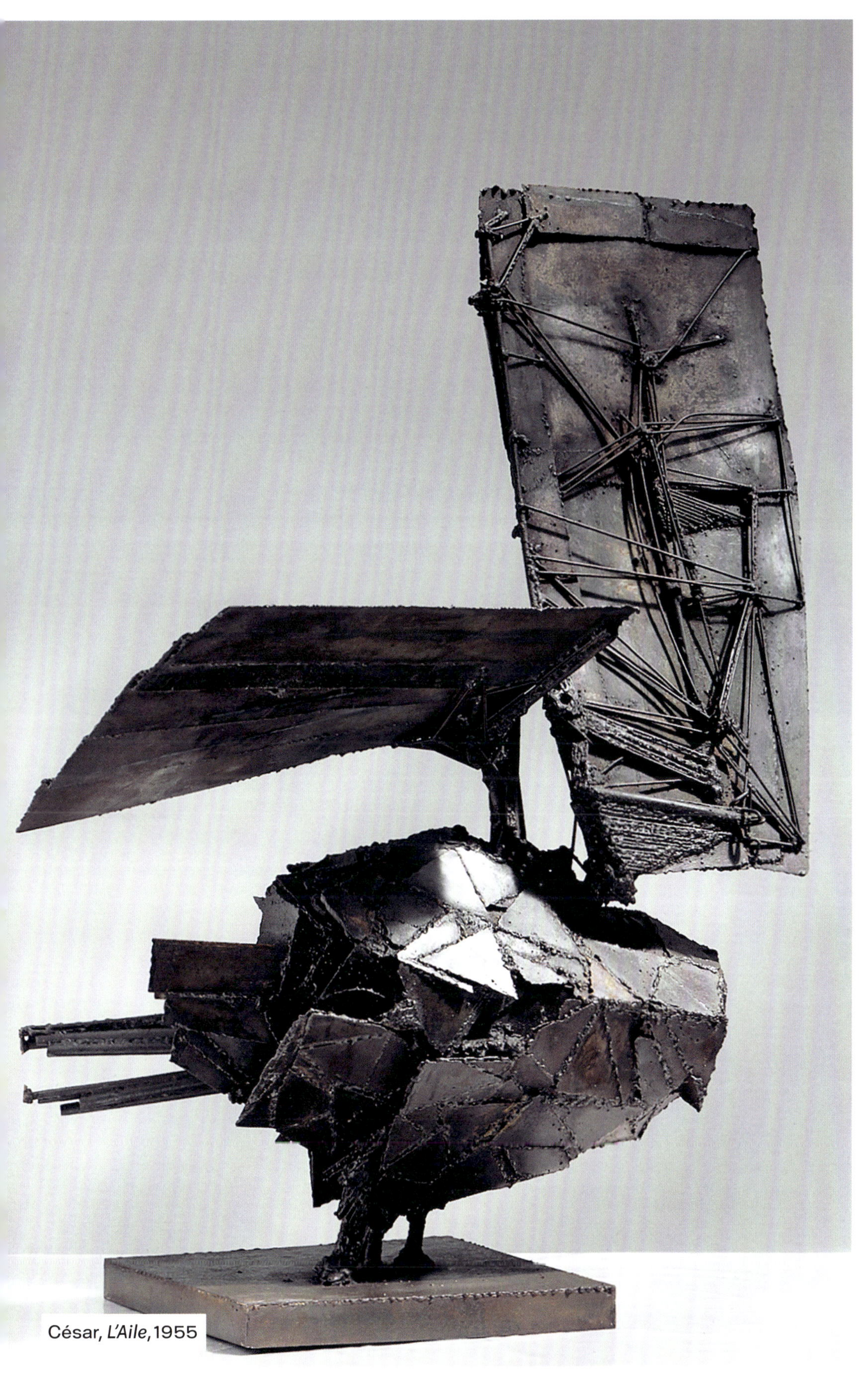

César, *L'Aile*, 1955

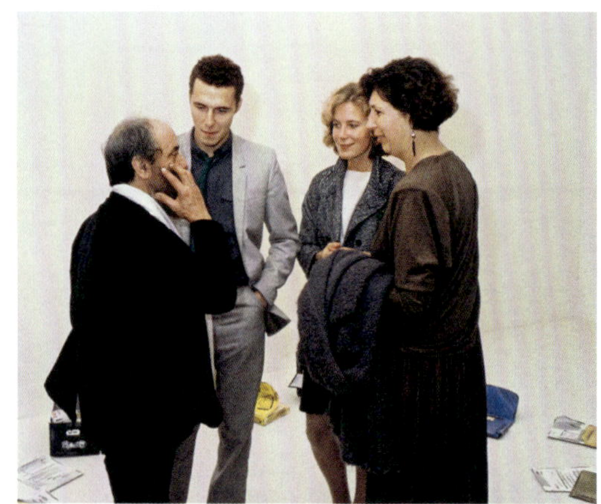

For the inauguration, the Fondation Cartier also hosted an exhibition devoted to the recent work of Julian Opie and another to the paintings of Lisa Milroy.
Above: César and Marie-Claude Beaud with the two artists

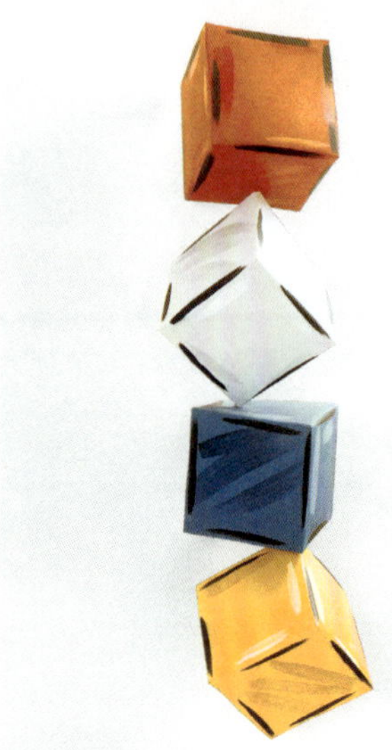

Julian Opie, *Coloured Boxes*, 1984
FC Collections (1985)

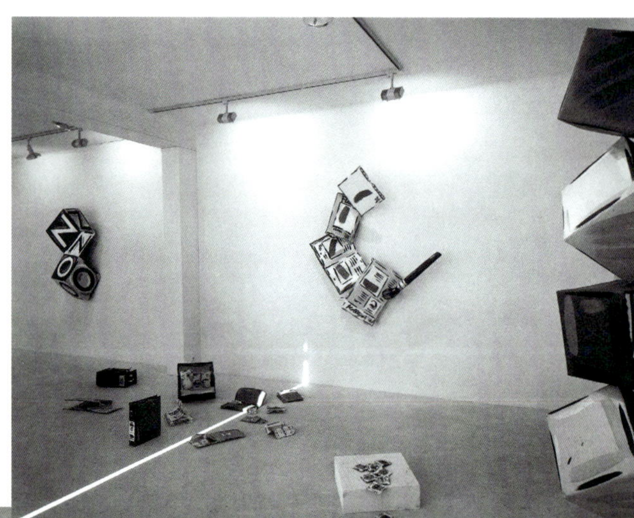

View of Julian Opie's exhibition

View of Lisa Milroy's exhibition

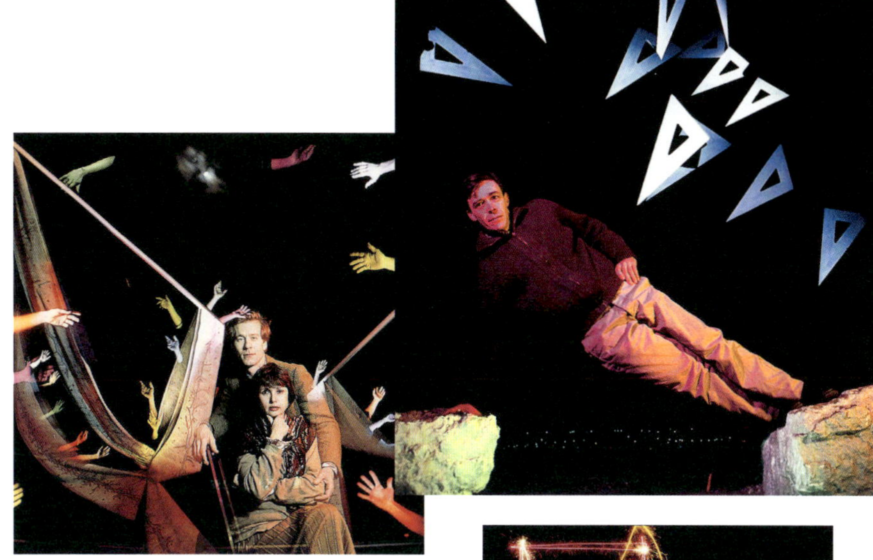

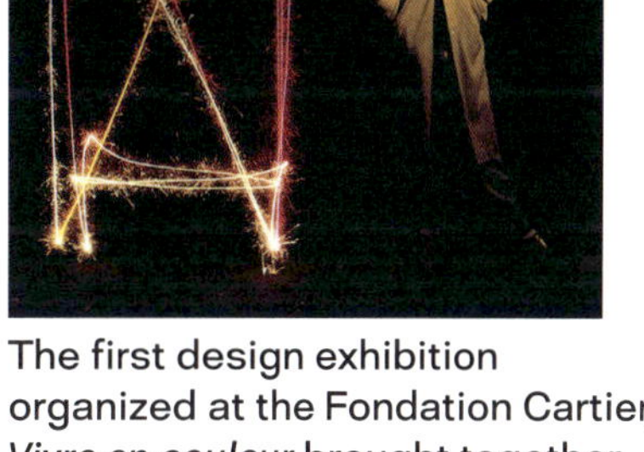

The first design exhibition organized at the Fondation Cartier, *Vivre en couleur* brought together young French designers.

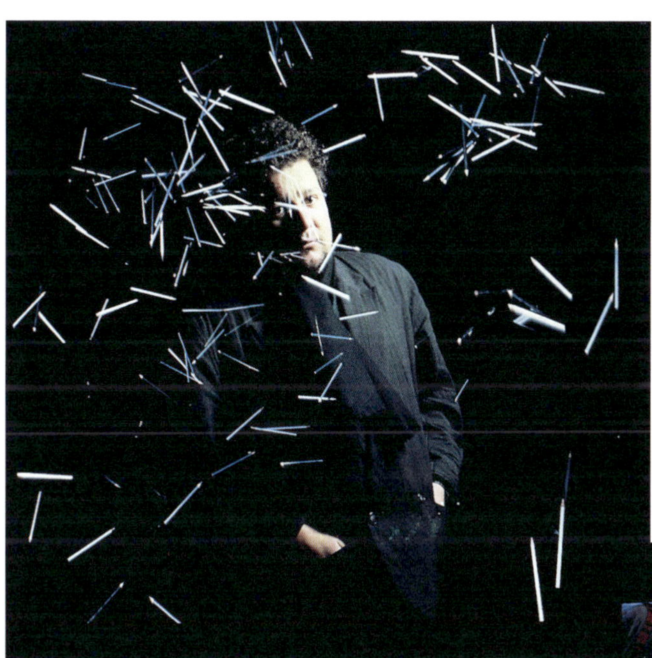

A series of portraits by Arnaud Baumann, created especially for the exhibition: Élisabeth Garouste and Mattia Bonetti, François Bauchet, Philippe Starck, Pascal Mourgue, Nestor Perkal, and the Totem Collective FC Collections (1985)

Histoire du Pot

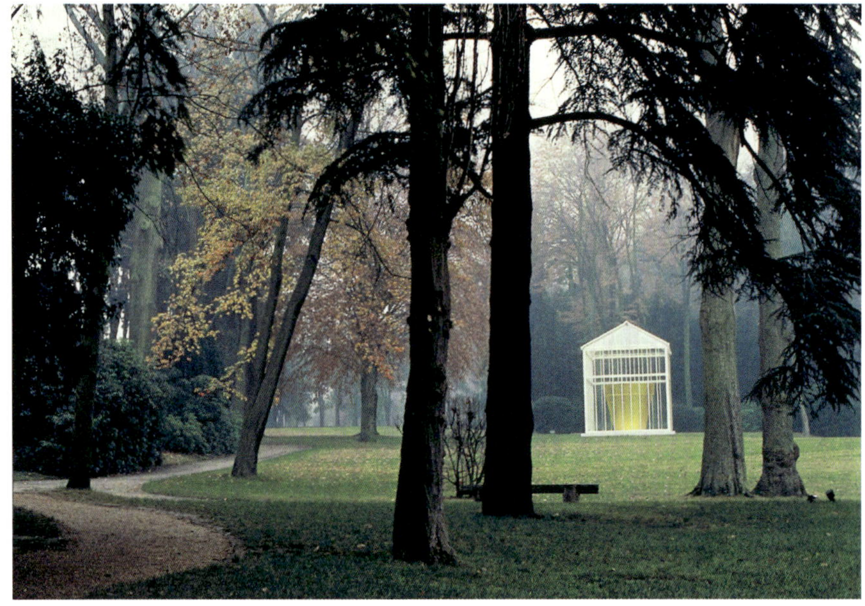

Jean Pierre Raynaud, *La Serre* and *Le Pot doré*, 1985. Commission for the park

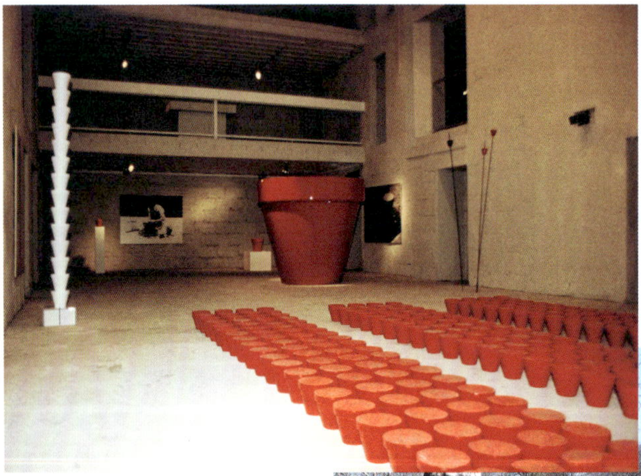

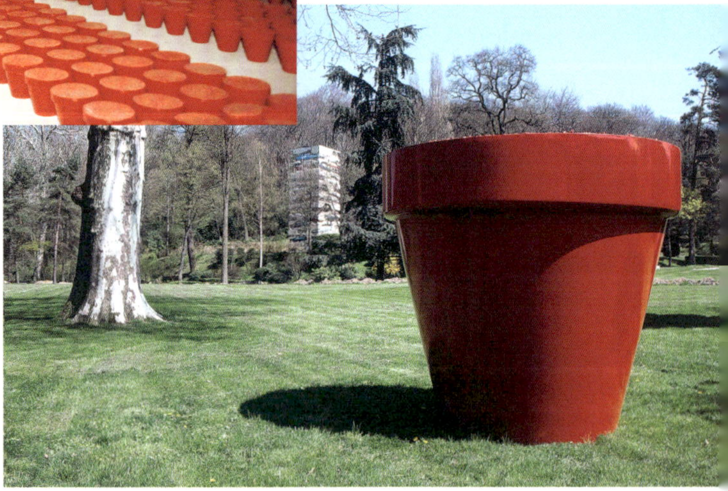

The exhibition *L'Histoire du Pot* stemmed from a desire
to explore Jean Pierre Raynaud's work, following the installation
of his sculpture *Le Pot doré* in the Fondation Cartier's park.

Jean Pierre Raynaud

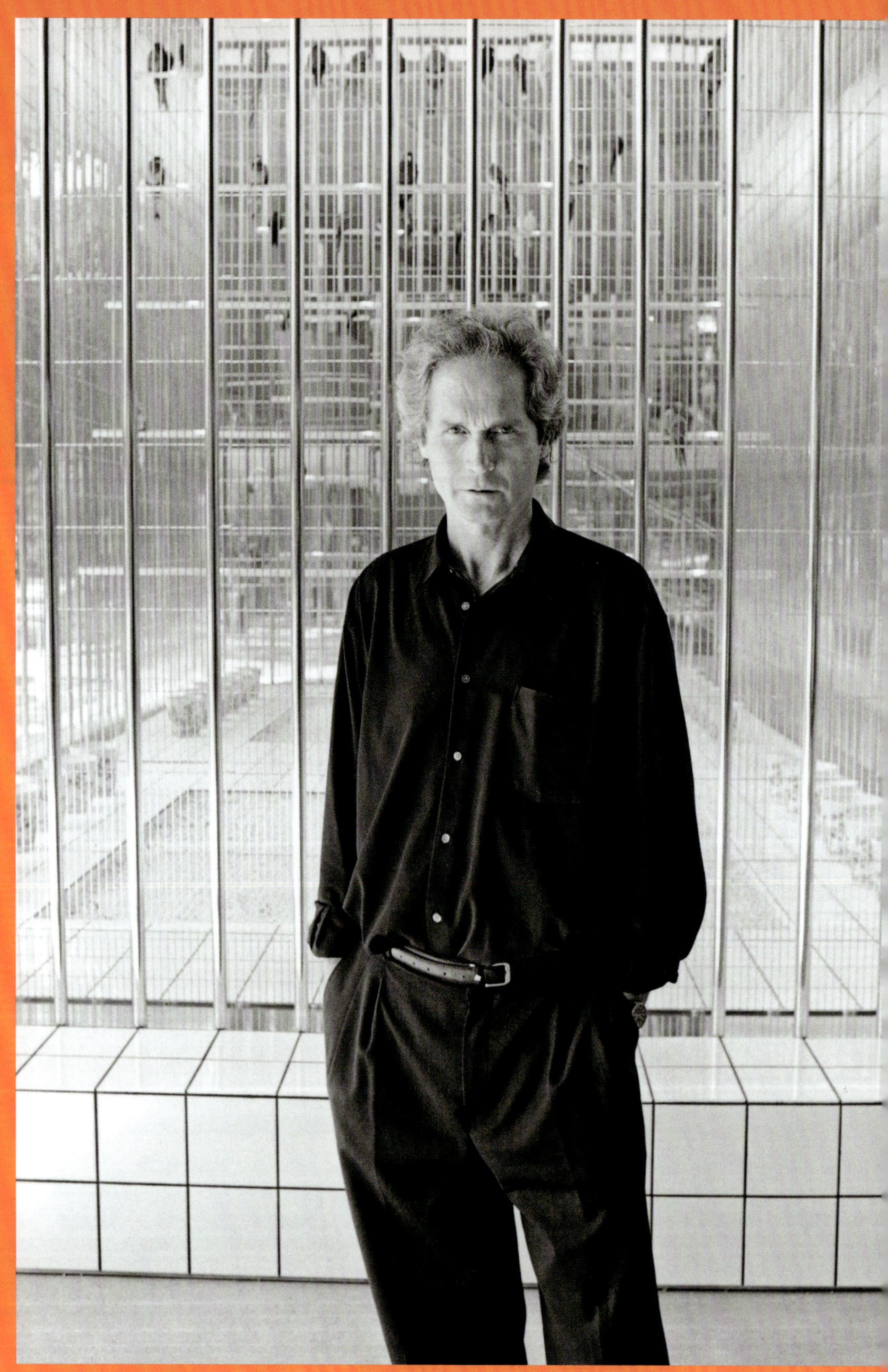

Jean Pierre Raynaud in front of his work *La Volière*, in the exhibition *Comme un oiseau*, 1996

Jean Pierre Raynaud

"One day, I went down to my garage and in a corner, I discovered things from my past: a few pots, a bag of cement, water, a pipe. There, in a very impulsive and incomprehensible gesture, I poured the cement into the pot, covered it and smeared it with paint. There was also a pot of vermilion red paint next to it, number 521, which I had bought at the BHV. At that moment, I had the feeling that I was discovering something in myself that freed me, that gave me life again. It is true to say that I was born on that day." (Excerpt from a radio interview, for the *Affaires culturelles* program on France Culture, February 23, 2023.)

In the early 1960s, and without really being aware of it, Jean Pierre Raynaud made his first artistic gesture. At the time, aged in his twenties, the young horticulture graduate had just completed twenty-eight months' military service, which had had a profound effect on him. The object used, a simple earthenware pot, drew him out of his torpor and quickly became an object of experimentation and a fundamental element in his artistic vocabulary. This pot—in turn filled with cement, molded in plastic, painted red, green, yellow, or blue, covered in gold leaf, exhibited on its own, or in multiple, even endless copies, produced at ordinary size or disproportionately enlarged—could be read as a symbol of the living and the inert, while at the same time, containing obvious links to nature or the plant world, without being fully restricted to either.

This pot was the starting point of a dialogue between Jean Pierre Raynaud and the Fondation Cartier pour l'art contemporain. In 1984, the Fondation Cartier, freshly founded and based in Jouy-en-Josas, invited the artist to present a solo exhibition of his works, and to produce a large format piece for its sculpture garden. The idea of a monumental pot immediately emerged and echoing the golden pots he had created in 1980, the artist decided that this sculpture would also be covered in gold leaf. At the exhibition opening in June 1985, a radiant, 3.5-meter pot was presented in a white greenhouse with glass walls. Once the exhibition ended, the pot remained in its greenhouse in the grounds of the Domaine du Montcel for several years. In 1994, when the Fondation moved to the Boulevard Raspail in Paris, Jean Pierre Raynaud did not want the piece to become just another work in a museum. He considered imploding or burying it, performing, in some way, a "ritual sacrifice" to have it disappear with grace. The Fondation Cartier encouraged the artist to imagine a less radical fate. Then began an astonishing journey for *Le Pot doré*: it was presented from May 31 to June 2, 1996, in Berlin, suspended from a crane, 30 meters above the Potsdamer Platz construction site. It was then installed, from October 16 to November 6, 1996, in the courtyard of the Hall of Supreme Harmony in the Forbidden City in Beijing. Built in the fifteenth century, this was the first time the Forbidden City had hosted the work of a contemporary artist. Finally, in March 1998, the pot was placed on the forecourt of the Centre Georges-Pompidou in Paris, at the top of a 10.5-meter stele covered in white marble. This event marked an important turning point in the history of *Le Pot doré*: the work's donation, fourteen years after its commissioning by the Fondation Cartier, to the Musée National d'Art Moderne.

While *La Serre* and *Le Pot doré* are the basis for the relationship between Jean Pierre Raynaud and the Fondation Cartier, there was another commission, no less spectacular. In 1996, the Fondation Cartier asked the artist to create a huge aviary as part of the exhibition *Comme un oiseau*. Made of ceramic and steel, it was filled with colorful Australian parakeets. A veritable tableau vivant, the work was in harmony with Jean Nouvel's building. Shortly after the exhibition, the Fondation Cartier acquired *La Volière* for its Collections.

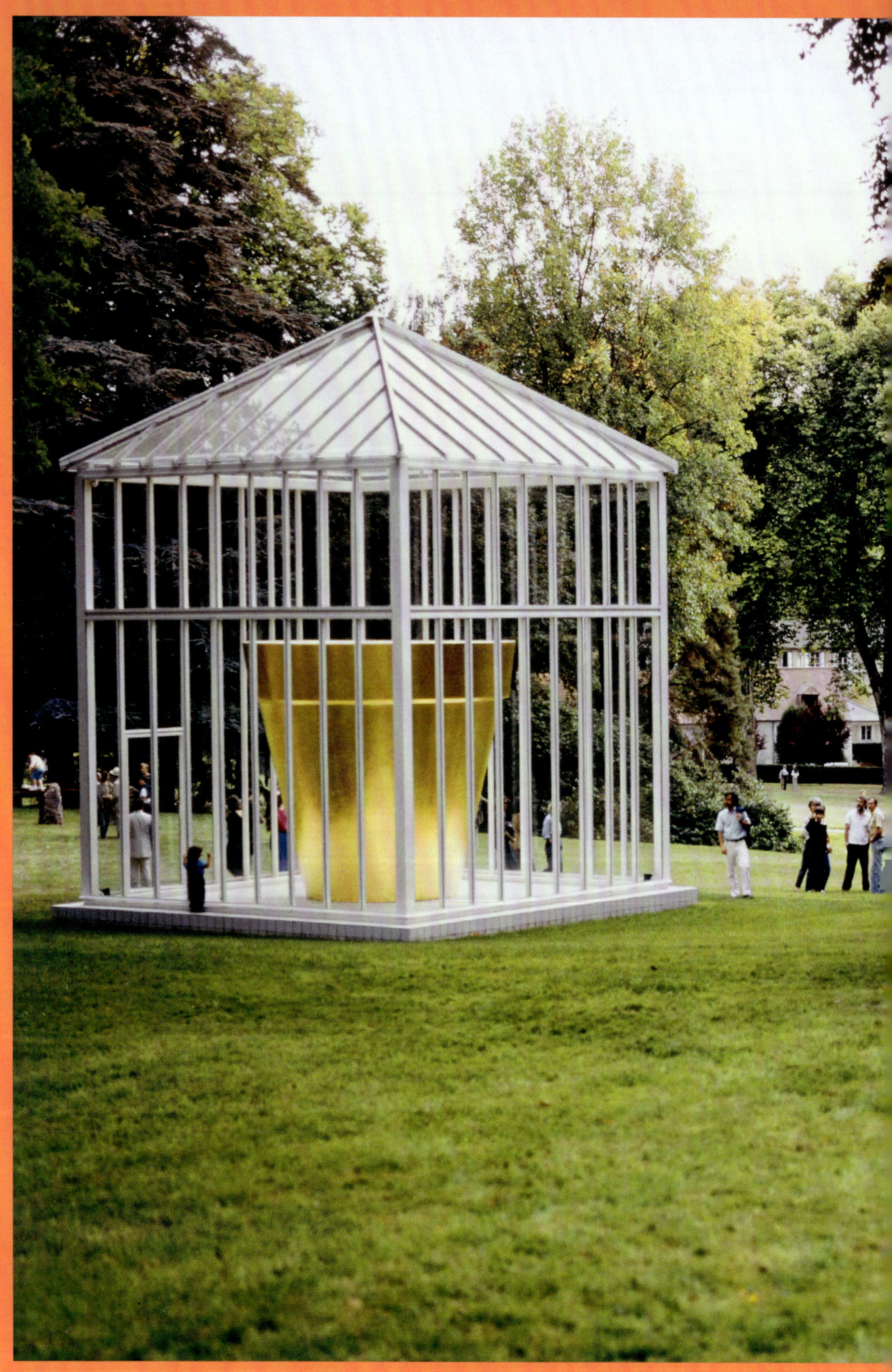

1985–1993   *La Serre* and *Le Pot doré* by Jean Pierre Raynaud were installed in the park of the Fondation Cartier at Jouy-en-Josas.

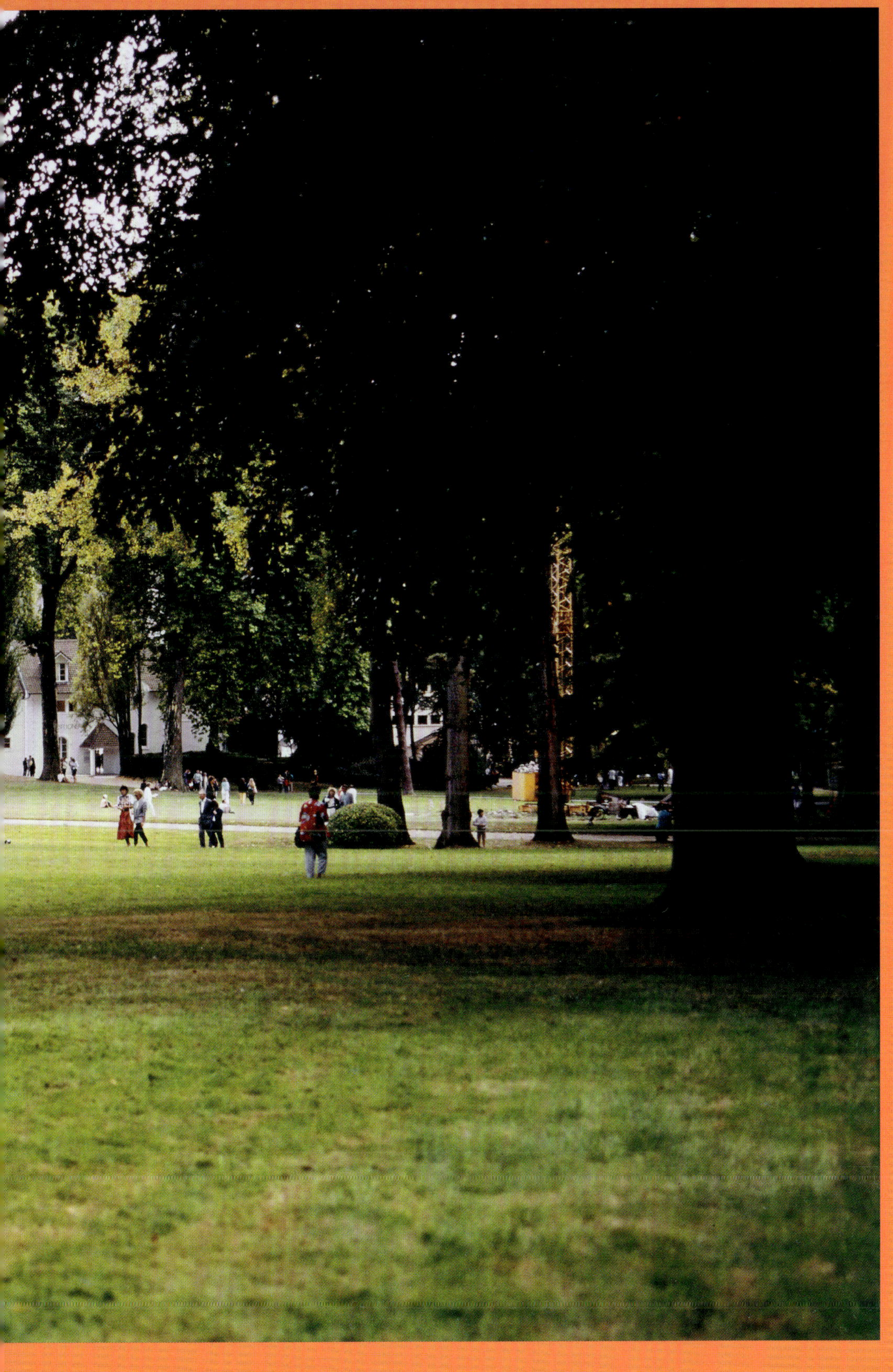

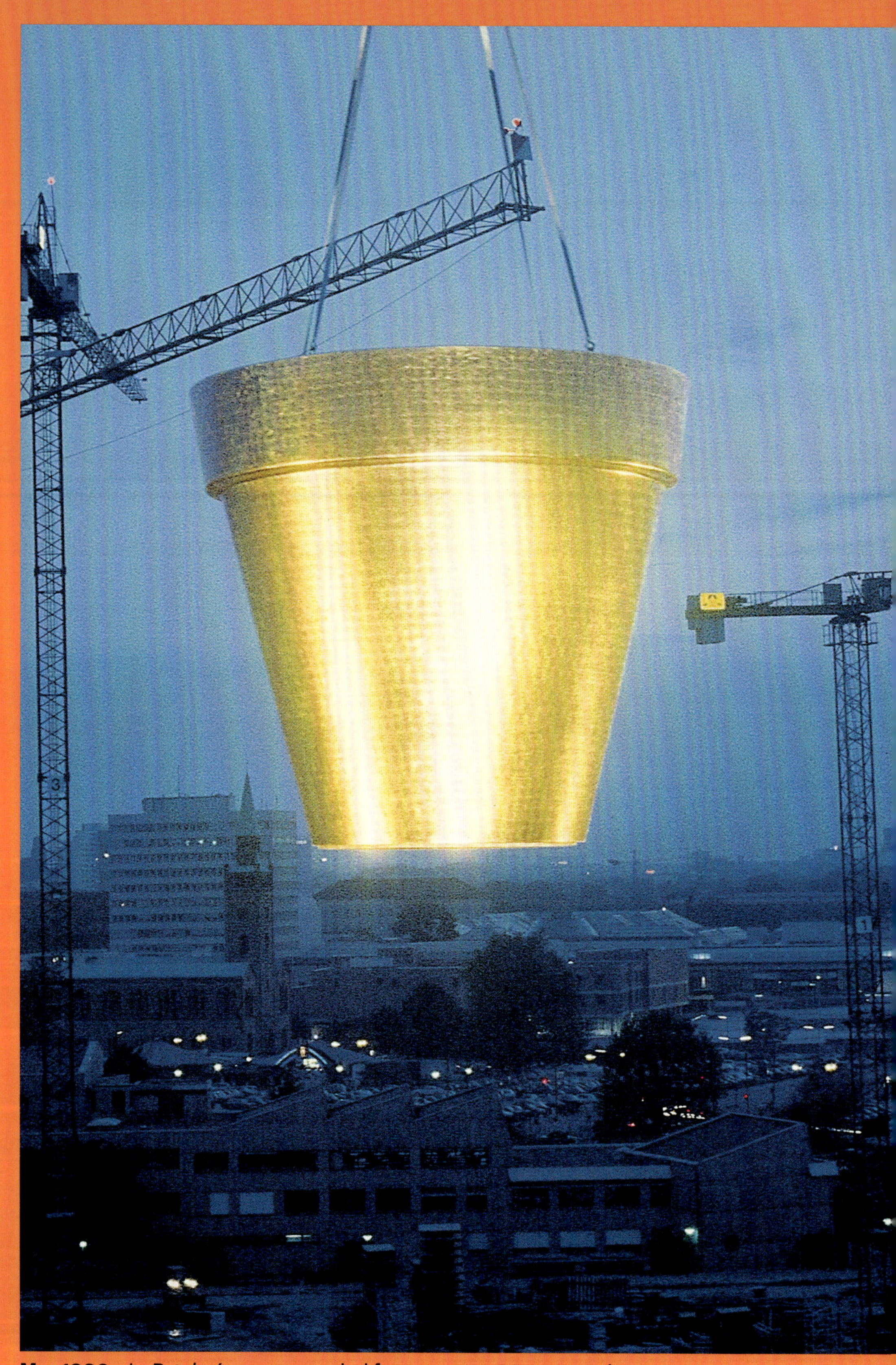

May 1996 *Le Pot doré* was suspended from a crane, 30 meters above the construction site at the Potsdamer Platz in Berlin.

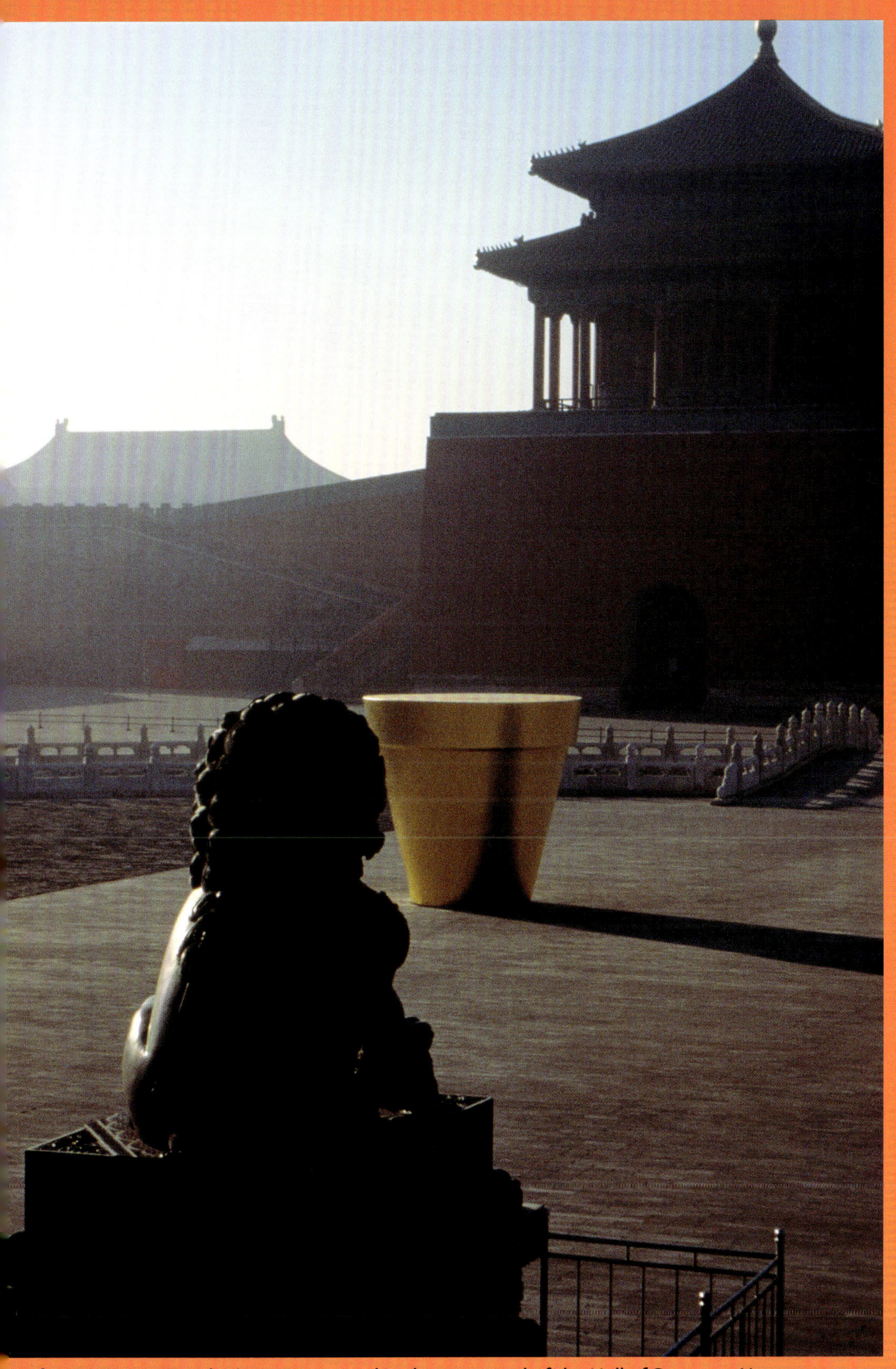

ctober 1996 *Le Pot doré* was presented in the courtyard of the Hall of Supreme Harmony the Forbidden City, Beijing.

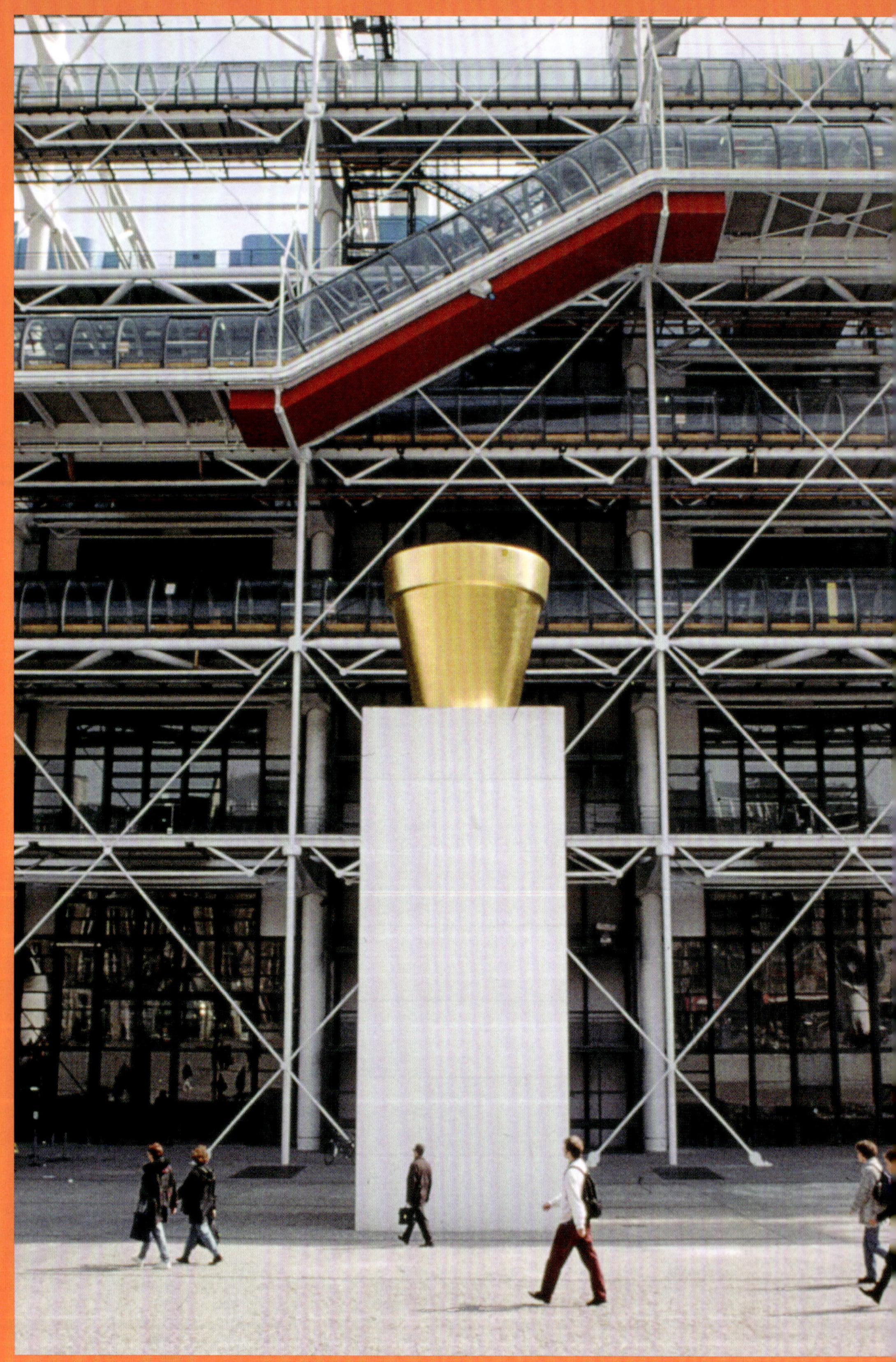

1998–2009   *Le Pot doré* had pride of place on the forecourt of the Centre Georges-Pompidou in Paris.

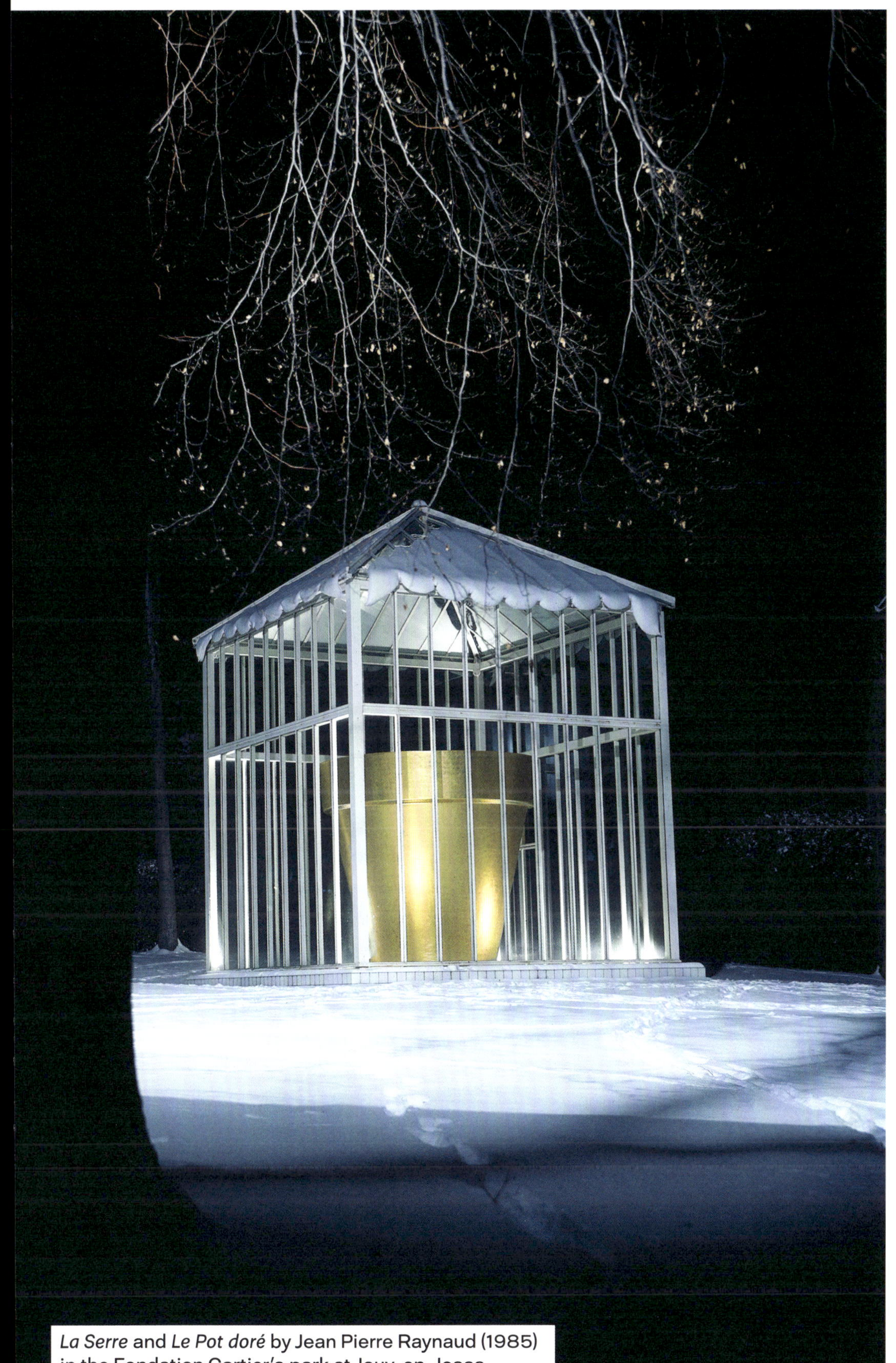

La Serre and *Le Pot doré* by Jean Pierre Raynaud (1985)
in the Fondation Cartier's park at Jouy-en-Josas

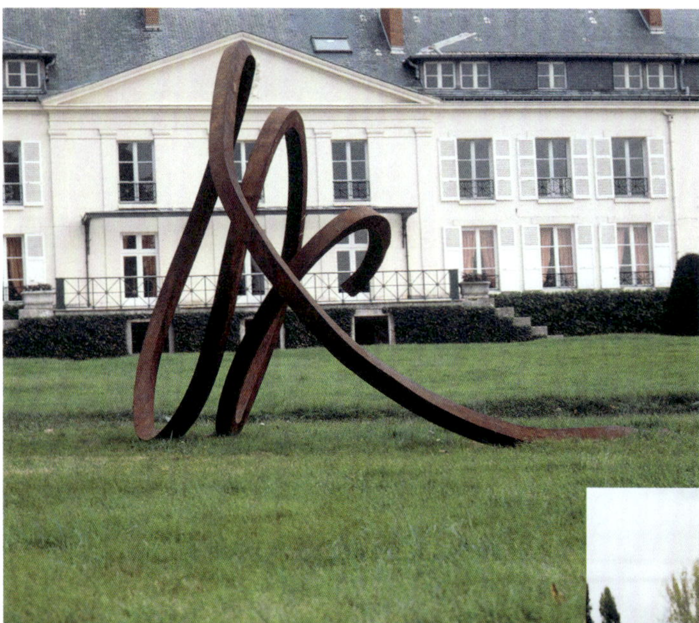

The exhibition *Sculptures, première approche pour un parc* was born from the desire to offer a first glimpse at the work of artists the Fondation Cartier had already commissioned or would like to commission for the site.
Bernar Venet, *Ligne indéterminée*, 1985

Richard Tuttle, *Earth of Granada*, 1985
FC Collections (1986)

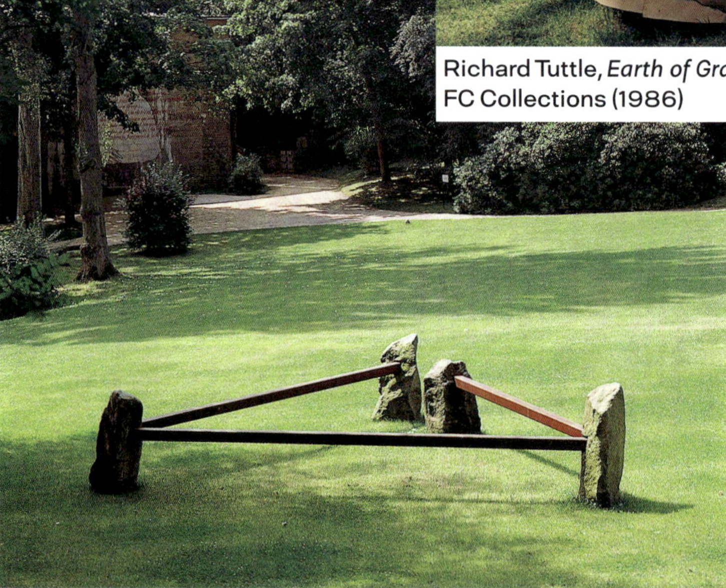

Keiji Uematsu, *Situation horizontale*, 1985
FC Collections (1986)

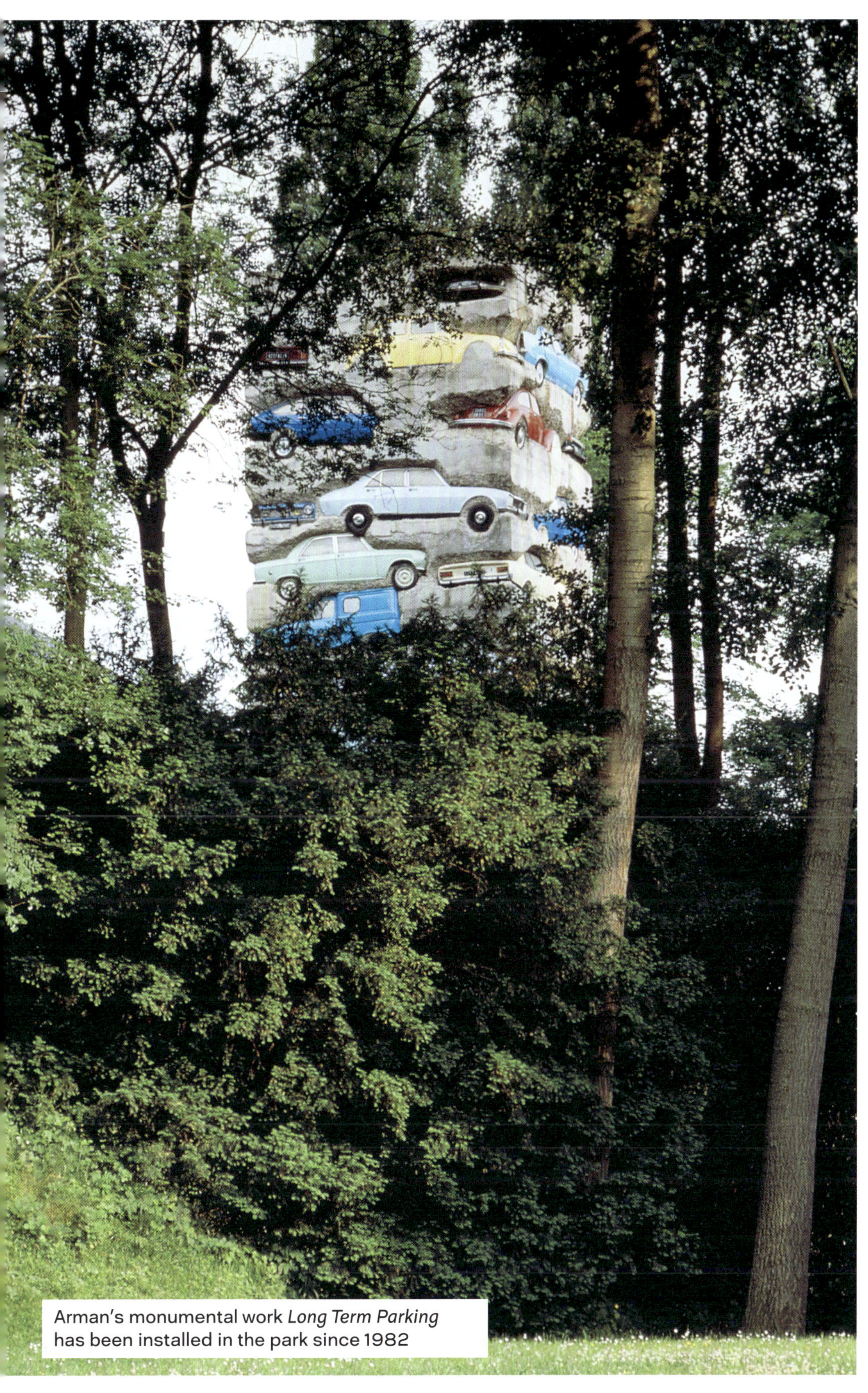

Arman's monumental work *Long Term Parking* has been installed in the park since 1982

Hommage au marquis de Bièvre

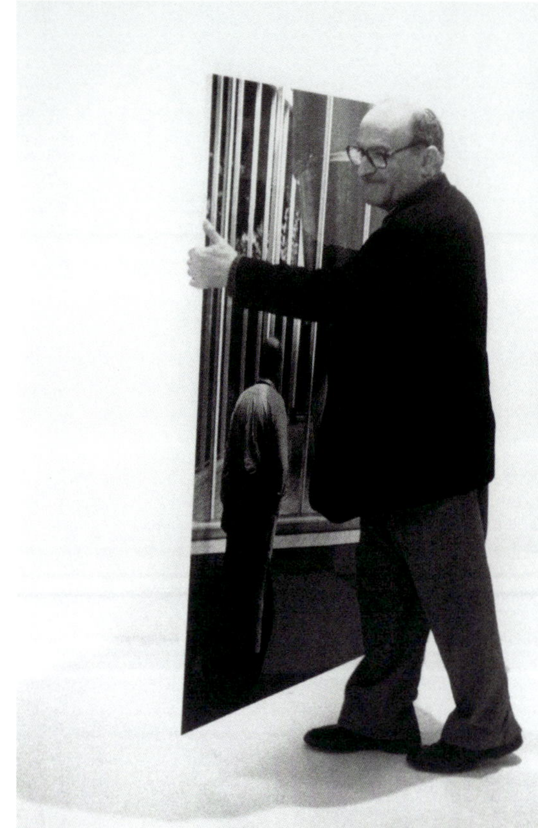

Raymond Hains during the installation
of the exhibition

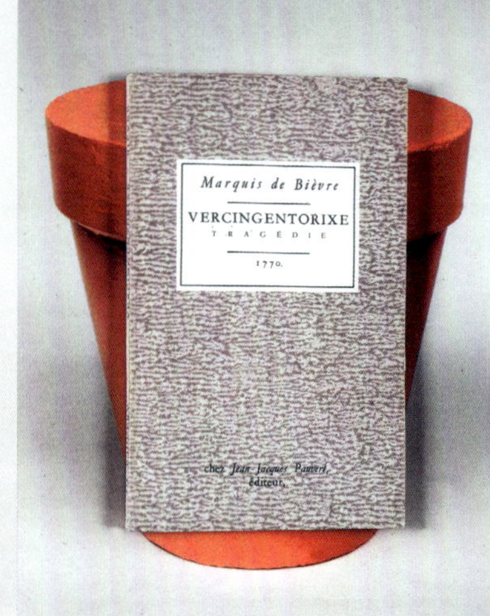

Raymond Hains, *Hommage
au marquis de Bièvre*, 1986
FC Collections (1987)

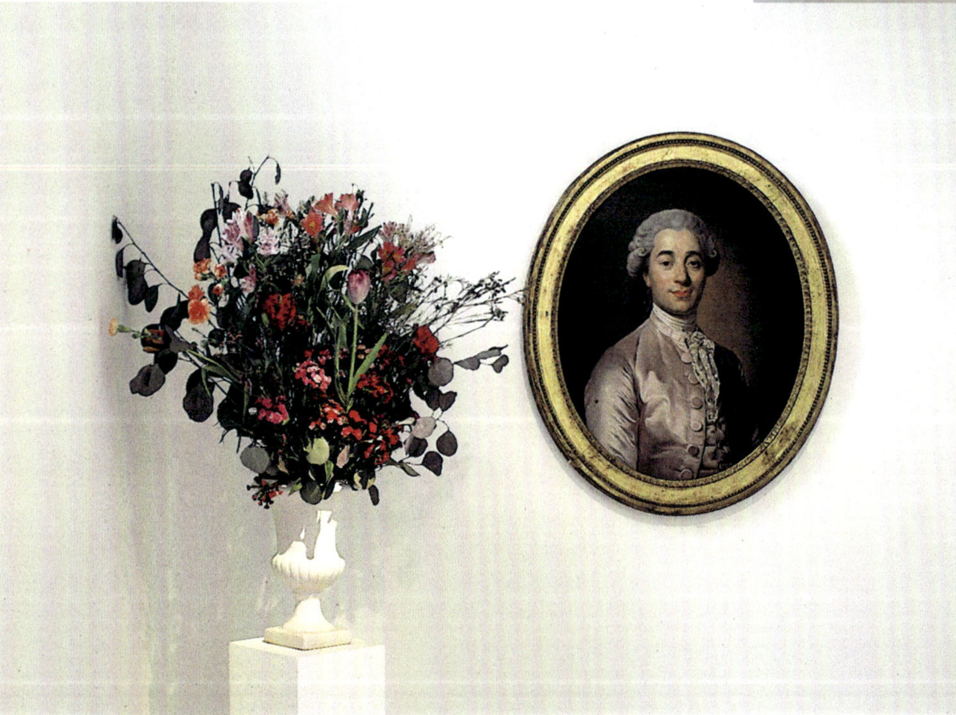

Raymond Hains presented a unique piece on the Bièvre Marquis
and the Bièvre Valley, in reference to the Fondation Cartier's site.

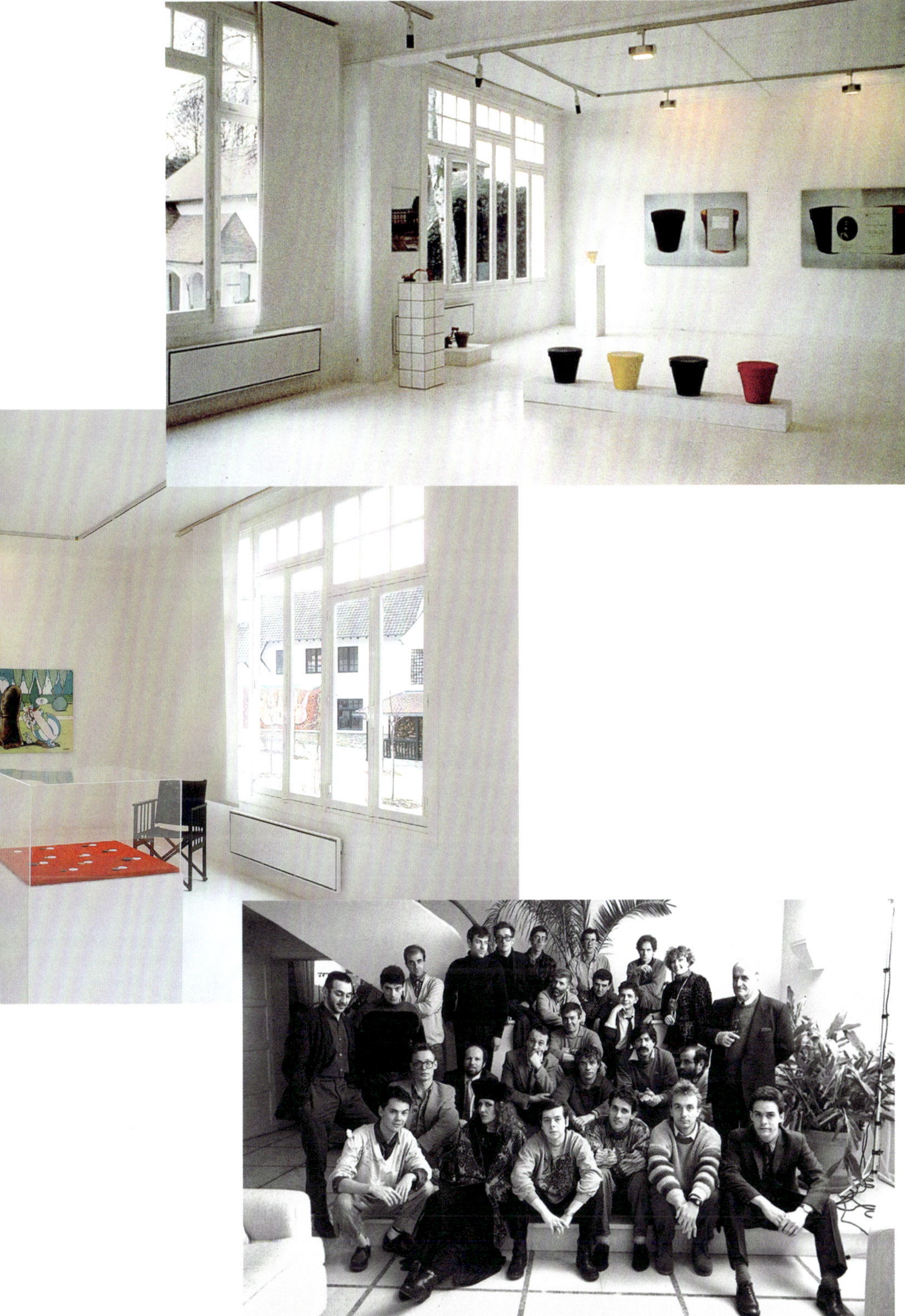

In parallel with the exhibition devoted to Raymond Hains,
the Fondation Cartier exhibited the work of seven sculptors
in *L'Art fun ou l'Enfance de l'art* and presented *Sur les murs*,
an exhibition of works created by 18 artists for its exterior spaces.
Above: the group of artists involved

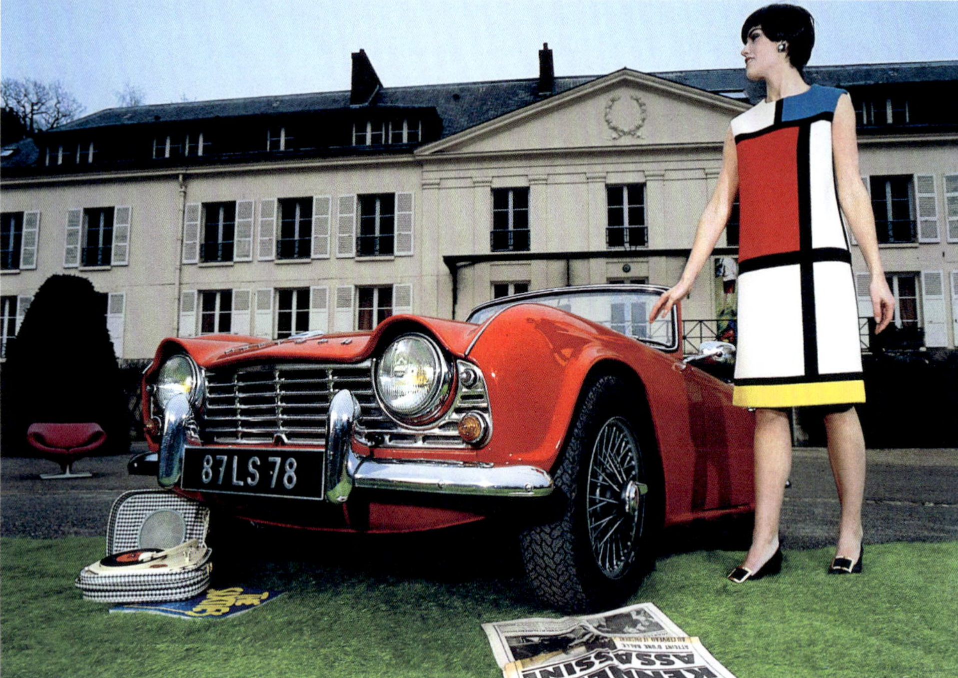

"Alain Dominique Perrin asked me
to create themed exhibitions, accessible
to a broad public. He wanted this popular
dimension. So I suggested exhibitions
on design, architecture, and fashion
with Courrèges." Marie-Claude Beaud

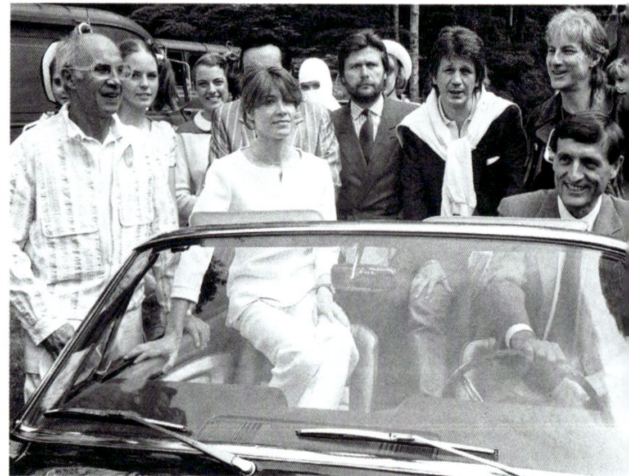

André Courrèges, Françoise Hardy,
Alain Dominique Perrin, Gérard Lenorman,
Hugues Aufray, and François Léotard at the
opening of the exhibition *Les Années 60*

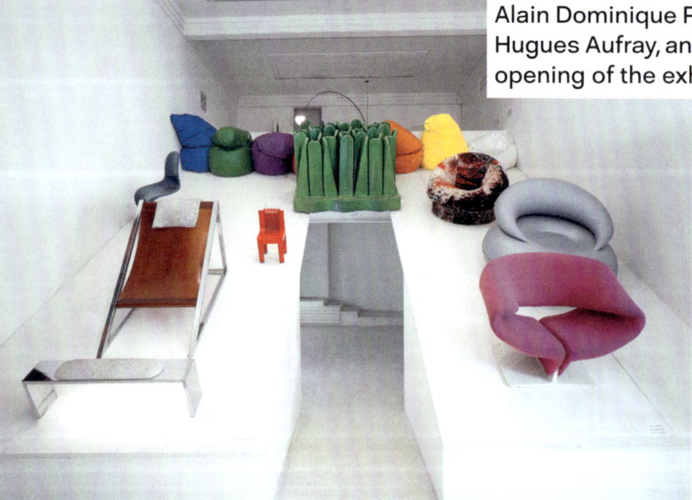

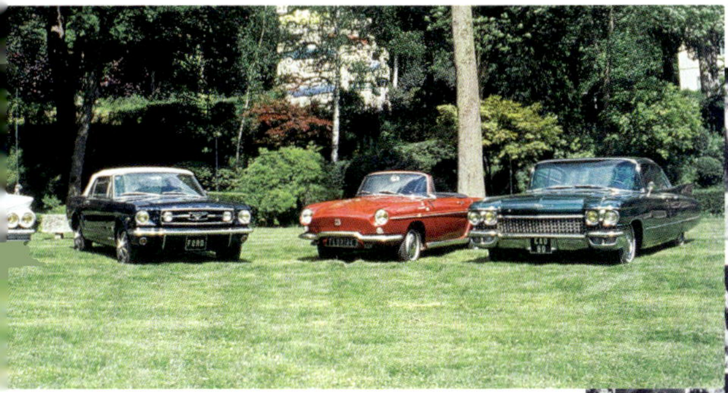

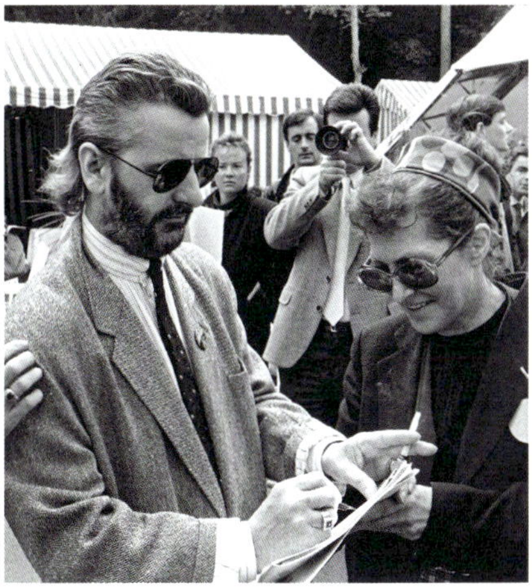

Ringo Starr at the exhibition opening

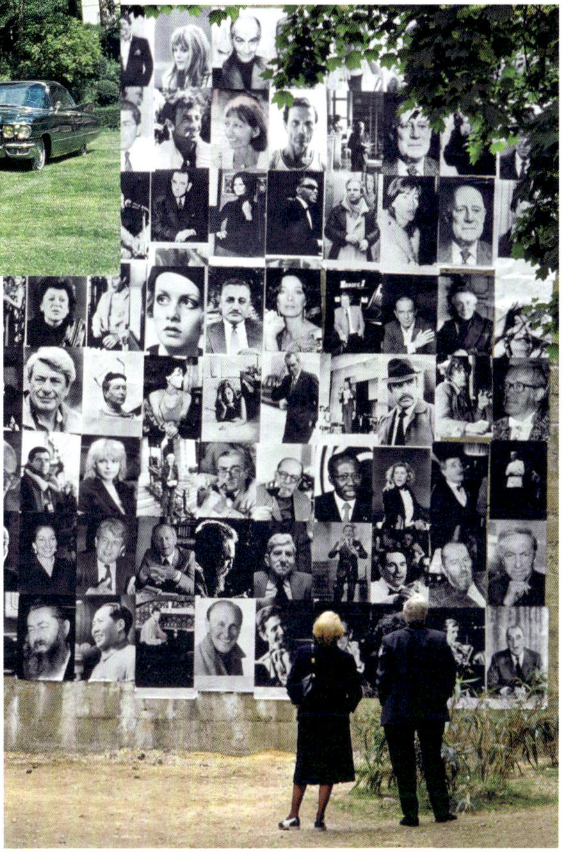

Installation created with archival photos
from *Paris Match*

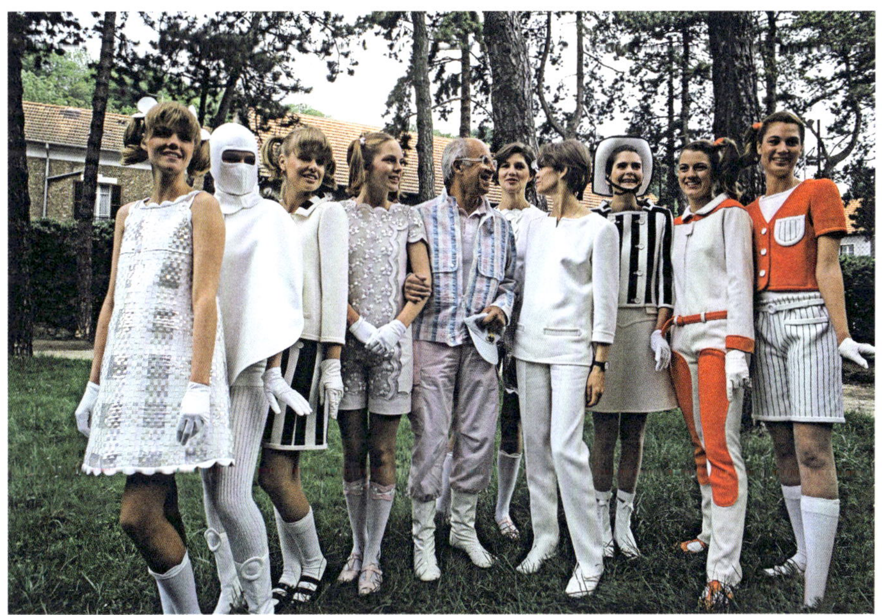

For the exhibition opening, the Fondation Cartier invited fashion
designer André Courrèges to create a fashion show in the park.
Above: André Courrèges, Françoise Hardy, and the models

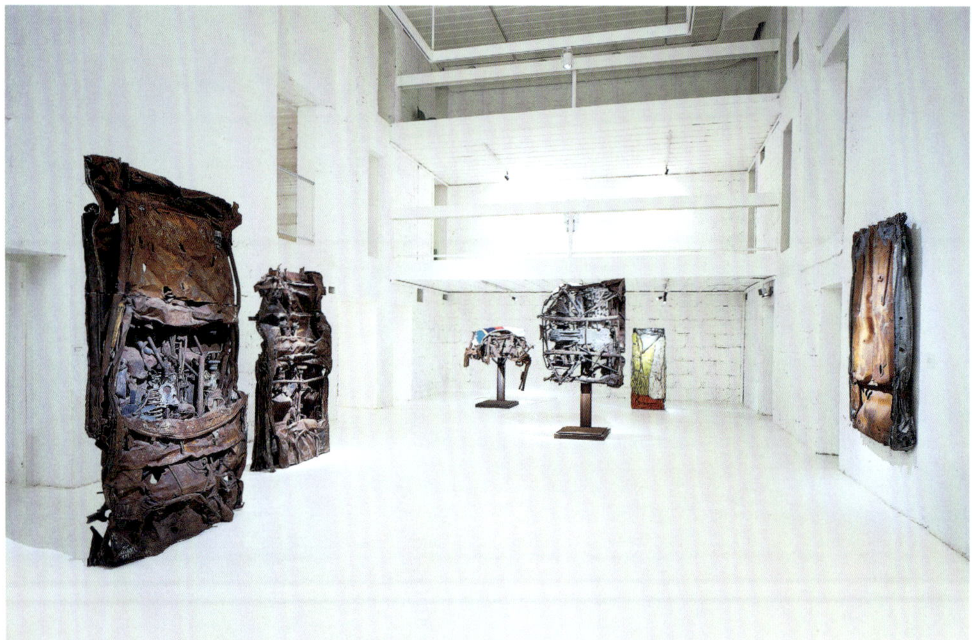

The exhibition *Les Championnes de César* presented a group of 24 compressions made in the Peugeot workshops from four 205 Turbo 16, former rally "champions" that César reduced to plates of no more than 30 cm thick.

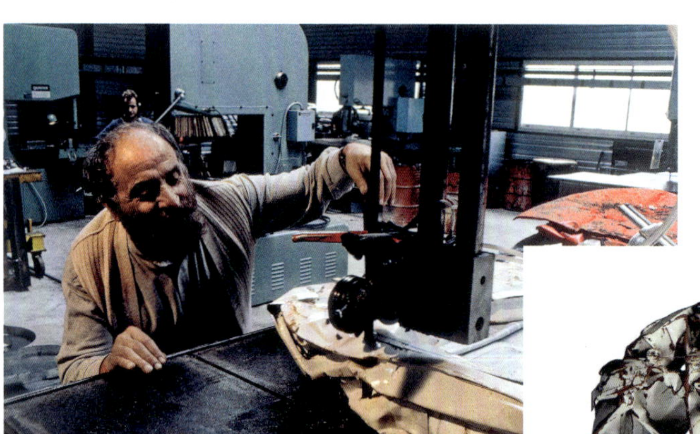

César at a Peugeot factory, 1986

César, *Championne corse no. 3*, 1986

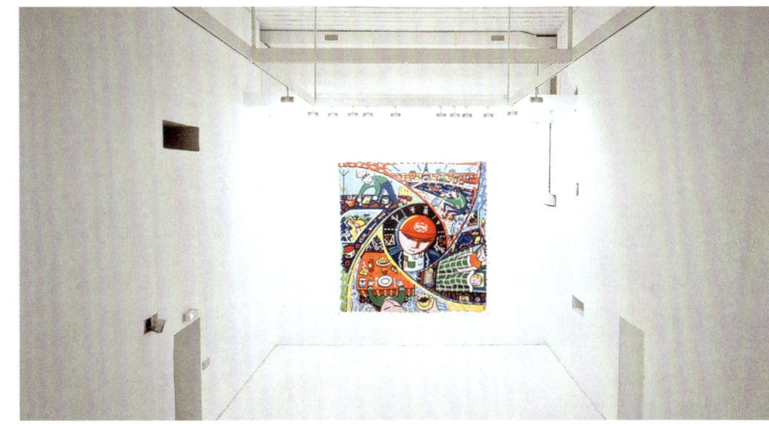

Under the title *Camouflage*, the Fondation Cartier organized three consecutive exhibitions between January and May 1987, dedicated to Dominique Gauthier, François Boisrond, and Shirley Jaffe. François Boisrond, *La Journée complète*, 1987. FC Collections (1987)

View of Dominique Gauthier's exhibition

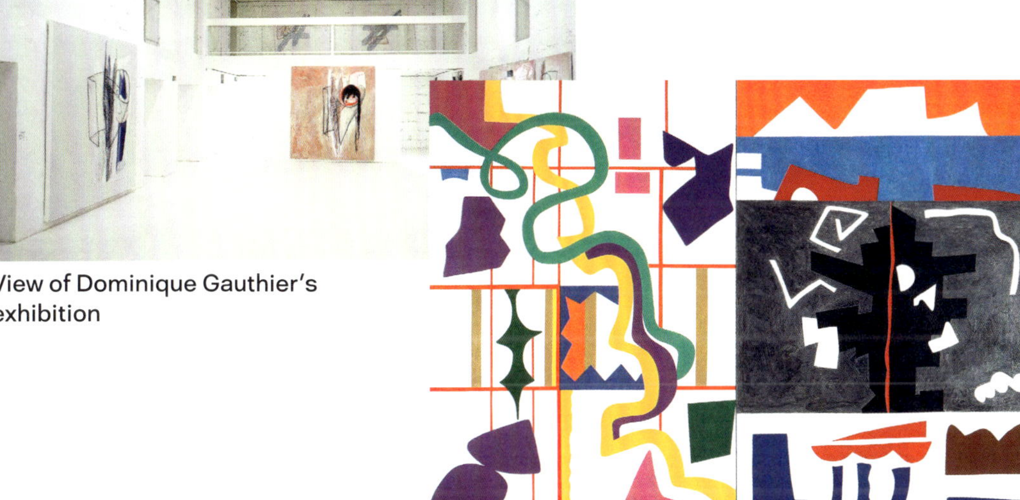

Shirley Jaffe, *Playground*, 1995. FC Collections (1996)

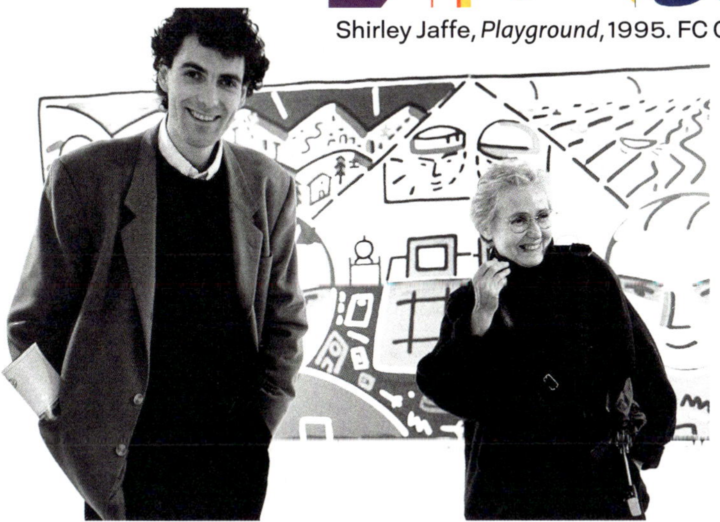

François Boisrond and Shirley Jaffe

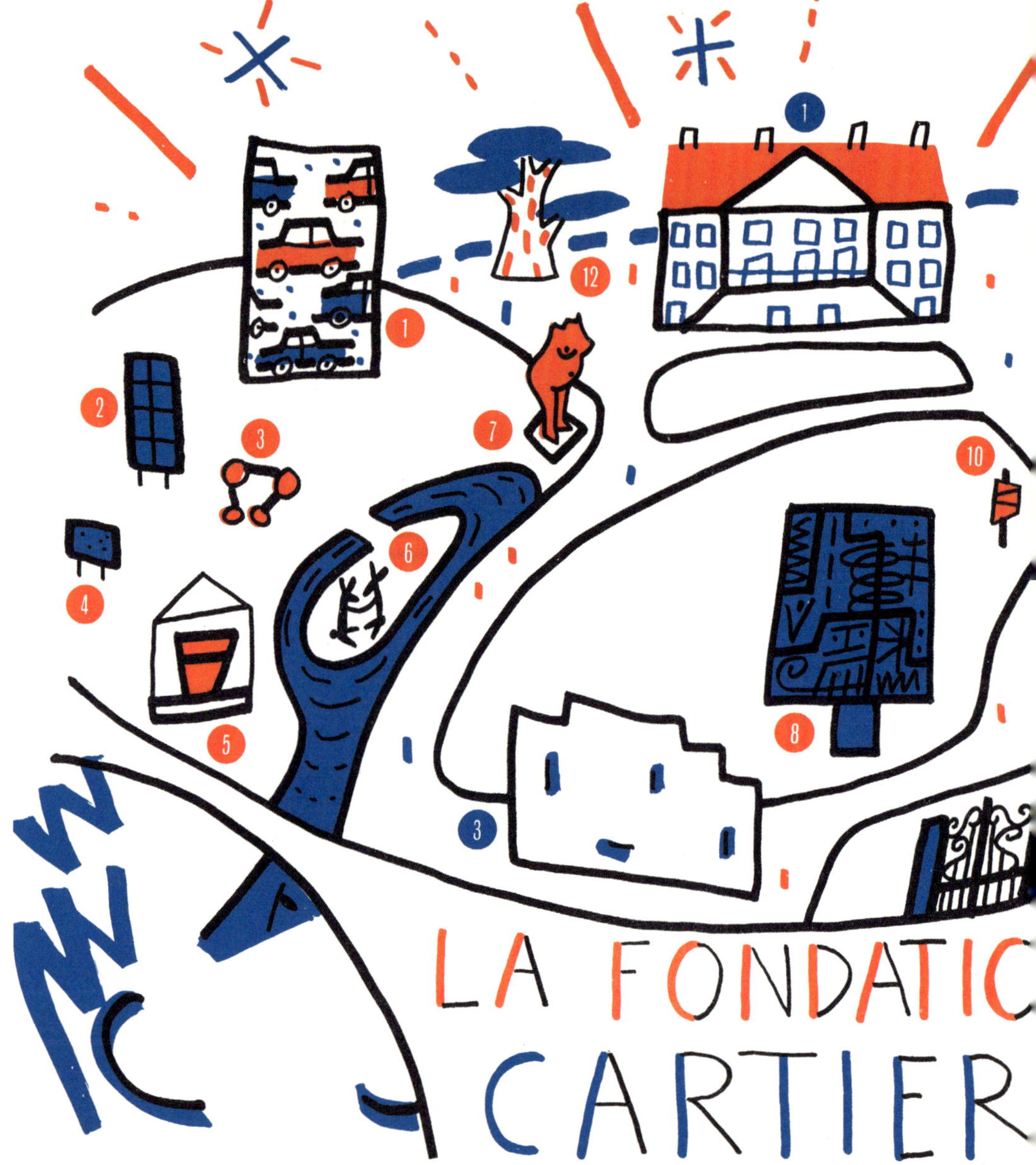
LA FONDATIO
CARTIER
Long Term Parking d'Arman
Le Totem de Pagés
Situation horizontale d'Uematsu
Naraha structure 85.A65
La serre de J.P. Raynaud
The boxing hares Flanagan
La Vénus de Villetaneuse
L'hommage à Eiffel
Le Pouce de Césa
Terre de grenade de Tu
L'endroit décisif (6 ifs) d'
Le déjeuner sous l'herbe de

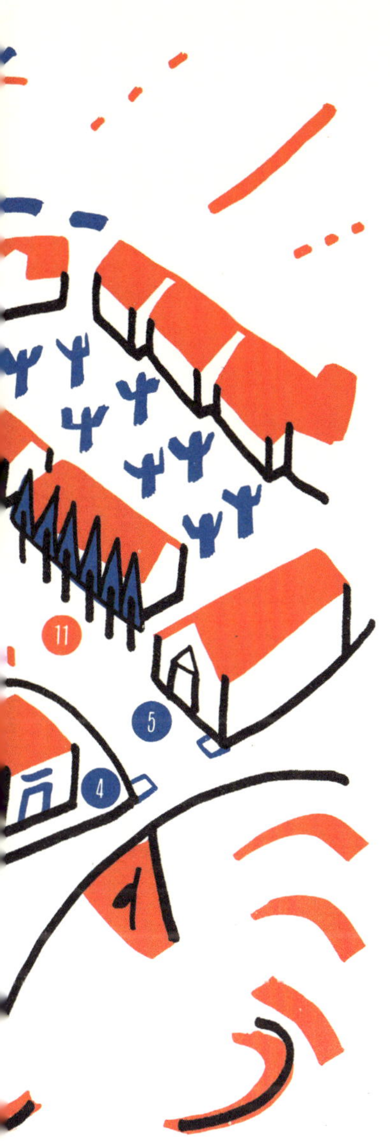

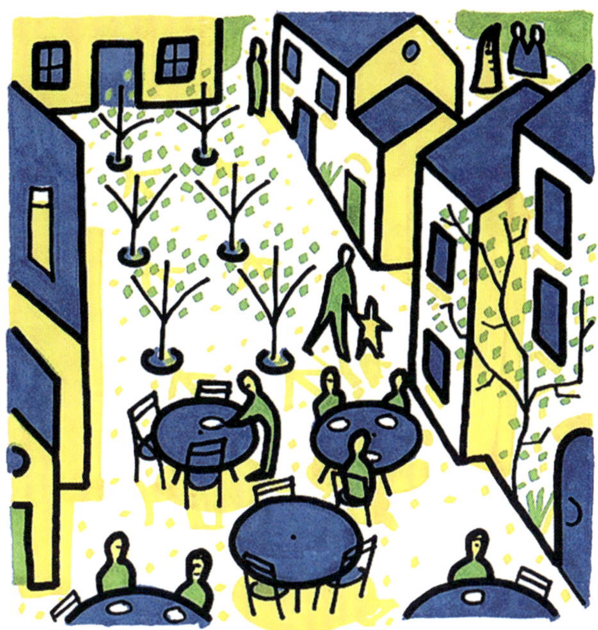

Drawings by François Boisrond for the Fondation Cartier: map of the exhibition spaces and the park, and an illustration for the Petit Café

LE CHATEAU
LE VILLAGE DES EXPOSITIONS
LE BUNKER
L'ACCUEIL
LES BUREAUX
LE PORTAIL XVIII°

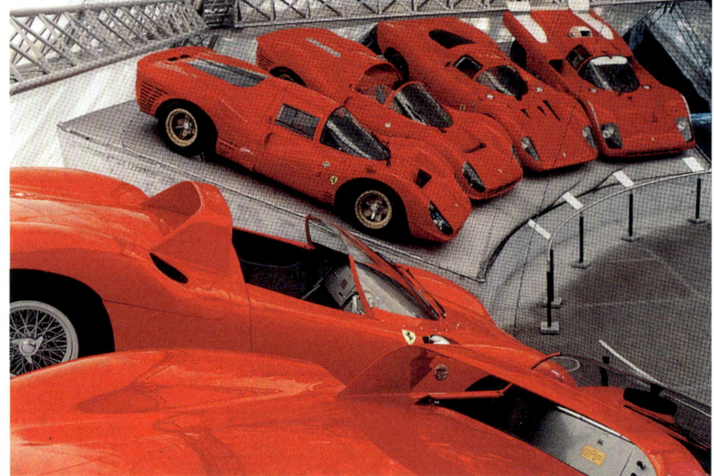

For its second themed summer exhibition,
the Fondation Cartier paid tribute to Enzo Ferrari.

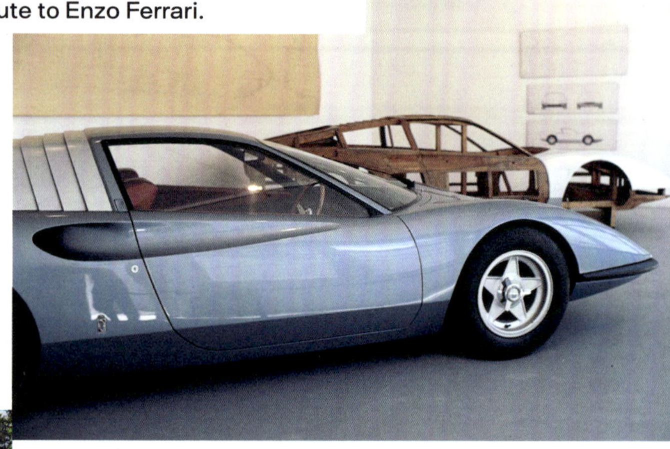

A special space was devoted to Pininfarina's
mechanics and design.

Andrée Putman was entrusted with the scenography of the exhibition
and design of the furniture elements.

Tribute to Ferrari

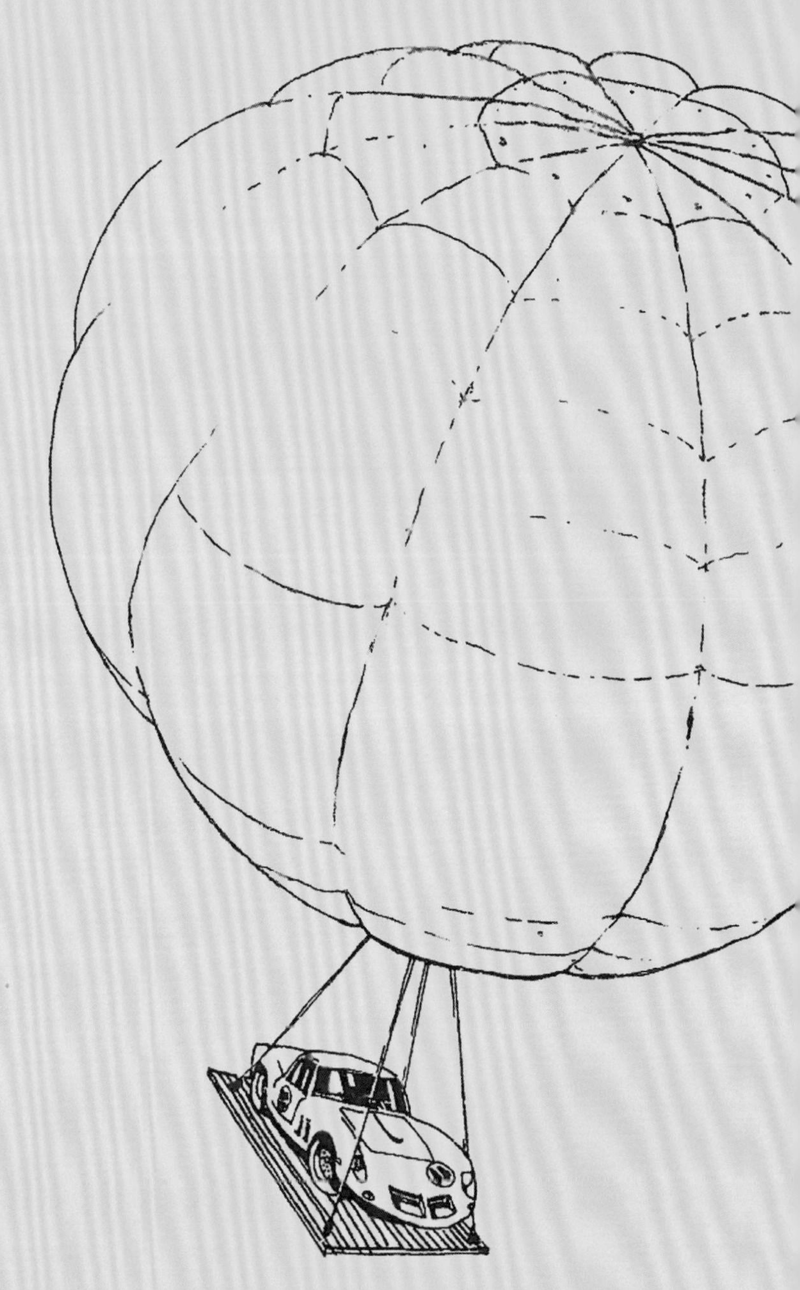

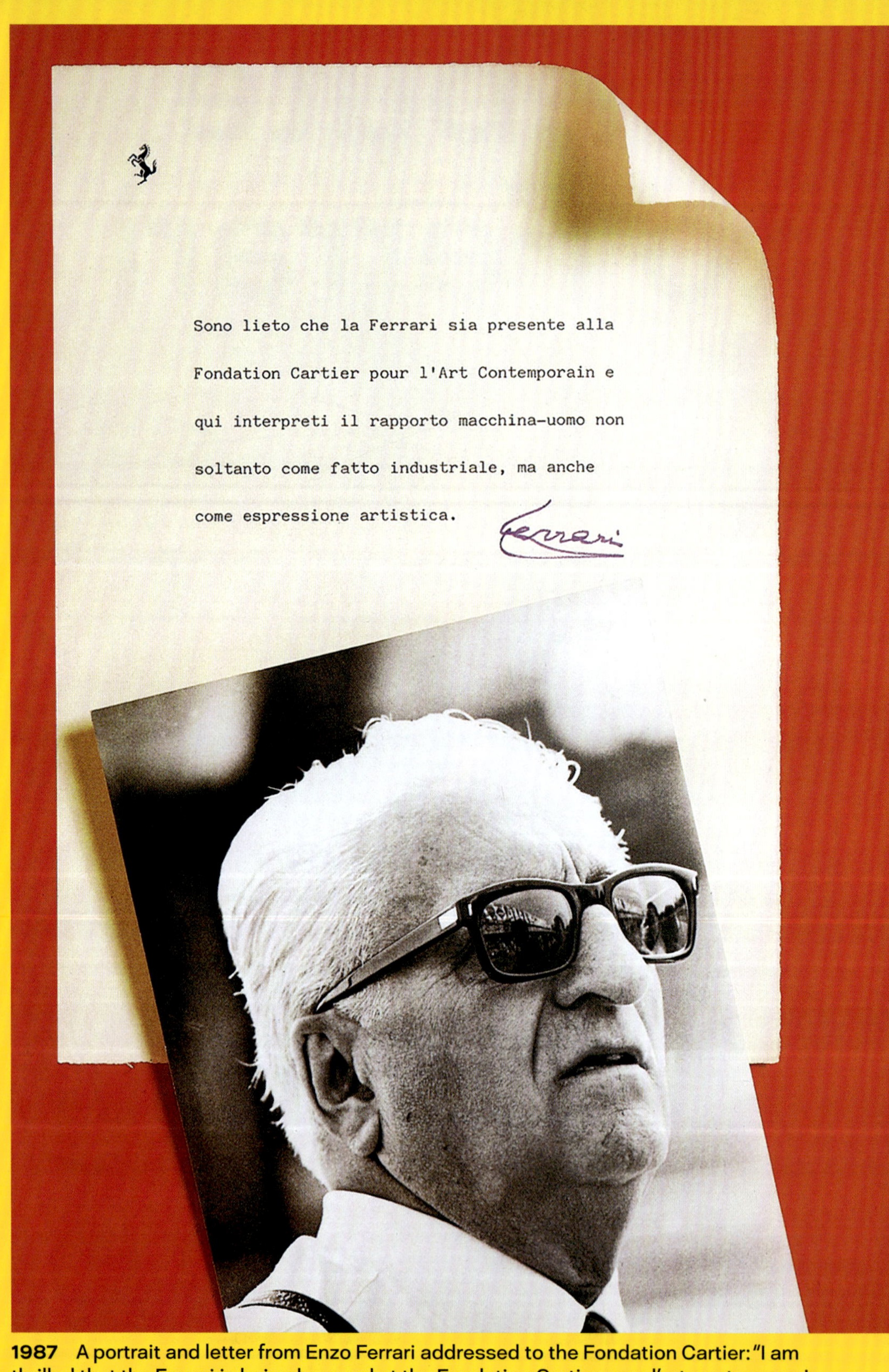

1987   A portrait and letter from Enzo Ferrari addressed to the Fondation Cartier: "I am thrilled that the Ferrari is being honored at the Fondation Cartier pour l'art contemporain and that the relationship between man and the machine is not only being shown from an industrial perspective, but also as a means of artistic expression."

Tribute to Ferrari

Summer 1987. The Fondation Cartier, opened almost three years earlier in Jouy-en-Josas, presented a major thematic exhibition, a tribute to the almost-ninety-year-old Enzo Ferrari, one of the greatest automobile engineers of the twentieth century. This Italian racing-car driver with a passion for technology and speed, was the founder of the Ferrari brand and of the famous Scuderia Ferrari racing team behind the prestigious red sports car, adorned with the prancing black horse. A few months earlier, Alain Dominique Perrin had spoken of him as "the greatest twentieth-century artist" when he asked Marie-Claude Beaud, the first Director of the Fondation Cartier, to organize the upcoming summer exhibition. Ferrari in a contemporary art foundation? This was something that had never been seen before and a far cry from what museums traditionally offered. But this was precisely what the founding President of this new arts and culture center wanted to do, to stand apart from others. For him, summer exhibitions should attract visitors around innovative themes. Thus, *Hommage à Ferrari* went off the beaten track, aimed at a wider audience, unaccustomed to the world of museums. To properly stage the myth Enzo Ferrari created, Marie-Claude Beaud invited interior architect and designer Andrée Putman to take on the project. Known for her black-and-white checkerboard creations and penchant for simplicity, Andrée Putman adapted to the vivid Ferrari red, and assisted by Bruno Moinard, designed a unique and striking experience. While she created the furniture for the exhibition, she notably suggested suspending some ten gleaming Ferraris from hot-air balloons in the Domaine du Montcel. Her idea was to make the sports coupés and convertibles lift off for a few moments, before coming back to land. While they didn't actually leave the earth, the cars attached to the hot-air balloons nevertheless gave the impression that they were just about to take off or had just landed. The bet was daring and worthy of the giant that is Ferrari. The few models exhibited captured the imagination of visitors as soon as they entered the Fondation Cartier. The rest of the exhibition was simple: all the exterior and interior spaces of the Domaine du Montcel were dedicated to the Ferrari universe, and visitors were led on a journey through its history by guides dressed in red jumpsuits. Under a pyramid were seventeen Ferrari models dating from 1953 to 1971, owned by collector Jacky Setton; in what was called "the bunker," the fascinating world of racing was presented to fans of sport and speed; while finally in "the village" of the Fondation, Pininfarina's engineering and design for Ferrari were showcased with the presentation of the Formula 1 prototypes Sigma 1969, Zaz 1979, Testarossa 1981, and Dino 206 GT 1967. Also in the village, the works commissioned by the Fondation Cartier from painter Valerio Adami and photographers Alain Bizos, Agnès Bonnot, Pierre-Olivier Deschamps, Pascal Dolémieux, Franco Fontana, Frank Horvat, Xavier Lambours, François Le Diascorn, Erica Lennard, and Jeanloup Sieff were displayed. Each offered their own take on Ferrari, whether focusing on the racing-circuit legend or the Maranello factory near Modena, or indeed anywhere else Ferrari can appear.

The exhibition was a great success. It was a major talking point and crowds flocked to see this *Hommage à Ferrari*. Even today, Alain Dominique Perrin likes to recall that people said he was mad for showing cars in a contemporary art foundation. He has no regrets. For the opening of the exhibition, Enzo Ferrari sent a congratulatory letter and video specially made for the occasion, thanking the Fondation Cartier for taking an artistic look at an industrial object.

The Fondation Cartier has always had a special connection to the automobile. The exhibitions *Les Années 60* and *Les Championnes de César* in 1986, *La Vitesse* in 1991, and *Rock'n'Roll 39–59* in 2007, all featured cars. In 2017, based on a proposal by Xavier Barral and Philippe Séclier, the exhibition *Autophoto* explored the links between photography and the automobile.

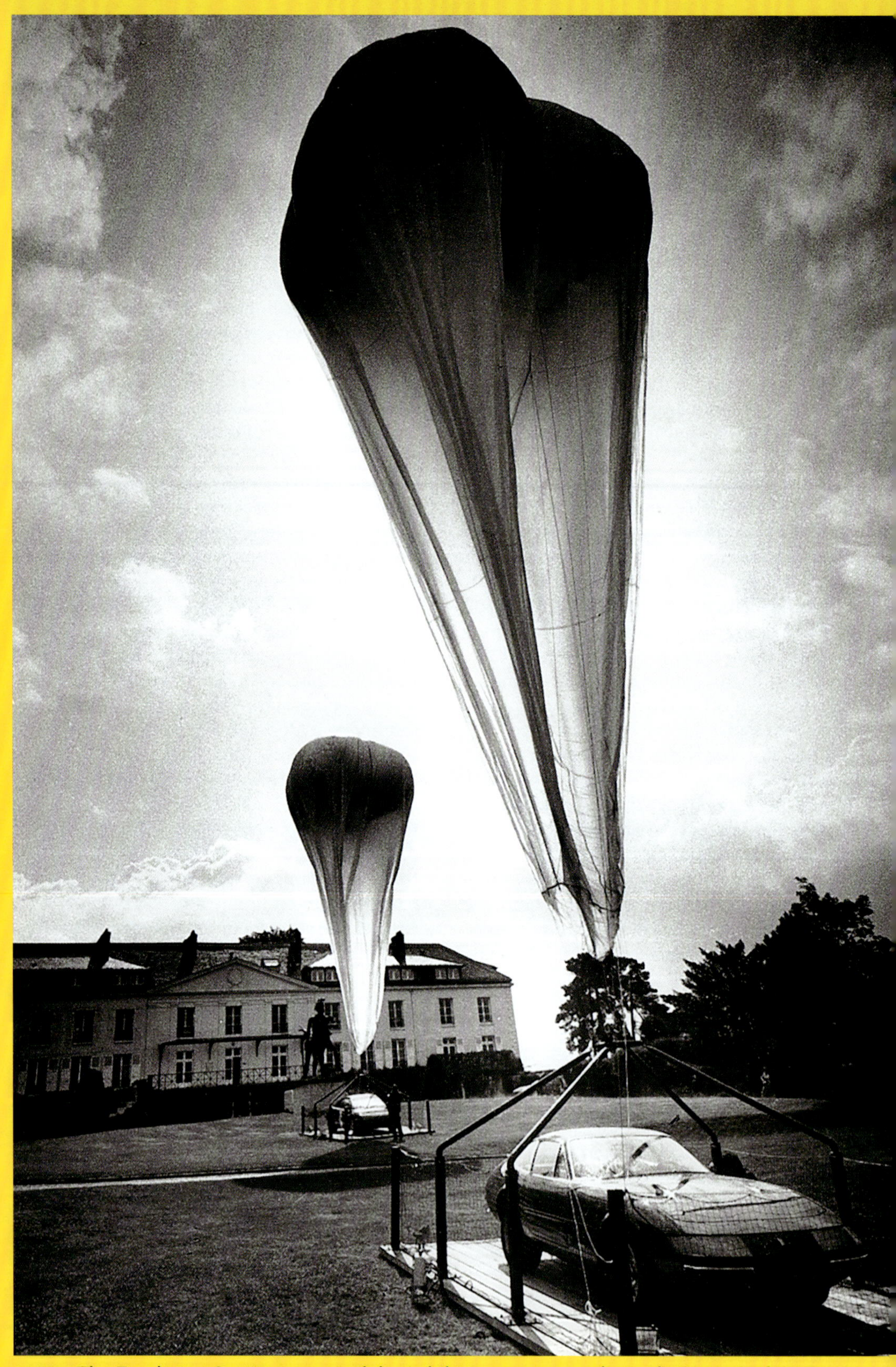

1987 The Fondation Cartier entrusted the exhibition scenography to designer Andrée Putman. Thanks to her original approach, she made the Ferrari into a veritable objet d'art.

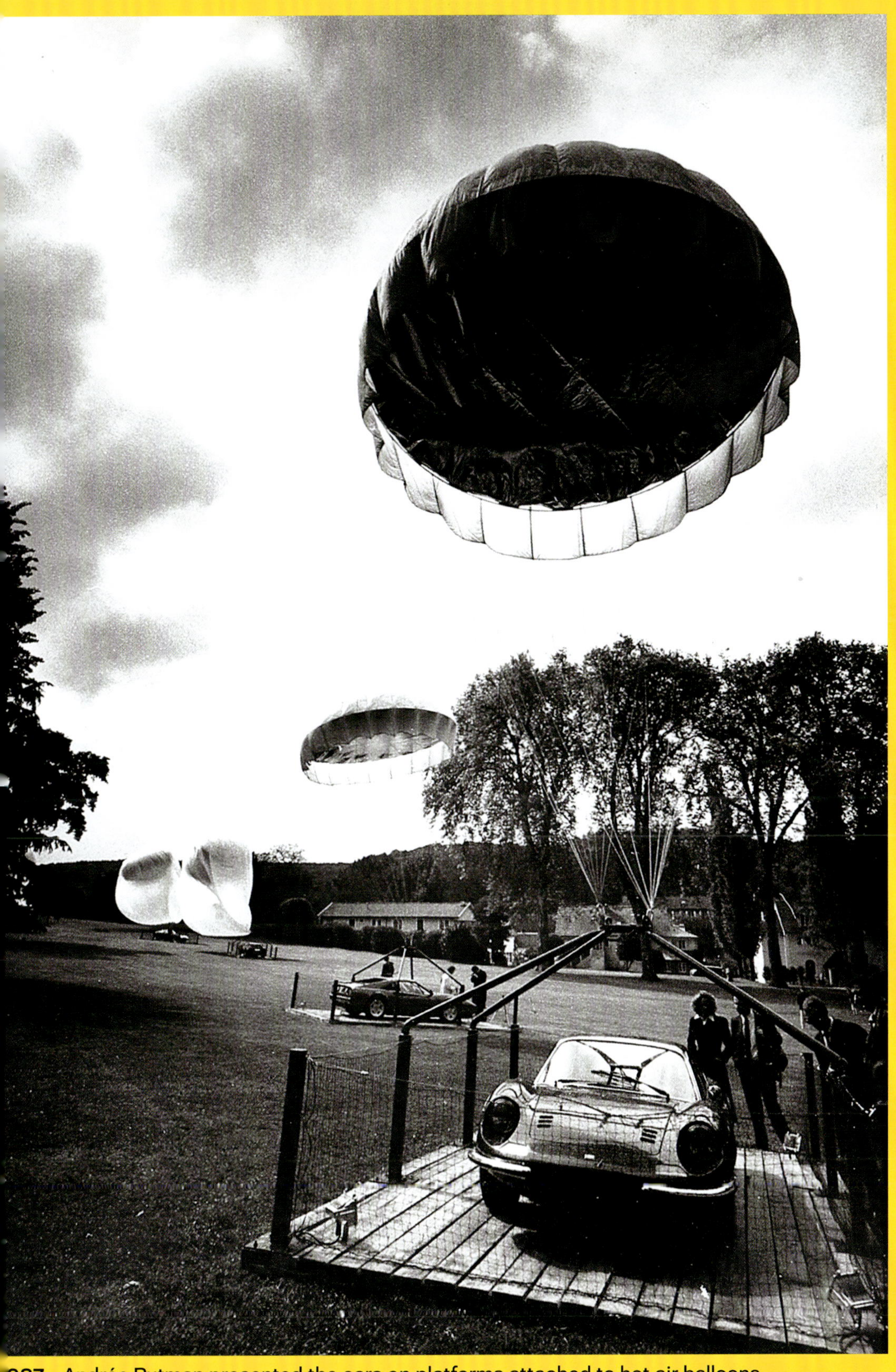

987 Andrée Putman presented the cars on platforms attached to hot air balloons, making it easy to imagine the Ferraris taking off and landing.

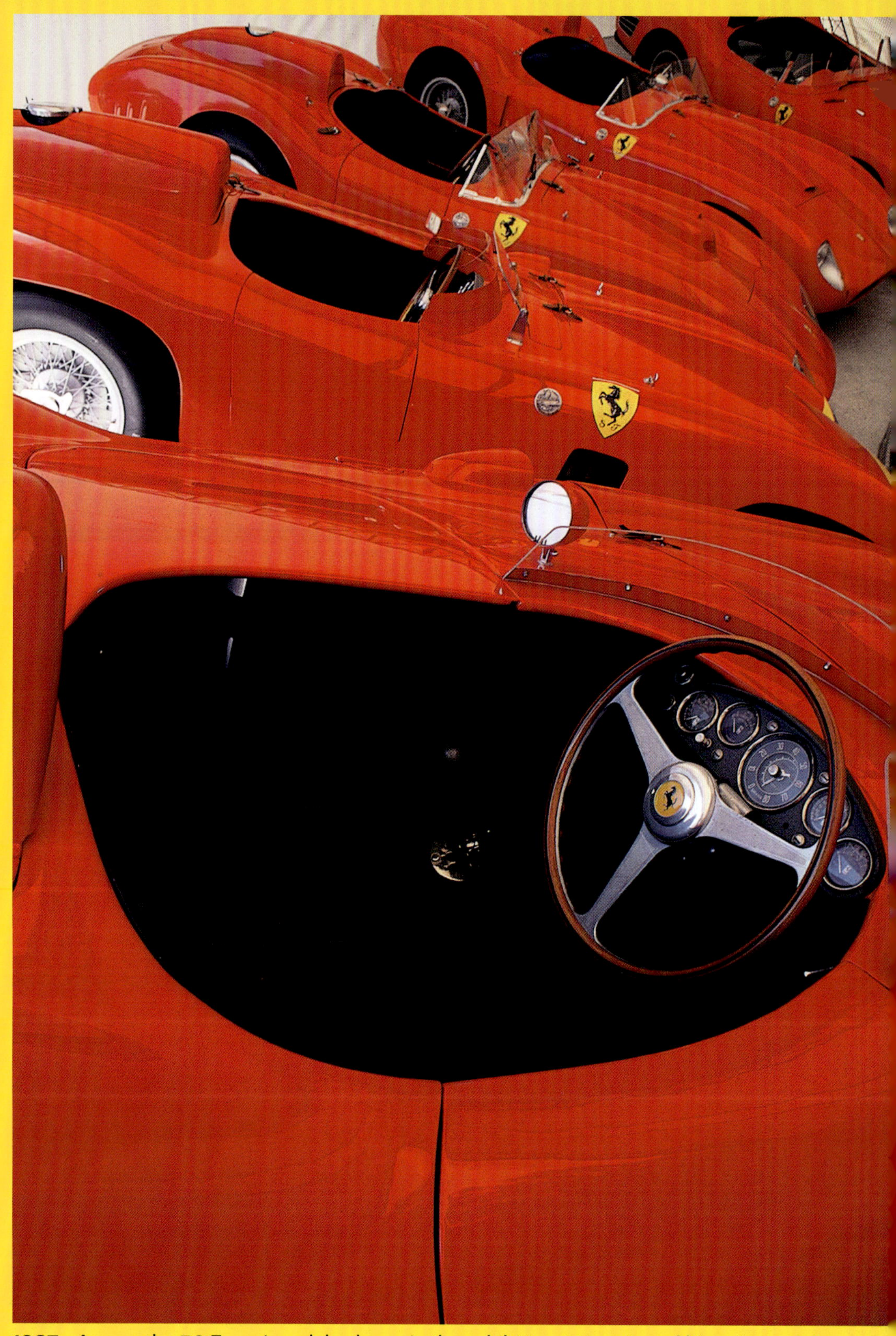

1987   Among the 50 Ferrari models shown in the exhibition, 17 iconic and historic models were displayed in the large pyramidal tent, installed in the Fondation Cartier's park.

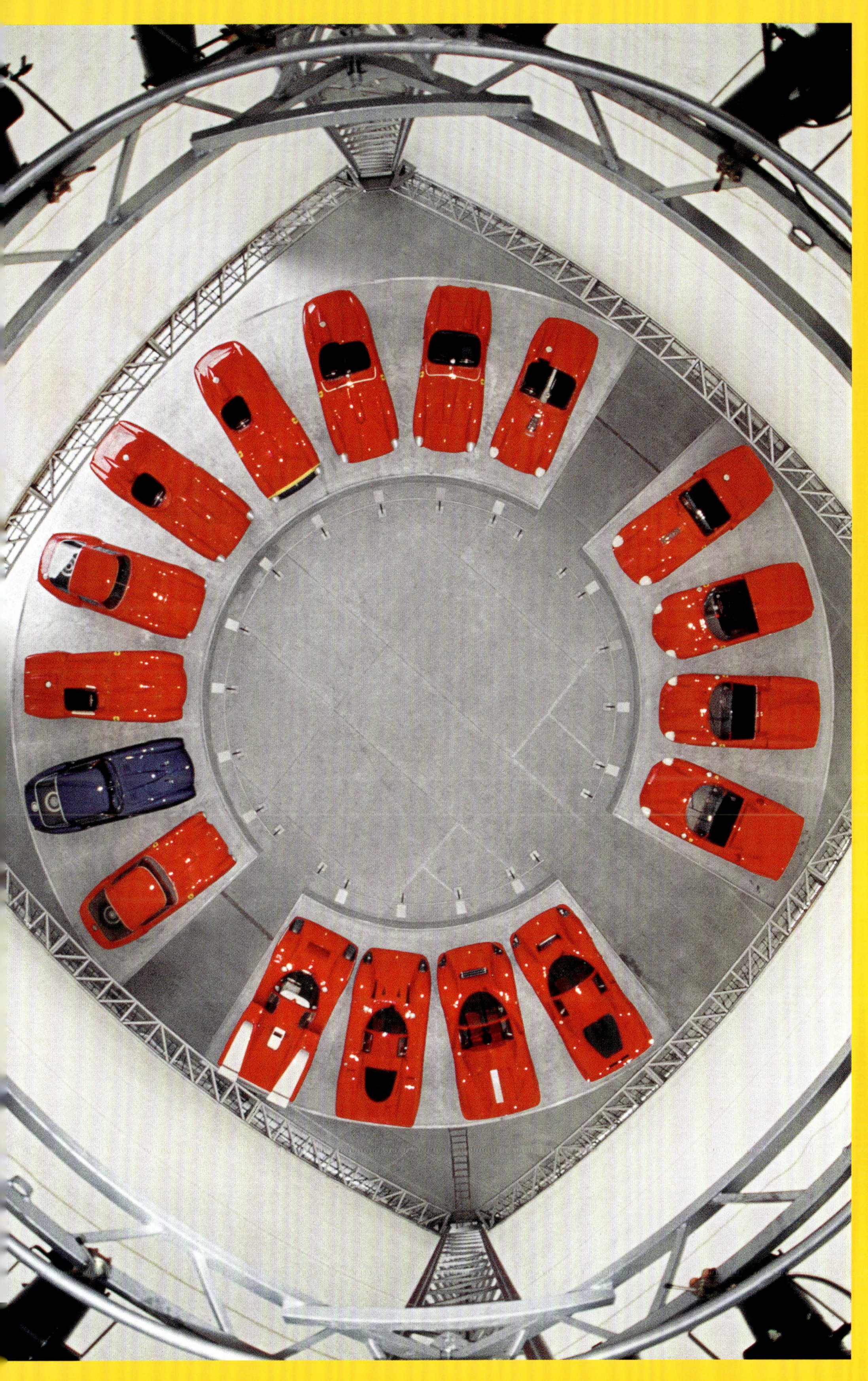

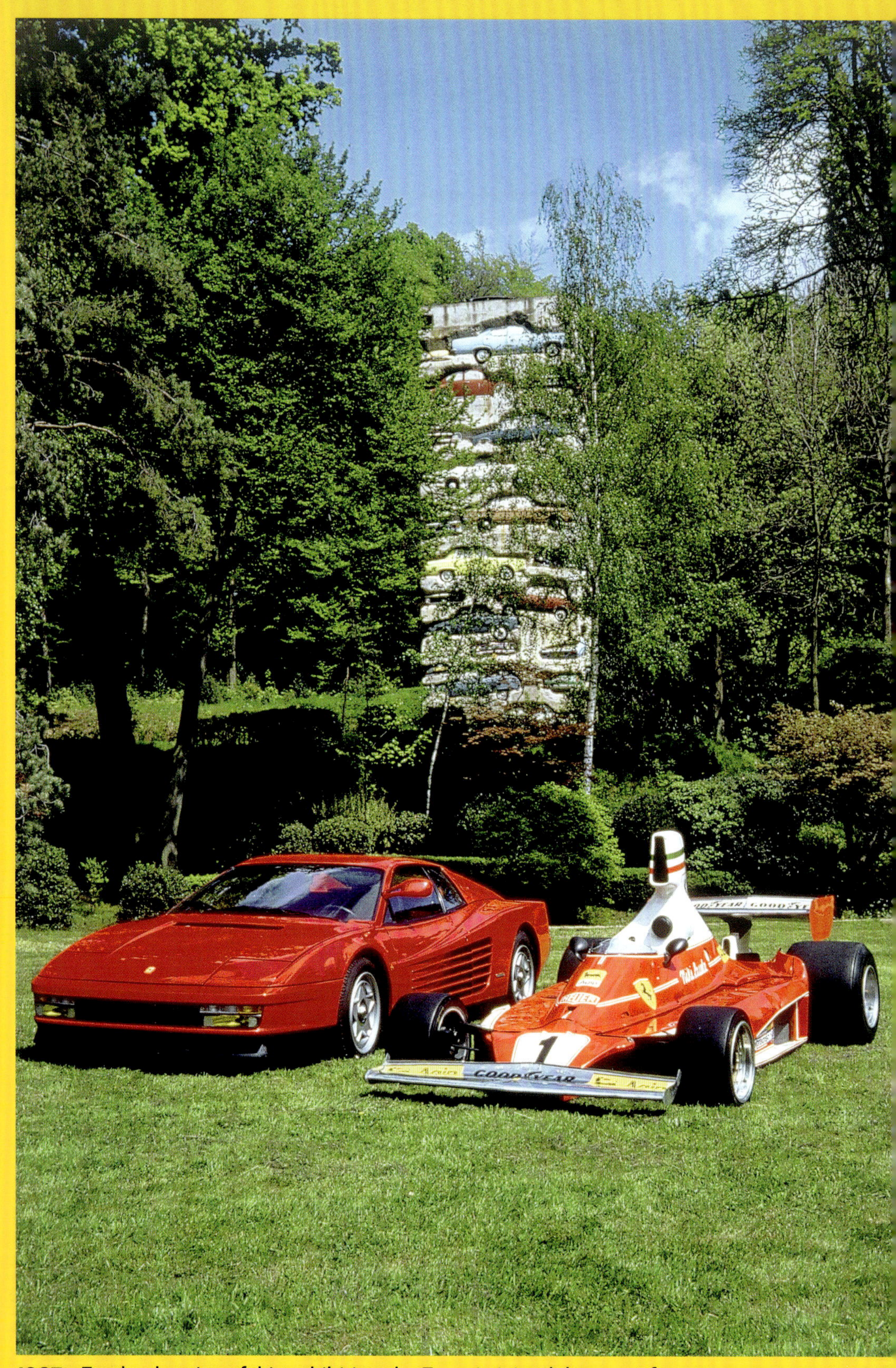

1987   For the duration of this exhibition, the Ferraris joined the cars of Arman's *Long Term Parking* (1982), also located in the Fondation's park.

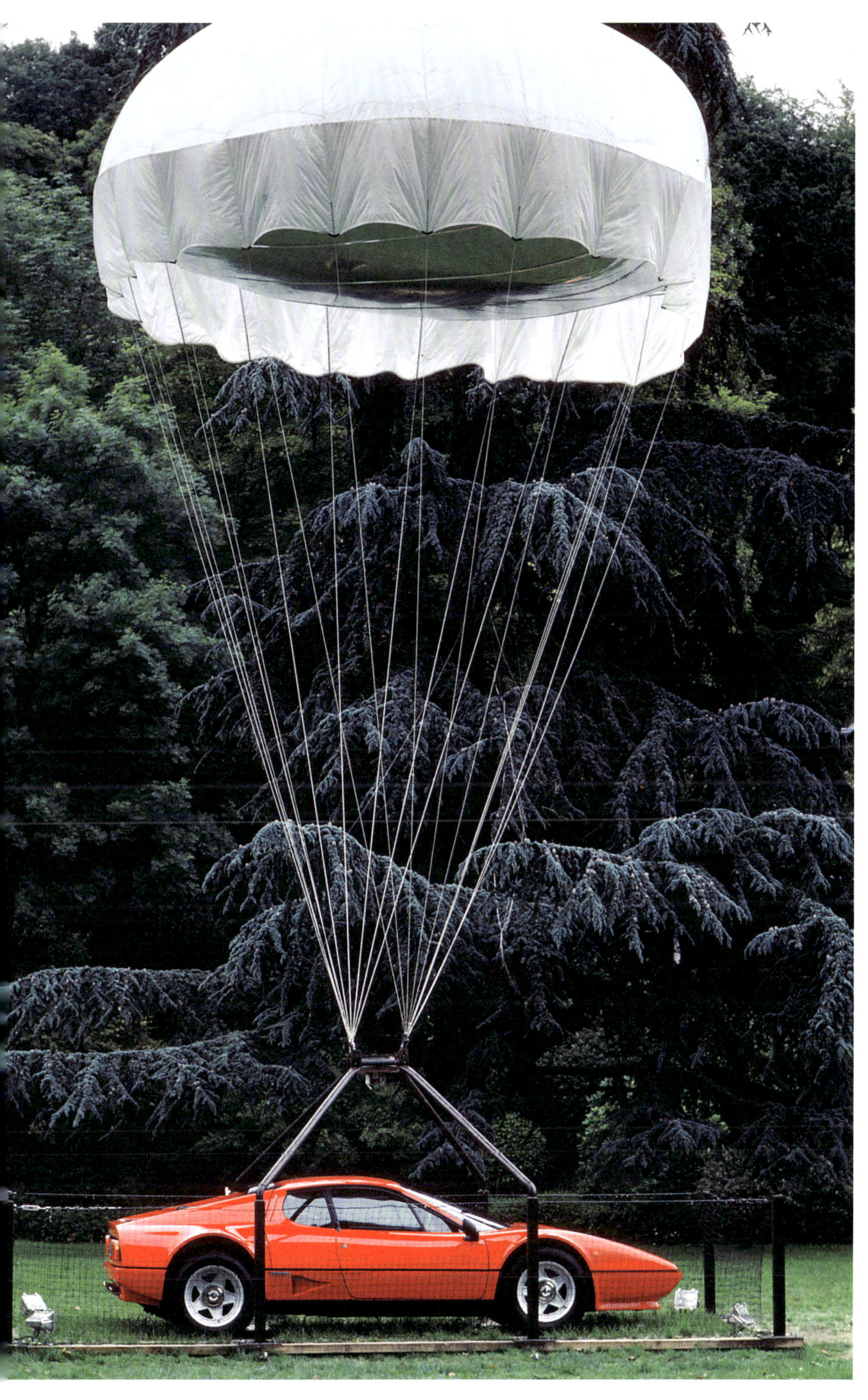

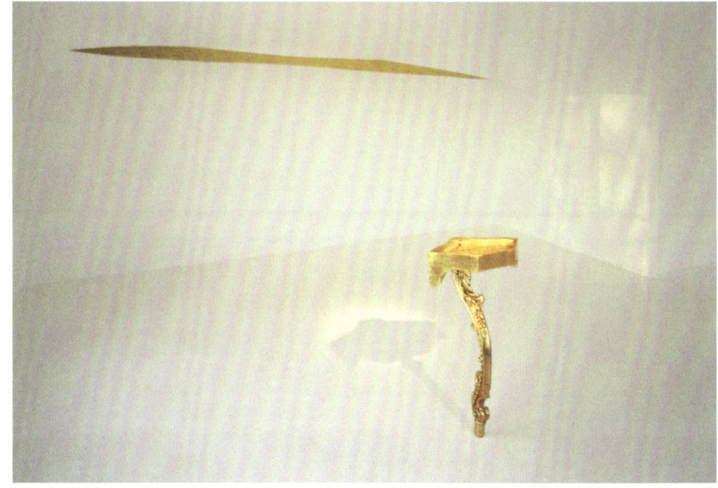

Marc Couturier, *Il ne reste plus qu'à demander à Dieu*, 1987
FC Collections (1987)

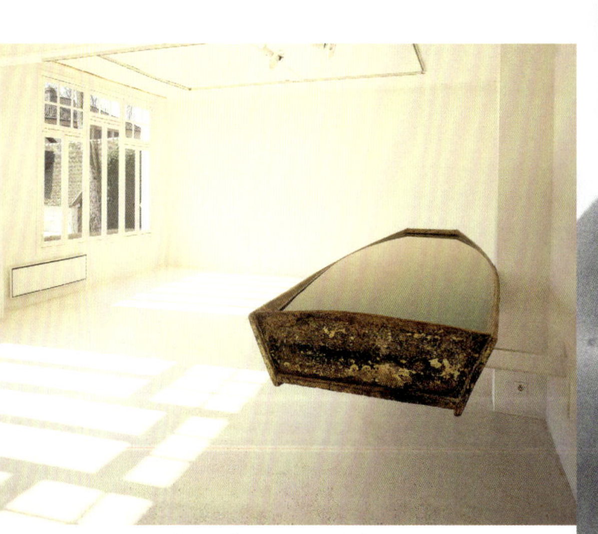

Marc Couturier, *Quand notre acuité
nous dépasse*, 1987

Marc Couturier in his studio
at Jouy-en-Josas, 1987: this residency
marked the beginning of a long
collaboration between the artist
and the Fondation Cartier.

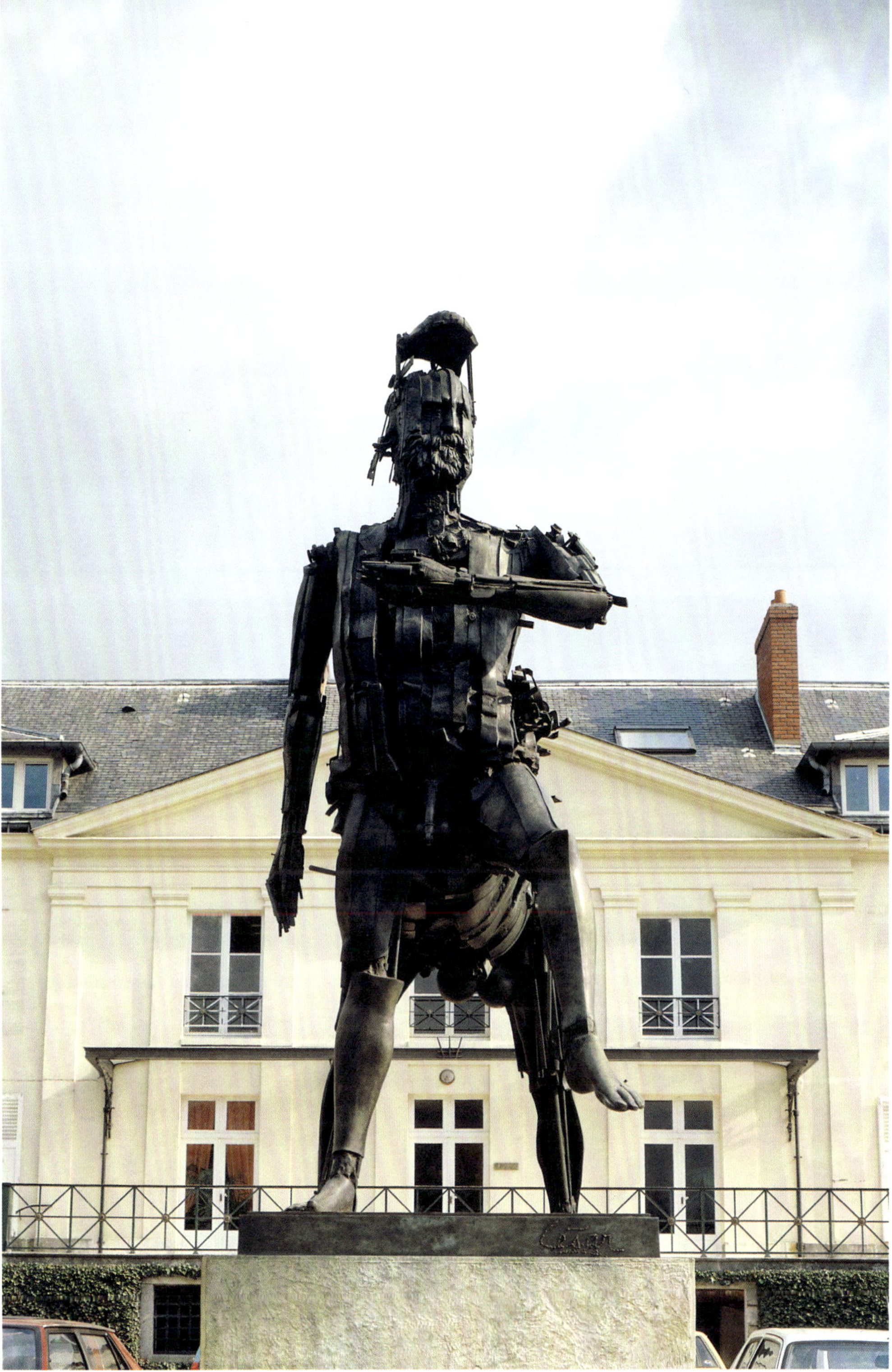

Between 1983 and 1985, César created the sculpture called *Le Centaure*, as a tribute to Pablo Picasso. First shown in the park of the Fondation Cartier in 1987, the work was then installed at the Carrefour de la Croix-Rouge (now Place Michel-Debré) in Paris in 1988.

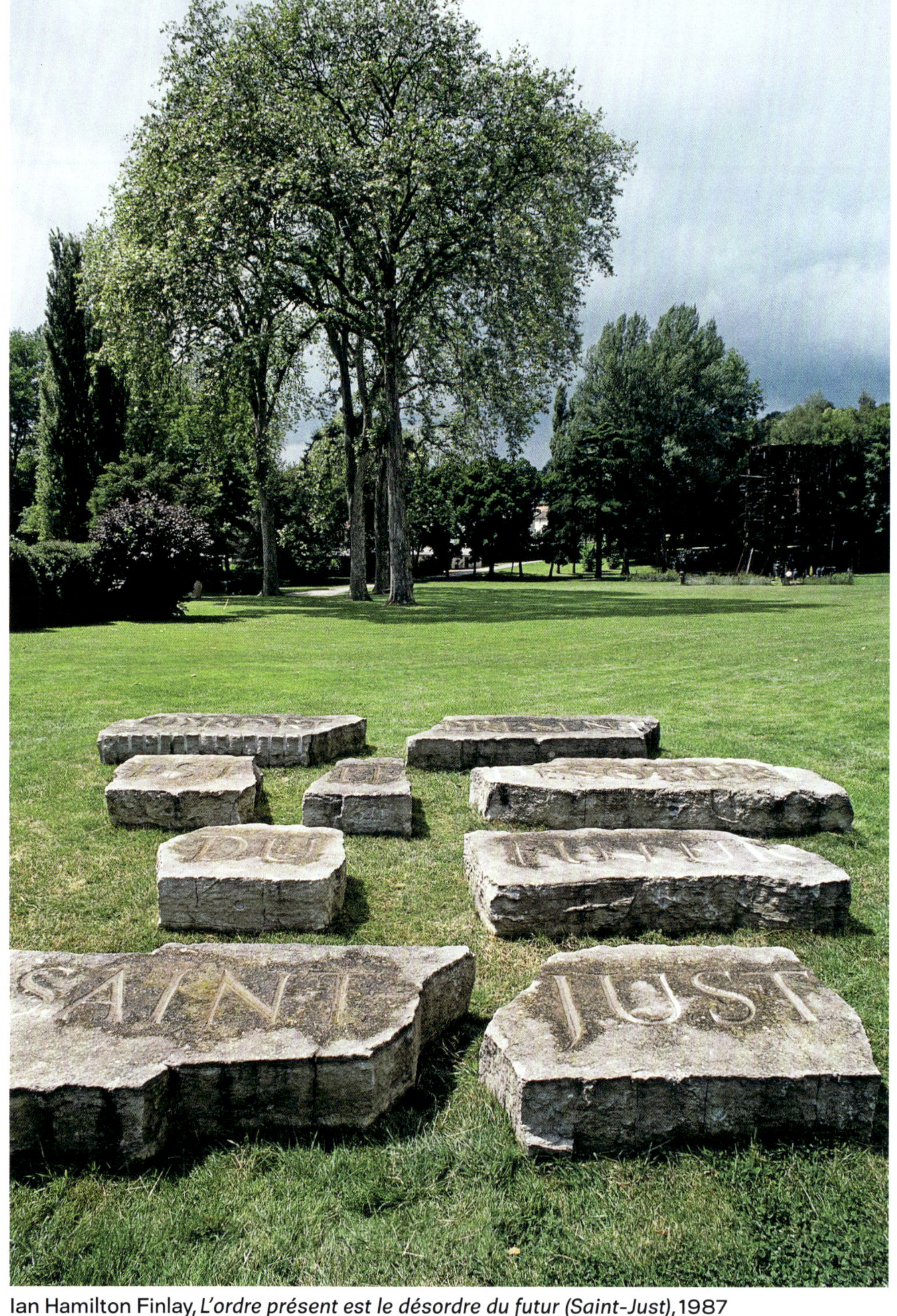

Ian Hamilton Finlay, *L'ordre présent est le désordre du futur (Saint-Just)*, 1987
FC Collections (1987). Created for the exhibition *Poursuites révolutionnaires* in 1987, and installed in the park of the Domaine du Montcel, it later moved to the garden of the Fondation Cartier in Paris.

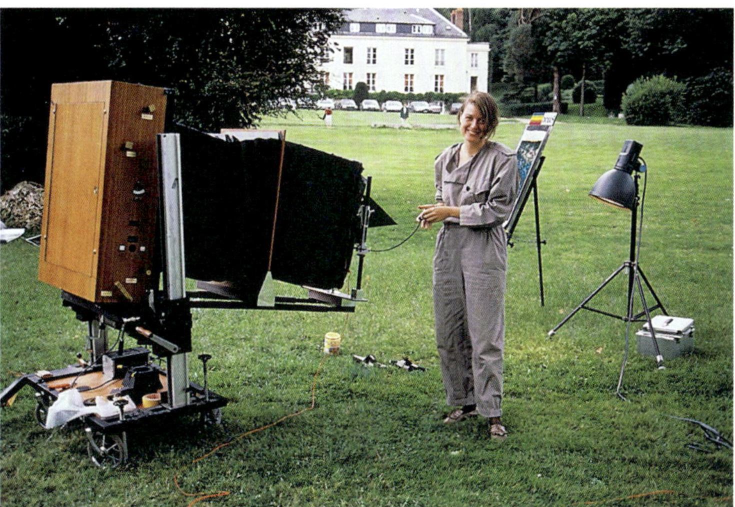

Photographer Ouka Lele created a group of portraits and still lifes
in the park of the Fondation Cartier using the largest Polaroid
camera in Europe, generating giant snapshots measuring
60 × 50 cm.

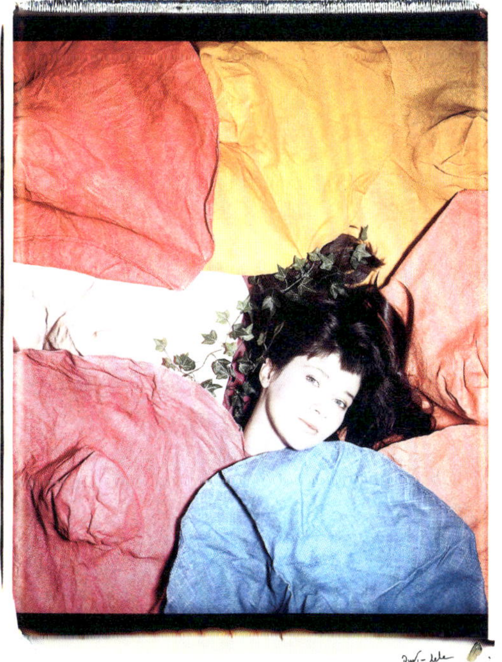

These photographs of fashion accessories
were taken by stylist Philippe Model,
who created the design of the exhibition.
FC Collections (1988)

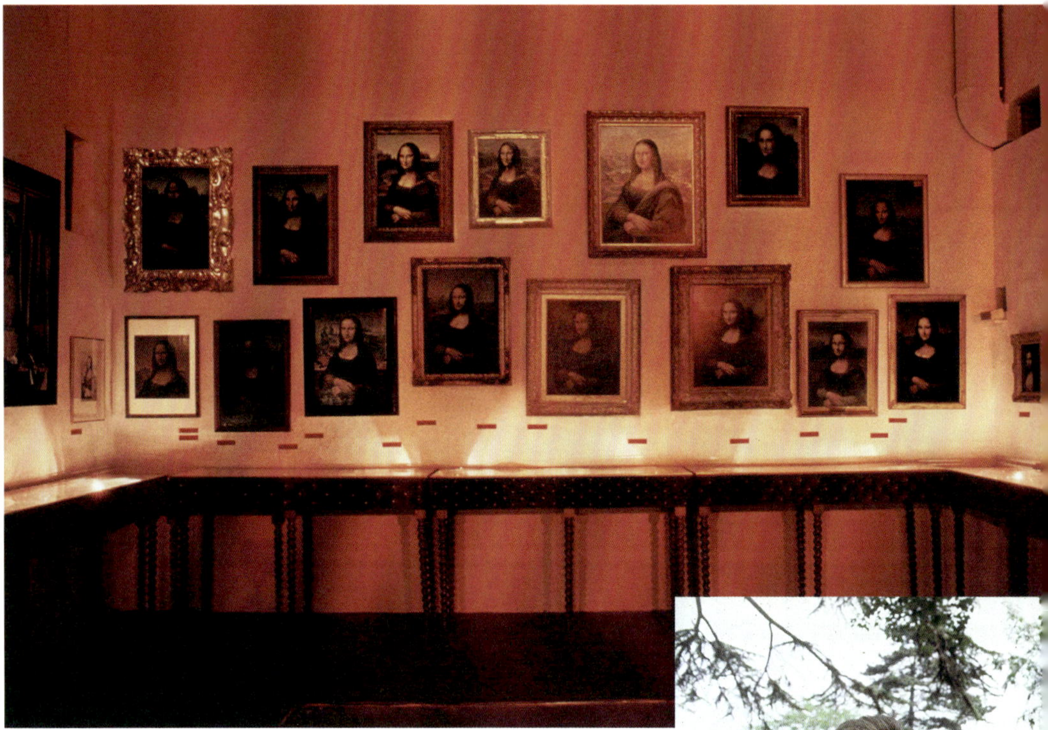

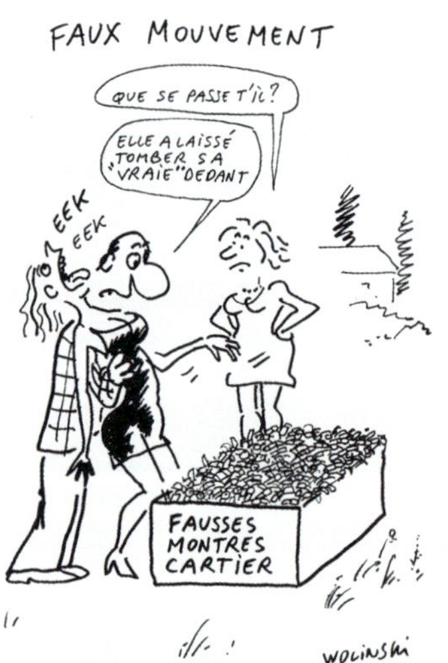

The exhibition *Vraiment faux* focused on fakes,
imitations, counterfeits, plagiarism, copies,
and trompe-l'oeil, in a scenography designed
by Élisabeth Garouste and Mattia Bonetti.

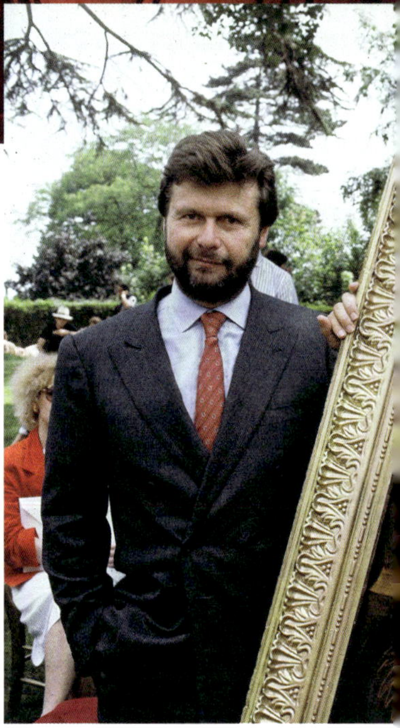

In response to a commission
by the Fondation Cartier, illustrator
Georges Wolinski created
36 drawings on the theme
of fakes.

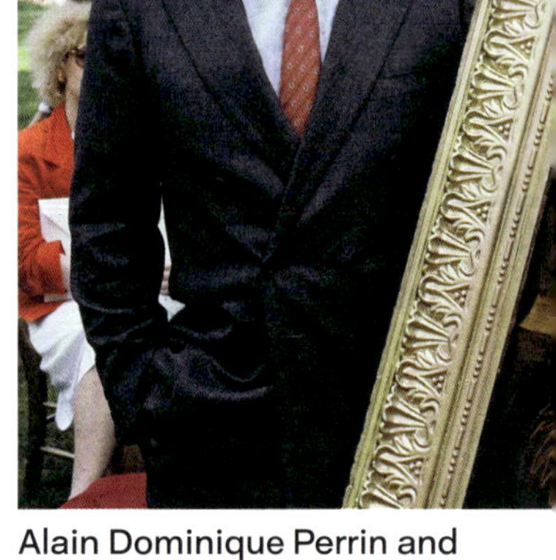

Alain Dominique Perrin and
a Margaret Thatcher lookalike
at the exhibition opening

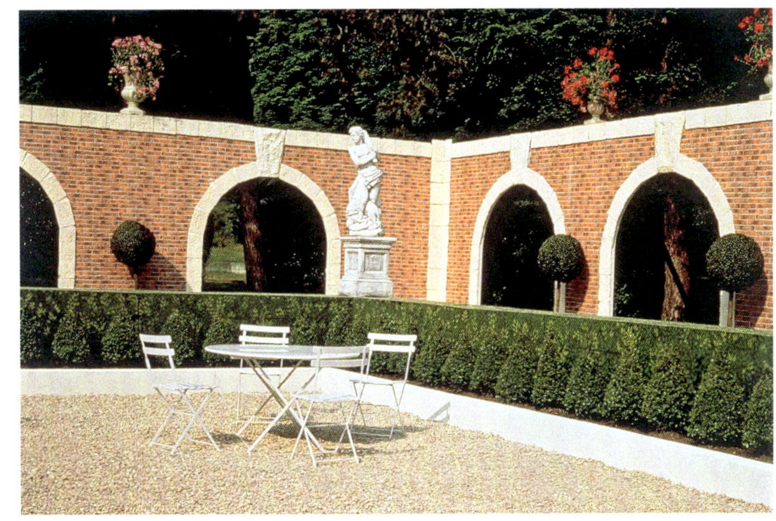

Élisabeth Garouste and Mattia Bonetti, *Le Jardin des illusions*, 1988

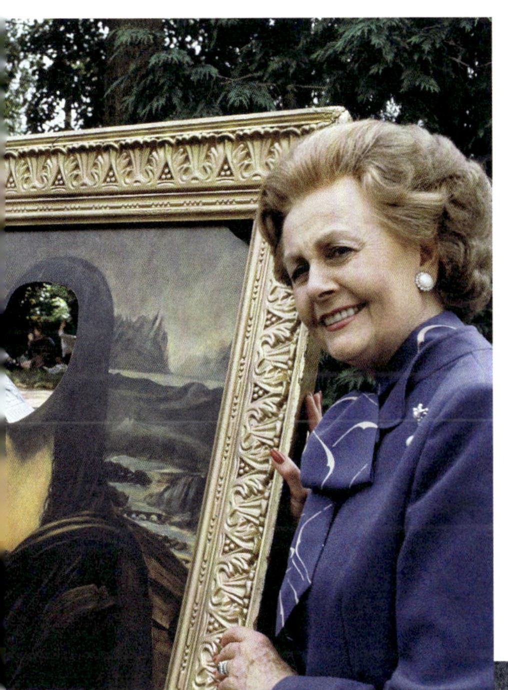

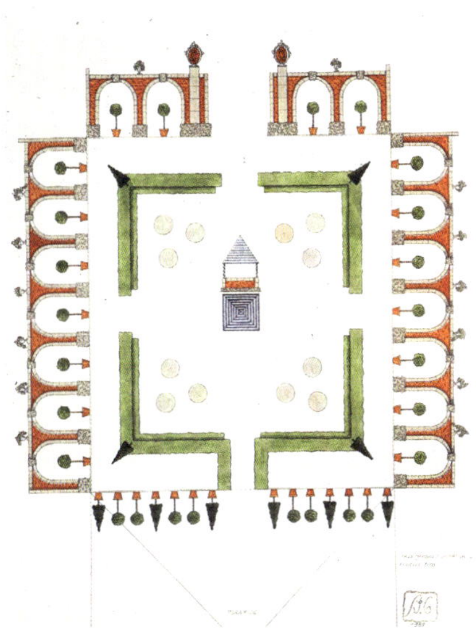

Élisabeth Garouste and Mattia
Bonetti, preparatory sketch
for *Le Jardin des illusions*, 1988

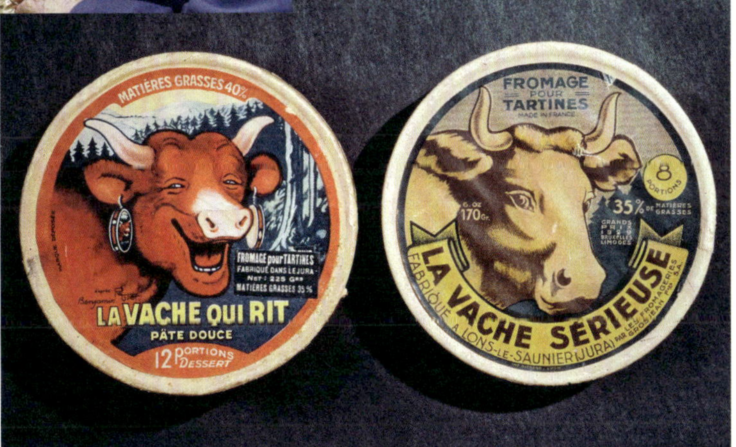

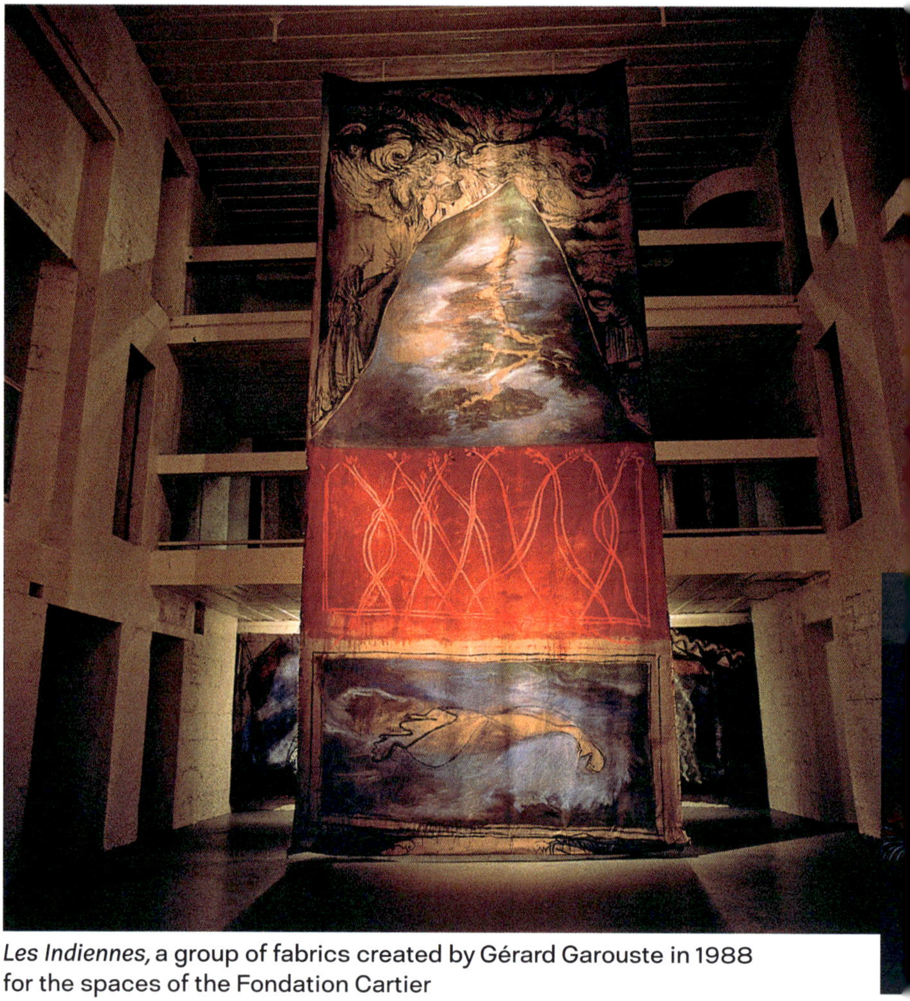

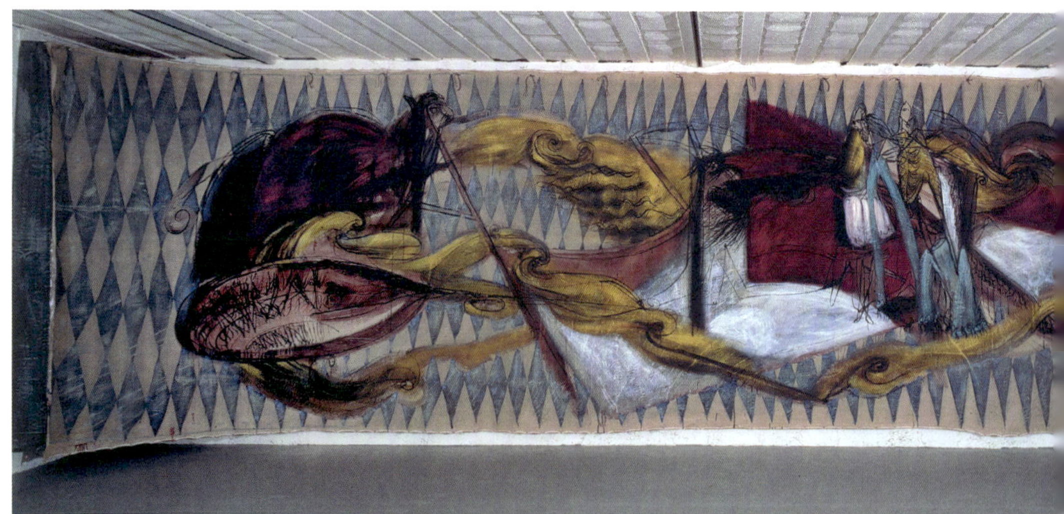

Les Indiennes, a group of fabrics created by Gérard Garouste in 1988
for the spaces of the Fondation Cartier

View of the exhibition at Jouy-en-Josas

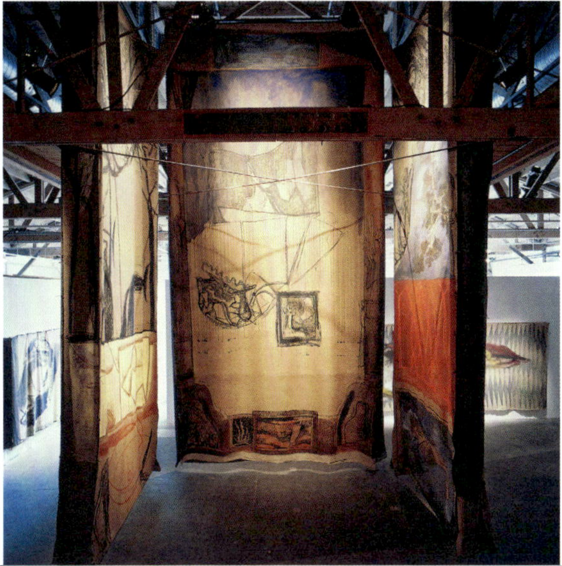

In 1990, this exhibition was presented
at the Santa Monica Museum of Art, California.

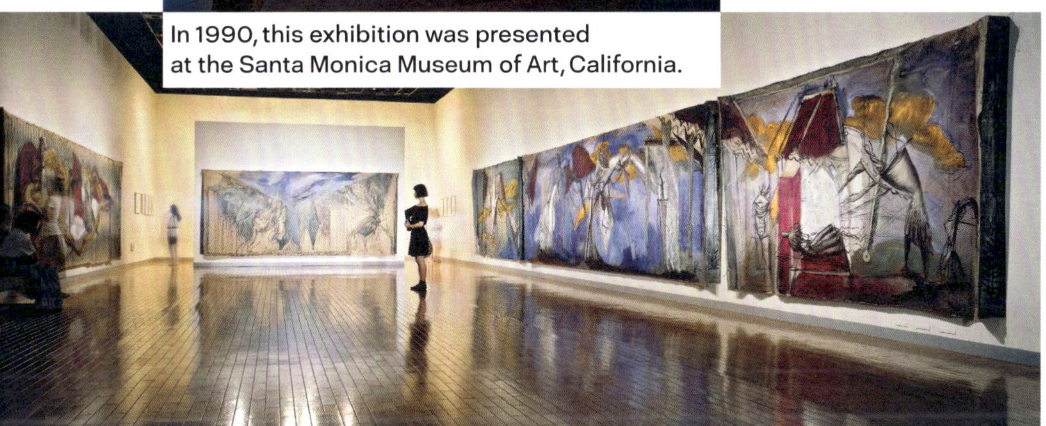

The same year, it traveled to the Touko Museum
of Contemporary Art in Tokyo.

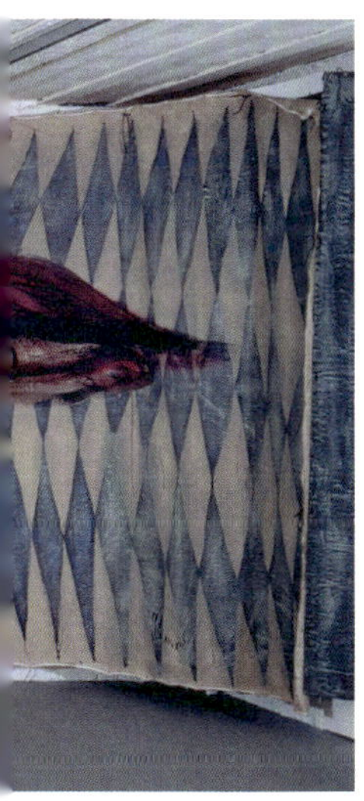

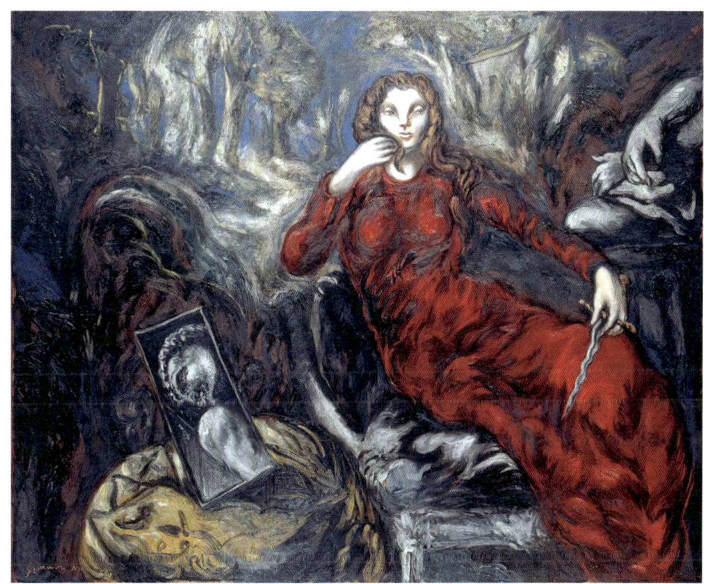

Gérard Garouste, *Lucrèce*, 1982
FC Collections (1987)

Under the title *Un, deux, trois... Sculptures*, the Fondation Cartier organized three exhibitions dedicated to sculpture: the group exhibitions *Solex-nostalgie* and *Aspects de la jeune sculpture européenne*, and *Ni rond, ni carré, ni pointu*, dedicated to Judith Bartolani and Claude Caillol.

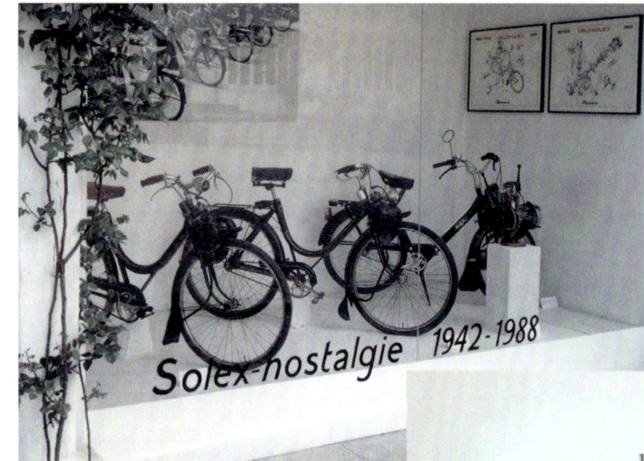

The year 1988 marked the demise of Solex: artists were given ten of the very last models to create an artwork.

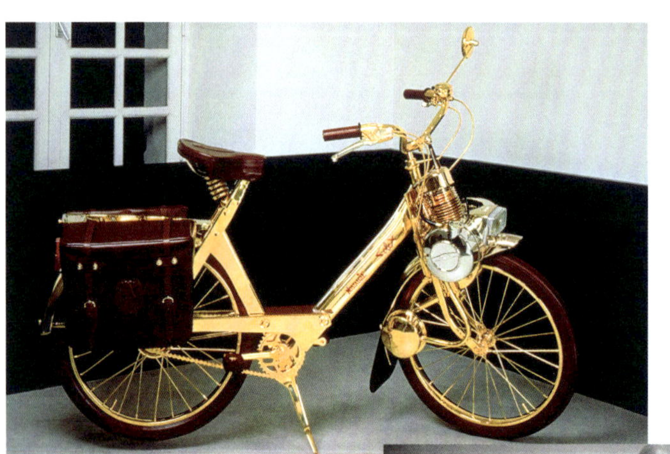

Présence Panchounette, *Le Vrai Classique du vide parfait*, 1989
FC Collections (1989)

Richard Baquié, 1989

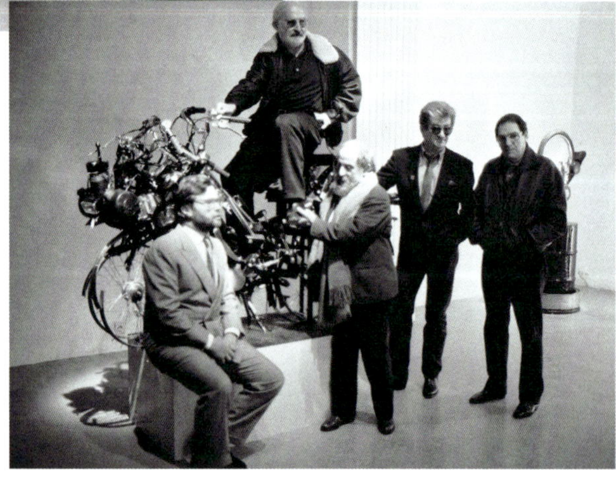

Alain Dominique Perrin, Arman, César, Eddy Mitchell, and Robert Hossein at the exhibition opening

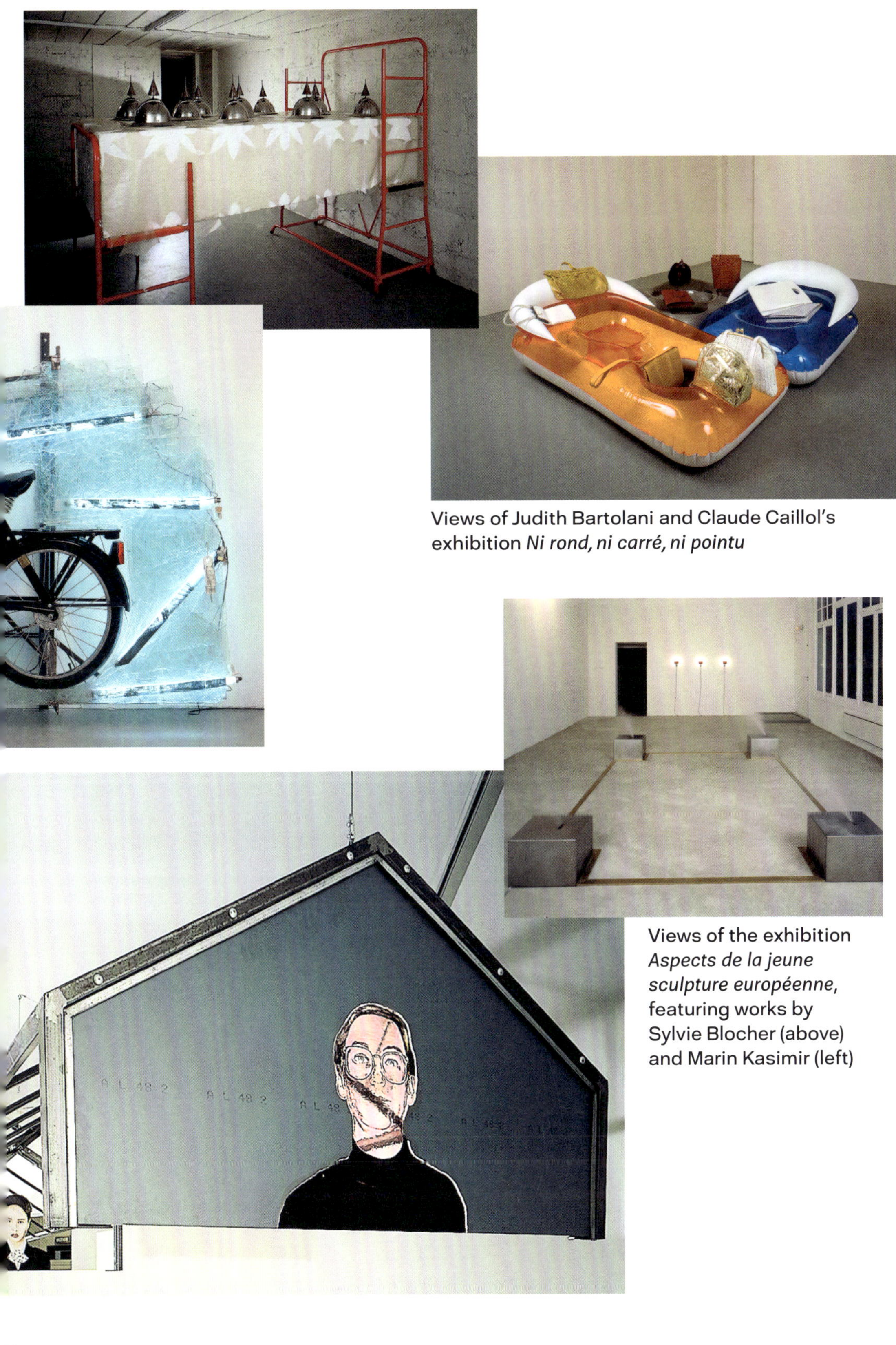

Views of Judith Bartolani and Claude Caillol's exhibition *Ni rond, ni carré, ni pointu*

Views of the exhibition *Aspects de la jeune sculpture européenne*, featuring works by Sylvie Blocher (above) and Marin Kasimir (left)

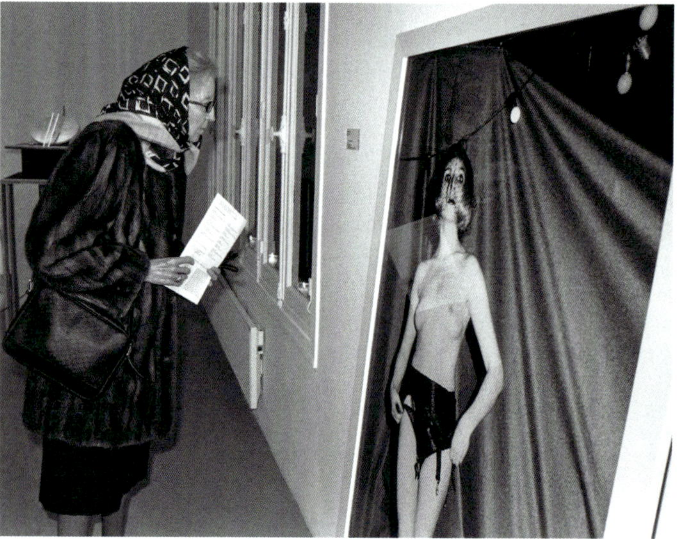

Sophie Calle, *Le Strip-tease*, 1989. FC Collections (1989)

The exhibition *Nos années 80* offered a panorama of French creation across the domains of architecture, design, painting, photography, sculpture, and video, and featured the works of 70 creators.

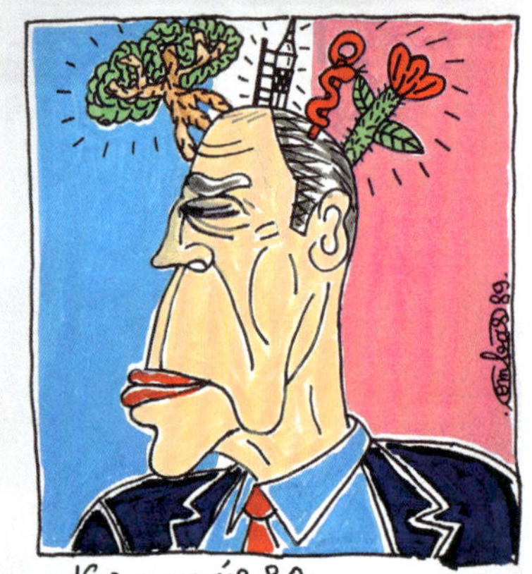

Robert Combas, *Nos années 80*, 1989. Commission for the exhibition poster. FC Collections (1989)

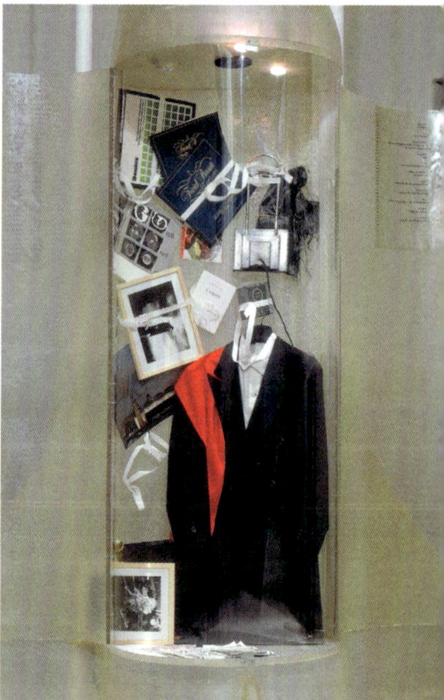

In the installation *Voyage au pays des stars*, François Bauchet, Sylvain Dubuisson, and Martin Szekely showed the universe of 18 well-known figures through a series of "cases." Above: Jean Nouvel by Sylvain Dubuisson

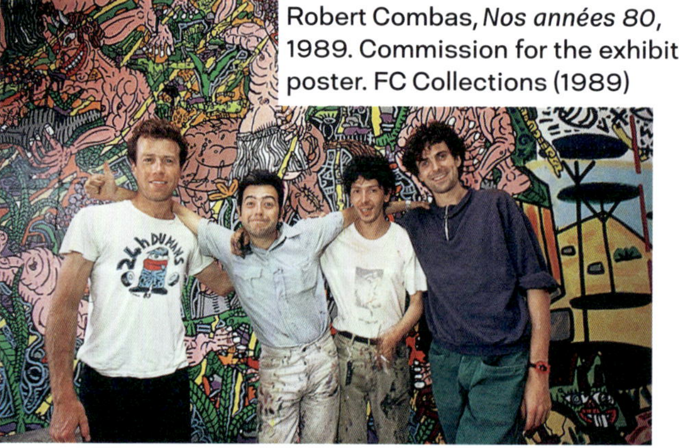

Following the exhibition *Nos années 80*, the Fondation Cartier brought together Rémi Blanchard, Hervé Di Rosa, Robert Combas and François Boisrond, photographed here in 1987 during the creation of a fresco in Parnac, France.

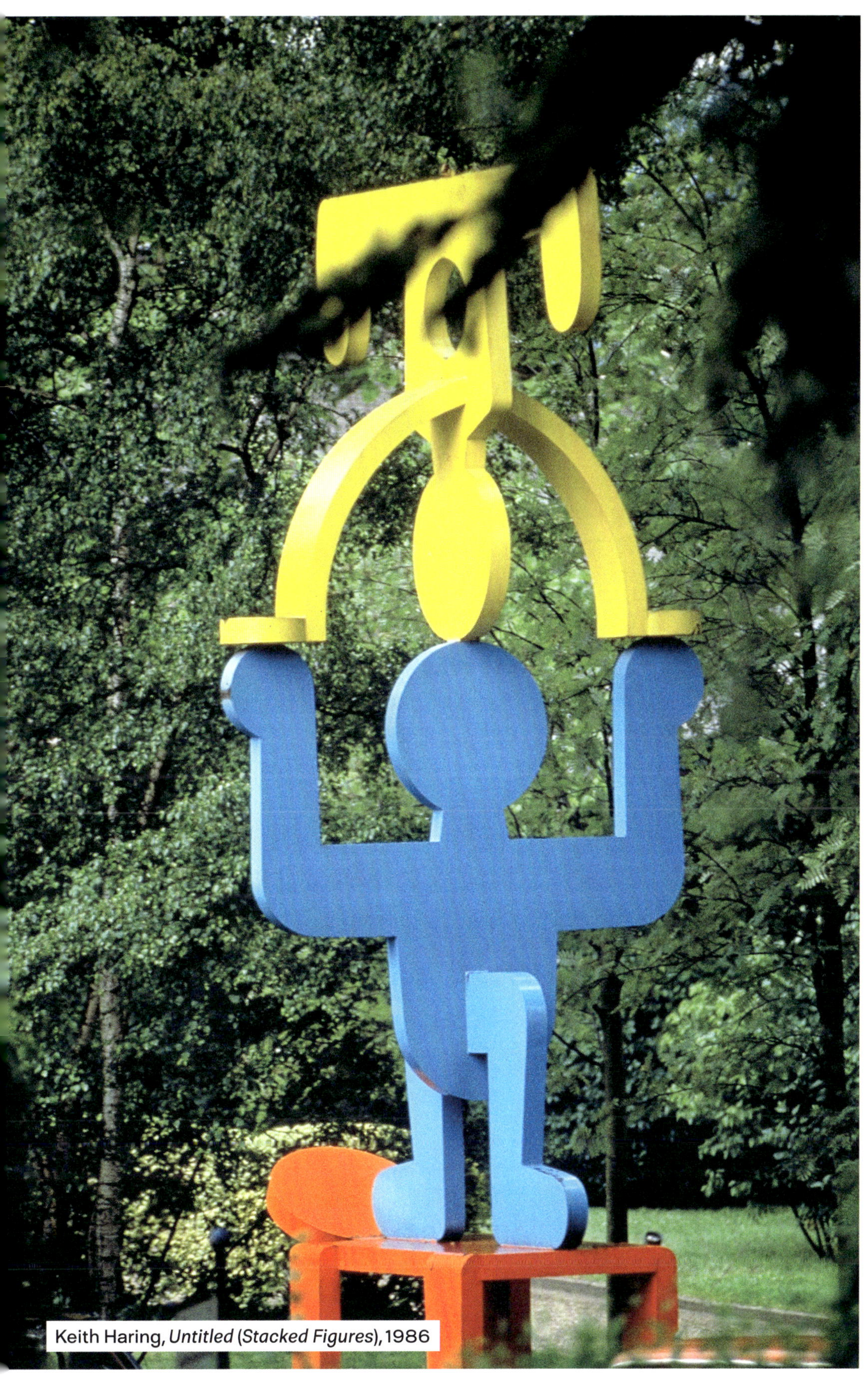

Keith Haring, *Untitled (Stacked Figures)*, 1986

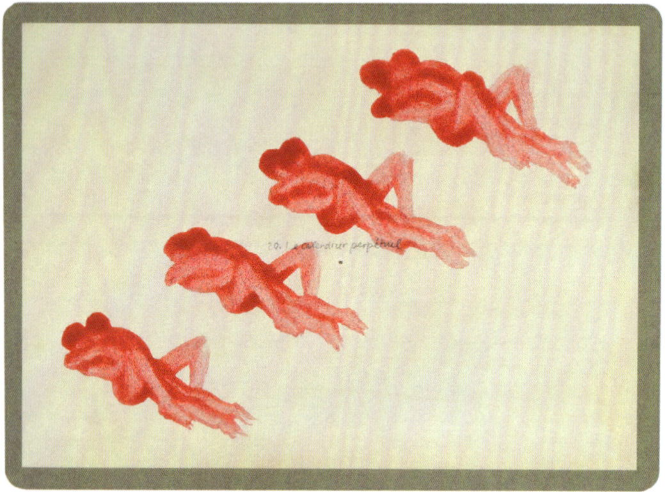

Lignes de mire – 1 presented the main groups of works belonging to the Collections of the Fondation Cartier.
Markus Raetz, *L'Amour*, 1980. FC Collections (1985)

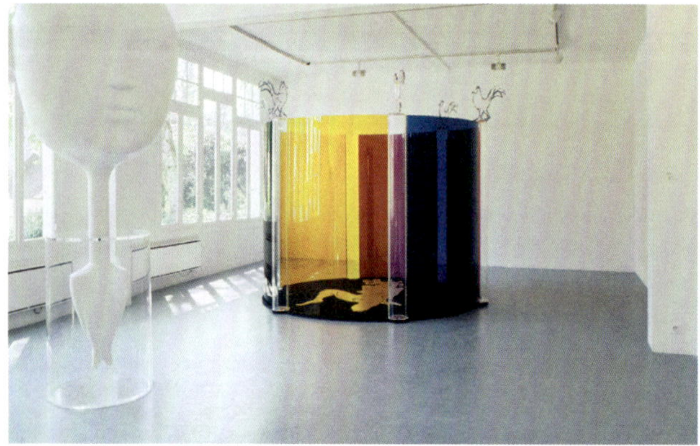

Alain Séchas, *La Grosse Tête*, 1986, and *Peep-Show*, 1988
FC Collections (1990)

James Turrell, *Skeet*, 1990
FC Collections (1990)

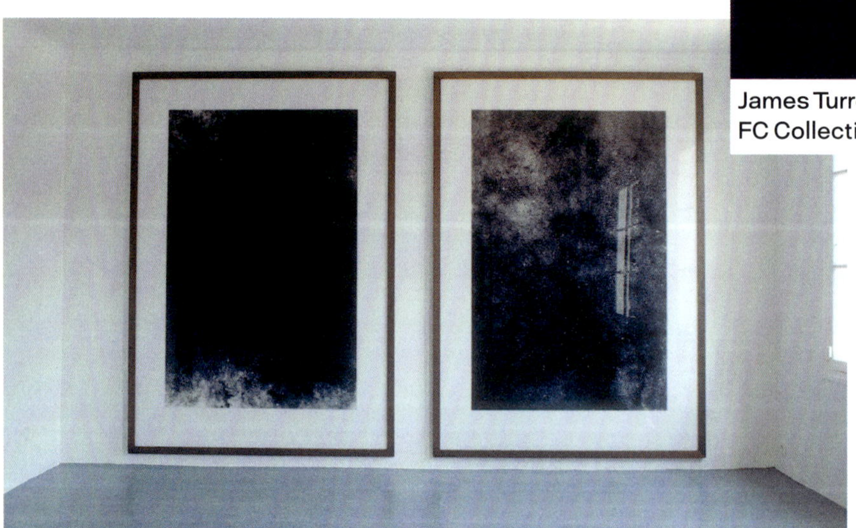

Thomas Ruff, *Les Étoiles : 17 h 38 mn,-30°*, and *17 h 15 mn,-30°*, 1990
FC Collections (1990)

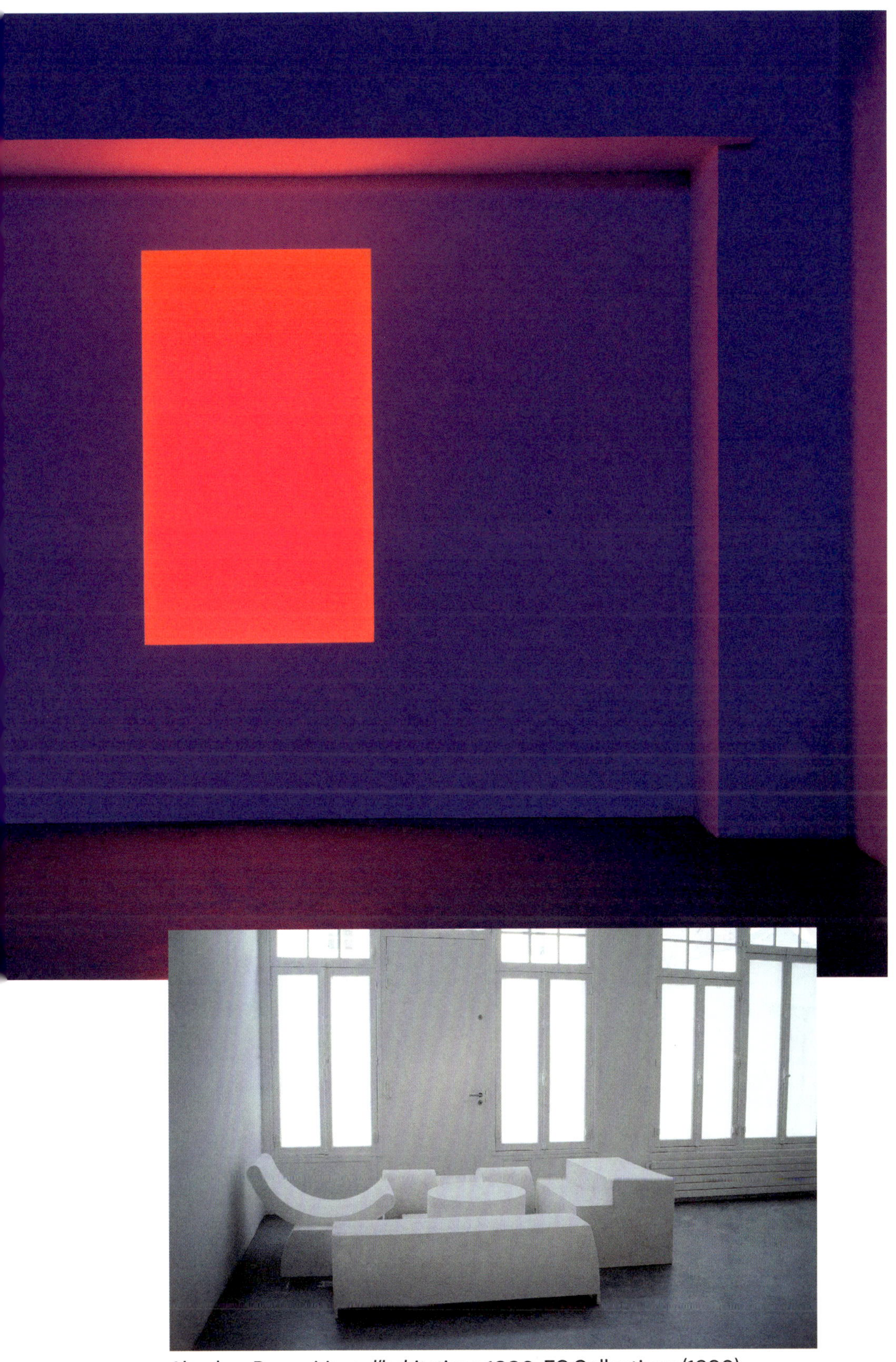

Absalon, *Propositions d'habitations*, 1990. FC Collections (1990)

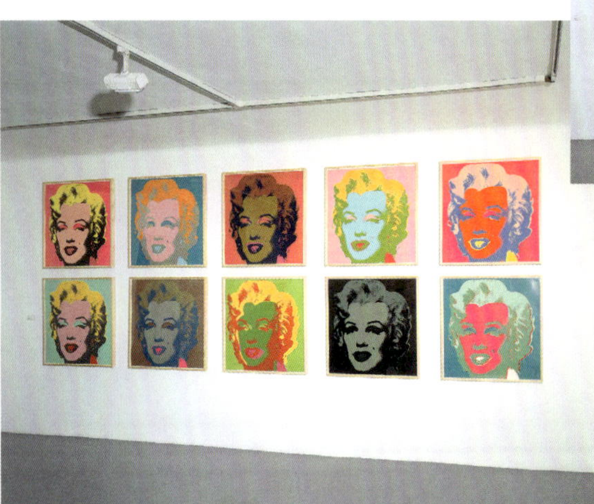

Pop : Andy Warhol, Les Estampes

Andy Warhol System : Pub-Pop-Rock brought together under this title, three major summer events: a presentation of prints by Andy Warhol (*Les Estampes*), an exhibition of works created by the artist between 1945 and 1962 (*Success is a Job in New York*), and an exhibition exploring the collaboration between Andy Warhol and The Velvet Underground (*Sur les traces acharnées du Velvet*).

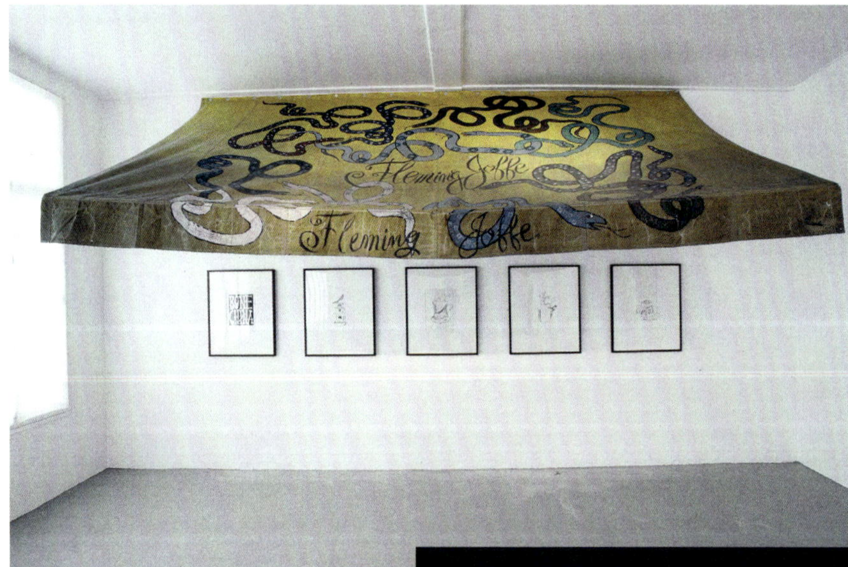

Pub : Success is a Job in New York

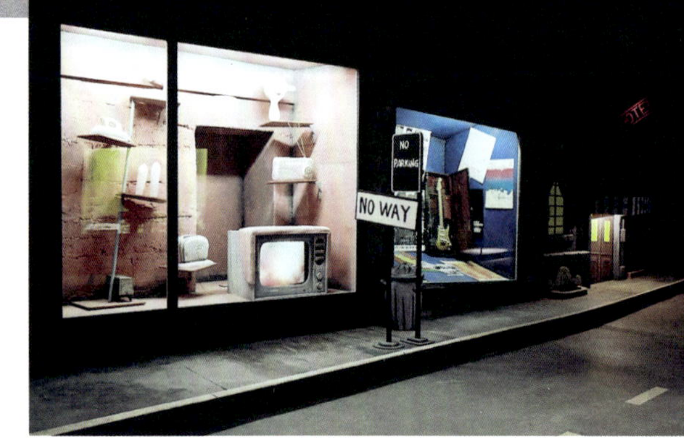

Rock : Sur les traces acharnées du Velvet, staged by David Rochline

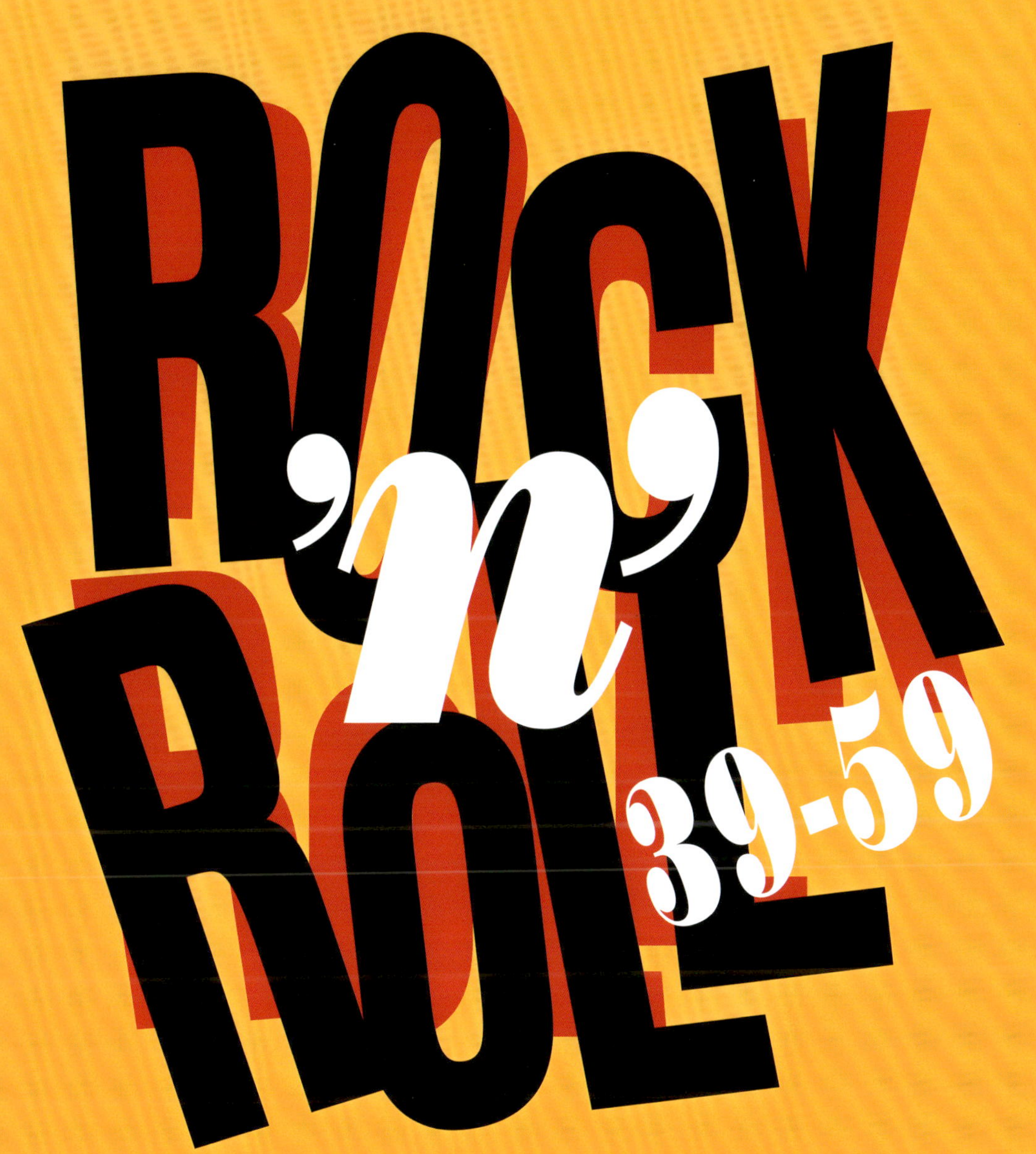

ROCK
'N'
ROLL
39-59

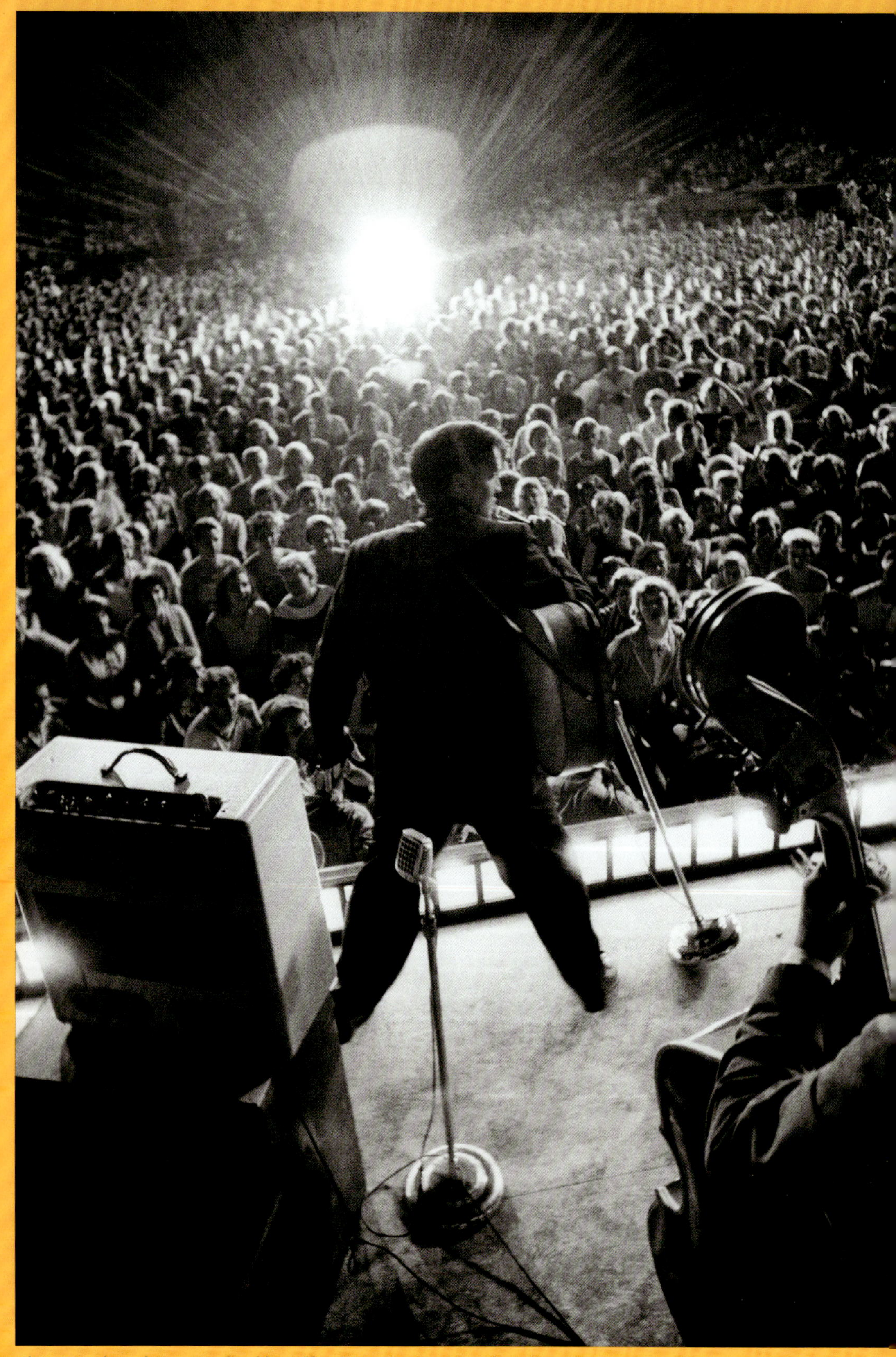

Elvis Presley photographed by Alfred Wertheimer performing a concert at Russwood Park in Memphis, Tennessee, in 1956

On the afternoon of June 15, 1990, the Fondation Cartier inaugurated the exhibition *Andy Warhol System : Pub-Pop-Rock* in Jouy-en-Josas. Guests that day could retrace the artist's history through his early illustrations and photographs, prints, and his collaboration with the rock group The Velvet Underground, whose first album he produced in 1966. On a stage set up in the park, microphones, keyboards, drums, and guitars stood in position. Pülnoc, a rock band from Prague, were to perform. But, to the audience's amazement, instead, two rock legends took the stage: Lou Reed and John Cale, founding members of The Velvet Underground, separated since 1968! One on guitar, the other on keyboards, they started playing "Style It Takes" from the album *Songs for Drella*, which they wrote in 1989 as a tribute to their friend and former mentor Andy Warhol, who had died in 1987. Then, for twenty minutes, they played songs from the album that told the story of the Andy they had known and who had introduced them to the singer Nico, from the days of the Factory. Then came a second surprise: Sterling Morrison and Moe Tucker, two other historic members of the group, joined them to perform "Heroin," one of their very first songs. In the Fondation Cartier's park, it was as if time had stopped; The Velvet Underground were back together!

The Fondation Cartier loves music and particularly enjoys creating events. In 2007, for the thirtieth anniversary of Elvis Presley's death, Alain Dominique Perrin, Fondation President, wanted to tell the story of rock's origins in the United States through a large, immersive exhibition in the building on Boulevard Raspail. Acting as curator, he sculpted the exhibition's main focuses, working closely with music producer and cocurator Gilles Pétard. *Rock'n'Roll 39-59* offered a sonic and visual journey through time. Exceptional guitars, posters, records, and rare period objects, including jukeboxes and a Cadillac Eldorado, plunged visitors into the musical origins of rock'n'roll, from rhythm and blues to country, as well as boogie-woogie. Individual stories of well-known musical figures were told, those of musicians including Bill Haley, Bo Diddley, Little Richard, Chuck Berry, and Elvis Presley,

Rock'n'Roll 39-59

along with lesser-known figures working behind the scenes, such as Sam Phillips, founder of Sun Records in Memphis, and the songwriting/producing duo of Jerry Leiber and Mike Stoller. Photography was central to the exhibition, particularly the work of Alfred Wertheimer who followed Elvis's early years, from 1956 to 1958, and previously unpublished images that William Eggleston shot in Buddy Holly's New Mexico recording studio in 2004. The exhibition also placed this musical phenomenon within the broader context of an important historical period in the United States, which saw the early stages of the civil rights movement, and the musical and artistic upheavals of the postwar generation.

On the evening of the *Rock'n'Roll 39-59* opening, the atmosphere at the Fondation Cartier was electric. Guests included Tina Turner, Dick Rivers, Eddy Mitchell, Jean Dujardin, and Jean-Pierre Raffarin. In the garden, Little Richard in a white suit and black glasses, appeared at a piano and played his greatest hits in his inimitable style in what was a truly memorable concert.

Music has been given a special place throughout the Fondation Cartier's history, rock in particular, but also, more generally, live performances. Created in 1994, and scheduled in parallel with the exhibition program, the Nomadic Nights invite artists from the contemporary scene to make use of the Fondation Cartier's exhibition spaces and garden. Music, dance, performances, and film screenings offer visitors an experience that complements the current exhibition. These evenings have seen performance by artists from the rock and underground scenes, including Patti Smith, John Cale, Chrysta Bell, and Stuart A. Staples—solo and with his band Tindersticks—Peaches, Chilly Gonzales, Boredoms, and Blixa Bargeld. The Fondation Cartier is a meeting place where the incredible and the unforgettable are always possible.

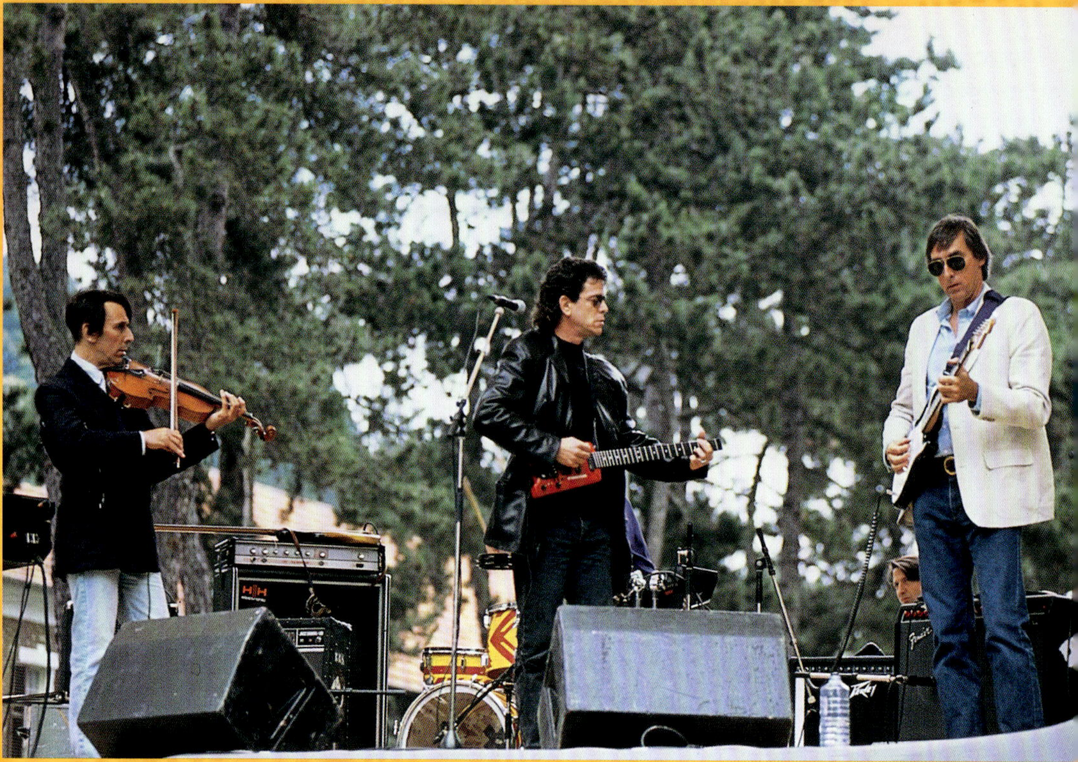

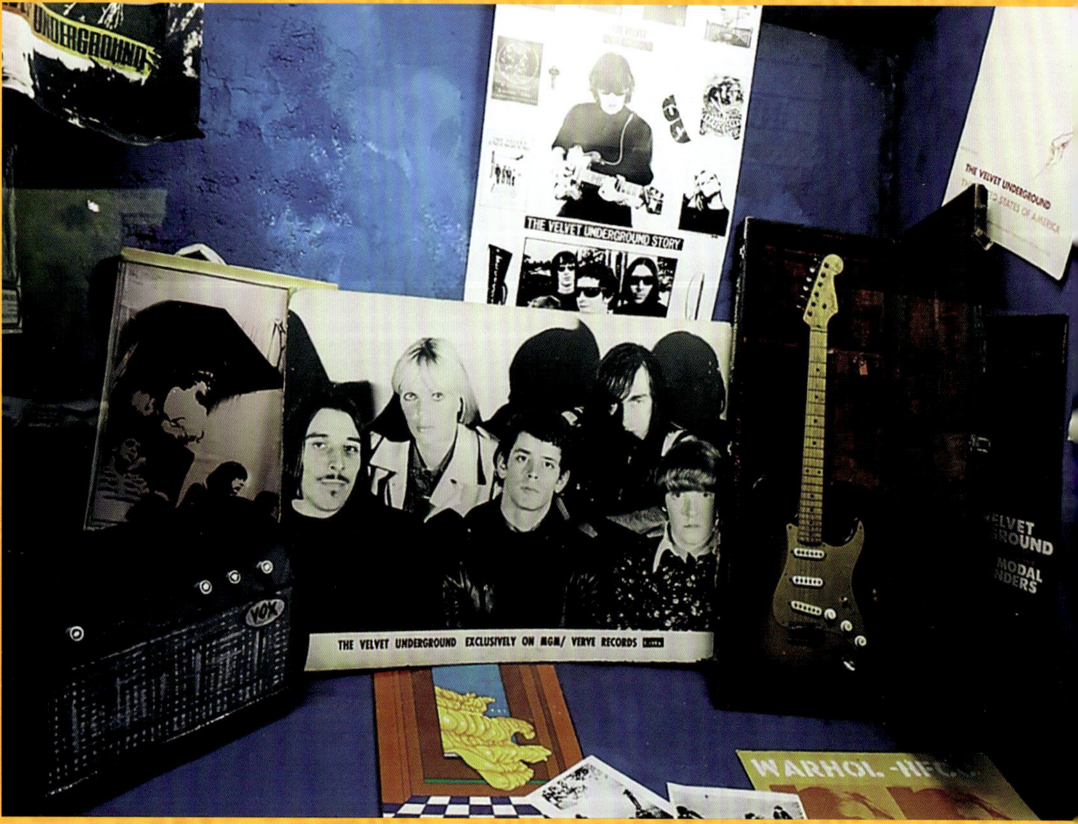

1990   John Cale, Lou Reed, Moe Tucker, and Sterling Morrison, historic members of The Velvet Underground, reunited for a unique concert at Jouy-en-Josas during the opening of the exhibition *Andy Warhol System : Pub-Pop-Rock*.

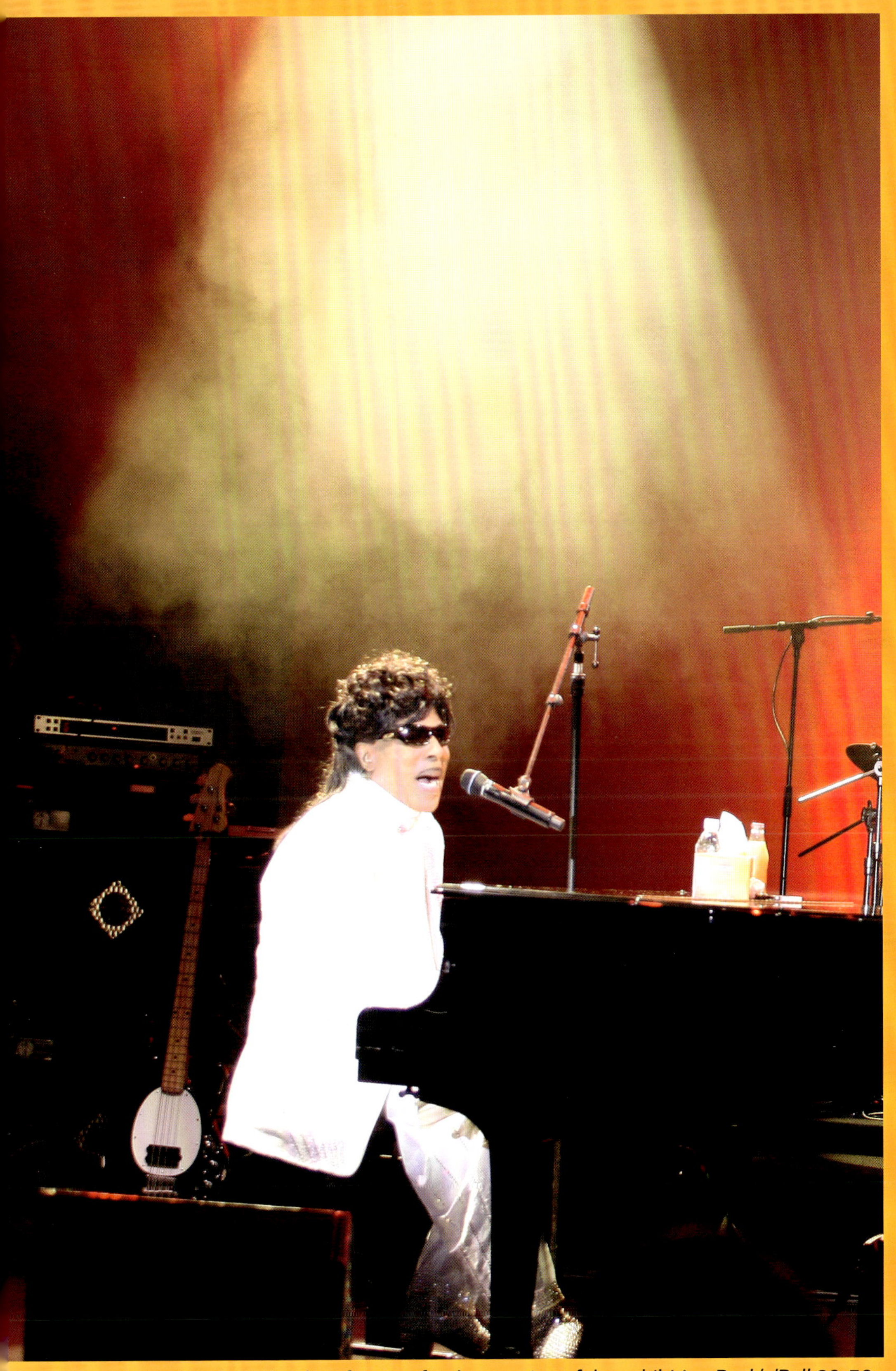

2007   Rock legend Little Richard performing for the opening of the exhibition *Rock'n'Roll 39-59*.

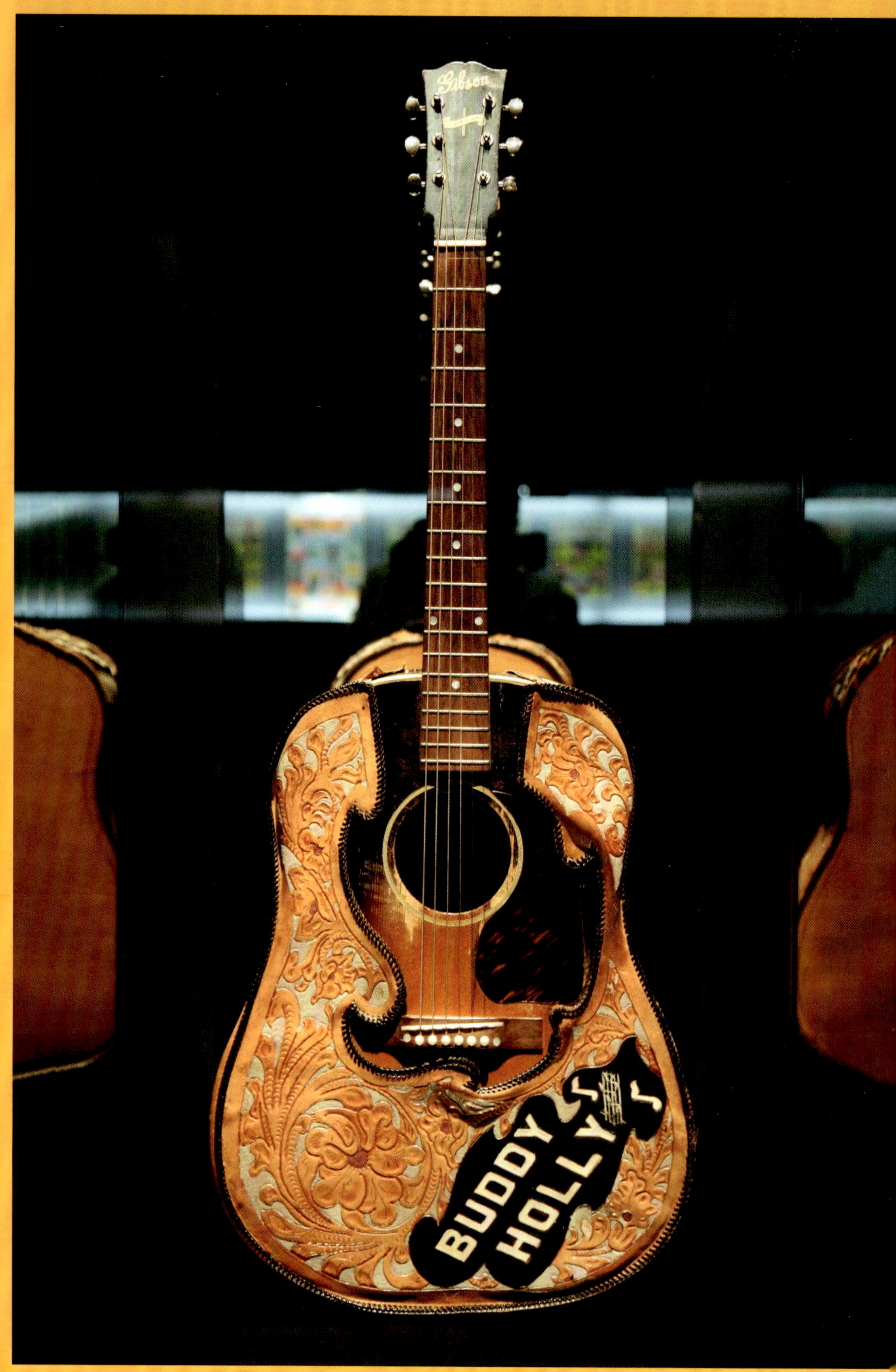

2007 Several iconic guitars were displayed as part of the exhibition *Rock'n'Roll 39-59*, including the legendary Gibson J-45 once owned by Buddy Holly.

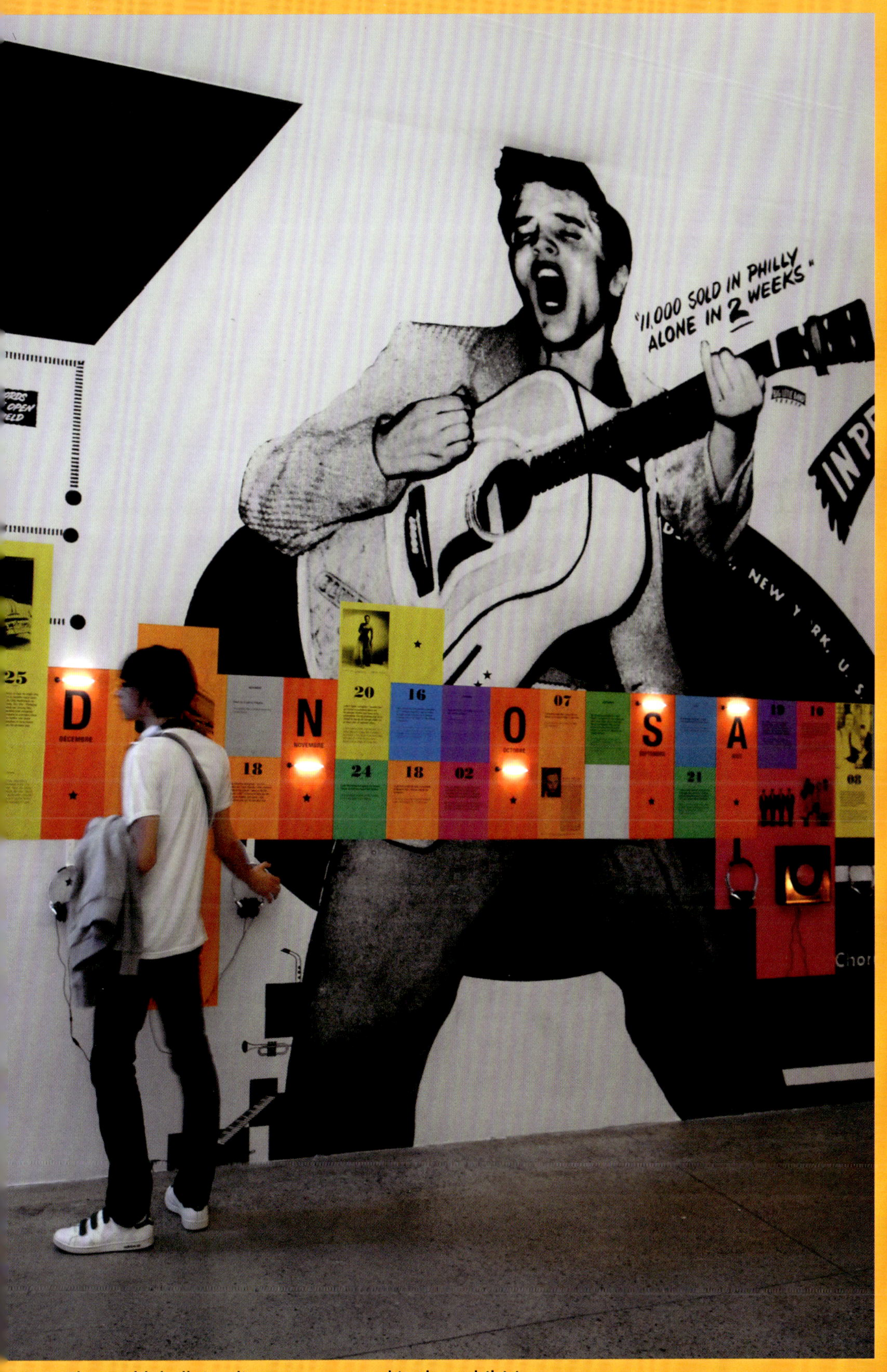

  The rock'n'roll timeline as presented in the exhibition

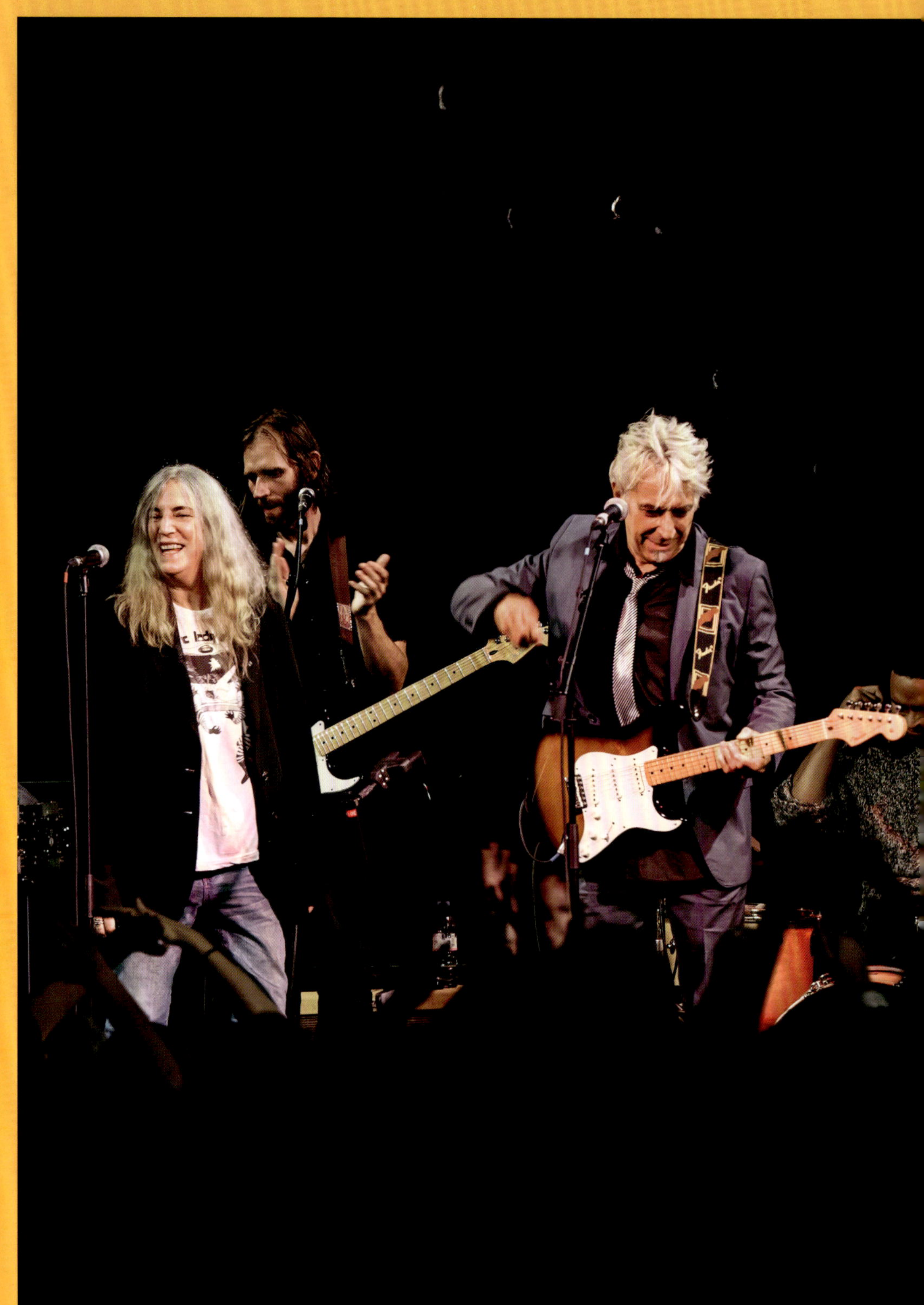

2014   For the Fondation Cartier's 30th anniversary, a special concert brought together Patti Smith and John Cale, one of the founding members of The Velvet Underground and producer of *Horses*, her most lauded album.

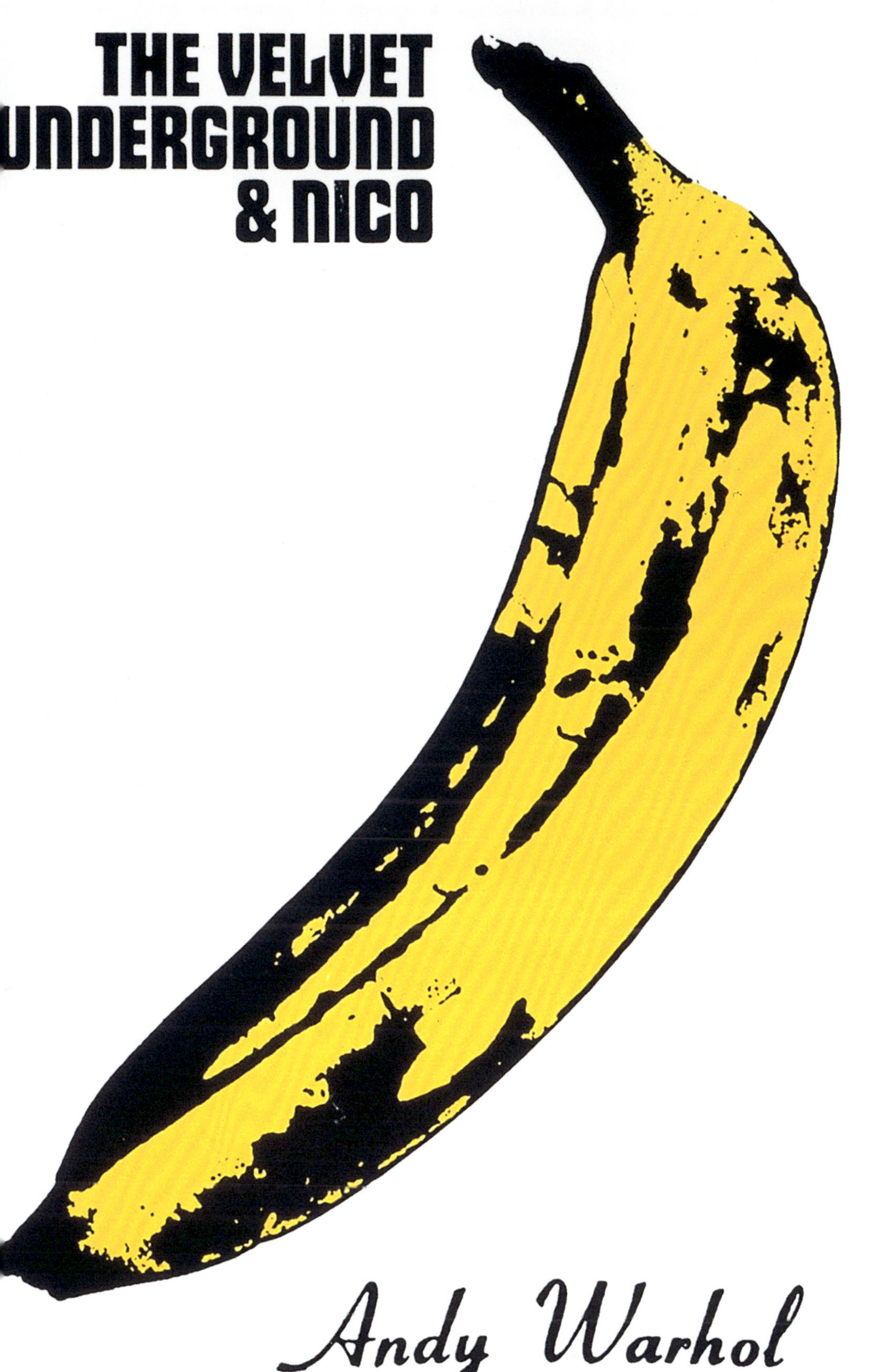

THE VELVET UNDERGROUND & NICO
Andy Warhol

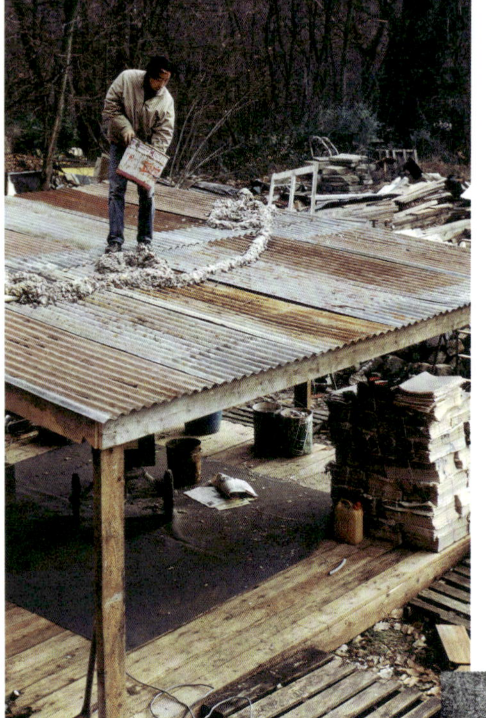

Huang Yong Ping decided to set up his studio in the "dump" behind the castle of the Fondation Cartier.

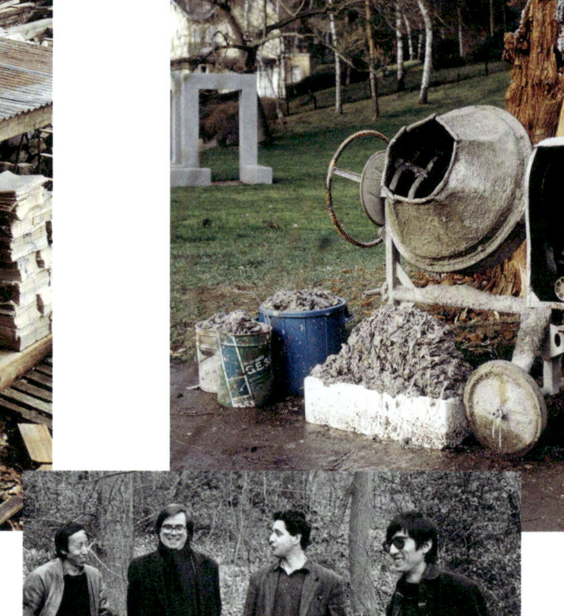

Huang Yong Ping, Michel Nuridsany, Jean de Loisy, and Fei Dawei

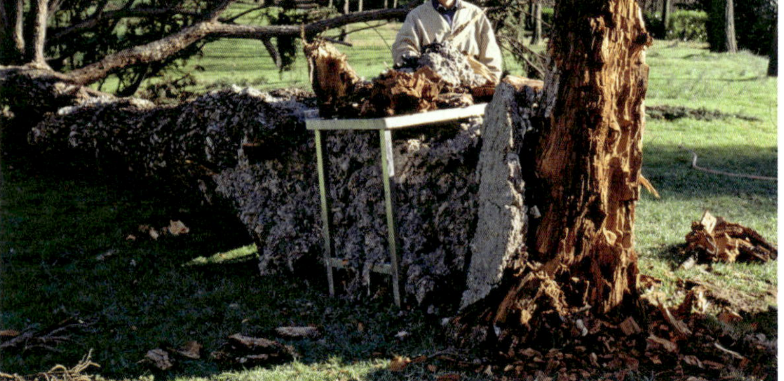

In January 1990, a tree in the park was blown down in a storm. Huang Yong Ping attempted to "heal" it.

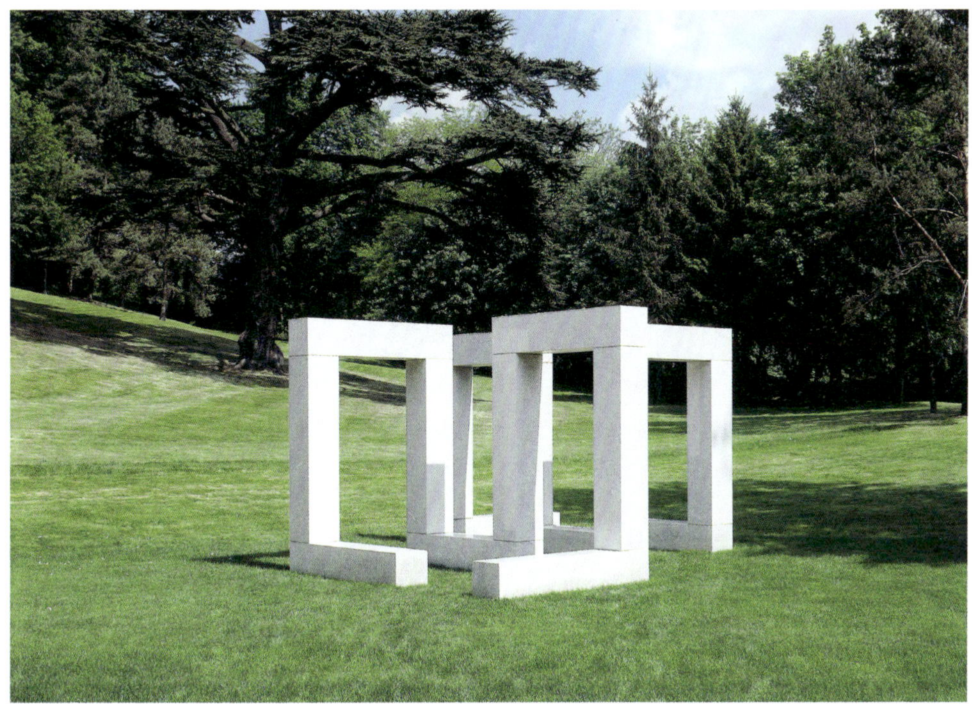

Max Bill, *Pavillon*, 1989. Commission for the park

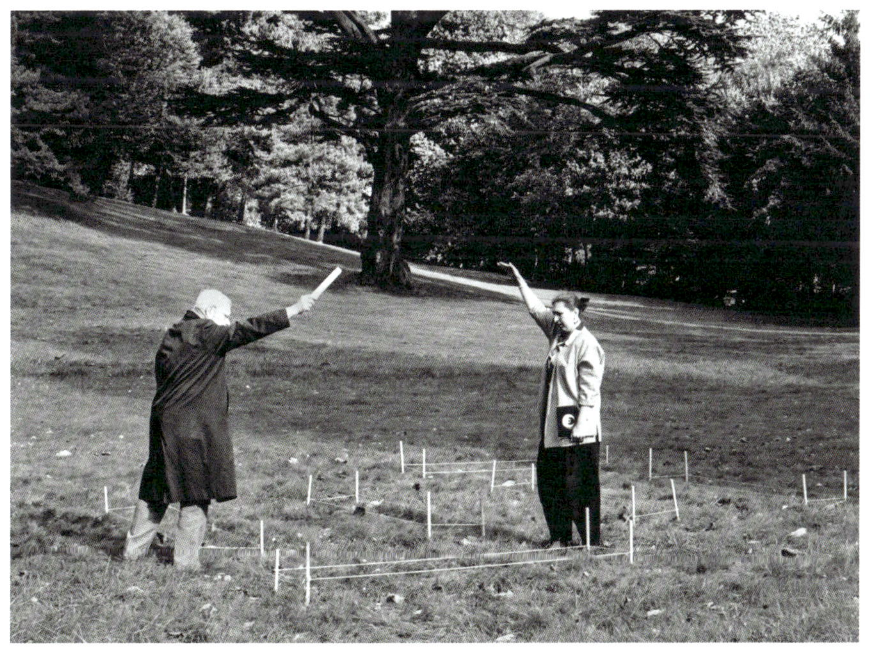

Max Bill and Marie-Claude Beaud preparing for the installation
of *Pavillon*, inaugurated on May 15, 1990.

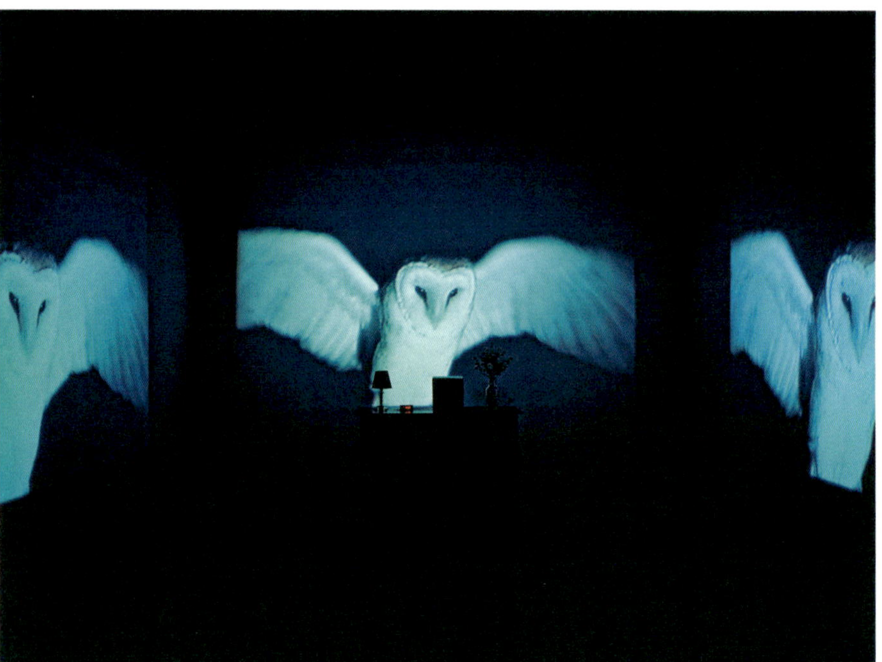

For his solo exhibition at the Fondation Cartier, Bill Viola presented three installations including, for the first time in Europe, *The Sleep of Reason* (1988).

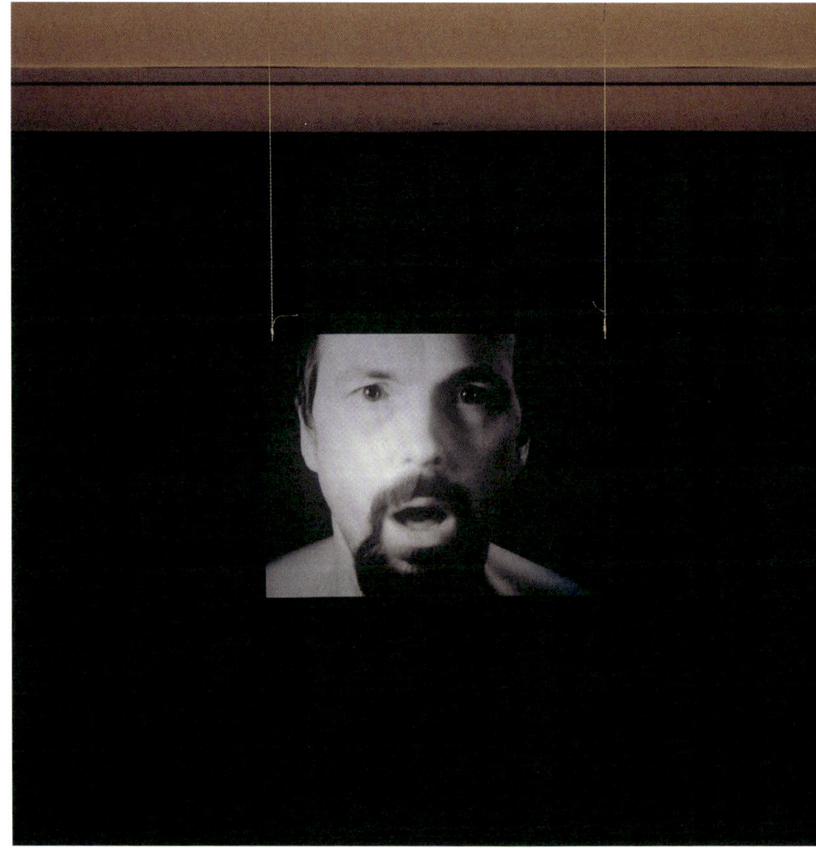

Bill Viola, *Nine Attempts to Achieve Immortality*, 1996
FC Collections (1996)

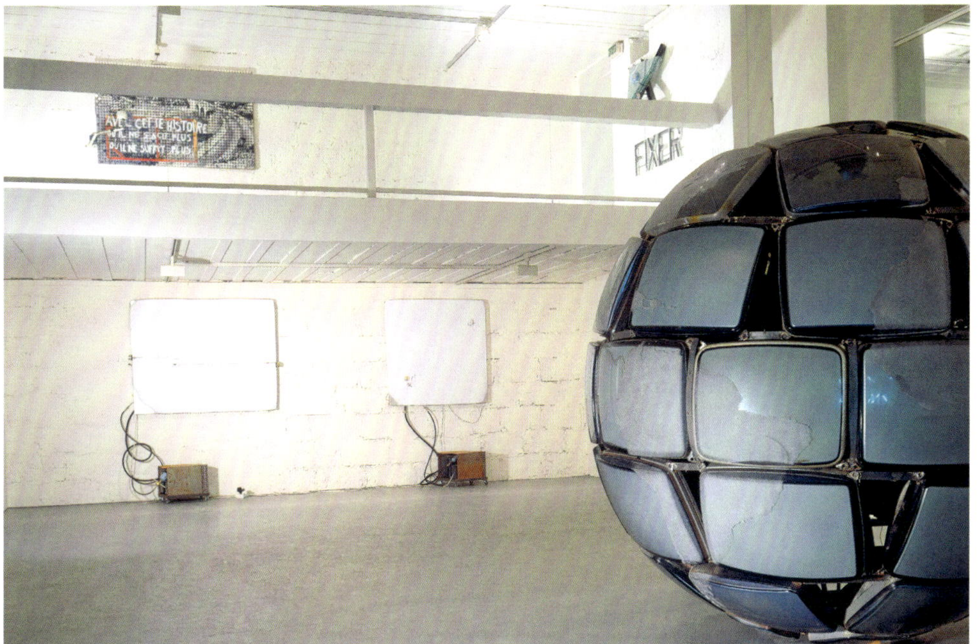

In 1991, the Fondation Cartier exhibited a selection of sculptures by Richard Baquié
some of which, including *Constats d'échec*, were bought for the Collections
of the Fondation Cartier.
Richard Baquié, *Réduction*, 1988

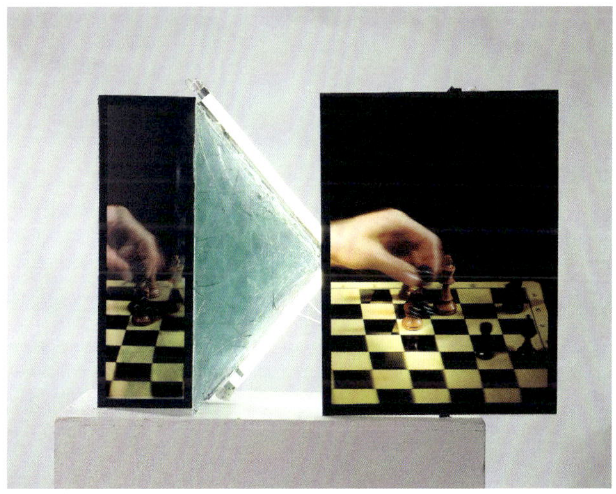

Richard Baquié, *Constats d'échecs*, 1989
FC Collections (1991)

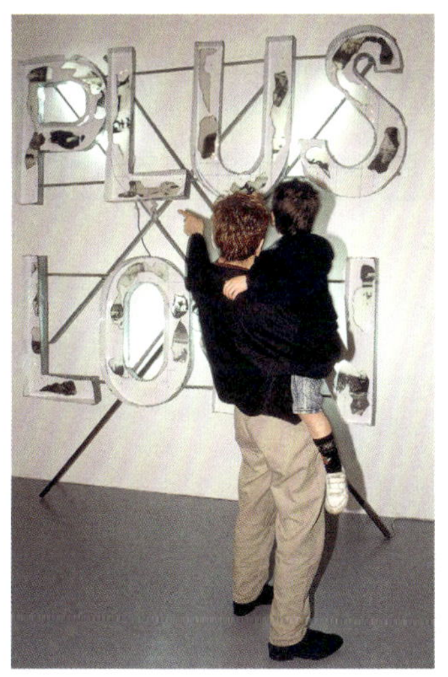

Richard Baquié, *Réduction*,
1988

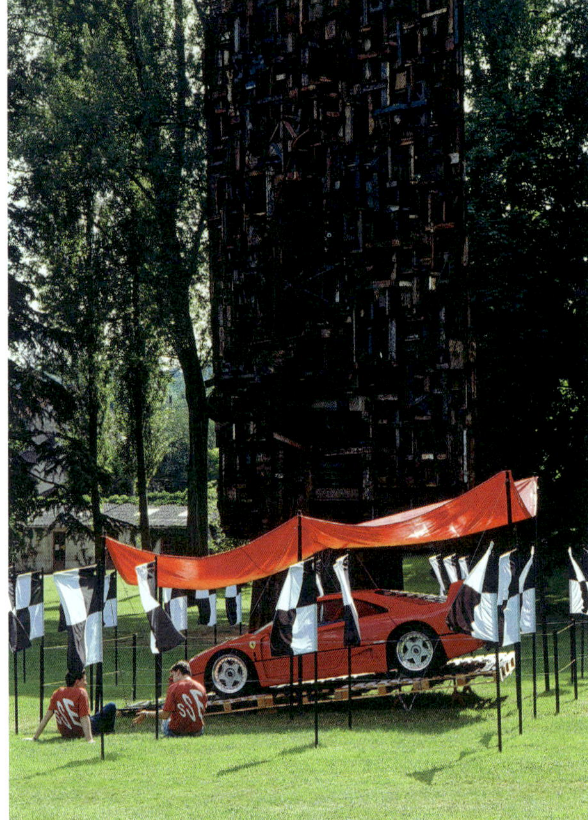

"Speed is certainly one of the major criteria for analyzing the transformations of the 20th century. An exhilarating development but one which also poses—if we are to listen to Paul Virilio, the mentor of this project—a great threat. Artists have constantly responded to, and even anticipated, this importance of speed." Jean de Loisy

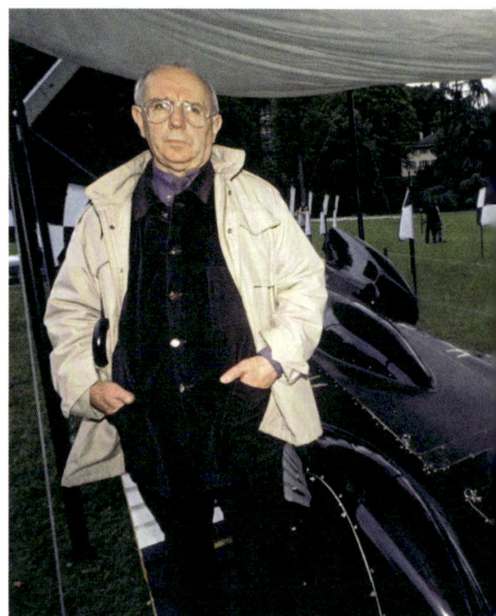

Paul Virilio at the opening of the exhibition *La Vitesse*

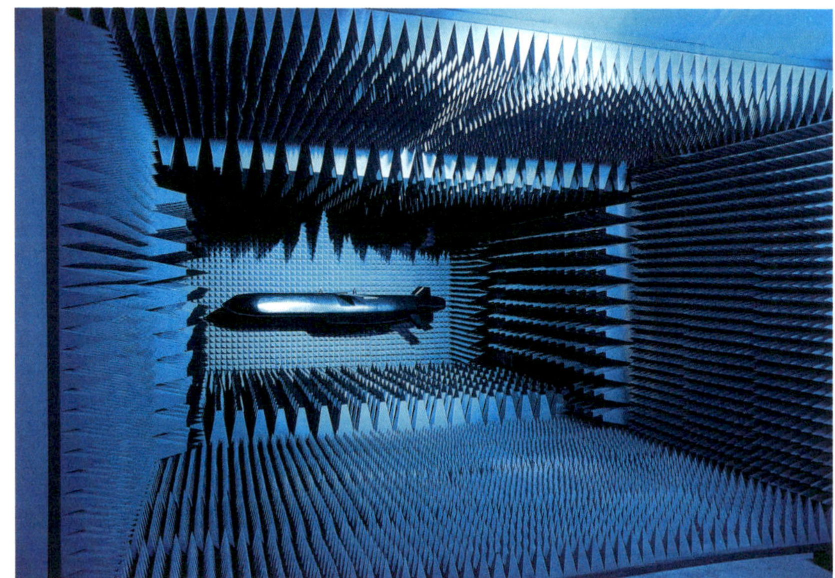

Apache missile in an anechoic chamber

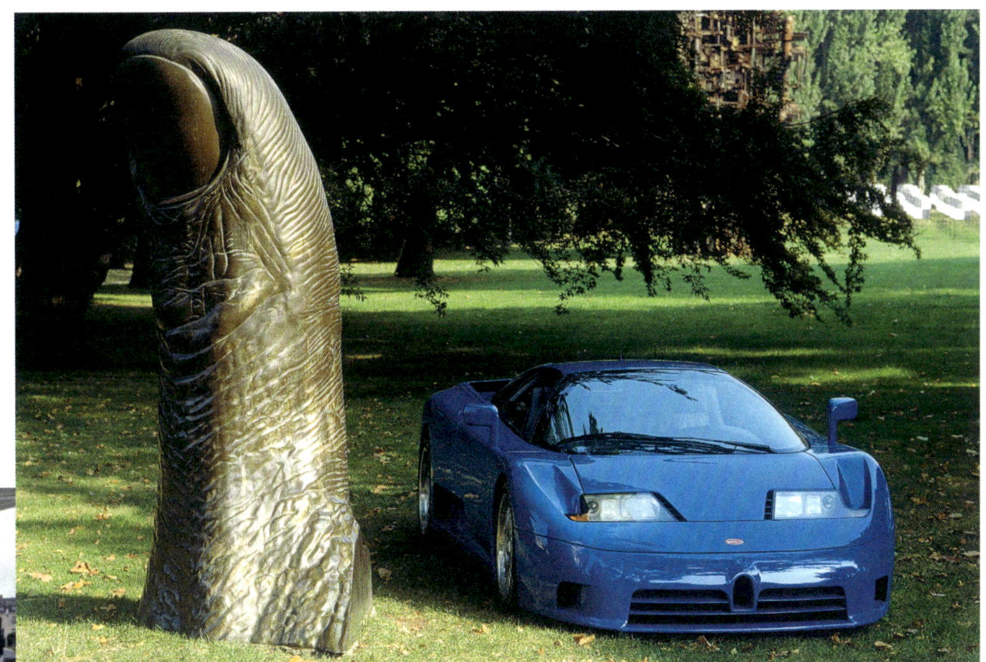

The very latest Bugatti EB110 was presented alongside
César's work *Le Pouce* (1966).

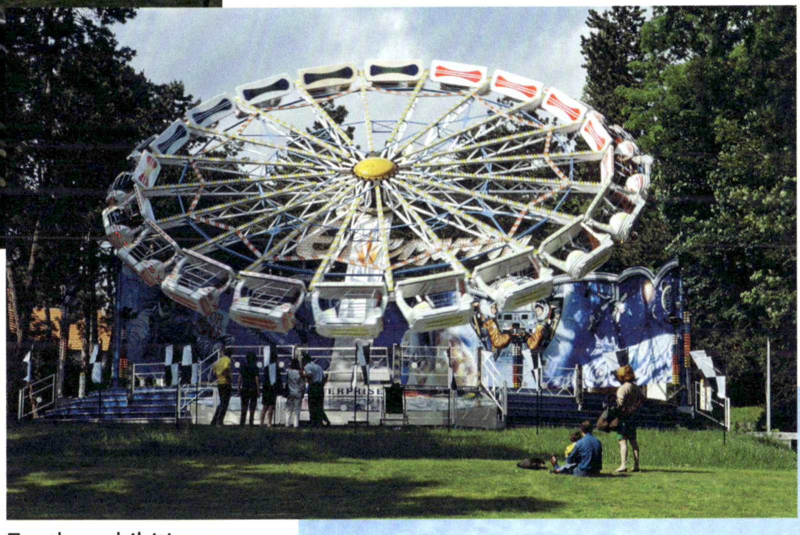

For the exhibition,
an *Enterprise* fairground
ride was installed
in the park.

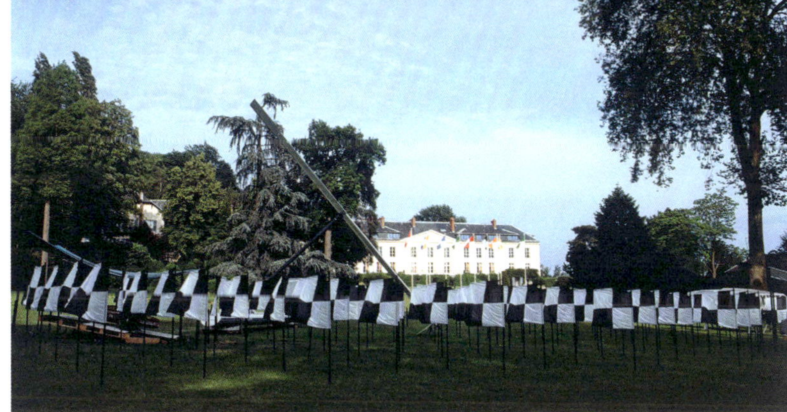

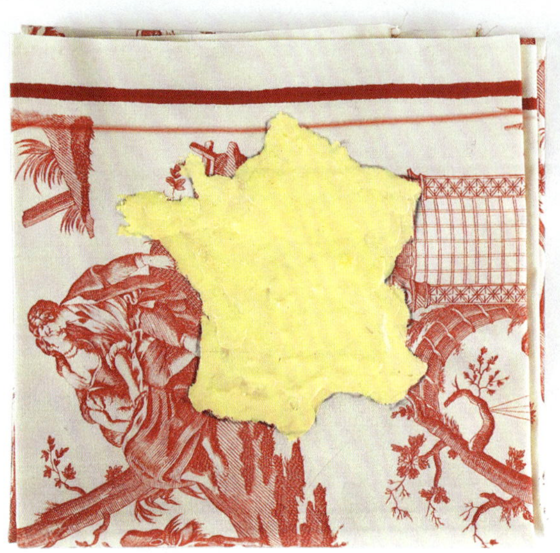

Too French brought together 21 French artists, whose work, beyond aesthetic and historical affiliations, evoked the colors and landscapes synonymous with France. The exhibition traveled to the Hong Kong Museum of Art, then the Hara Museum of Contemporary Art in Tokyo the following year. Jean-Michel Othoniel, *Carte de France sur toile de Jouy*, 1991

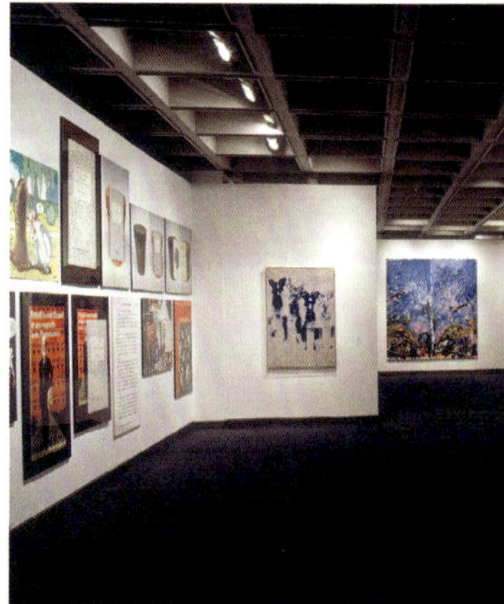

Works by Raymond Hains, Yves Klein, and Joan Mitchell

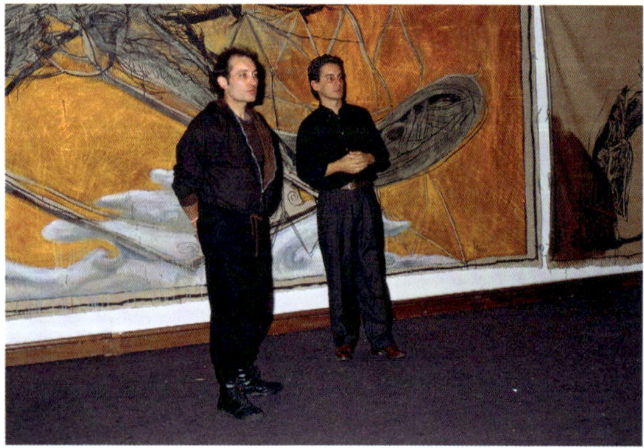

Marc Couturier and Hervé Chandès at the Hong Kong Museum of Art in front of *Indienne* by Gérard Garouste (1988)

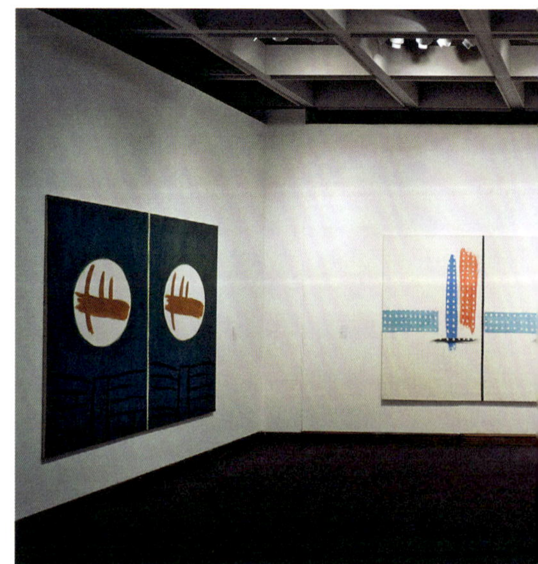

Bernard Piffaretti, *Untitled*, 1987-1989
Shirley Jaffe, *Summer Flower* and *The Center*, 1990

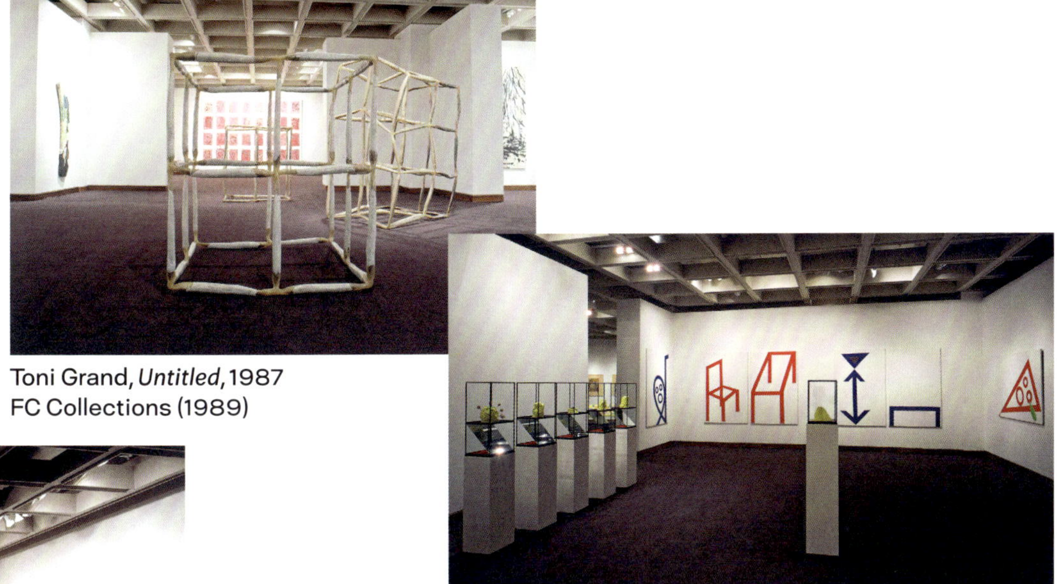

Toni Grand, *Untitled*, 1987
FC Collections (1989)

Works by Jean-Michel Othoniel and Emmanuel Pereire

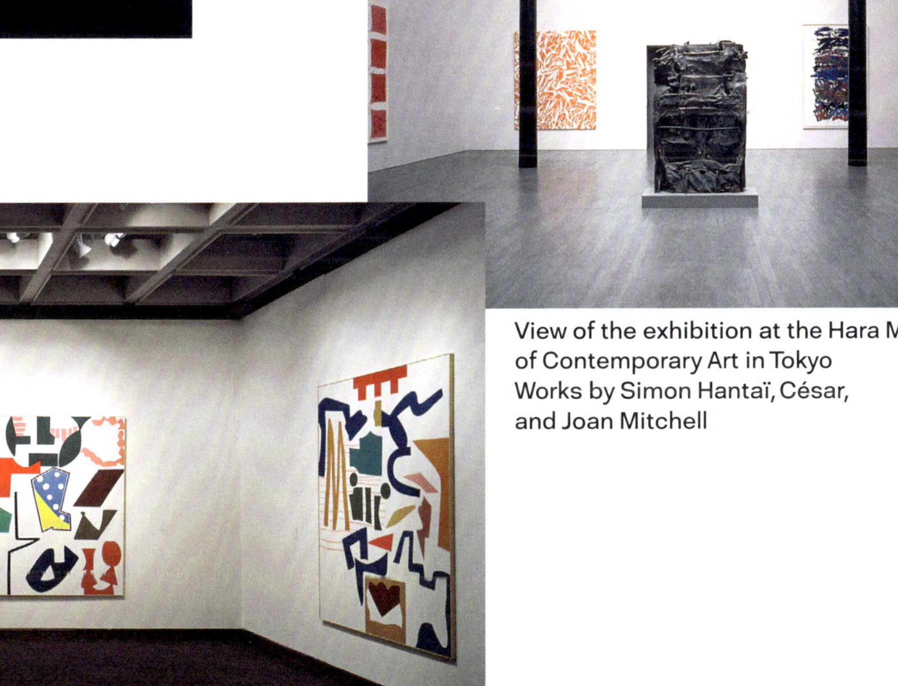

View of the exhibition at the Hara Museum
of Contemporary Art in Tokyo
Works by Simon Hantaï, César,
and Joan Mitchell

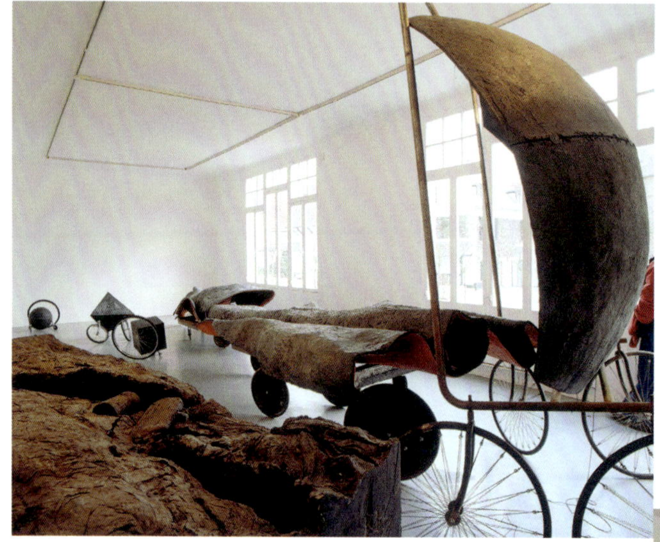

With *Machines d'architecture*, the Fondation Cartier invited 13 international architects to present works specially designed for the exhibition spaces.
Raoul Bunschoten, *The Skin of the Earth*, 1990

Liz Diller and Ricardo Scofidio, *Para-site*, 1989

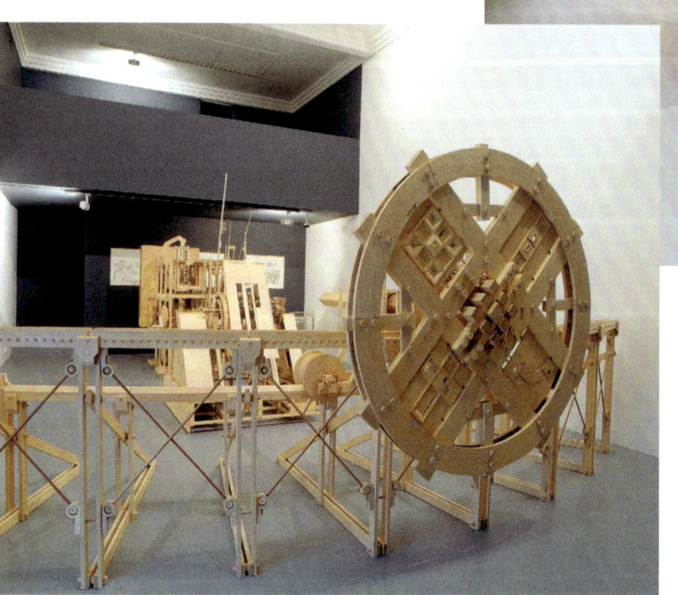

Meton Gadelha, *The Anarchitomy of tec-ture*, 1985

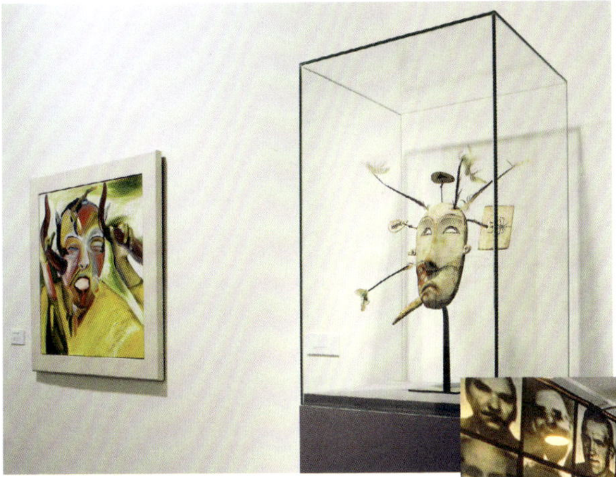

Through the works of over 80 artists, *À visage découvert* offered a glimpse of faces of all kinds, from antique and non-European art, up until contemporary art.

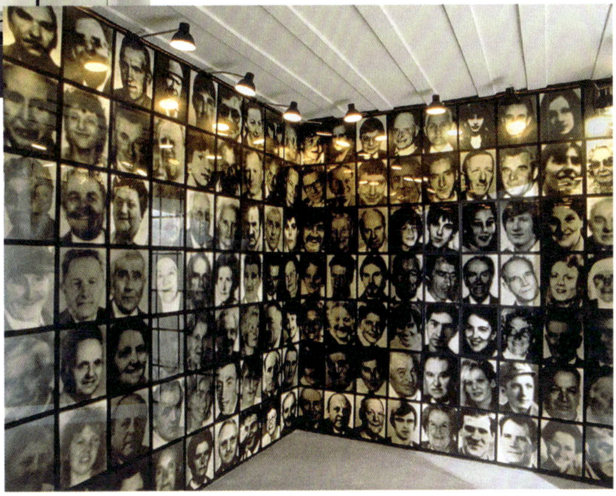

Christian Boltanski, *Les Suisses morts*, 1989

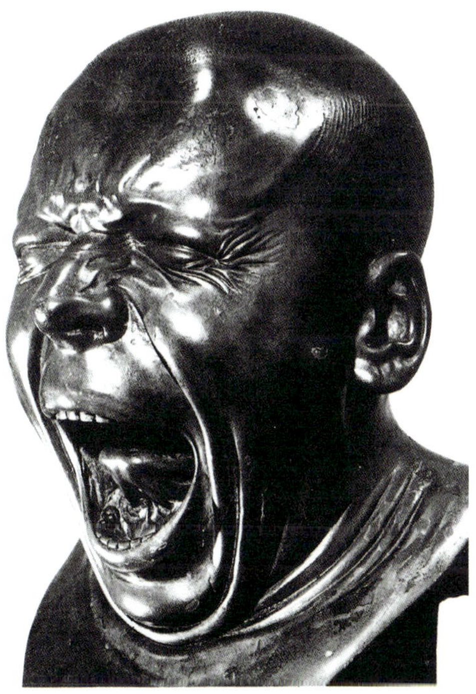

Franz Xaver Messerschmidt, *Le Bâilleur*,
c. 1777–1783

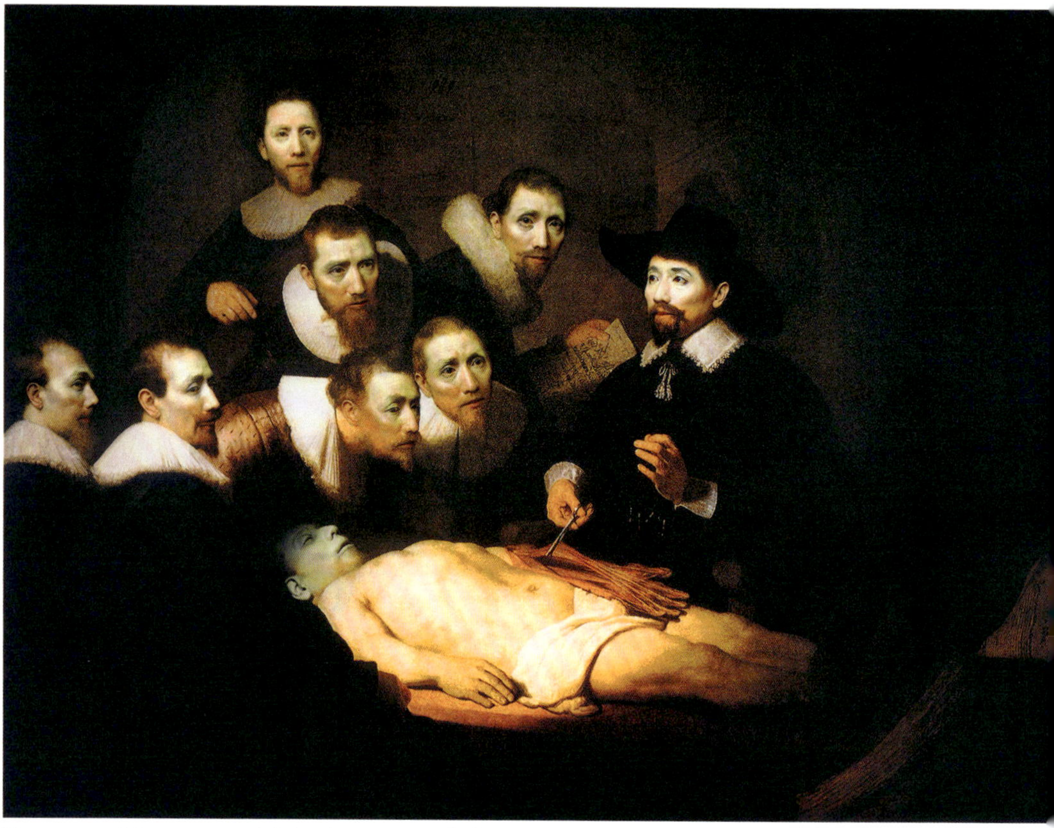

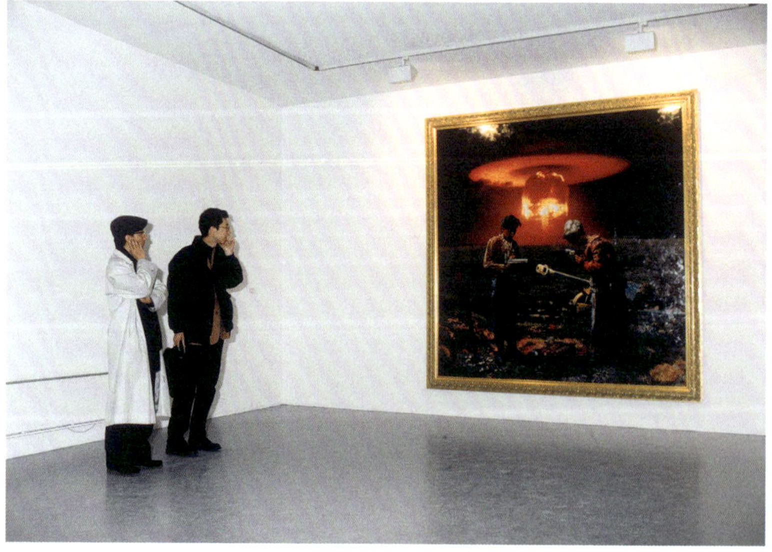

Yasumasa Morimura exhibited a group of photographs inspired by masterpieces of Western and Japanese art. Yasumasa Morimura, *9 visages*, 1993

Yasumasa Morimura, *Brothers (A Late Autumn Prayer)*, 1991

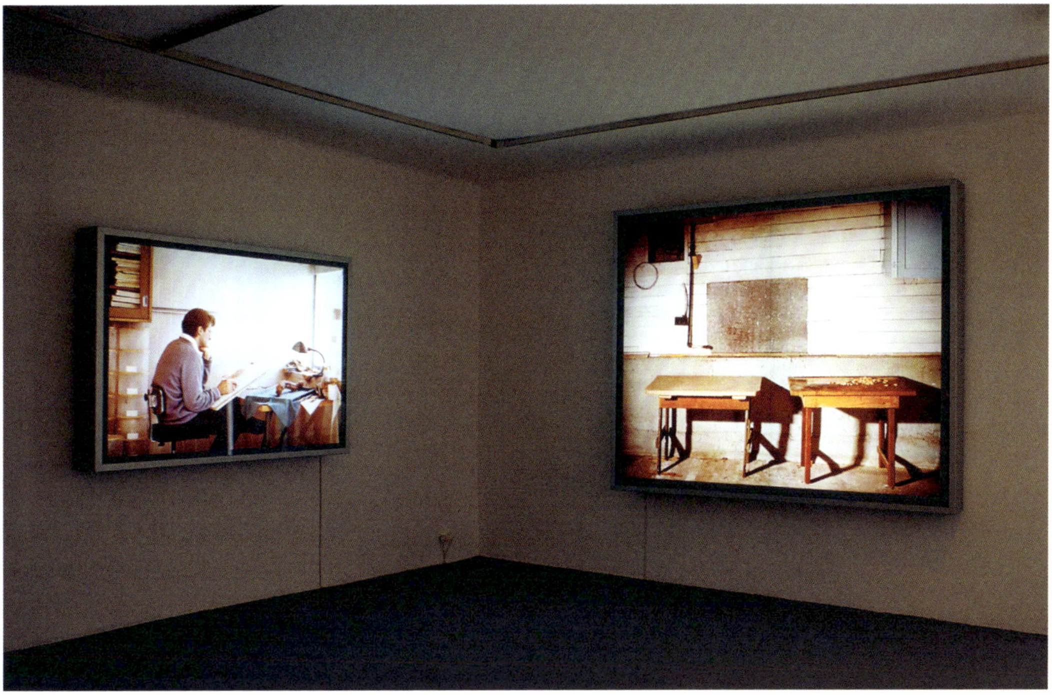

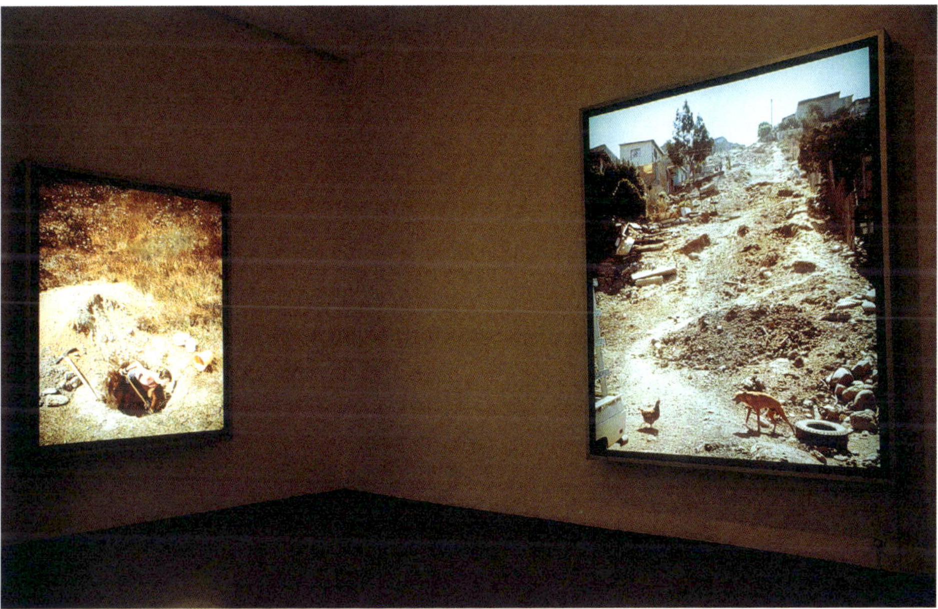

The exhibition of Jeff Wall's work brought together a group of seven
pieces from different periods.

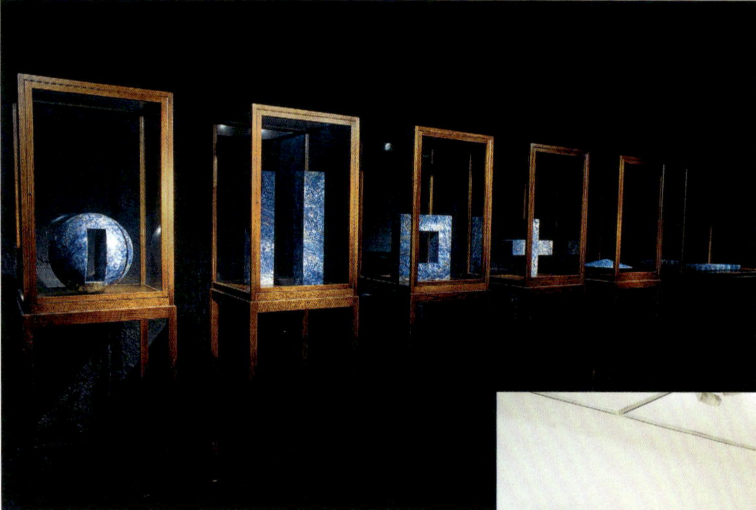

James Lee Byars, *The Path of Luck*, 1989

With a selection of works from the 19th century to the early 1990s, *Azur* bore witness to the paradoxical representations of the infinite and the absolute by a range of artists.

Gustave Courbet, *Mer calme à Palavas*, 1857
Gerhard Richter, *Seestück*, 1975

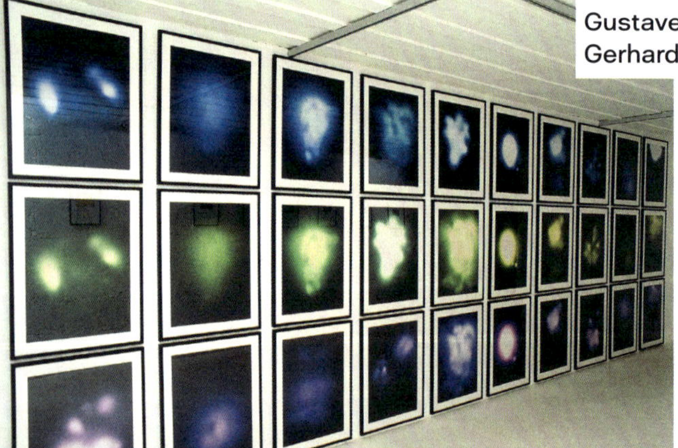

Sigmar Polke, *Blue, Uranium Green*, and *Purple*, 1992

James Turrell, *Skeet*, 1990
FC Collections (1990)

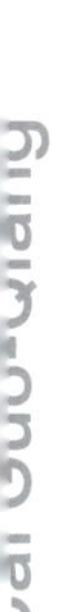

During his residency, Cai Guo-Qiang orchestrated several explosions, including the work *The Earth Has Its Black Hole Too: Project for Extraterrestrials No. 16.* FC Collections (1997)

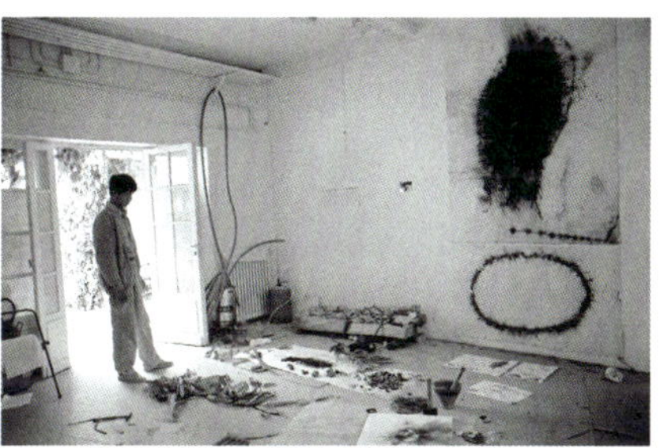

Cai Guo-Qiang working on *The Idea Book*, 1993

Cai Guo-Qiang in his studio; on the wall: *Normandy's Halo: Project for Extraterrestrials No. 19*, 1993

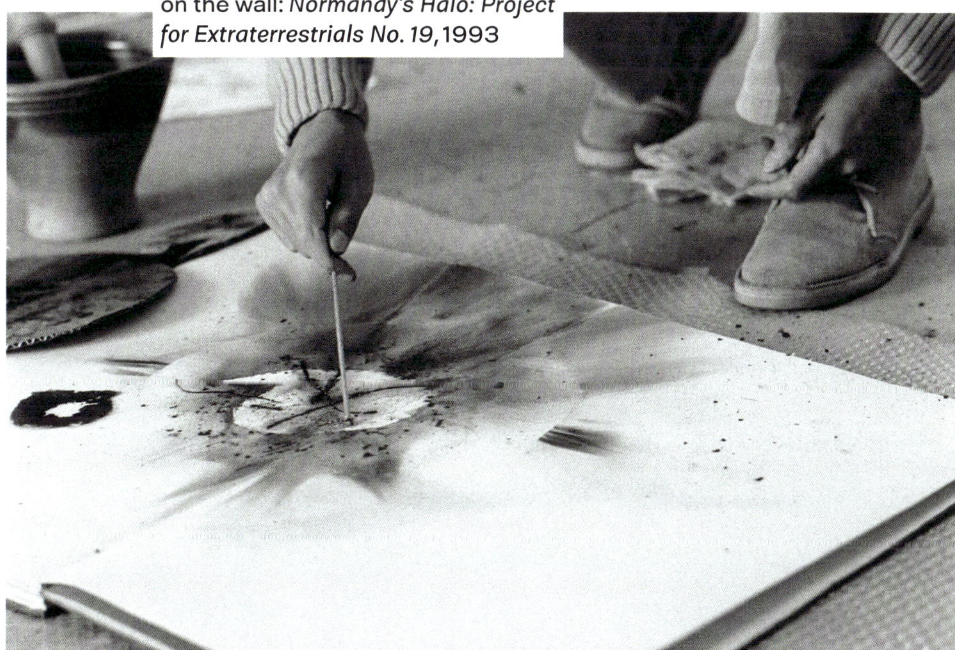

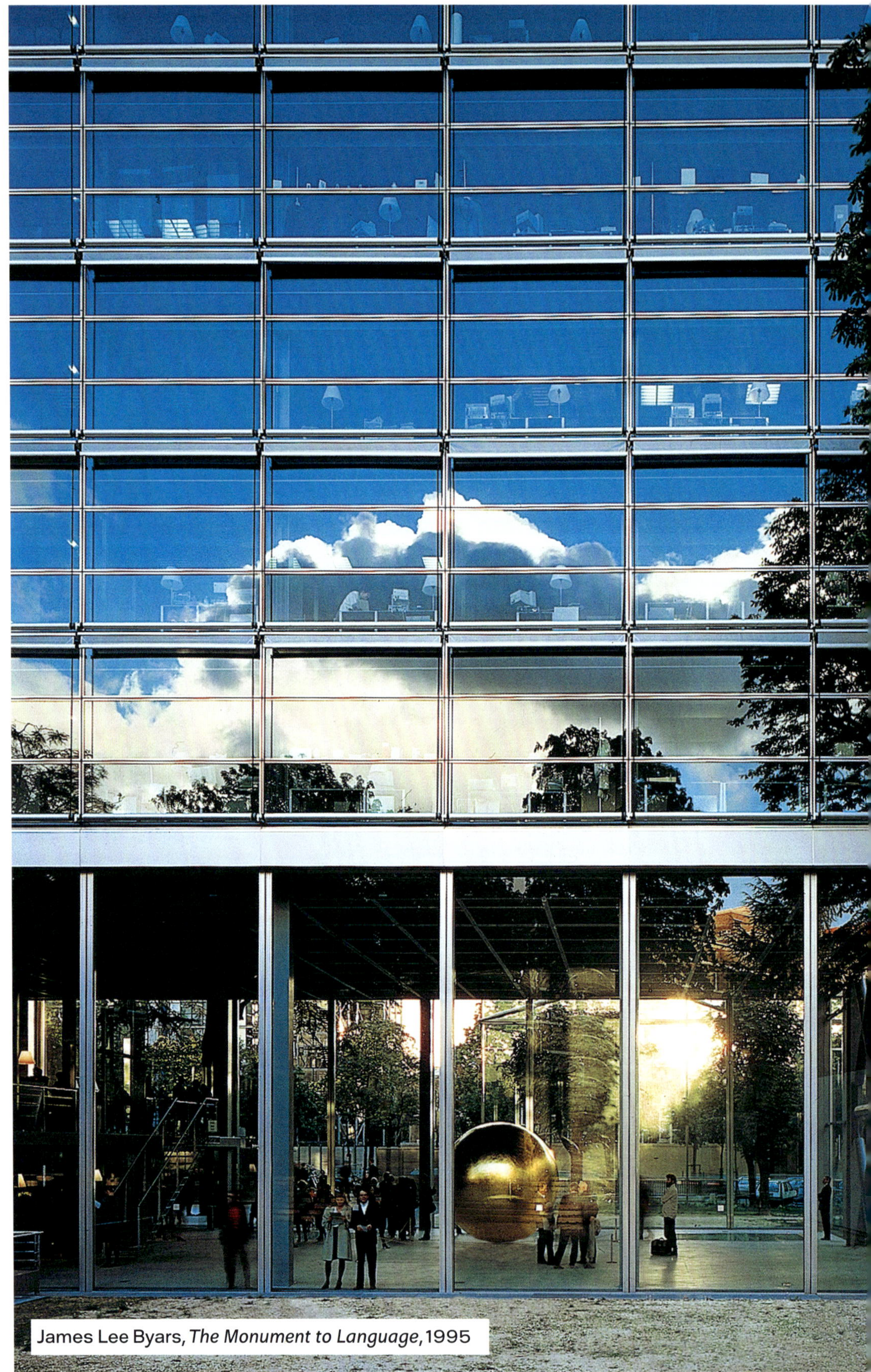

James Lee Byars, *The Monument to Language*, 1995

1994–2003

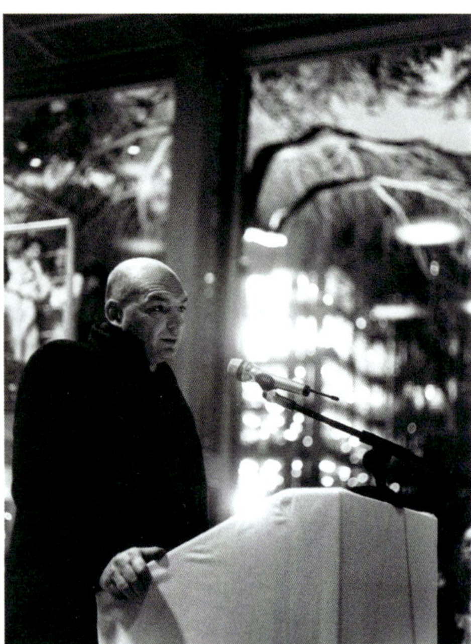

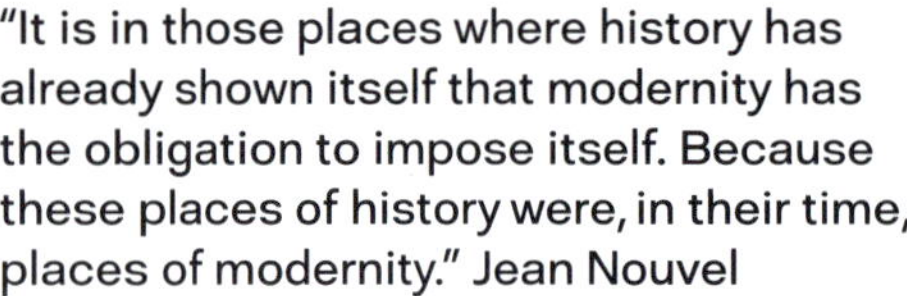

"It is in those places where history has already shown itself that modernity has the obligation to impose itself. Because these places of history were, in their time, places of modernity." Jean Nouvel

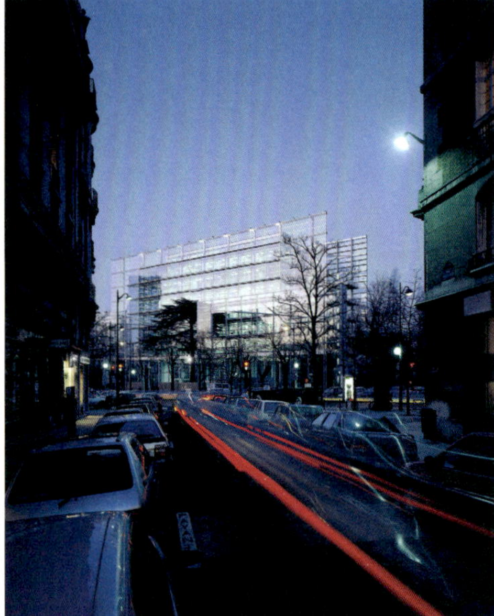

In 1994, the Fondation Cartier moved into the glass and metal building especially designed for it by Jean Nouvel, in the 14th arrondissement of Paris. A true "Parisian monument," this new site harmoniously combines 1,200 m² of exhibition spaces and six floors of office space.

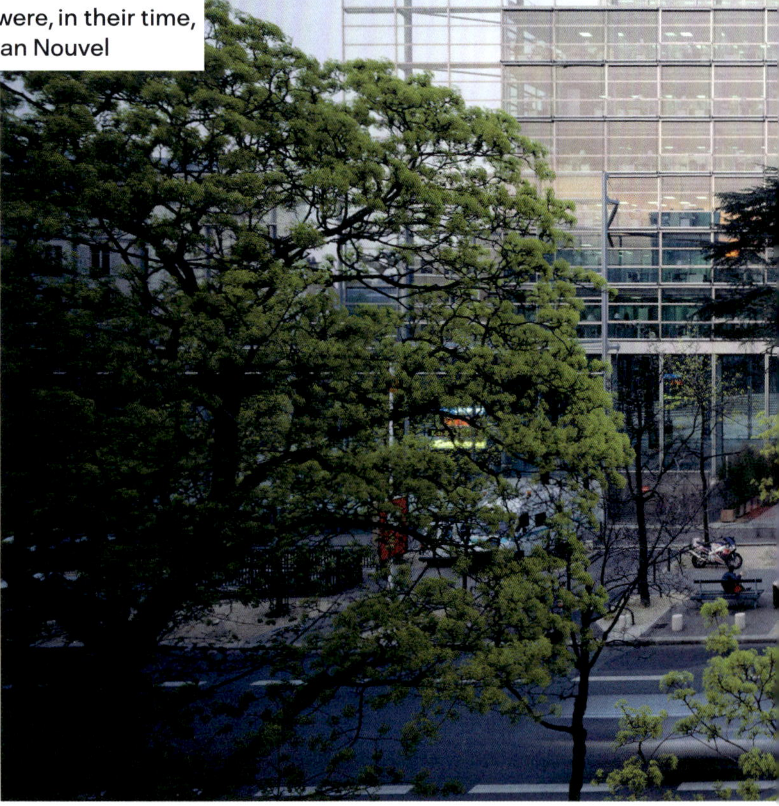

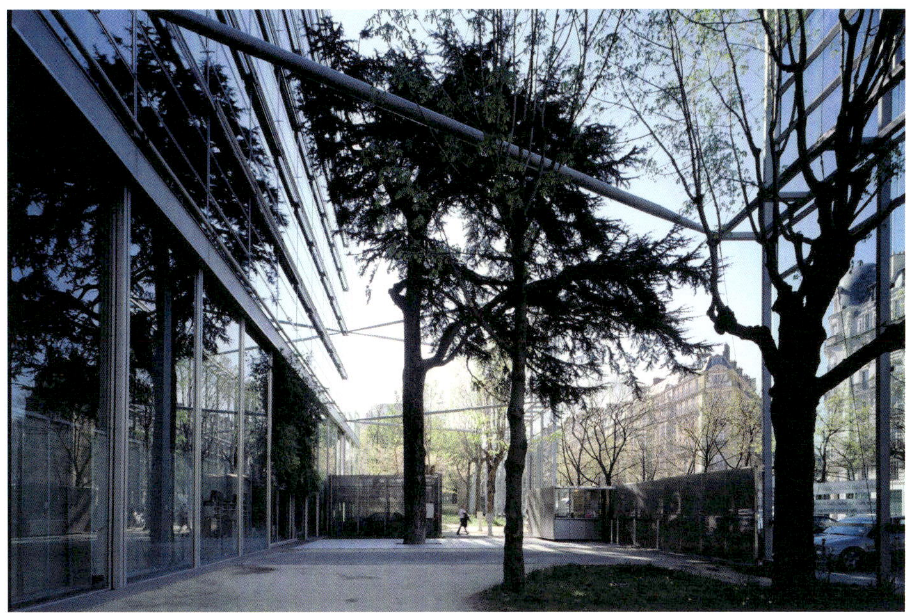

"It was Chateaubriand, in 1823, who planted the famous cedar of Lebanon at 261 Boulevard Raspail, which, for me, is the real monument here."
Jean Nouvel

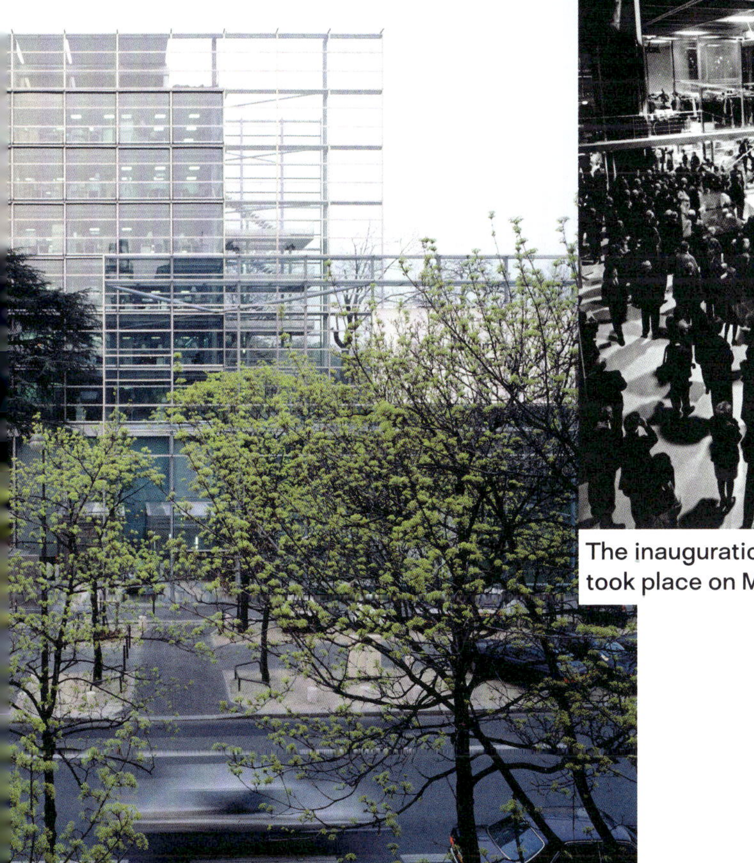

The inauguration of the building took place on May 10, 1994.

In response to a commission from the Fondation Cartier for its new garden on Boulevard Raspail, Lothar Baumgarten created *Theatrum Botanicum* featuring some 35 tree species and almost 200 French plant species, planted or sown in a specific order.

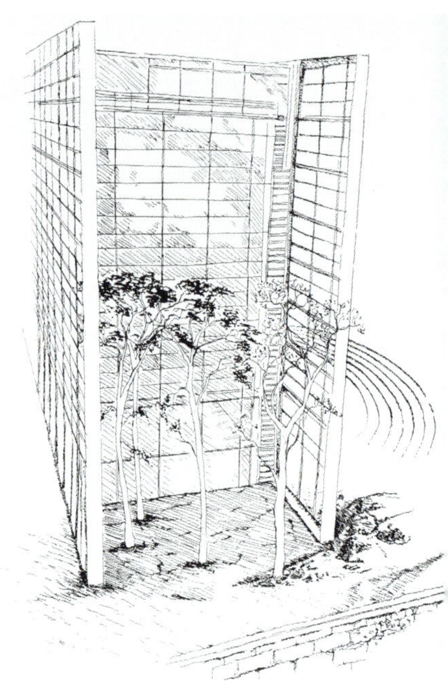

Lothar Baumgarten, preparatory sketch for the *Theatrum Botanicum*, 1994

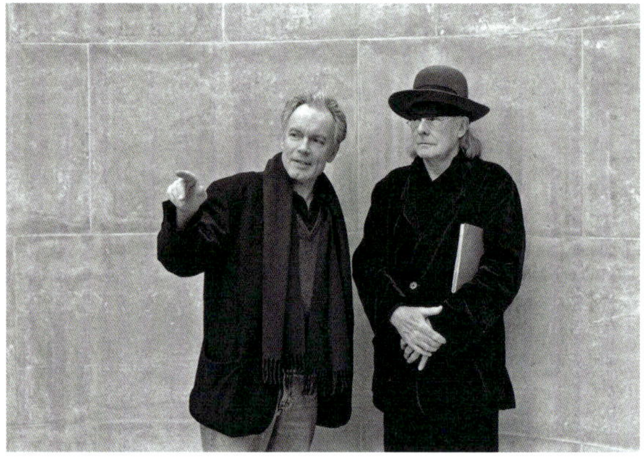

Lothar Baumgarten and James Lee Byars in 1995

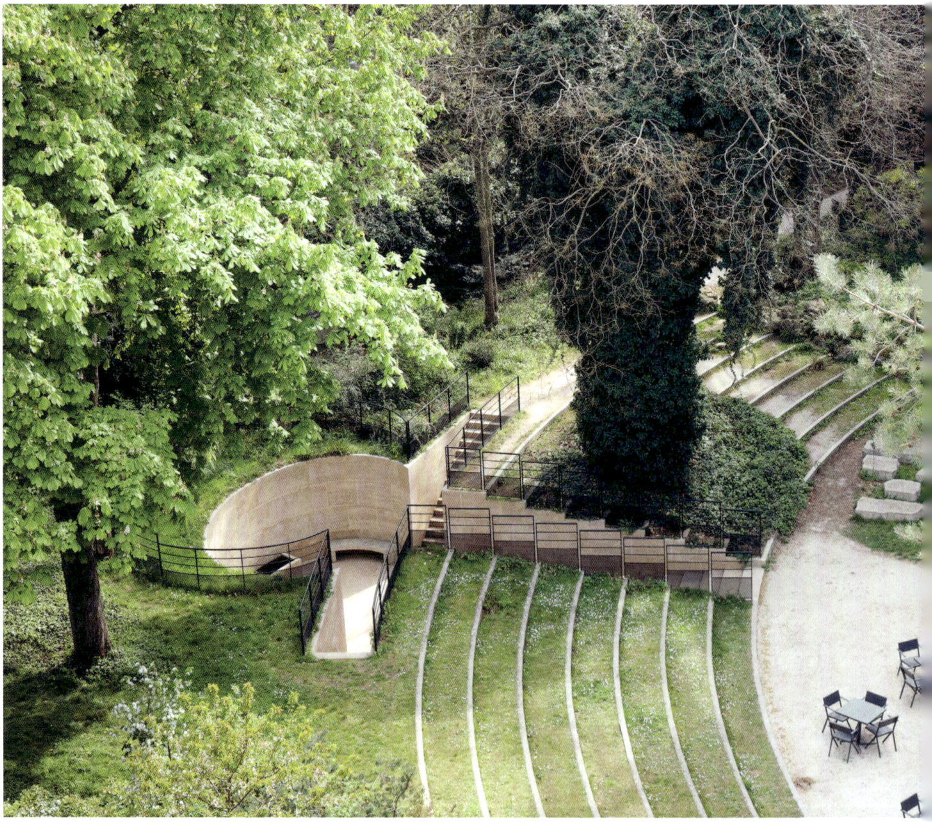

At the rear of the building, the garden evolves into a sandy expanse, accommodating an amphitheater whose shallow steps are covered with grasses and weeds.

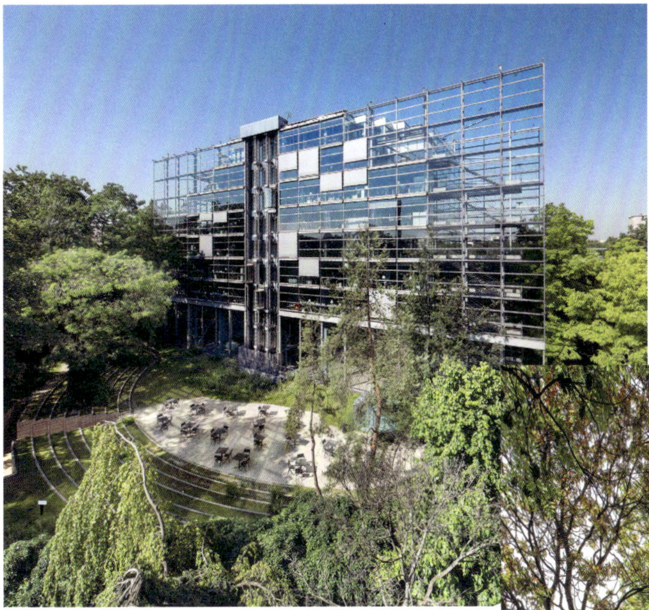

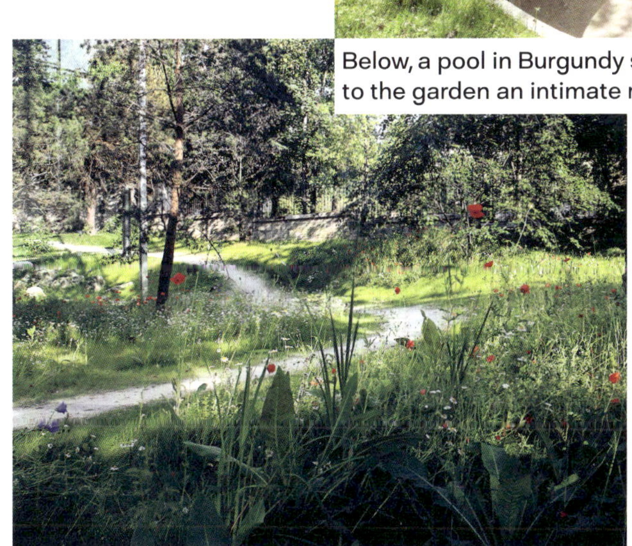

"Space transforms into a reflected surface; the park serves as a setting for the building and the building shows off the foliage."
Lothar Baumgarten

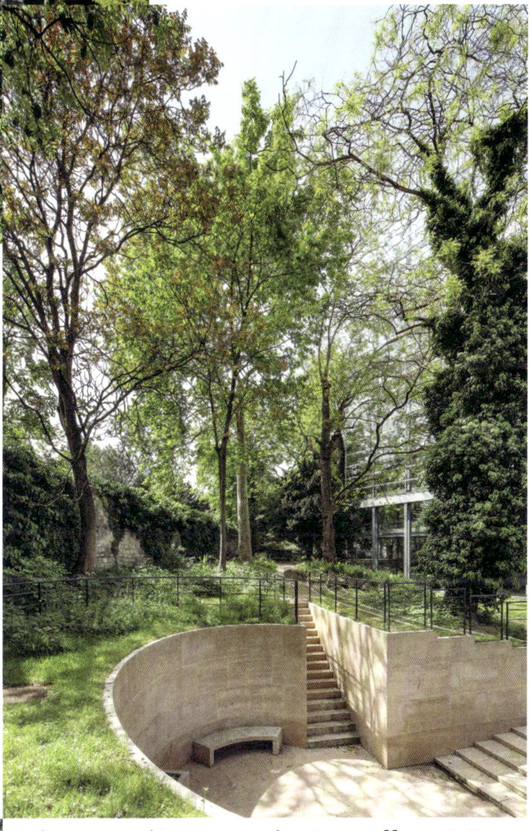

Below, a pool in Burgundy stone offers visitors to the garden an intimate retreat.

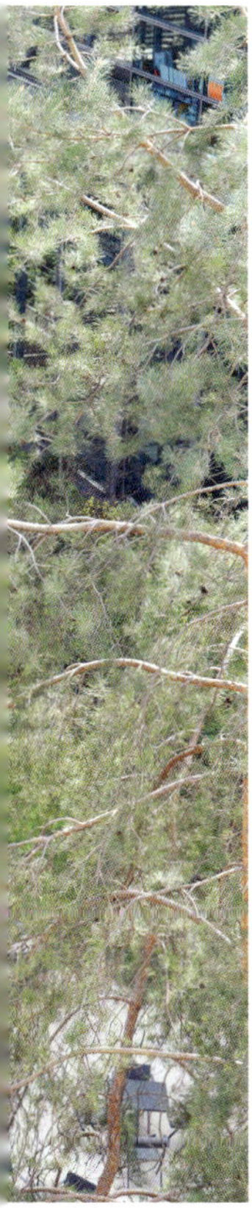

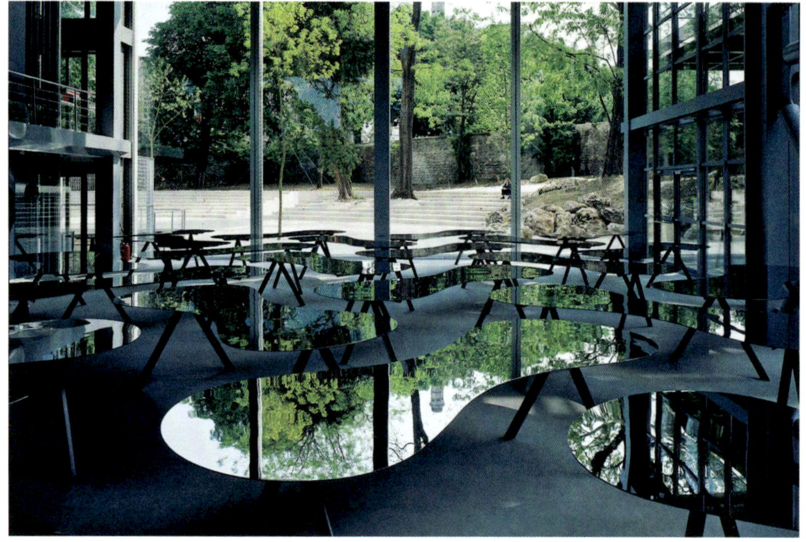

When its new Parisian venue opened to the public, the Fondation Cartier explored three fields of contemporary creation: design with Ron Arad, sculpture with Richard Artschwager, and video with Pierrick Sorin. The garden surrounding Jean Nouvel's building was still being created.
Ron Arad, *Table*, 1994. FC Collections (2019)

Richard Artschwager, *L'Arbre chez lui, Question Mark – Three Periods* and *Pyramid II*, 1994. FC Collections (1994)

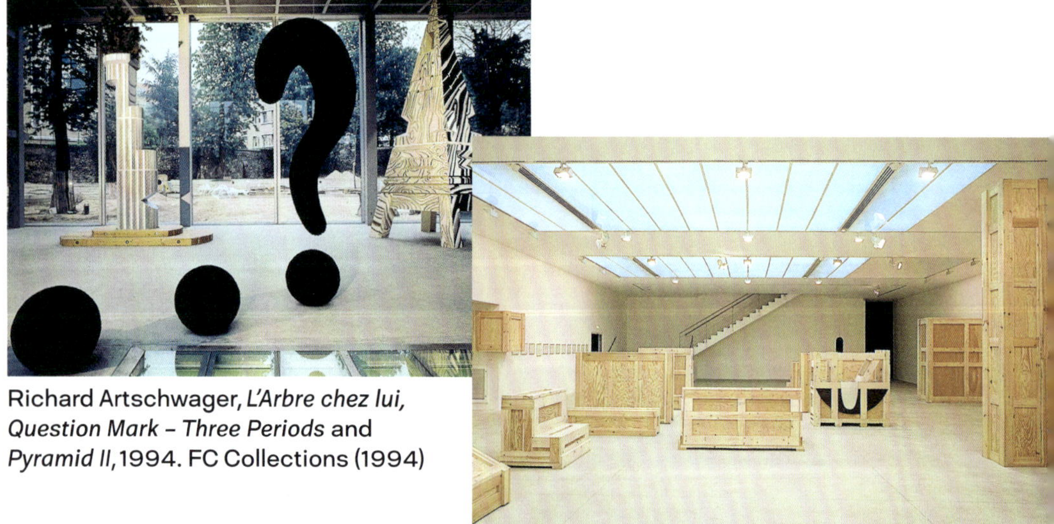

Richard Artschwager, *Archipelago, 8 Crates*, 1994
FC Collections (1994)

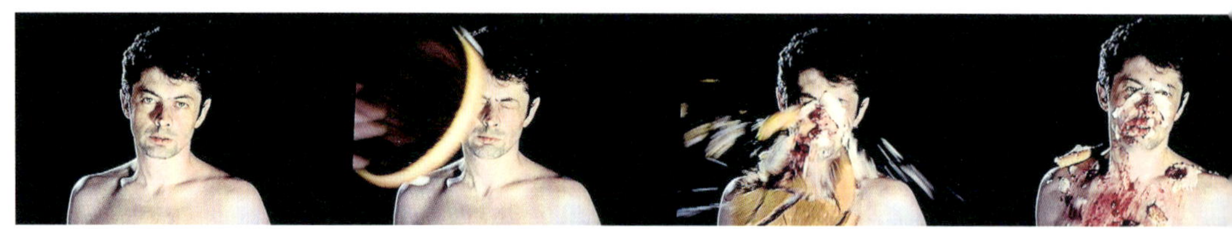

Pierrick Sorin, *La Bataille des tartes*, 1994. FC Collections (1994)

For his second exhibition at the Fondation Cartier, Raymond Hains made use of names, places, circumstances, and events to create a new ensemble of visual puns. The title *Les 3 Cartier* refers to the Saint-Malo navigator Jacques Cartier who discovered Canada in 1534, to the Cartier saga, and especially to Jacques Cartier in whose London office, General de Gaulle wrote the appeal of June 18, 1940. In French, it also evokes, in its pronunciation, the former Parisian department store, Aux Trois-Quartiers.

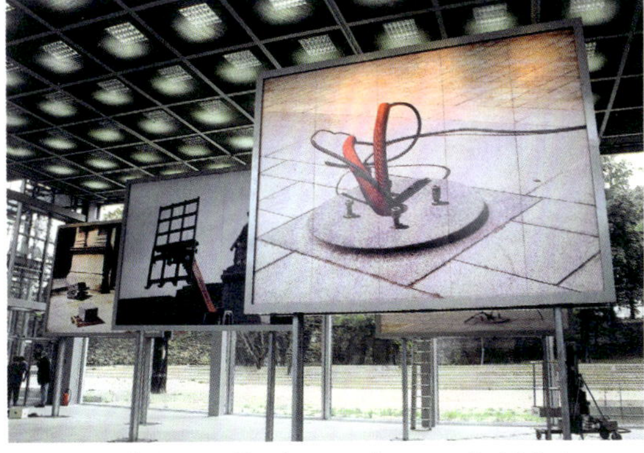

Raymond Hains, *Sculpture de trottoir*, 1994

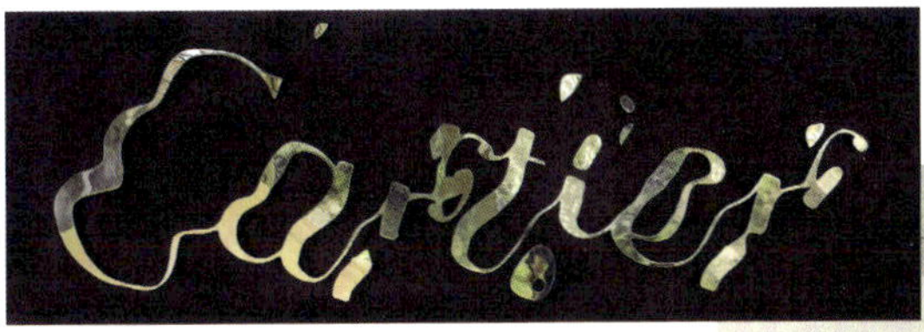

Raymond Hains, *Hommage à Jacques Cartier 1884–1942*, 1994
FC Collections (1994)

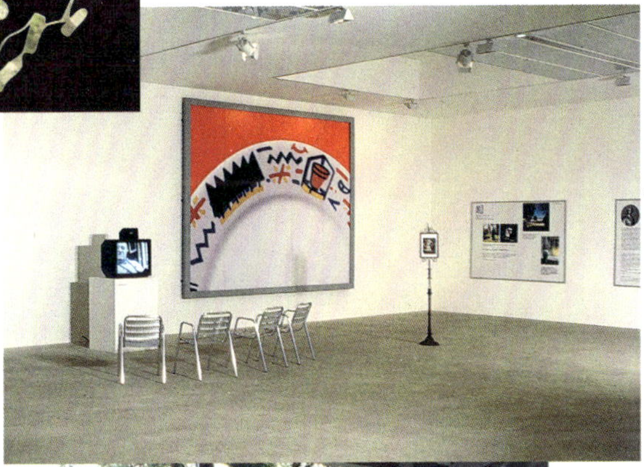

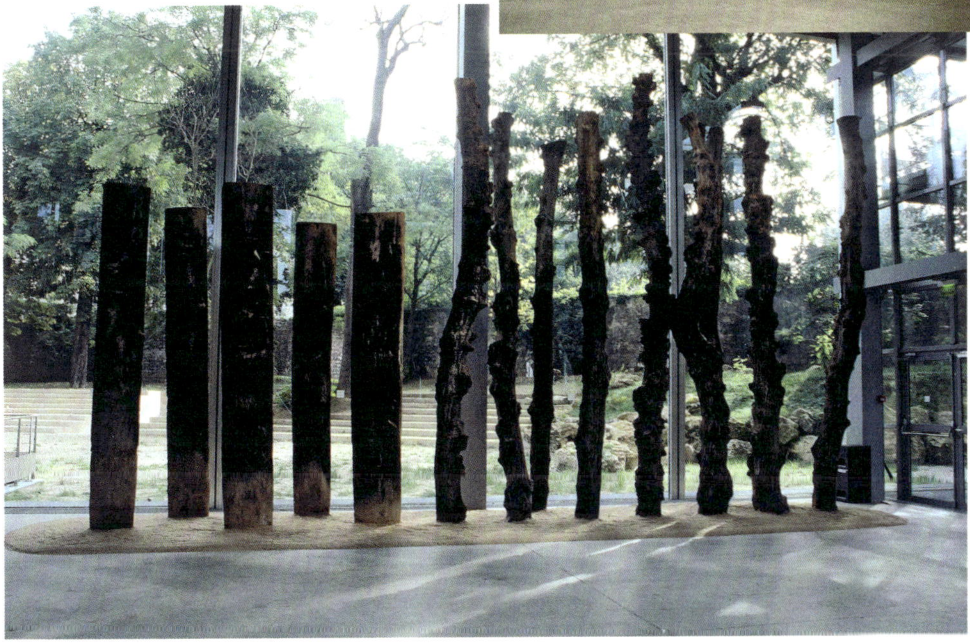

Raymond Hains, *15 Brise-lames de Saint-Malo, plage du Sillon*, 1994
FC Collections (1994)

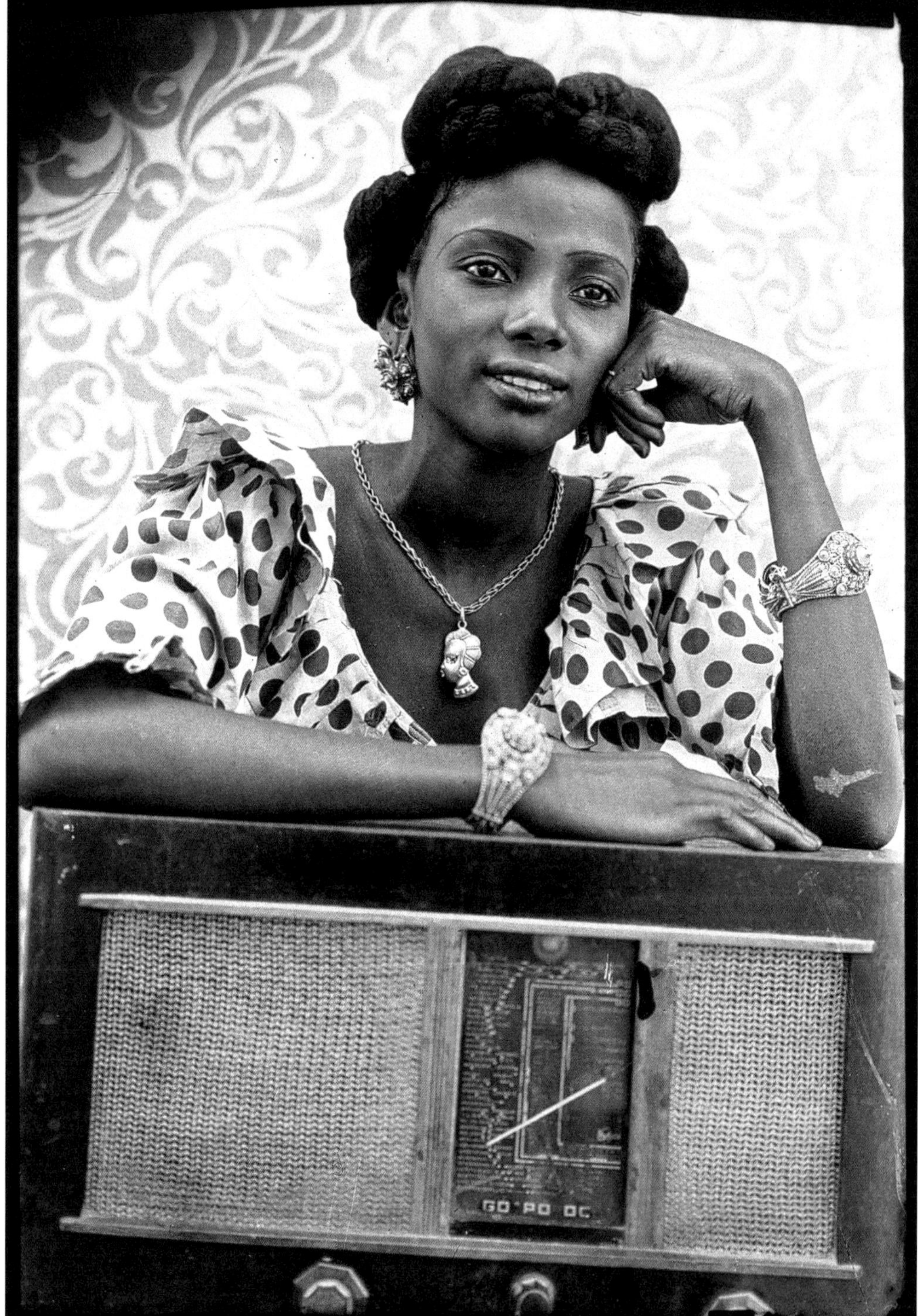

The Fondation Cartier presented the first solo exhibition of Seydou Keita, bringing together some 40 never-before-seen photos, taken in the 1950s and 1960s.
Seydou Keita, *Untitled, Bamako*, 1949–1964. FC Collections (1995)

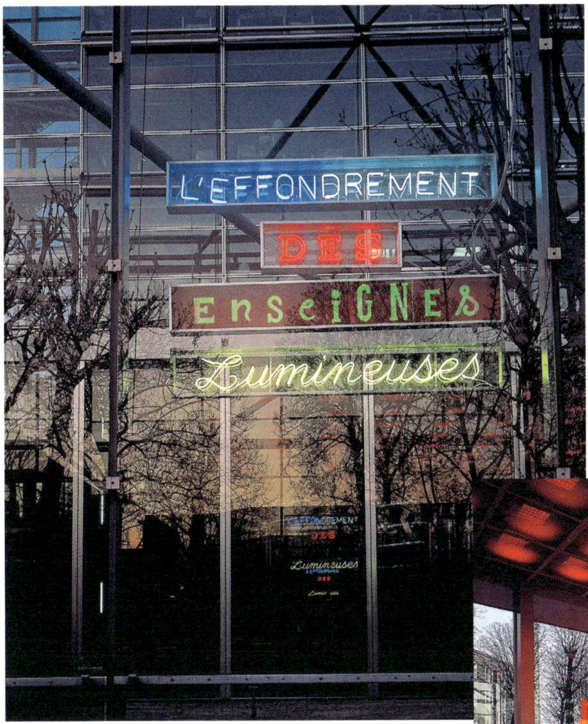

Jean-Michel Alberola,
Enseigne extérieure, 1995

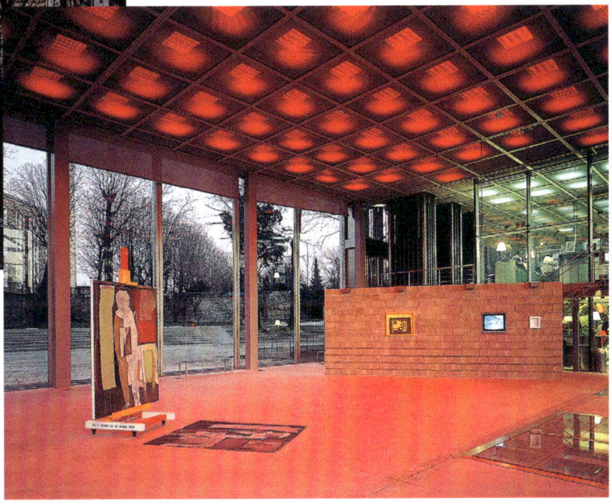

For the exhibition *L'Effondrement des enseignes lumineuses*, Jean-Michel Alberola presented a group of works, encompassing painting, sculpture, and installation.

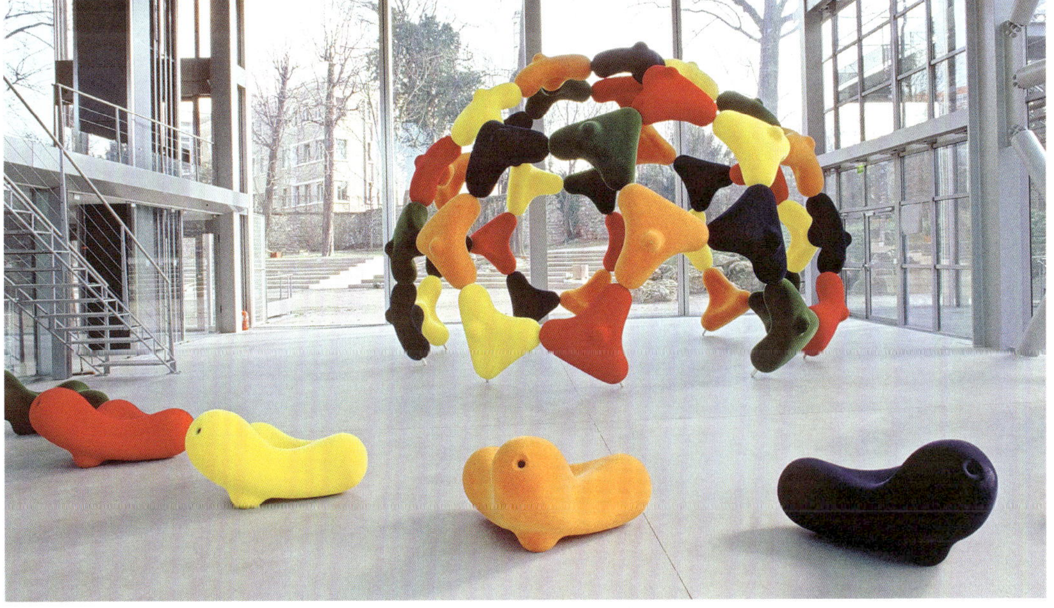

View of Marc Newson's exhibition *Bucky, de la chimie au design*

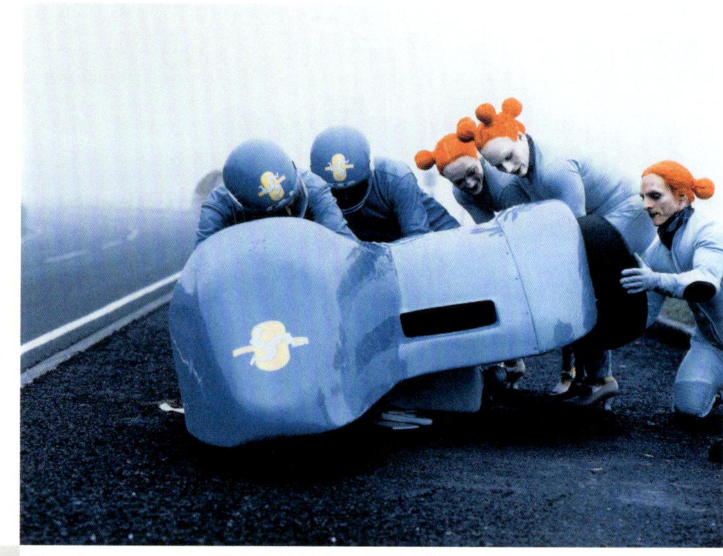

Matthew Barney, *CREMASTER 4: Triple Option*, 1994
FC Collections (1995)

The Fondation Cartier, coproducer of the film *CREMASTER 4*, organized Matthew Barney's first solo exhibition in Europe.

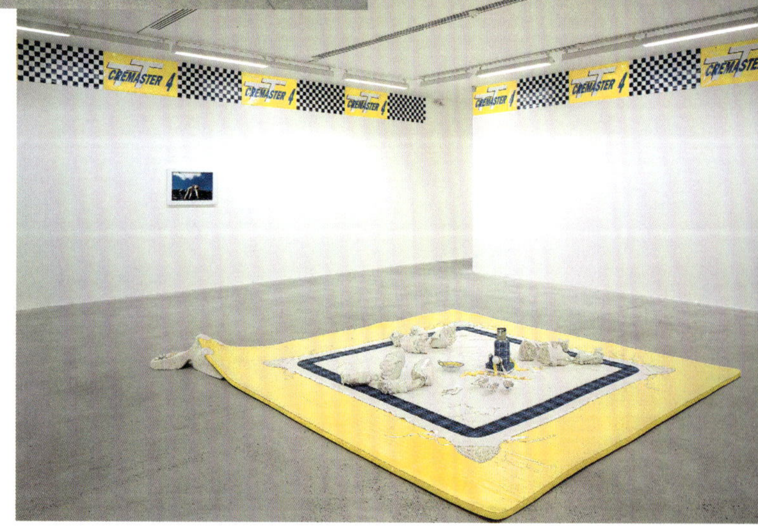

View of the installation *CREMASTER 4: Field of the Ascending Fearie*, 1995. FC Collections (1995)

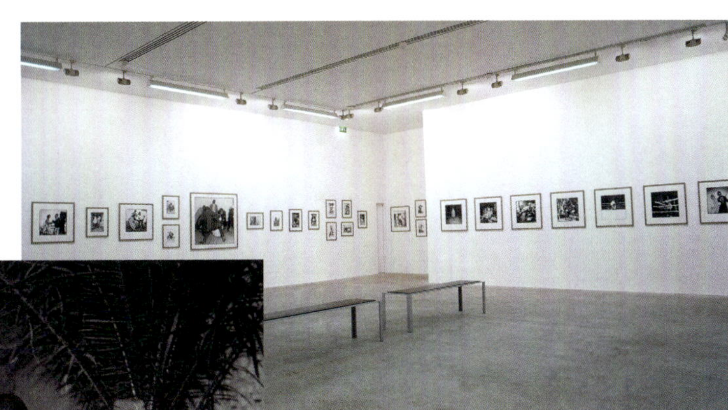

View of Malick Sidibé's exhibition

Malick Sidibé, *Nuit de Noël (Happy Club),* 1963
FC Collections (2004)

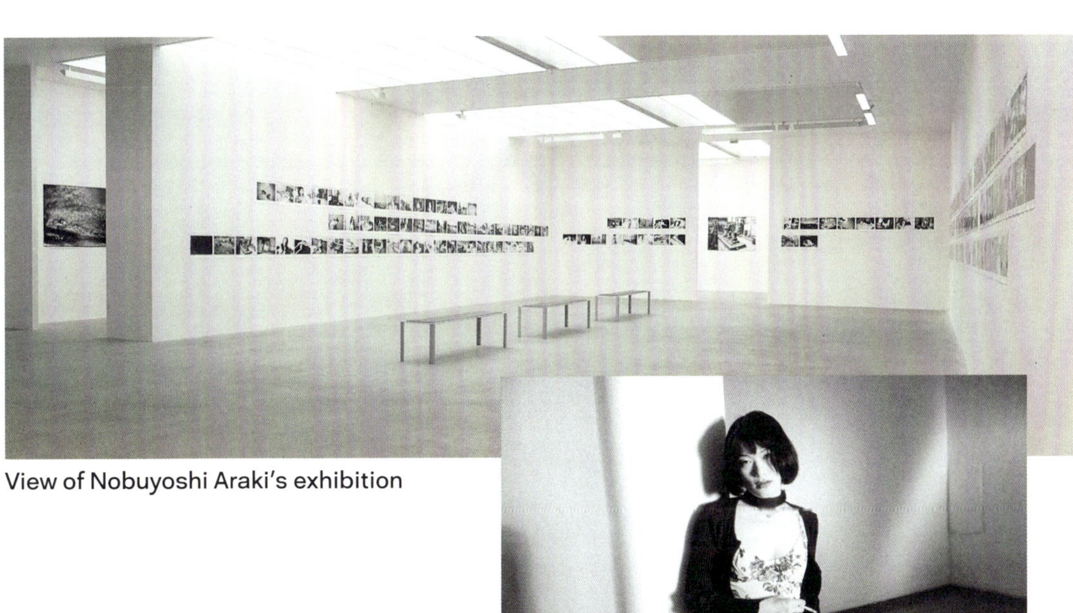

View of Nobuyoshi Araki's exhibition

Nobuyoshi Araki, *Journal intime #21,* 1994
FC Collections (1995)

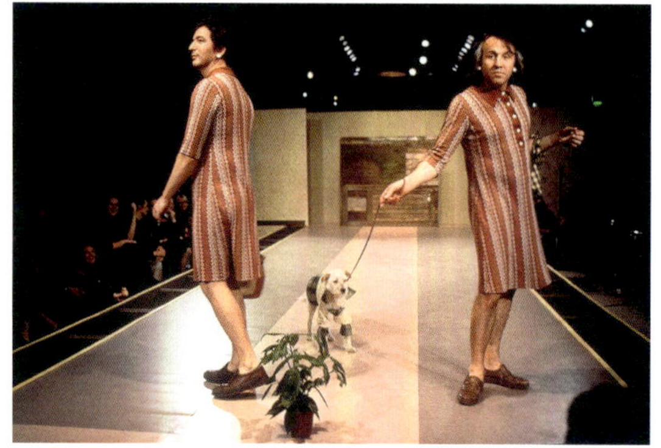

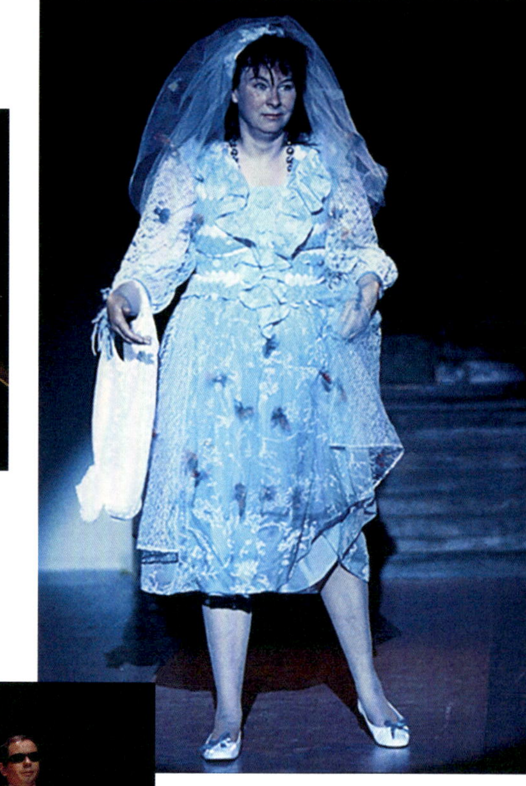

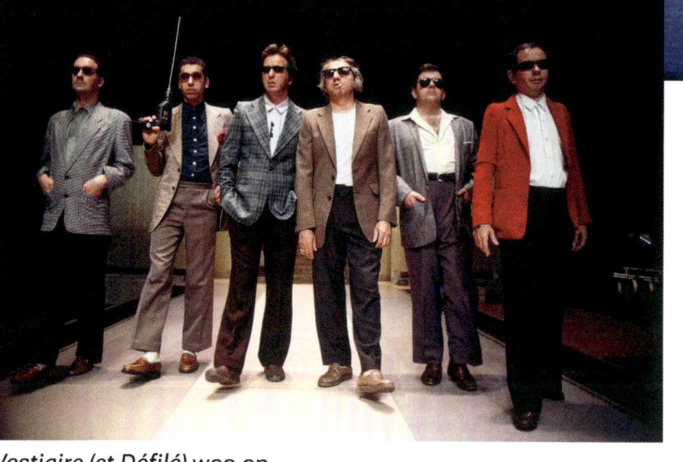

Vestiaire (et Défilé) was an exhibition conceived by Macha Makeïeff as a space of openness and encounters. Over the course of several Nomadic Nights, she and Jérôme Deschamps invited artists from the French comedy troupe Les Deschiens to produce a performance-fashion show.

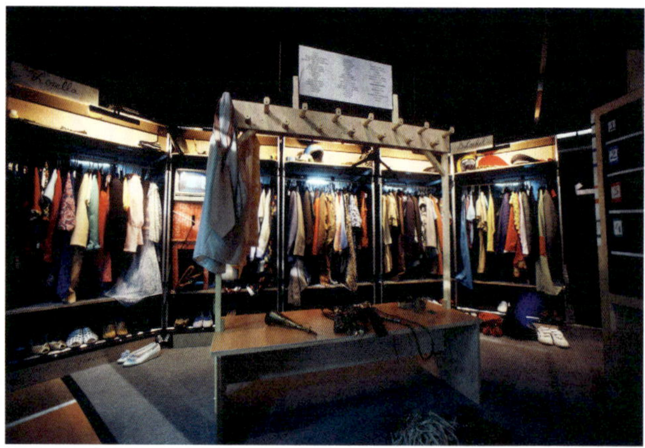

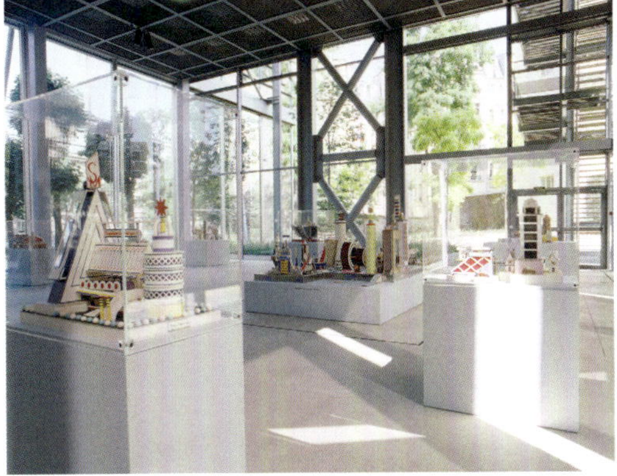

Presented on the ground floor, the imaginary sculptures of Bodys Isek Kingelez, or his "extreme maquettes" entered into a dialogue with the work of Jean Tinguely, on display at the same time.

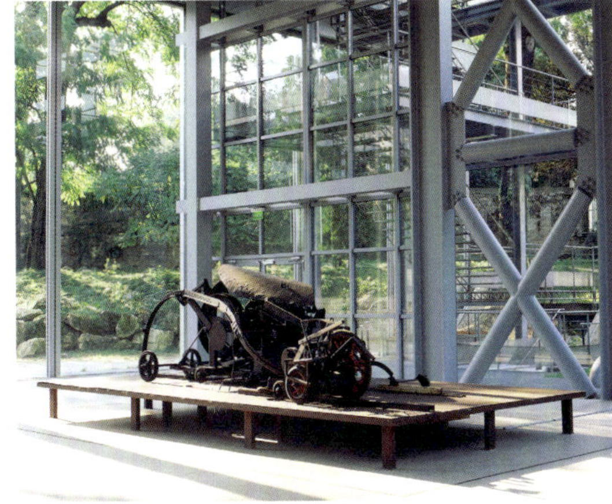

Jean Tinguely, *Tombeau de kamikaze*, 1969

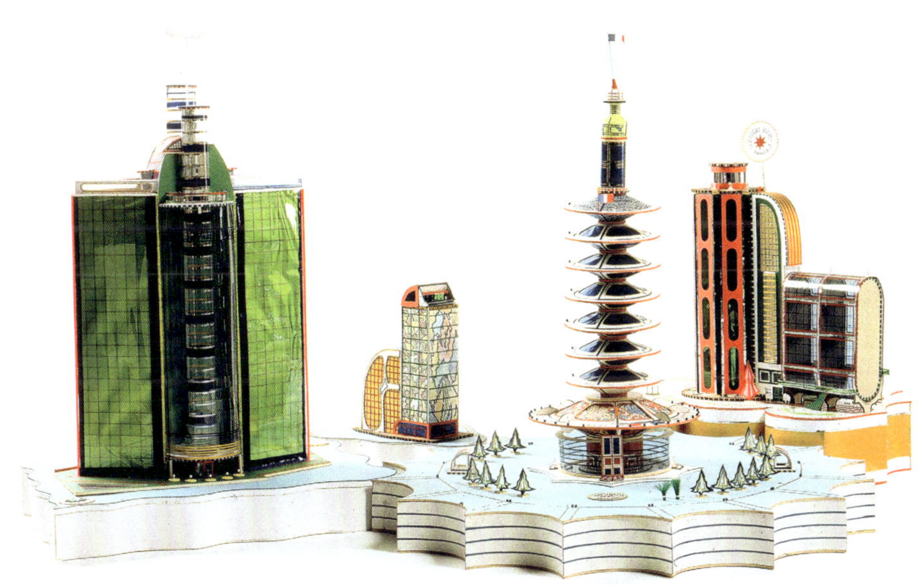

Bodys Isek Kingelez, *Hommage à Jean Nouvel*, 1995
FC Collections (1996)

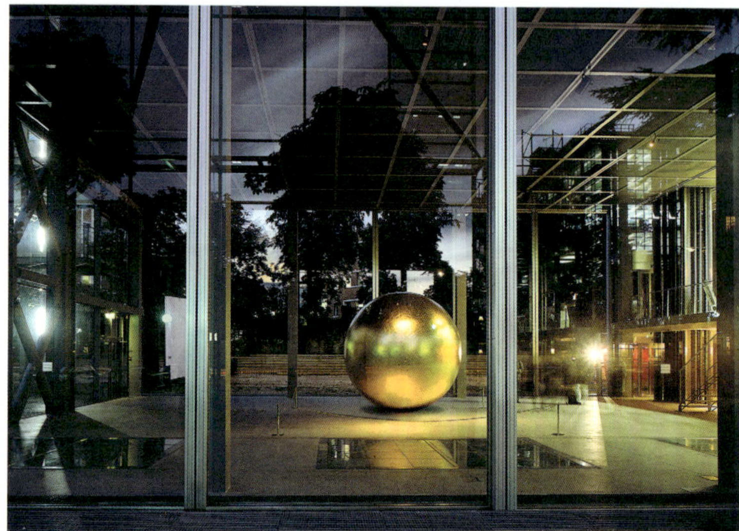

James Lee Byars, *The Monument to Language*, 1995
FC Collections (1995)

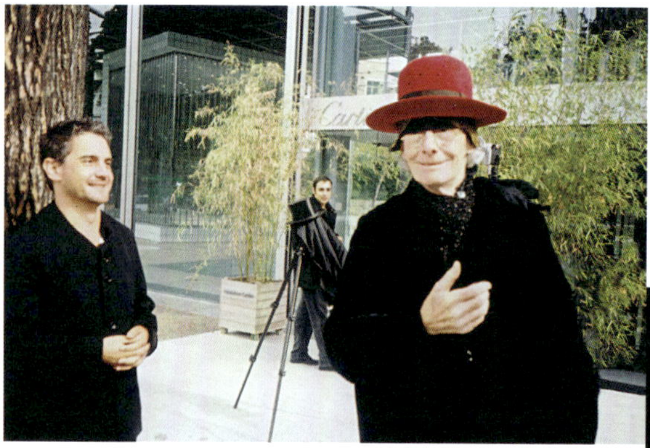

Hervé Chandès and James Lee Byars, 1996

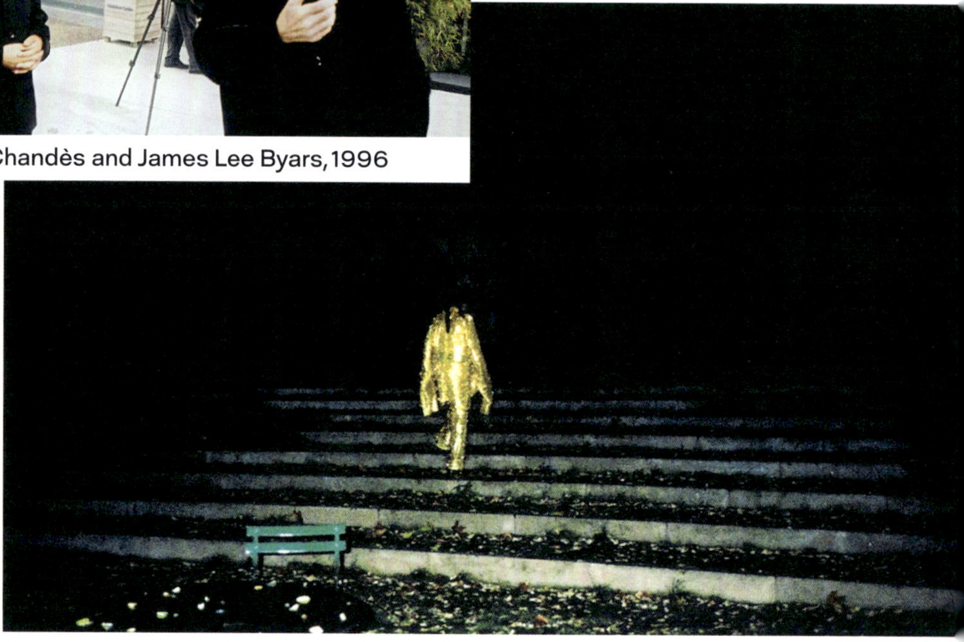

One year after the exhibition, on September 17, 1996, James Lee Byars
returned to the Fondation Cartier to create a performance titled *Amour*,
which would be his last public appearance.

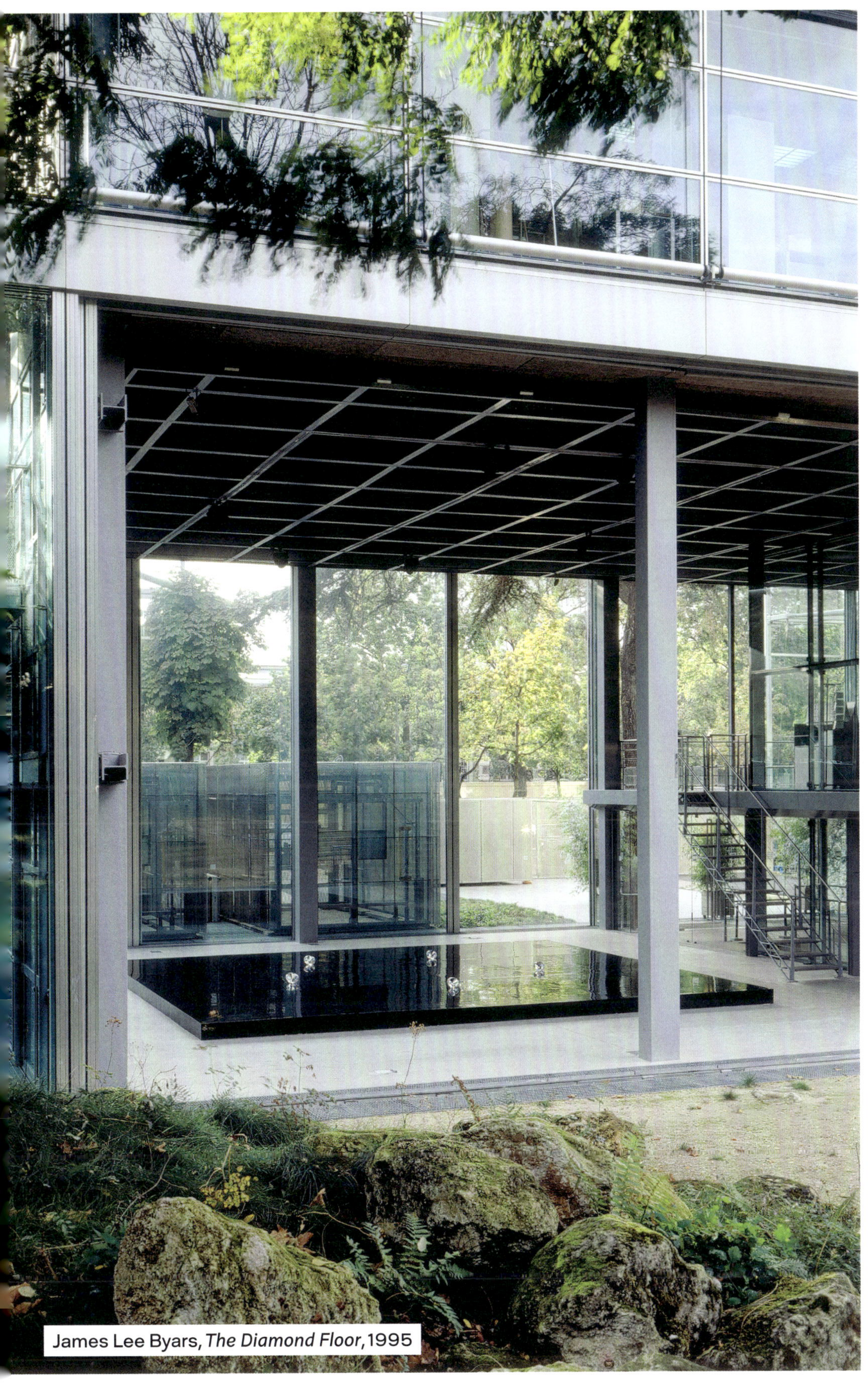

James Lee Byars, *The Diamond Floor*, 1995

Vija Celmins, *Night Sky #11*, 1995. FC Collections (1996)

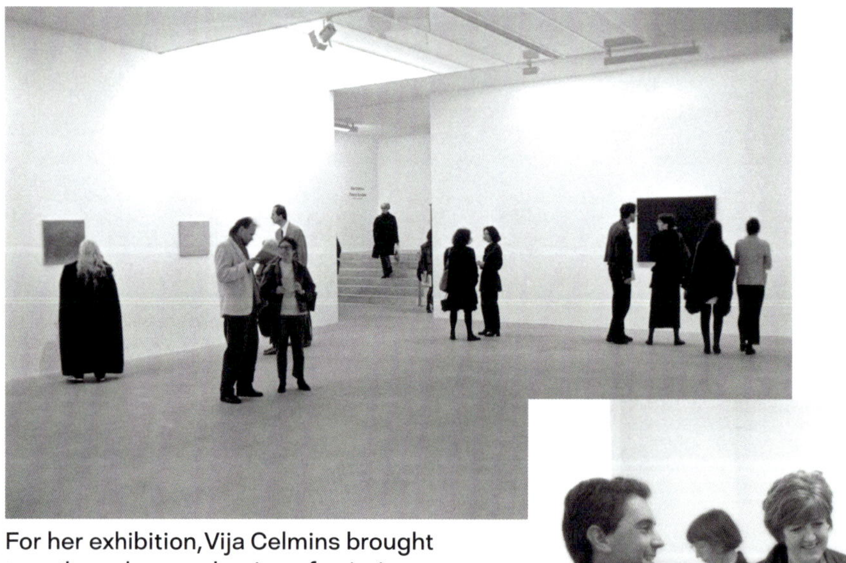

For her exhibition, Vija Celmins brought together a large selection of paintings and drawings evoking unlimited and infinite spaces.

Hervé Chandès, Vija Celmins, and James Lingwood at the exhibition opening

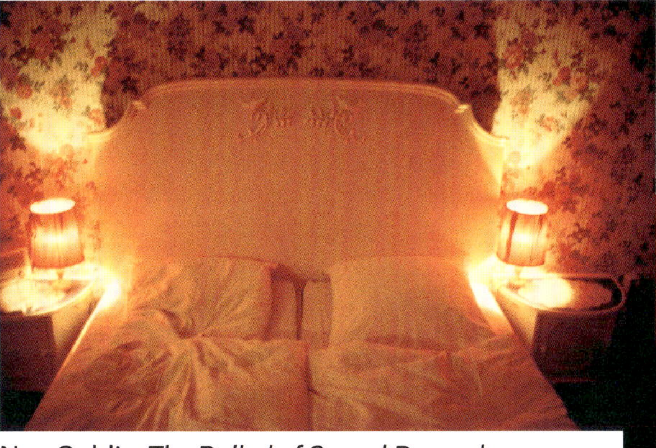

Nan Goldin, *The Ballad of Sexual Dependency*, 1979–1995. FC Collections (1996)

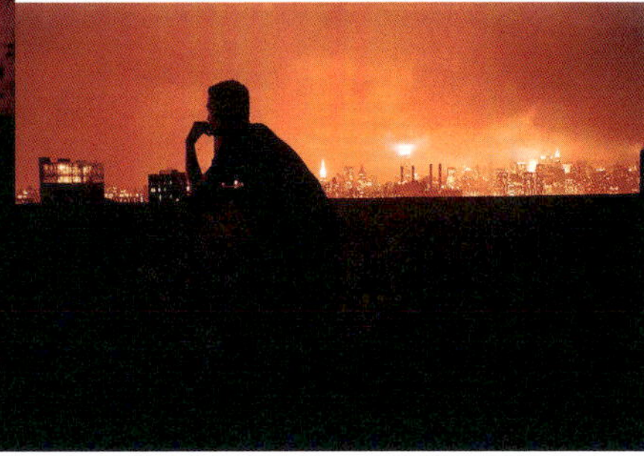

Wolfgang Tillmans, 1990–1995: *Paul, New York*, 1994. FC Collections (1995)

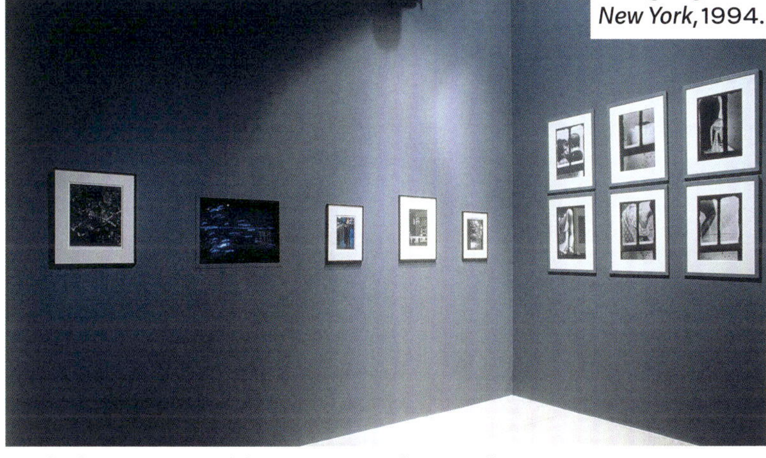

Works by Berenice Abbott, Raymond Depardon, Louis Faurer, and Merry Alpern

"One of the exhibitions that I really liked in terms of the understanding of what constitutes the spaces of the Fondation Cartier was *By Night*. Here, the entire ground floor was plunged into darkness, completely shutting out daylight for three months, this was part of the game." Jean Nouvel

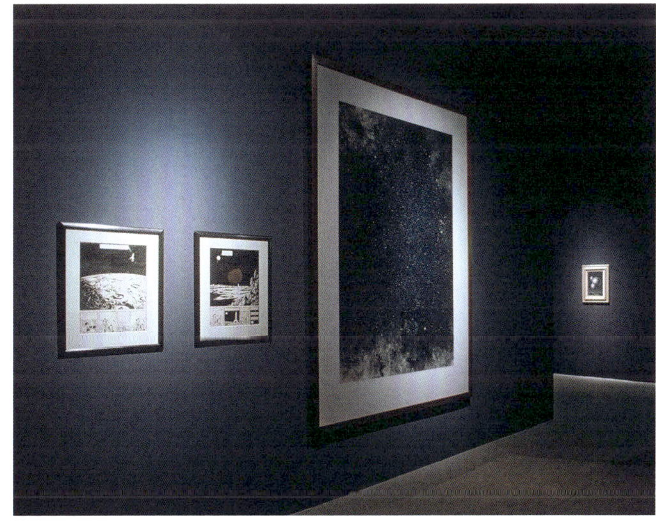

Works by Hergé, Thomas Ruff, and René Magritte

Tatsuo Miyajima

Running Time (U-CAR) and Time Go Round

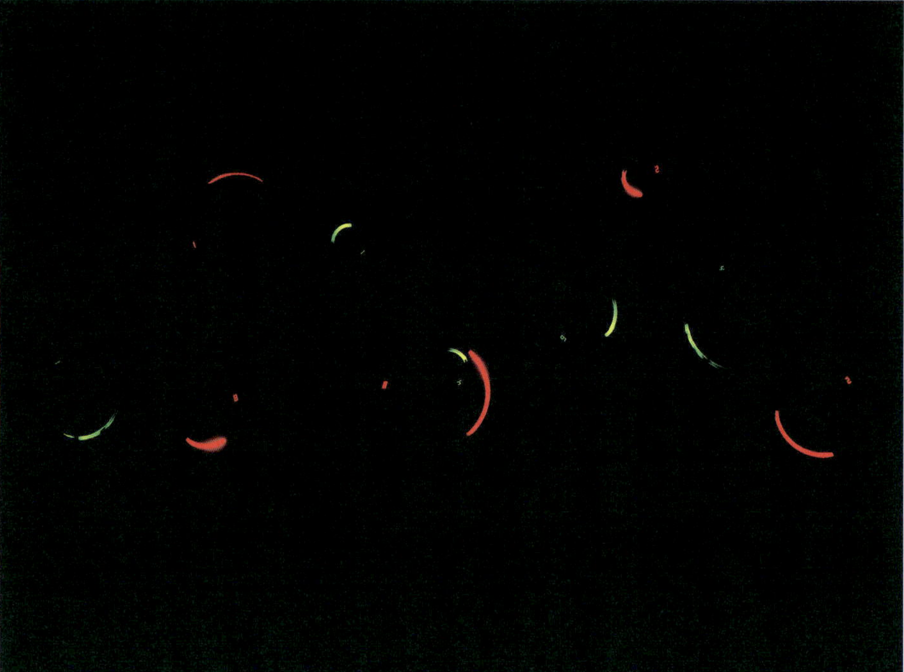

For his first solo exhibition in Paris, Tatsuo Miyajima presented his works *Running Time (U-CAR)*, made in 1993, and *Time Go Round*, produced specially for the Fondation Cartier in 1995.
Tatsuo Miyajima, *Time Go Round*, 1995
FC Collections (1995)

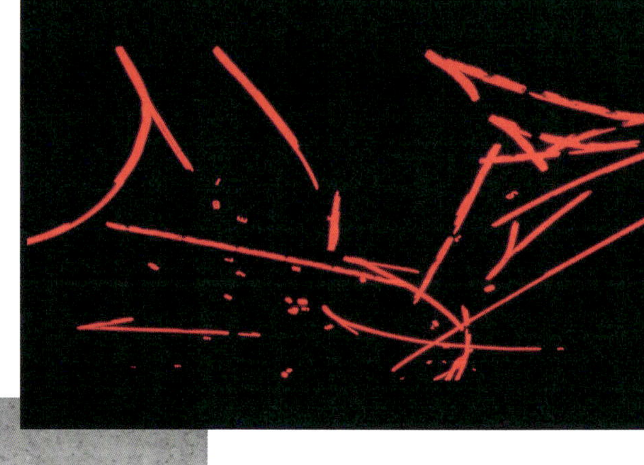

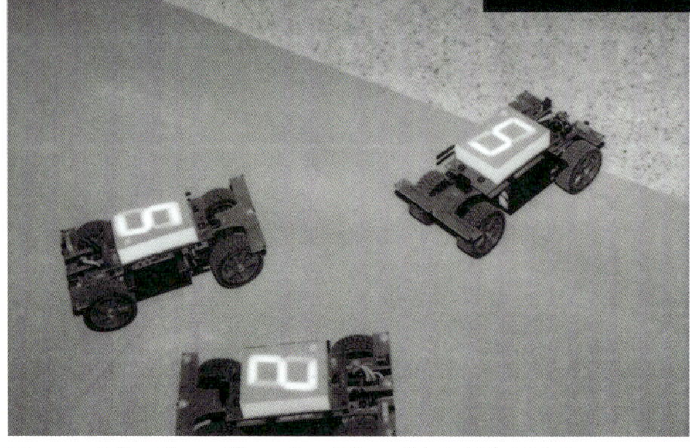

Tatsuo Miyajima, *Running Time (U-CAR)*, 1993

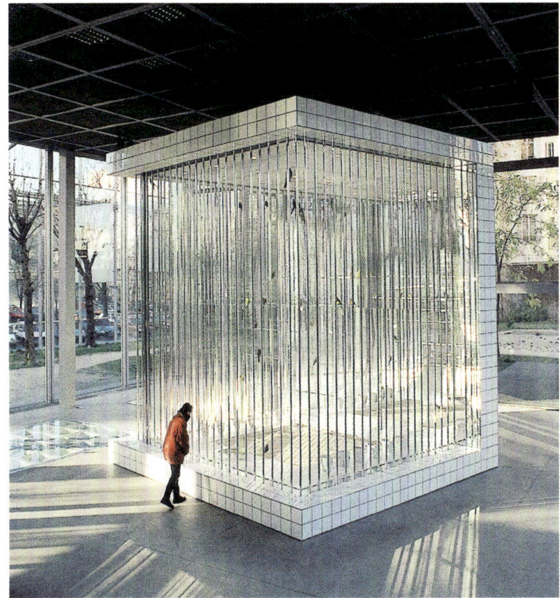

Jean Pierre Raynaud, *La Volière*, 1996
FC Collections (1996)

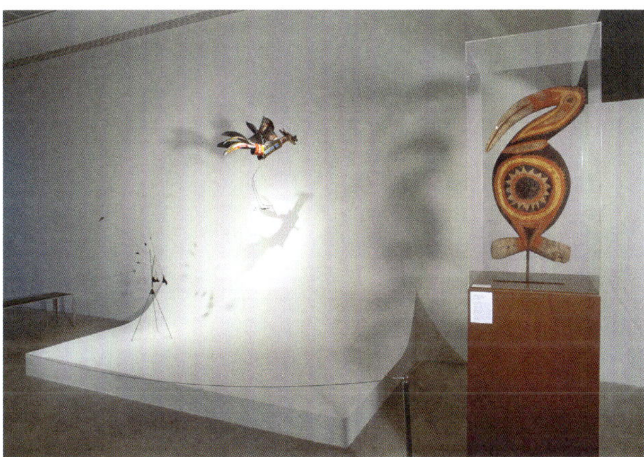

Alexander Calder, *L'Autruche*, 1945 and
La Touraine, c. 1960. Maprik bird, Abelam culture,
New Guinea

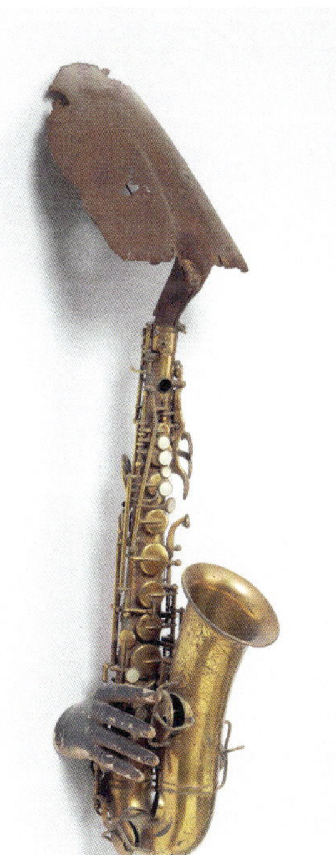

David Hammons, *Bird*, 1973

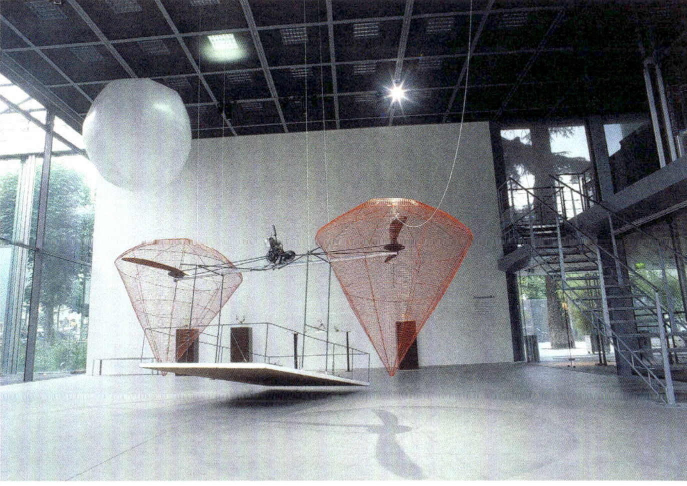

Panamarenko, *Bernouilli*, 1995

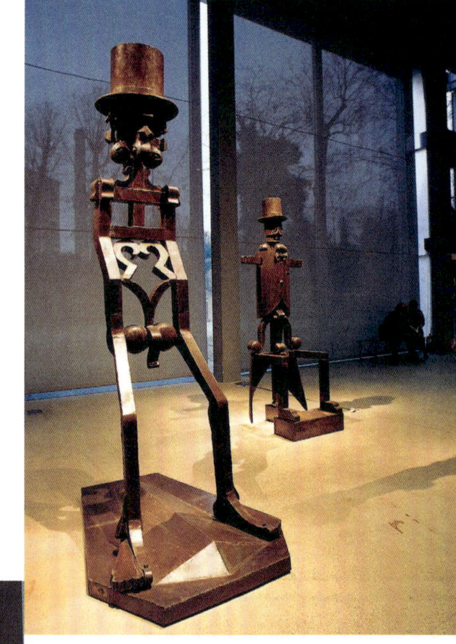

Patrick Vilaire, *Baron Samedi*, 1992
and *Baron Lacroix*, 1989

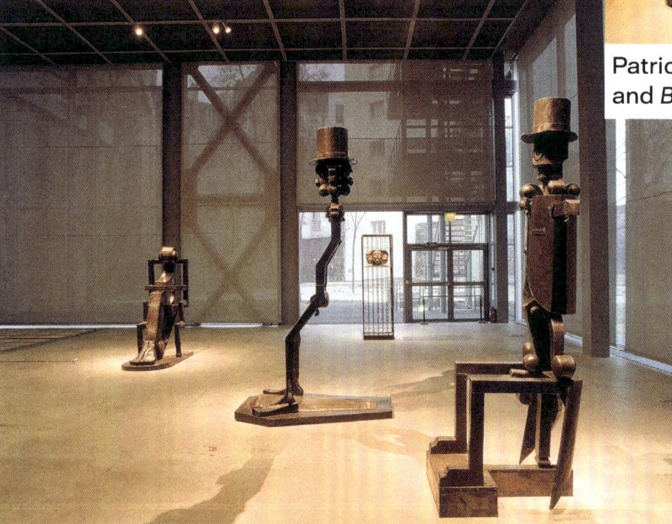

For his first solo exhibition at the Fondation Cartier,
Patrick Vilaire presented seven monumental sculptures.
Seven works with a single subject: death.

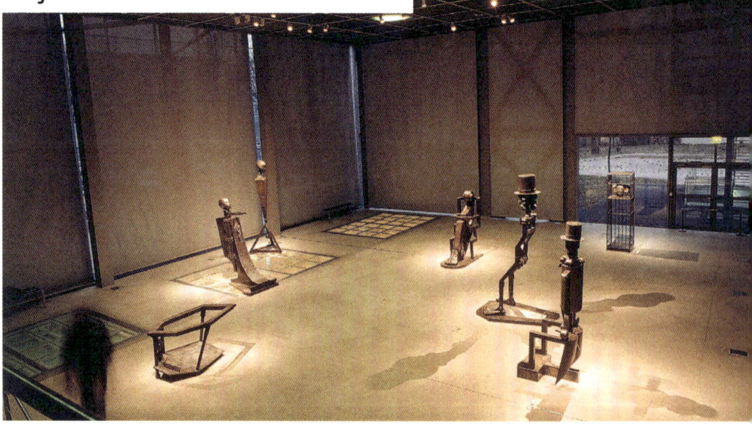

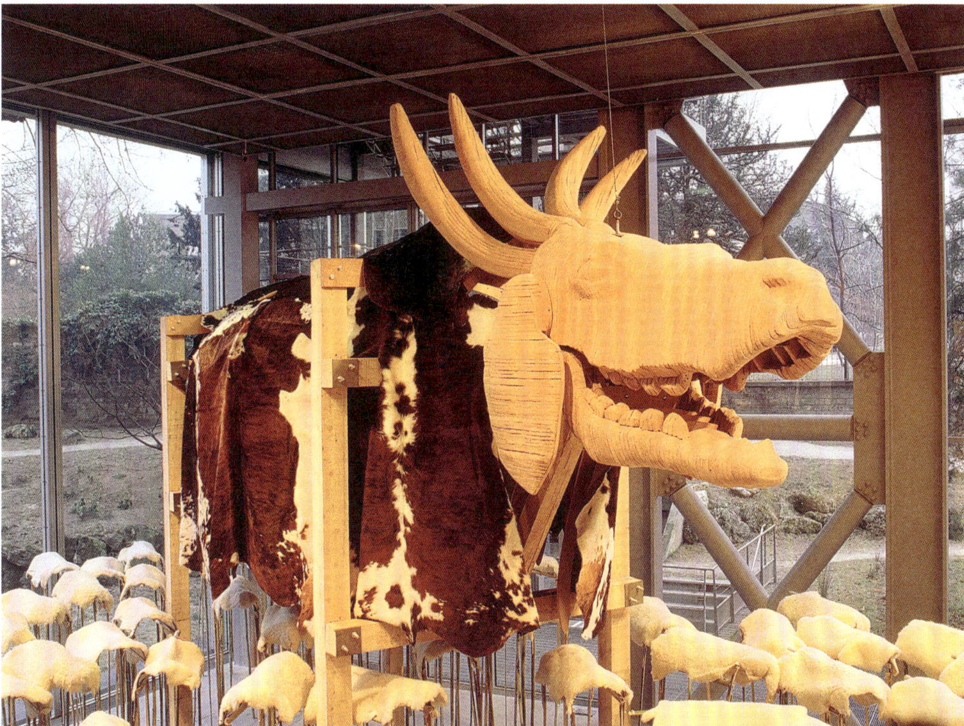

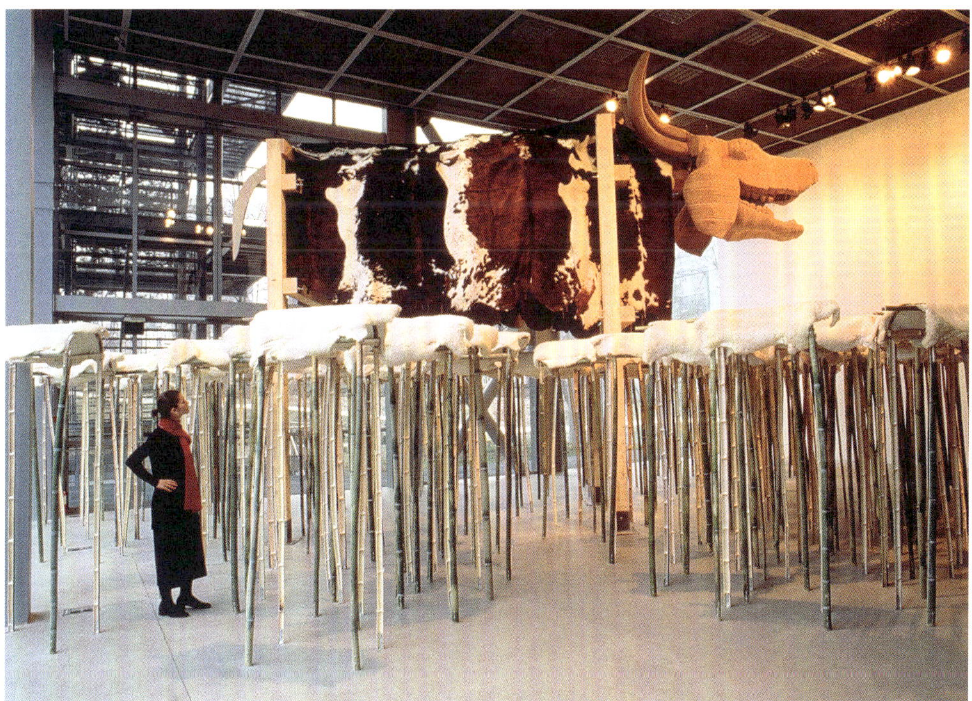

Specially created for the Fondation Cartier, the installation *Péril de mouton* was designed as an invitation to move in and around the installation.

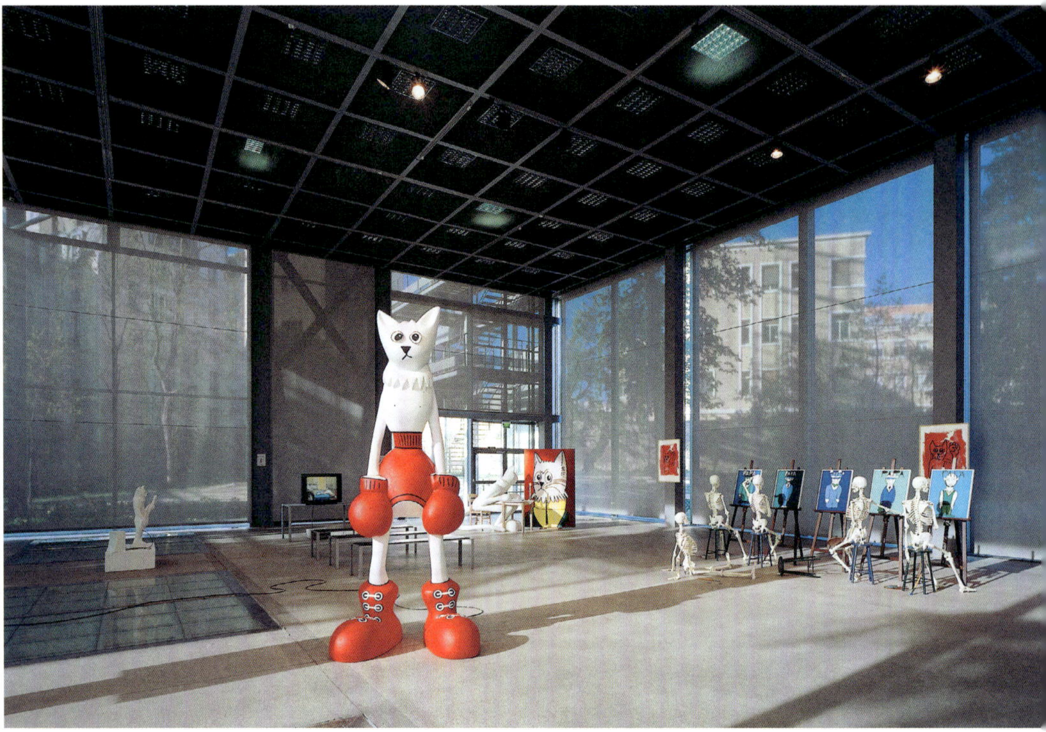

Alain Séchas, *El Pacificador*, 1996

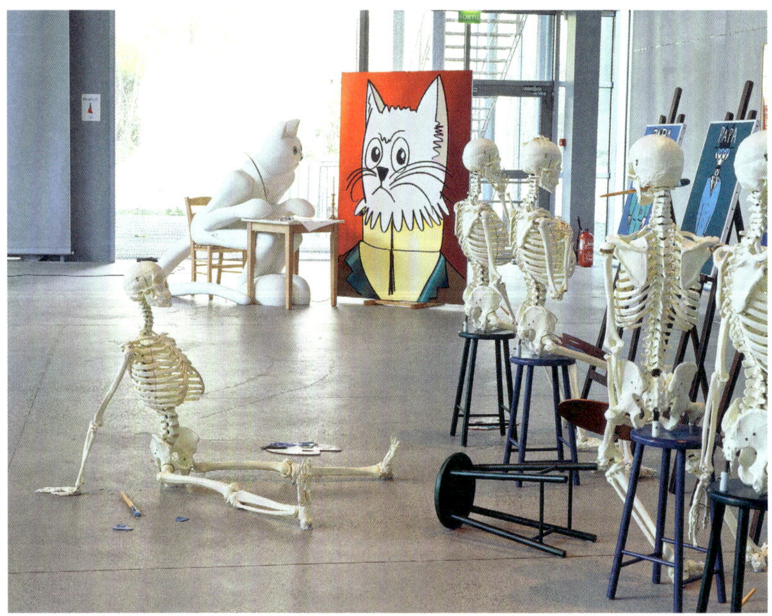

Alain Séchas, *Les Papas*, 1995. FC Collections (1997)

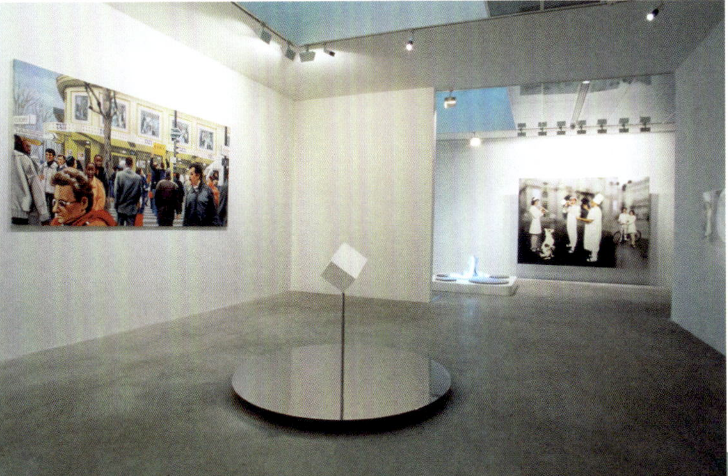

The exhibition *Coïncidence(s)* questioned
the links between reality and fiction
thanks to the works of 14 artists. Above:
works by François Curlet, Didier Marcel,
Franck Scurti, and Xavier Veilhan

Xavier Veilhan, *Les Haltérophiles*, 1997
FC Collections (1998)

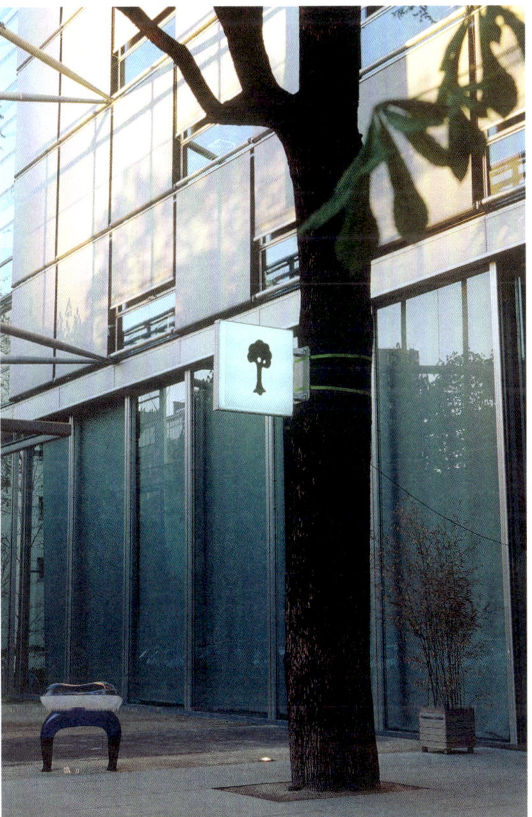

Works by Judith Bartolani and Claude Caillol,
and by François Curlet

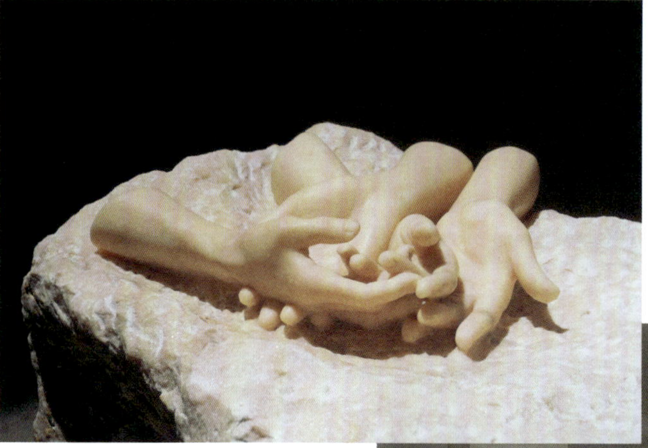

Louise Bourgeois,
Untitled (no. 2), 1996

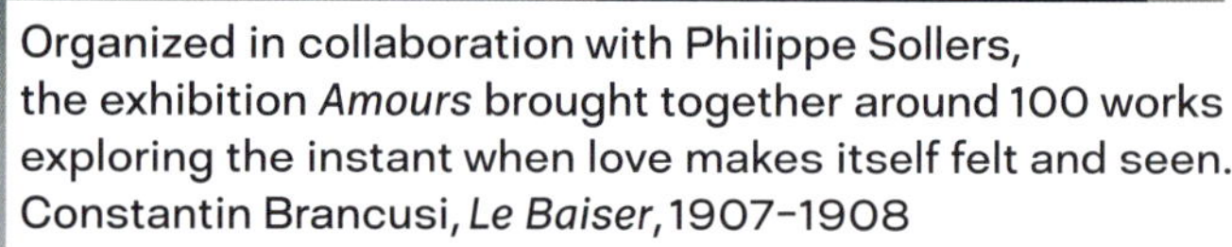

Organized in collaboration with Philippe Sollers,
the exhibition *Amours* brought together around 100 works
exploring the instant when love makes itself felt and seen.
Constantin Brancusi, *Le Baiser*, 1907-1908

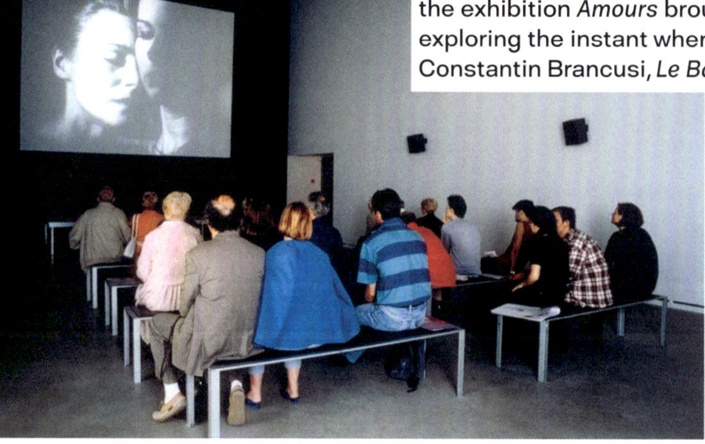

A projection room hosted a montage of film excerpts curated
by André S. Labarthe titled *Amours, mensonges et météo*.
Monitors placed among the works also projected several films
specially made for the occasion, notably by Olivier Assayas,
Claire Denis, and Hal Hartley.

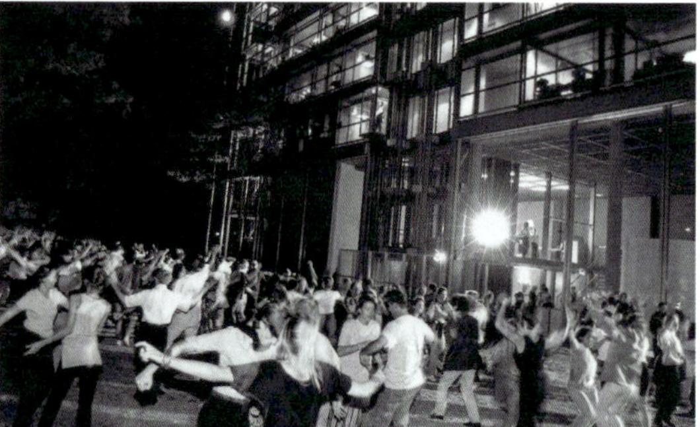

Nomadic Night, *Le Bal moderne*, June 5, 1997

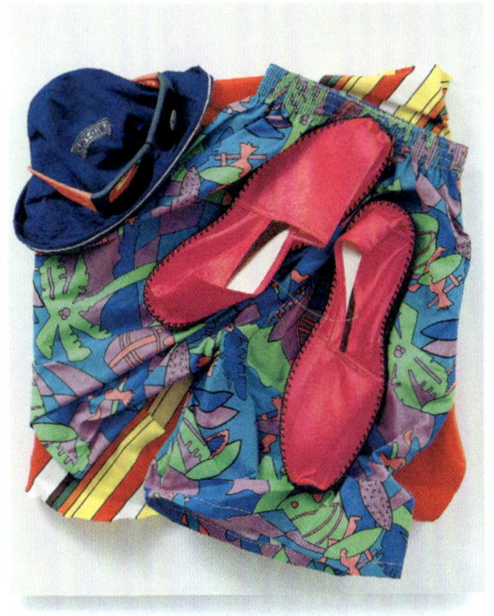

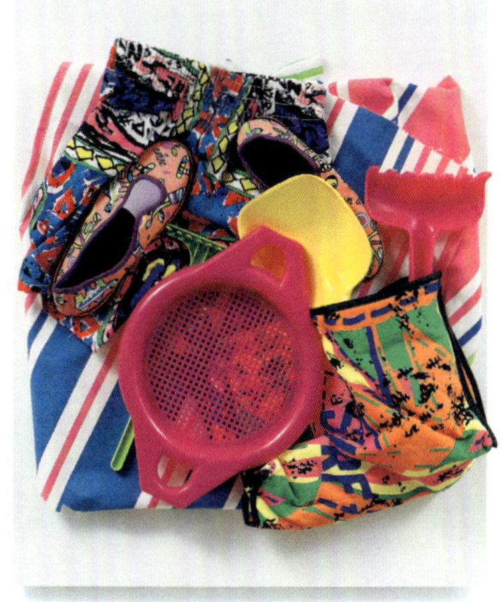

Gérard Deschamps, *Un arbre*, 1989
FC Collections (1998)

Gérard Deschamps, *Navy-Club*, 1988
FC Collections (1998)

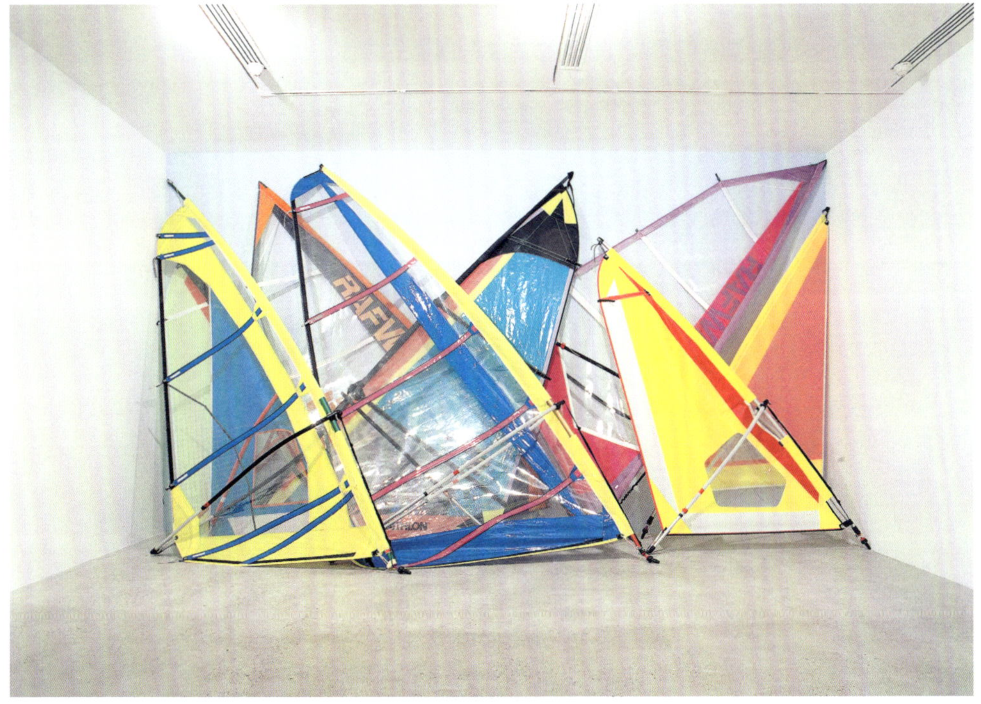

The exhibition *Homo Accessoirus* brought together some 30 works by Gérard
Deschamps, a mixture of colorful textiles hanging from the ceiling or sewn into patchwork.
Gérard Deschamps, *Voiles de planches*, 1998. FC Collections (1998)

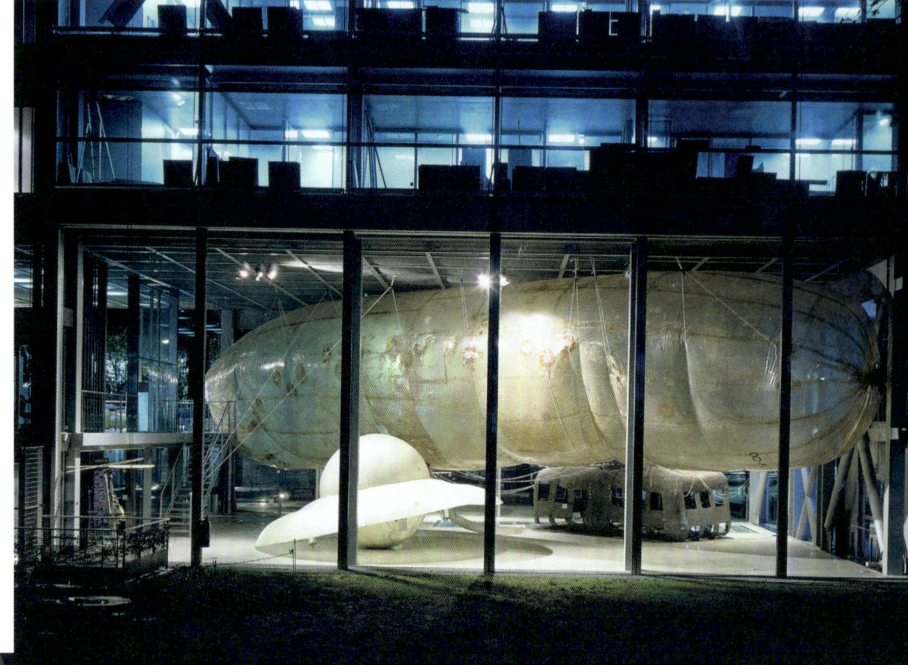

Panamarenko, *Bing of the Ferro Lusto*, 1997, and *The Aeromodeller*, 1971

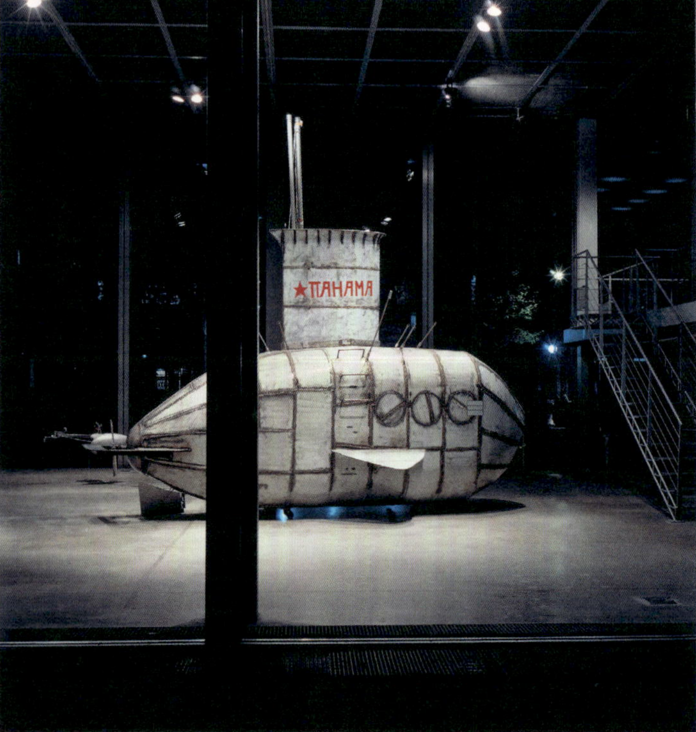

Panamarenko, *Panama, Spitsbergen, Nova Zemblaya*, 1996
FC Collections (1998)

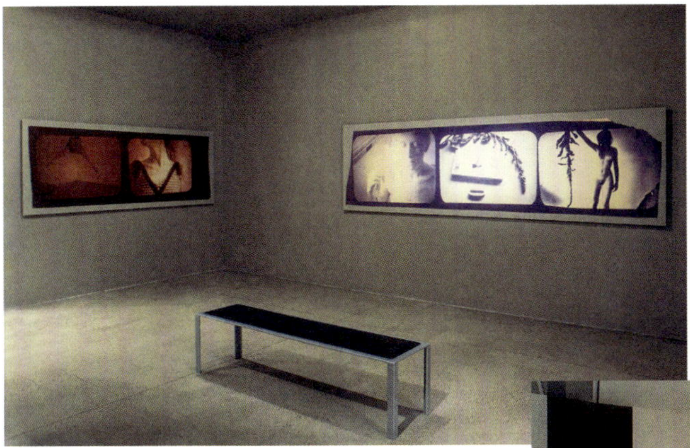

Showcasing the work of Francesca Woodman to a broad public, this exhibition presented some 100 photographs, a dozen large formats on blue or sepia-colored paper, as well as the original layout for the book *Some Disordered Interior Geometries* (1981).

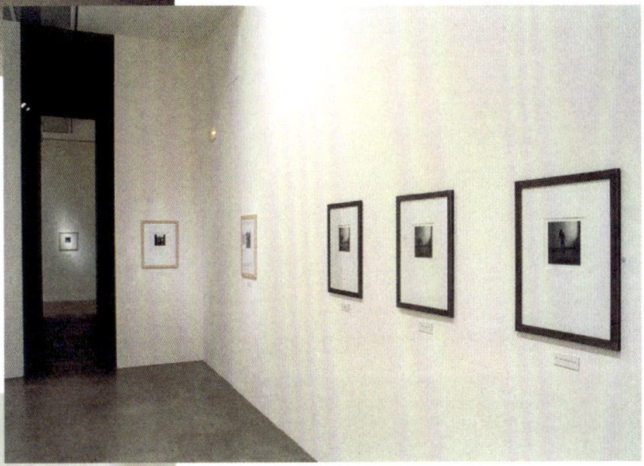

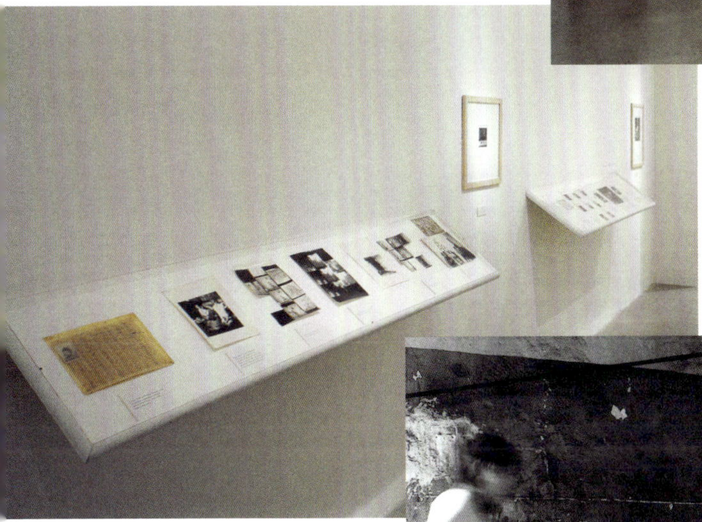

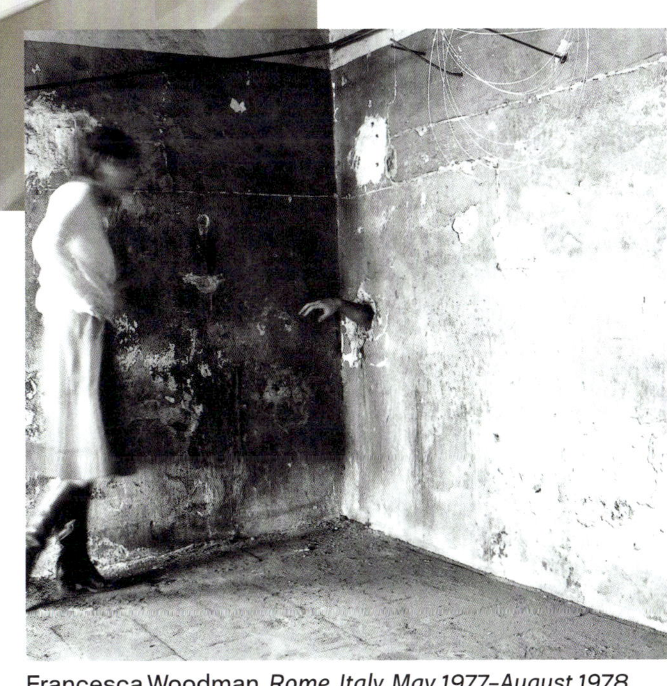

Francesca Woodman, *Rome, Italy, May 1977–August 1978*
FC Collections (1998)

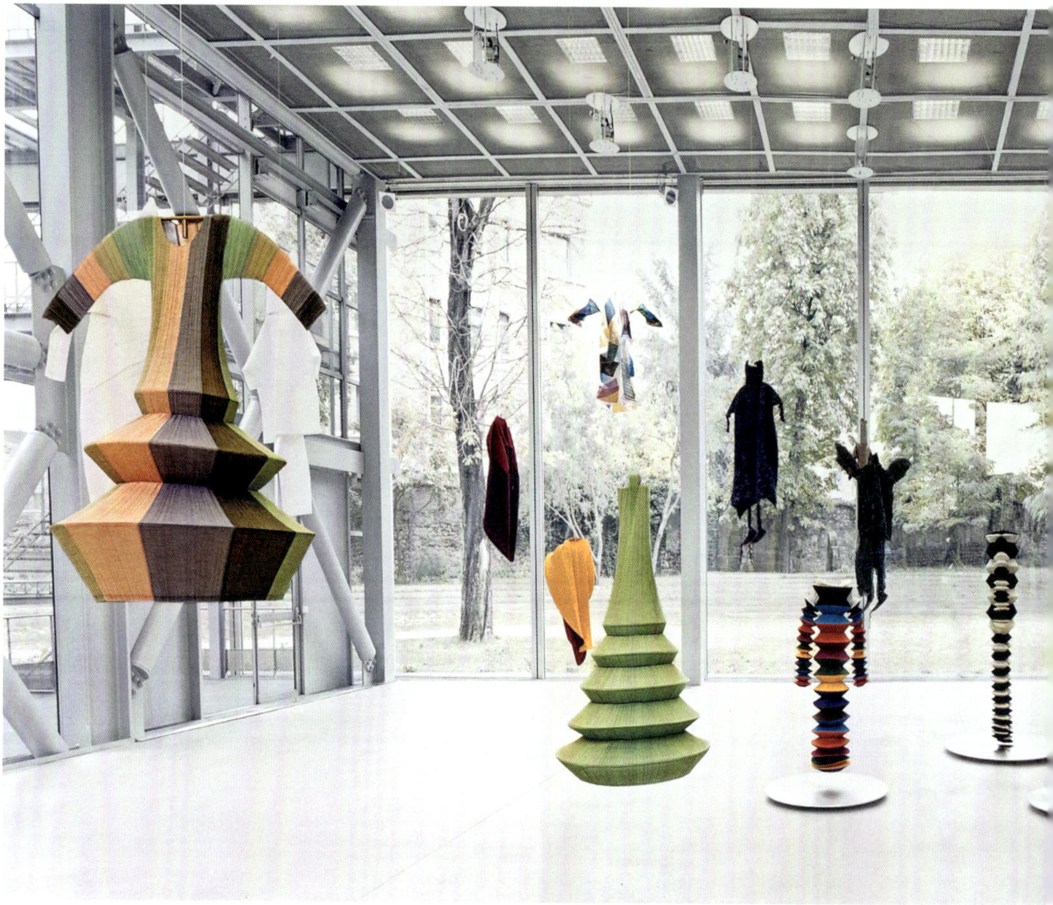

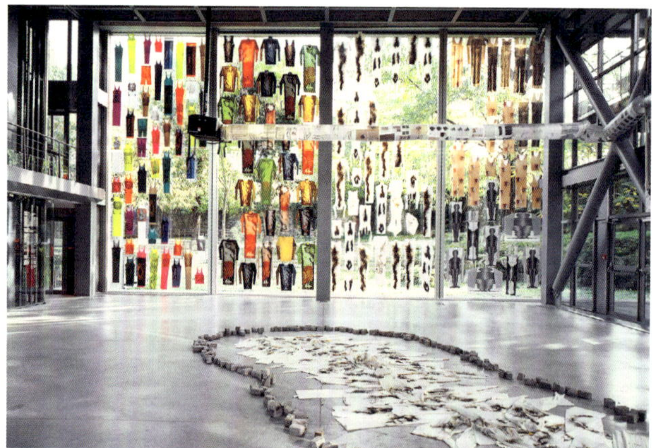

Issey Miyake, *Jumping*, 1998. Installation of clothing in motion

For his exhibition, Issey Miyake presented almost 200 items of clothing from the Pleats Please Issey Miyake collection, created in collaboration with artists Nobuyoshi Araki (1997), Yasumasa Morimura (1996), Cai Guo-Qiang (1998), and Tim Hawkinson (1998). The dresses, pants, and jumpsuits all became elements of a colorful stained glass piece, thus fostering a dialogue with Jean Nouvel's architecture.

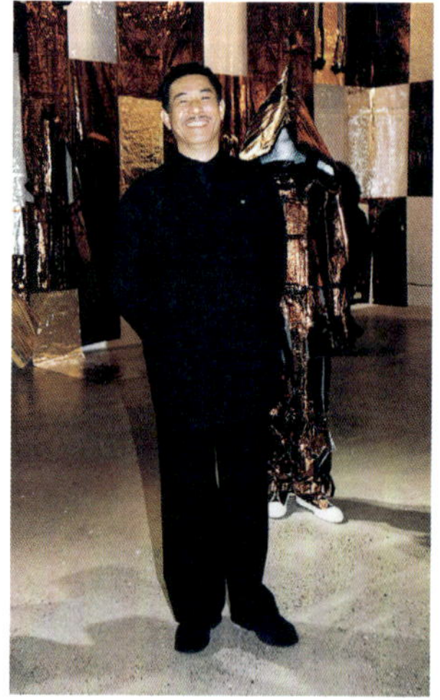

Issey Miyake at the exhibition opening

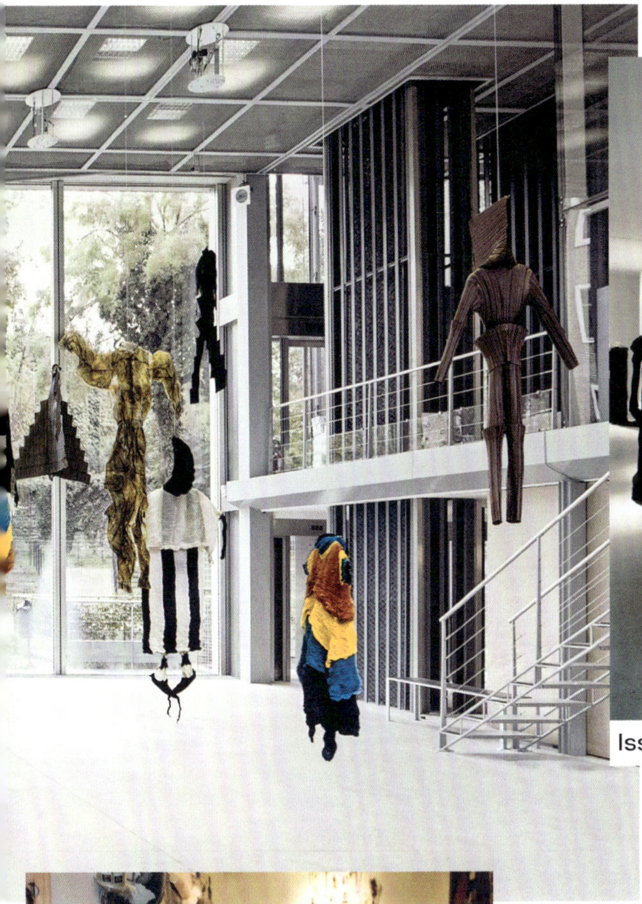

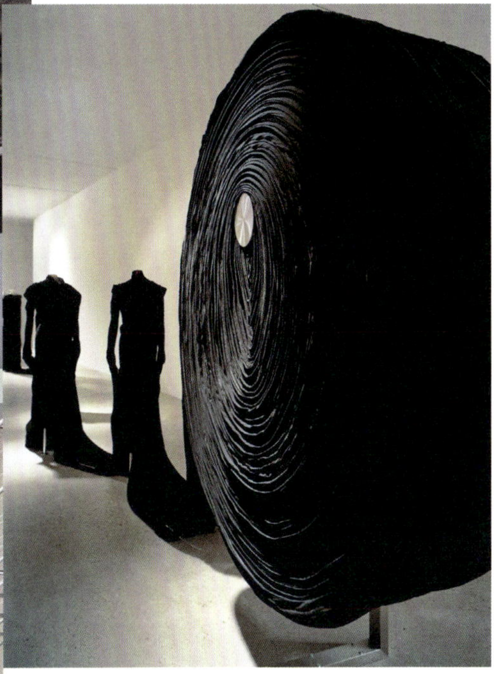

Issey Miyake, *Just Before*, 1998

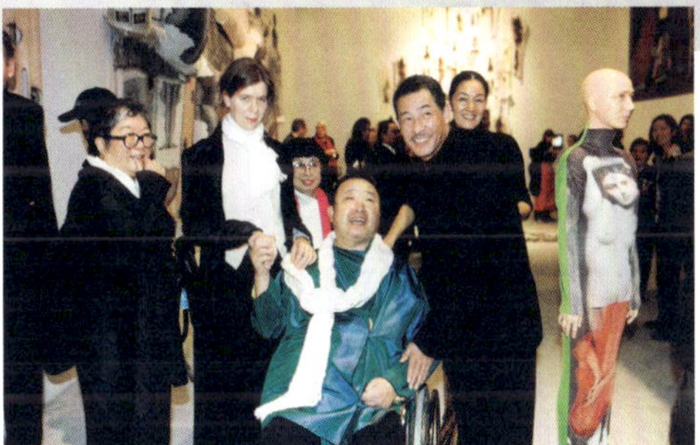

Nam June Paik and Issey Miyake at the opening of the exhibition *Issey Miyake Making Things* at the Ace Gallery, New York, November 1999

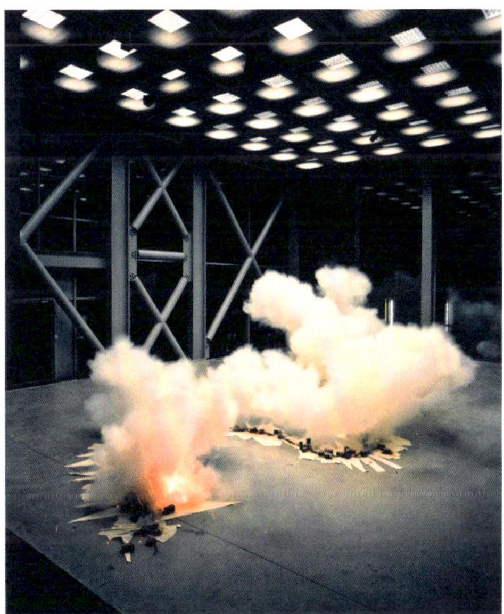

On October 5, 1998, a few days before the opening of the exhibition, Cai Guo-Qiang orchestrated an in-situ explosion, making use of Issey Miyake's creations: *Dragon-Explosion on Issey Miyake Pleats Please.*

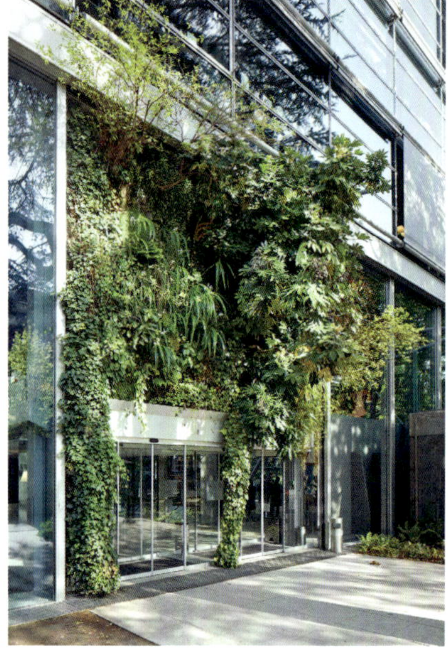

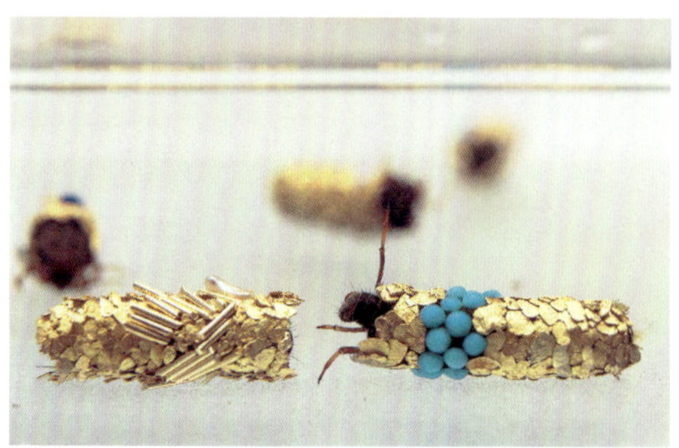

Hubert Duprat, *Larves aquatiques de trichoptères avec leur étui*, 1980–1998

Bringing together art and nature, the exhibition *Être nature* played on the visual ambiguity between the beauty that arises from the artist's gesture and that of nature. Patrick Blanc created his first *Mur végétal* for Jean Nouvel's building.

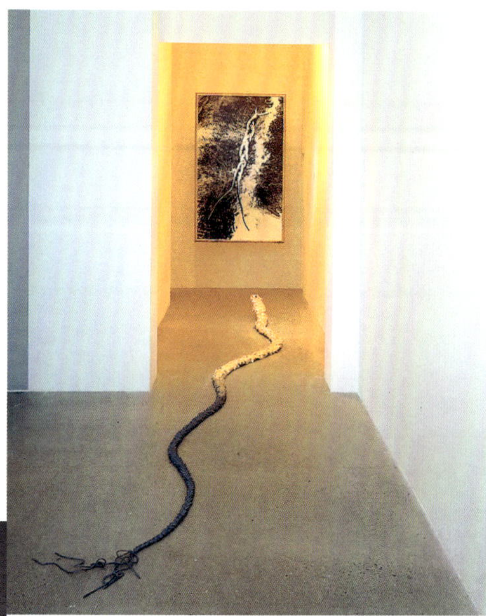

Tunga, *Trança*, 1984

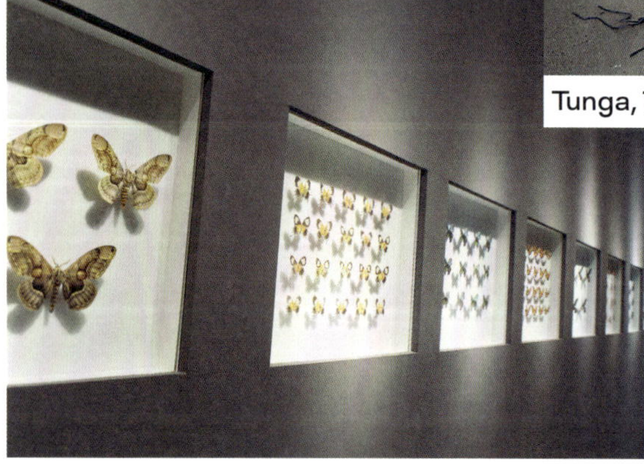

Nature Démiurge, Anne and Jacques Kerchache Collection

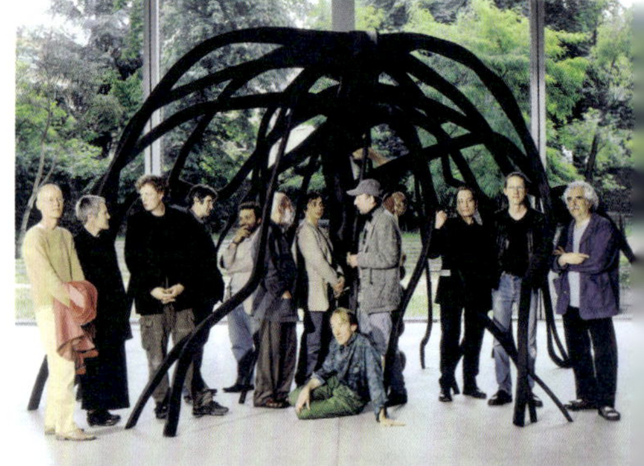

Wolfgang Laib, Ann Hamilton, Olaf Nicolai, Giuseppe Penone, Hubert Duprat, Frans Krajcberg, Tunga, Patrick Blanc, Jacques Kerchache, Marc Couturier, Tim Hawkinson, and Peter Campus under Frans Krajcberg's *Skulpturengruppe* (1973)

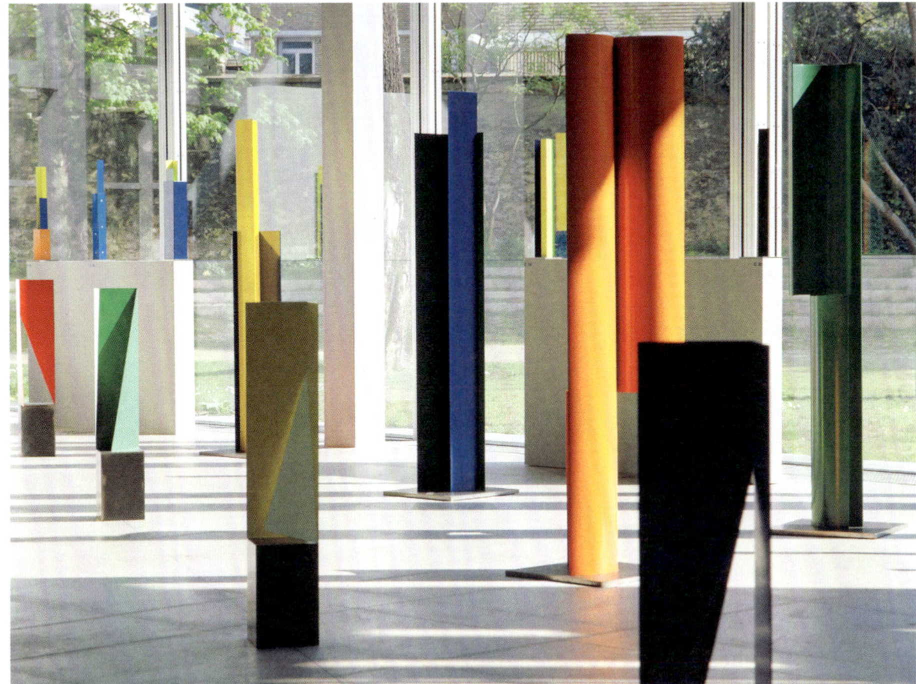

With a scenography designed by Jean Nouvel, the exhibition *Métamorphose* showcased more than eighty of Gottfried Honegger's most recent paintings and sculptures.

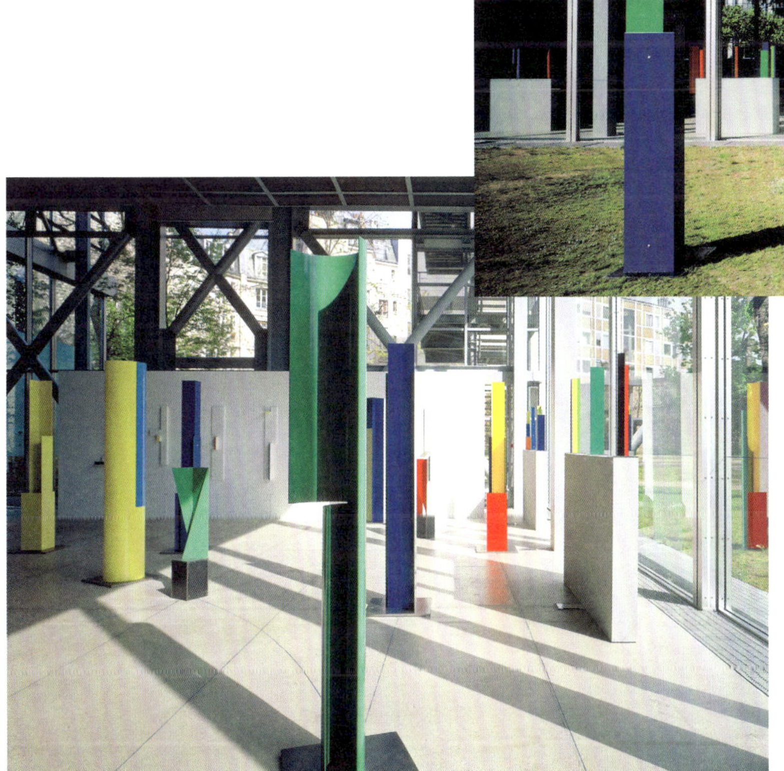

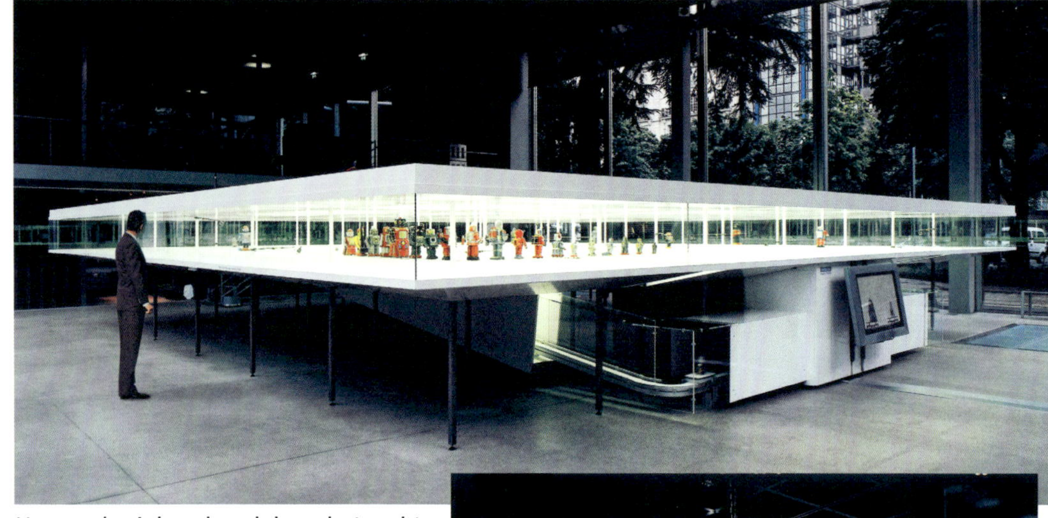

Un monde réel explored the relationship between the imagination and action, known and unknown territories, the experience of reality and fiction. Diller + Scofidio, *Master/Slave*, 1999, with robots from the collection of Rolf Fehlbaum in Basel

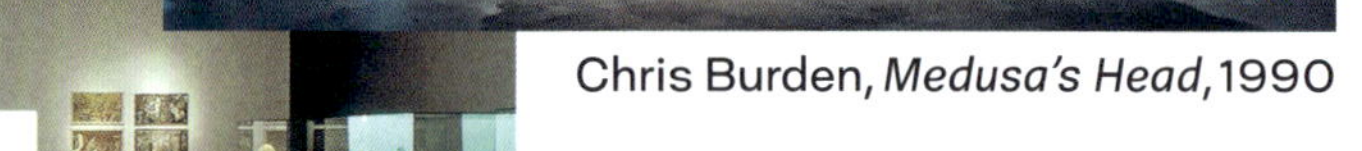

Chris Burden, *Medusa's Head*, 1990

View of the exhibition, featuring the works of James Lee Byars, Bodys Isek Kingelez, Vincent Beaurin, and Fabrice Domercq

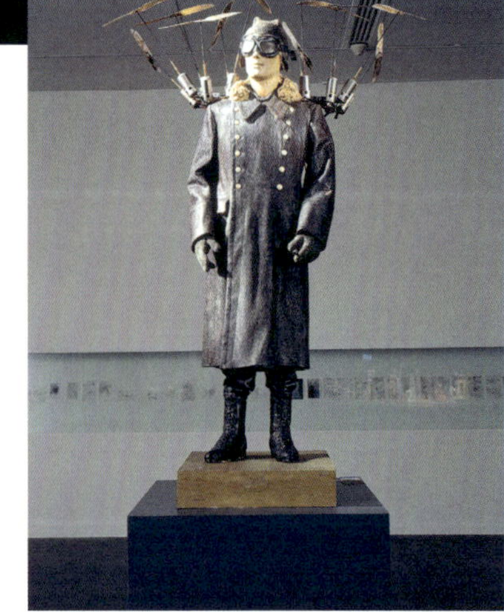

Panamarenko, *Pepto Bismo*, 1996

MŒBIUS

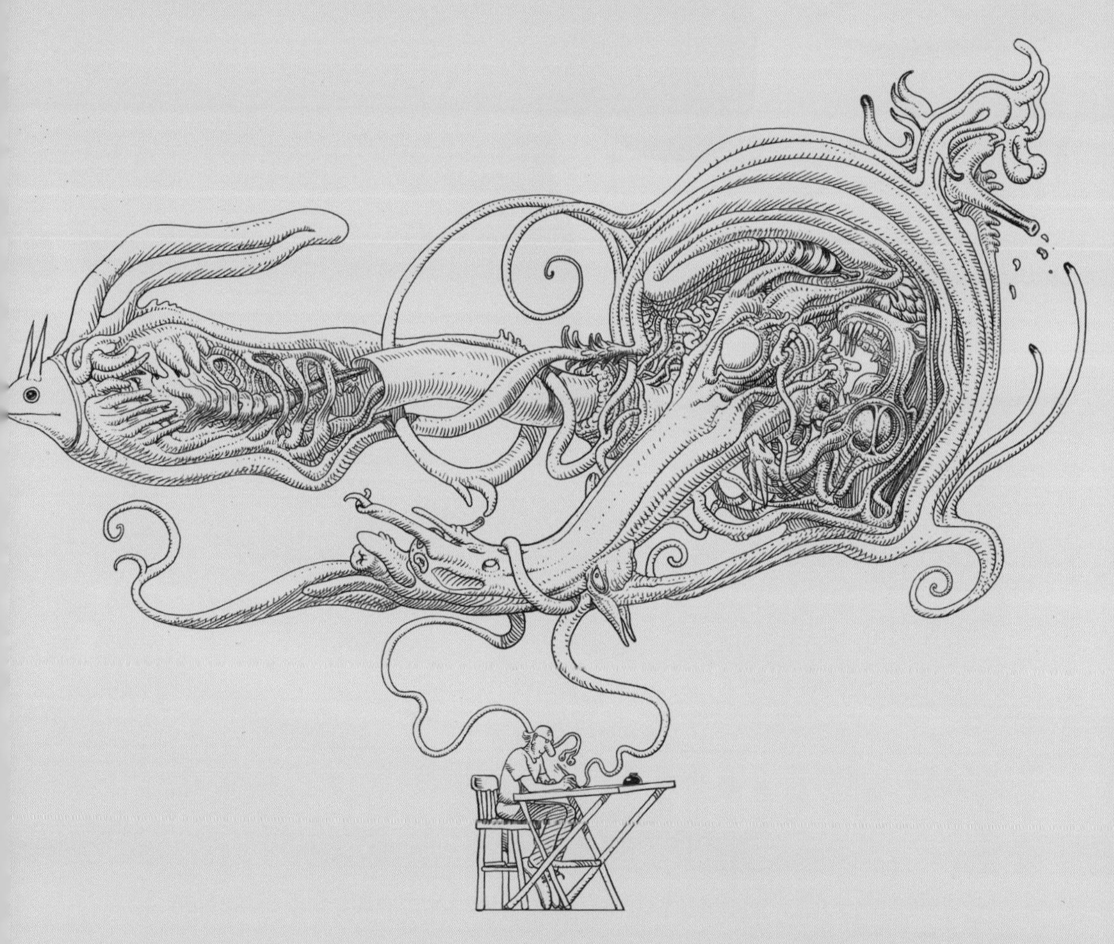

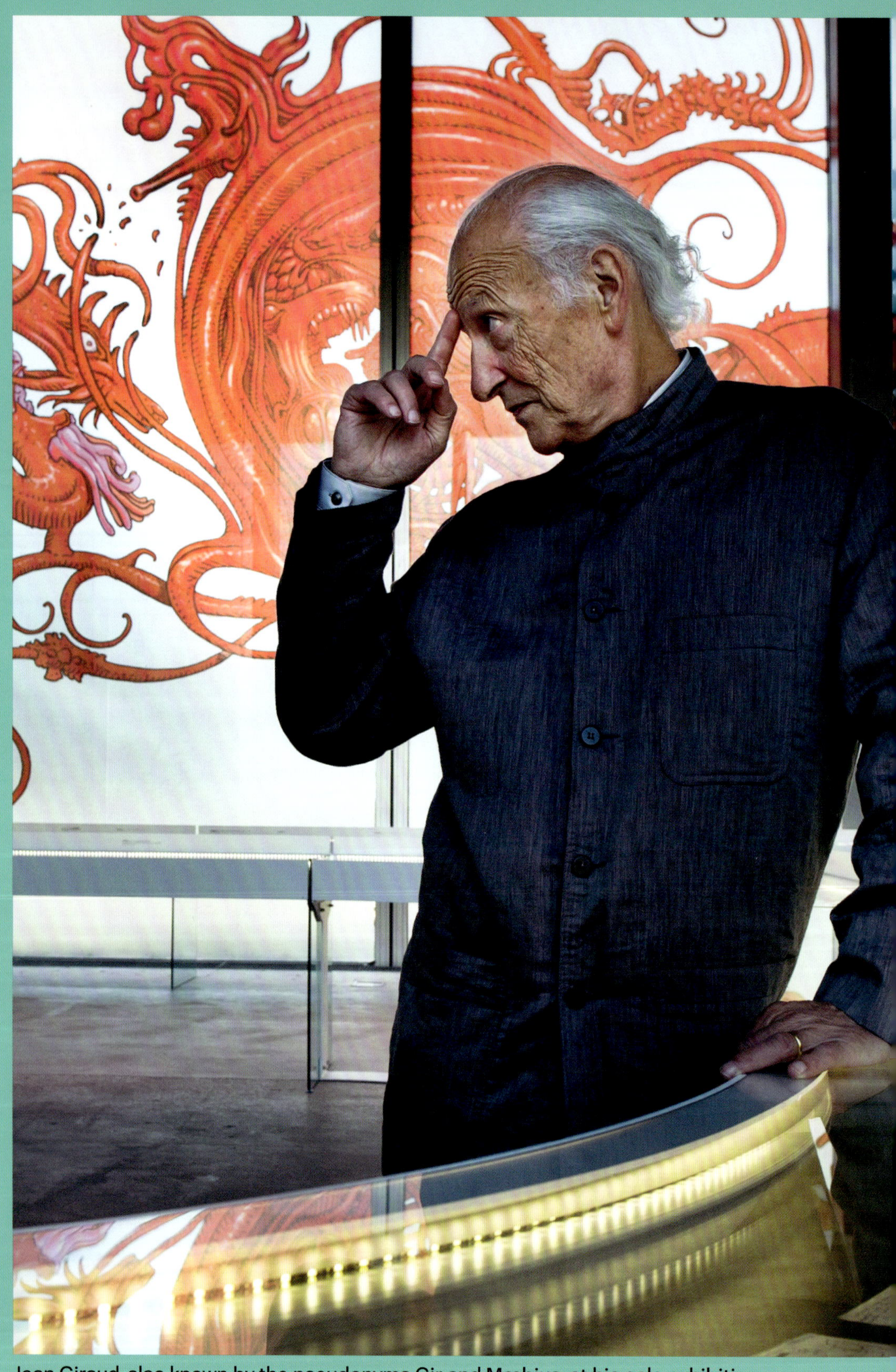

Jean Giraud, also known by the pseudonyms Gir and Mœbius, at his solo exhibition *Mœbius-Transe-Forme* in 2010

Mœbius

His pencil line was quick and precise, his inventiveness limitless, and his freedom absolute. Jean Giraud, Gir, or Mœbius, depending on how or whether he signed his creations—the realistic ones of the American West in the *Blueberry* series, launched with Jean-Michel Charlier in 1965, or the fantastical dream worlds as in *Arzach* (1976), *The Airtight Garage* (1979), or *The Incal* (1981)—transgressed the anonymity of the author and the illustrator, making him an icon of the comic world. The transgression was such that his name, pseudonyms, and style not only earned themselves a unique place in the world of the ninth art, but also in the history of art.

The Fondation Cartier first presented his works in the exhibition *Un monde réel* in 1999, alongside artists Chris Burden, James Lee Byars, Diller + Scofidio, Bodys Isek Kingelez, Andrei Ujică, Panamarenko, Jean-Michel Alberola, Vincent Beaurin, and Fabrice Domercq. Two groups of Mœbius's work were included, one comprising drawings taken from a notebook, and the other, a series of fourteen watercolors. During the exhibition, Mœbius held a live discussion with astronaut Jean-Pierre Haigneré on the Mir space station. Another conversation between the artist and philosopher and urban planner Paul Virilio was also published. Alongside the exhibition and its catalog, a rare reproduction of forty color drawings, signed by Mœbius, was copublished by the Fondation Cartier and Éditions Stardom. This small book, *Une jeunesse heureuse* (1999), along with two notebooks acquired following the exhibition by the Fondation Cartier for its Collections, convey a great deal about the artist's worlds.

Metamorphosis is among the major themes running through Jean Giraud's work. It is omnipresent in his comics but also in the film projects on which he collaborated with Luc Besson, James Cameron, and Ridley Scott. As an artist, he played with it, immersed himself in it, and explored all its possibilities, inventing landscapes and characters in perpetual transformation. Metamorphosis was a part of his daily life and preoccupied him to the point that it became the center of his solo exhibition at the Fondation Cartier in 2010. Designed and constructed by Jean Giraud himself with the active participation of Mœbius Production, *Mœbius-Transe-Forme* offered visitors a journey into the heart of his work, making use of all the Fondation Cartier's spaces, from the bookstore to the bay windows overlooking Boulevard Raspail and the garden, extending from the ground floor to the basement. The exhibition was truly comprehensive. It was that of an artist in his own right, as Hervé Chandès, Director of the Fondation Cartier and the exhibition's curator, wanted. For the first time within a contemporary art institution, Mœbius was able to summon his pantheon of heroes: Blueberry, Arzach, Major Grubert, John Difool, Stel and Atan, without forgetting his own double, who appeared at an early stage in his comic strips, and who continued to mutate as time passed and worlds evolved. The exhibition unfurled like a long Möbius strip: sketches, comic strips, paintings, ideas for the underwater creatures in the film *Abyss* (1989), and drawings of lands straight from the artist's imagination, presented his ongoing reflections on reality and fiction, on humans and their creative capacities, on the laws of nature and the origin of the universe, on metaphysics, dreams, and trance. It also allowed the public to test a three-dimensional experience with *La Planète Encore* (2010), an animated film coproduced especially for the exhibition by the Fondation Cartier and Mœbius Production, with the animation studio BUF, based on the short story *The Aedena Cycle*, first published in 1990. This exhibition was the last and only major celebration of this builder of worlds, social critic, and philosopher on the human condition, before his death in 2012. For more than fifty years, Mœbius, a "free artist" as he described himself, never ceased to wonder and to make others wonder, leaving an unforgettable legacy and influencing generations of illustrators, cartoonists, and writers.

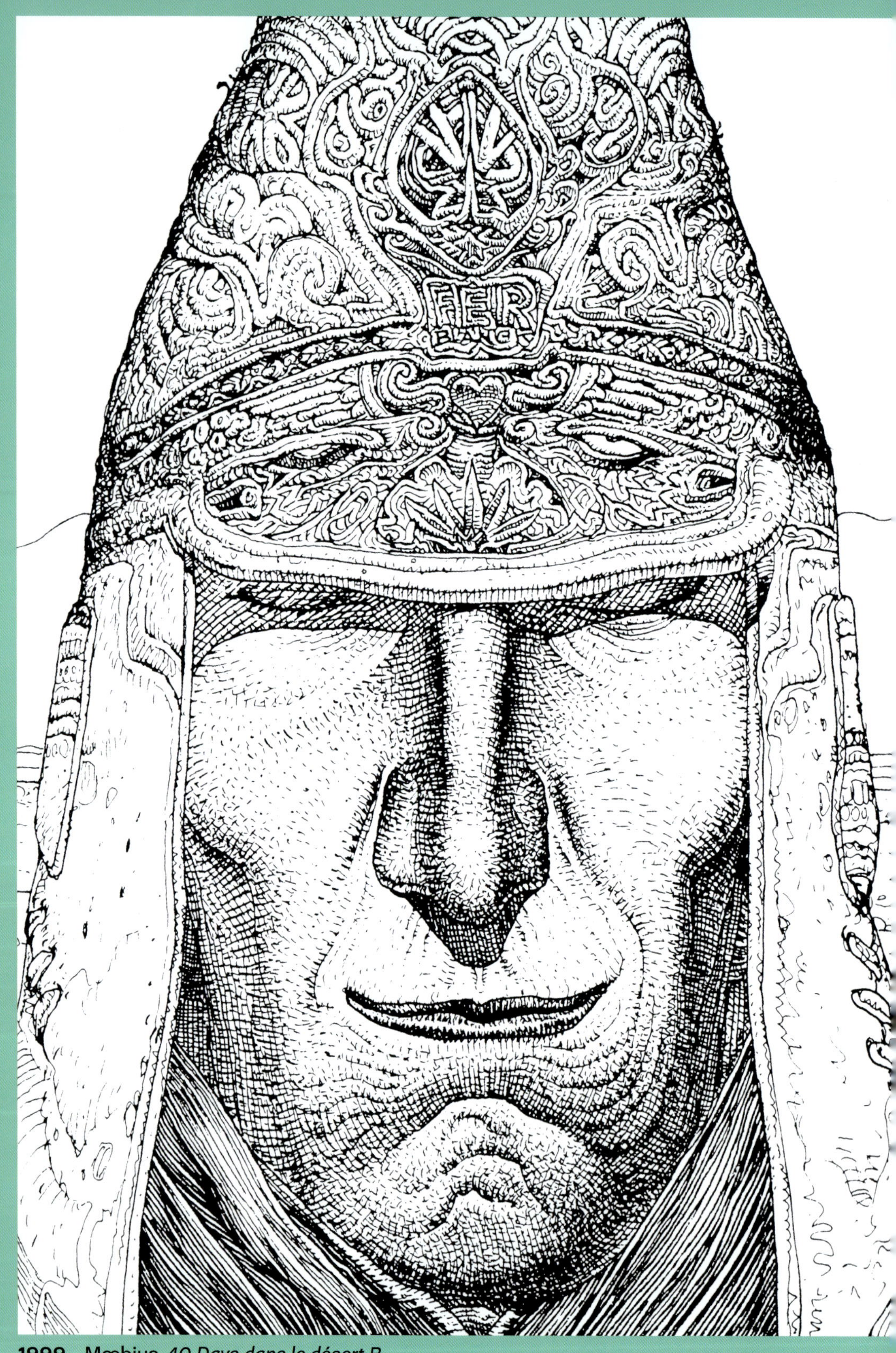

1999   Mœbius, *40 Days dans le désert B*

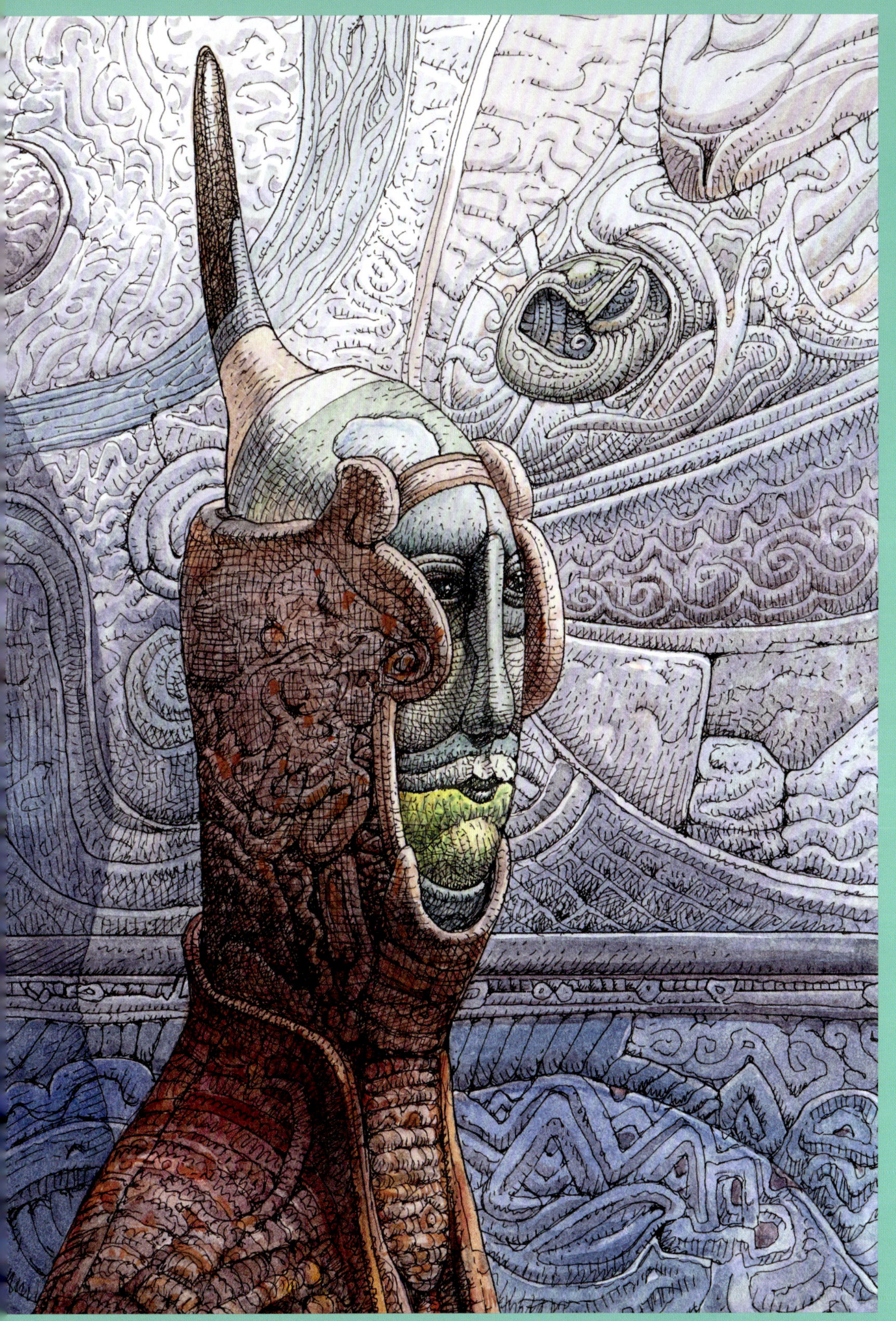

999   The exhibition *Un monde réel* was the chance to present 183 drawings
aken from Mœbius's sketchpads and notebooks, as well as a group of 14 watercolors,
itled *Souvenirs de 2001* (1999). Mœbius, *Untitled, Carnet no. 1,* 1999. FC Collections (1999)

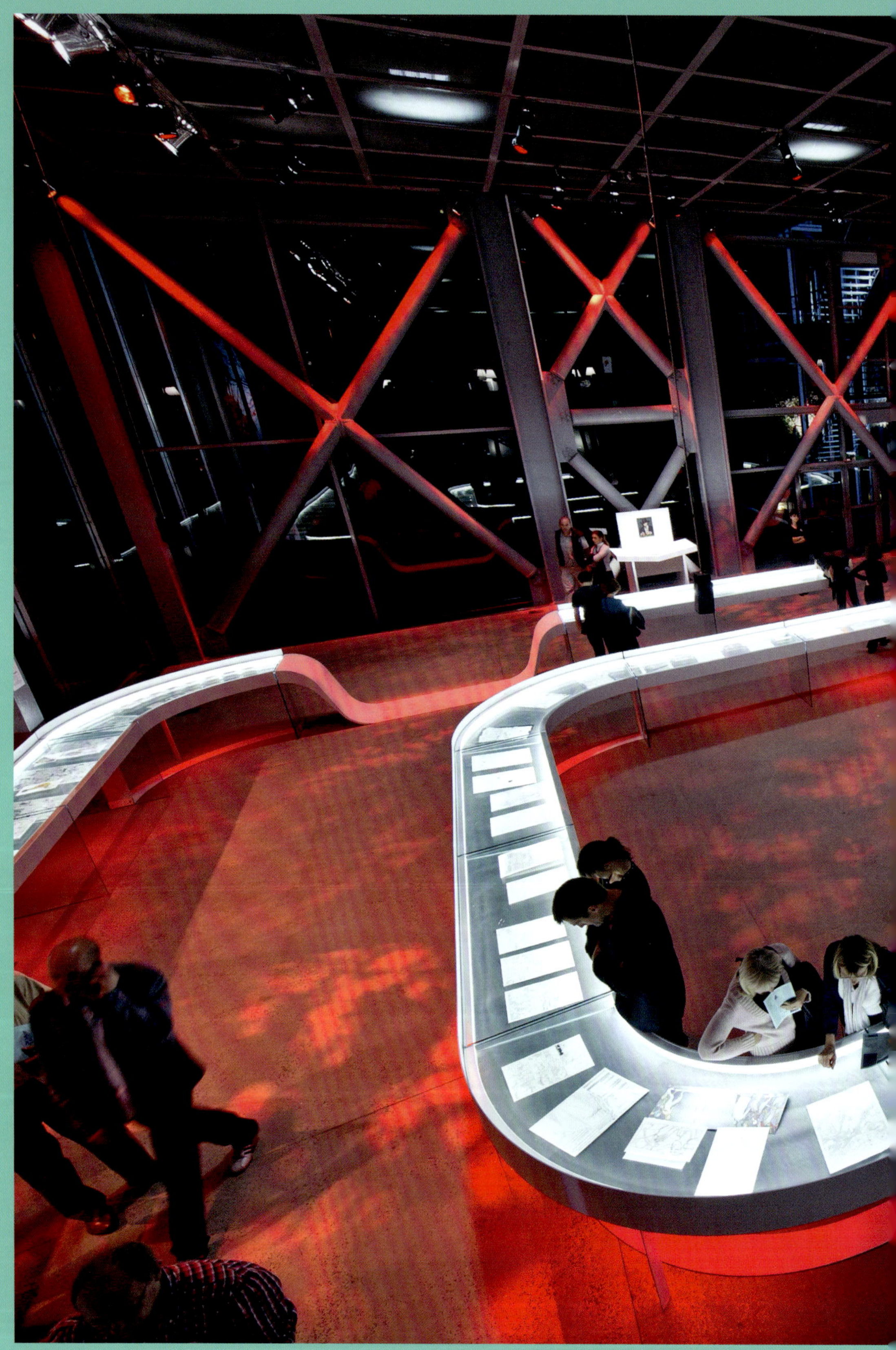

2010   Featuring over 400 documents and drawings, the exhibition
Mœbius-Transe-Forme was the first large solo exhibition devoted to the artist.

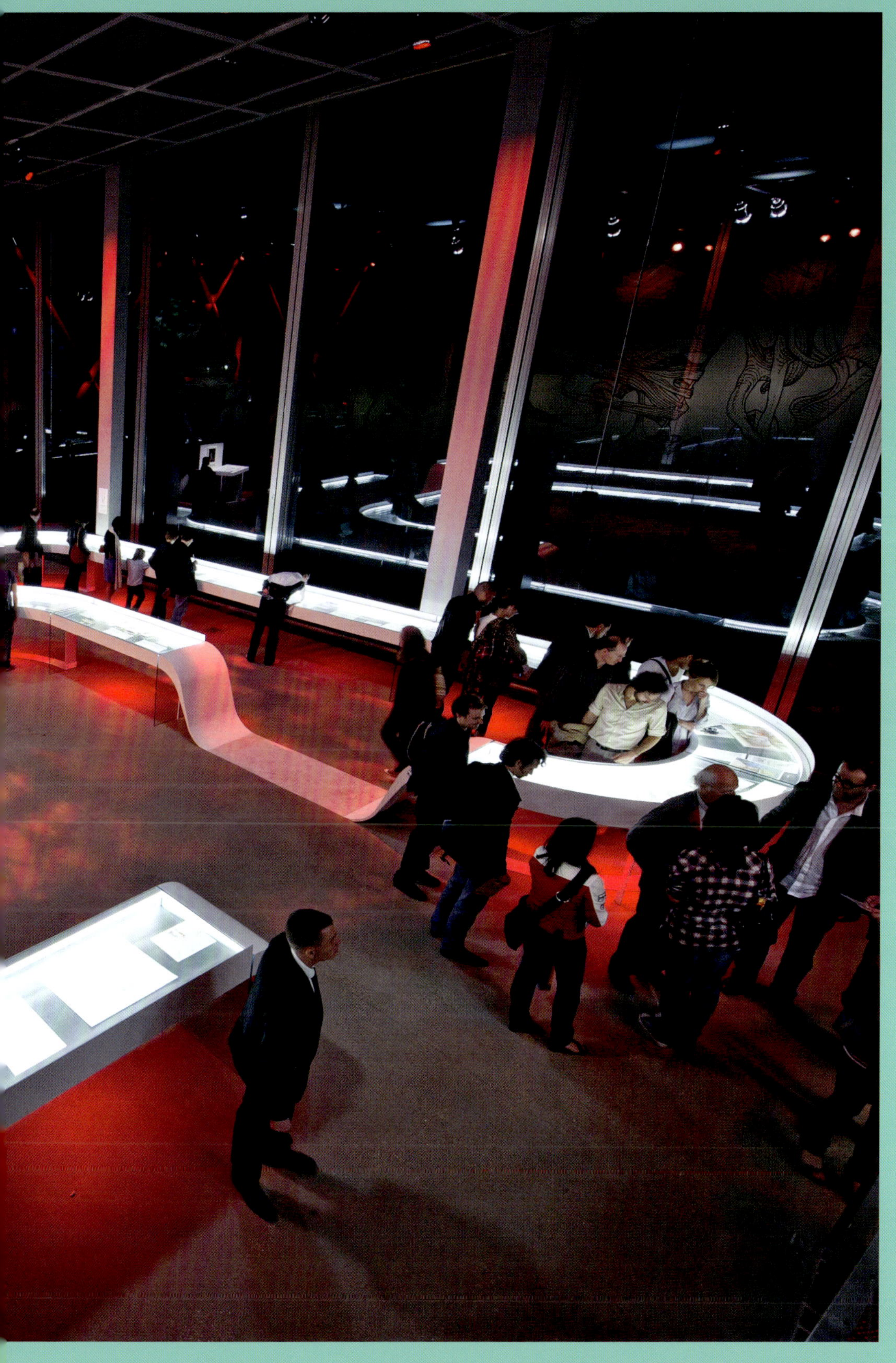

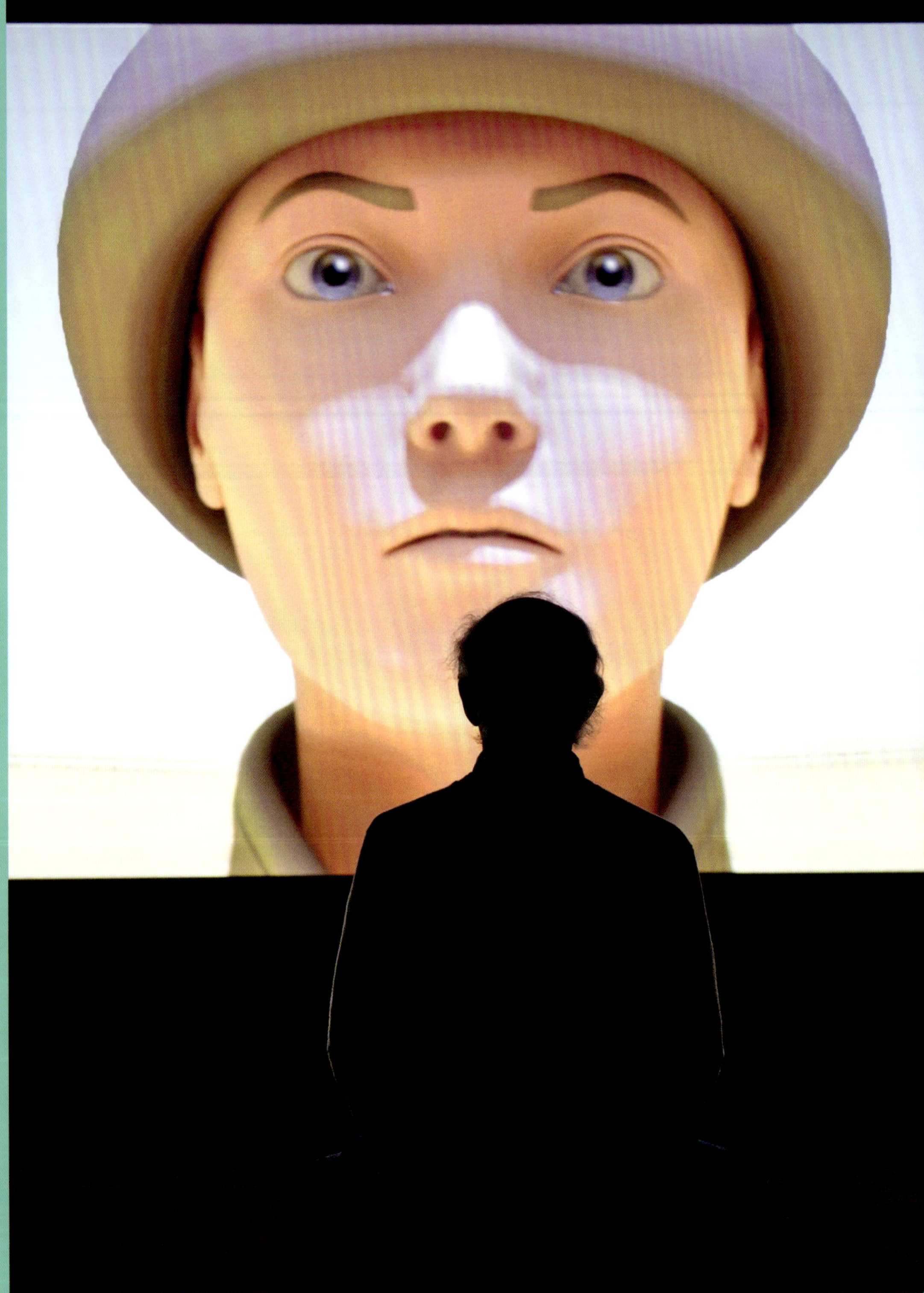

2010 *La Planète Encore* is a 3-D film adapted from the comic strip *The Aedena Cycle* (1990), created with the studio BUF and coproduced by the Fondation Cartier and Mœbius Production for the exhibition.

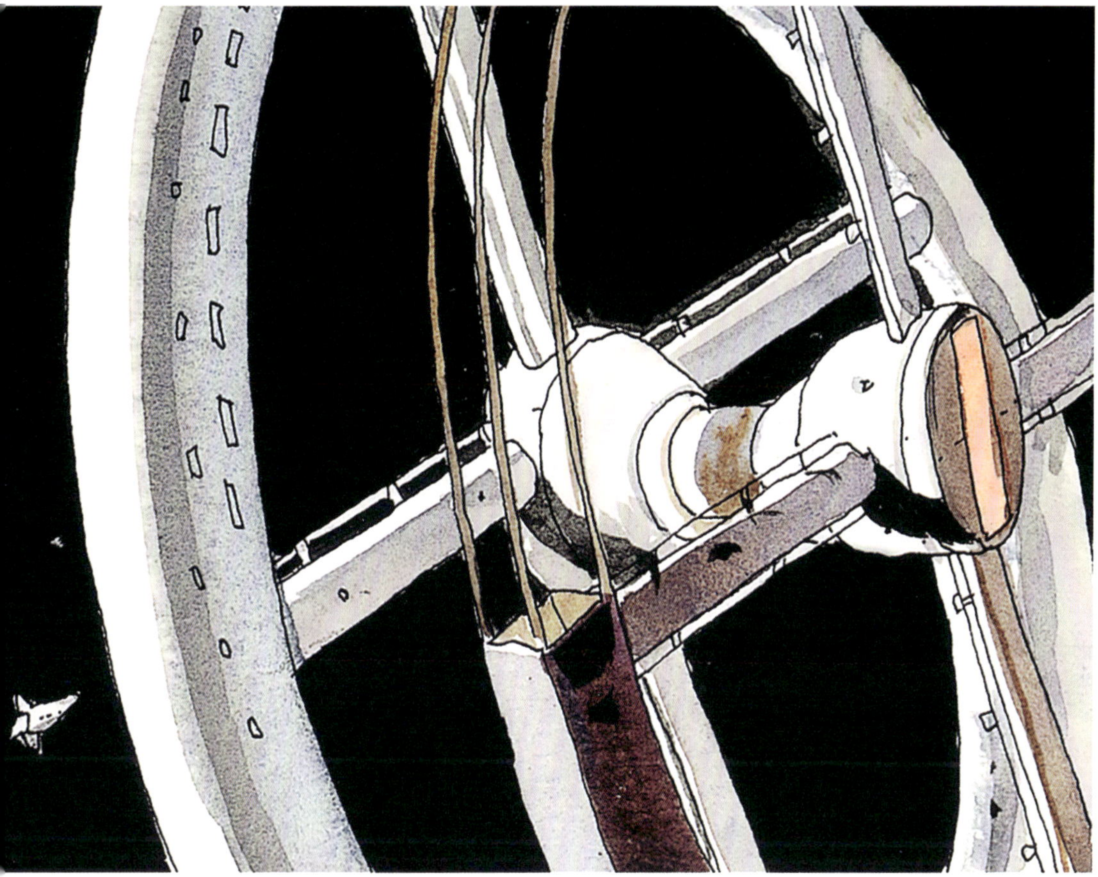

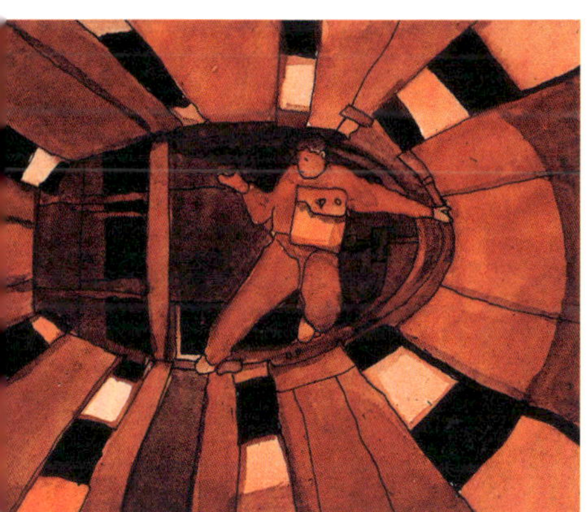

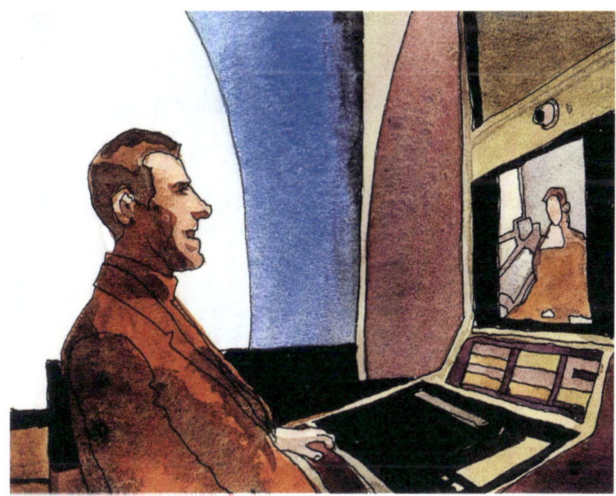

Mœbius, *Souvenirs de 2001*, 1999: a series of watercolors illustrating the conversation between Paul Virilio and Andrei Ujică, published in the catalog of the exhibition *Un monde réel* (1999).

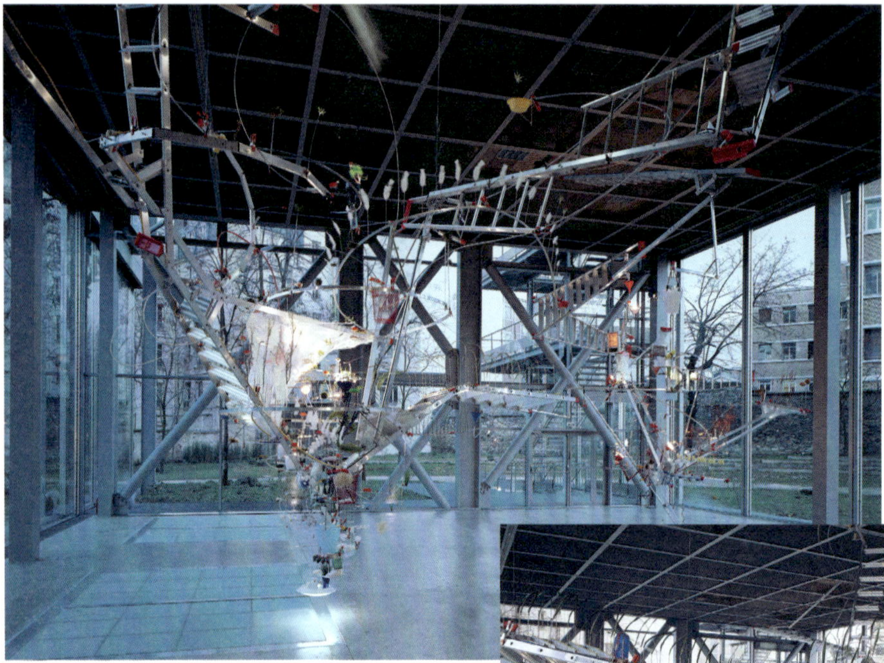

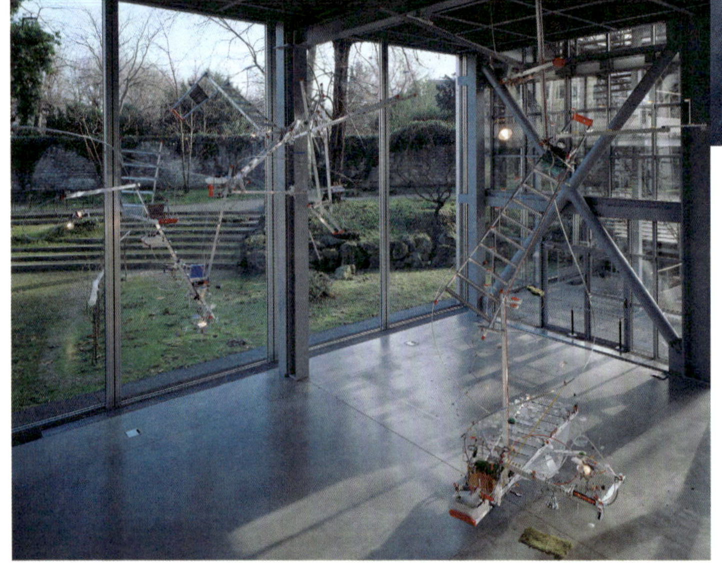

For her first solo exhibition in France,
Sarah Sze was invited to create *Everything
That Rises Must Converge*, an installation
composed of ladders and countless small
objects, arranged over the two rooms
of the ground floor exhibition spaces.

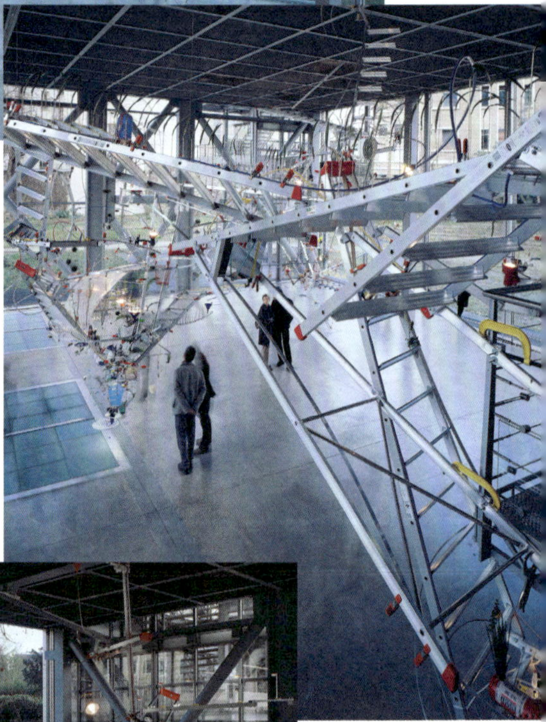

Sarah Sze, *Everything That Rises Must Converge*, 1999
FC Collections (2000)

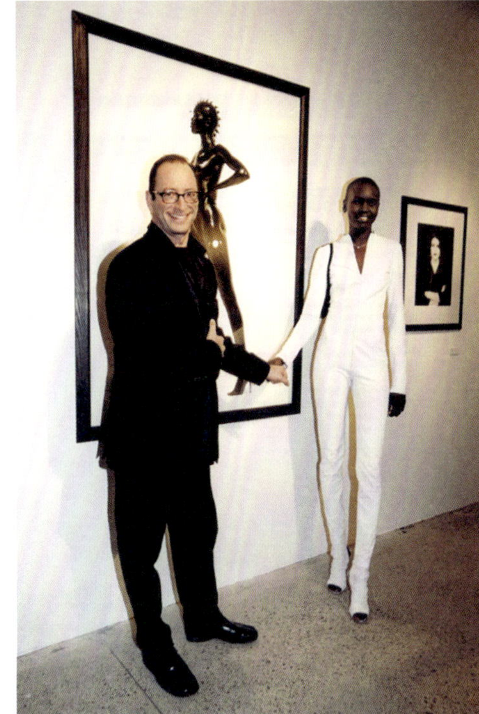

Herb Ritts and Alek Wek
at the exhibition opening

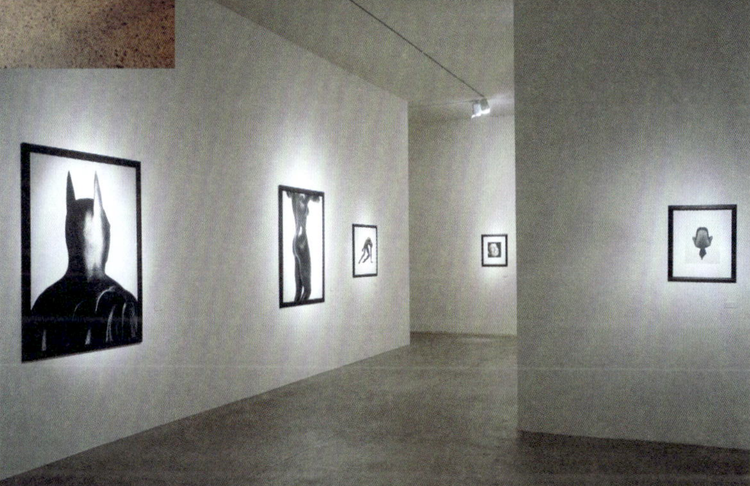

The exhibition comprised some 100 photographs by Herb Ritts,
some of which had never been seen before.

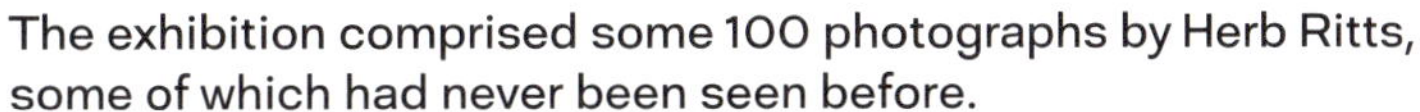

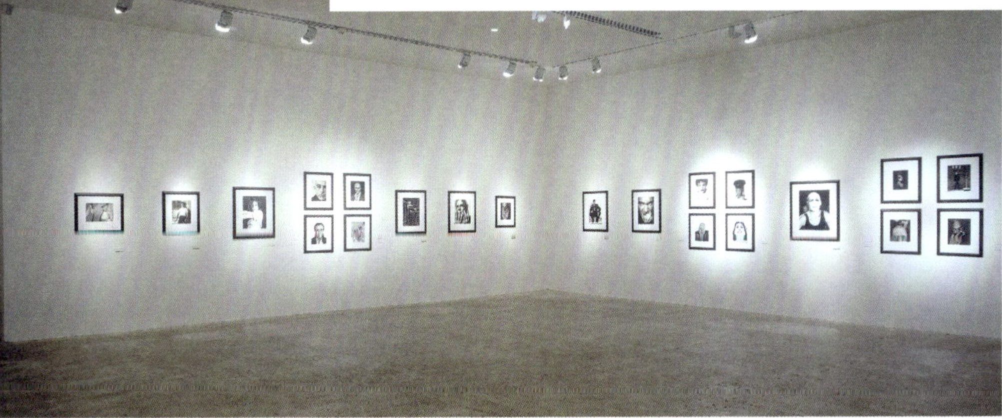

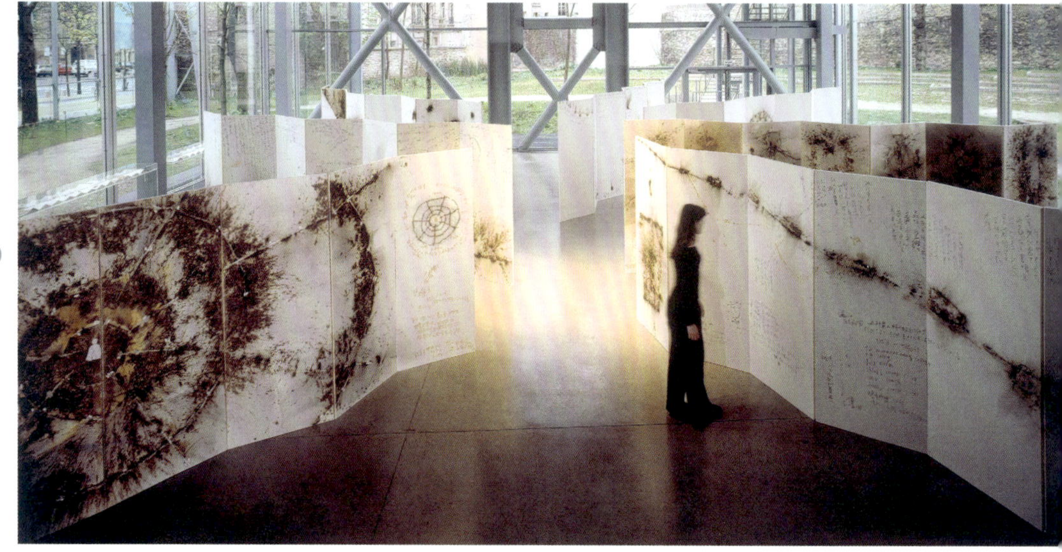

Cai Guo-Qiang, *Primeval Fireball – The Project for Projects*, 2000

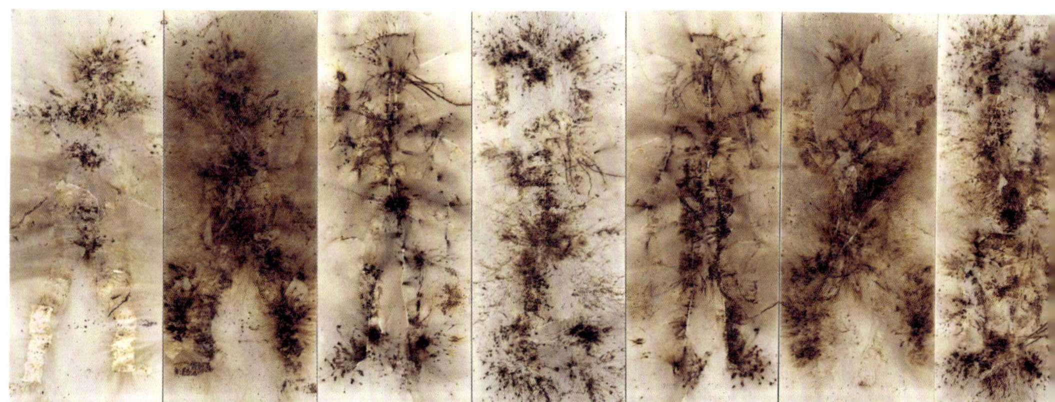

Cai Guo-Qiang, *The Vague Border at the Edge of Time/Space Project*, 1991
FC Collections (2000)

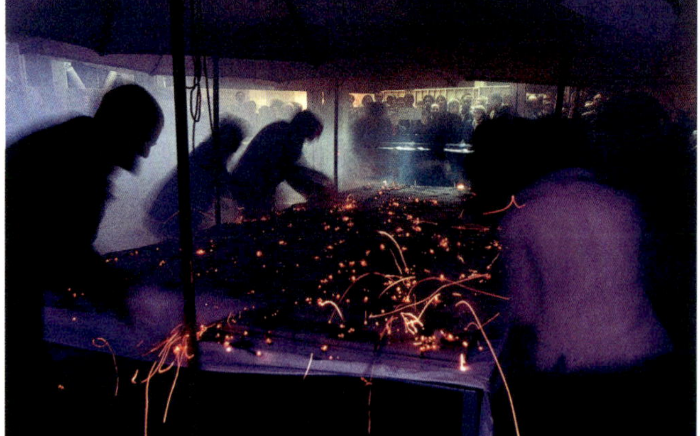

On April 20, 2000, Cai Guo-Qiang orchestrated
an explosion on the catalogs of his exhibition.

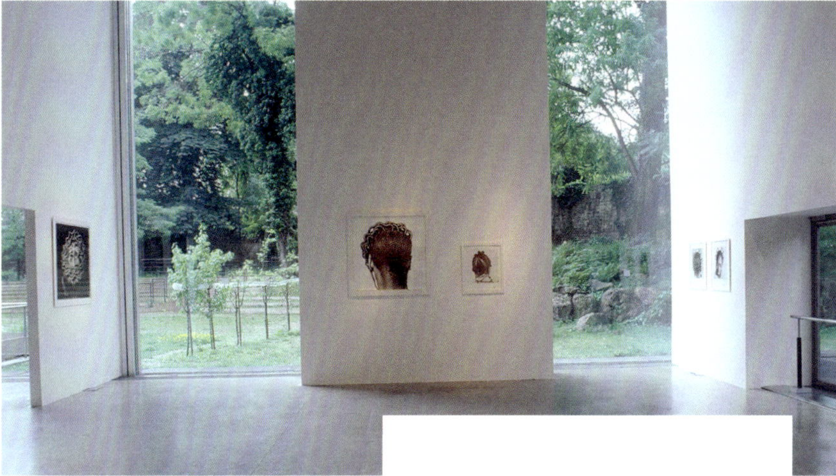

For the first time outside Nigeria, J.D. 'Okhai Ojeikere presented 64 *Hair Style* photographs at the Fondation Cartier.

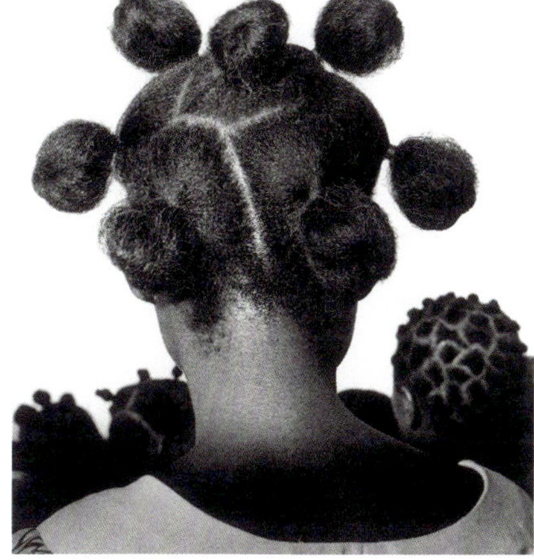

J.D. 'Okhai Ojeikere, *Mkpuk Eba*,1974
FC Collections (1999)

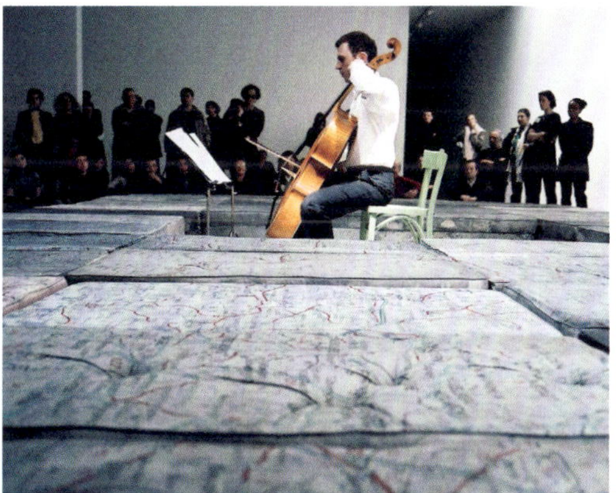

Nomadic Night with Mauricio Kagel and Benjamin Carat, May 4, 2000

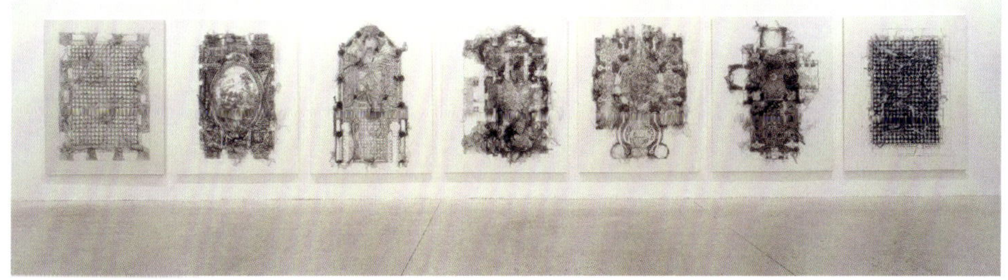

The Fondation Cartier exhibited four of artist Guillermo Kuitca's recent series, including this group of seven canvases from *L'Encyclopédie* series.

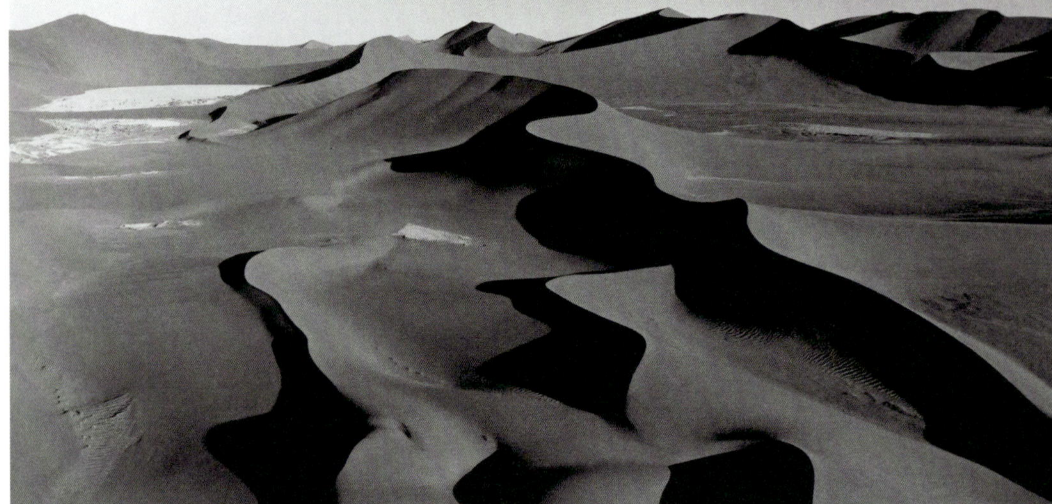

The exhibition *Le Désert* confronted 19th-century photographs with commissions from ten artists. The Fondation Cartier invited six of them to travel to desert regions in Egypt, Mali, Australia, and the United States. Balthasar Burkhard, *Namibie #1*, 2000. FC Collections (2002)

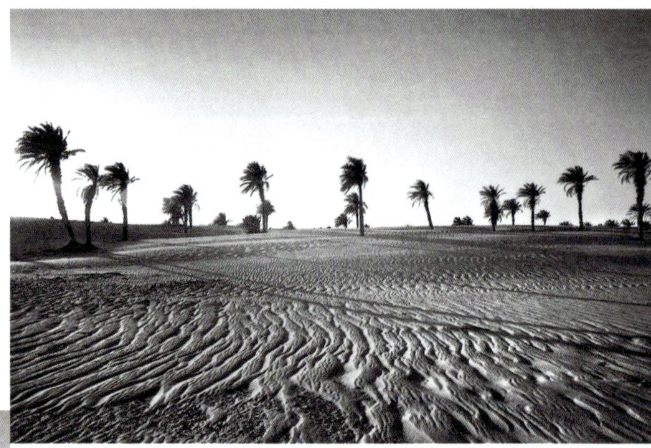

Raymond Depardon, *Déserts*, 2000

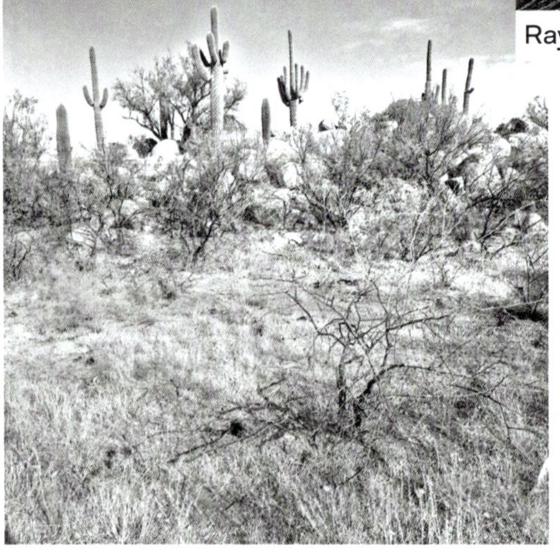

Lee Friedlander, *Sonora*, *The Desert* series, 1991–1995. FC Collections (1997)

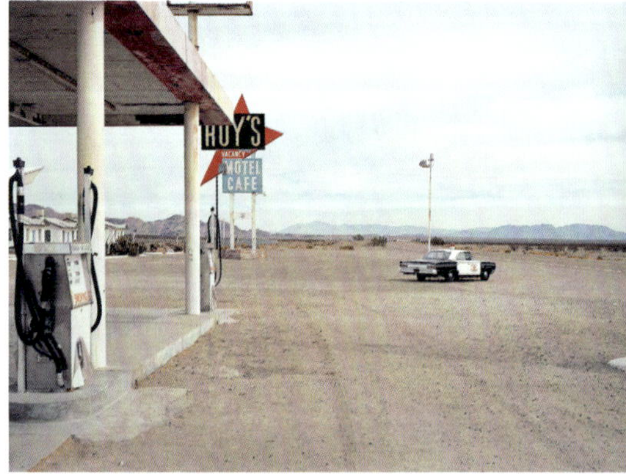

William Eggleston, *Déserts de Californie, de l'Arizona et de l'Utah*, 2000
FC Collections (2000)

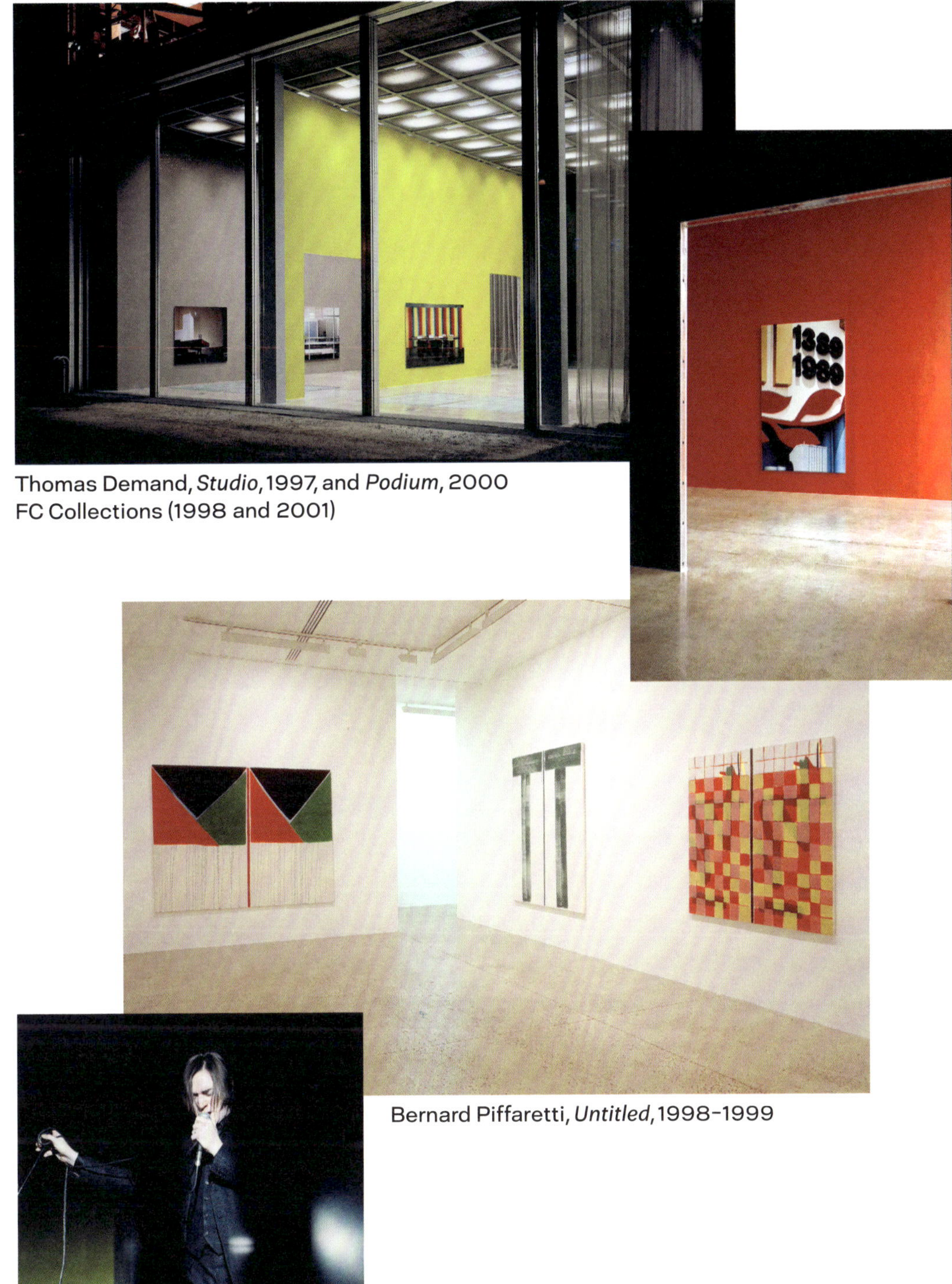

Thomas Demand, *Studio*, 1997, and *Podium*, 2000
FC Collections (1998 and 2001)

Bernard Piffaretti, *Untitled*, 1998–1999

Nomadic Night with Blixa Bargeld,
Speech, February 1, 2001

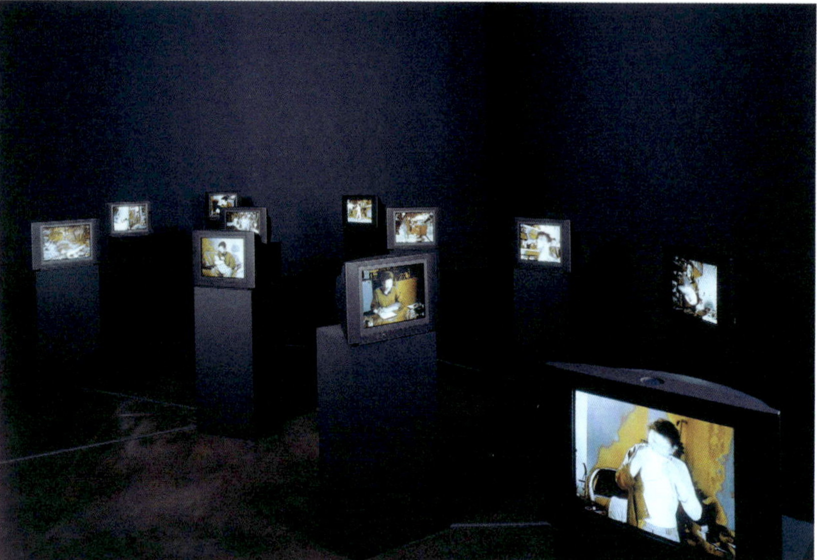

The exhibition title—*261 Bd Raspail, Paris XIV*—the actual address of the Fondation Cartier, expressed Pierrick Sorin's desire to appropriate the site, to inhabit it, and make it into an "apartment of images," thanks to a selection of video installations.

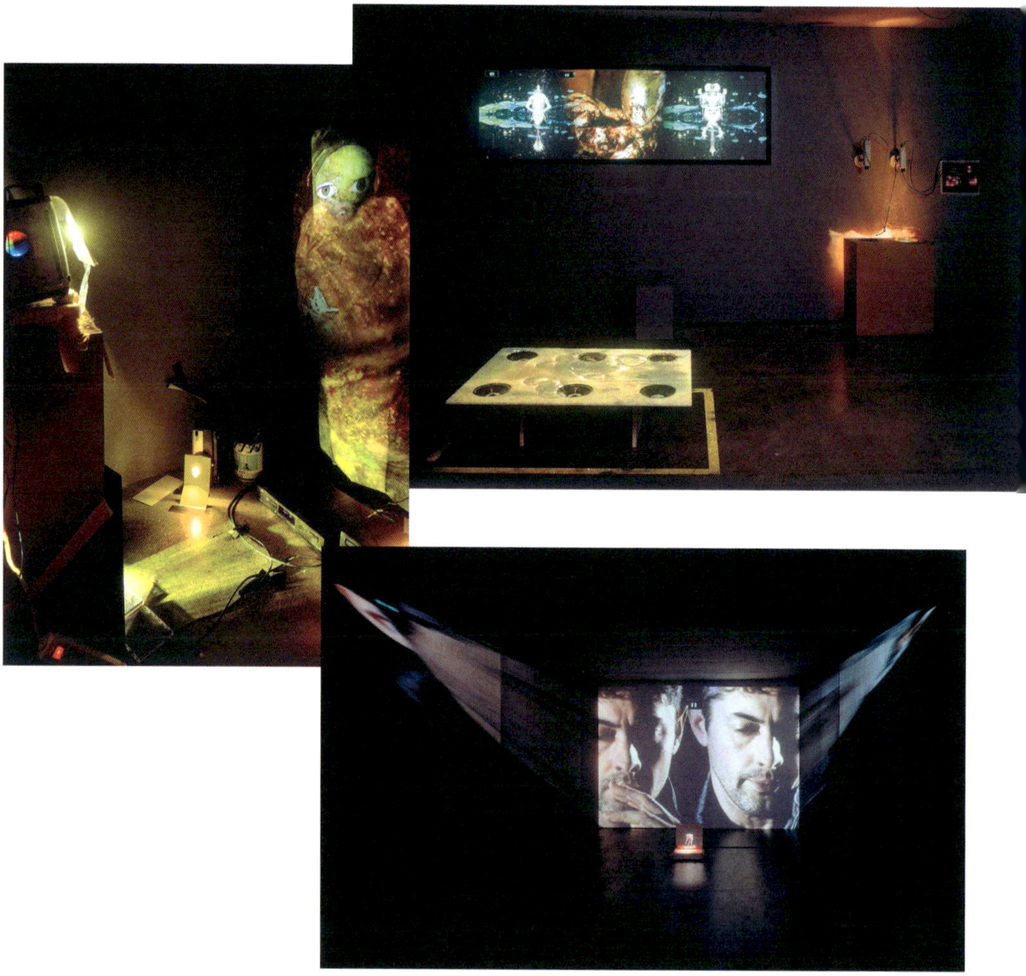

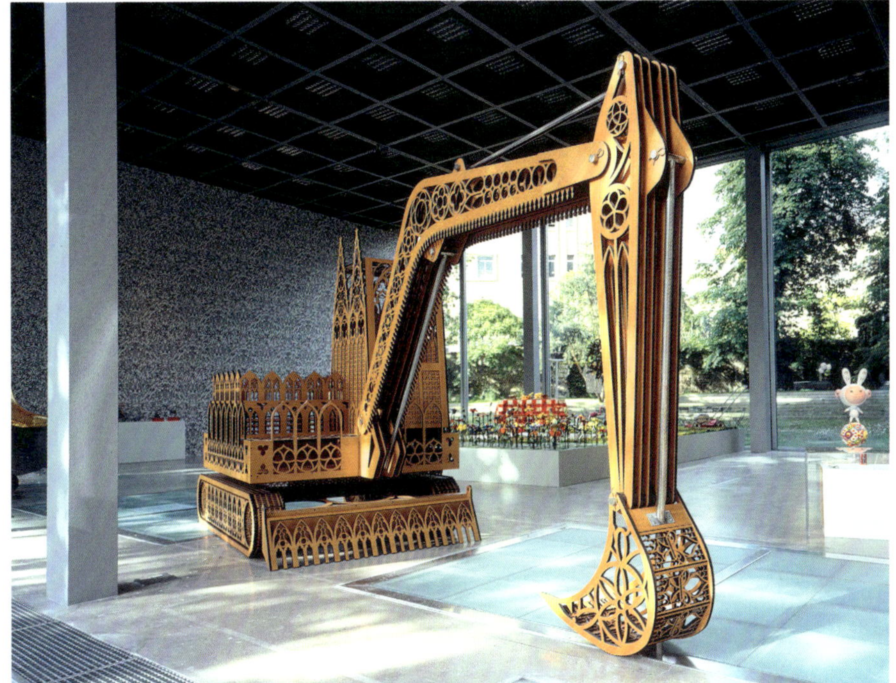

With 130 works by 37 artists from all over the world on display for the first time or specially commissioned for the occasion, this exhibition aimed to illustrate the modernity of popular art, and to underline the way in which it infiltrates contemporary art, and how the two intertwine.
Wim Delvoye, *Caterpillar*, 2001. FC Collections (2001)

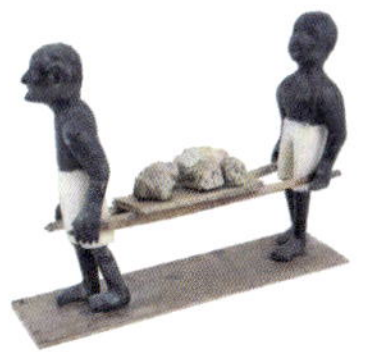

Antônio de Oliveira, *Porteurs de pierres*, 1980s

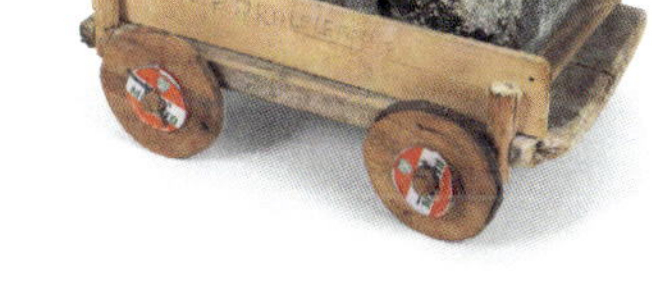

Arthur Bispo do Rosário, *Parallélépipède*, n.d.

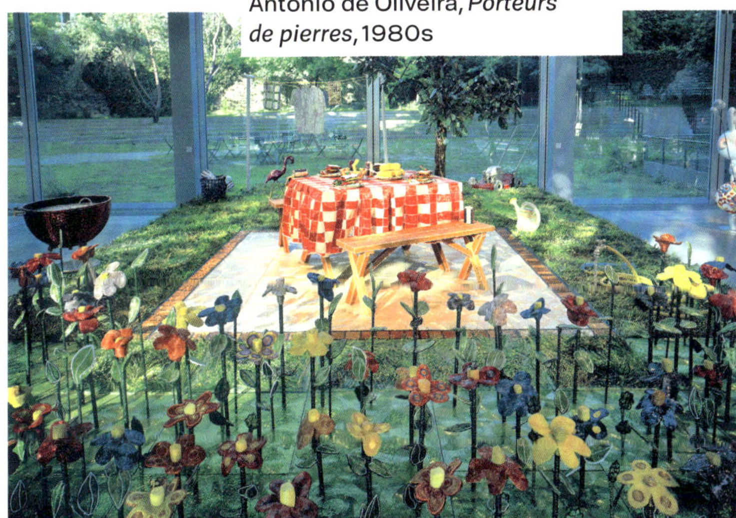

Liza Lou, *Back Yard*, 1996-1999. FC Collections (2002)

This exhibition brought together, for the first time in France, William Eggleston's most significant works, from his first black-and-white prints to the series of photographs commissioned by the Fondation Cartier and shot in Kyoto.

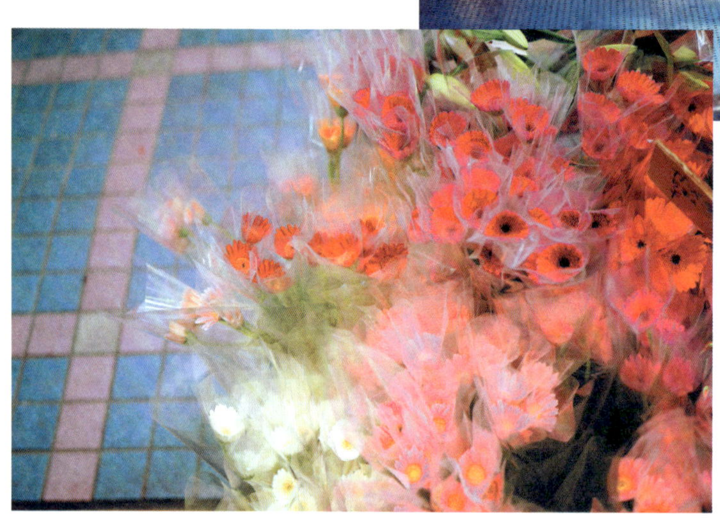

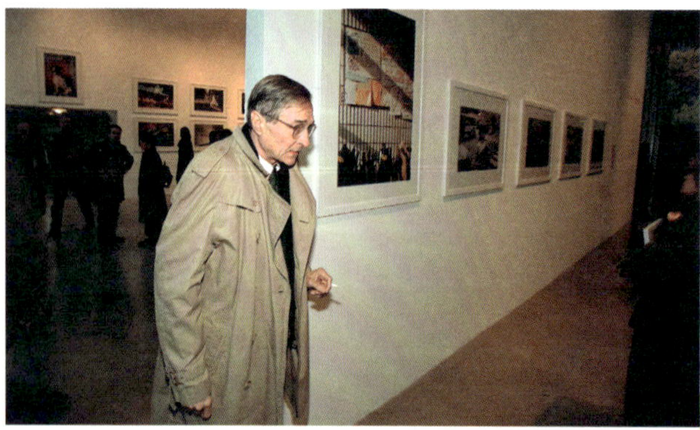

William Eggleston, *Kyoto* series, 2001. FC Collections (2002)

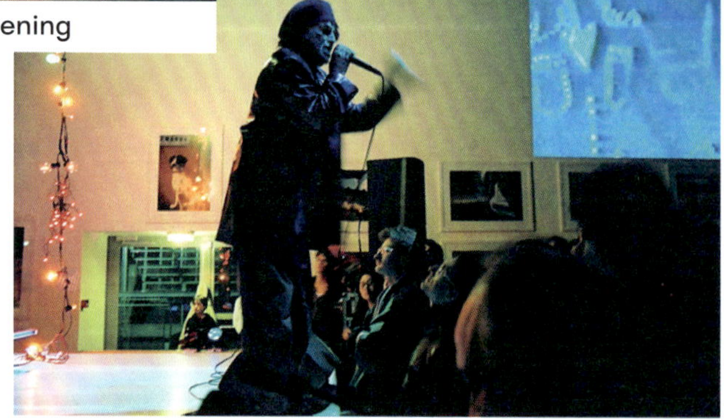

William Eggleston at the exhibition opening

Nomadic Night with Suicide, February 14, 2002

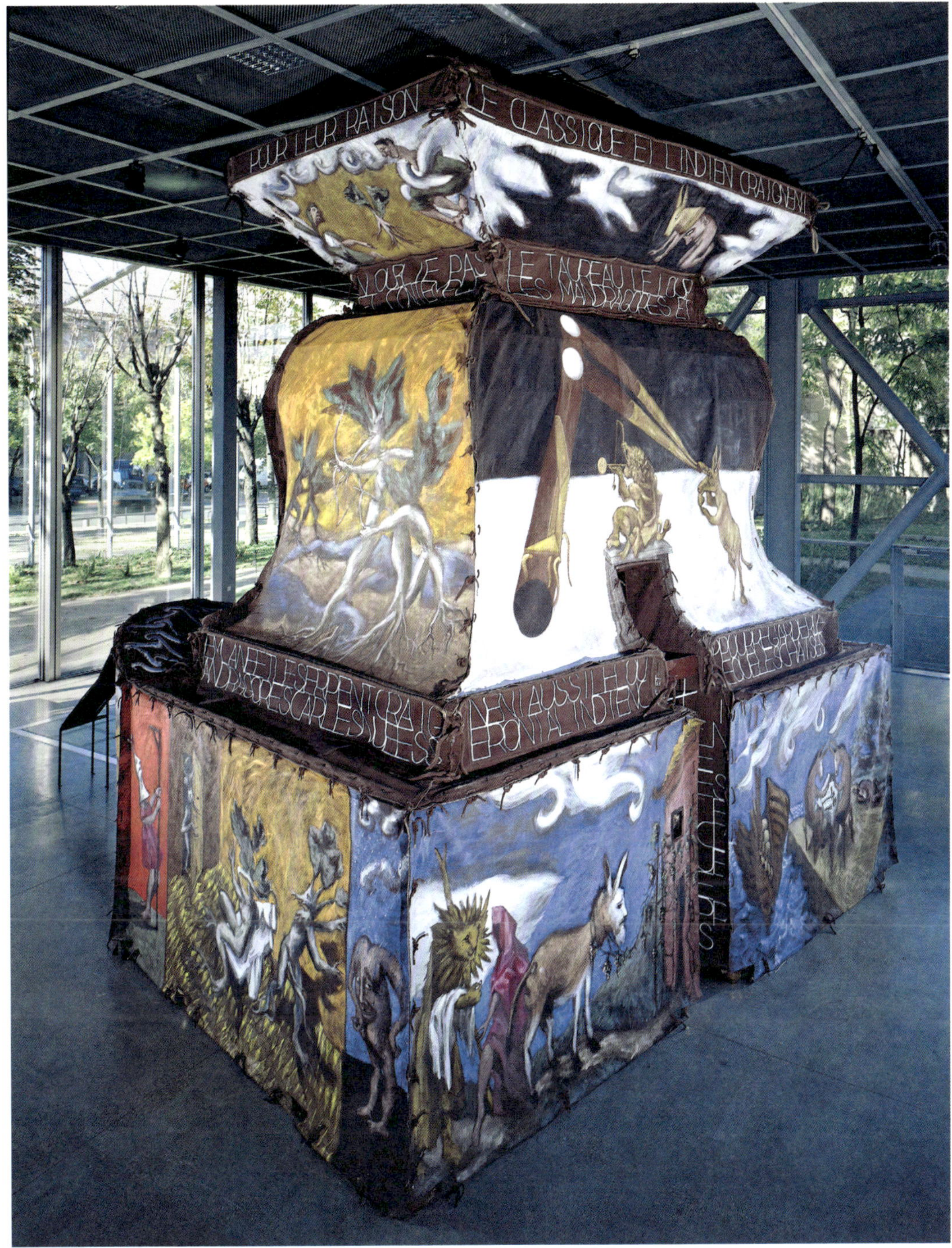

A monumental installation by Gérard Garouste, *Ellipse* was entirely created for the spaces of the Fondation Cartier, halfway between a tent and the follies that decorated 18th-century gardens. The canvases from which it was made evoked the *Indiennes* presented at Jouy-en-Josas in 1988. Gérard Garouste, *Ellipse*, 1999–2001

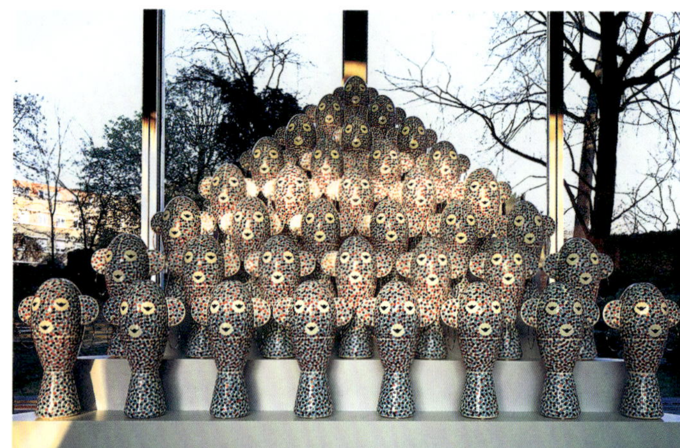

Alessandro Mendini,
Vases visages, 2002

With exhibition design by Alessandro Mendini, *Fragilisme* featured
his works alongside those of Vincent Beaurin and Fabrice Domercq.
Alessandro Mendini, *Tête géante* and *Petite cathédrale*, 2002
and Vincent Beaurin, *Montagne*, 2002

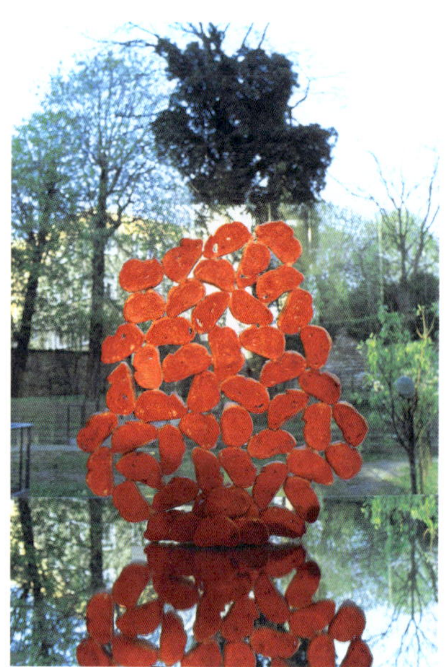

Fabrice Domercq, *Untitled*, 2001

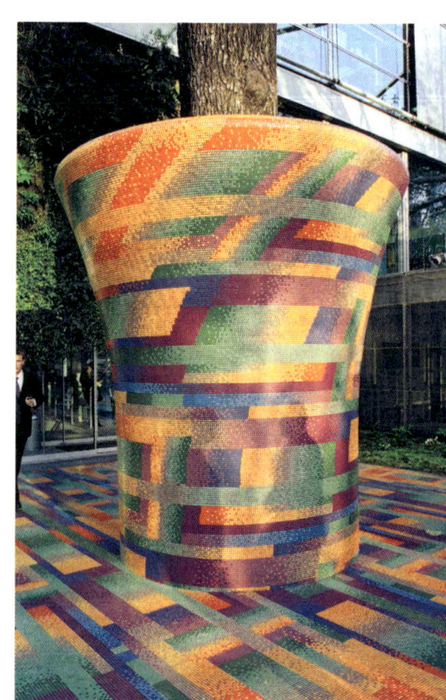

Alessandro Mendini,
Pot pour le cèdre, 2002

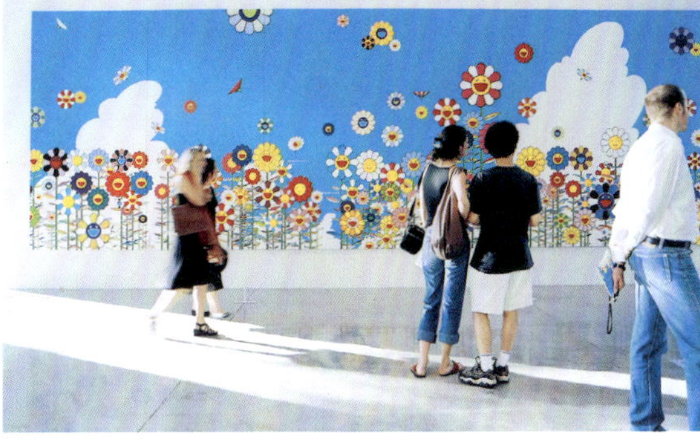

For his first exhibition in Europe, Takashi Murakami chose to show sculptures, paintings, and wallpapers specially created for the occasion. Takashi Murakami, *Kawaii! Vacances d'été*, 2002

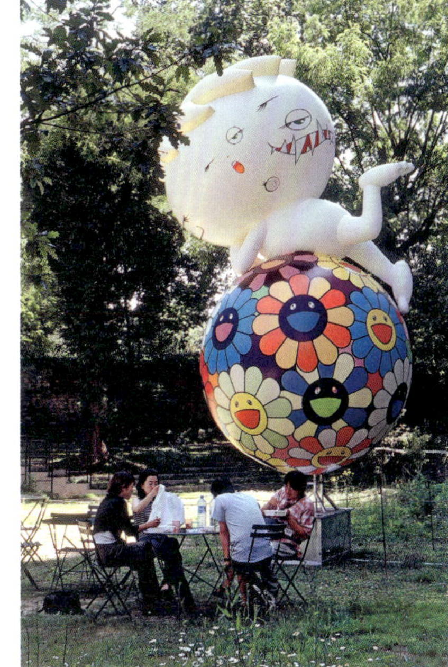

Takashi Murakami, *Napping/Ovale*, 2002

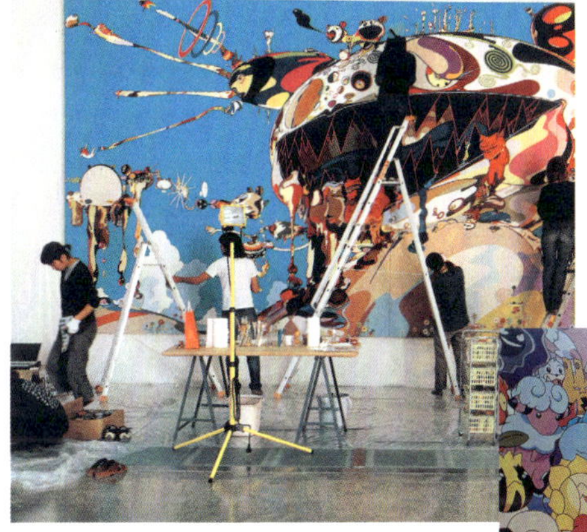

The exhibition being installed

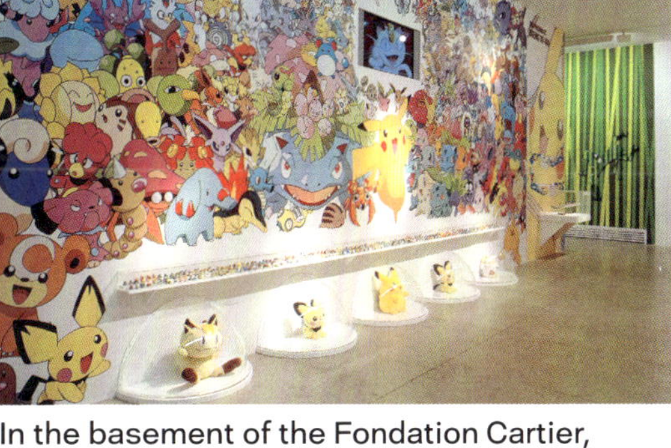

In the basement of the Fondation Cartier, Takashi Murakami designed the exhibition *Coloriage*, a panorama of contemporary Japanese creation, bringing together the works of almost 20 artists.

Nomadic Night with Gaspard Yurkievich, *Aurore Overnight, Girls Band*, July 4, 2002

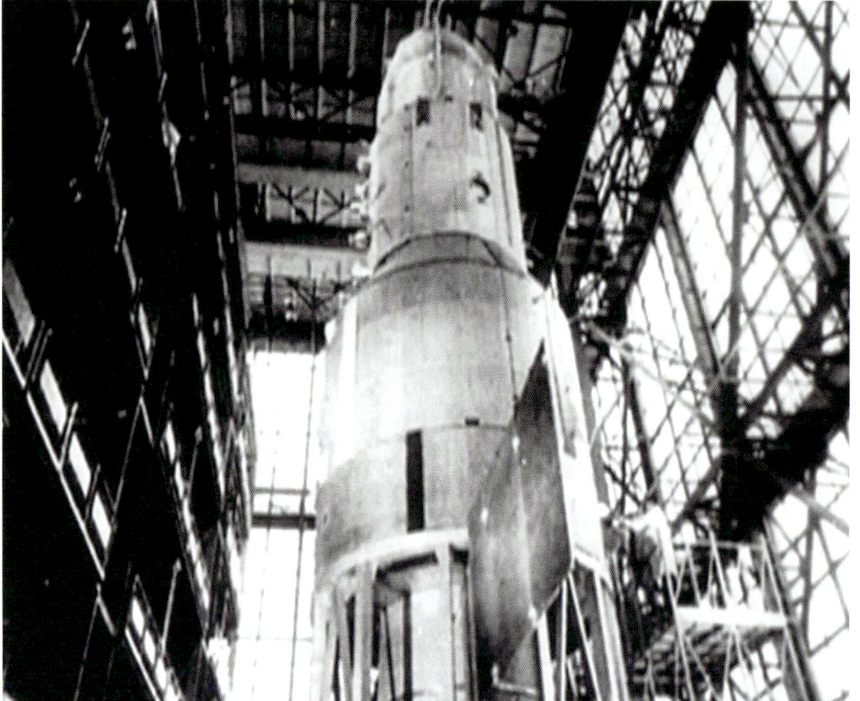

"Exploring the accident. All accidents, from the most banal to the most
tragic, from natural catastrophes to industrial and/or scientific disasters,
but also fortunate accidents, a stroke of luck or love at first sight.
The accident comes with an element of surprise. It stuns us. The first time.
The unexpected. The unknown quantity." Paul Virilio, exhibition curator
Artavazd Pelechian, *Notre siècle*, 1990
FC Collections (2003)

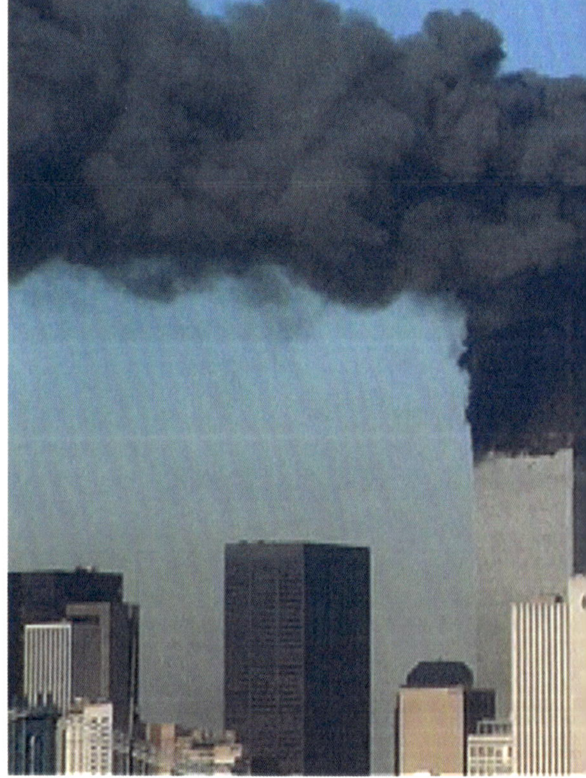

Tony Oursler, *9/11*, 2001

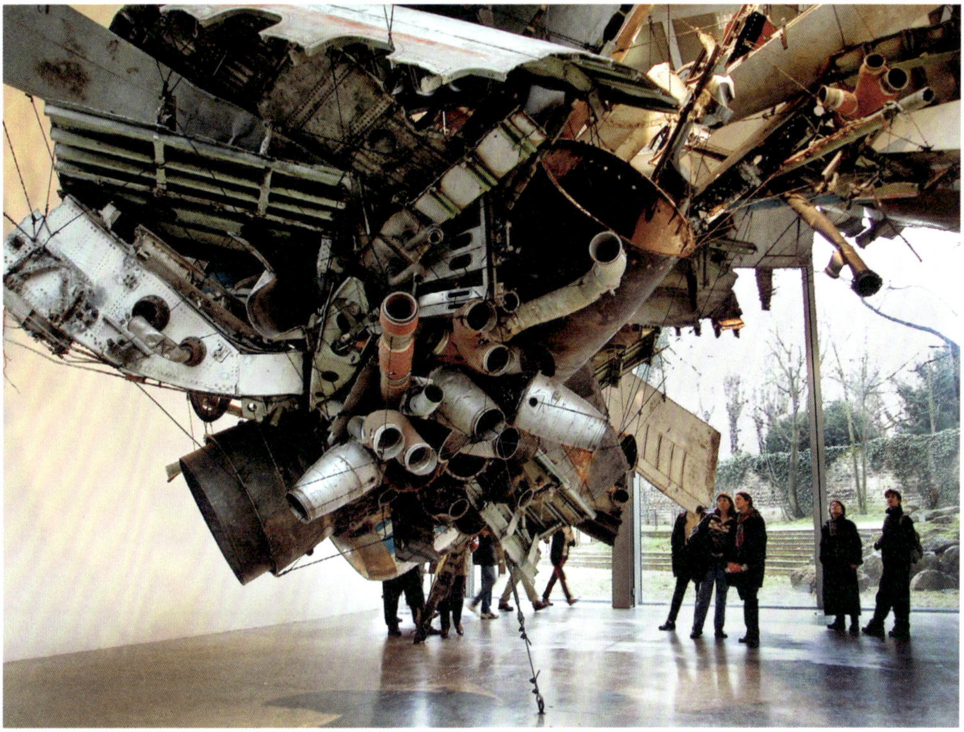

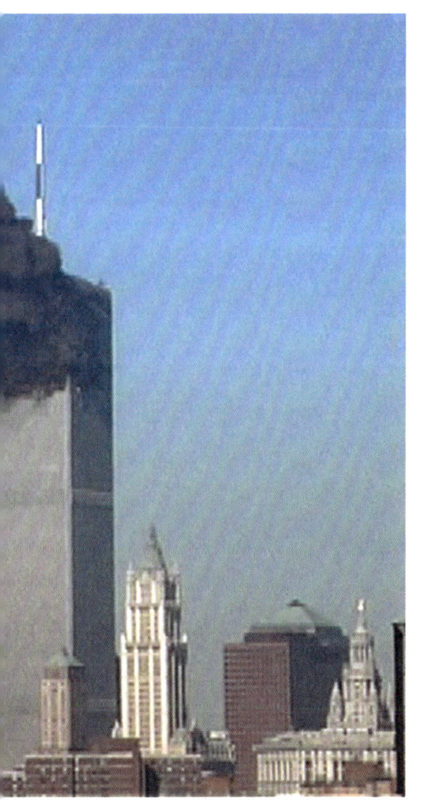

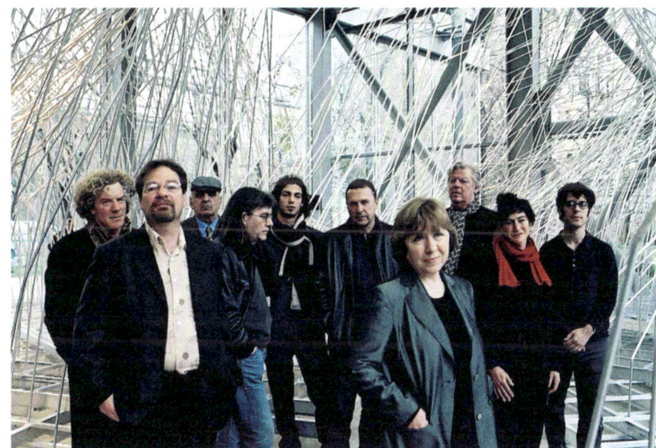

Nancy Rubins, *MoMA & Airplane Parts*, 1995

Peter Hutton, Dominic Angerame, Artavazd Pelechian, Andrei Ujică, Alexis Rochas, Wolfgang Staehle, Svetlana Alexievitch, Lebbeus Woods, Nancy Rubins, and Stephen Vitiello in front of *The Fall* by Lebbeus Woods (2002)

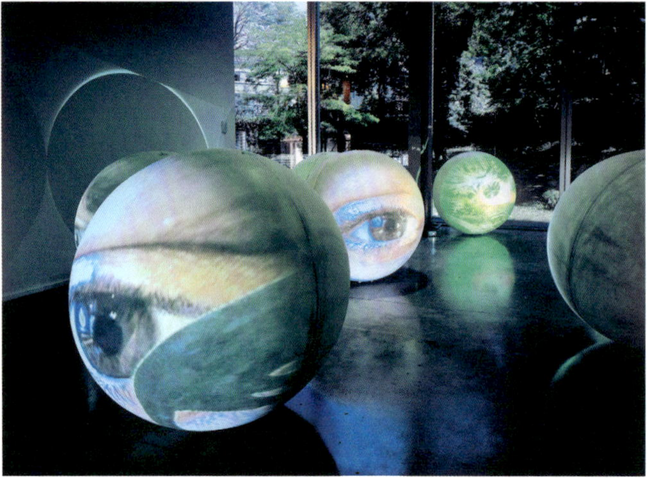

Tony Oursler, *Mirror Maze (Dead Eyes Live)*, 2003
FC Collections (2003)

"The exhibition was invented—with the invaluable help of Davi Kopenawa—as an experimental system that would put cultural discordance to work … through the confrontation of a selection of international artists and a group of Yanomami shamans from Watorikɨ, a Yanomami village in the Brazilian Amazon."
Bruce Albert, exhibition curator

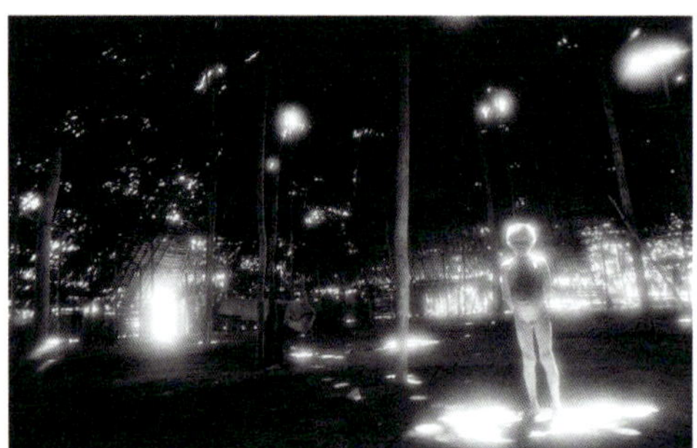

Claudia Andujar, *La Maison, Wakatha u*, 1974–1976. FC Collections (2021)

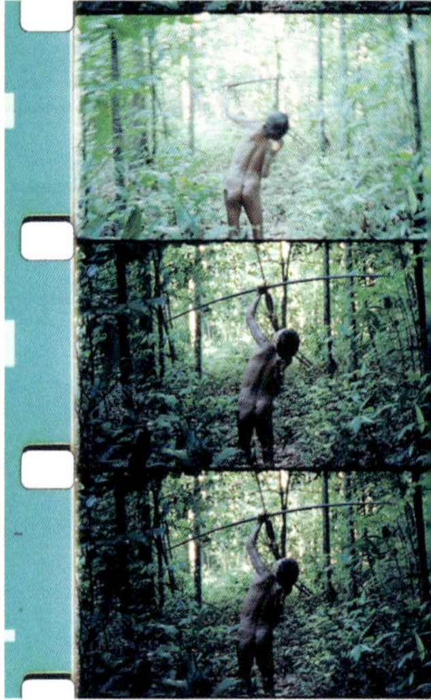

Raymond Depardon, still from the film *Chasseurs et Chamans*, 2002
FC Collections (2005)

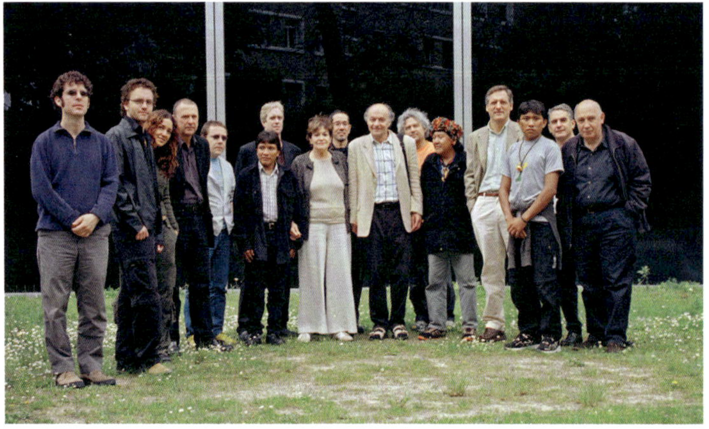

Stephen Vitiello, Jan Gerber, Adriana Varejão, Wolfgang Staehle, Vincent Beaurin, Joseca Mokahesi, Tony Oursler, Claudia Andujar, Naoki Takizawa, Volkmar Ziegler, Gary Hill, Davi Kopenawa, Bruce Albert, Dário Kopenawa, Hervé Chandès, and Raymond Depardon

CLAUDIA

THE YANOMAMI STRUGGLE

ANDUJAR

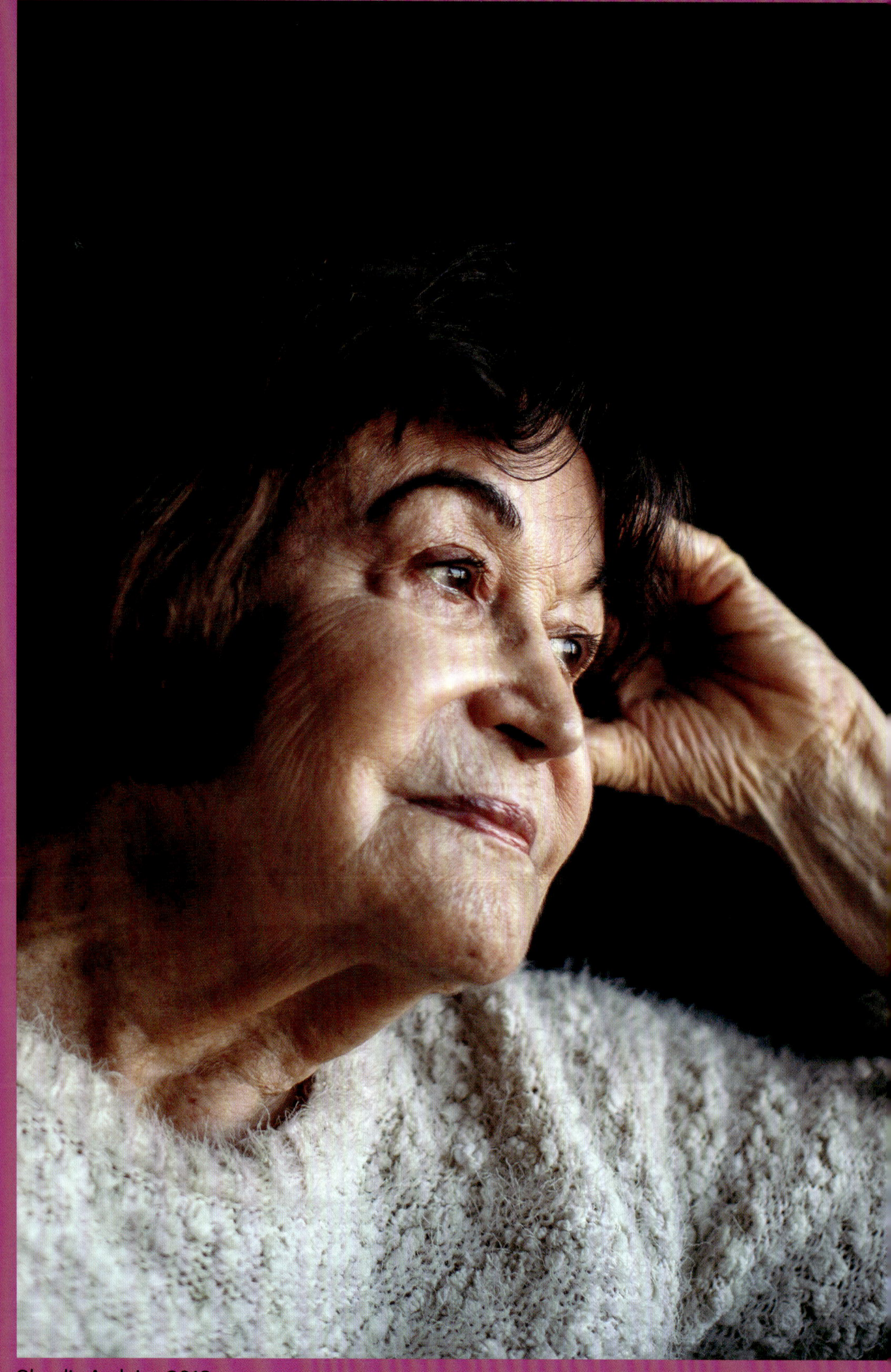

Claudia Andujar, 2019

Claudia Andujar
The Yanomami Struggle

To talk about Claudia Andujar, her career as a photographer, and commitment as an artist, also means talking about the Yanomami, a community of hunter-gatherers living in the heart of the Amazon rainforest, between the northwest of Brazil and Venezuela. Brazilian Claudia Andujar first met them in 1971, when she was working on a report on the Amazon for the magazine *Realidade*. Fascinated, she decided to undertake an in-depth photographic study of the Yanomami's world, which allowed her to discover their way of life, but also to denounce the damage caused by their interaction with white people. In 1978, with Italian missionary Carlo Zacquini and French anthropologist Bruce Albert, she founded the Comissão Pró-Yanomami (CCPY) and embarked on a campaign lasting almost fifteen years, culminating in the official delimitation of the Yanomami's territory, recognized by the Brazilian government in 1992. With Davi Kopenawa, shaman and spokesperson for the Yanomami, and recipient in 2019 of the "Alternative Nobel Prize," the Right Livelihood Award, she continues to travel the world in support of the Yanomami cause and the Amazon forest they call home.

Hervé Chandès, Director of the Fondation Cartier met Claudia Andujar during a trip to Brazil in the mid-1990s. The photographer showed him her work on the Yanomami, revealing the depth of her commitment. Two years later, she visited the Fondation Cartier team, accompanied by Bruce Albert. The latter spoke of his experience of the Yanomami, with whom he has worked and stayed regularly since 1975. He explained the cosmological philosophy and shamanic vision of these inhabitants of the Amazon. For Hervé Chandès, the Fondation Cartier needed to give the Yanomami a space in which to speak. The idea of an exhibition was conceived with Bruce Albert. Presented in 2003, the exhibition *Yanomami, Spirit of the Forest* told the story of an encounter: one that had taken place a few months earlier between the inhabitants of the Yanomami village of Watoriki and some ten international artists, including Raymond Depardon, Tony Oursler, Adriana Varejão, and of course, Claudia Andujar. *Yanomami, Spirit of the Forest* thus inaugurated a series of collective exhibitions highlighting the Yanomami through the work of Claudia Andujar and the drawings produced at her invitation by artists from the community. At the Fondation Cartier in Paris, these include *Native Land, Stop Eject* (2008), *Histoires de voir, Show and Tell* (2012), *América Latina 1960–2013* (2013), and *Trees* (2019), but their work was also shown in *Trees* at the Power Station of Art in Shanghai (2021), *Les Vivants* (*Living Worlds*) at the Tripostal in Lille (2022), and *Siamo Foresta* at Triennale Milano (2023).

In 2020, the Fondation Cartier devoted a solo exhibition to Claudia Andujar. Initially devised by Thyago Nogueira for the Instituto Moreira Salles in Brazil, Claudia Andujar's exhibition *The Yanomami Struggle* naturally found its place at the Fondation Cartier in Paris. Through more than three hundred photographs, an audiovisual installation, historical documents, and drawings by Yanomami artists such as André Taniki, Joseca Mokahesi, Ehuana Yaira, and Kalepi Sanöma, this exhibition reflected Claudia Andujar's political commitment and her major contribution to photographic art. The importance of this exhibition was such that it was also presented at The Shed in New York in 2023, in an expanded version. Claudia Andujar's photographs were again accompanied by drawings by Yanomami artists, as well as films by Yanomami directors, including Morzaniel Iramari, Roseane Yariana, Aida Harika, and Edmar Tokorino. As they did at the Fondation Cartier in 2020, in New York, Claudia Andujar and Davi Kopenawa continued the story of their fight for the Yanomami and for environmental justice, two essential struggles that the Fondation Cartier is committed to. Invited by Columbia University, Davi Kopenawa also spoke of his fight, accompanied by his son Dário Kopenawa.

Today, the Collections of the Fondation Cartier bring together a large body of photographs by Claudia Andujar, along with numerous drawings and paintings by Yanomami artists.

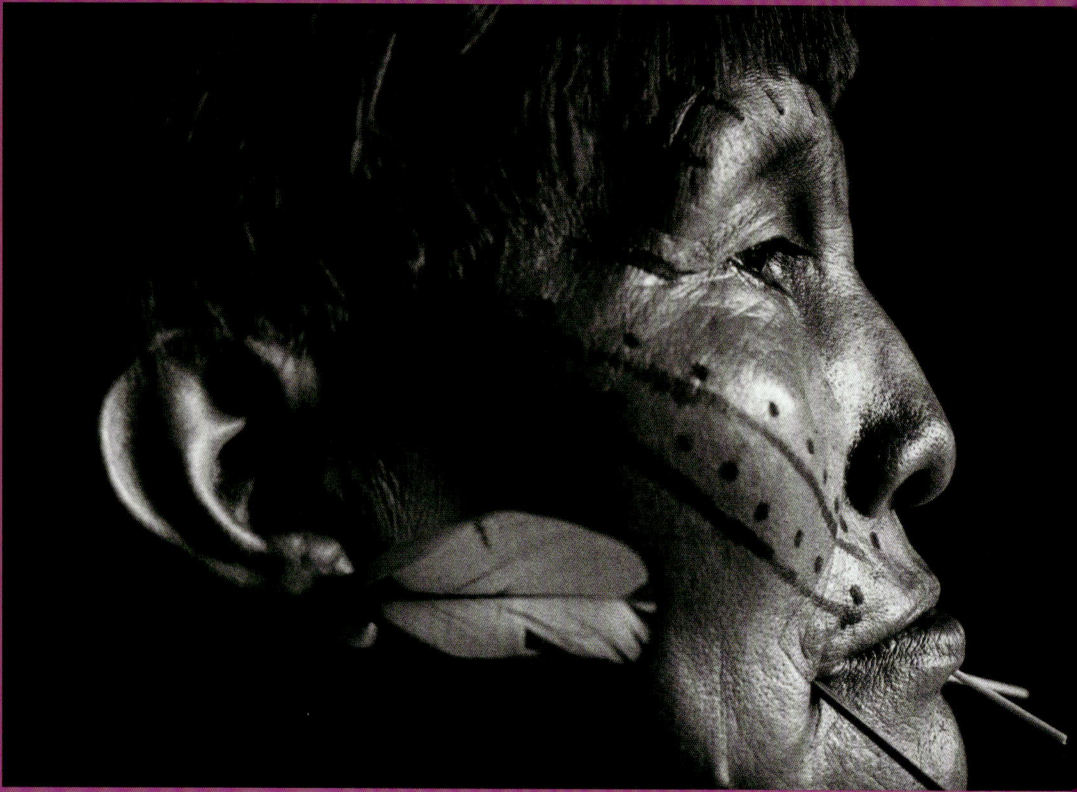

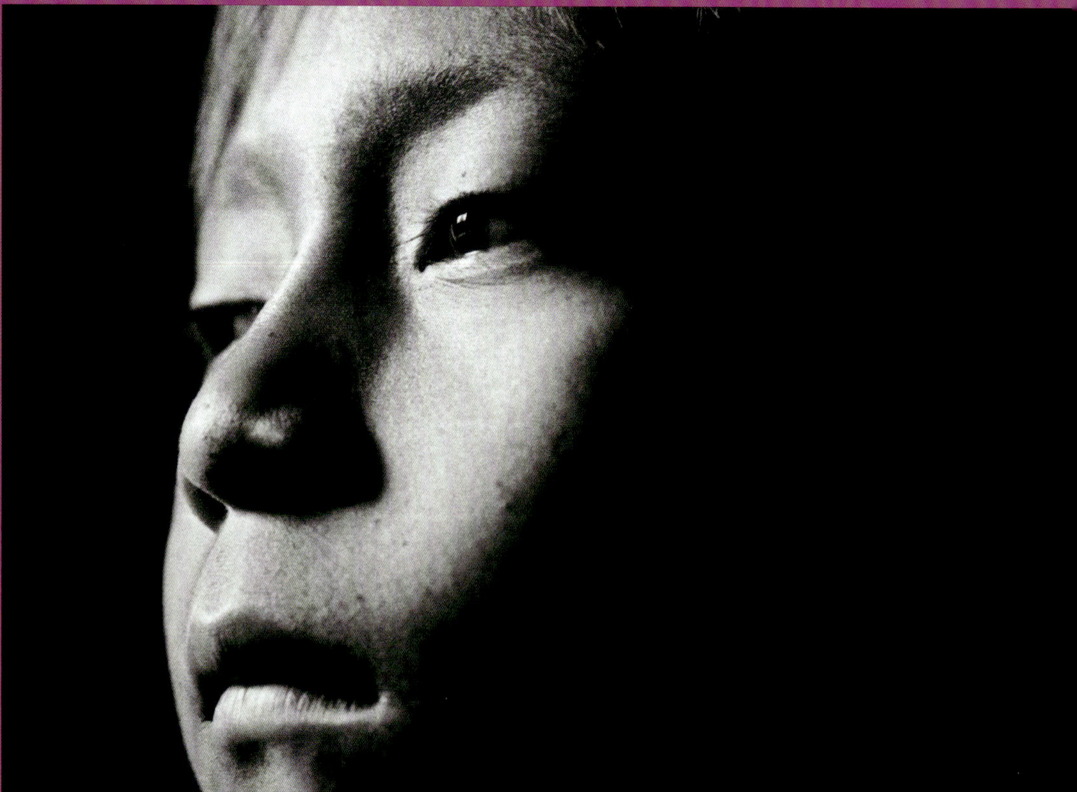

1976   Five years after her first encounter with the Yanomami, Claudia Andujar created the *Identité, Wakatha u* series. FC Collections (2004–2006)

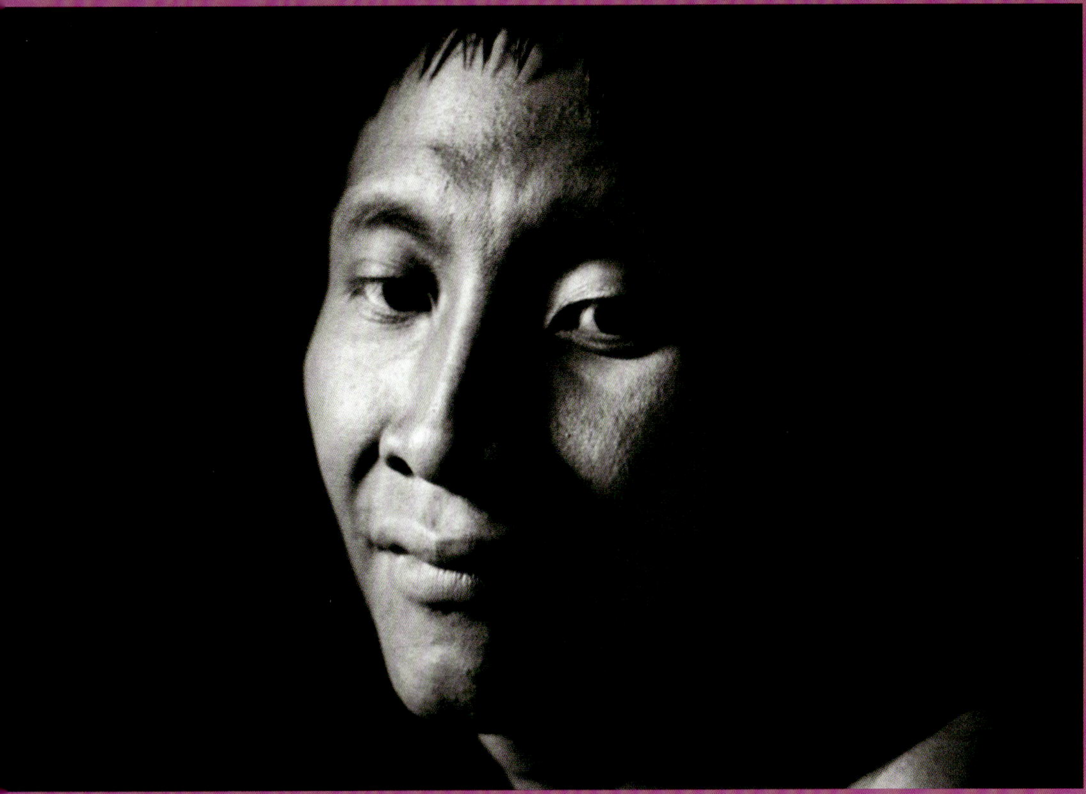

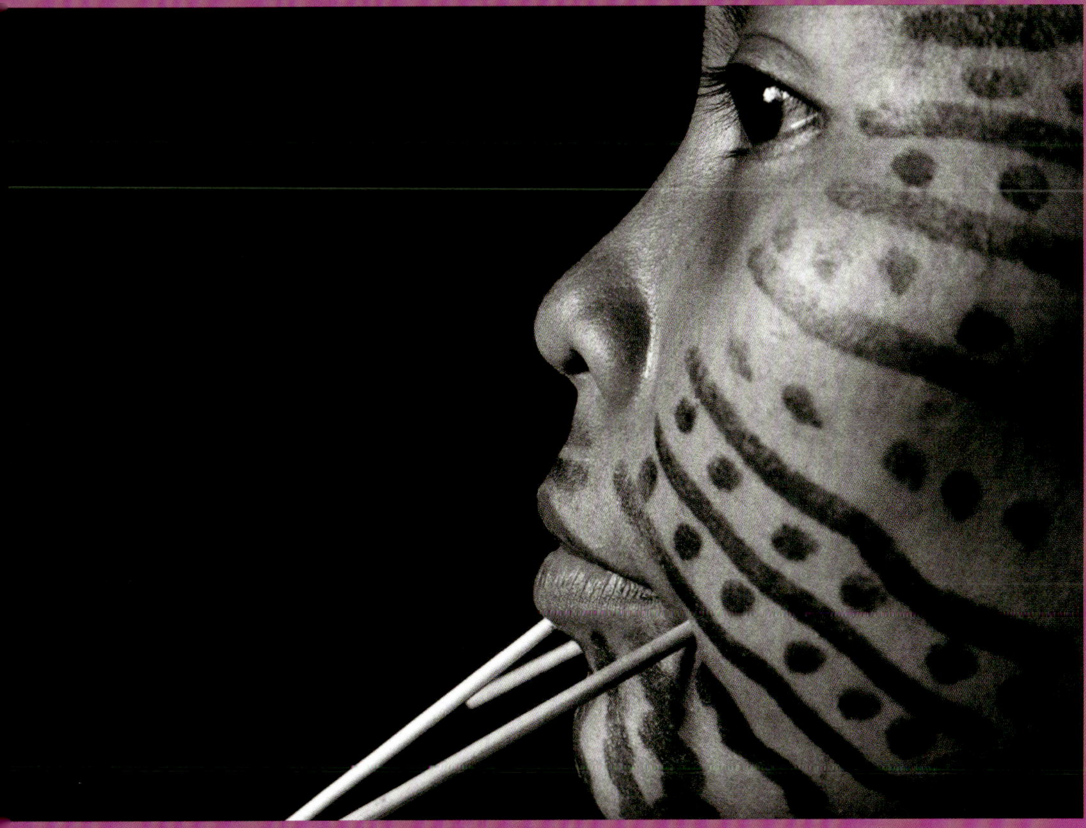

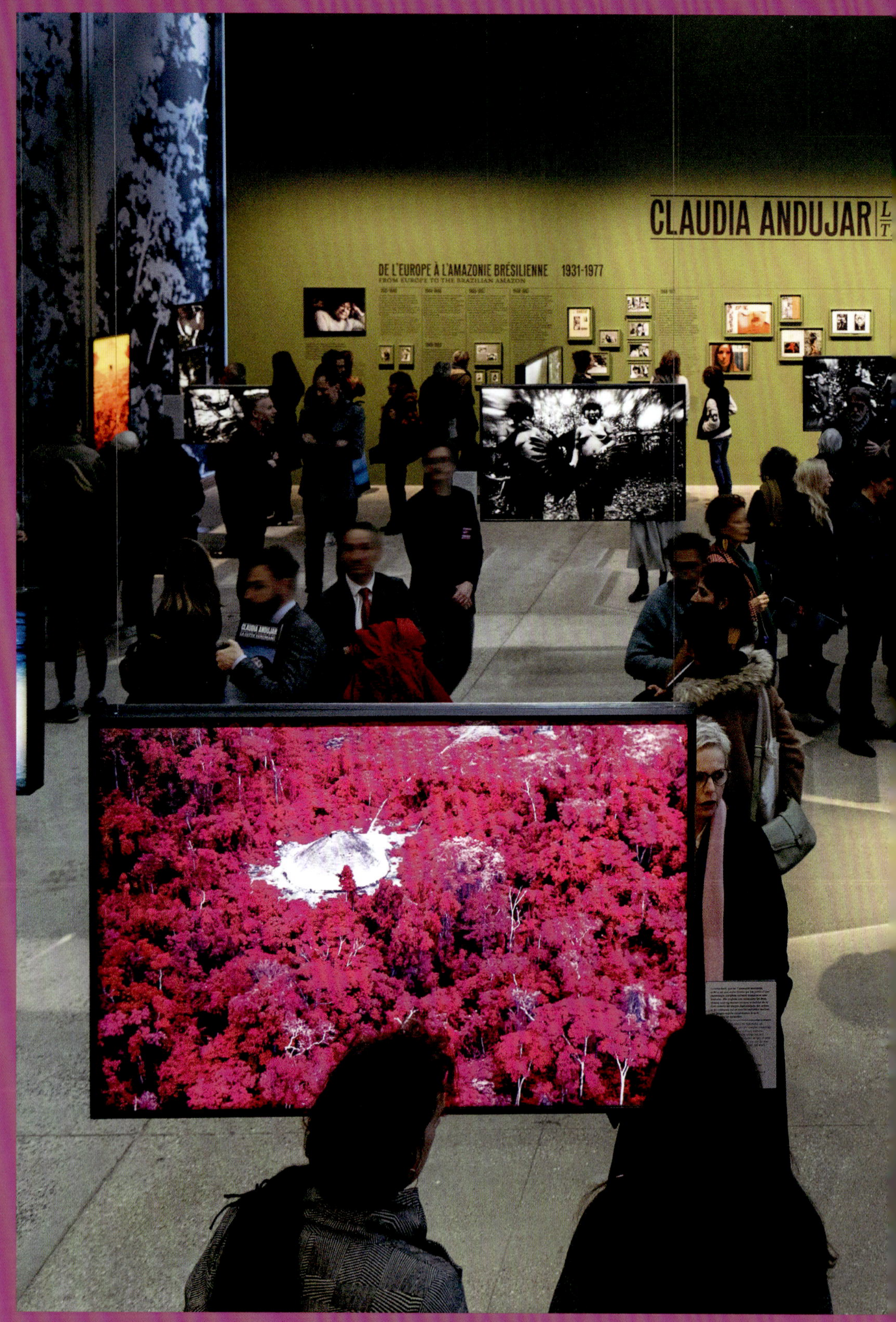

2020   With over 300 photographs, an audiovisual installation, and drawings by Yanomami artists, Claudia Andujar's exhibition, *The Yanomami Struggle* revealed both the Brazilian photographer's aesthetic approach and political convictions.

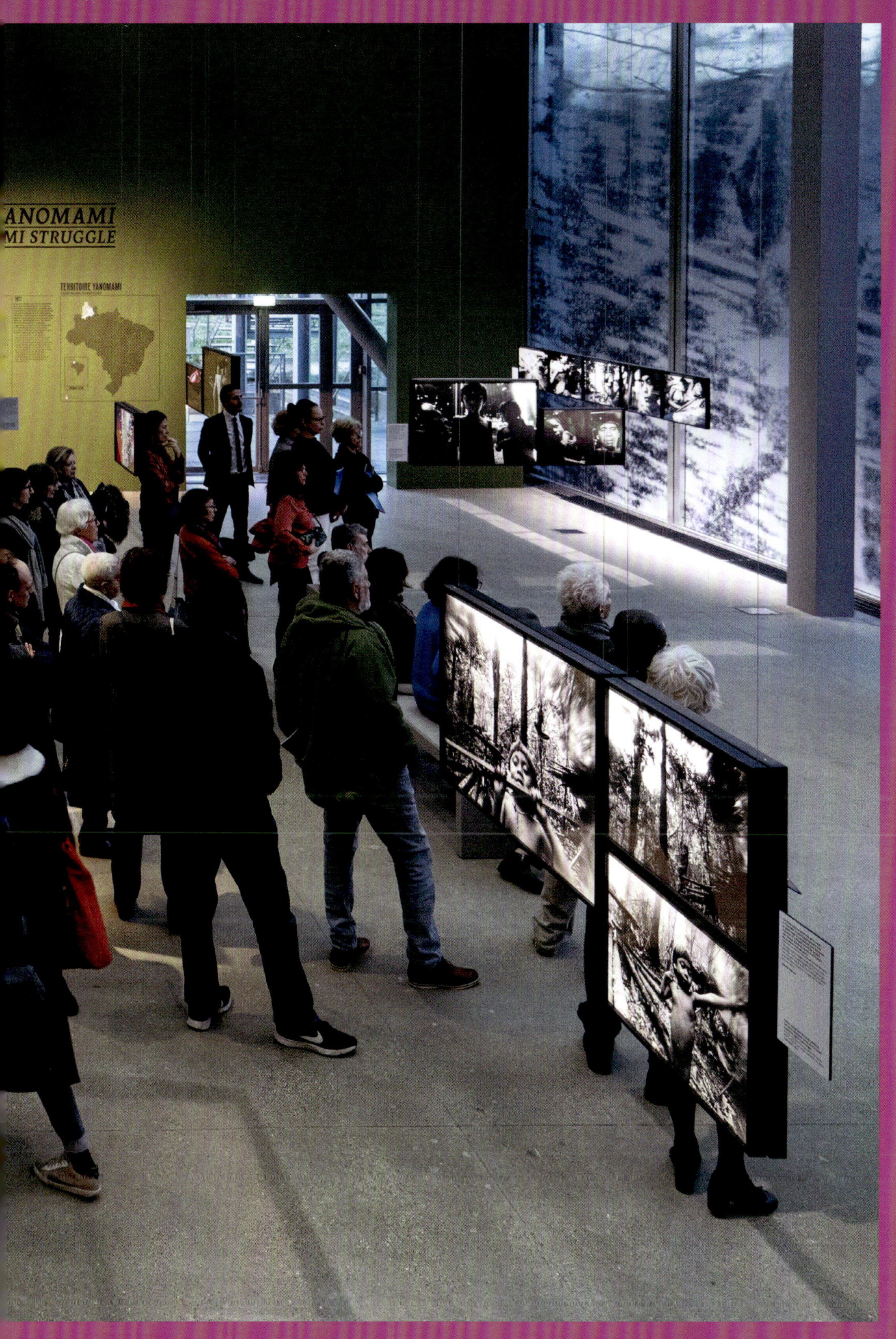
ANOMAMI
MI STRUGGLE
TERRITOIRE YANOMAMI

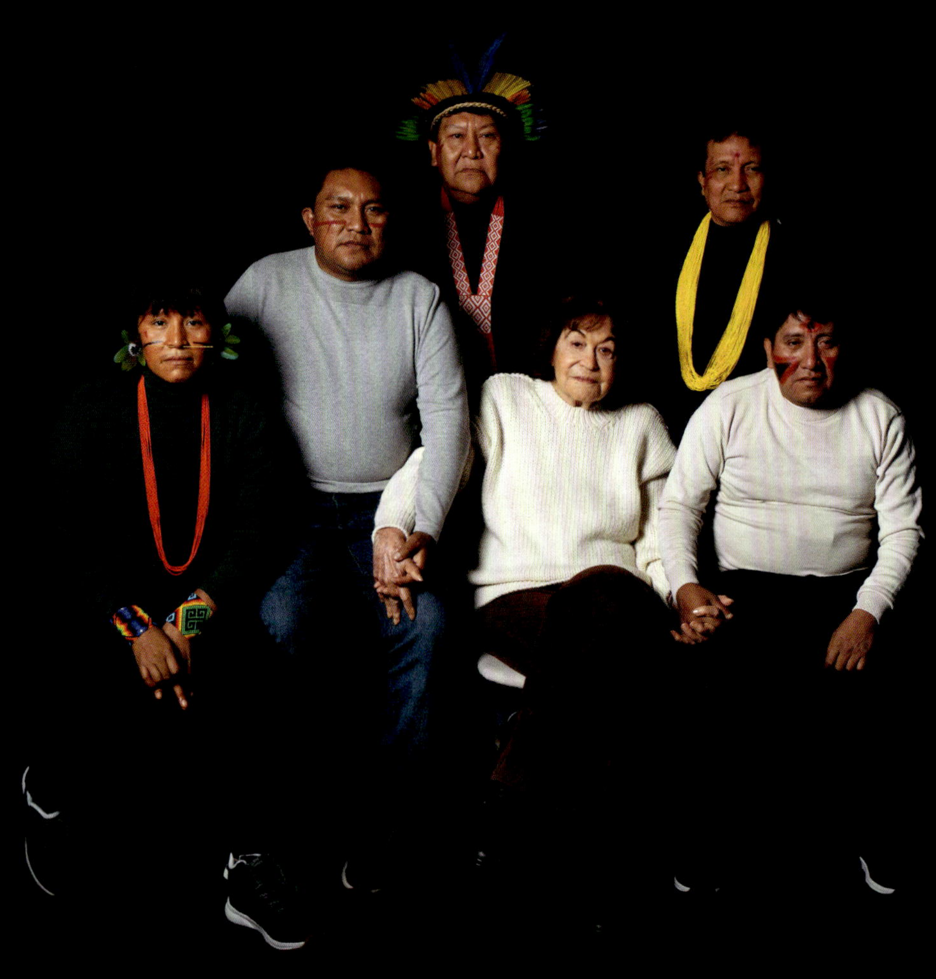

2023   After being shown in six countries, the exhibition *The Yanomami Struggle* traveled to The Shed in New York. Ehuana Yaíra, Dário and Davi Kopenawa, Claudia Andujar, Morzaniel Ɨramari, and Joseca Mokahesi were all present for the opening.

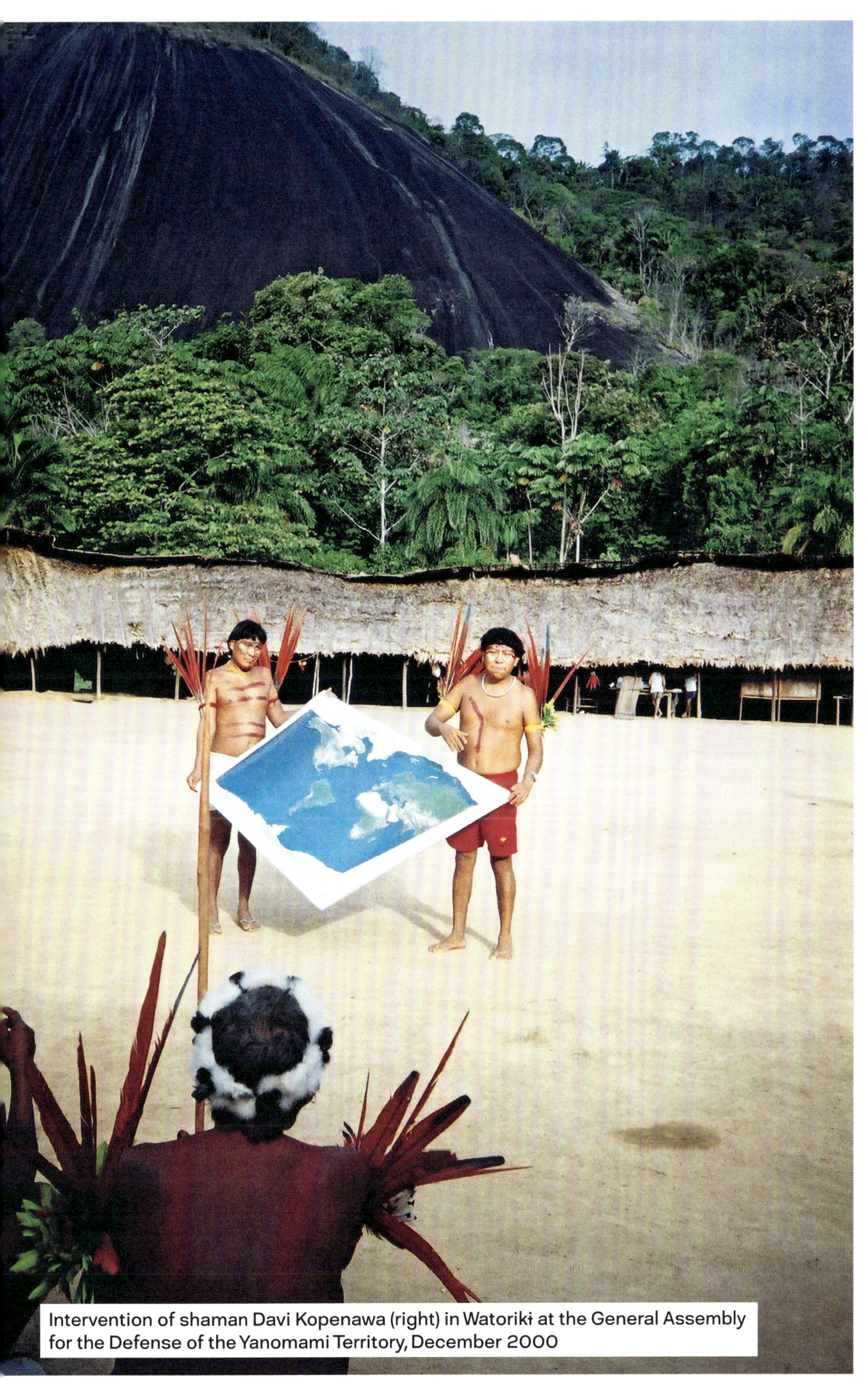

Intervention of shaman Davi Kopenawa (right) in Watorikɨ at the General Assembly for the Defense of the Yanomami Territory, December 2000

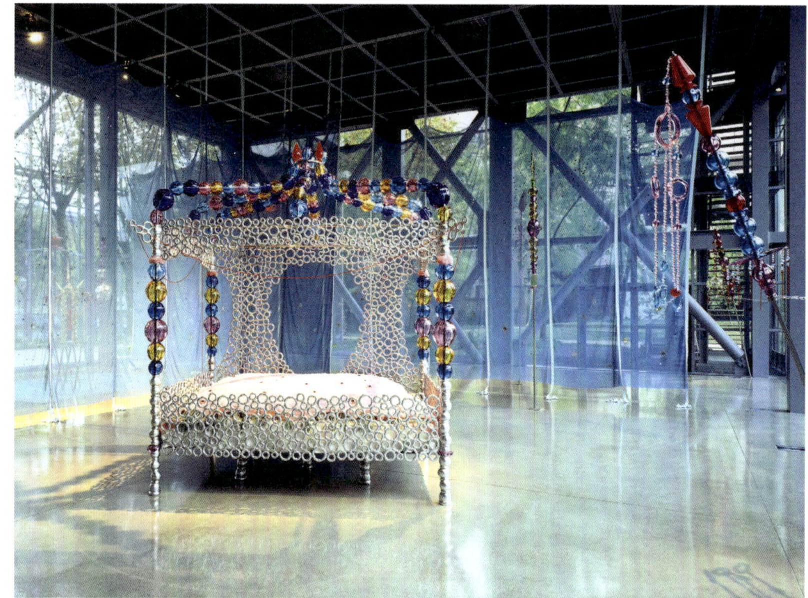

Jean-Michel Othoniel, *Mon lit*, 2003

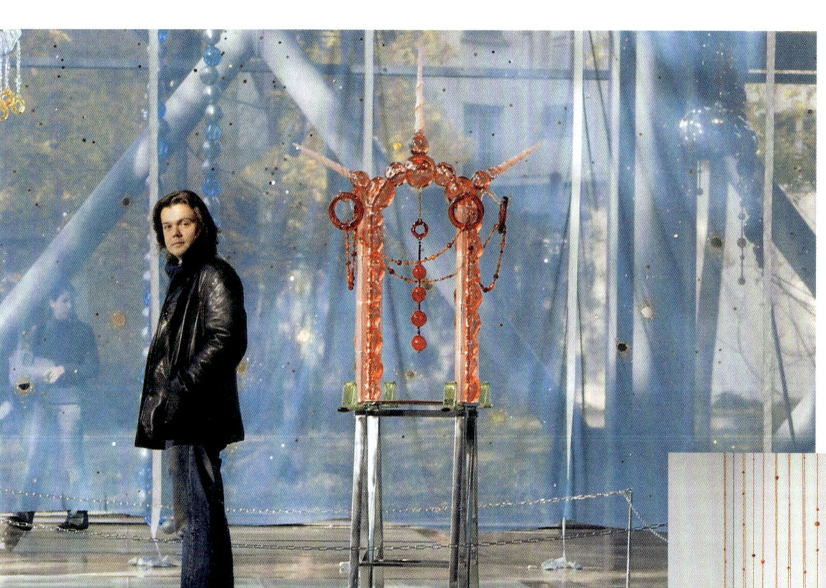

Jean-Michel Othoniel at the exhibition opening near his work *L'Unicorne*, 2003. FC Collections (2004)

Jean-Michel Othoniel,
Paysage amoureux, 1997
FC Collections (1998)

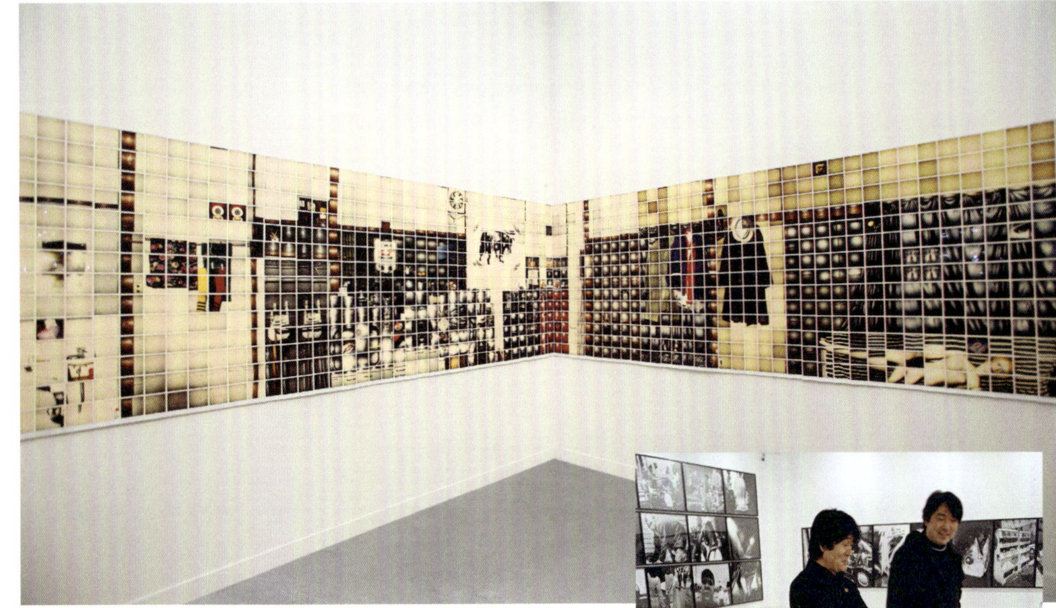

Daido Moriyama, *Polaroid, Polaroid* (detail), 1997
FC Collections (2004)

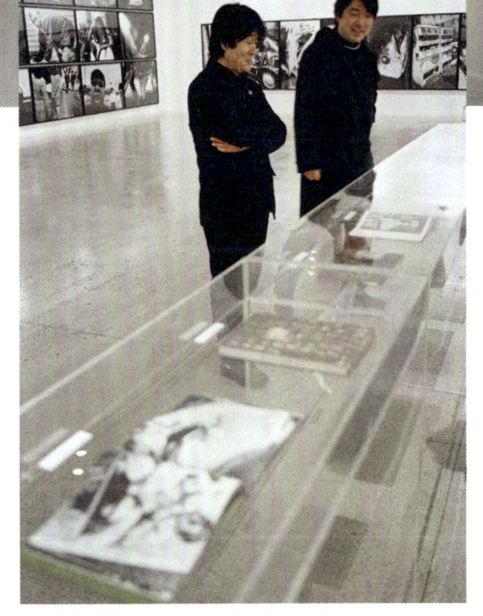

Daido Moriyama during the
installation of his exhibition

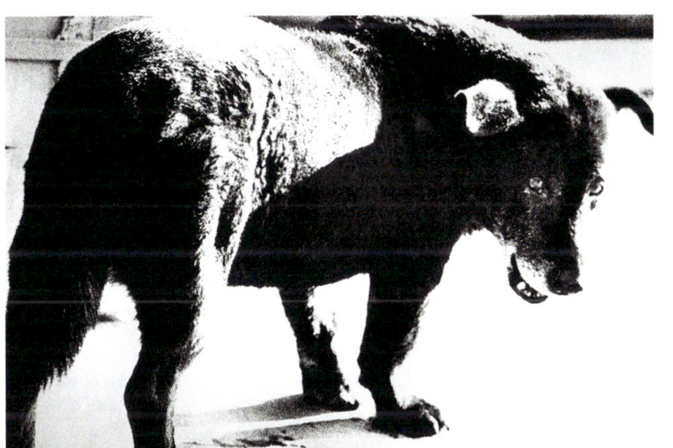

Daido Moriyama, *Stray Dog, Misawa*, 1971
FC Collections (2004)

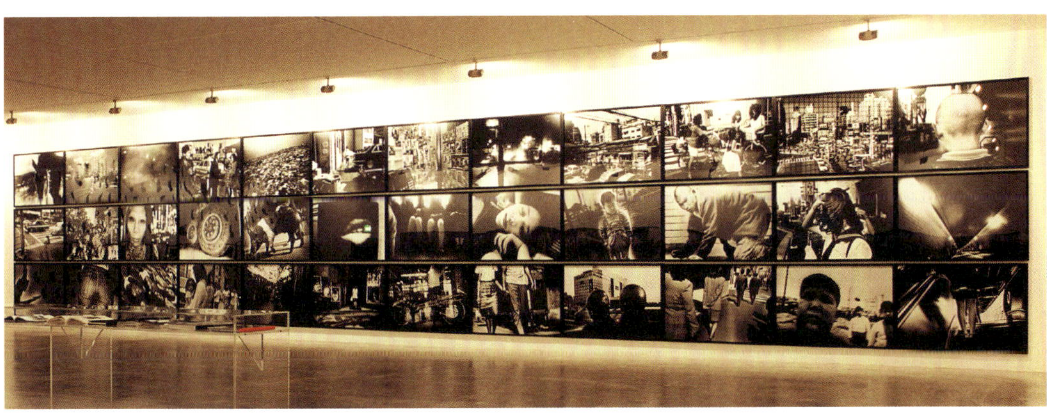

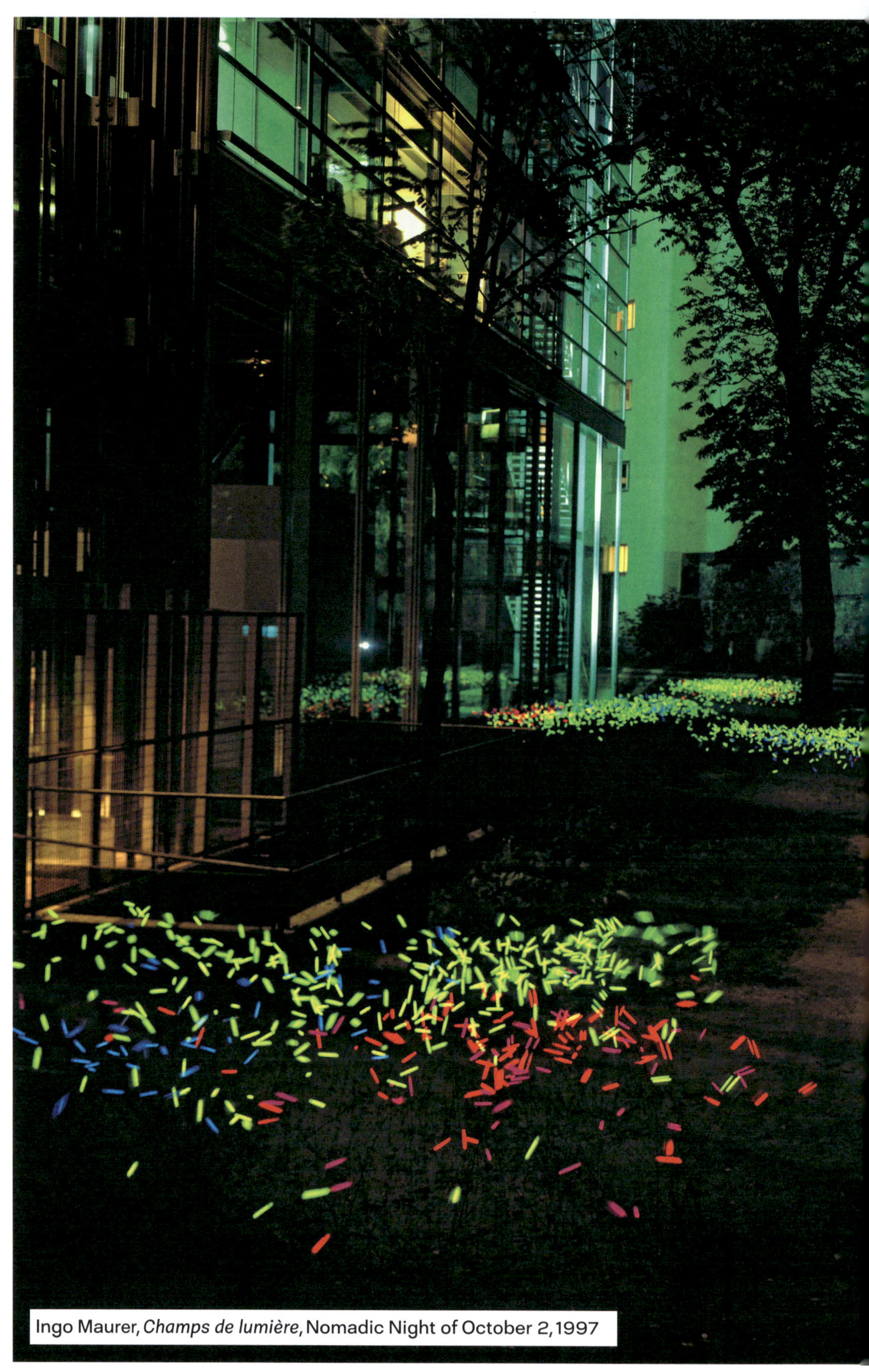

Ingo Maurer, *Champs de lumière*, Nomadic Night of October 2, 1997

2004–2013

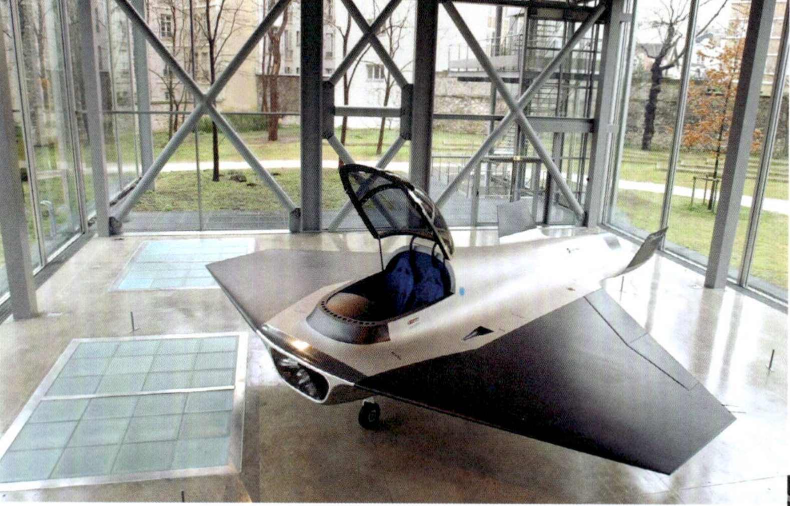

The Fondation Cartier gave carte blanche to Australian designer
Marc Newson: for the exhibition, he conceived *Kelvin 40*, a jet plane.
FC Collections (2004)

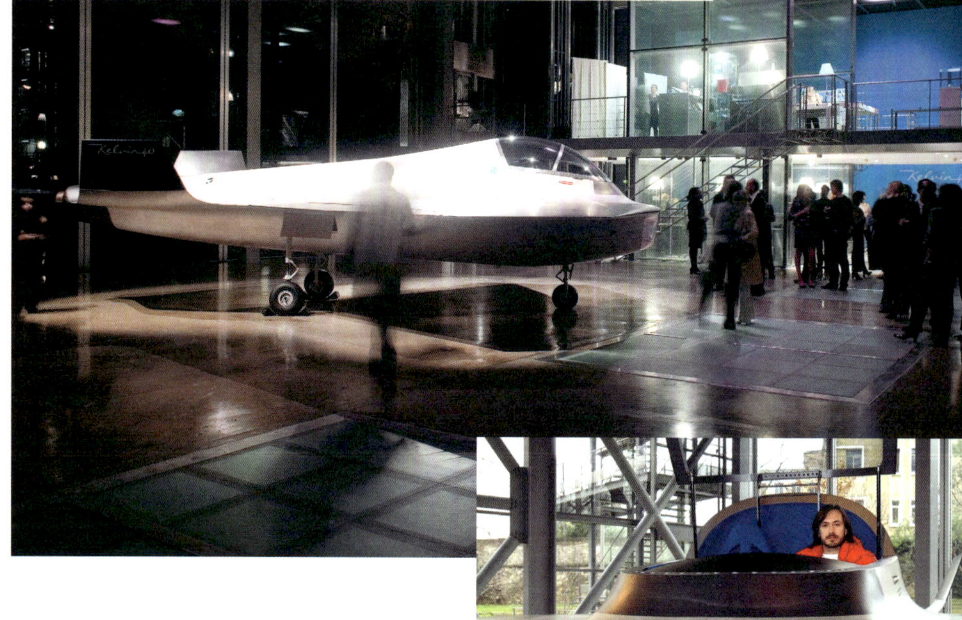

Marc Newson at the exhibition opening

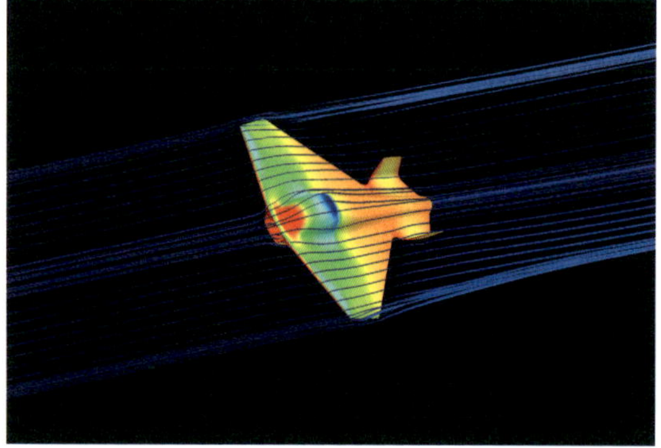

Aerodynamic study and technical development
for *Kelvin 40*, 2003

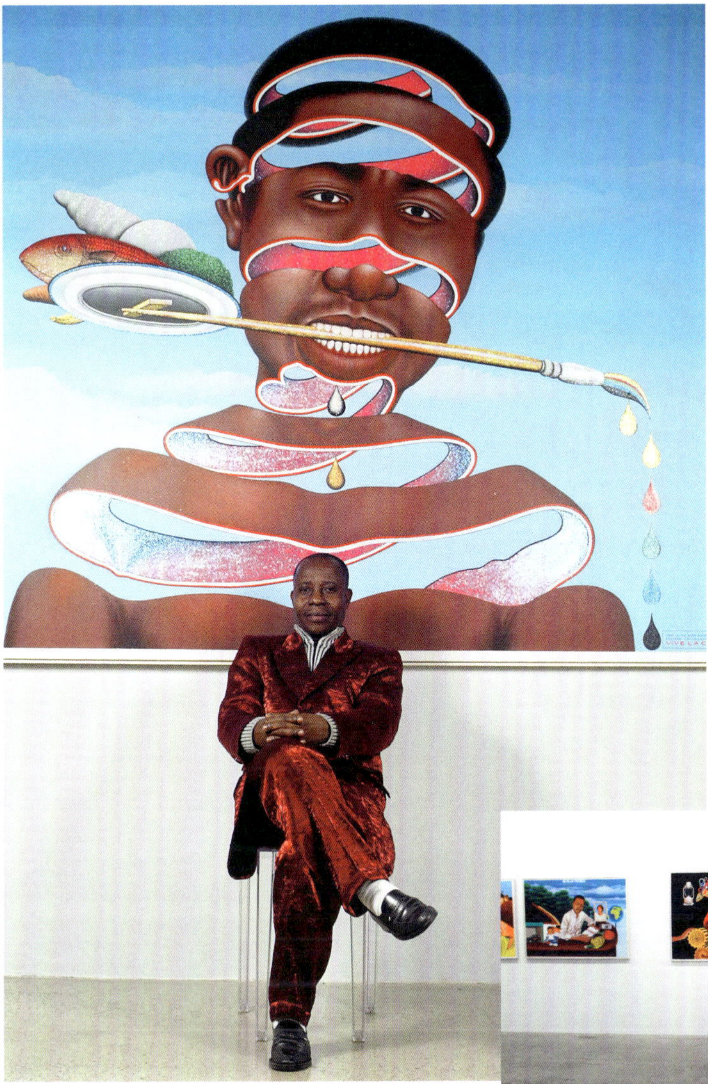

Chéri Samba at the exhibition opening,
in front of his canvas *J'aime la couleur*, 2004

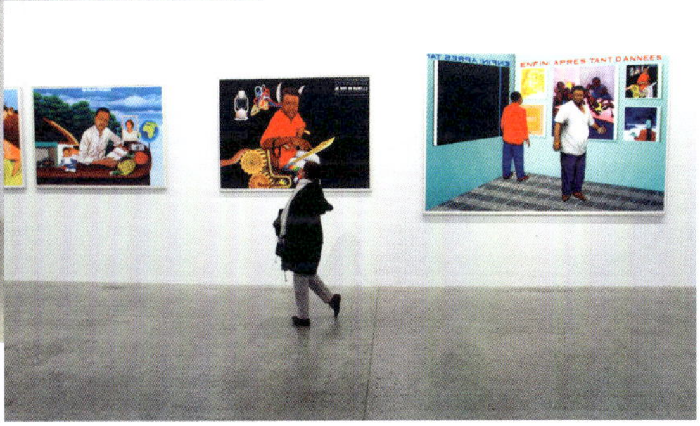

The exhibition *J'aime Chéri Samba*
featured 35 paintings by the artist.

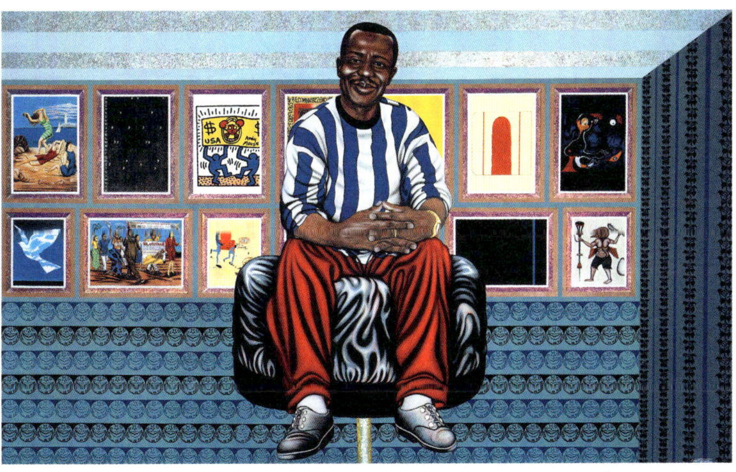

Chéri Samba, *Aussi… au plafond*, 2002. FC Collections (2002)

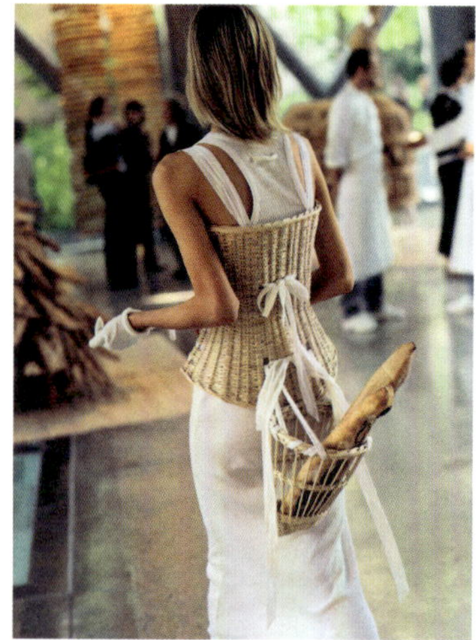

Exhibition opening

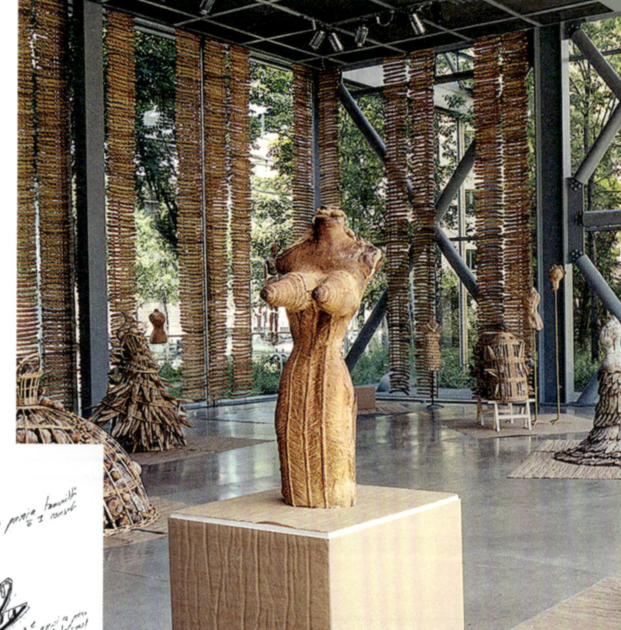

Pain Couture by Jean Paul Gaultier was a commission by the Fondation Cartier. This exhibition of ephemeral dresses brought together two completely different worlds: the reality of the bakery and the magic of fashion design.

Jean Paul Gaultier, preparatory sketch for the exhibition

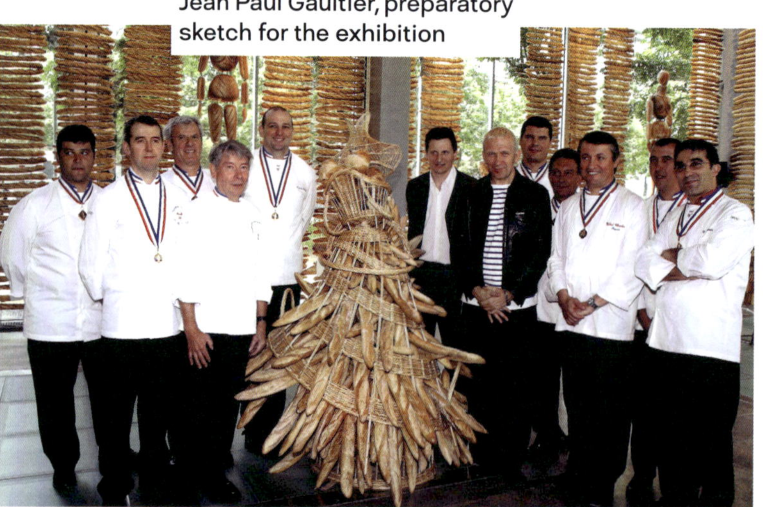

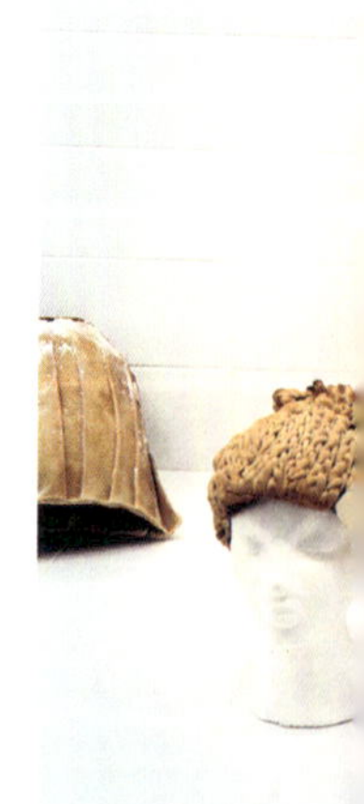

Fourteen members of the "Meilleurs Ouvriers de France" (Best French artisans) and three members of the "Compagnons du Devoir" (Craftsmen's guild) created bread accessories and the baguettes used to make the dresses.

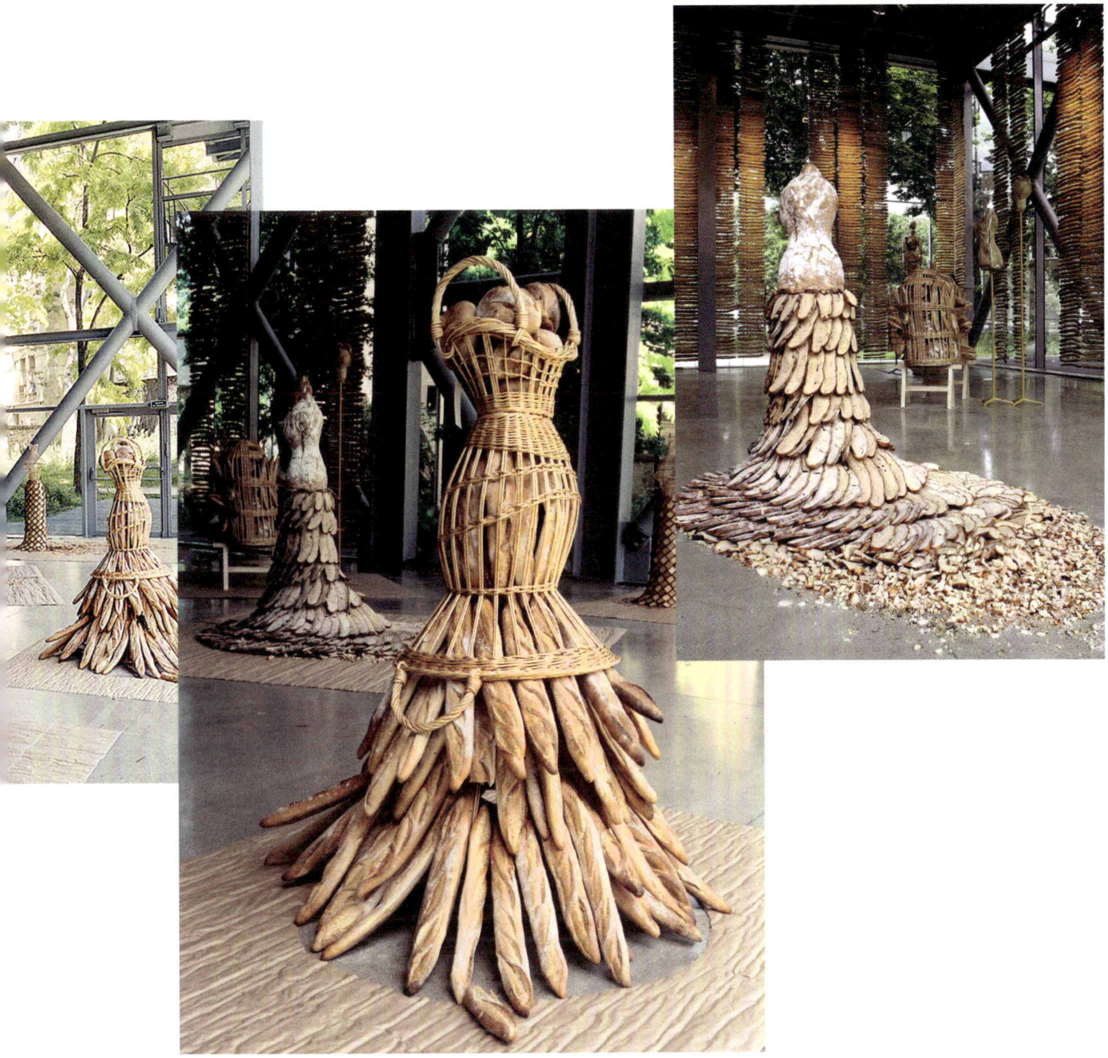

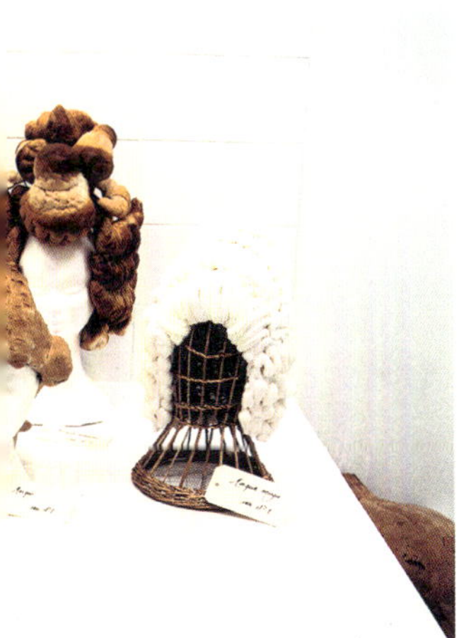

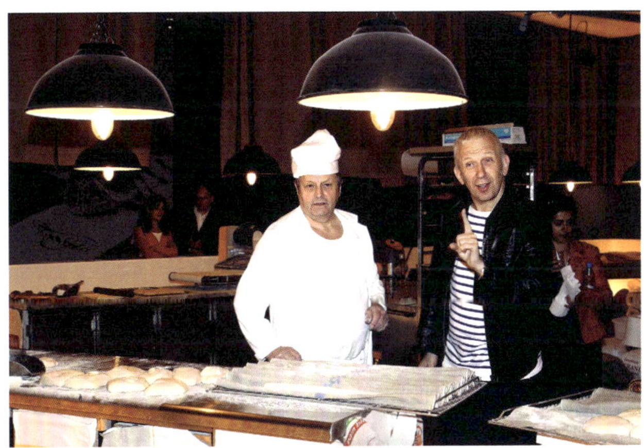

A "couture-boulangerie" laboratory was set up
in the Fondation Cartier basement. Here visitors could
watch the different stages involved in making bread,
which was then sold in the exhibition.

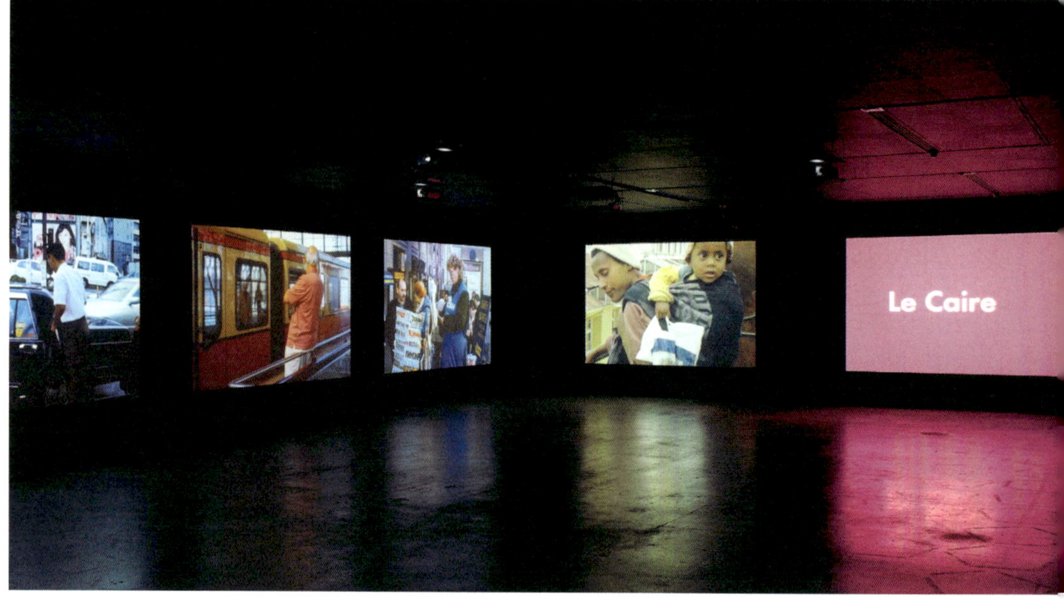

7×3 was an exhibition of films bringing together seven short films
by Raymond Depardon, devoted to seven large cities: Rio de Janeiro,
Shanghai, Tokyo, Berlin, Moscow, Addis Ababa, and Cairo.

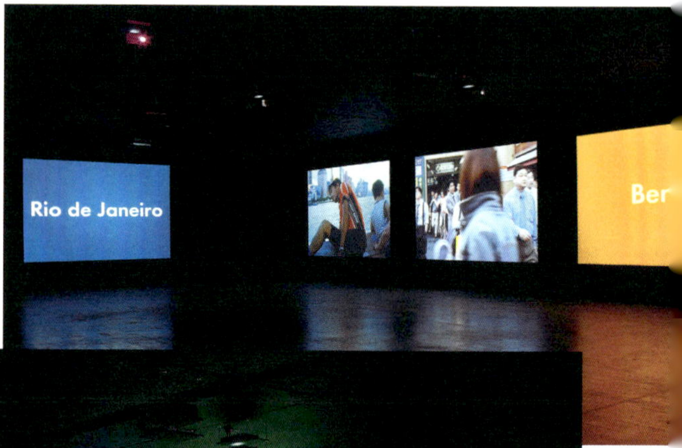

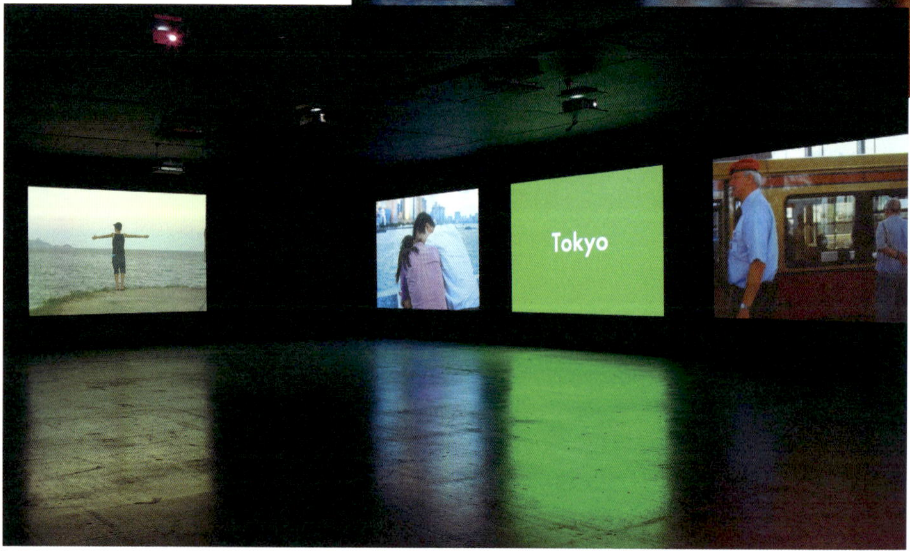

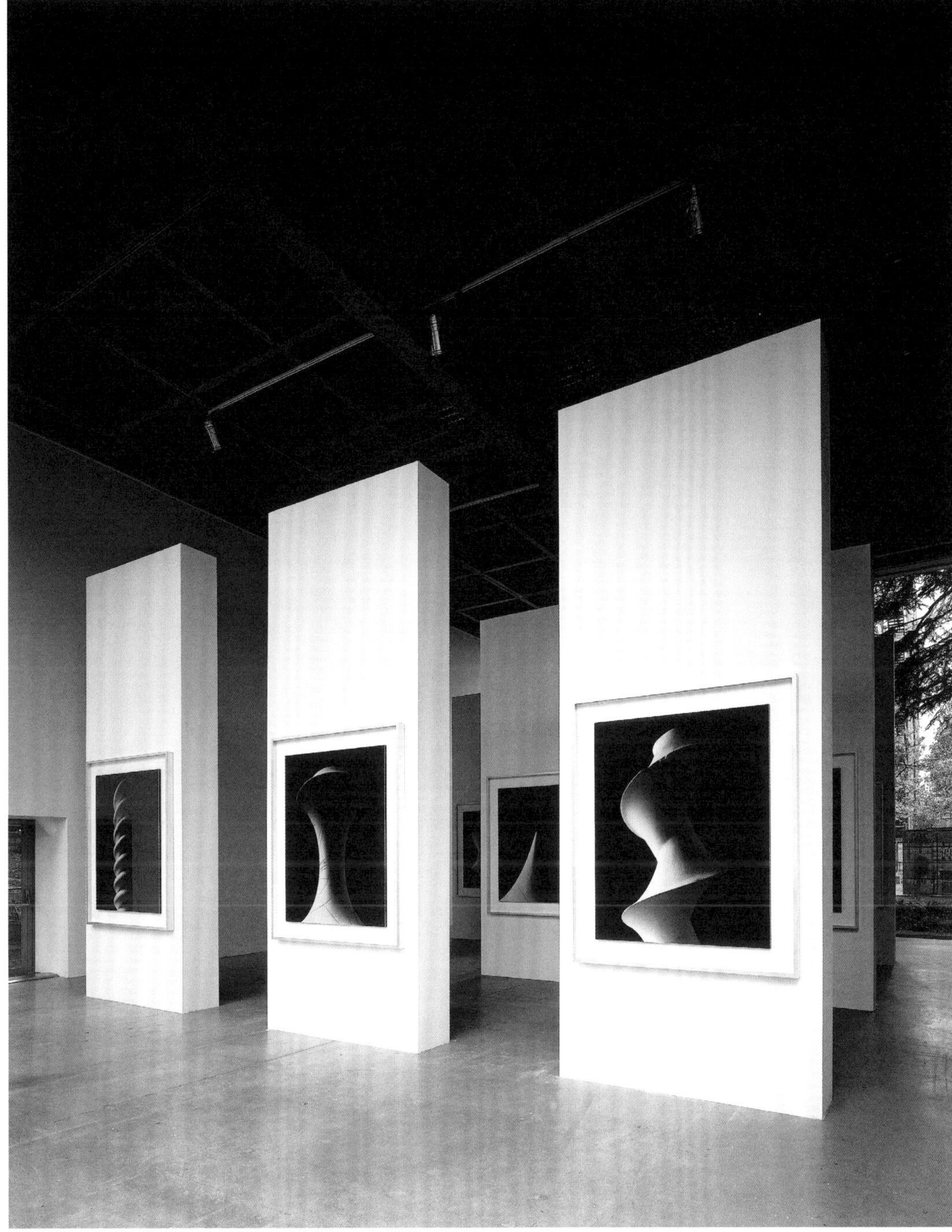

This exhibition, designed by Hiroshi Sugimoto, presented a group of 19 prints from the series *Mathematical Forms* and *Mechanical Forms*, paying tribute to Marcel Duchamp's *Large Glass* and to Jean Nouvel's building. Like a mise en abyme, Hiroshi Sugimoto also photographed the exhibition. Hiroshi Sugimoto, *Mathematical Forms*, 2004. FC Collections (2005)

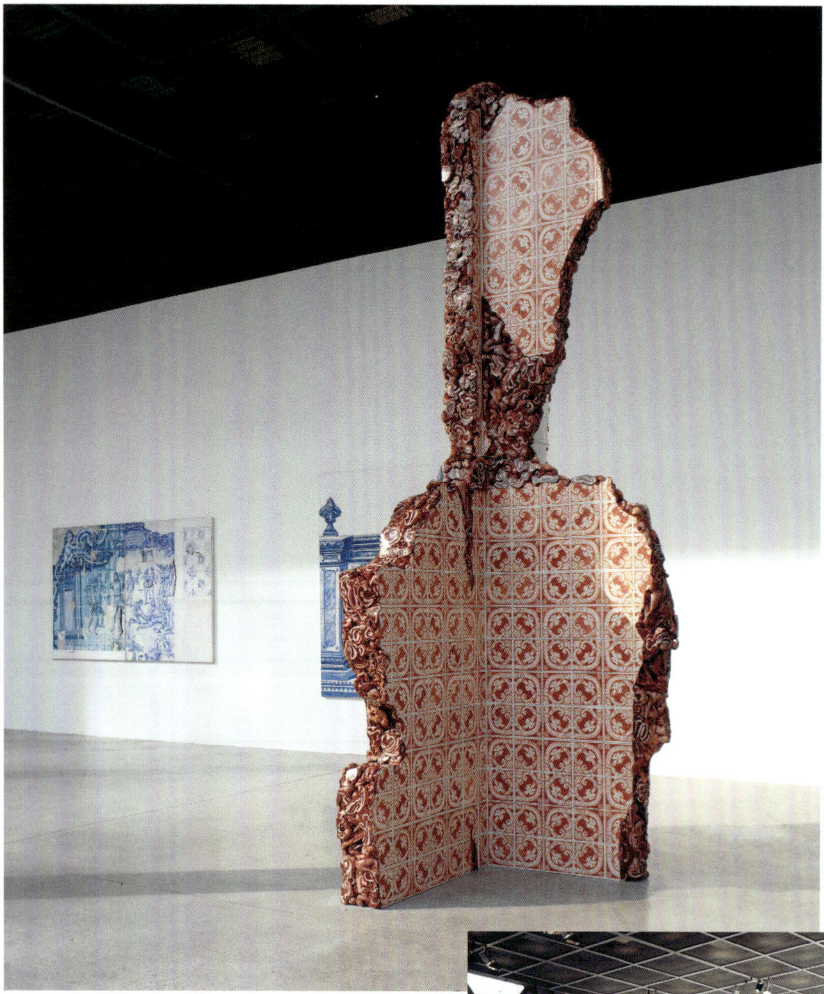

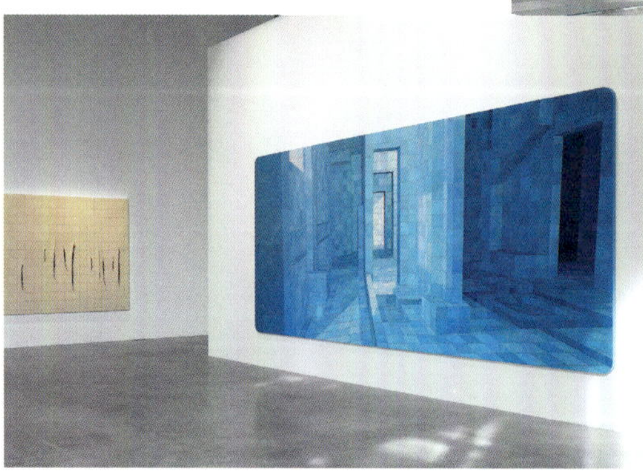

Adriana Varejão, *Linda da Lapa*, 2005
FC Collections (2005)

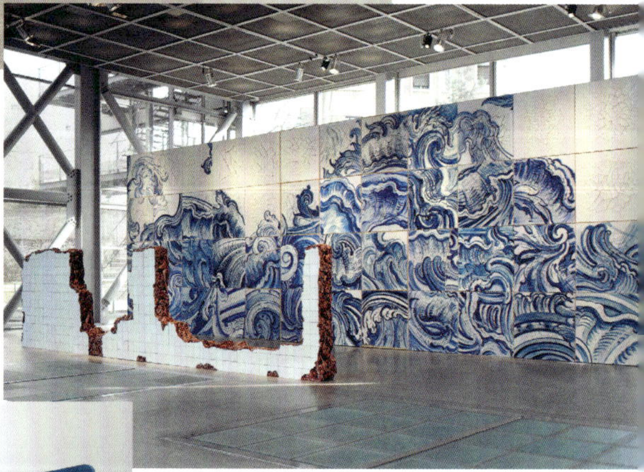

Adriana Varejão, *Linda do Rosário*, and
Celacanto provoca maremoto, 2004

Adriana Varejão, *Parede com incisões
a la Fontana*, 2002, and *O Sedutor*, 2004

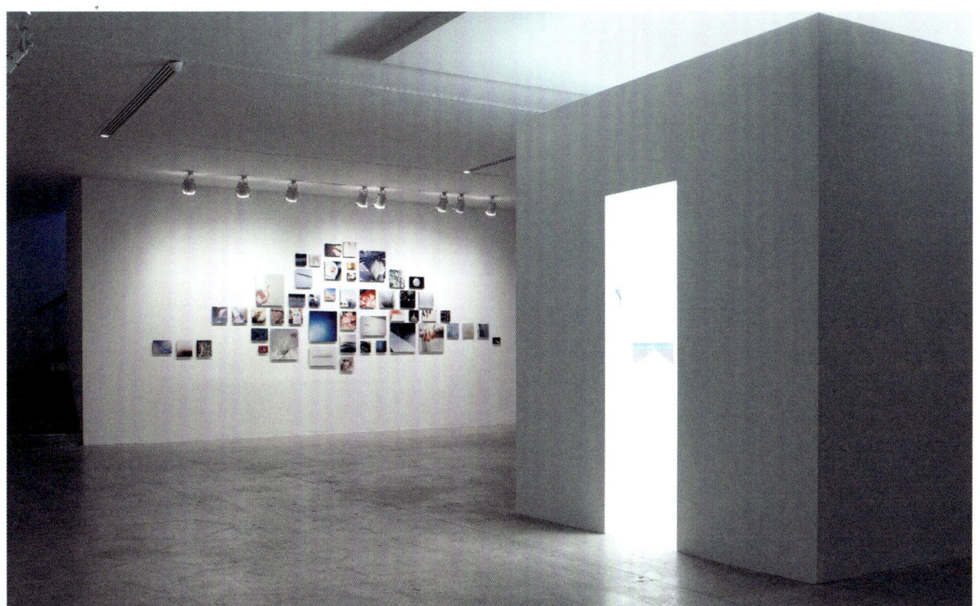

Rinko Kawauchi featured a large selection of photographs from the *Aila* series (2000-2004) and presented the following series for the first time: *The Eyes, the Ears* (2002-2004) and *Cui Cui* (1992-2005), a slideshow of 232 photographs belonging to the Collections of the Fondation Cartier.

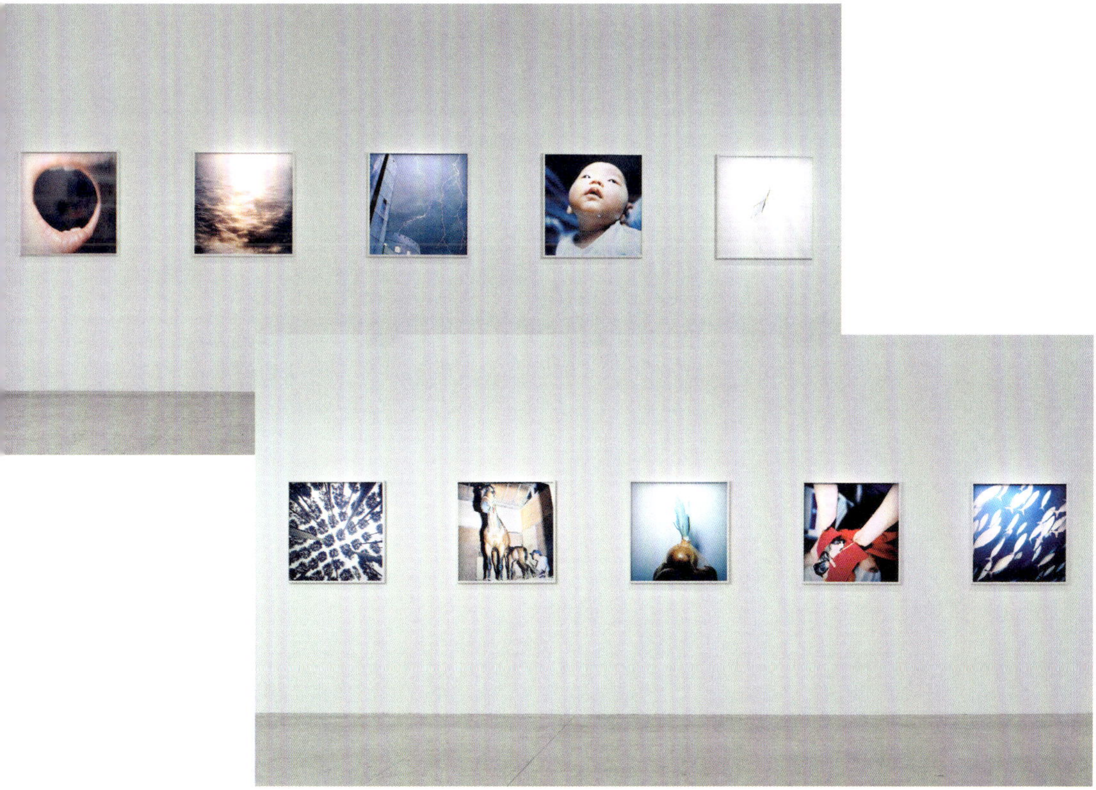

Rinko Kawauchi, *Aila* series, 2000-2004

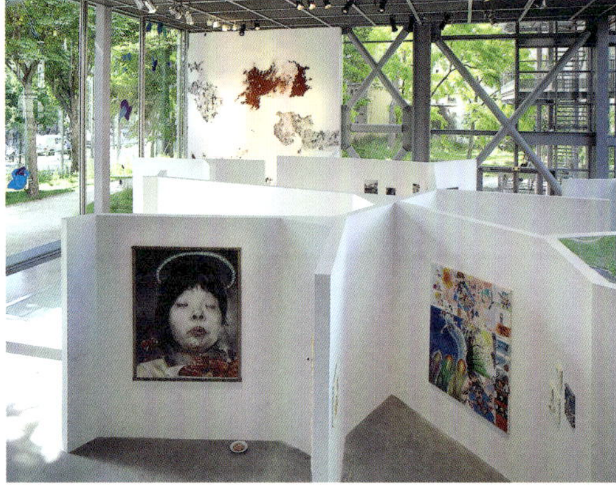

J'en rêve brought together the works of 58 artists, either still students or freshly graduated, selected by a jury of internationally renowned artists including Christian Boltanski, Fabrice Hyber, and Nan Goldin.

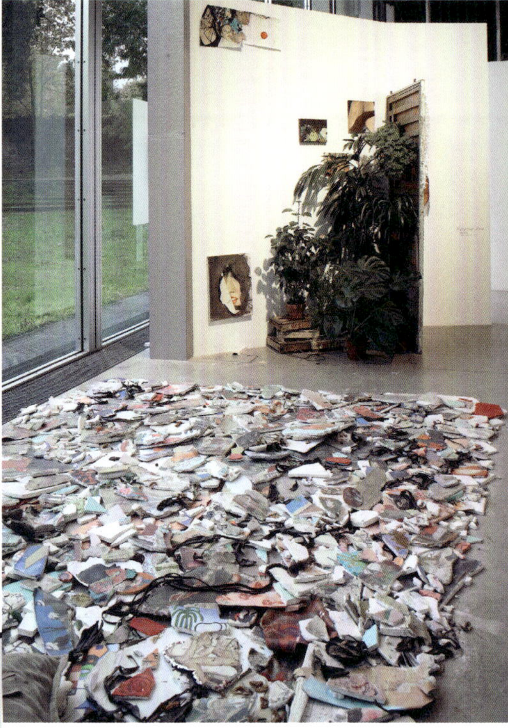

Catalina León, *Almohadon con fuente*, 2005

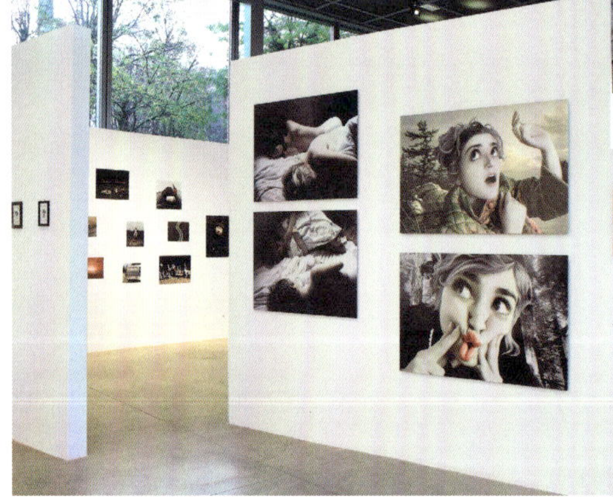

Flavia Da Rin, *Untitled*, 2001–2005
FC Collections (2005)

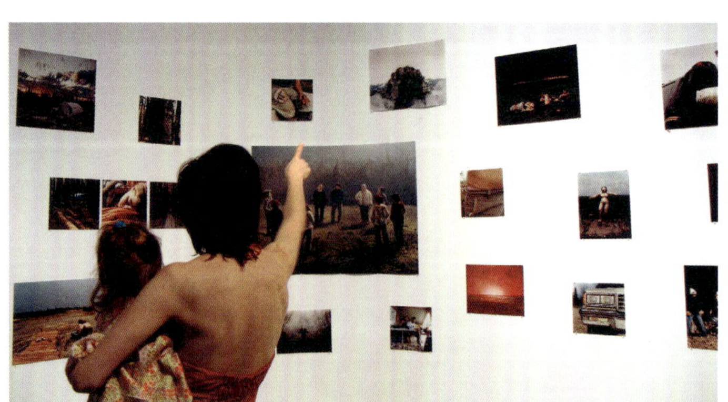

Works by Peter Harkawik

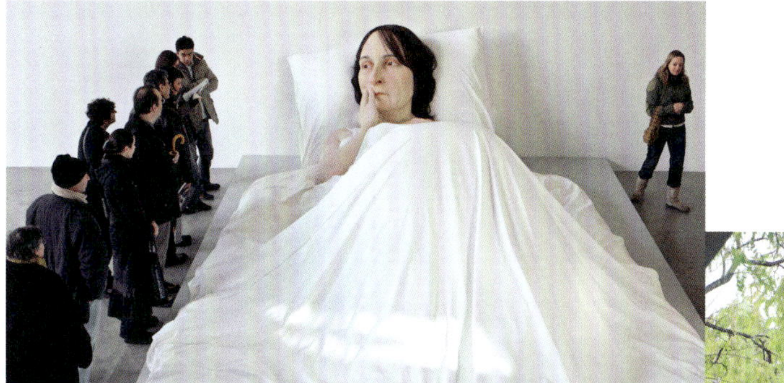

Ron Mueck, *In Bed*, 2005
FC Collections (2006)

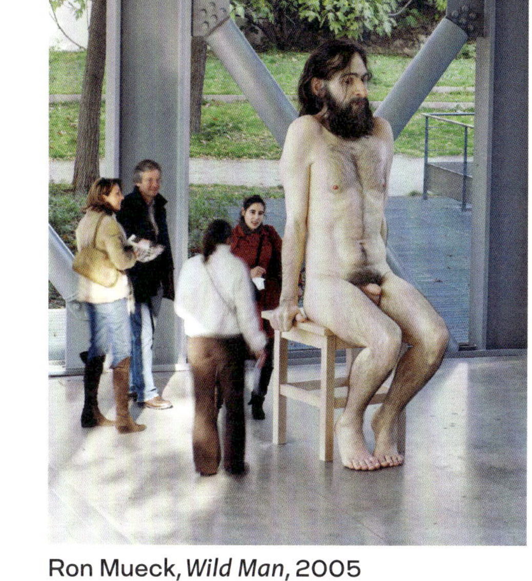

Ron Mueck, *Wild Man*, 2005

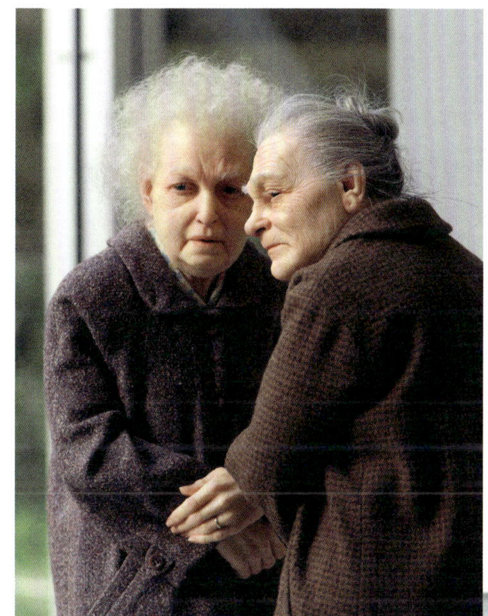

Ron Mueck, *Two Women*, 2005

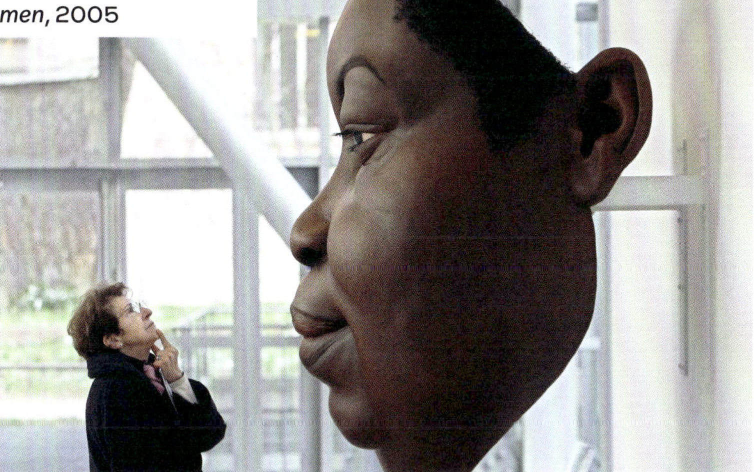

Ron Mueck, *Mask III*, 2005

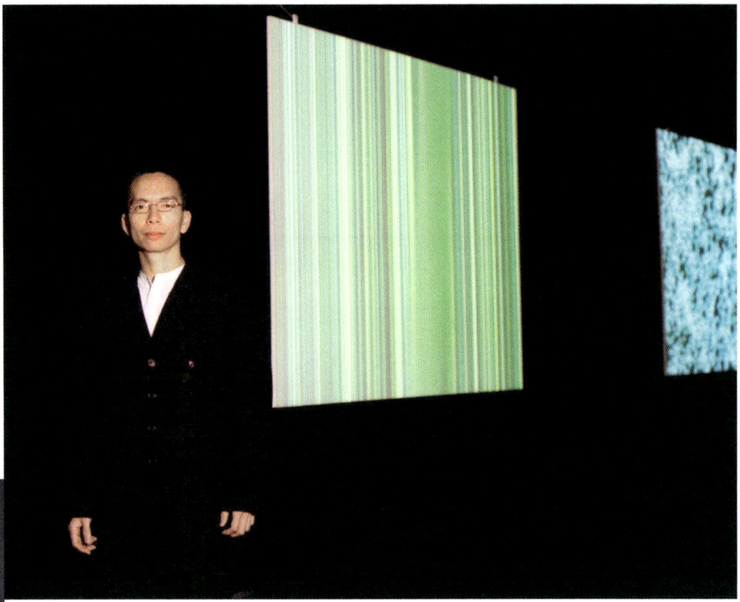

John Maeda at the exhibition opening

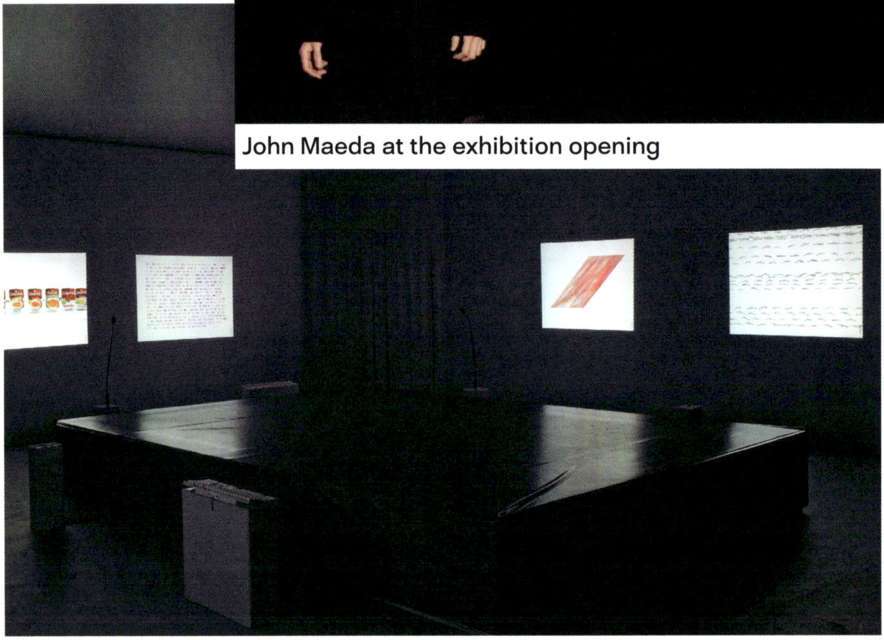

John Maeda, *Eye'm Hungry*, 2005

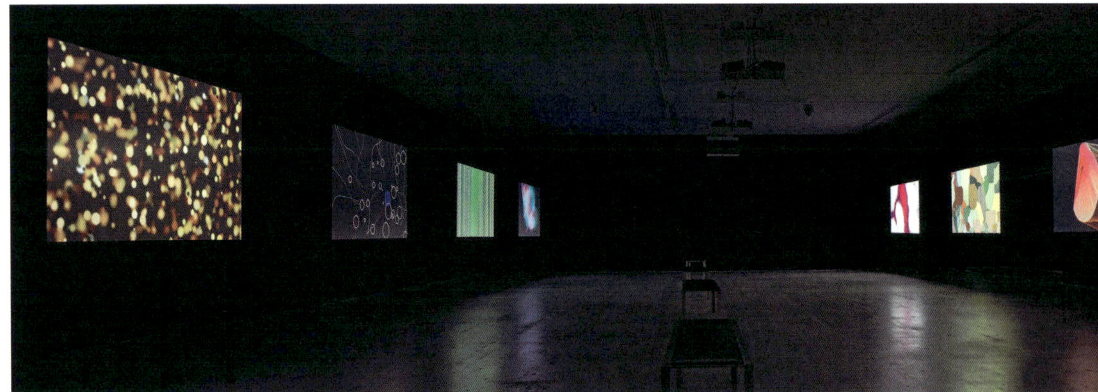

John Maeda, *Nature*, 2005. FC Collections (2006)

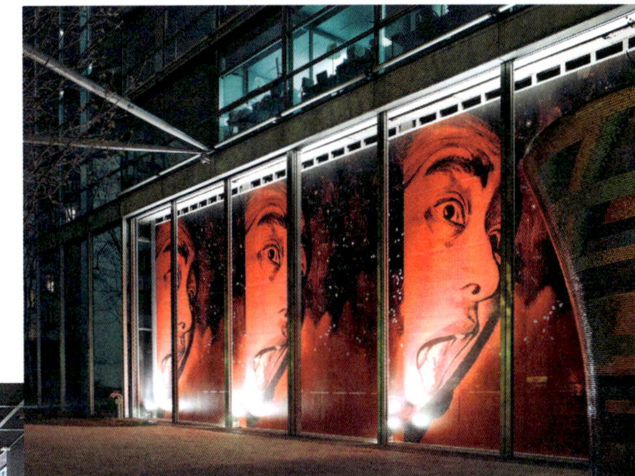

The Fondation Cartier presented the first exhibition devoted to the paintings of Tadanori Yokoo outside Japan.

Tadanori Yokoo, *Jules Verne's Ocean*, 2006 and *Le Bain d'or*, 2005

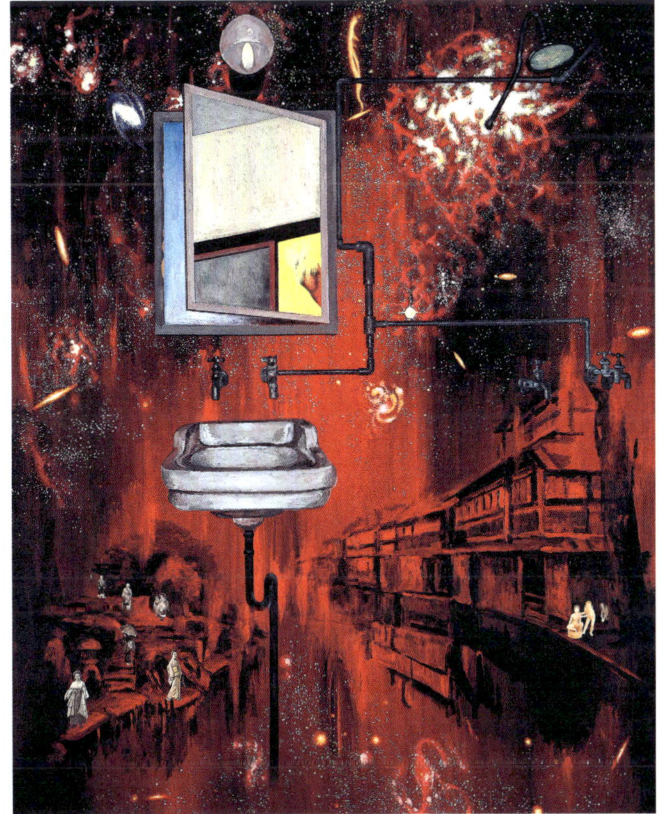

Tadanori Yokoo, *Water Circulation*, 1999 FC Collections (2023)

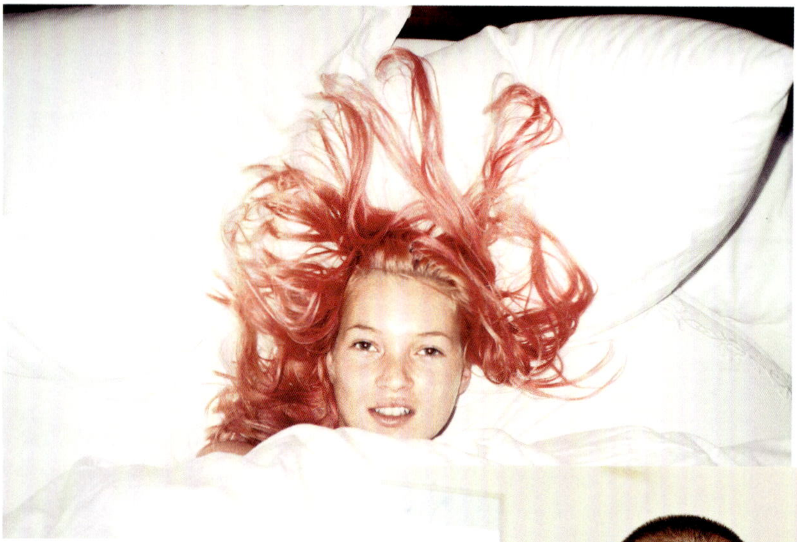

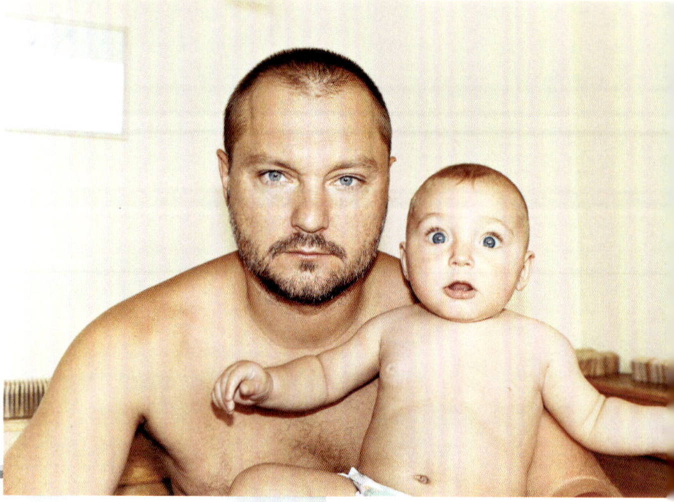

Juergen Teller, *Young Pink Kate*,
London, 1998, and *Vater und
Sohn, Bubenreuth*, 2005
FC Collections (2006)

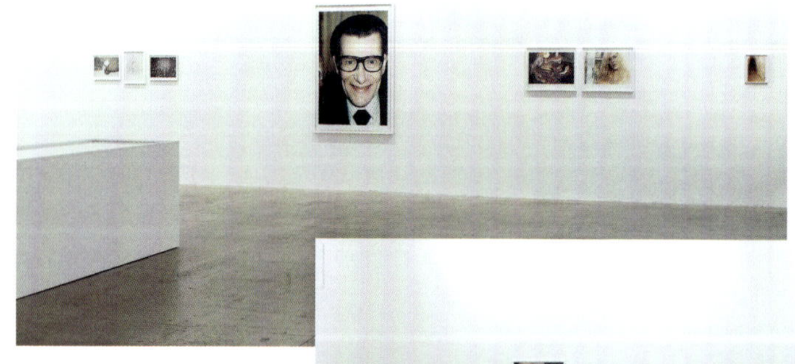

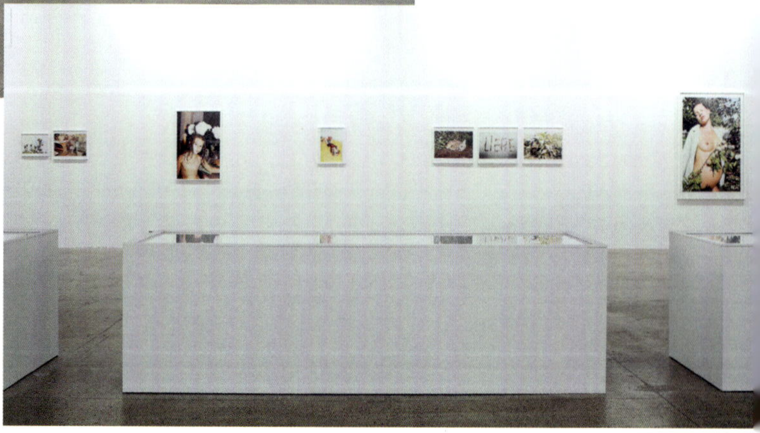

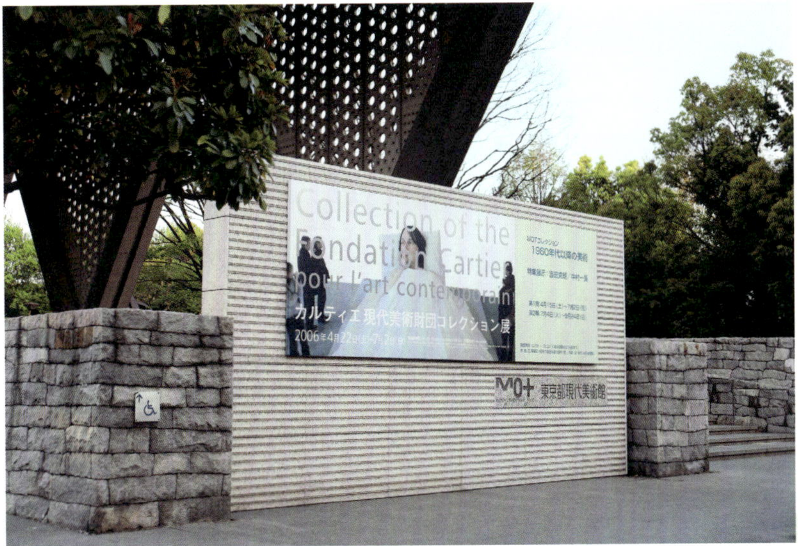

The Fondation Cartier showcased some of the most remarkable works in its Collections at the Museum of Contemporary Art in Tokyo (MOT).

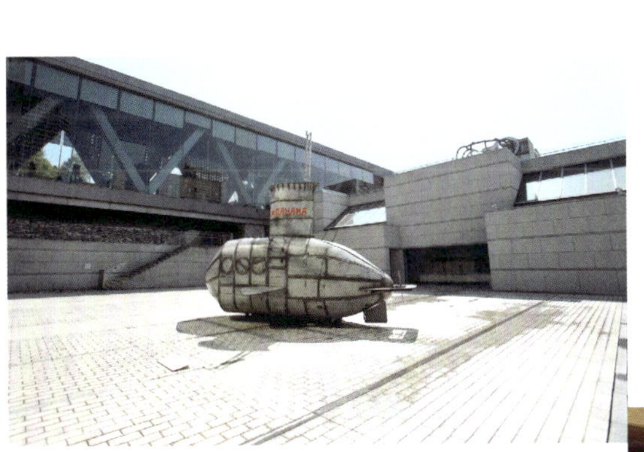

Panamarenko, *Panama, Spitsbergen, Nova Zemblaya*, 1996. FC Collections (1998)

Marc Couturier, *Vous êtes ici*, 2002
FC Collections (2003)

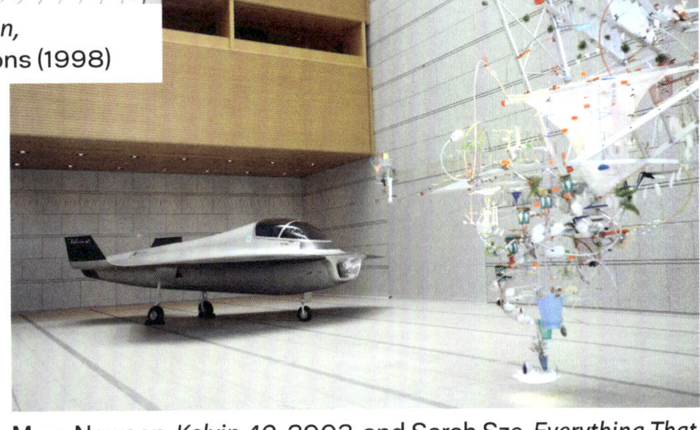

Marc Newson, *Kelvin 40*, 2003, and Sarah Sze, *Everything That Rises Must Converge*, 1999. FC Collections (2004 and 2000)

L'île et Elle

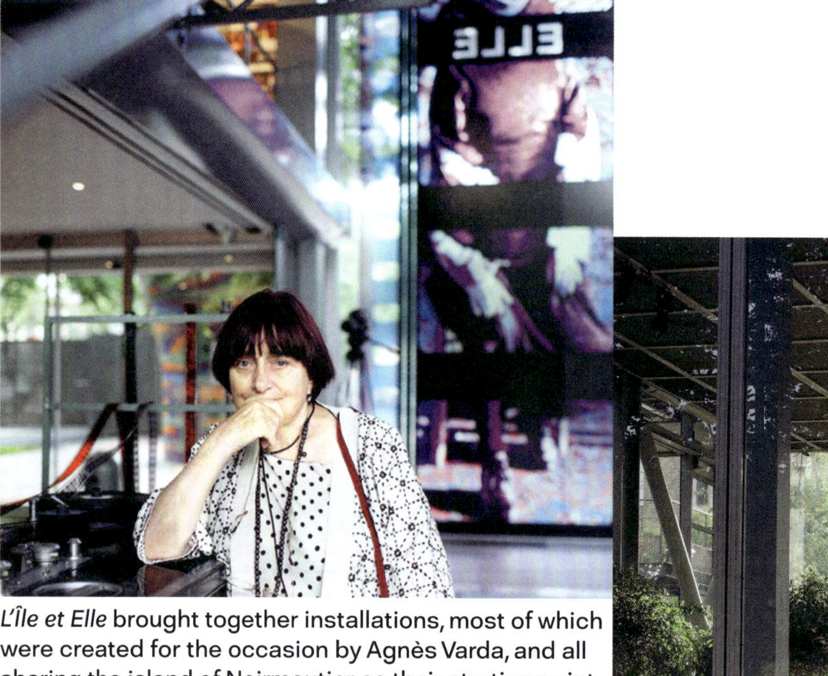

L'Île et Elle brought together installations, most of which were created for the occasion by Agnès Varda, and all sharing the island of Noirmoutier as their starting point.

Agnès Varda, *La Cabane de l'Échec*, 2006

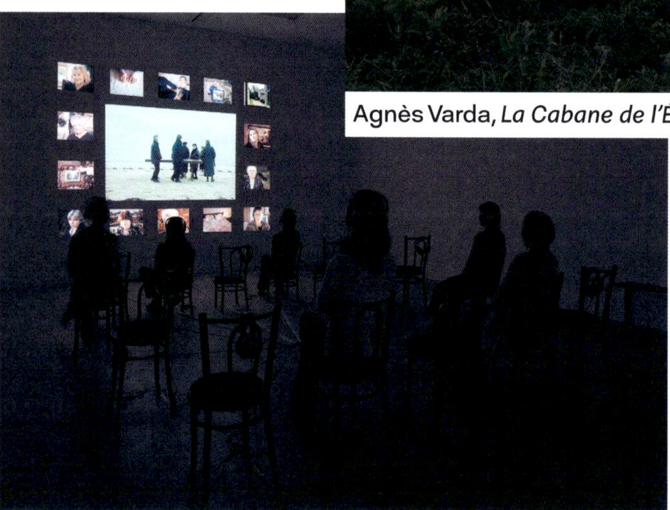

Agnès Varda, *Les Veuves de Noirmoutier*, 2004–2005
FC Collections (2017)

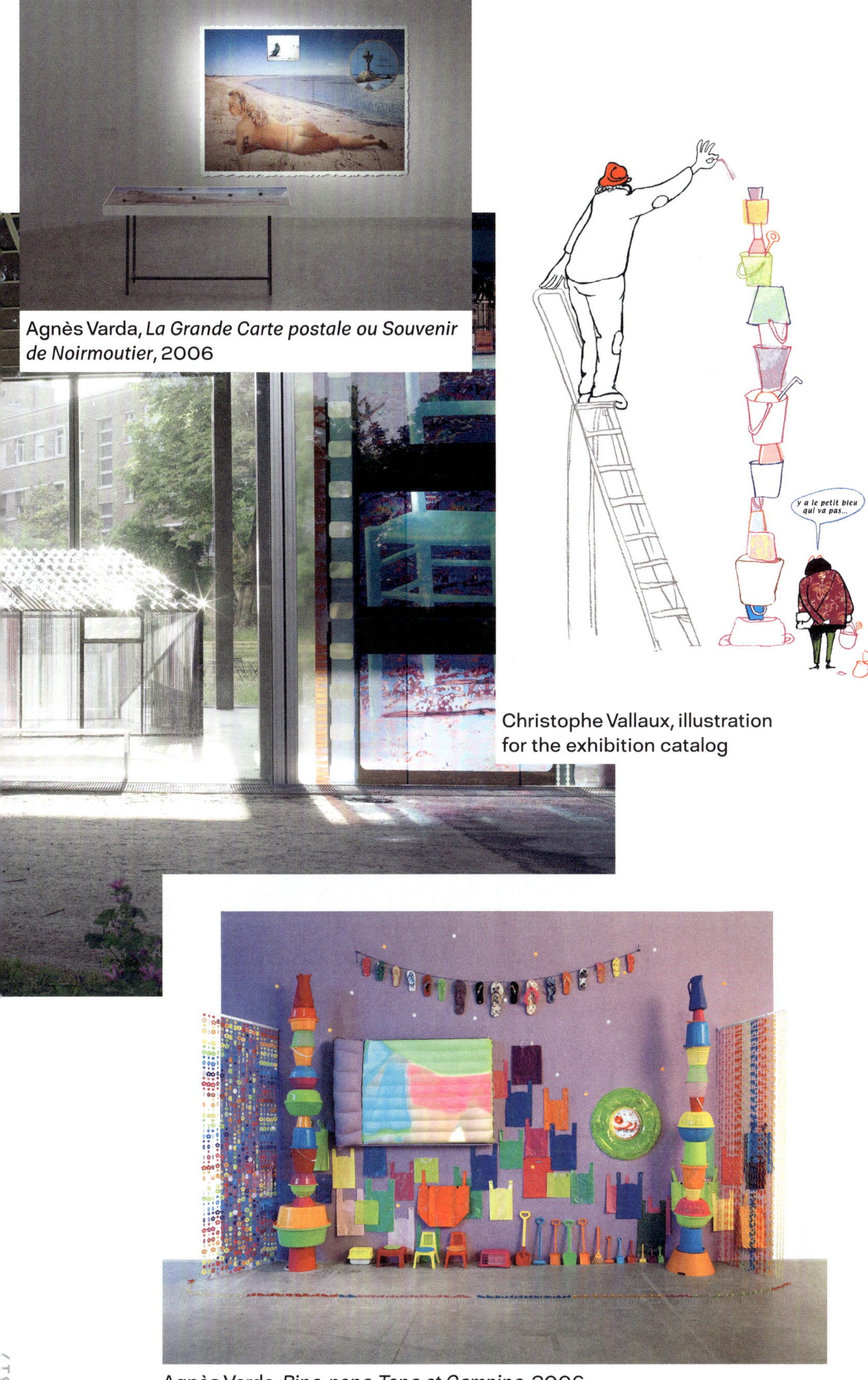

Agnès Varda, *La Grande Carte postale ou Souvenir de Noirmoutier*, 2006

Christophe Vallaux, illustration for the exhibition catalog

Agnès Varda, *Ping-pong, Tong et Camping*, 2006

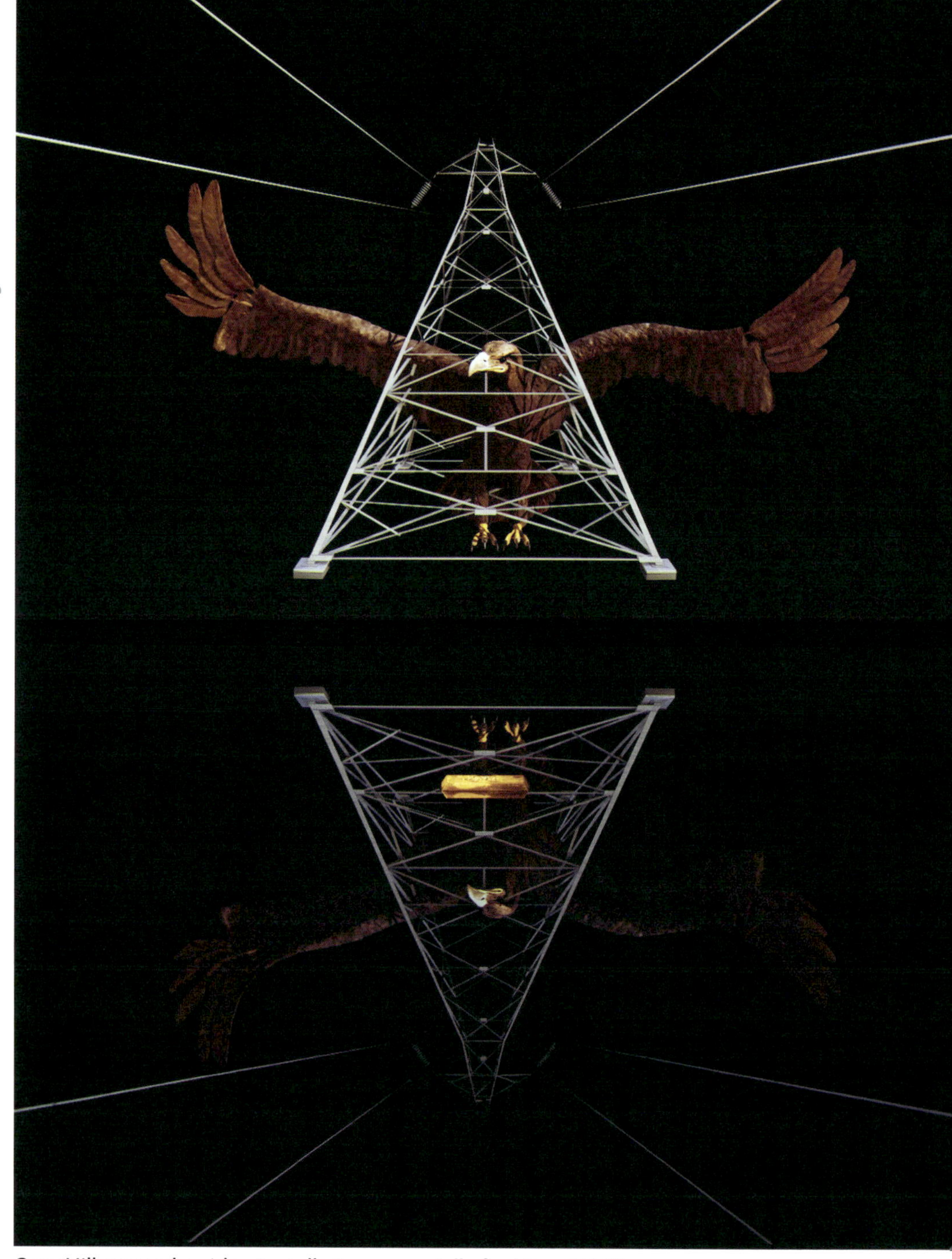

Gary Hill created a video installation especially for his exhibition:
Frustrum, 2006. FC Collections (2007)

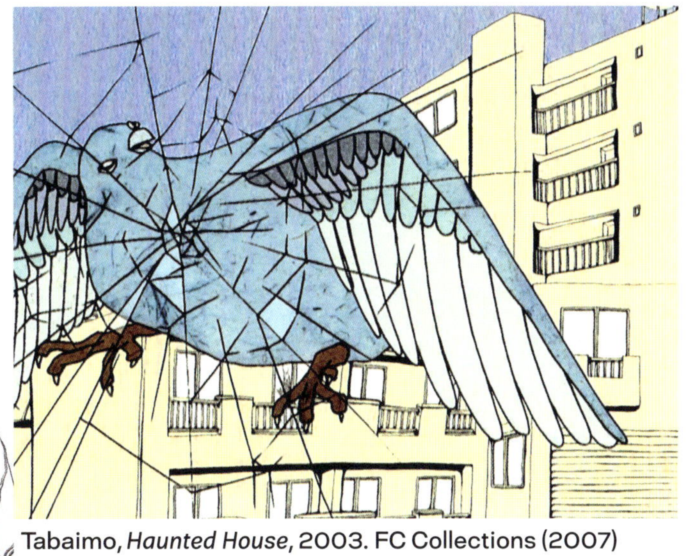

Tabaimo, *Haunted House*, 2003. FC Collections (2007)

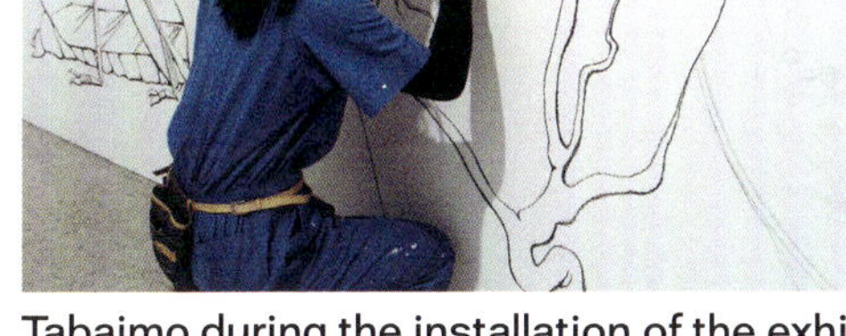

Tabaimo during the installation of the exhibition

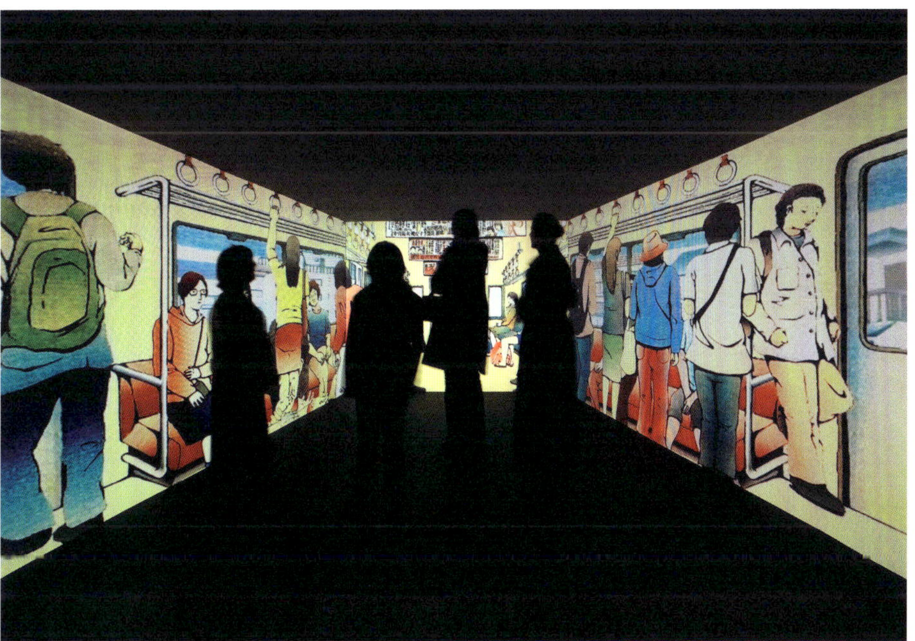

The Fondation Cartier presented the work of Tabaimo for the first time in Europe. Tabaimo, *Japanese Commuter Train*, 2001. FC Collections (2007)

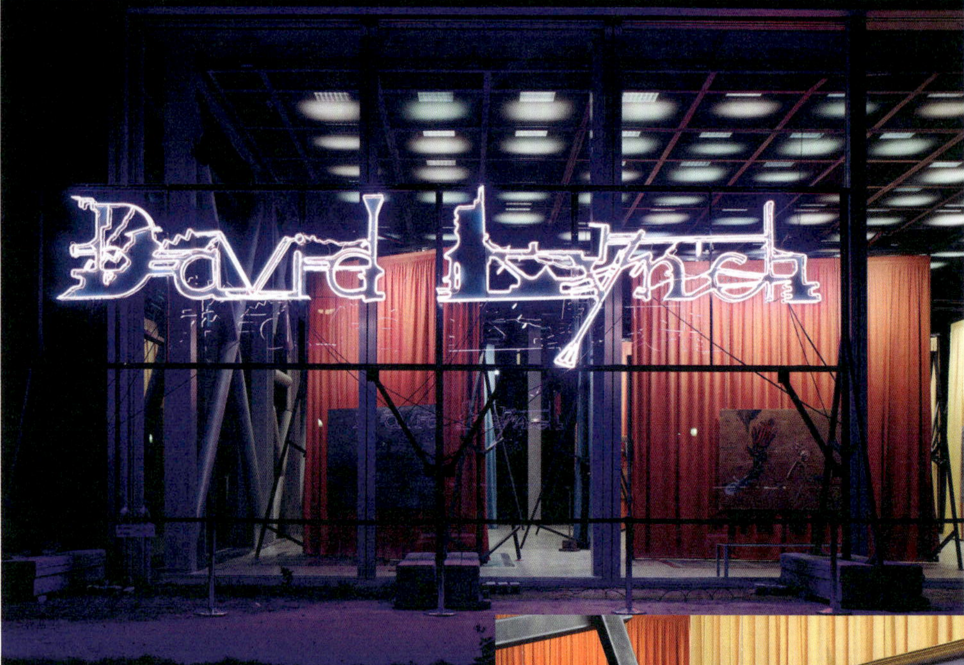

With a scenography designed by David Lynch himself, this exhibition featured a vast ensemble of works created between 1960 and 2007: paintings and photographs, as well as countless drawings, sketches, and notes, all meticulously kept by the artist since his adolescence.

David Lynch, *Well, I Can Dream, Can't I?*, 2003
FC Collections (2007)

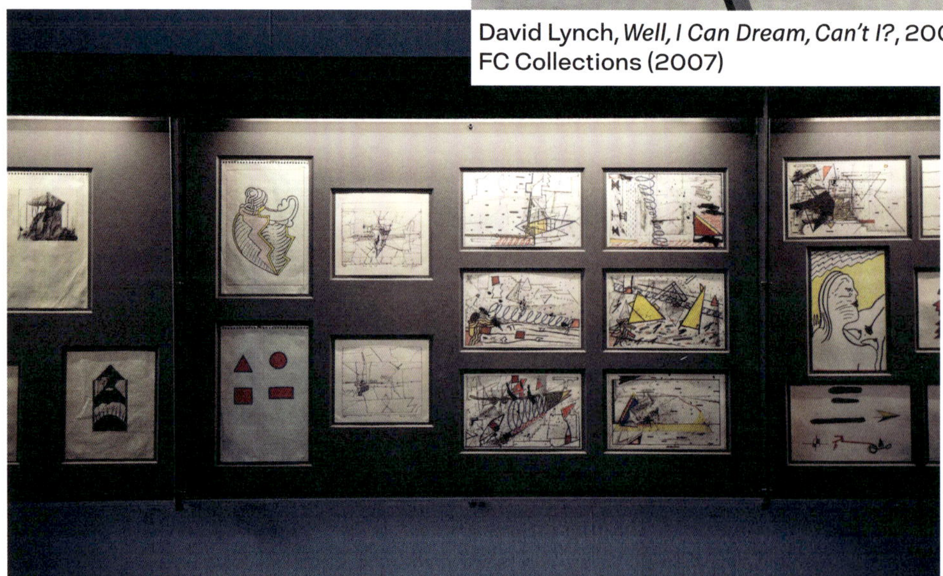

David Lynch, *Binder Works #1* and *#2*, 1970-2006
FC Collections (2007)

daviD
LyncH.

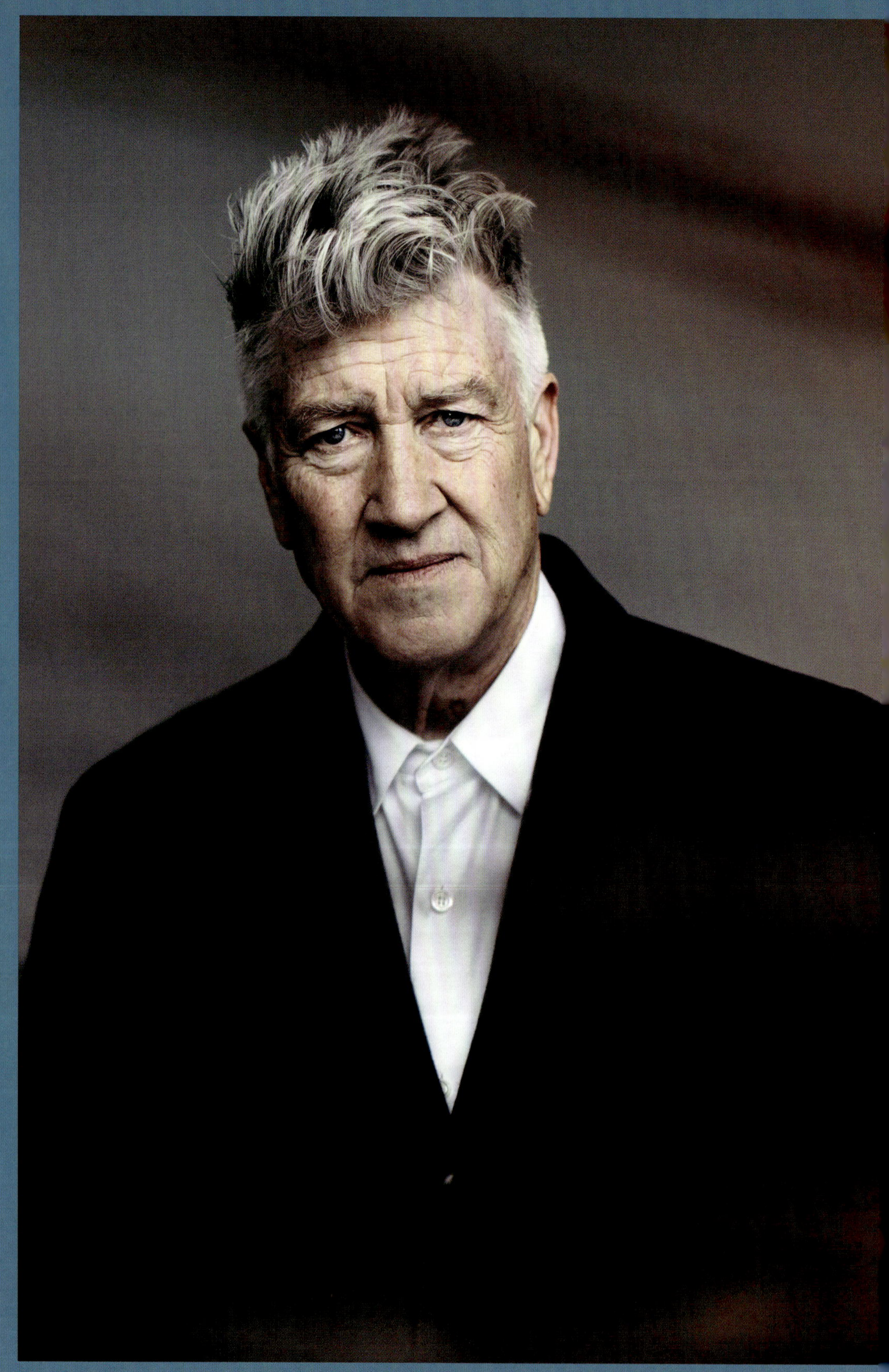

David Lynch, 2013

David Lynch

Two black and white striped armchairs are positioned in a living room-like space with blue walls covered in yellow marks. On the floor, the blood-red carpet is dotted with black. Behind each of the seats, two rooms papered with botanical motifs draw the viewer toward other corners of a house that we imagine to be immense and strange. This small, enigmatic drawing by David Lynch was the starting point for the installation recreating the artist's imagined living room in three dimensions, presented as part of the exhibition *The Air is on Fire* in 2007, at the Fondation Cartier. Conceived and staged by the artist himself, the exhibition offered the public a veritable immersion into his personal universe: paintings, photographs, drawings, sketches, notes, and experimental short films, made between 1960 and 2006, all revealed a life devoted to creation in every form. By showing a number of hitherto lesser-known works, David Lynch shed light on the genesis and evolution of his obsessions and aesthetics, initially seen in his visual work, and later in his filmography. A few months later, the exhibition *The Air is on Fire* was presented at Triennale Milano, then in Moscow in 2009, and in Copenhagen in 2010.

Since that time, the Fondation Cartier and David Lynch have enjoyed a continual dialogue in response to the simple desire to do things together: exhibitions, publications, concerts, and films. Over the years, a range of projects have followed. In 2011, the Fondation Cartier asked him to create the exhibition design for *Mathematics, A Beautiful Elsewhere*. David Lynch took possession of Jean Nouvel's building and created a strange and fascinating universe with *The Library of Mysteries* by mathematician Misha Gromov, the mathematical exercises of the mischievous Takeshi Kitano, as well as a host of robots developed by Pierre-Yves Oudeyer and his collaborators at INRIA, endowed with artificial intelligence and curiosity, whose faces recalled that of the baby in Lynch's 1977 film *Eraserhead*. David Lynch also produced a sound creation for the exhibition, comprising a recording of singer and poet Patti Smith reciting a text by mathematician Misha Gromov. He also shared the stage with her, performing in a remarkable concert at the Fondation Cartier a few days after the exhibition opening.

In 2009, David Lynch imagined a work of art incorporating precious and semiprecious stones that couldn't be used in making jewelry and supplied by Cartier. The artist created a unique piece, *Jeweled Triangle* (2009), which was exhibited in the spaces of the Fondation Cartier in 2012, alongside works by artists Alessandro Mendini, Beatriz Milhazes, and Takeshi Kitano.

The Fondation Cartier and David Lynch have also collaborated on several books, successively publishing *The Air is on Fire* (2007), *Snowmen* (2007), *Works on Paper* (2011), *Nudes* (2017), and *Digital Nudes* (2021). The Fondation has also supported his cinematic explorations, coproducing the short film *What Did Jack Do?* (2017), in which the artist-director himself played the role of a detective questioning a small, lovestruck monkey.

Over the course of all these years, David Lynch has consistently and methodically devoted himself to an artistic activity in a timeless space. In 2006, while preparing the exhibition *The Air is on Fire*, the Director of the Fondation Cartier Hervé Chandès introduced him to Idem Paris, an art printer in the Montparnasse district. David Lynch dived into the world of lithographic stones, which between 2006 and 2024, resulted in the creation of almost two hundred and fifty prints where the obsessions permeating his life can be seen, in a predominantly black-and-white aesthetic.

As for the mysterious living room, it became the central element of the exhibitions *Les Habitants* (Paris, 2014), *Les Visitants* (Buenos Aires, 2017), and *Les Citoyens* (Milan, 2021), designed by Argentinian painter Guillermo Kuitca and honoring the Collections of the Fondation Cartier, which now include many works by David Lynch.

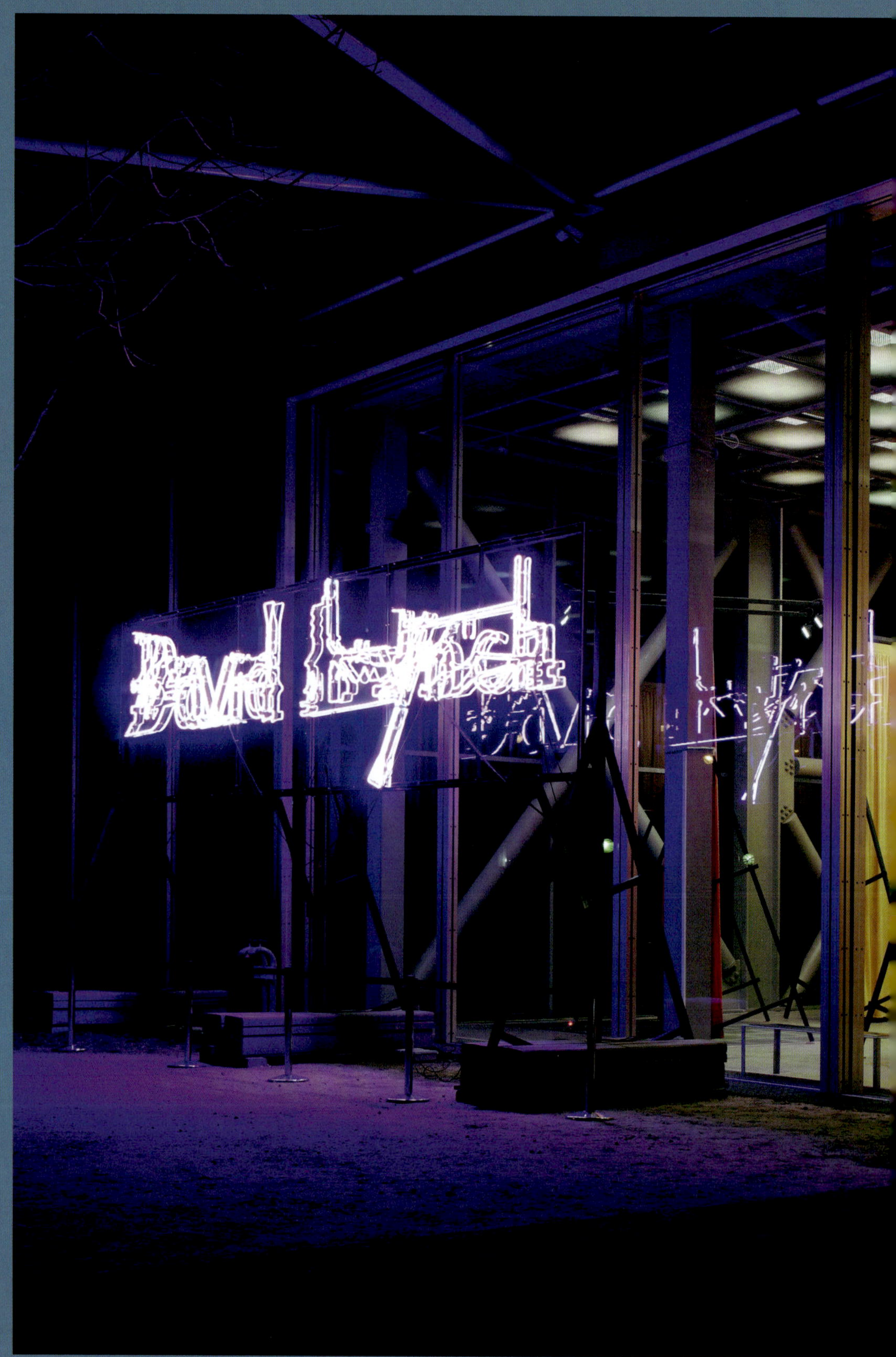

2007 David Lynch presented and staged a large number of his works in the exhibition *The Air is on Fire*.

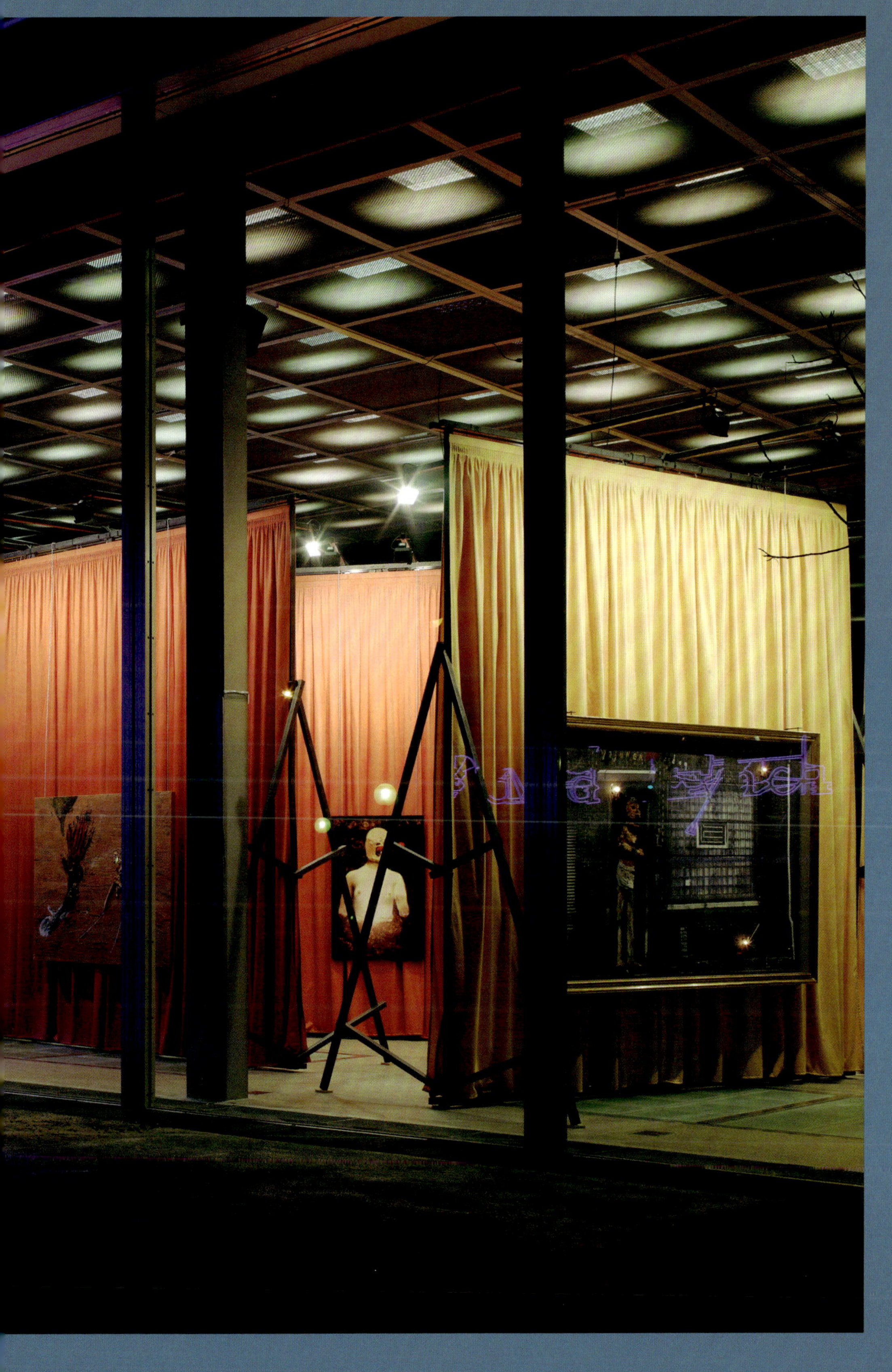

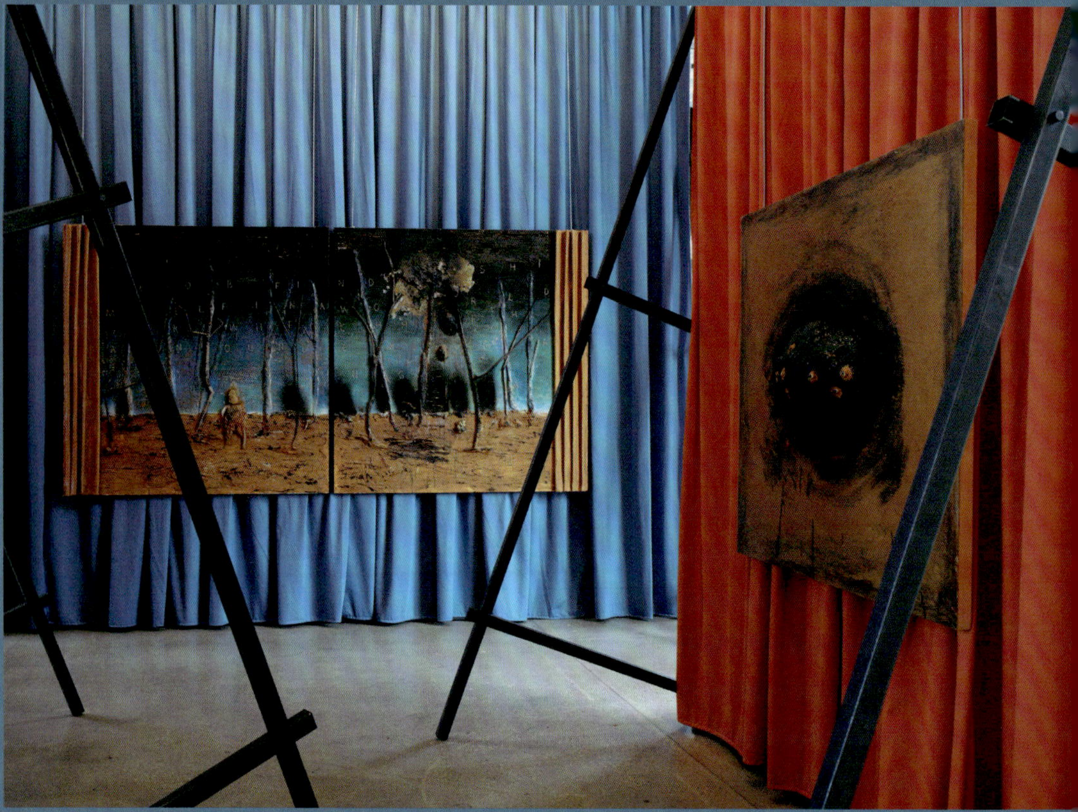

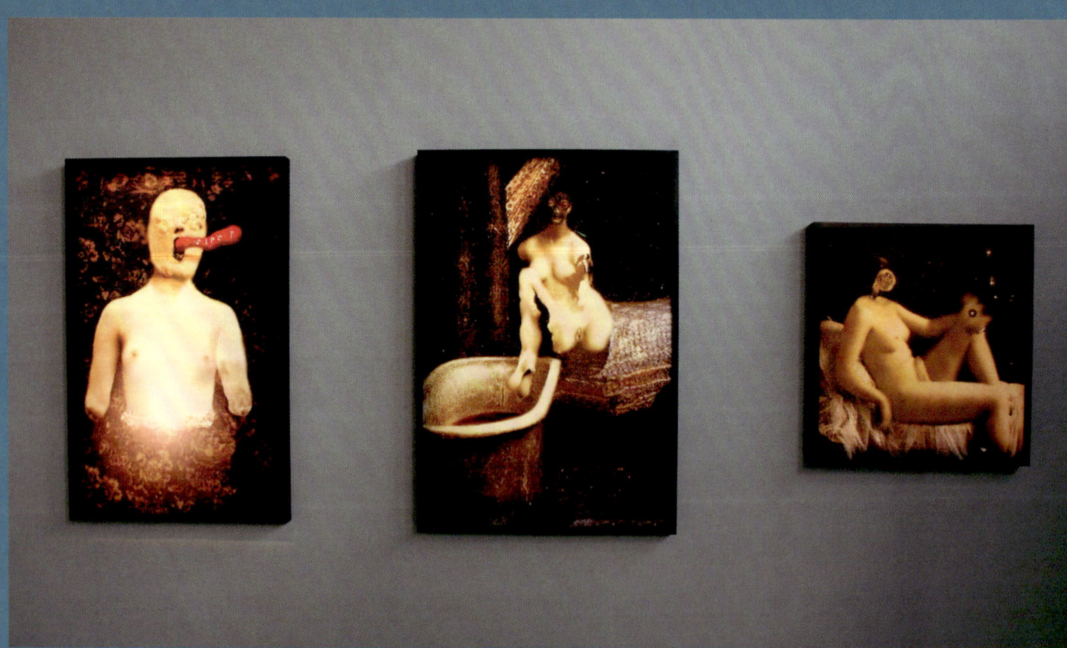

2007   Views of the exhibition *The Air is on Fire*

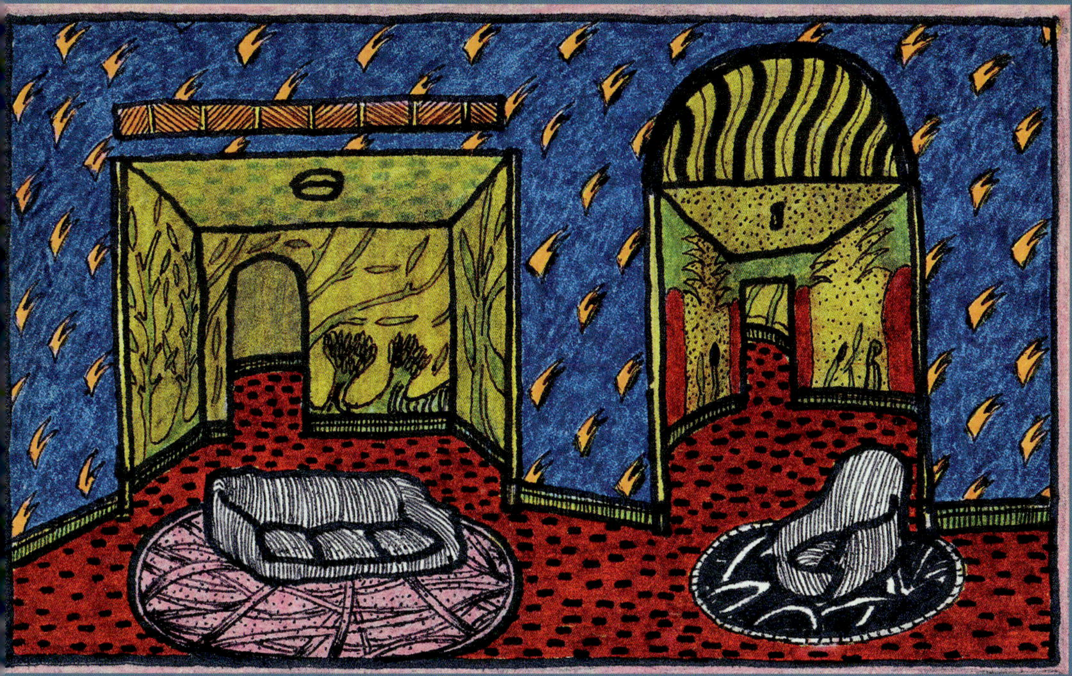

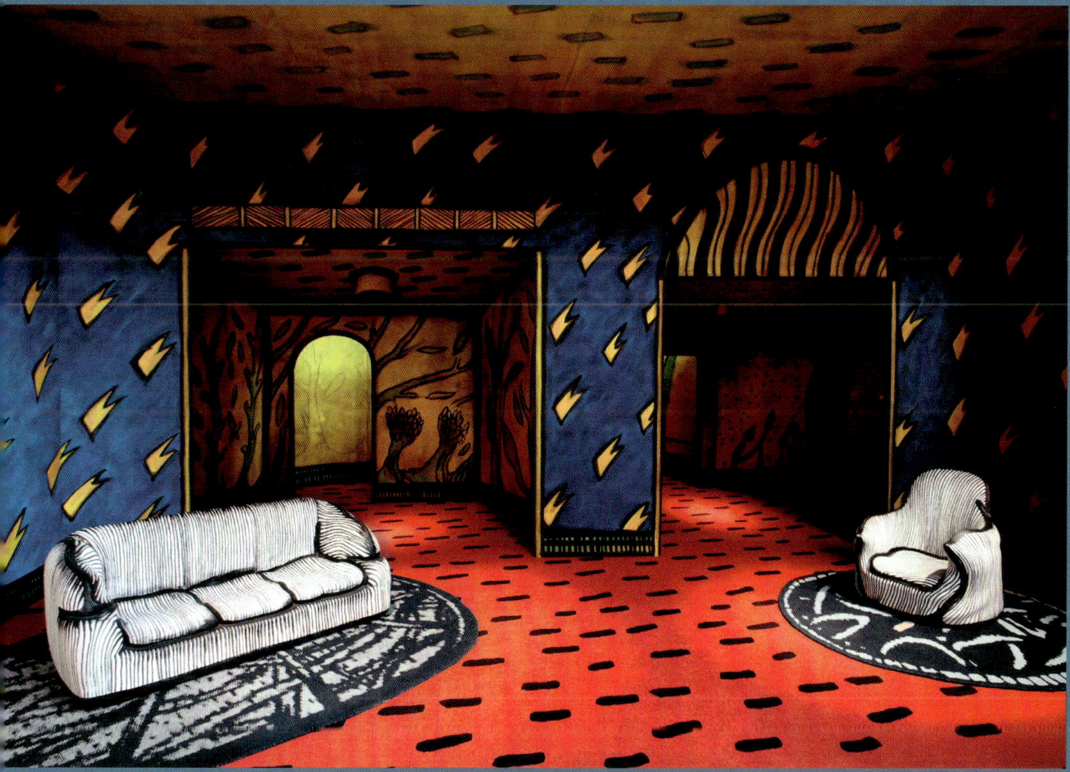

2007   For his exhibition *The Air is on Fire*, David Lynch created an installation based on his drawing *Untitled (Drawing for an Interior)*, n.d. FC Collections (2007)

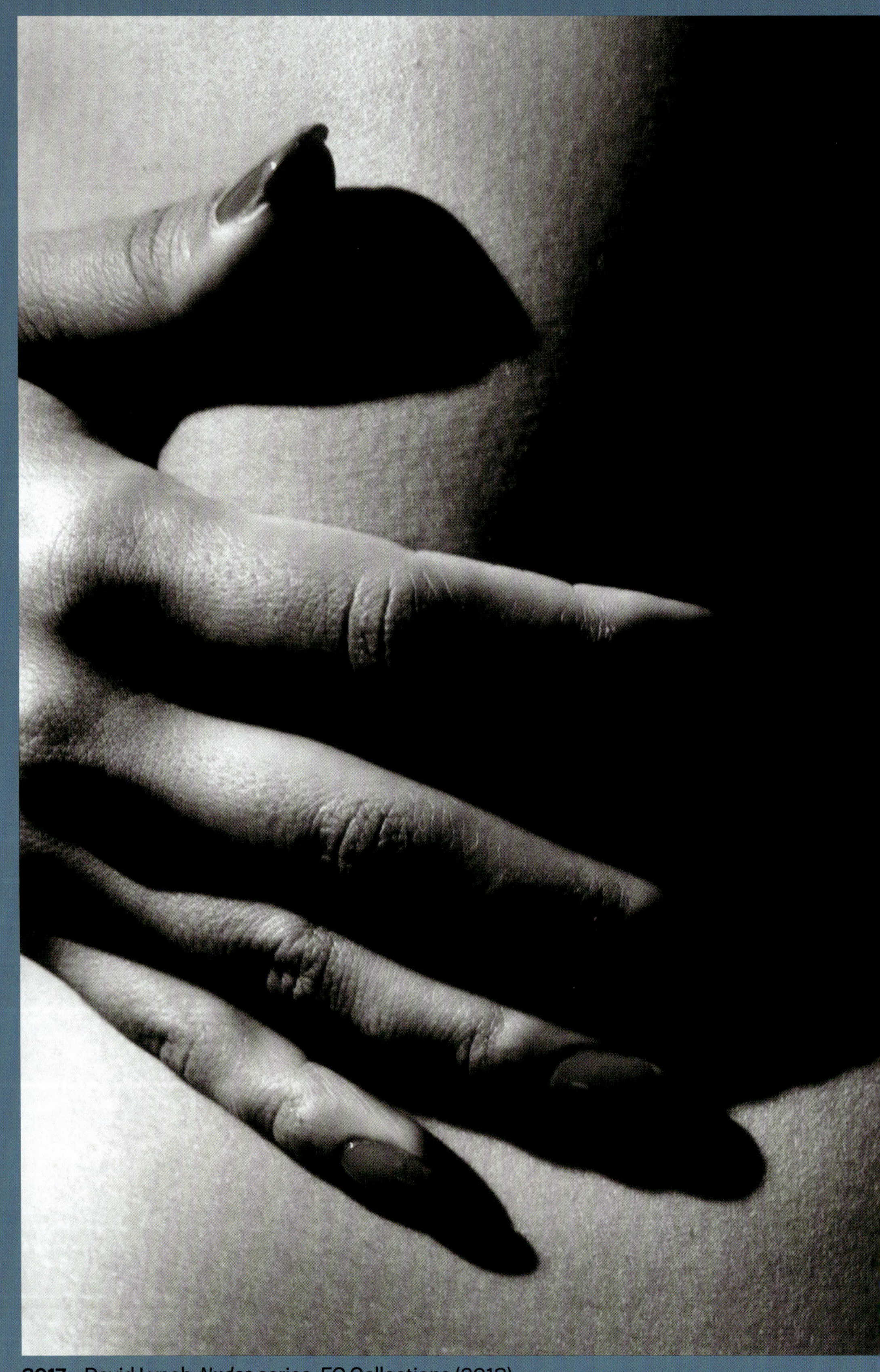

2017   David Lynch, *Nudes* series. FC Collections (2018)

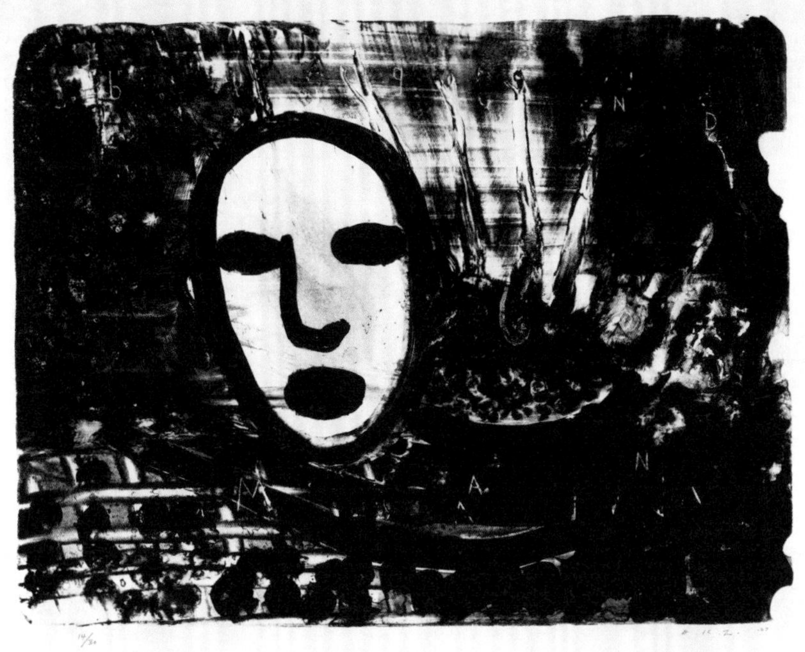

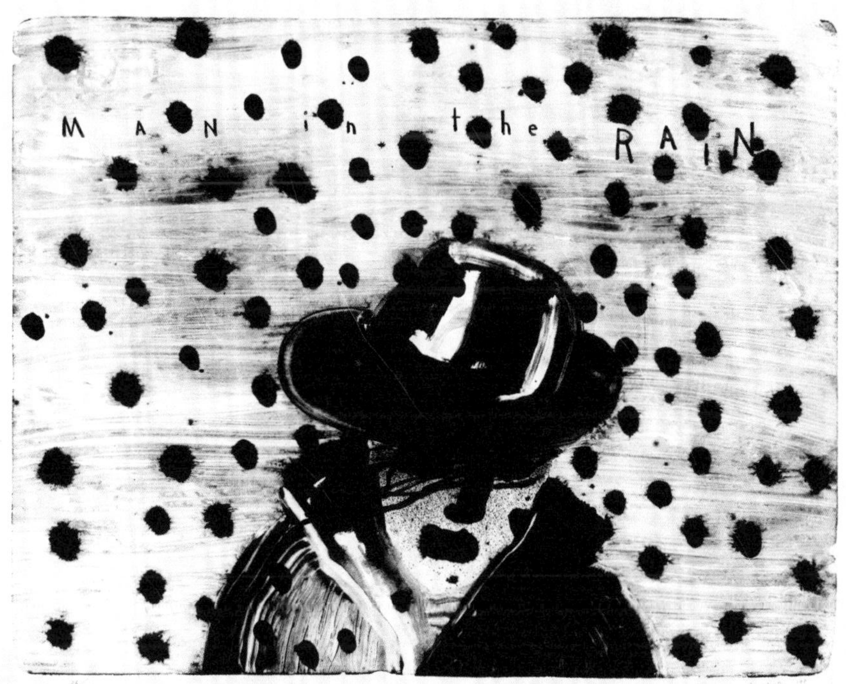

David Lynch, *Man in the Rain* and *Bug and Man*, 2008. FC Collections (2011)

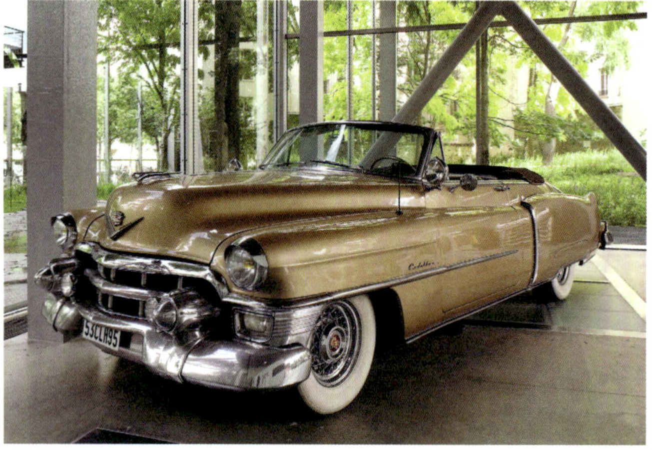

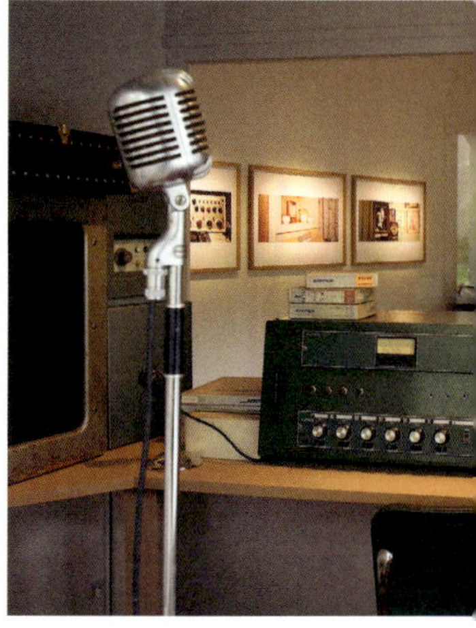

Rock'n'Roll 39-59 explored a key period in the history of the United States. Through the genesis and beginnings of rock'n'roll, it retraced the key stages in an unprecedented cultural revolution.

Reconstitution
of a recording studio

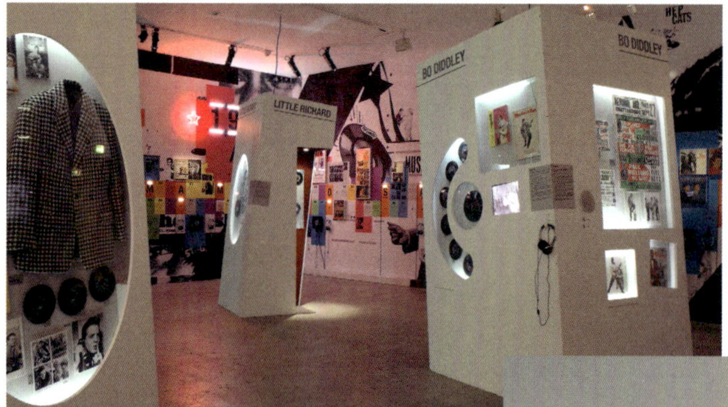

In the basement, the exhibition featured a genealogy of this musical "melting pot" through a look at the different musical genres that influenced it.

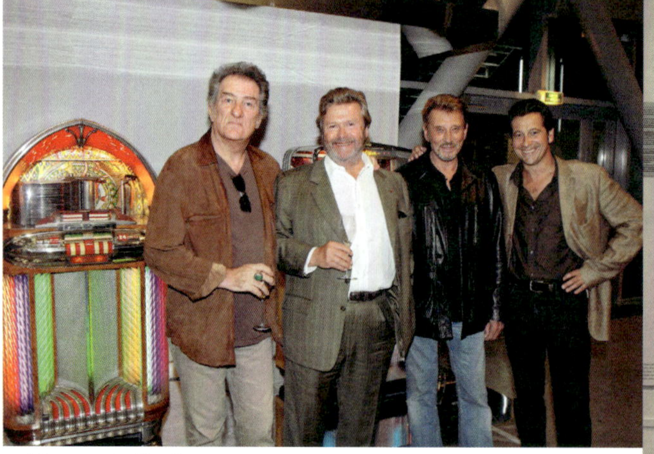

Eddy Mitchell, Alain Dominique Perrin, Johnny Hallyday, and Laurent Gerra at the exhibition

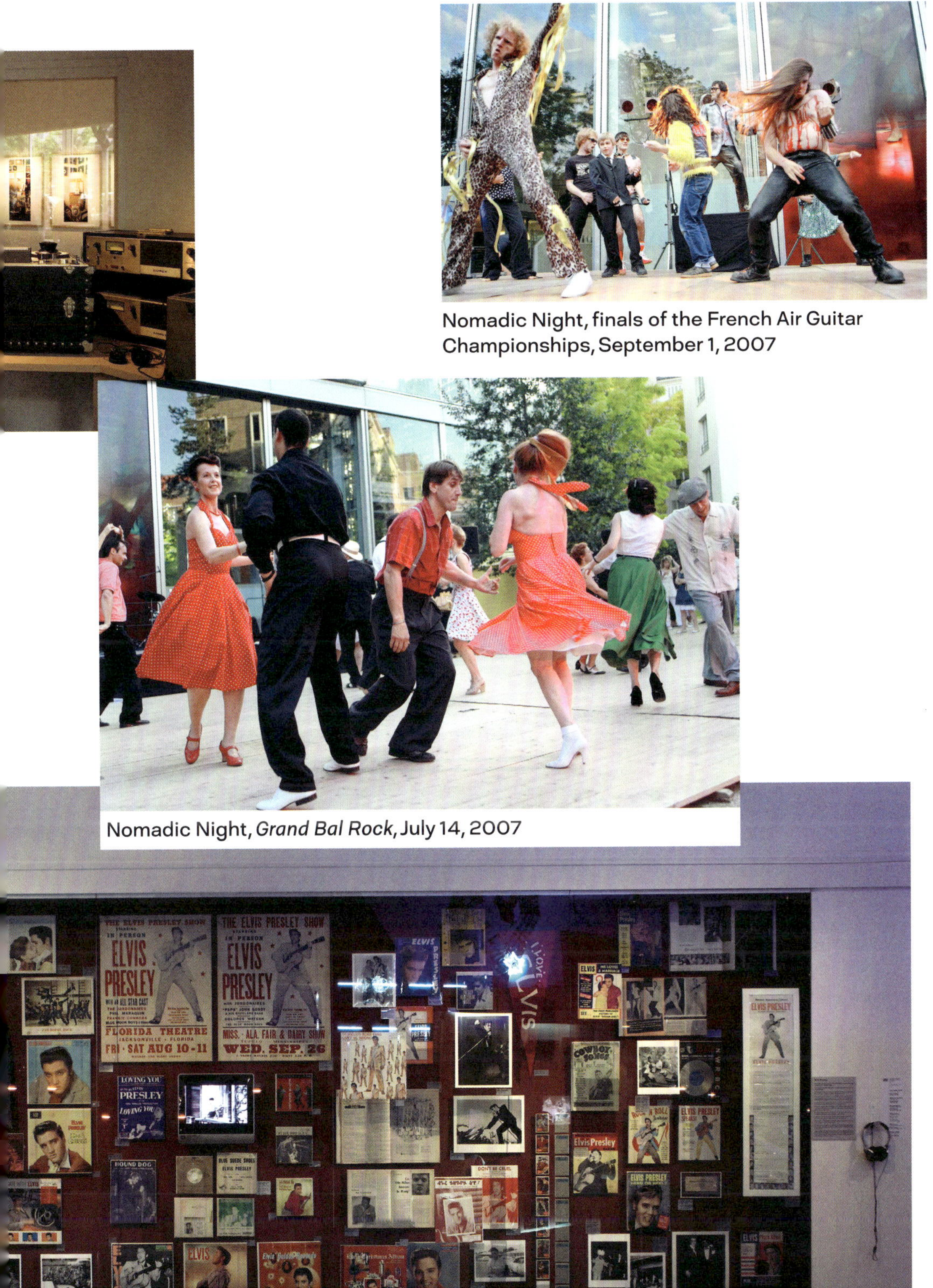

Nomadic Night, finals of the French Air Guitar
Championships, September 1, 2007

Nomadic Night, *Grand Bal Rock*, July 14, 2007

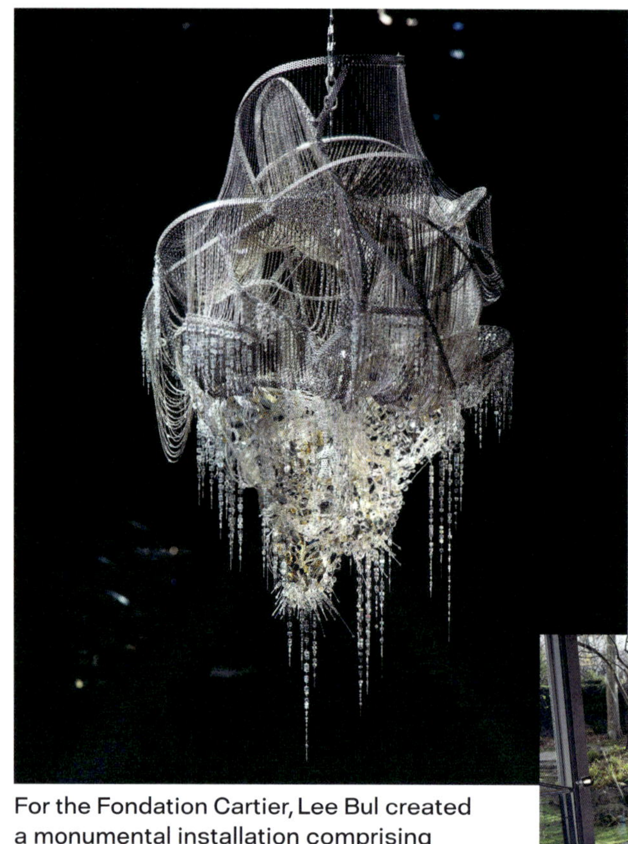

For the Fondation Cartier, Lee Bul created
a monumental installation comprising
a dozen crystal and aluminum sculptures.
Lee Bul, *Sternbau No. 4*, 2007

Lee Bul, *Heaven and Earth*, 2007

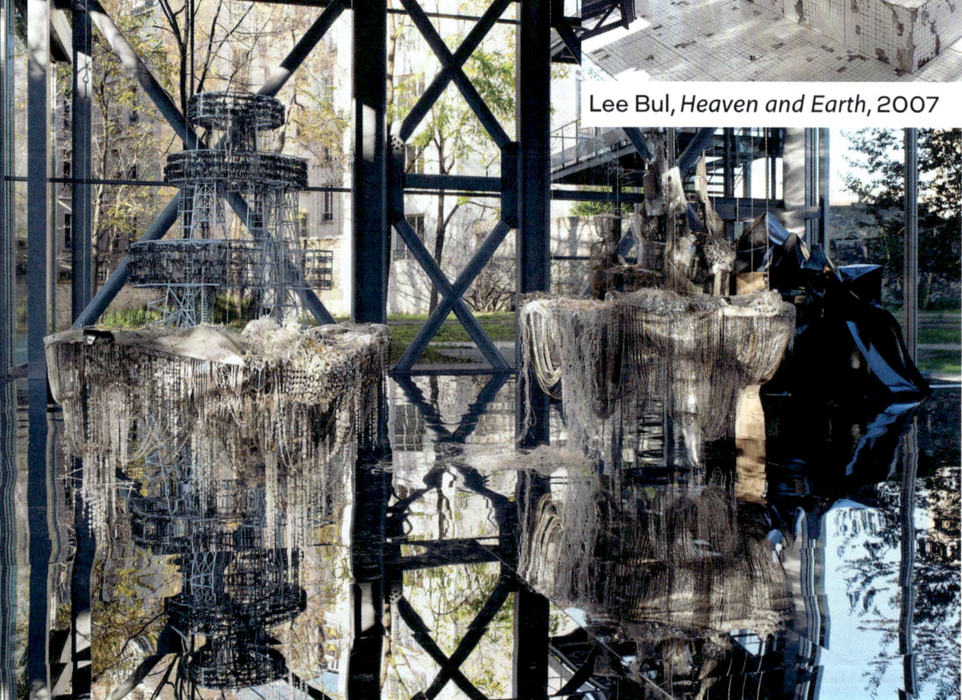

Lee Bul, *After Bruno Taut (A Formal Feeling Comes)*, 2006, and
After Bruno Taut (Beware the Sweetness of Things), 2007

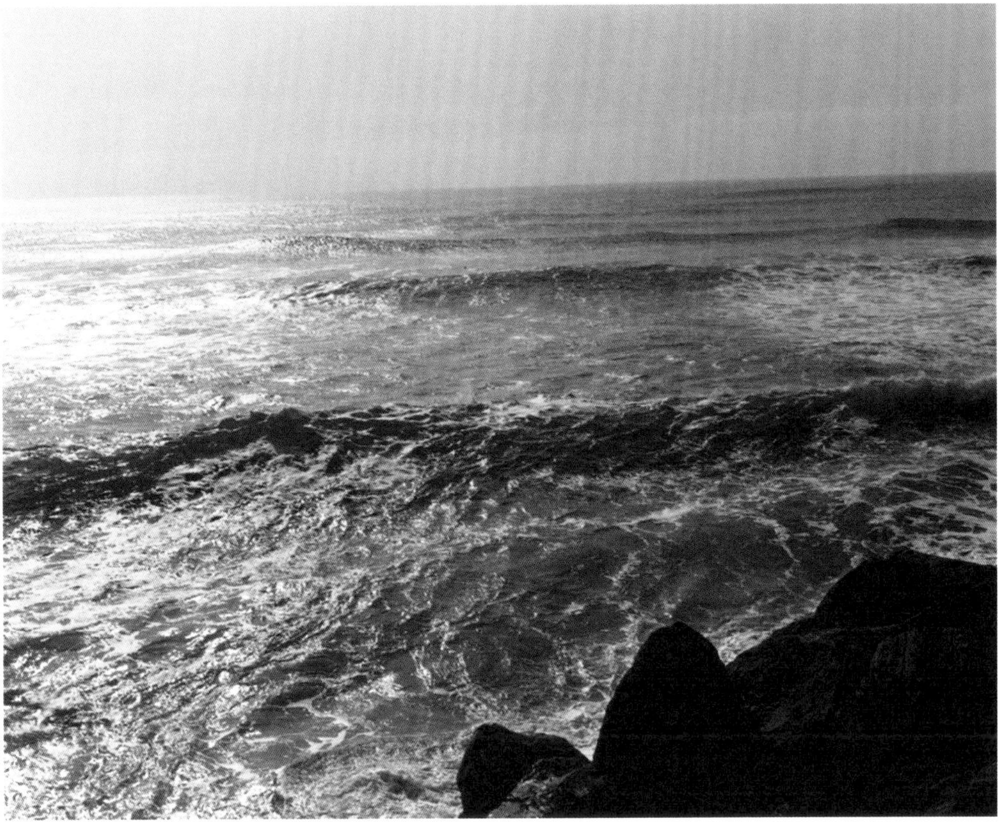

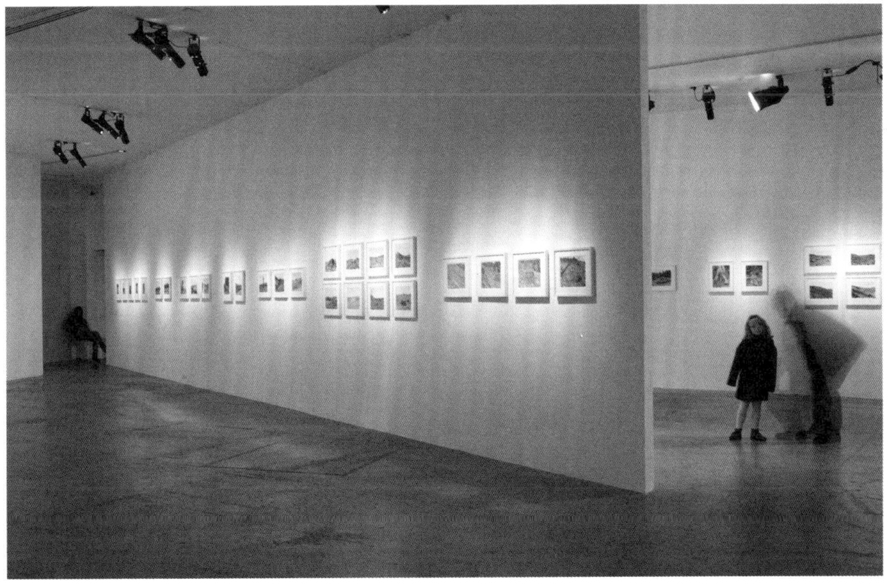

Robert Adams, *Time Passes*, 1990-1992. FC Collections (2008)

The exhibition *On the Edge* featured some 150 photographs from three series by Robert Adams: *West from the Columbia* (1990-1992), *Time Passes* (1990-1992), and *Turning Back* (1999-2003).

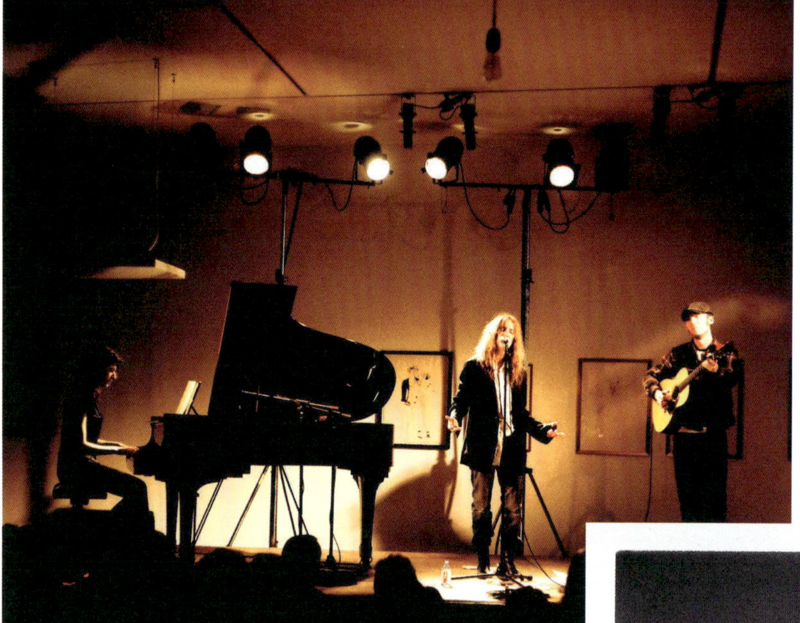

Land 250, Patti Smith's first solo exhibition, brought together a selection of photographs, drawings, and films dating from 1967 to 2007. Above: Patti Smith accompanied by Jesse and Jackson Smith during the *Virginia Woolf* Nomadic Night evening, March 28, 2008

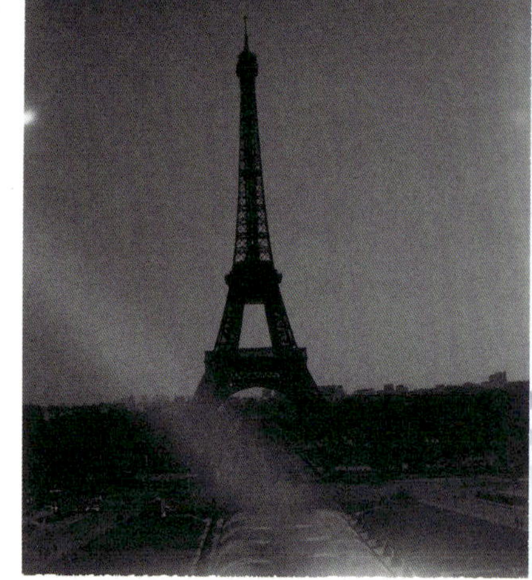

Patti Smith, *Untitled*, n.d.
FC Collections (2008)

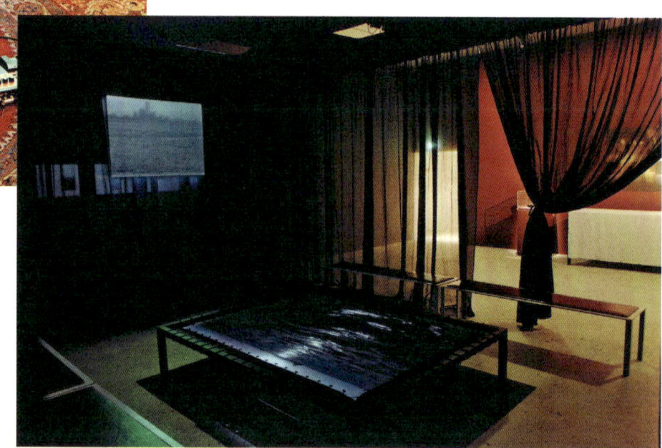

Patti Smith, *The Coral Sea Room*, 2008
FC Collections (2008)

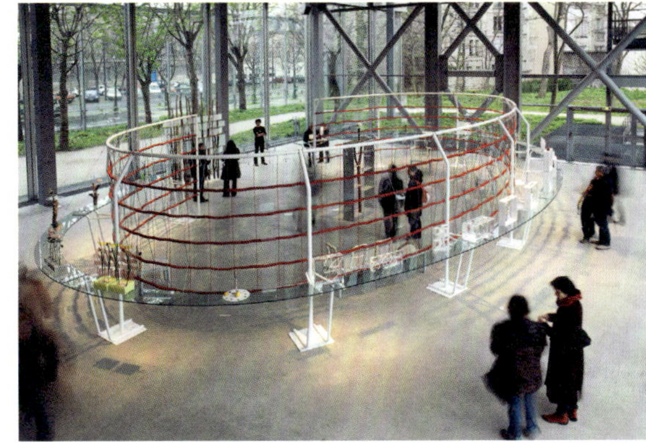

Designer Andrea Branzi imagined two monumental installations specially for the Fondation Cartier's exhibition spaces. Andrea Branzi, *Ellipse*, 2008 FC Collections (2008)

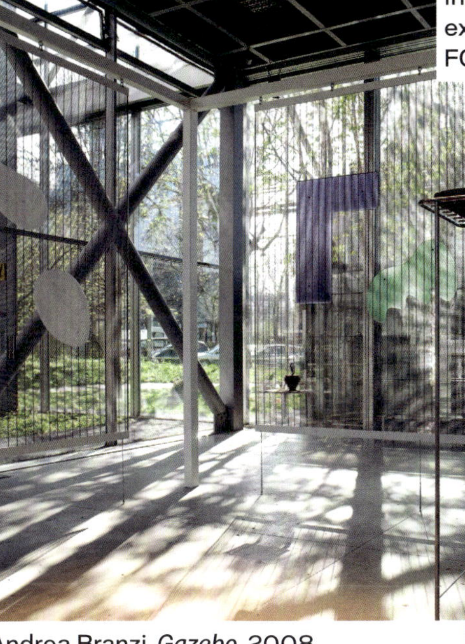

Andrea Branzi, *Gazebo*, 2008 FC Collections (2008)

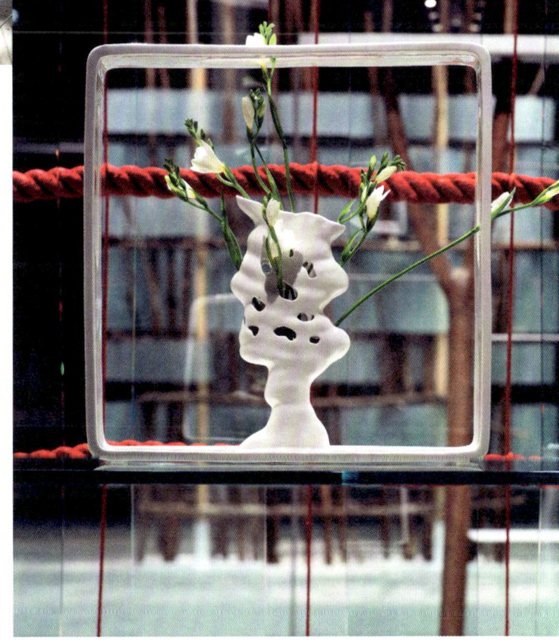

Andrea Branzi, *Portali* vase, 2007, positioned in the center of the installation *Ellipse*, 2008. FC Collections (2008)

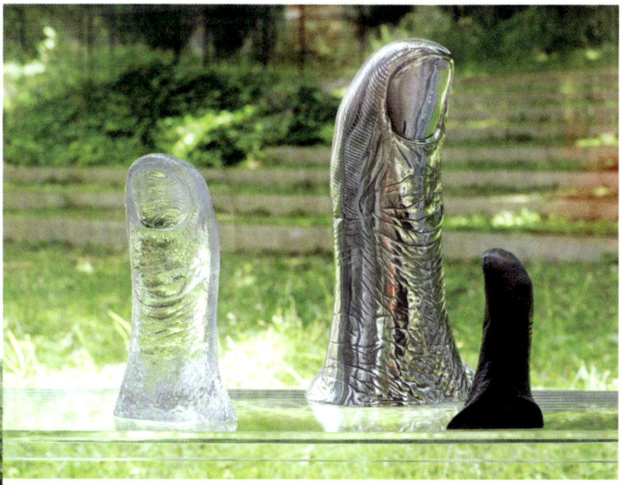

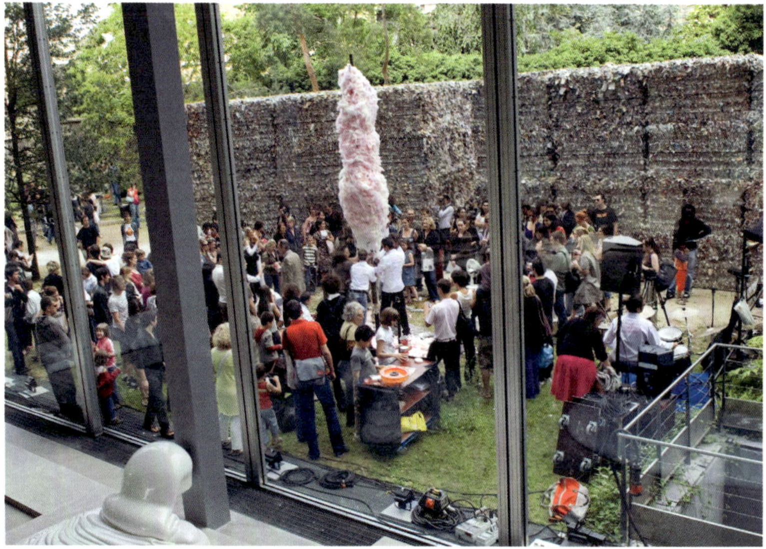

César, *Pouces*, 1967–1989

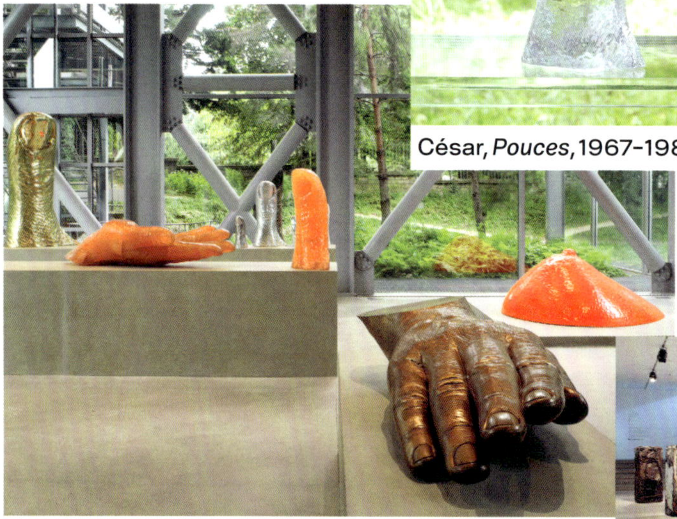

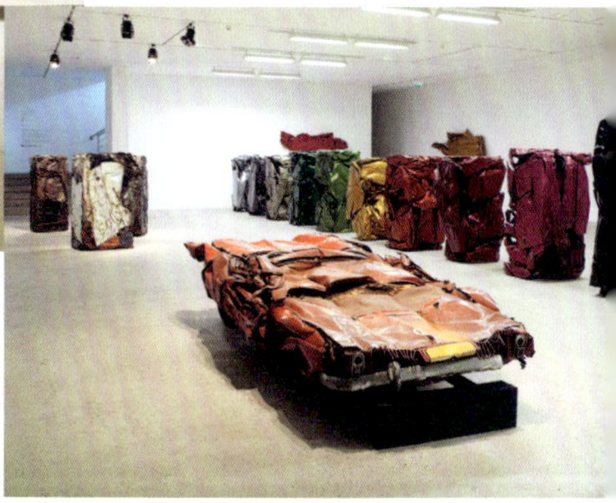

The architect of the Fondation Cartier and a friend
of César, Jean Nouvel selected and designed
an exhibition showcasing some 100 works that were
among the artist's most significant: his iron bestiary,
compressions, imprints, and expansions.

Nomadic Night *César salades… un happening en sucre filé :
la plus grande barbe à papa du monde*, with François Martin
and Nicolas Petit, July 20, 2008

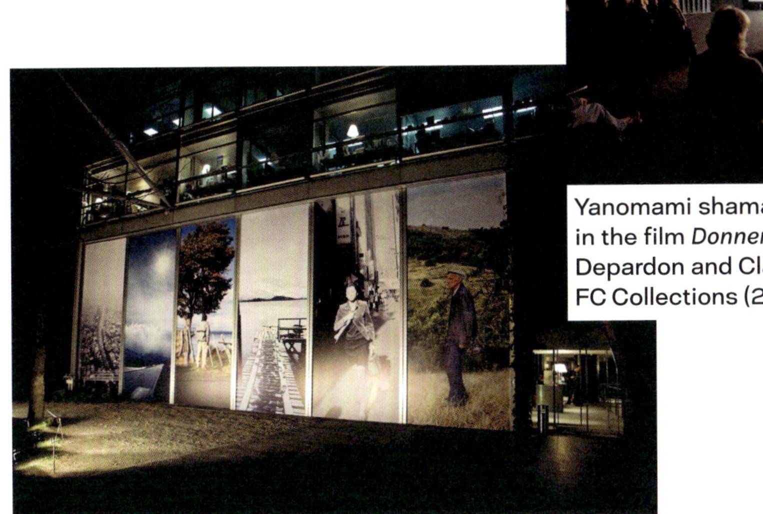

Yanomami shaman Davi Kopenawa
in the film *Donner la parole* by Raymond
Depardon and Claudine Nougaret, 2008
FC Collections (2009)

Born from an encounter between Raymond Depardon
and Paul Virilio, the exhibition *Native Land, Stop Eject*
offered a reflection on the notions of rootedness and
exile, as well as related issues of identity.

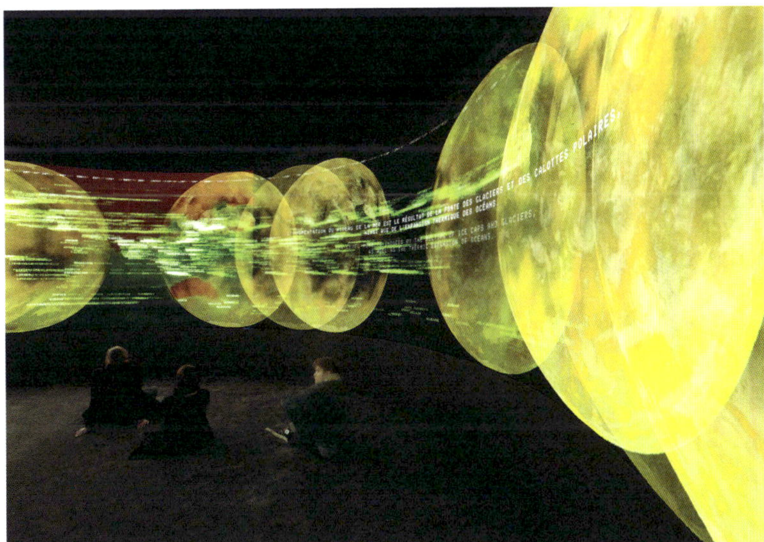

Prompted by an idea from Paul Virilio, *EXIT* is an immersive
installation showing the complex relationships between the different
economic, political, and climatic factors at the origin of population
displacements. It is built around a set of dynamic maps generated
from data collected from approximately one hundred international
organizations. In 2015, the work was updated for COP21 in Paris,
in response to the worrying evolution of data since its creation.
Diller Scofidio + Renfro, Mark Hansen, Laura Kurgan, and Ben Rubin,
in collaboration with Bruce Albert, François Gemenne, and
François-Michel Le Tourneau, *EXIT*, 2008. FC Collections (2012)

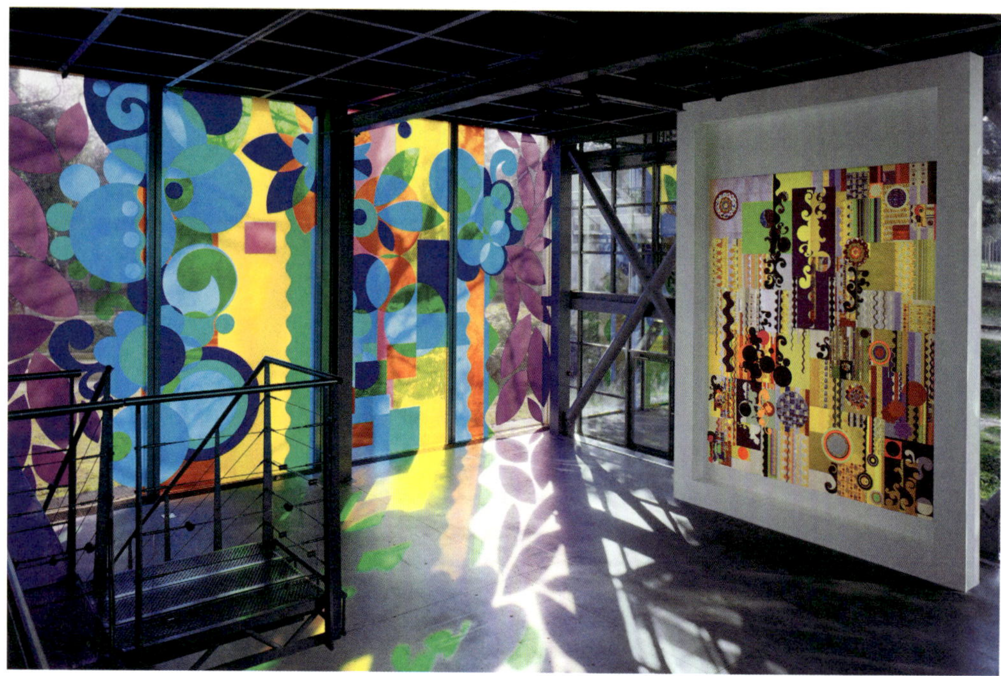

Beatriz Milhazes presented a selection of a dozen large-format paintings, a collage specially created for her exhibition, and two works displayed on the facades of the building. Beatriz Milhazes, *Samambaia*, 2009 (stained glass windows) and *Milk Mel*, 2008-2009 (collage). Commissions for the exhibition

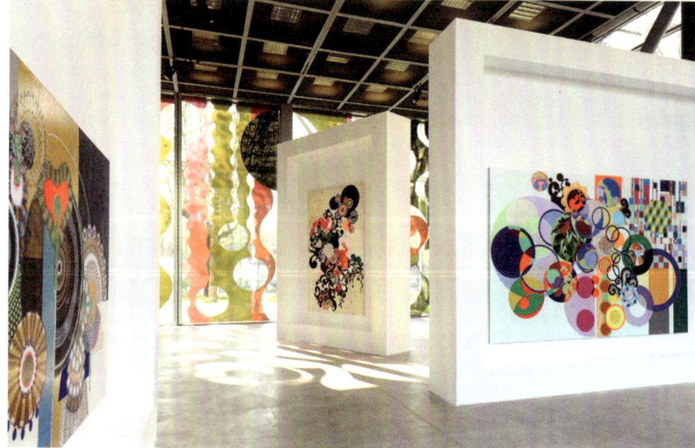

Beatriz Milhazes, *O Beijo*, 1995, *Ovo de Páscoa*, 2003, and *Sinfonia Nordestina*, 2008
Stained glass windows: *Casa de Baile*, 2009, commission for the exhibition

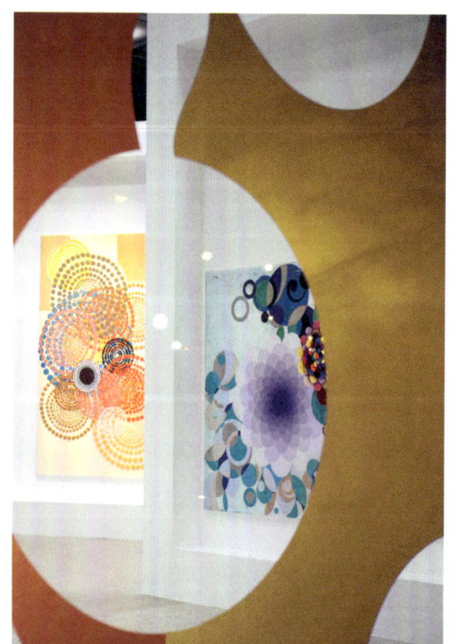

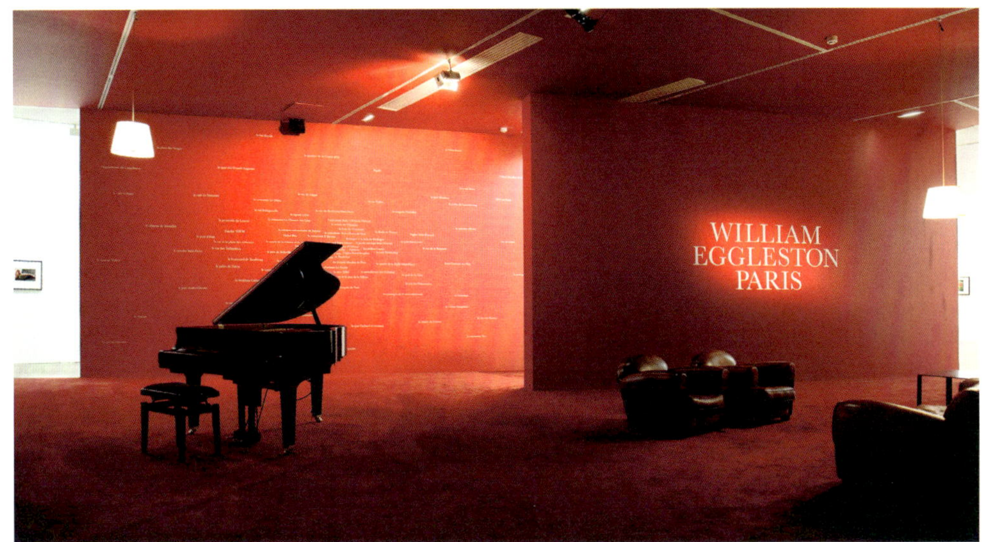

Between 2006 and 2008, William Eggleston embarked on an ambitious photographic project exploring the city of Paris at the invitation of the Fondation Cartier.

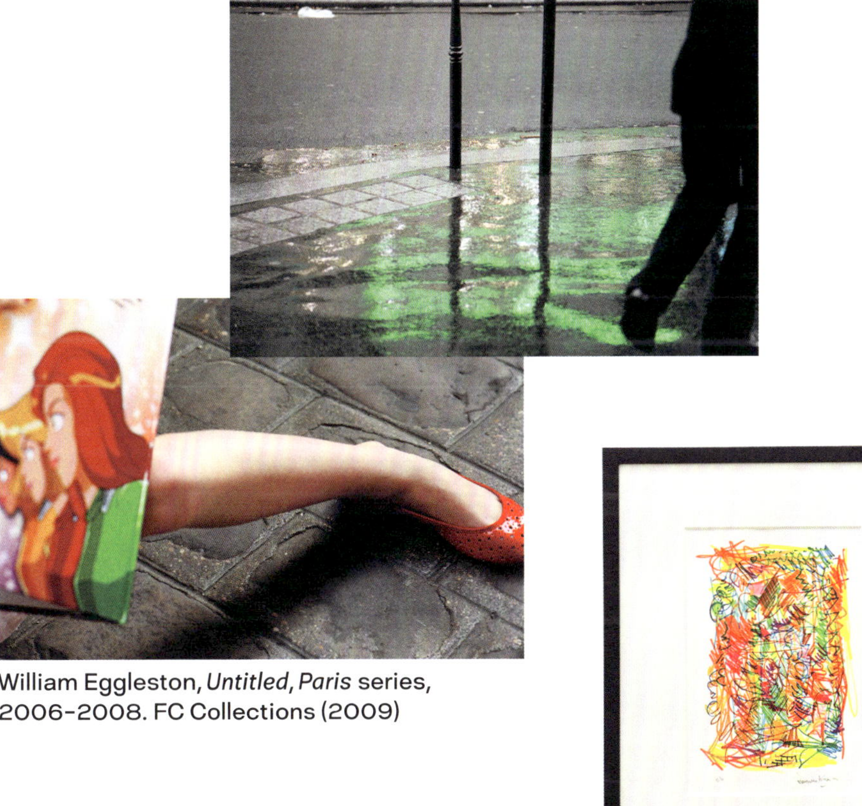

William Eggleston, *Untitled*, *Paris* series, 2006-2008. FC Collections (2009)

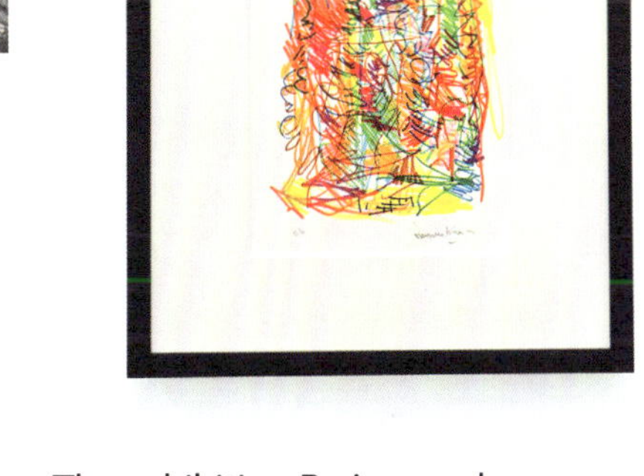

The exhibition *Paris* was also an opportunity to discover these photographs in dialogue with the artist's drawings. William Eggleston, *Untitled*, *Paris* series, 2006-2008

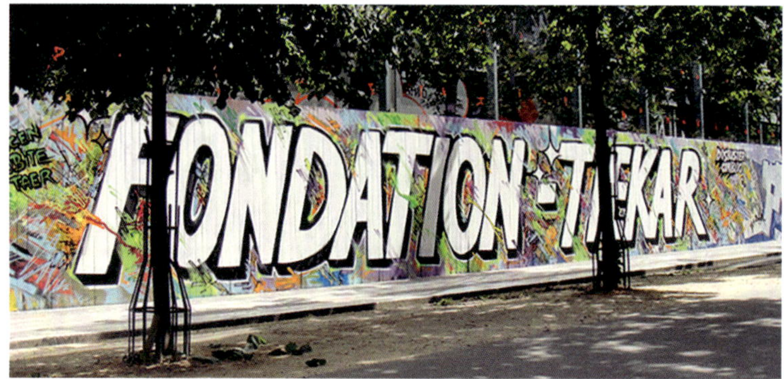

The exhibition *Born in the Streets—Graffiti* allowed the public to discover an art form omnipresent in cities and the extraordinary vitality of an artistic movement in perpetual evolution.
The fence of the Fondation Cartier on Boulevard Raspail.

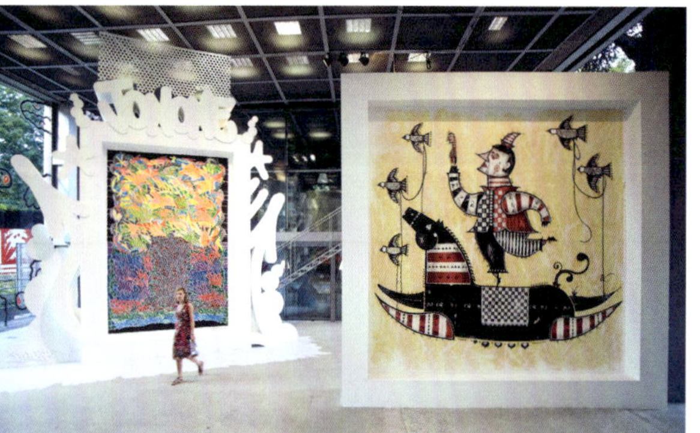

JonOne, *This Tree Has Been Planted a Long Time Ago*, 2009, and Vitché, *Untitled*, 2009

Seen, *Hand of Doom* (recreated for the exhibition), 2009

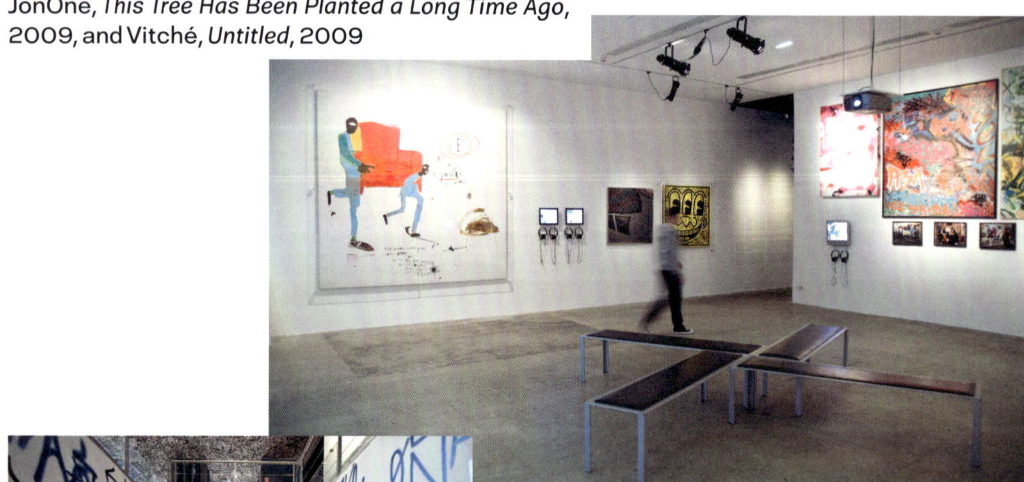

Jean-Michel Basquiat, *Light Blue Movers*, 1987 (left)

Cripta, 2009

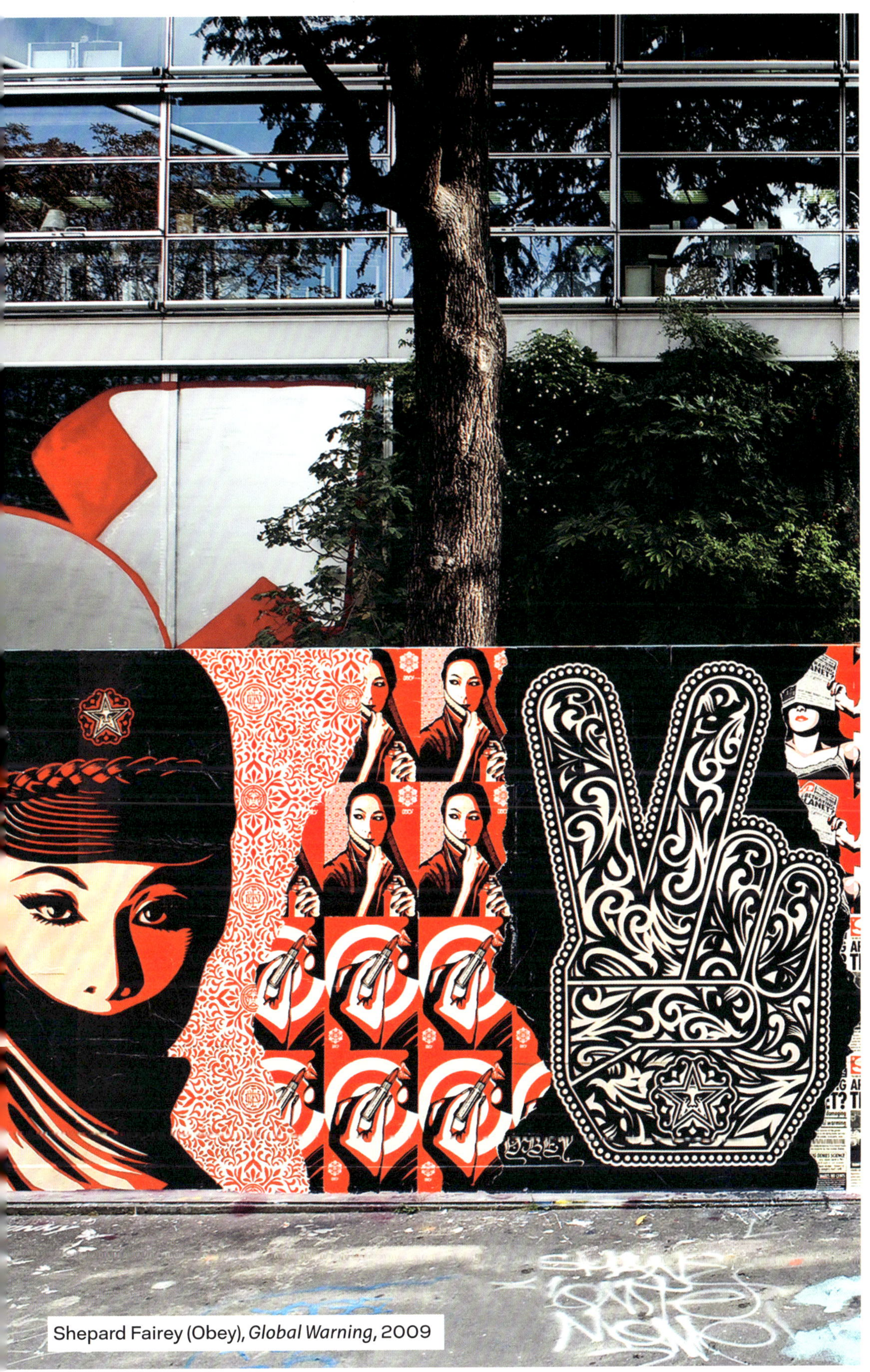

Shepard Fairey (Obey), *Global Warning*, 2009

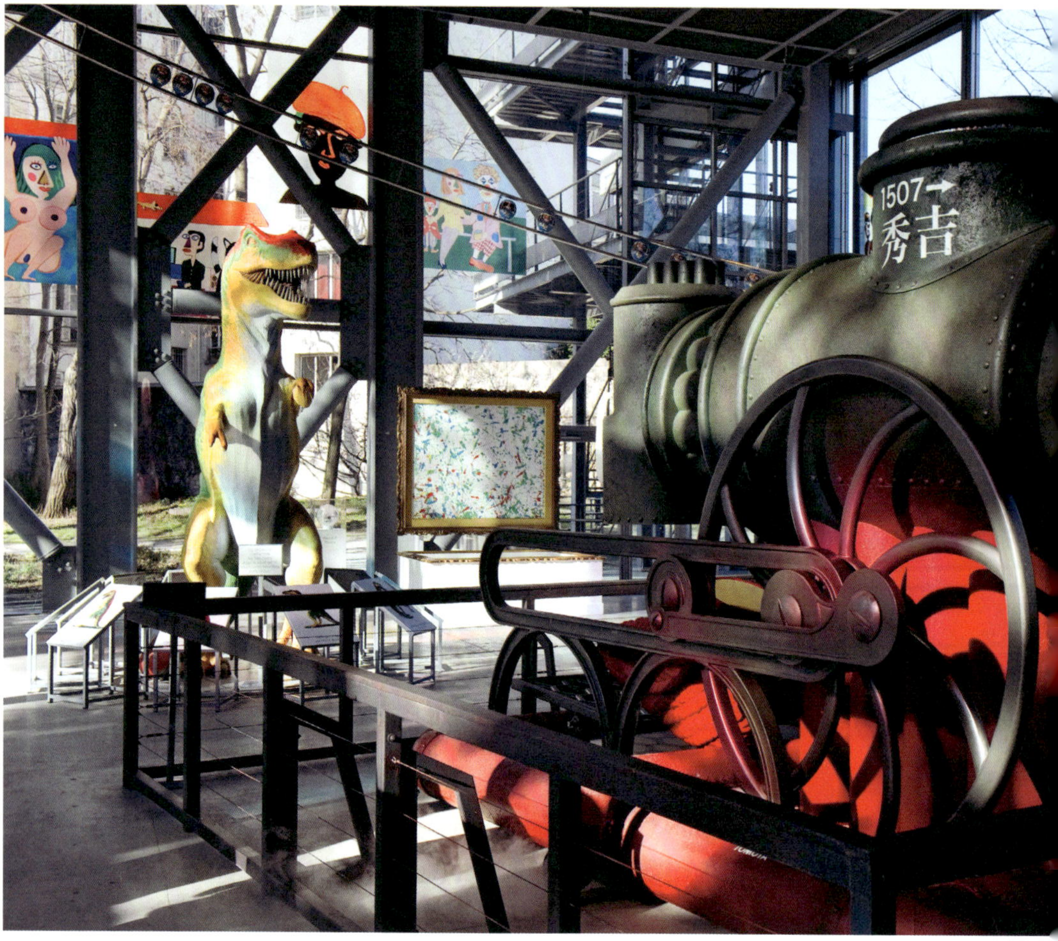

In the exhibition *Gosse de peintre* specially conceived for the Fondation Cartier, Takeshi Kitano displayed an endearing and impertinent world, where childhood souvenirs held a very special place. Takeshi Kitano, *"Hideyoshi," machine à coudre modèle Kitano*, 2009. FC Collections (2013)

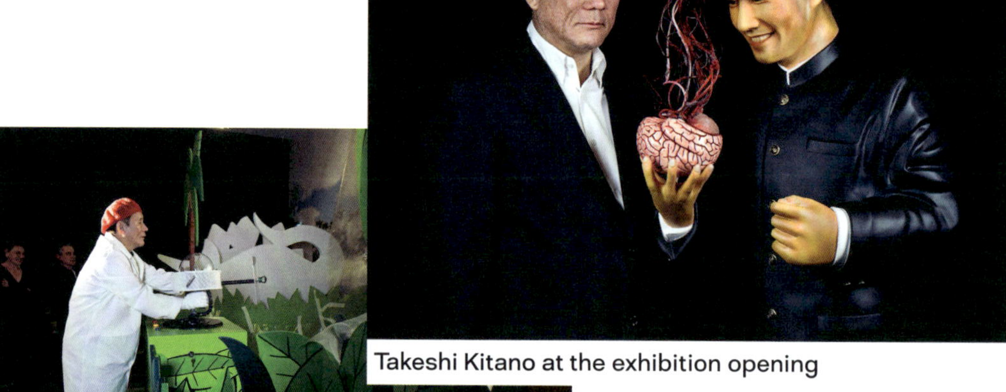

Takeshi Kitano at the exhibition opening

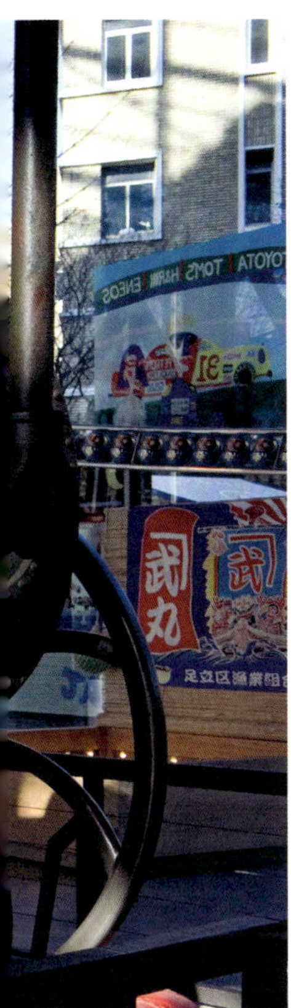

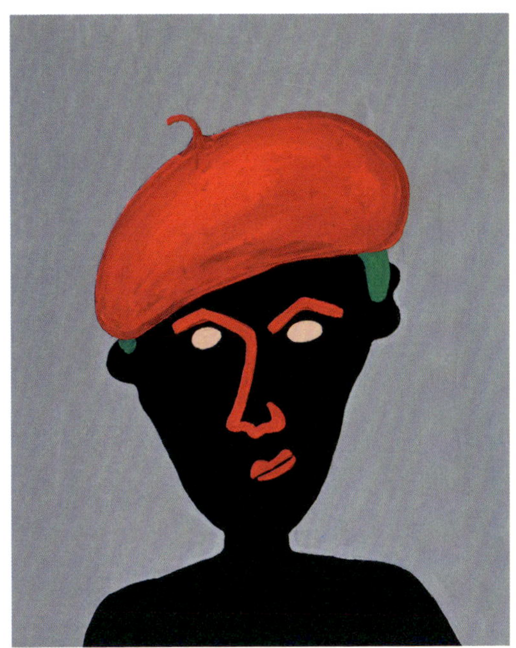

Takeshi Kitano, *Untitled*, 2008
FC Collections (2010)

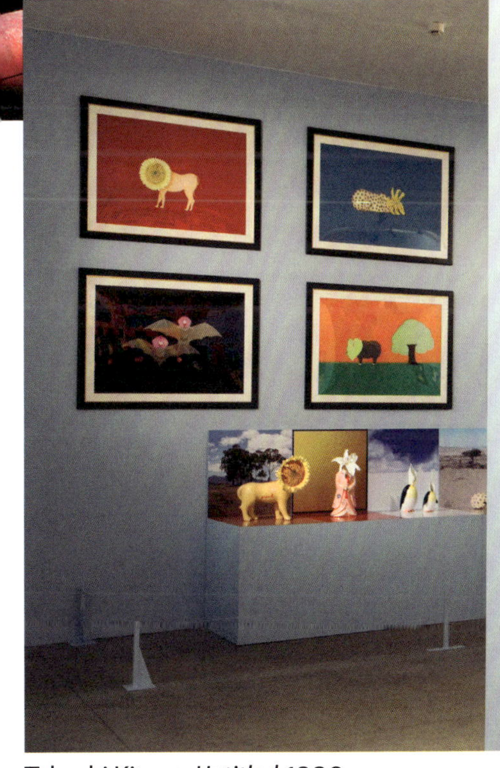

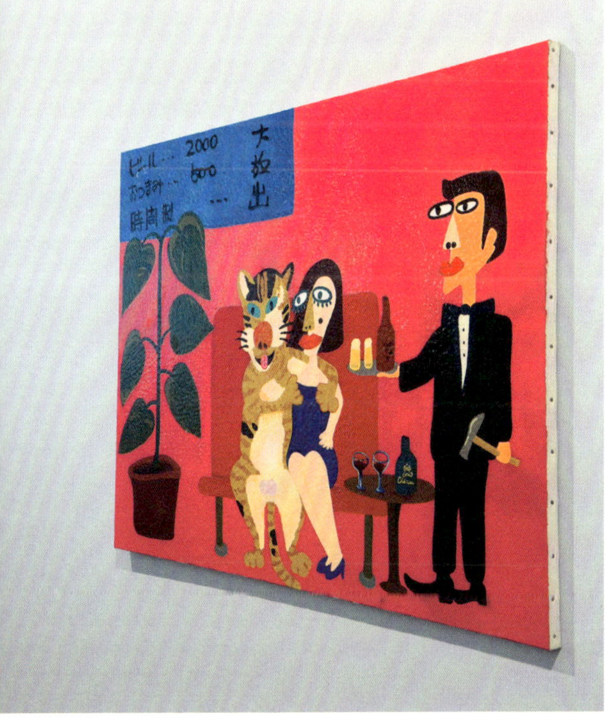

Takeshi Kitano, *Untitled*, 1996
FC Collections (2010)

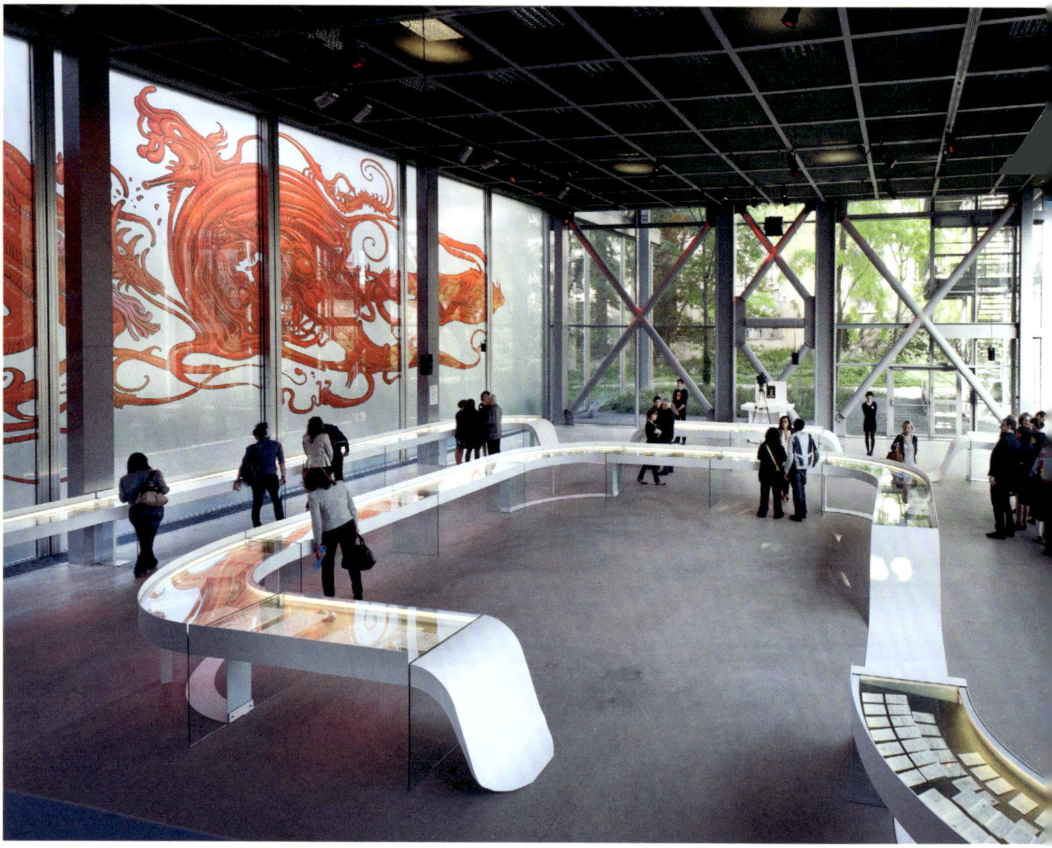

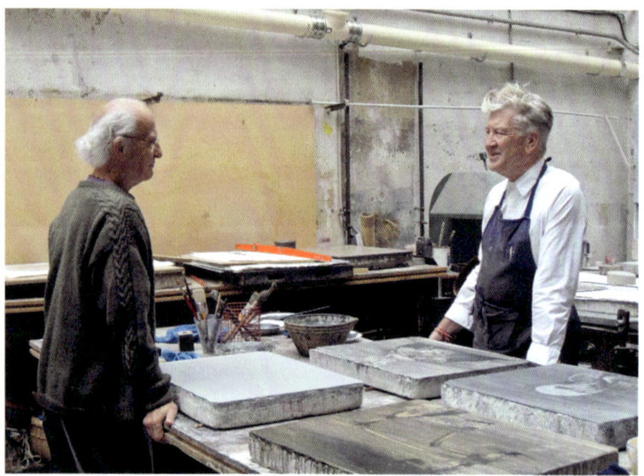

Featuring over four hundred works—sketches, cartoon storyboards, and paintings—as well as a 3-D animated film, specially created for the occasion, *Mœbius-Transe-Forme* was the first large-scale exhibition devoted to the artist.

At the invitation of the Fondation Cartier, Mœbius produced a lithograph at the Idem workshop in Paris in October 2010, and while there, met with David Lynch.

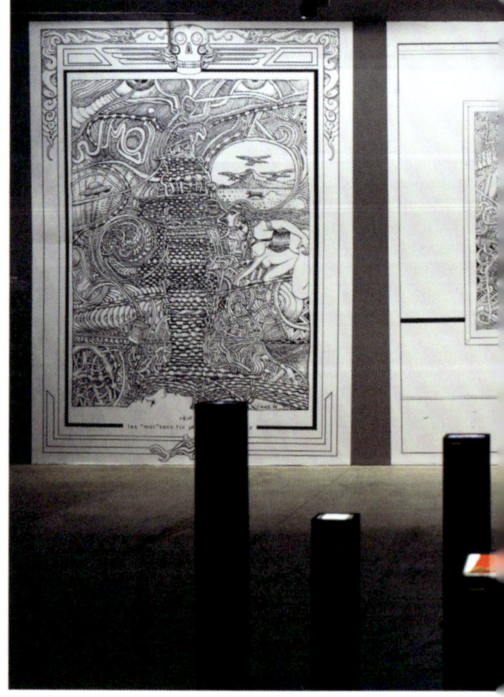

Mœbius, monumental reproductions of illustrations from the book *Le chasseur déprime*, 2008

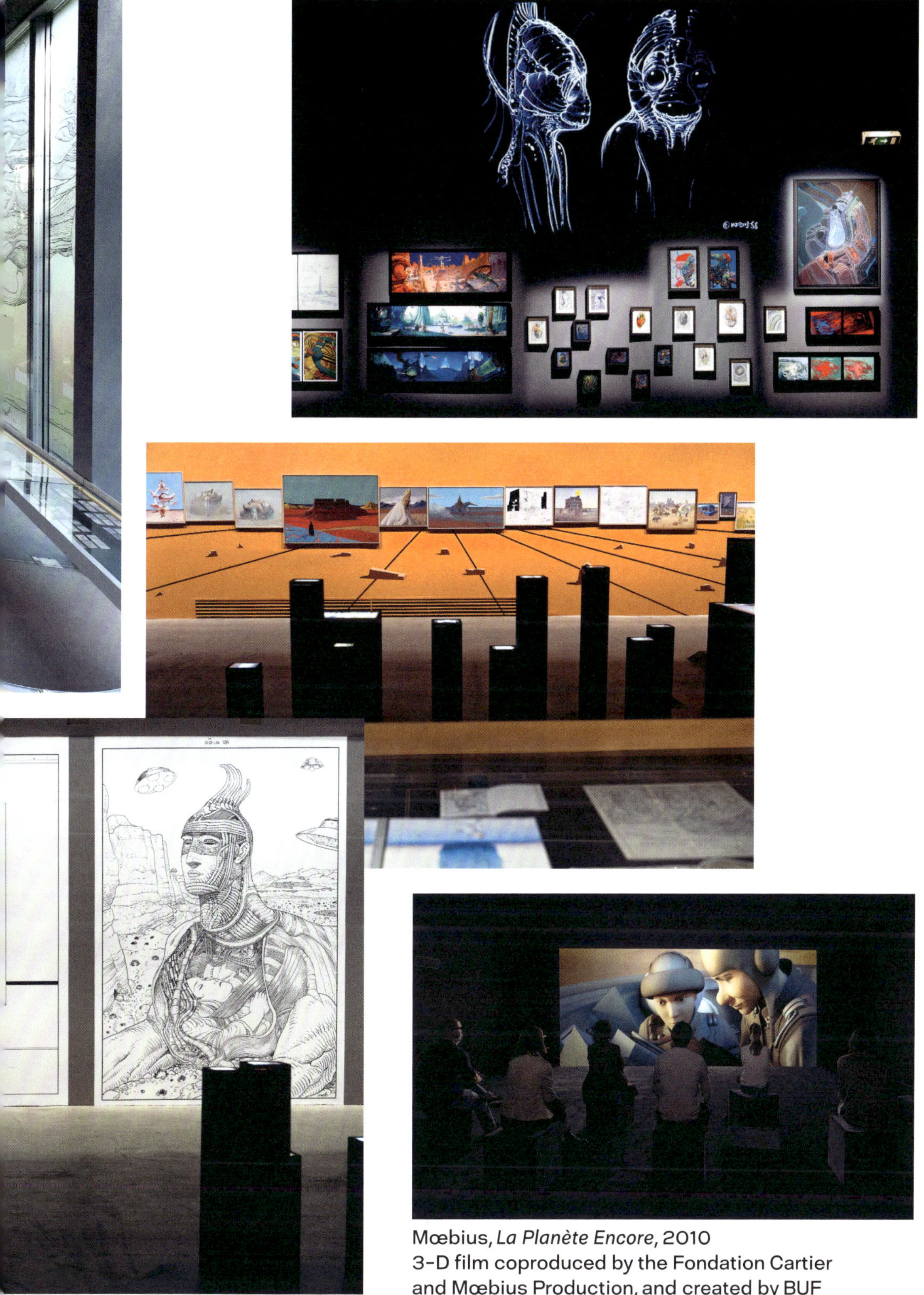

Mœbius, *La Planète Encore*, 2010
3-D film coproduced by the Fondation Cartier
and Mœbius Production, and created by BUF

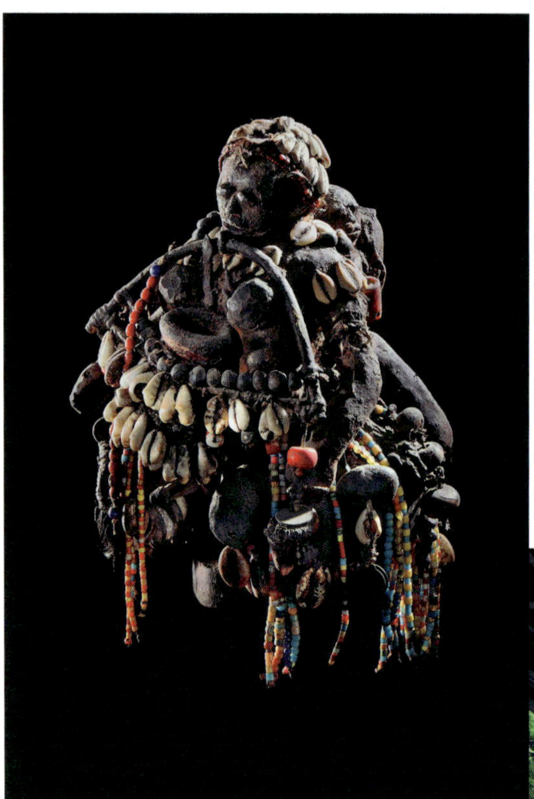

Fon voodoo sculpture, Benin

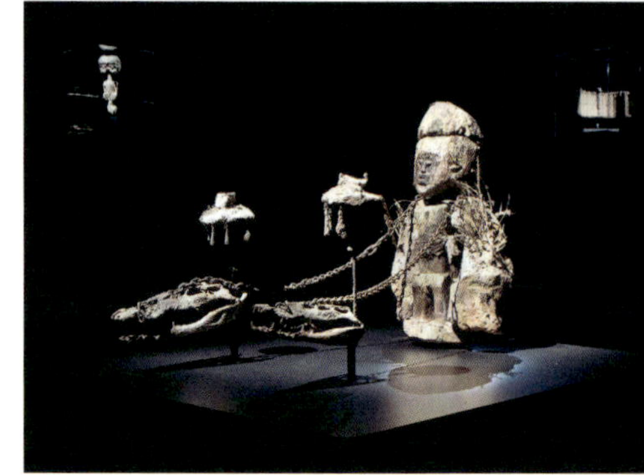

Chariot de la mort, Fon voodoo idol, Benin

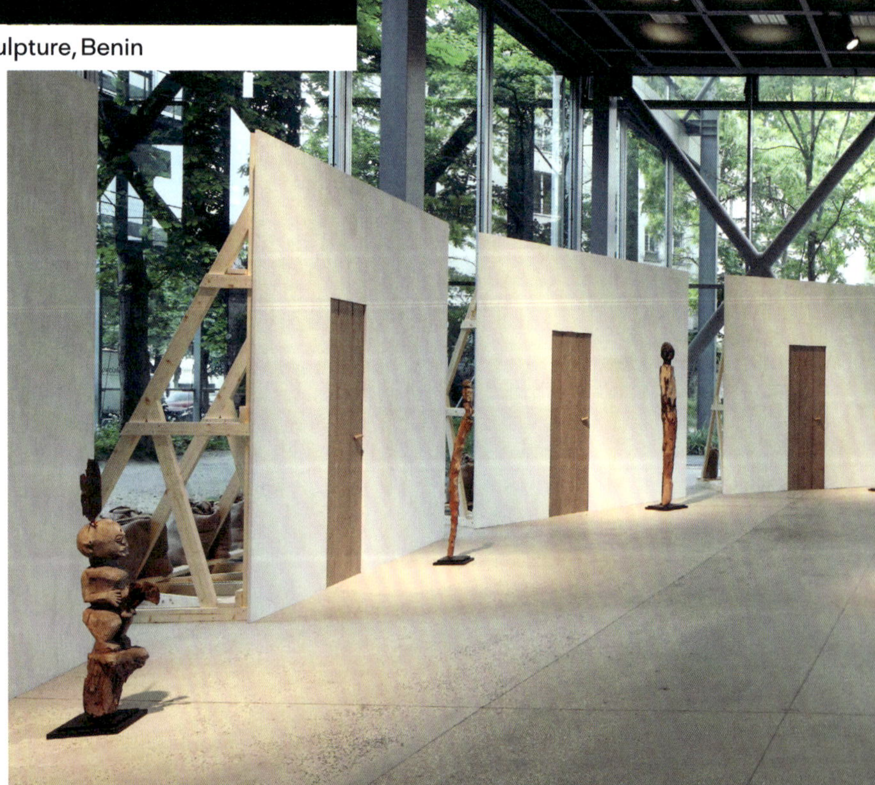

With the exhibition *Vodun: African Voodoo*, the Fondation Cartier presented to the public for the first time a remarkable group of voodoo idols from the collection of Anne and Jacques Kerchache, with a scenography designed by Enzo Mari.

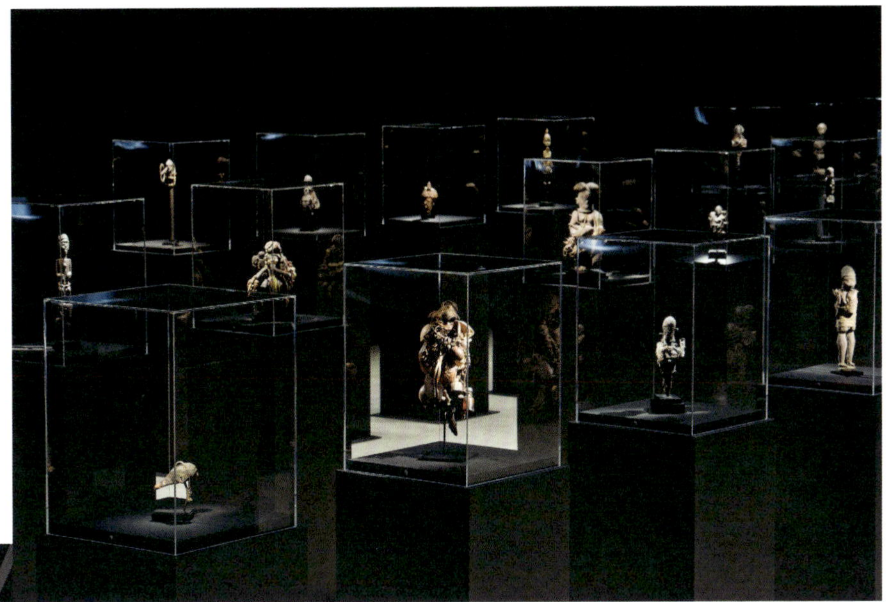

"After first encountering the venues, the exteriors of the houses, the lower level spaces are then defined by the exhibited works. The condition of man, the desire to escape death is inscribed on the 48 columns." Enzo Mari

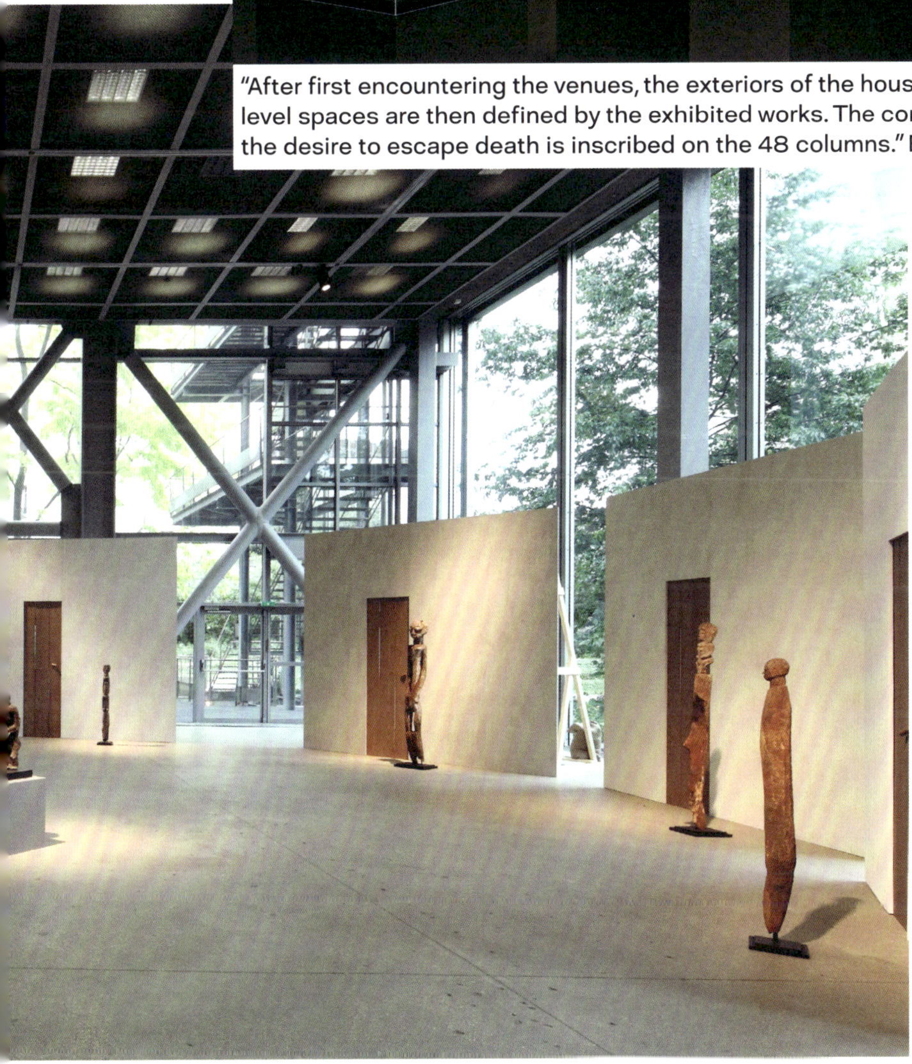

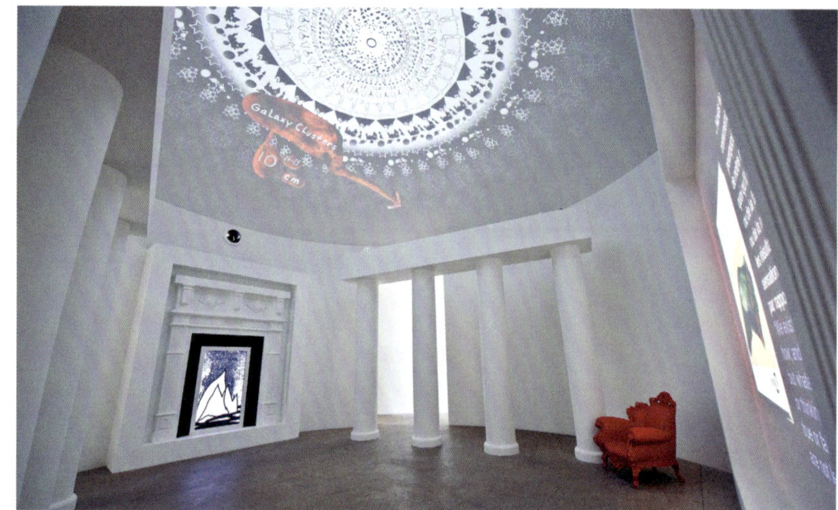

For the unusual exhibition *Mathematics, A Beautiful Elsewhere*,
the Fondation Cartier opened its doors to the mathematical community
and called on artists to travel with them on this adventure.
David Lynch, in collaboration with Misha Gromov, *The Library of Mysteries*,
2011. FC Collections (2012)

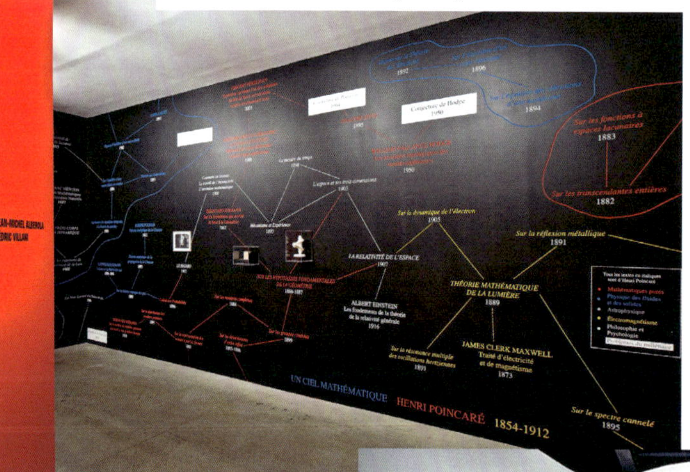

Jean-Michel Alberola, *Un ciel mathématique – Henri Poincaré*,
2011. FC Collections (2012)

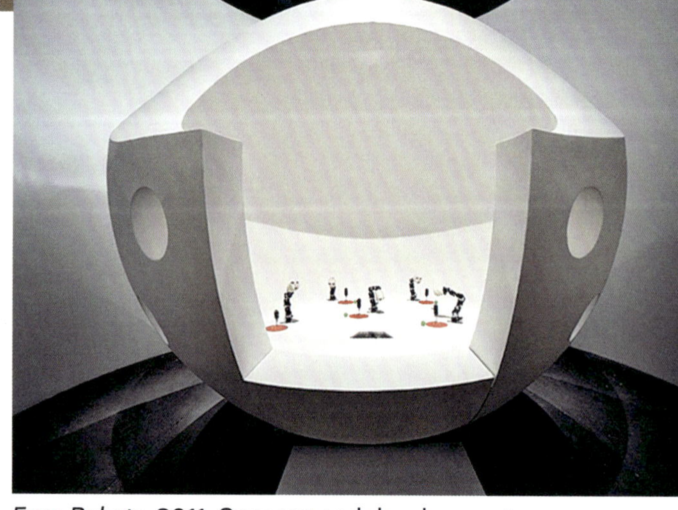

Ergo-Robots, 2011. Concept and development:
INRIA Bordeaux Sud-Ouest and Pierre-Yves Oudeyer
Scenography and design of the objects: David Lynch

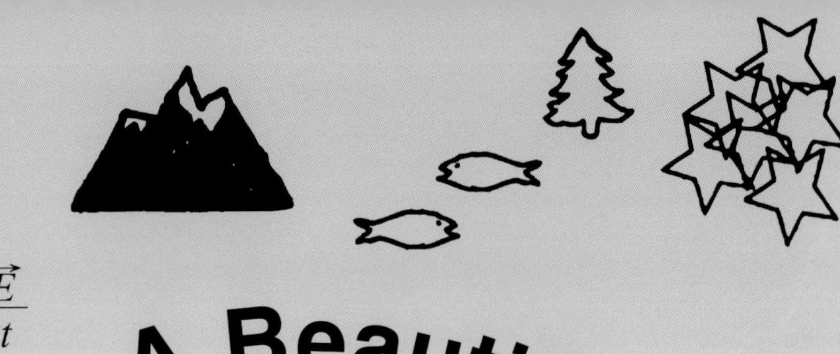

$$\times \vec{E} = -\frac{\partial \vec{B}}{\partial t}$$

$$\times \vec{B} = \frac{\vec{J}}{\varepsilon_0} + \frac{1}{c^2}\frac{\partial \vec{E}}{\partial t}$$

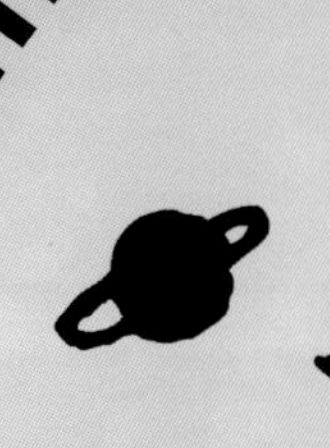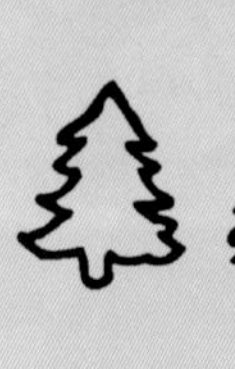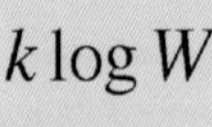

$$\forall n \in \mathbb{N},$$
$$n = \triangle + \triangle + \triangle$$
$$n = \square + \square + \square + \square$$
$$n = \pentagon + \pentagon + \pentagon + \pentagon + \pentagon$$

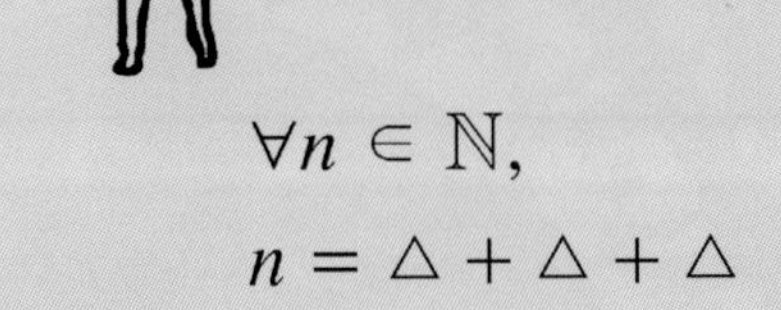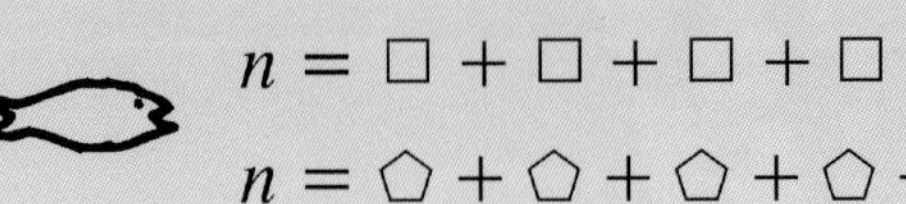

$$S = k \log W$$

$$\frac{1}{4}\iiint dv\, dv_*\, d\sigma\, B(v - v_*, \sigma)\left(f_*' f' - f f_*\right)\log\frac{f_*' f'}{f f_*} \geq 0$$

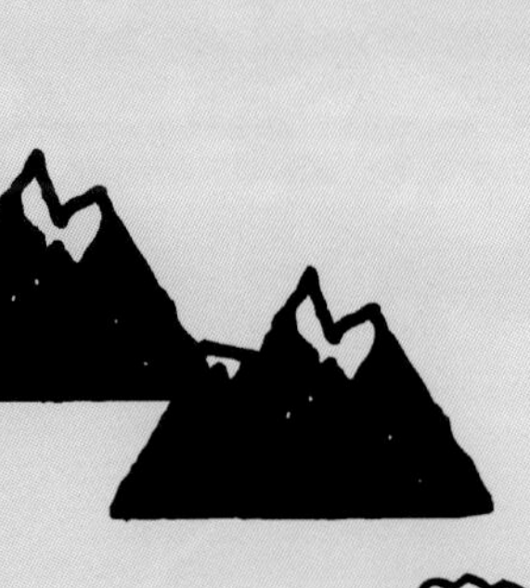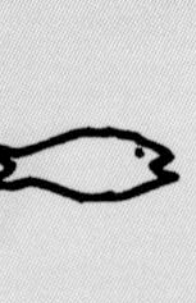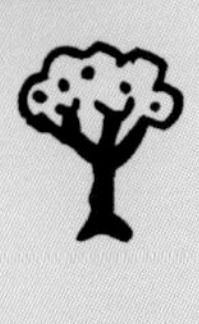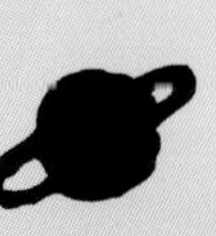

$$\frac{\partial X}{\partial t} = f(X, Y) + \mu\nabla$$

$$\frac{\partial Y}{\partial t} = g(X, Y) + \nu\nabla$$

$$+\mu\nabla^2 X$$

$$+\nu\nabla^2 Y$$

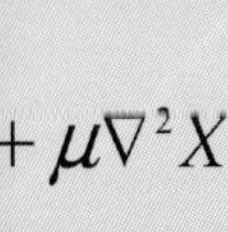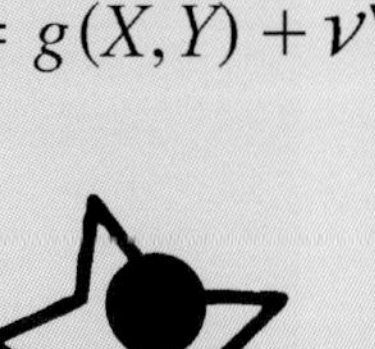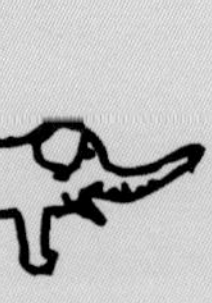

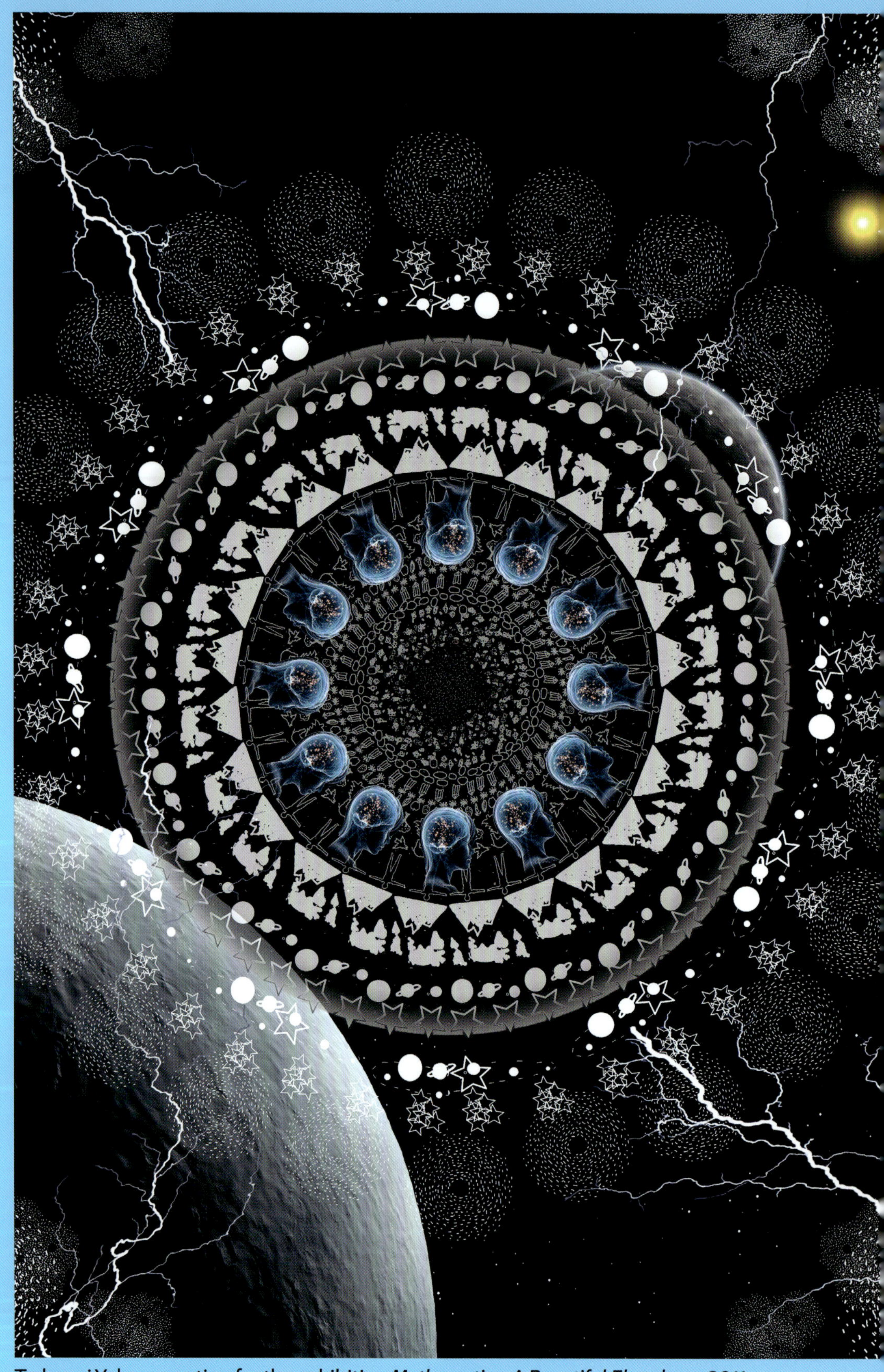

Tadanori Yokoo, creation for the exhibition *Mathematics, A Beautiful Elsewhere*, 2011

Mathematics A Beautiful Elsewhere

In 2011, a community of mathematicians and artists inaugurated an exhibition at the Fondation Cartier designed to be a journey to the heart of mathematical thought and creation. *Mathematics, A Beautiful Elsewhere*, which owes its title to a formula expressed by mathematician Alexander Grothendieck in his autobiographical work *Récoltes et Semailles* (1986), was the result of meetings and exchanges that had begun three years earlier. In November 2008, the Director of the Fondation Cartier Hervé Chandès and astrophysicist Michel Cassé decided to organize an exhibition around mathematics, to move it out of research laboratories and classrooms, and present it to a wider audience in a new light. They then met mathematician Nicole El Karoui who told them that "to do mathematics is to abstract." Everything began with this statement. A few months later, the IHES (Institut des Hautes Études Scientifiques) joined the project, thanks to the director at the time, the great mathematician Jean-Pierre Bourguignon. With his guidance, Hervé Chandès and Michel Cassé began meeting mathematicians from all over the world and from diverse mathematical fields: Sir Michael Atiyah, Alain Connes, Misha Gromov, Cédric Villani, and Don Zagier, as well as students Giancarlo Lucchini and Carolina Canales González who, like many other scientists, joined the project as it evolved.

The year 2010 marked a turning point in the adventure of the exhibition in the making. The small circle of mathematicians began exchanging ideas with artists close to the Fondation Cartier. In February, a few days before the opening of Takeshi Kitano's exhibition at the Fondation Cartier, Cédric Villani and Jean-Pierre Bourguignon had a conversation with this multifaceted artist, who was subsequently invited to take part in the project. Over the course of that year, the exhibition's three curators, Hervé Chandès, Michel Cassé, and Jean-Pierre Bourguignon, initiated other meetings. David Lynch, inspired by the thought and philosophy of mathematicians, and taking zero as a starting point, designed the exhibition spaces on the ground floor, featuring an ensemble of images and installations. Artists including Raymond Depardon and Claudine Nougaret, Patti Smith, Hiroshi Sugimoto, Tadanori Yokoo, Beatriz Milhazes, and Jean-Michel Alberola joined the adventure, immersing themselves in the fascinating world of mathematics. Over the following months, mathematicians and artists shared their mutual curiosity to compose an exhibition that allowed visitors to see, listen, play, and wonder at the beauty of mathematics. With Misha Gromov's *Library of Mysteries*, David Lynch showcased a selection of major works chosen by the mathematician for the essential place they hold in the history of thought. Next to this library, in a large, barely opened egg, were the "ergo-robots," a tribe of young robotic creatures endowed, thanks to the efforts of Pierre-Yves Oudeyer and his INRIA collaborators, with an artificial intelligence and curiosity that enabled them to create their own language. Raymond Depardon and Claudine Nougaret produced the documentary *Au Bonheur des Maths* for the exhibition, giving a voice to the mathematicians who collaborated on the project, while Jean-Michel Alberola filmed the hand of Cédric Villani transcribing the proof of Cercignani's conjecture with chalk on a blackboard. Also featuring the contributions of Patti Smith, Beatriz Milhazes, Hiroshi Sugimoto, and Takeshi Kitano, alongside the experiments on matter carried out by the CERN within the Large Hadron Collider (LHC) and the mapping of the primordial universe recorded by the Planck satellite, the exhibition offered the public a veritable change of scenery, a beautiful elsewhere.

While mathematics had been included in some of the Fondation Cartier's earlier exhibitions—*La Vitesse* in 1991 and *Étant donné: Le Grand Verre* by Hiroshi Sugimoto in 2004—*Mathematics, A Beautiful Elsewhere* was the first exhibition to fuse art and science so audaciously.

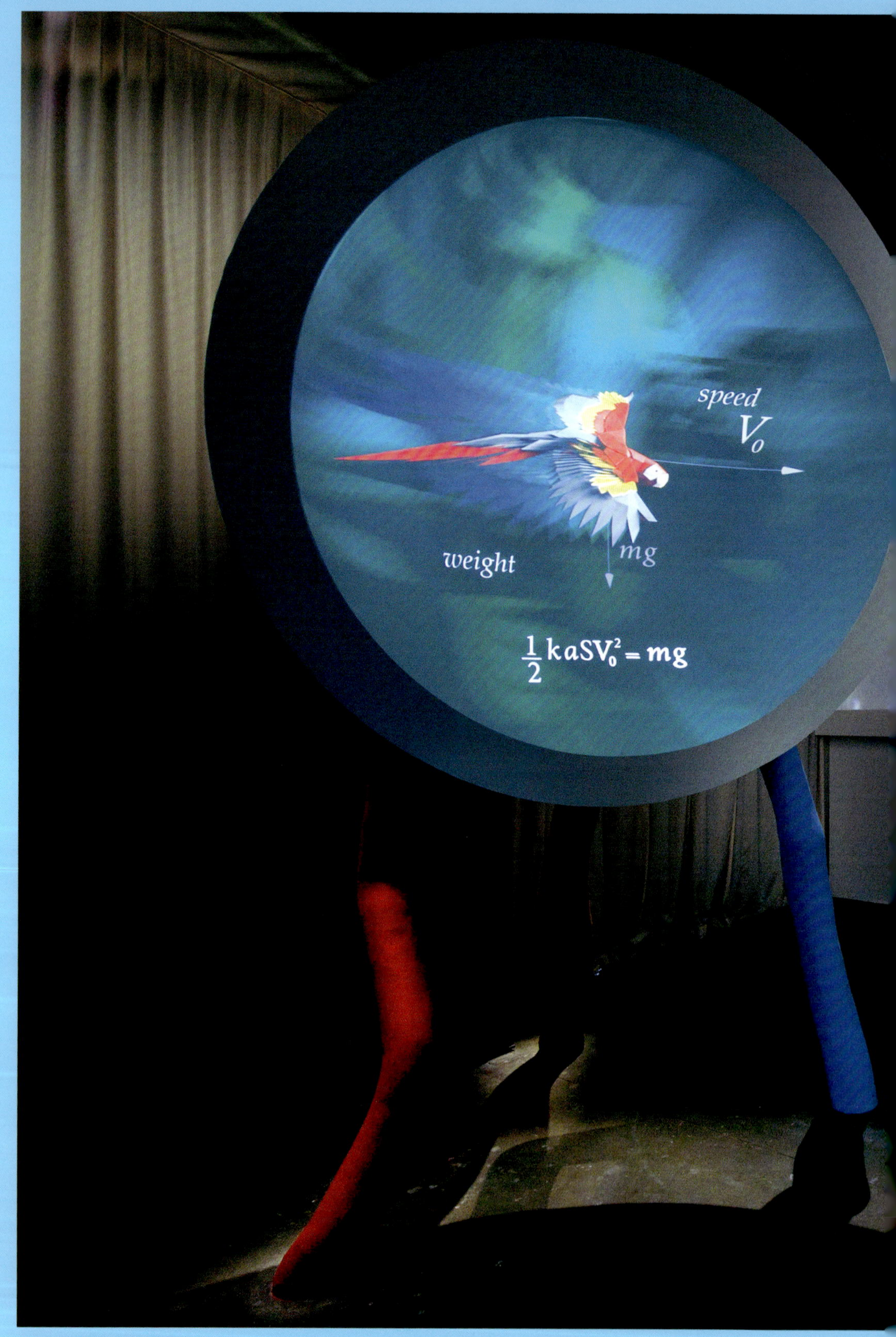

2011 Beatriz Milhazes and BUF, *Les Paradis mathématiques*. View of the exhibition *Mathematics, A Beautiful Elsewhere* with the scenography designed by David Lynch

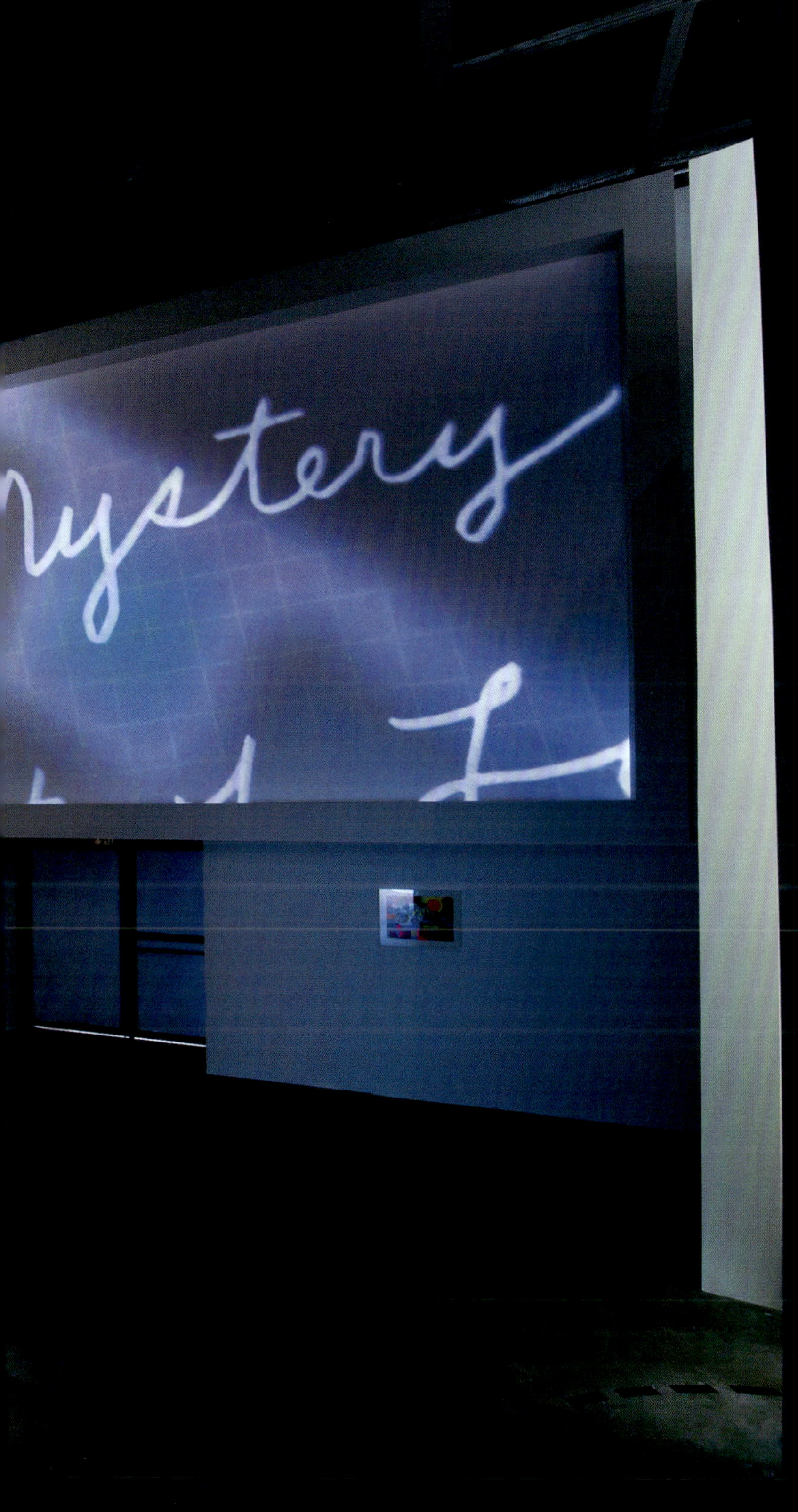
mystery

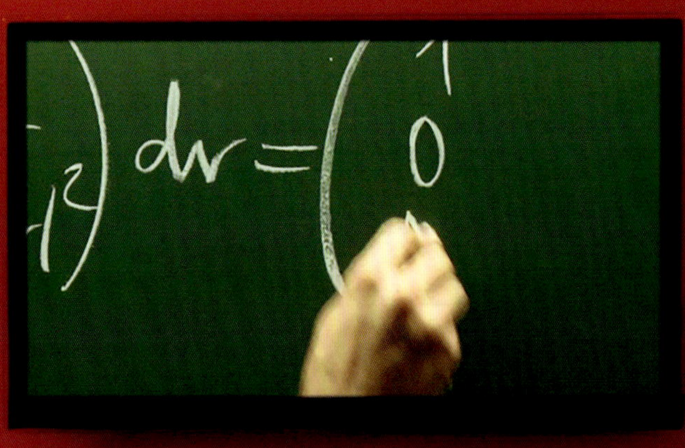

2011   Jean-Michel Alberola, *La Main de Cédric Villani (la conjecture de Cercignani)*
Commission for the exhibition

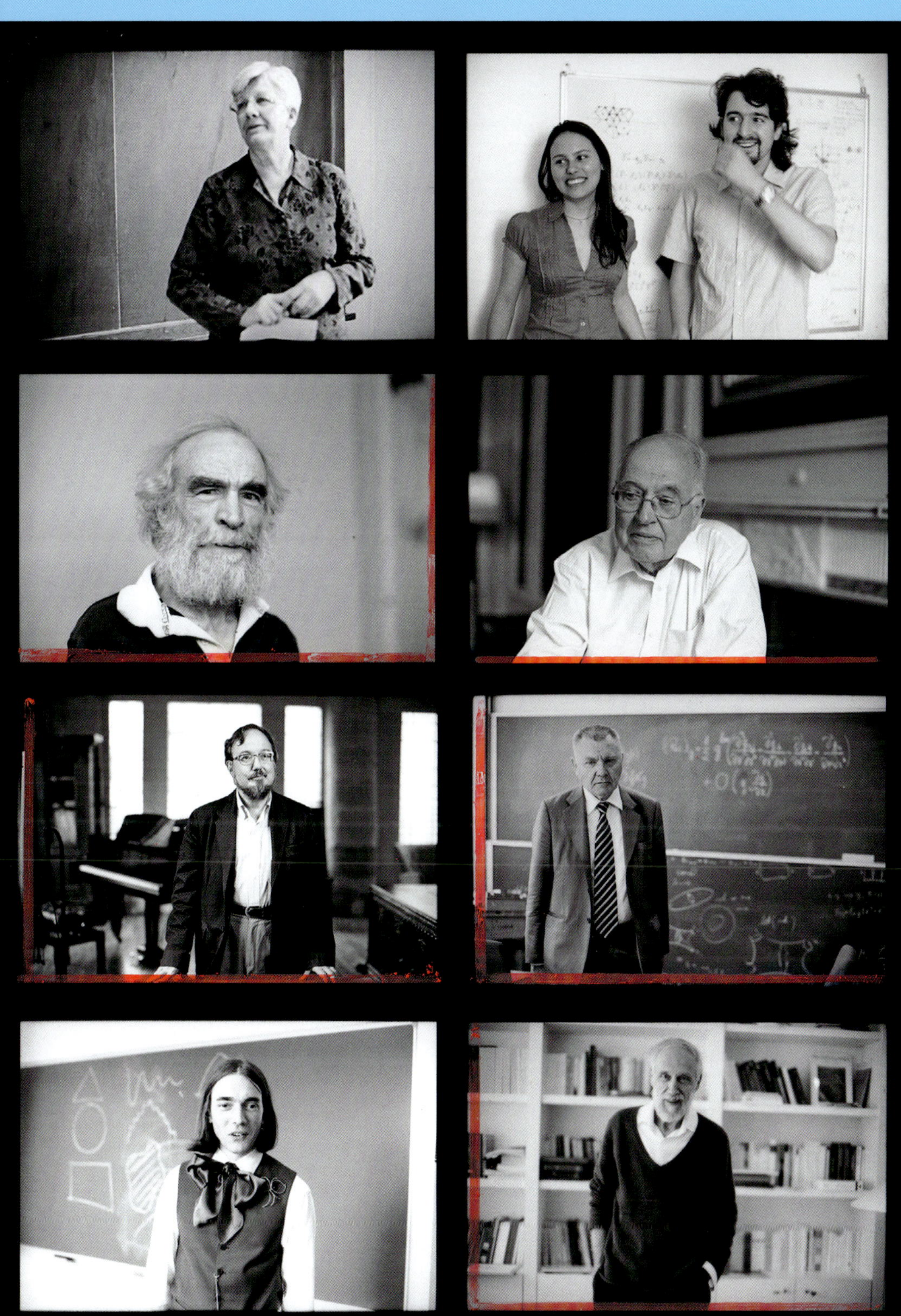

2011   Making of Raymond Depardon and Claudine Nougaret's film *Au Bonheur des Maths*, shot for the exhibition with mathematicians Nicole El Karoui, Carolina Canales González and Giancarlo Lucchini, Misha Gromov, Sir Michael Atiyah, Don Zagier, Jean-Pierre Bourguignon, Cédric Villani, and Alain Connes. Photographs by Raymond Depardon

LA RÉPONSE EST 2011
LES RÈGLES DU JEU DE TAKESHI KITANO

1. LES NOMBRES DOIVENT ÊTRE ÉCRITS DANS L'ORDRE :
   1, 2, 3, 4, …, ET AINSI DE SUITE.

2. ENTRE LES NOMBRES, ON PEUT METTRE N'IMPORTE QUEL OPÉRATEUR,
   COMME +, −, ×, ÷, √, !, ETC.

3. L'INSTALLATION EST EN QUELQUE SORTE UNE COMPÉTITION :
   PLUS LA FORMULE EST COURTE, MEILLEURE ELLE EST.

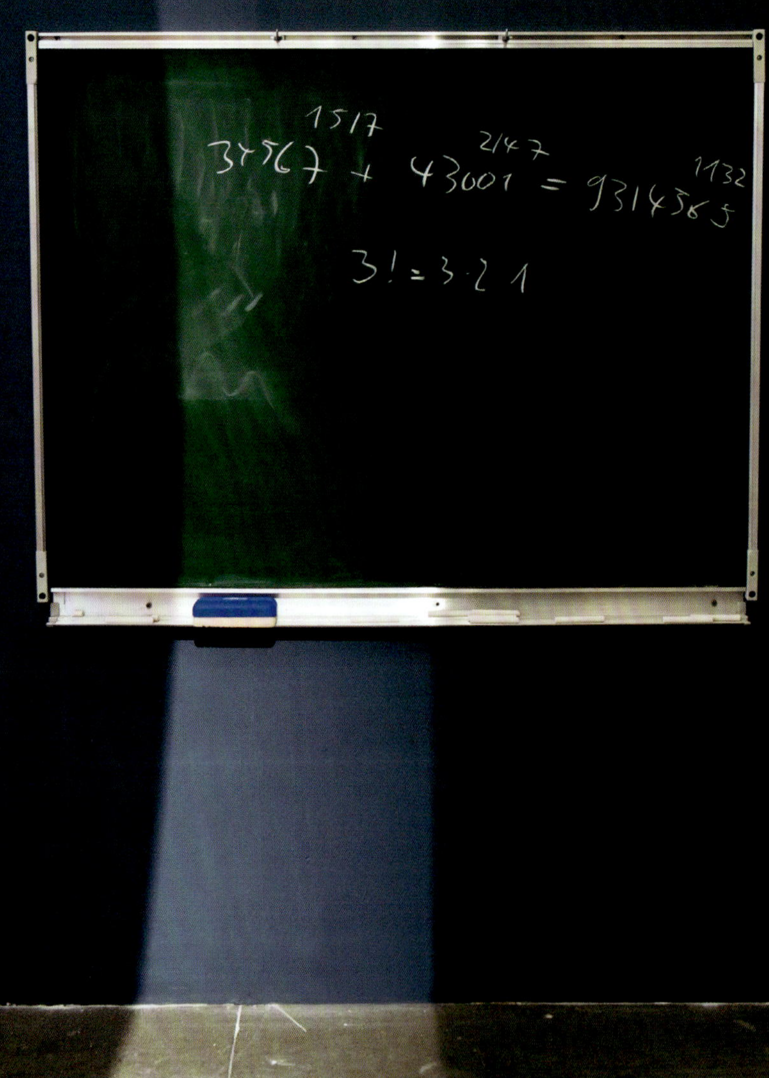

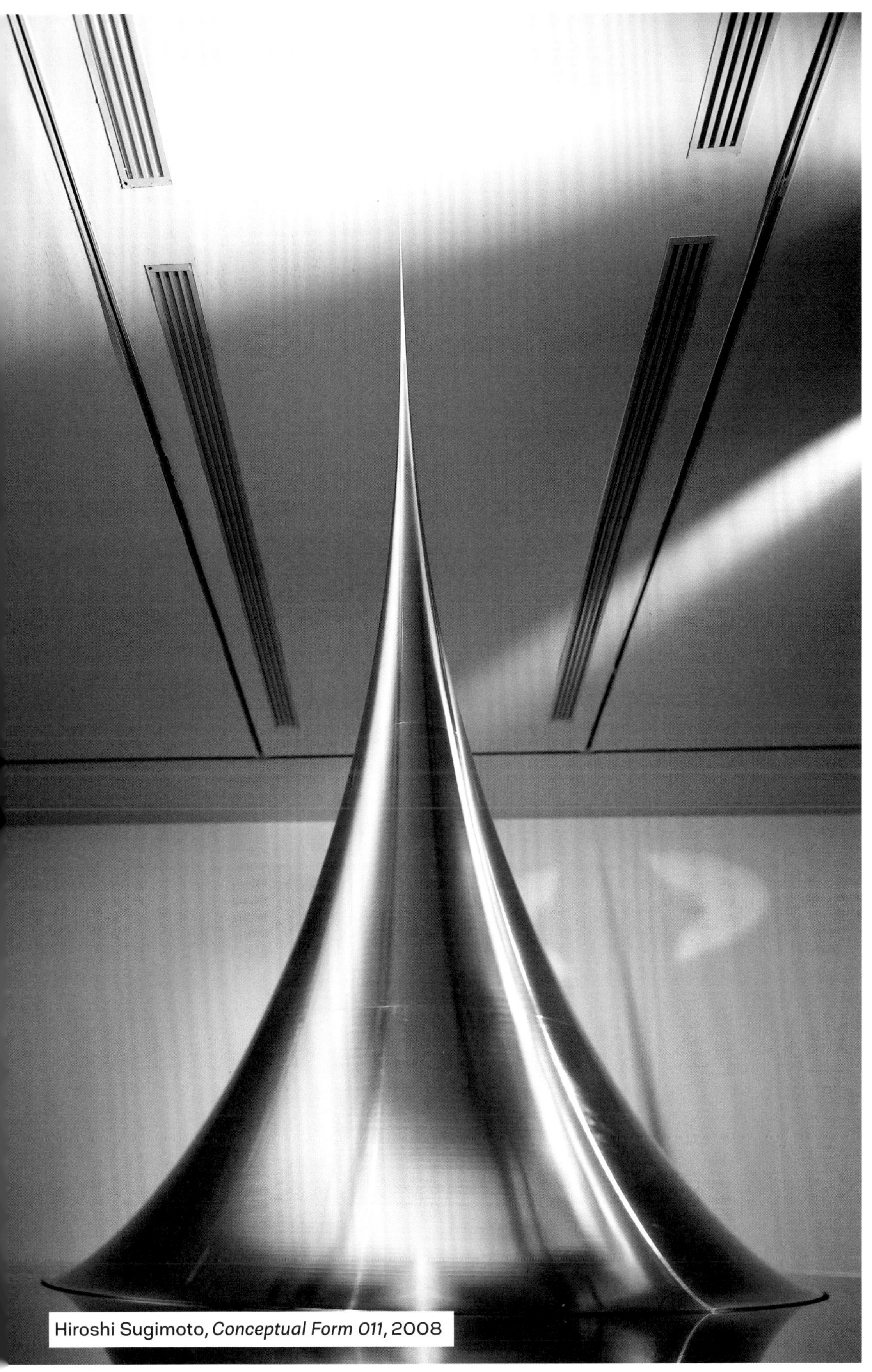

Hiroshi Sugimoto, *Conceptual Form 011*, 2008

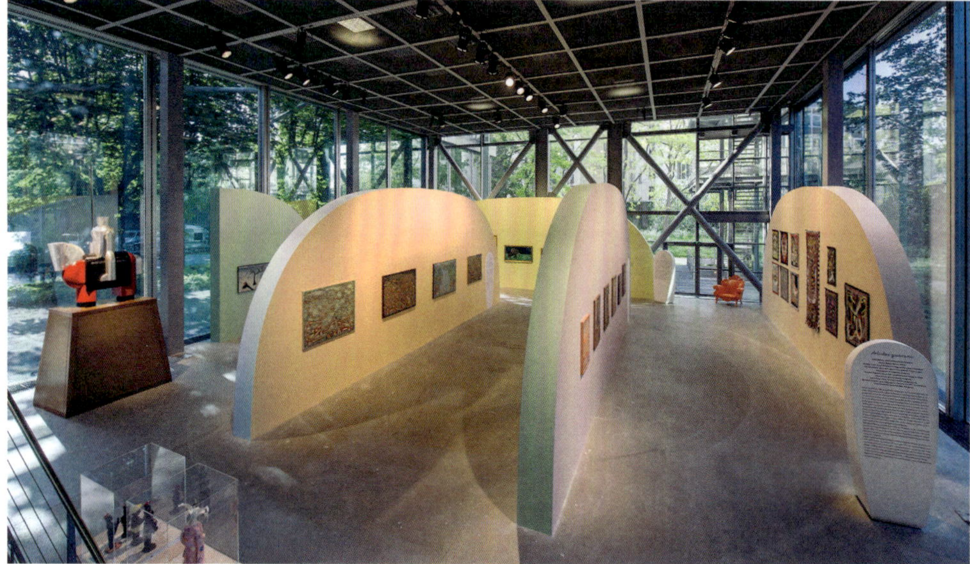

With a scenography designed by Alessandro Mendini, almost 300 works by 50 artists from all over the world reflected the profoundly personal vision of their creators, inspired by an anthology of stories, myths, folklore, and magic.

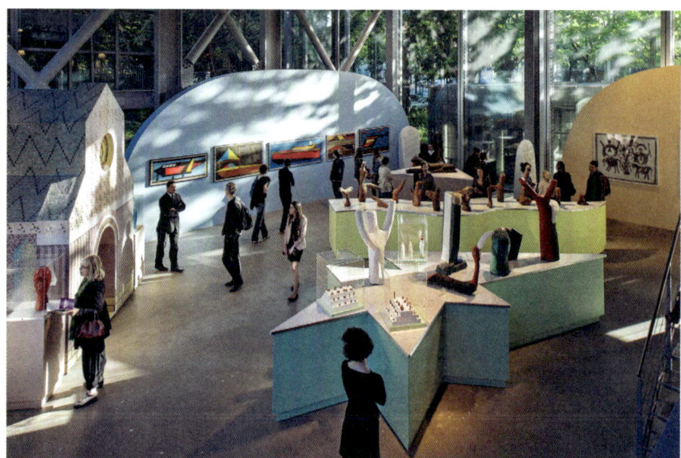

"The exhibition design is conceived as a setting, simple but precious, intended to contain, protect, and showcase a unique art that has a direct connection with the ultra-sensitive heart." Alessandro Mendini

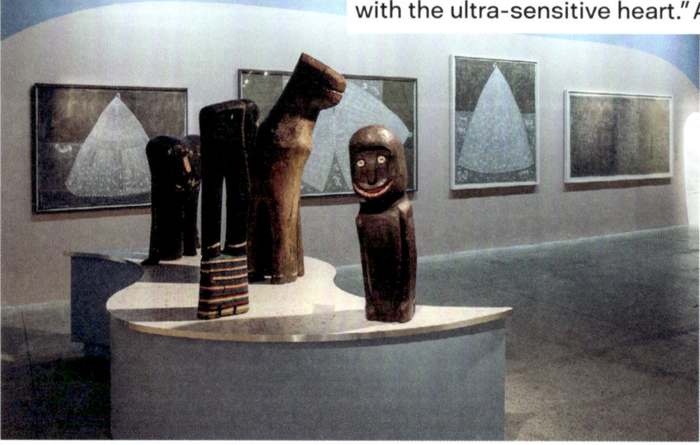

Works by Nino, Jivya Soma Mashe, and Ratna Raghia Dushalda

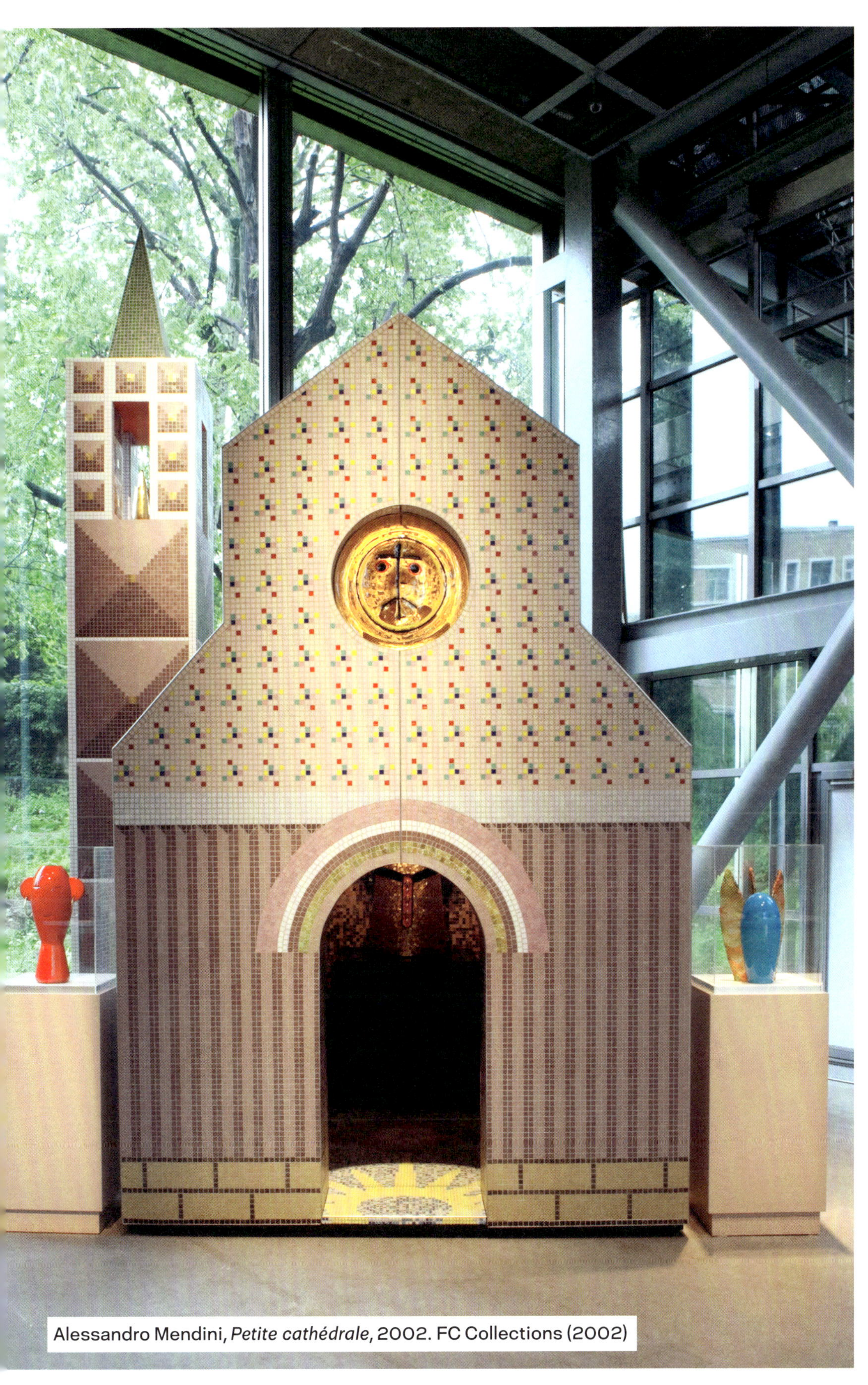

Alessandro Mendini, *Petite cathédrale*, 2002. FC Collections (2002)

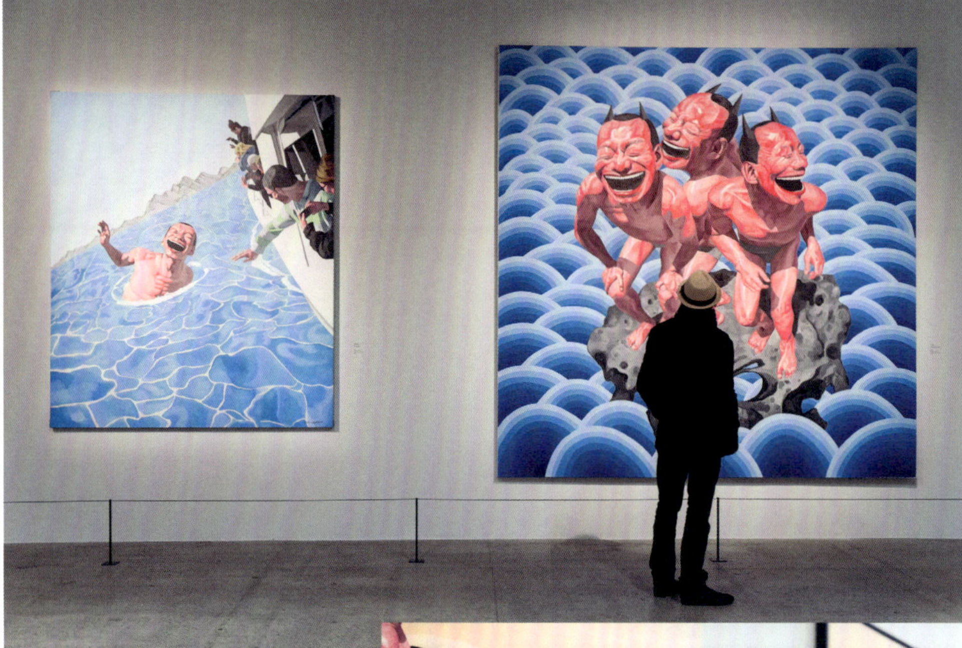

Yue Minjun, *Bystander*, 2011,
and *Isolated Island*, 2010

Yue Minjun at the exhibition opening

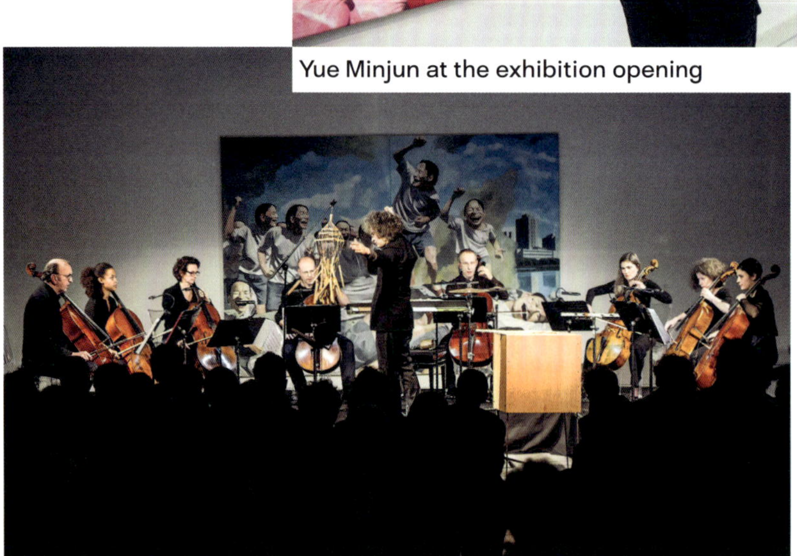

Concert by the ensemble Nomos for the Nomadic Night with Jean-Pierre
and Friends, based on a proposal by Jean-Pierre Drouet, February 11, 2013

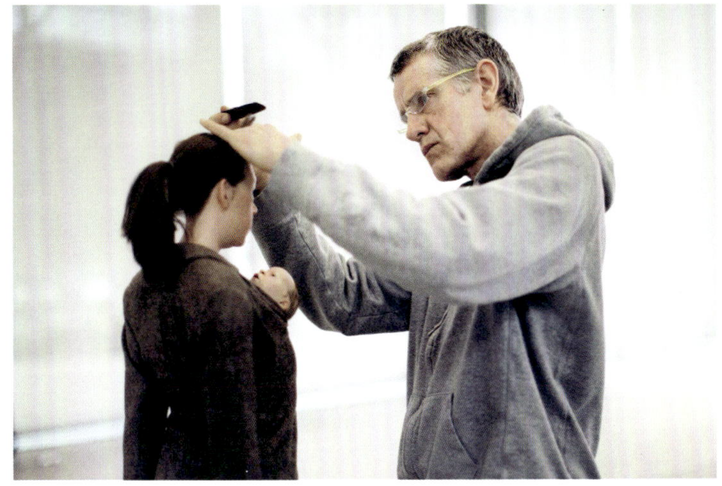

Ron Mueck working on *Woman with Shopping*, 2013, during the installation of the exhibition. FC Collections (2013)

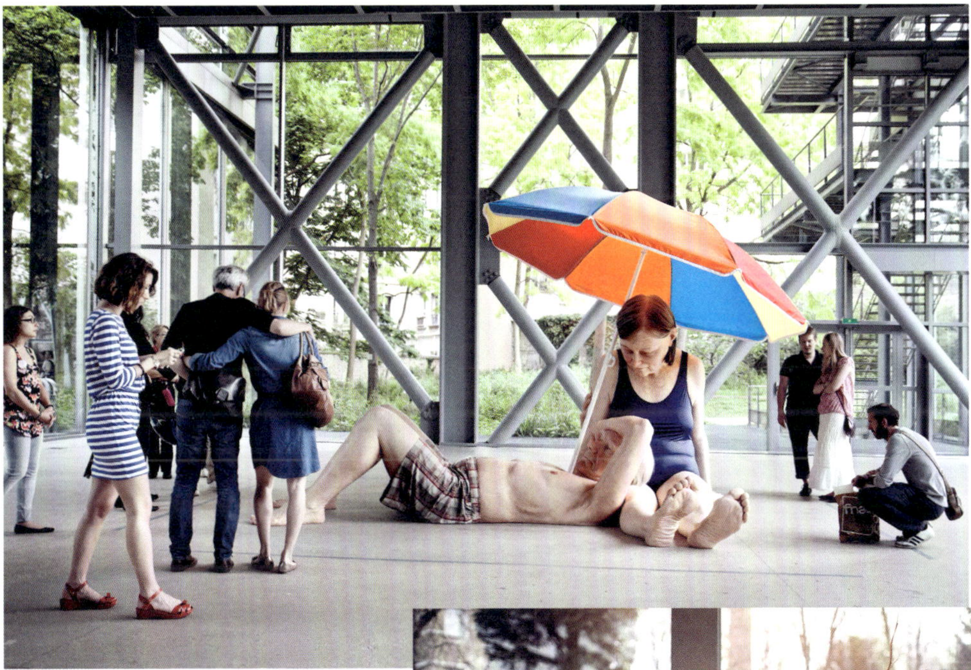

Ron Mueck, *Couple Under an Umbrella*, 2013

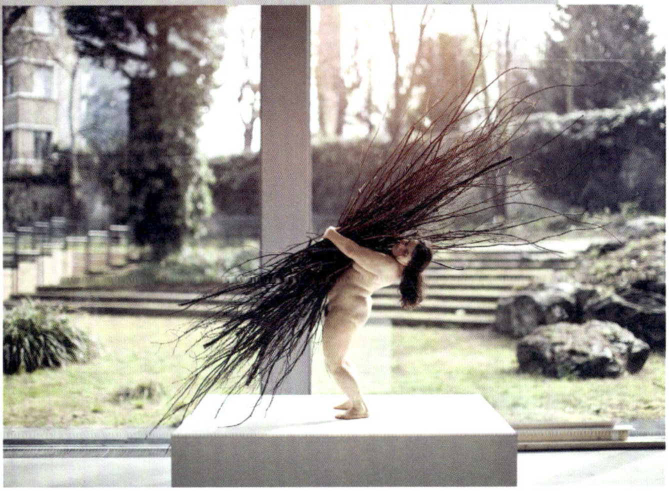

Ron Mueck, *Woman with Sticks*, 2009-2010
FC Collections (2013)

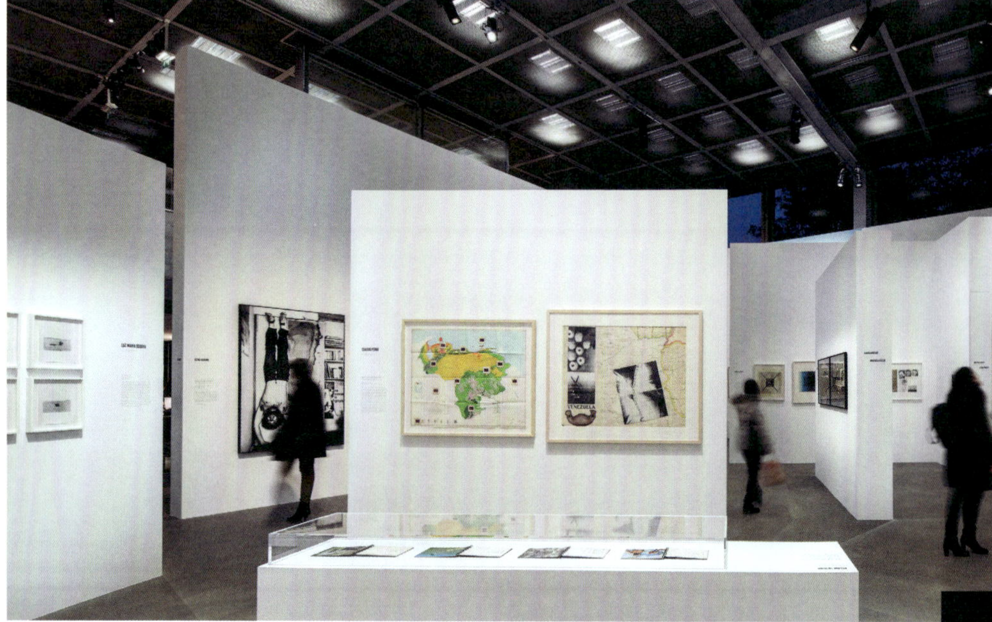

Featuring over 70 artists from 11 different countries, the exhibition *América Latina 1960-2013* offered a new perspective on Latin American photography through the prism of the relationship between text and image.

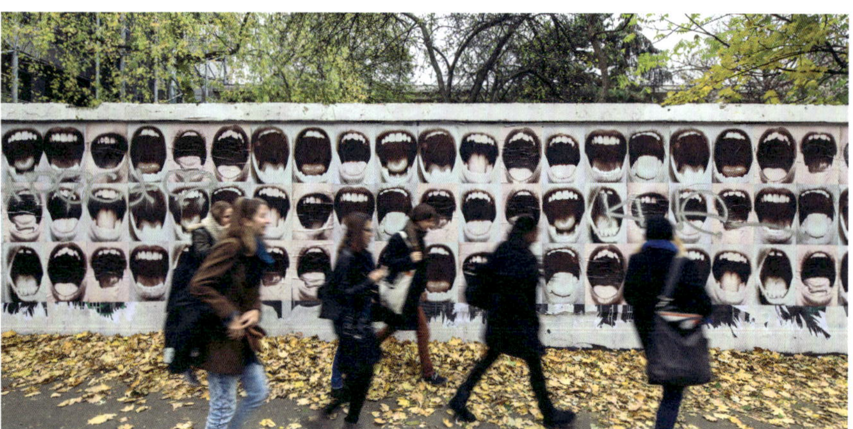

Photographer Graciela Sacco produced a collage from her *Bocanada* series on the wall of the École Spéciale d'Architecture, located just opposite the Fondation Cartier.

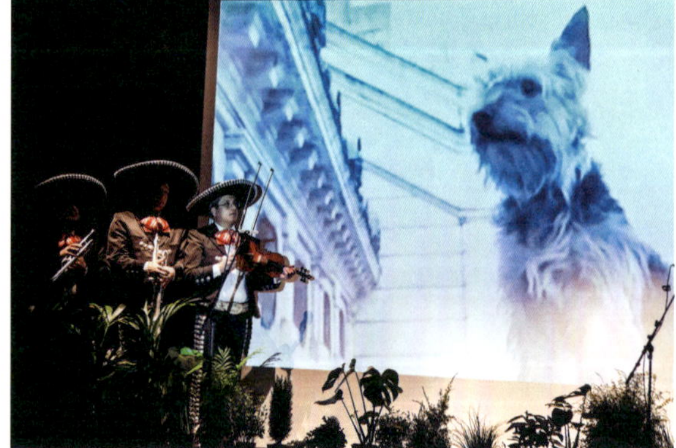

Nomadic Night with Lázaro Valiente, March 17, 2014

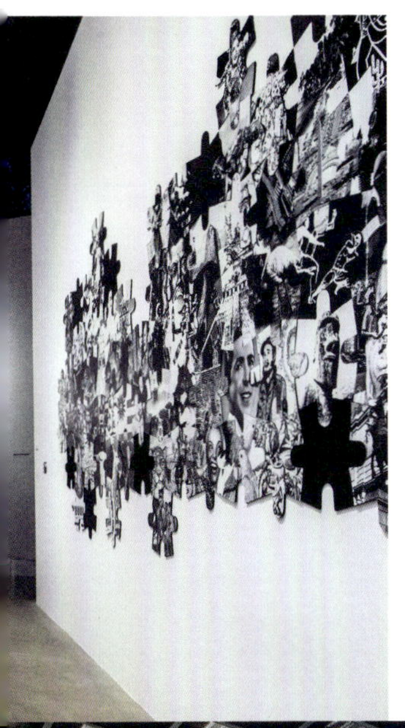

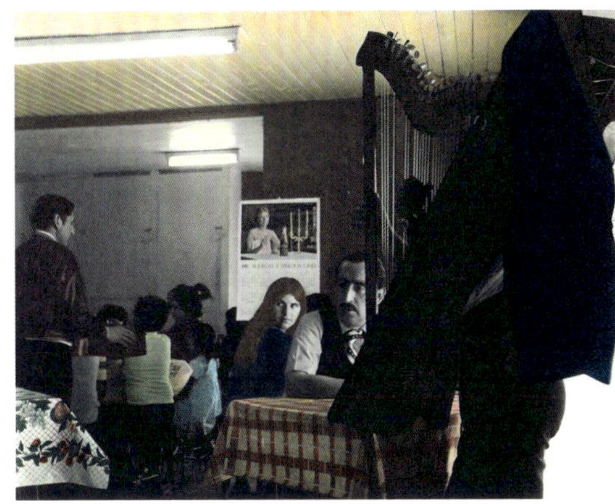

Leonora Vicuña, *Mercado de Valdivia, Chile*, 1980
FC Collections (2013)

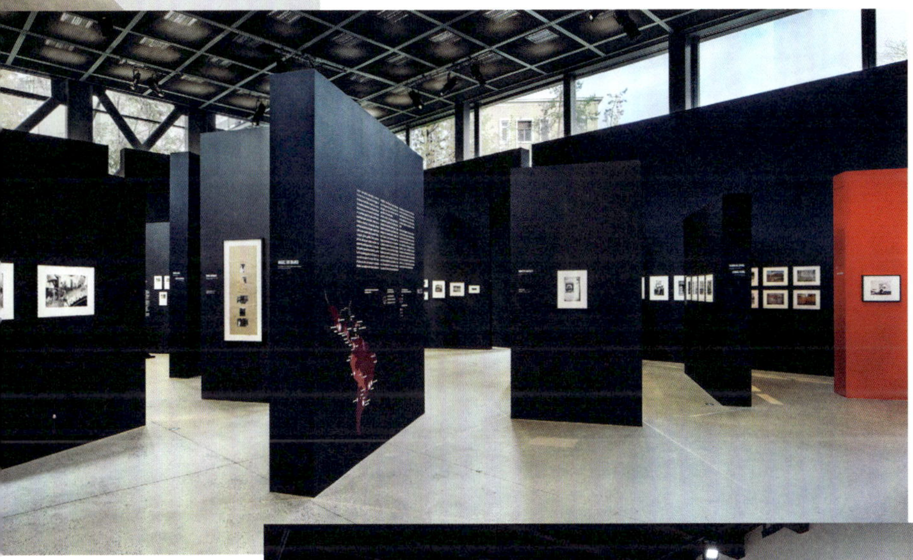

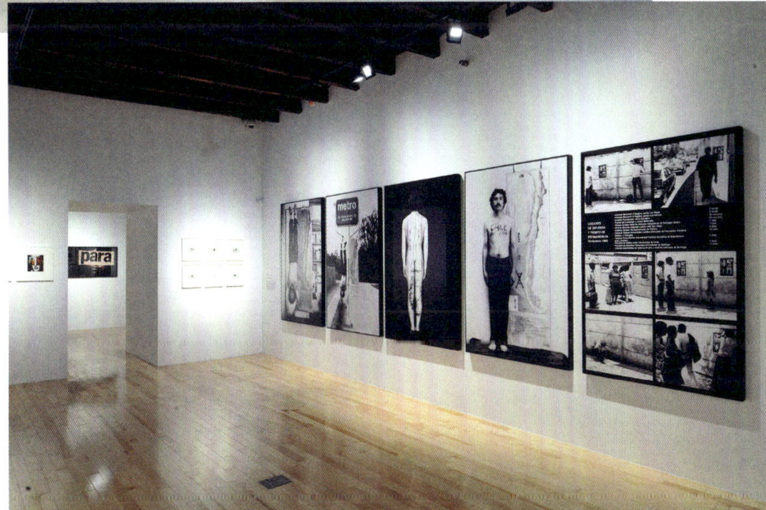

One month after its presentation in Paris, the exhibition was
shown at the Museo Amparo, in Puebla, Mexico.

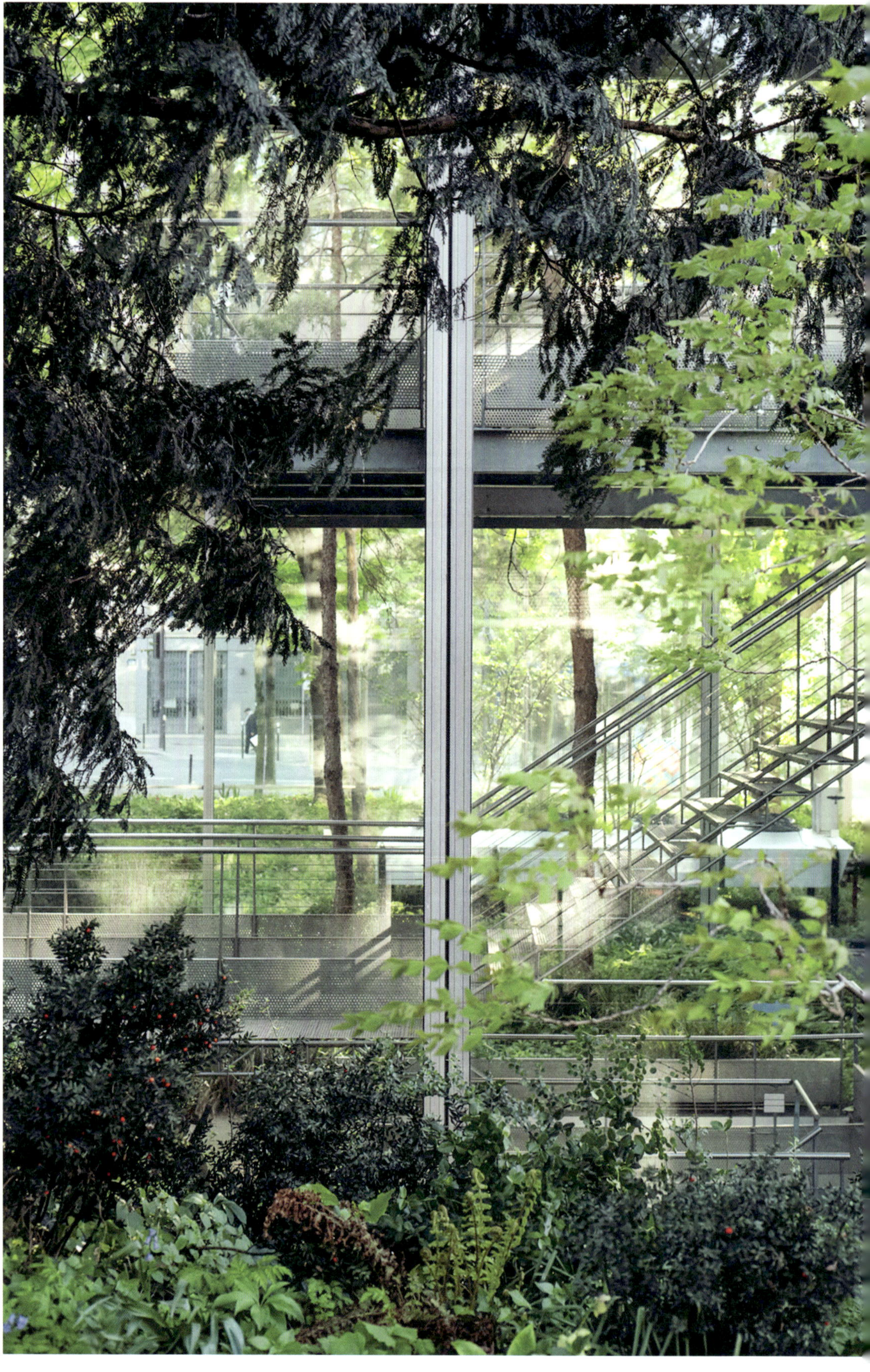

2014–2024

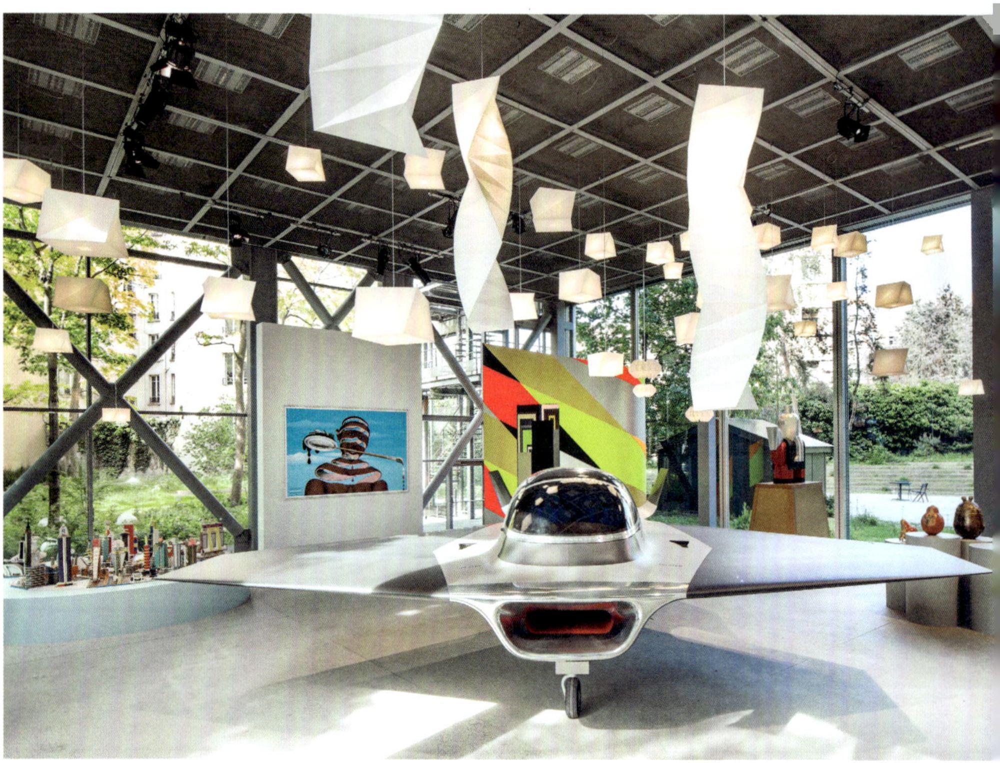

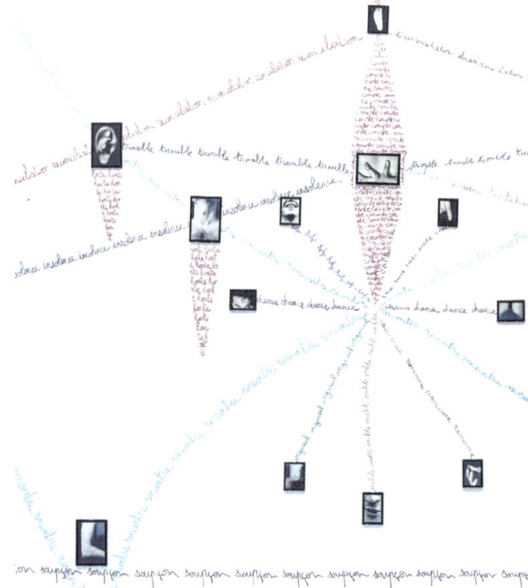

"The Collections of the Fondation Cartier are based on artworks, pieces of exhibitions, and relationships with artists. This is what constitutes its identity: bringing together artworks, the authors of these works, and the relationship between the Fondation and the artists, and between the artworks and the place." Hervé Chandès

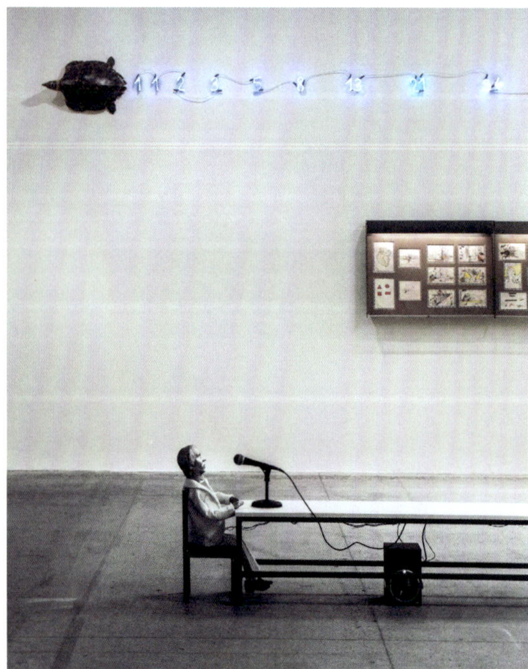

Annette Messager, *Mes ouvrages* (detail), 1988. FC Collections (1996)

Mario Merz, *La Tartaruga* (detail), 1975, and Dennis Oppenheim, *Table Piece* (detail), 1975 FC Collections (1997 and 2001)

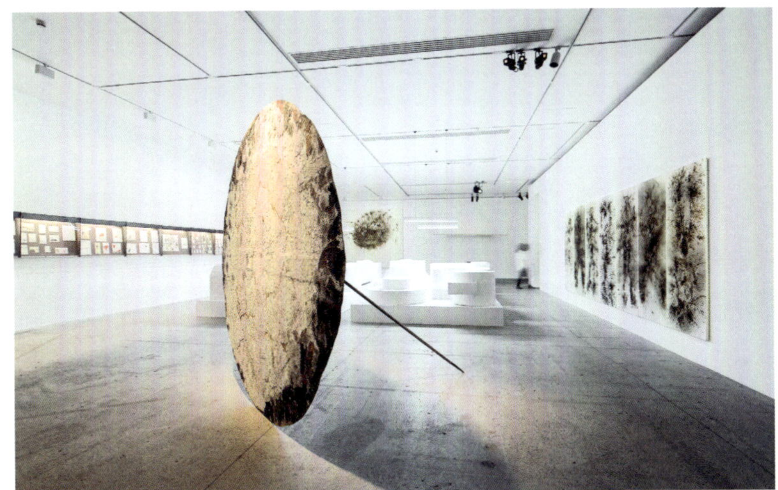

Judith Bartolani, *Grand disque*, 1983, and Cai Guo-Qiang,
The Vague Border at the Edge of Time/Space Project, 1991
FC Collections (1990 and 2000)

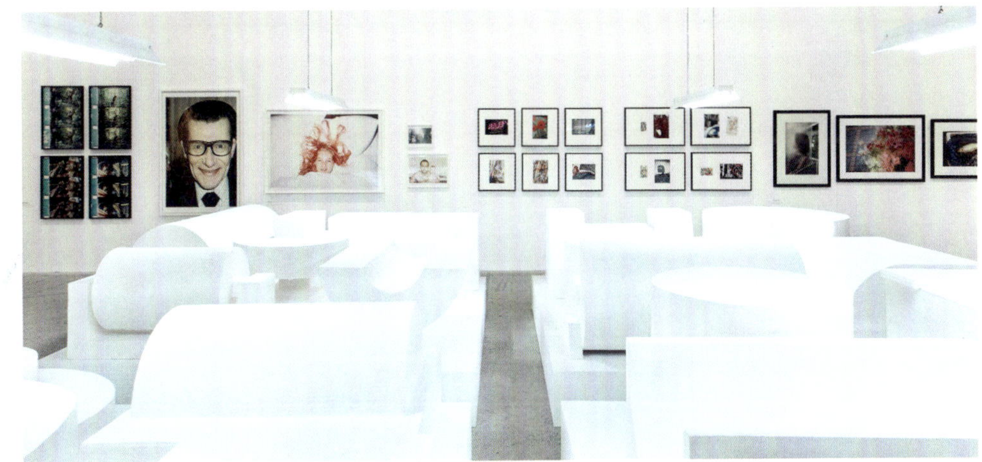

Absalon, *Propositions d'habitations* (detail), 1990. FC Collections (1990).
On the wall: photographs by Raymond Depardon, Juergen Teller, and William Eggleston

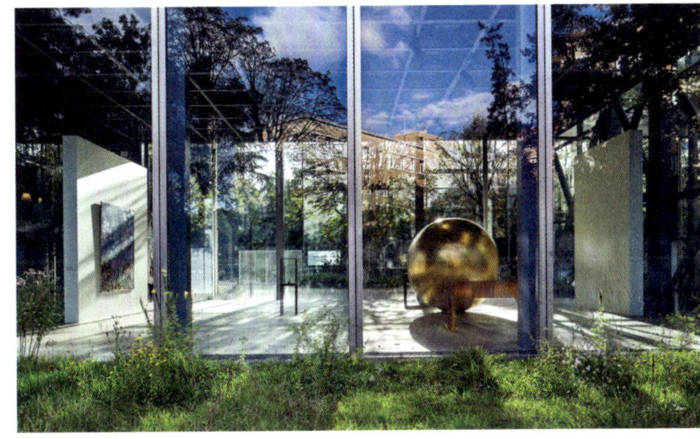

James Lee Byars, *The Monument to Language*, 1995
FC Collections (1995)

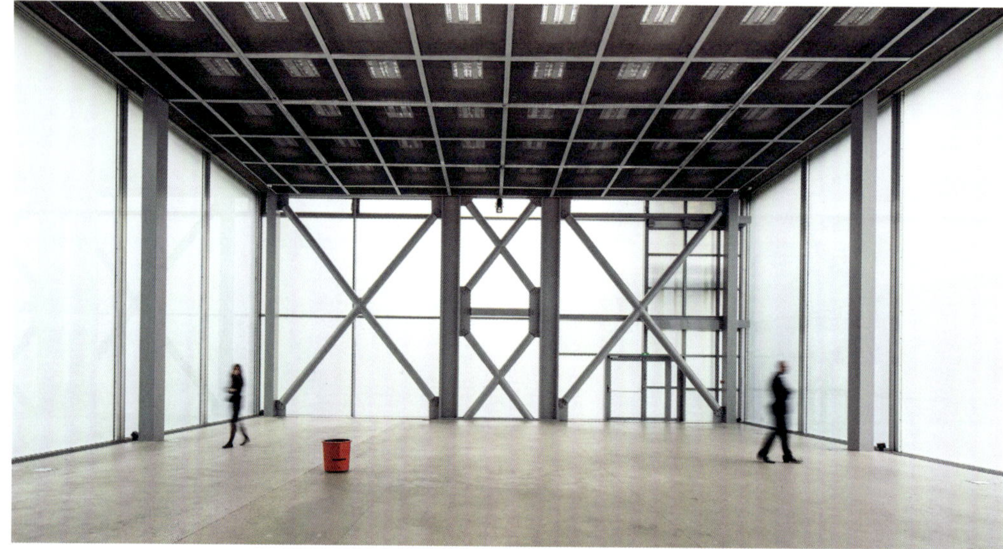

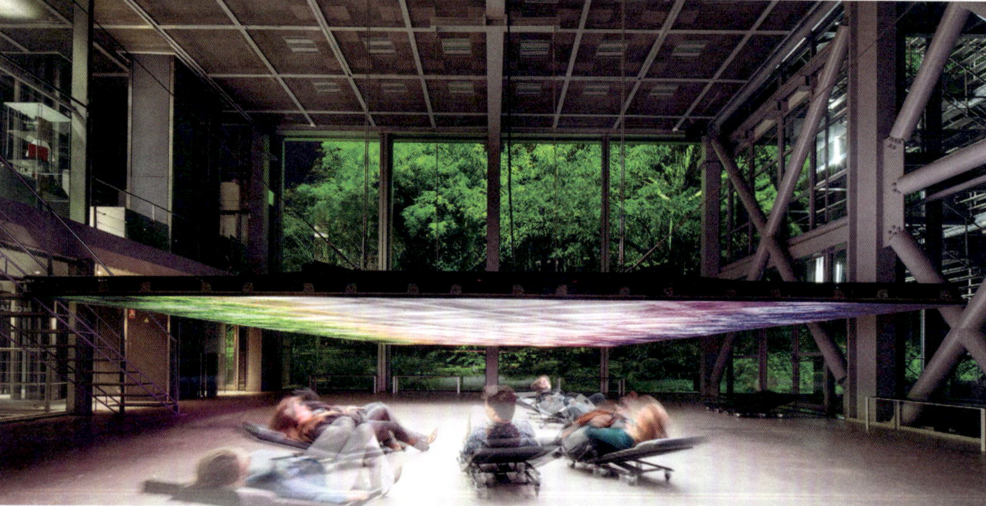

"*Musing on a Glass Box* empties the ground floor spaces to better exhibit them. The project begins with a single, mischievous leak from the ceiling. A response ensues with the aid of a bucket, a chorus, sensors, robotics, remote communications, video, and real-time sound processing." Diller Scofidio + Renfro

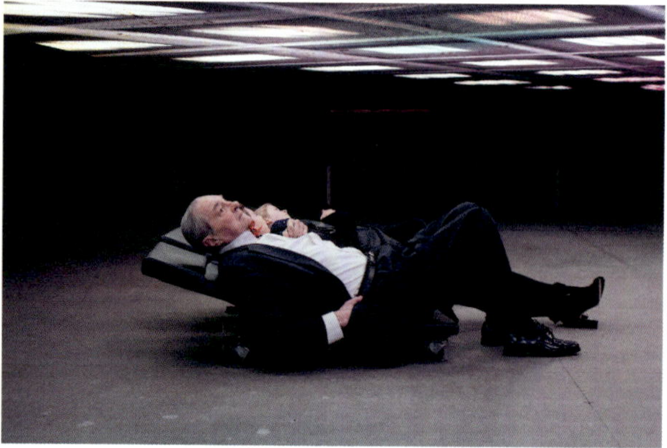

William Eggleston at the exhibition opening

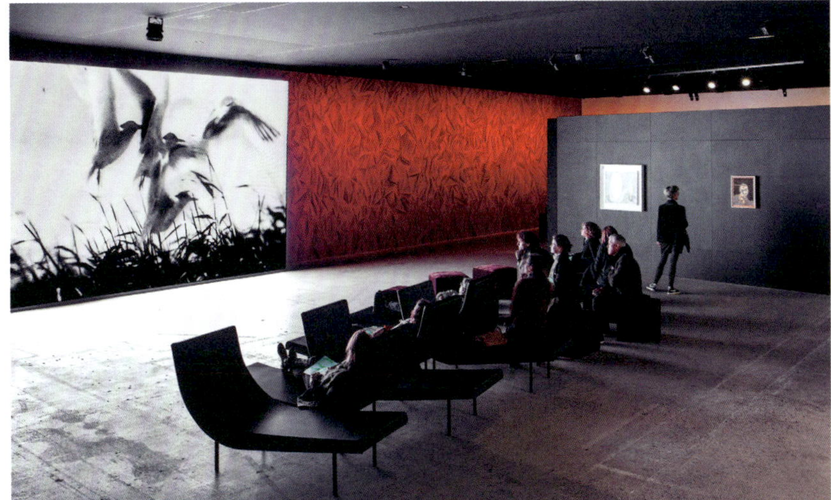

In *Les Habitants*, Guillermo Kuitca shone a light on the connections between his artworks and those of Tarsila do Amaral, Francis Bacon, Vija Celmins, David Lynch, Artavazd Pelechian, and Patti Smith. Artavazd Pelechian, *Les Habitants*, 1970. FC Collections (2015)

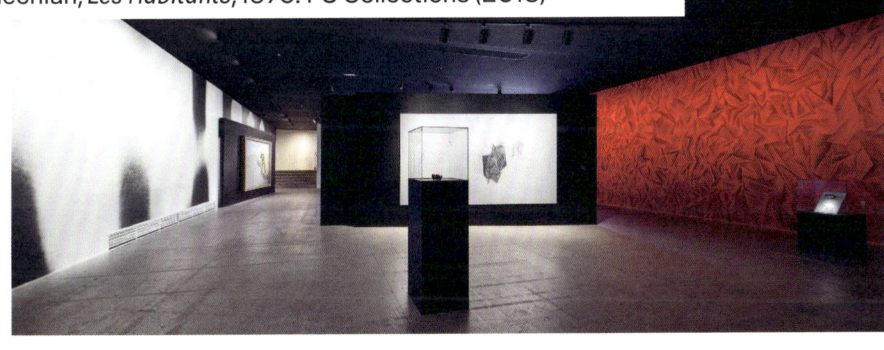

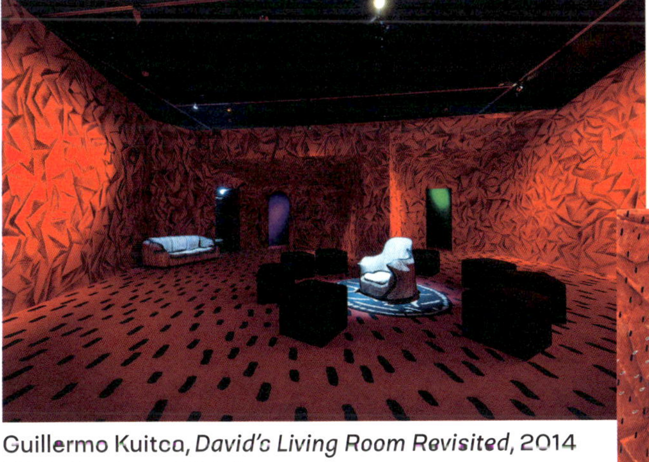

Guillermo Kuitca, *David's Living Room Revisited*, 2014
FC Collections (2018)

David Lynch, *Sun Is Gone*, 2014
FC Collections (2016)

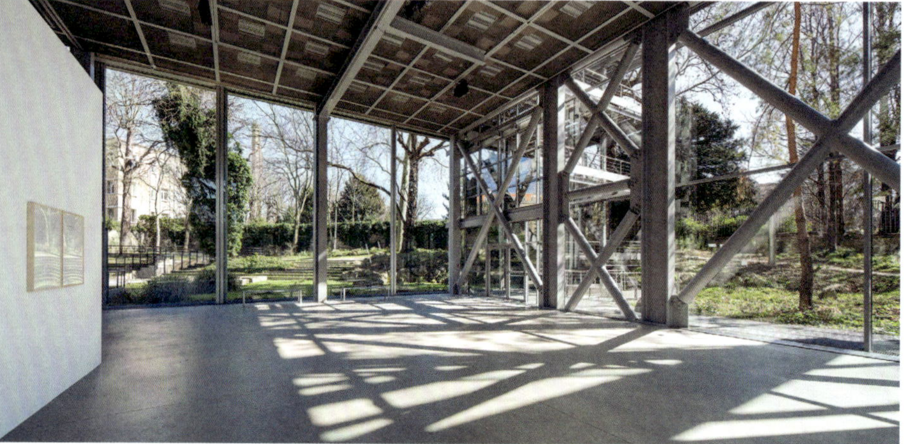

For his exhibition, Bruce Nauman installed four loudspeakers on the Fondation Cartier's ground floor, broadcasting two sound recordings on a loop: *For Children/Pour les enfants*, 2015

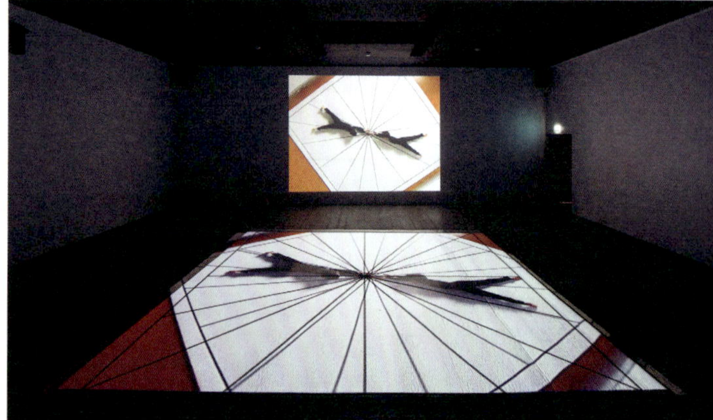

Bruce Nauman, *Untitled 1970/2009*

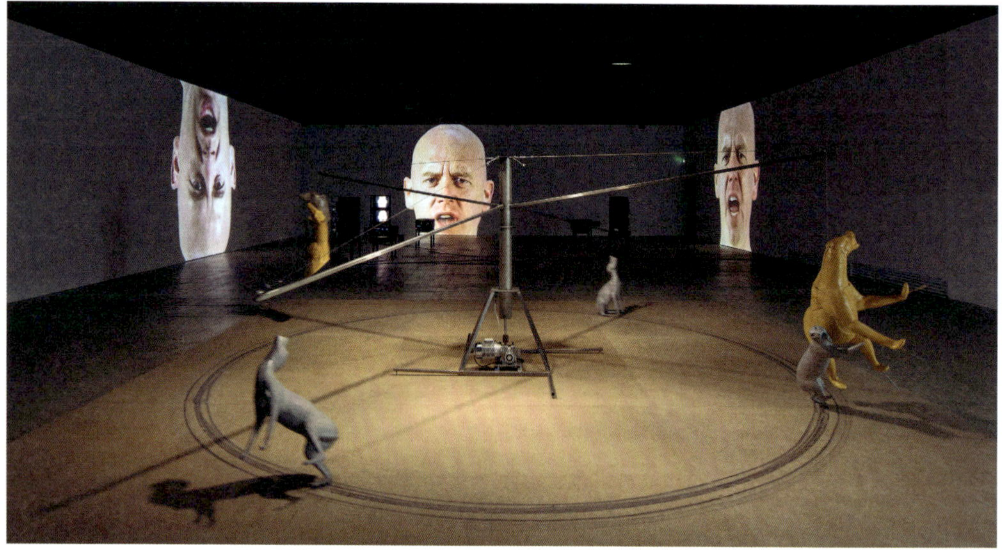

Bruce Nauman, *Carousel (Stainless Steel Version)*, 1988 and *Anthro/Socio (Rinde Facing: Camera)*, 1991

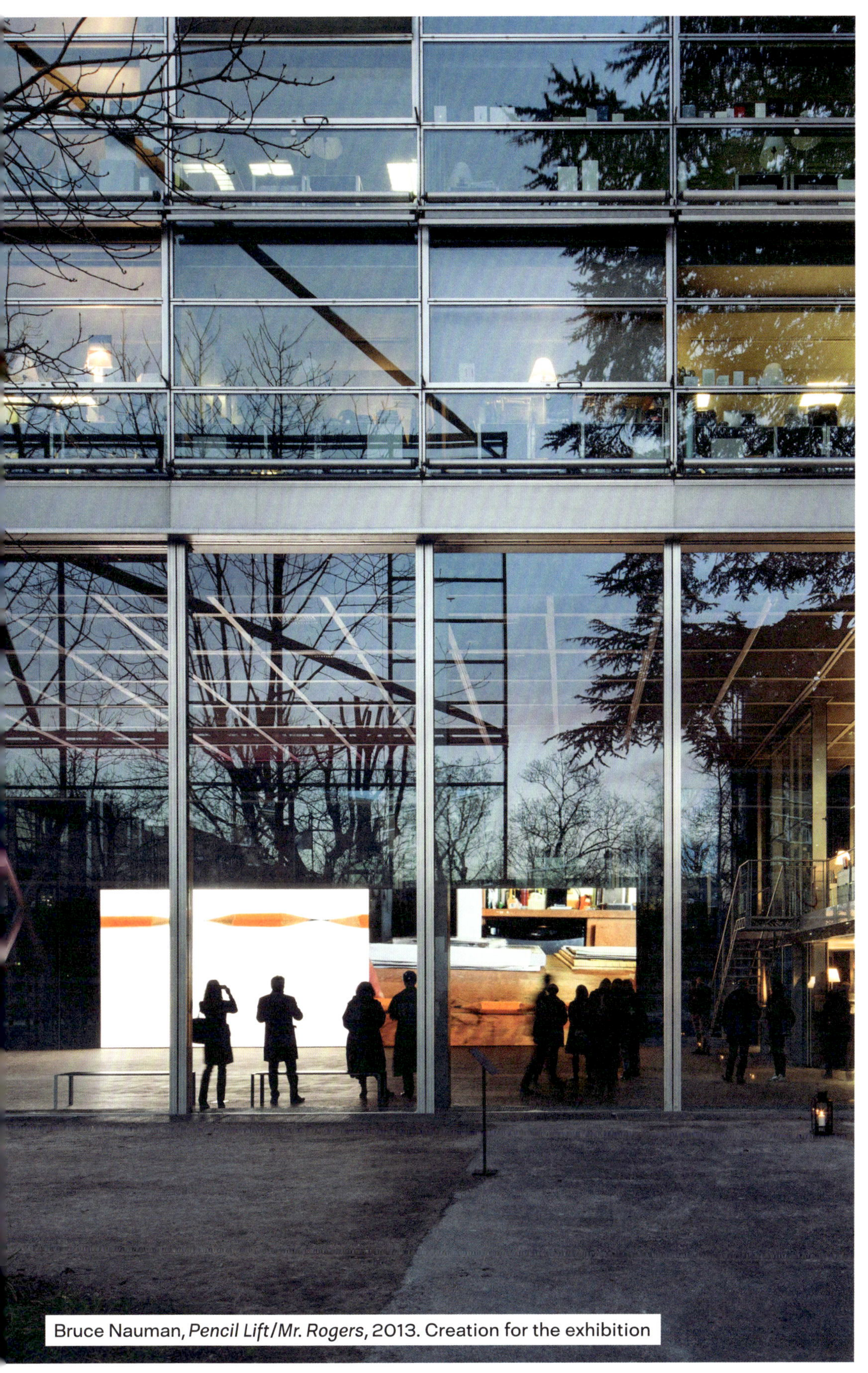

Bruce Nauman, *Pencil Lift / Mr. Rogers*, 2013. Creation for the exhibition

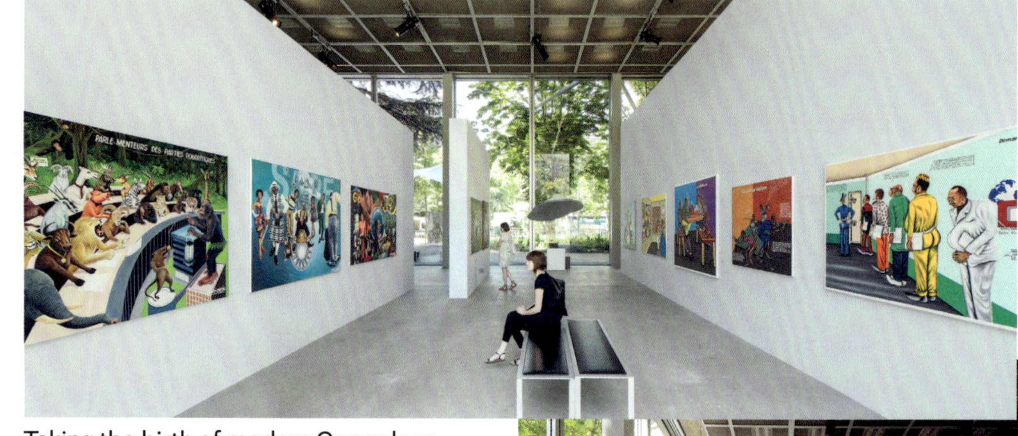

Taking the birth of modern Congolese painting in the 1920s as its starting point, the exhibition explored almost a century of artistic production in the Democratic Republic of the Congo. Works by Chéri Chérin and Cheik Ledy

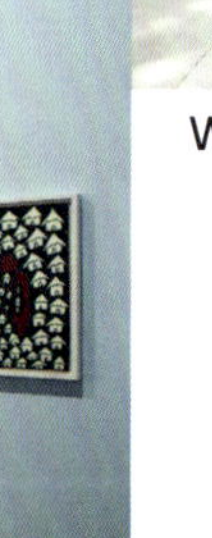

Works by Pierre Bodo

Works by
Mode Muntu

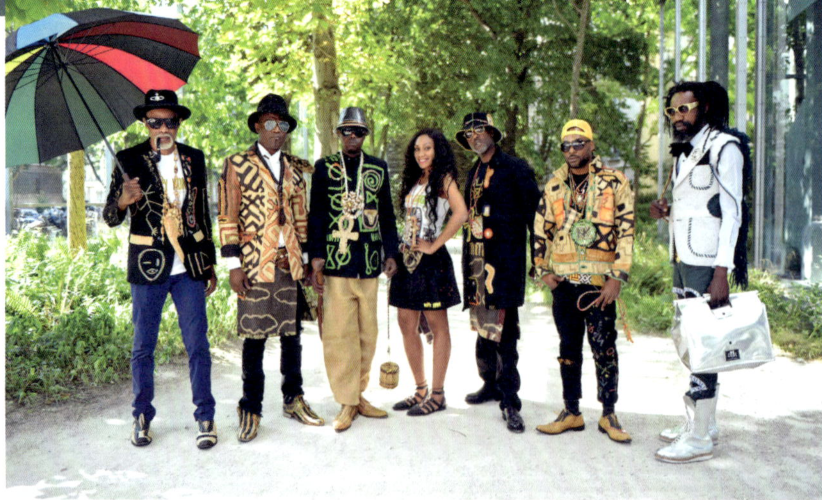

Sapeurs from the Association Culturelle Moderne et Traditionnelle Africaine at the exhibition opening

BEAUTÉ CONGO

1926 — 2015

CONGO KITOKO

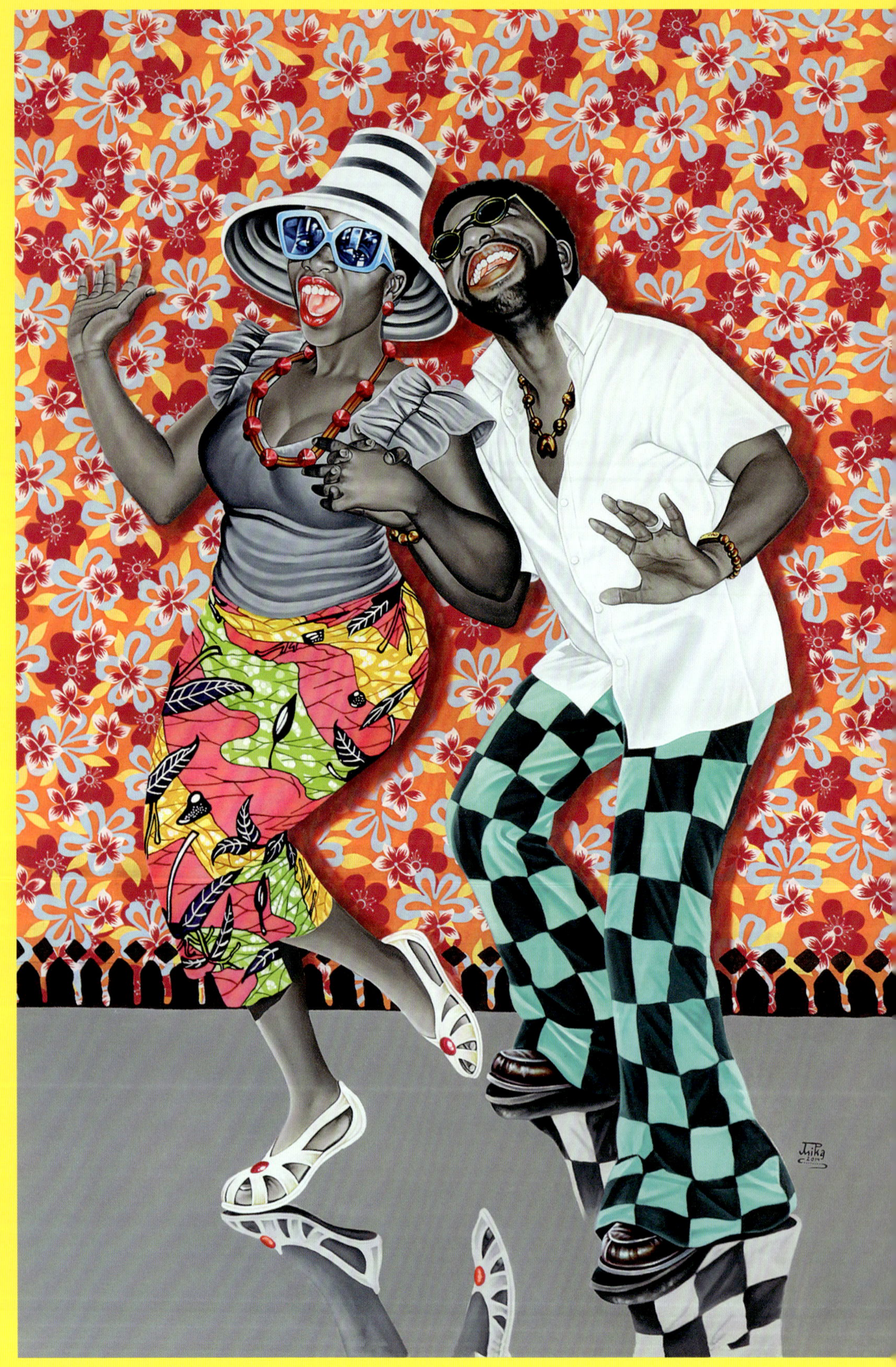

JP Mika, *Kiese na kiese*, 2014

Beauté Congo
– 1926–2015 –
Congo Kitoko

Early July 2015. The Fondation Cartier was a hive of activity. In just three weeks, the rich exhibition *Beauté Congo – 1926–2015 – Congo Kitoko* would be installed within the glass walls of the Fondation Cartier's building on Boulevard Raspail. Along with photography, video, comics, sculpture, and music, painting—the heart of the exhibition—bore witness to ninety years of Congolese artistic production, masterful and teeming with life and yet little known to the public. The artists and precursors to modern painting, such as Djilatendo and Albert and Antoinette Lubaki, the artists of the Atelier du Hangar of Pierre-Romain Desfossés, including Bela, Kayembe, and Mwenze Kibwanga, as well as contemporary artists such as Pierre Bodo, Chéri Chérin, Kiripi Katembo, Bodys Isek Kingelez, JP Mika, Moke, Mode Muntu, and Chéri Samba, all told the story of their country, history, and society. "This art is not bound to anything", explains André Magnin in the catalog's introduction. "Visitors need no instructions on how to enjoy it, apart from a certain open-mindedness that will allow them to make it their own, in their own way. The reward for me is if the exhibition takes them on a fantastic voyage, one on which they'll find their own way", concluded the optimistic curator.

The Nomadic Nights program that accompanied *Beauté Congo* over several months, was filled with exceptional events. Fashion came to the exhibition with the elegant "sapeurs" and "pagneuses" taking to the catwalk to the rhythm of Congolese music. Numerous concerts, notably by singer Papa Noël and the group Kasai Allstars, musical and ambulatory performances including *Fanfare Funérailles* by Papy Ebotani, readings and discussions with writers such as In Koli Jean Bofane and Fiston Mwanza Mujila, as well as dance with Jolie Ngemi, attracted a novice and curious public, as well as true connoisseurs.

The hoped-for "reward" was immediate: the public came in their droves and the exhibition was prolonged for two months. It must be said that *Beauté Congo* touched on all areas of creation and was in line with the major summer thematic exhibitions the Fondation Cartier had planned since its inception in 1984. It was also a means of reinforcing its ongoing commitment to African art.

From a very early stage, in fact, the Fondation Cartier has taken an interest in every kind of art from all over the continent. Since the 1990s, it has honored the great traditions of street photography and studio portraiture, devoting solo exhibitions to a number of photographers such as Seydou Keita (1994) and Malick Sidibé (1995 and 2017), both from Mali, as well as to the Nigerian J.D. 'Okhai Ojeikere (2000): for all of them, Paris and the Fondation Cartier was the first place they exhibited outside Africa. In 1995, it showcased the imaginary cities of Congolese sculptor Bodys Isek Kingelez. In 2004, almost fifteen years after Chéri Samba's residency in Jouy-en-Josas, the exhibition *J'aime Chéri Samba* presented thirty-five paintings by the Congolese artist. Group exhibitions have also provided opportunities to present works by African artists: the drawings of Ivorian Frédéric Bruly Bouabré in *Azur* (1993) and *Comme un oiseau* (1996), the paintings of Mode Muntu in *By Night* (1996), or those of Moke in *Un art populaire* (2001), the drawings of Senegalese Mamadou Cissé in *Histoires de voir, Show and Tell* (2012), as well as the work of Congolese Pierre Bodo in *The Great Animal Orchestra* (2016). Over the years and exhibitions, the Fondation Cartier has supported all these artists by acquiring numerous works for its Collections.

While always committed to contemporary African art, the Fondation Cartier is also passionate about other forms of art. In 2011, the *Vodun: African Voodoo* exhibition revealed the astonishing collection of Benin voodoo statuettes in the collection of Anne and Jacques Kerchache.

For forty years, the Fondation Cartier has cast an attentive gaze at the African continent. It has constantly supported and introduced its artists, thus contributing to their international recognition, and quite simply celebrating the beauty—*kitoko*—of African art.

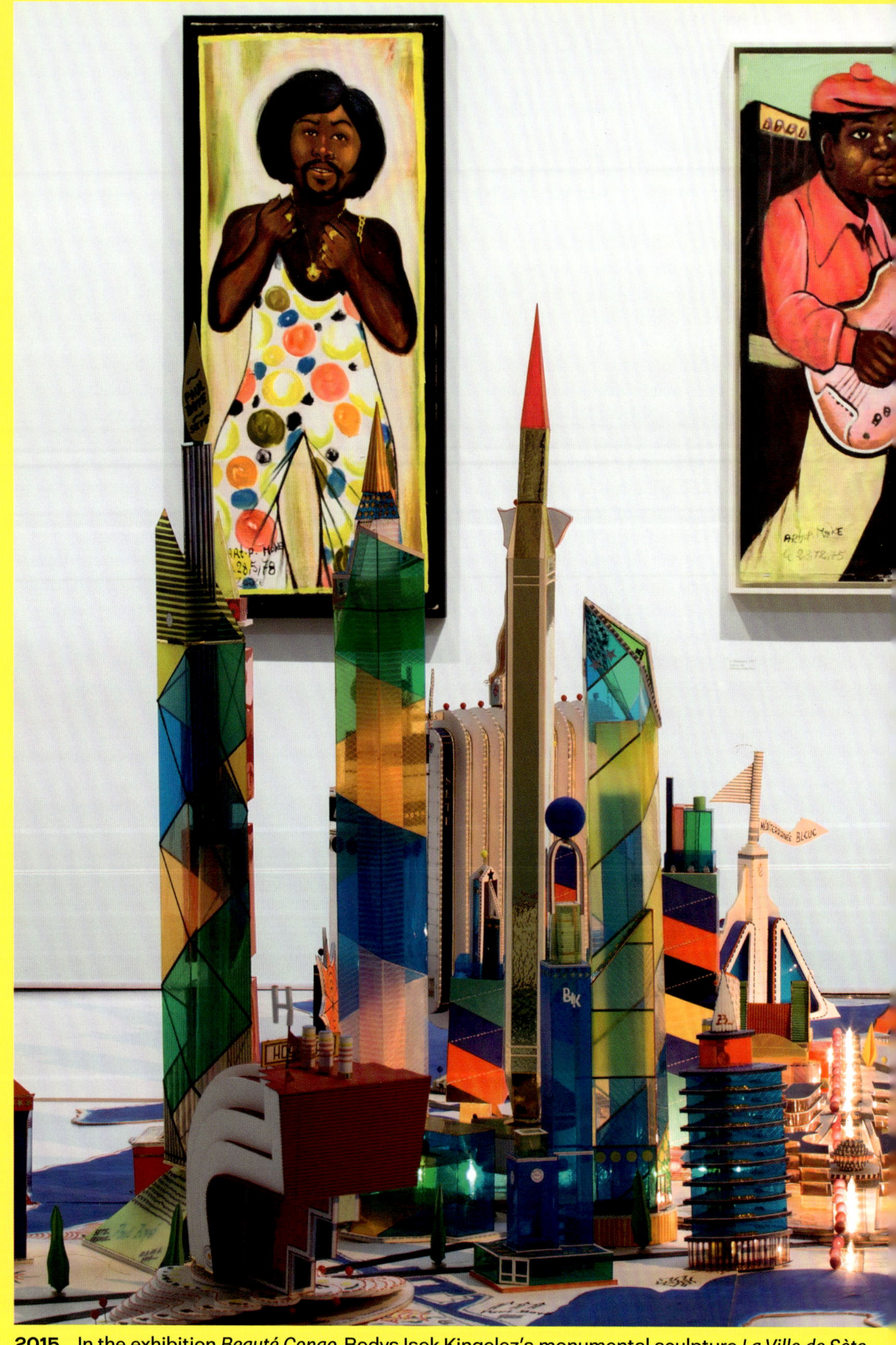

2015 In the exhibition *Beauté Congo*, Bodys Isek Kingelez's monumental sculpture *La Ville de Sète en 3009* (2000) was shown alongside paintings by Moke, *Sinatra* (1978) and *L'Orchestre* (1975).

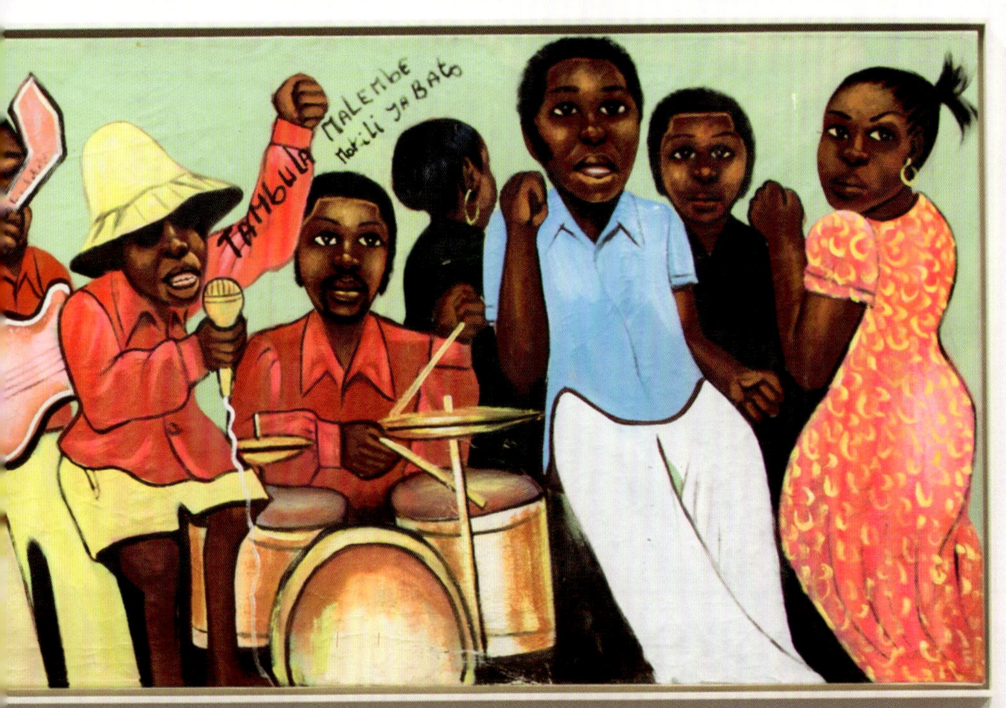

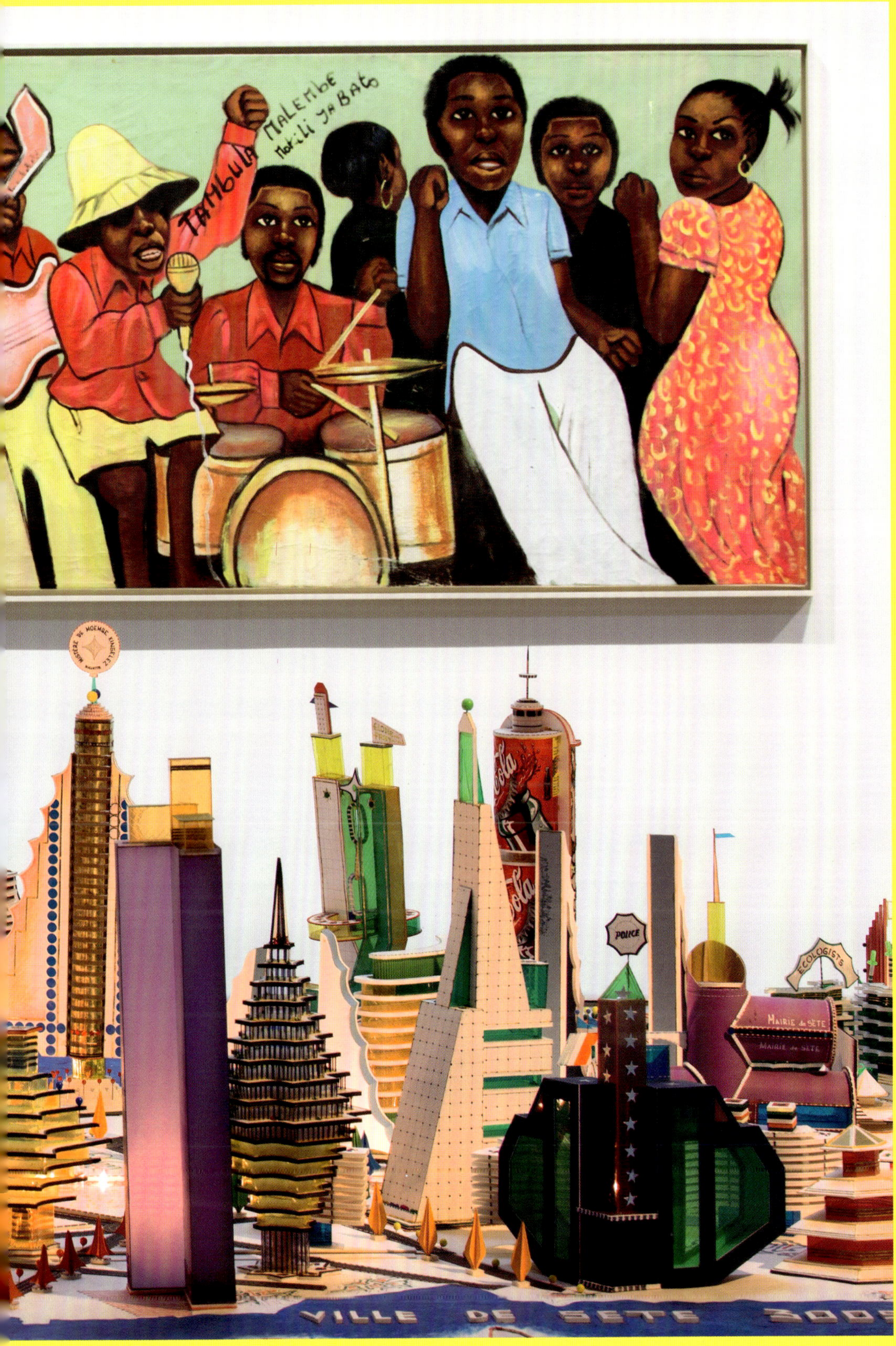

TAMBULA
MALEMBE
Mokili ya bato

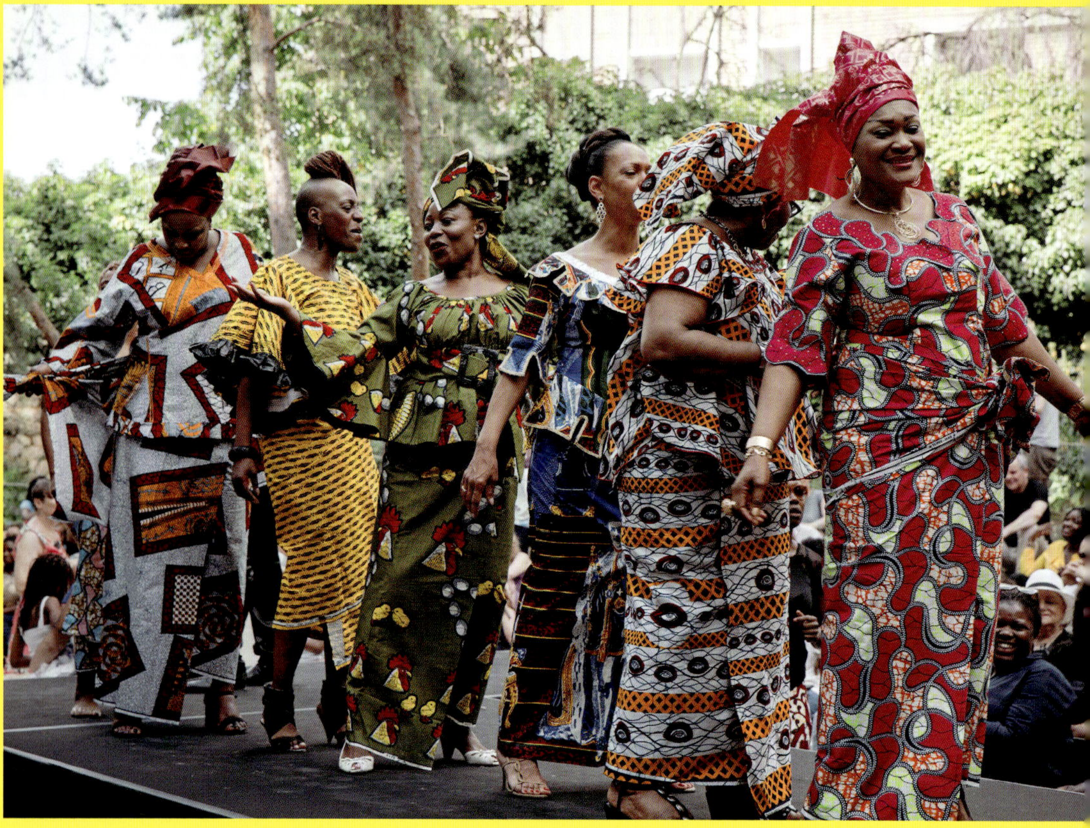

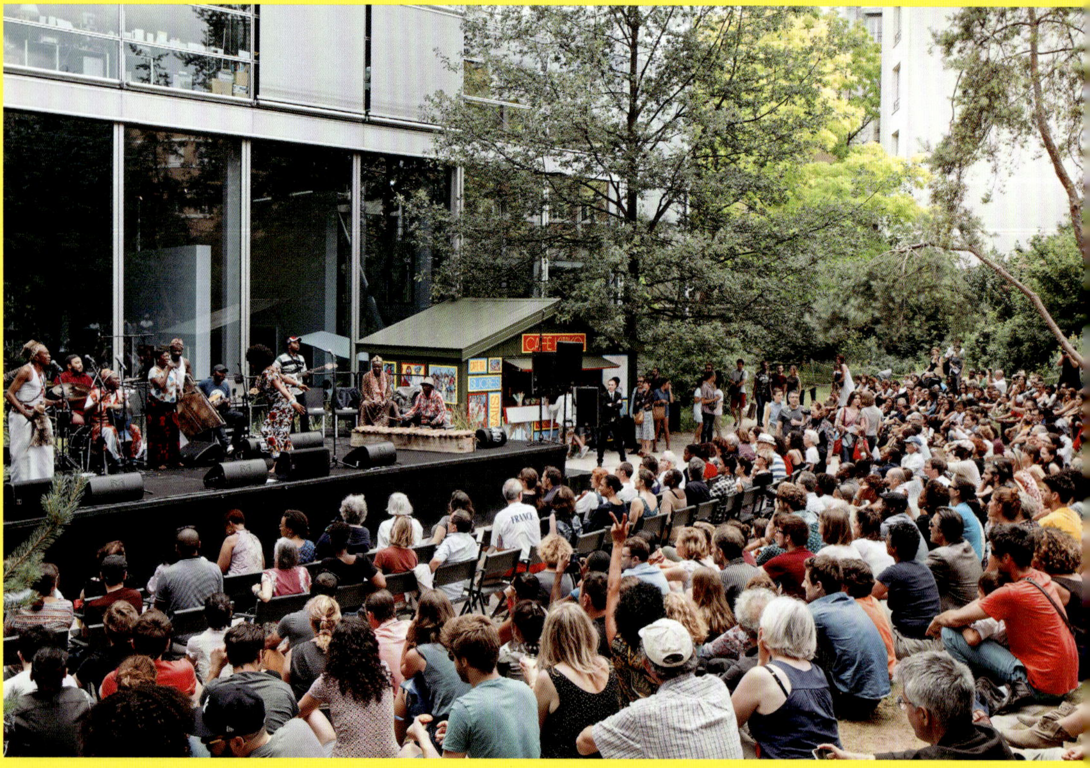

2015   On July 18 and 19, the Nomadic Nights invited Césarine Sinatu Bolya and the association Mémoires Vives Congo Afrique for a fashion show of wax cloths, followed by a concert in the garden by Congolese group Kasai Allstars.

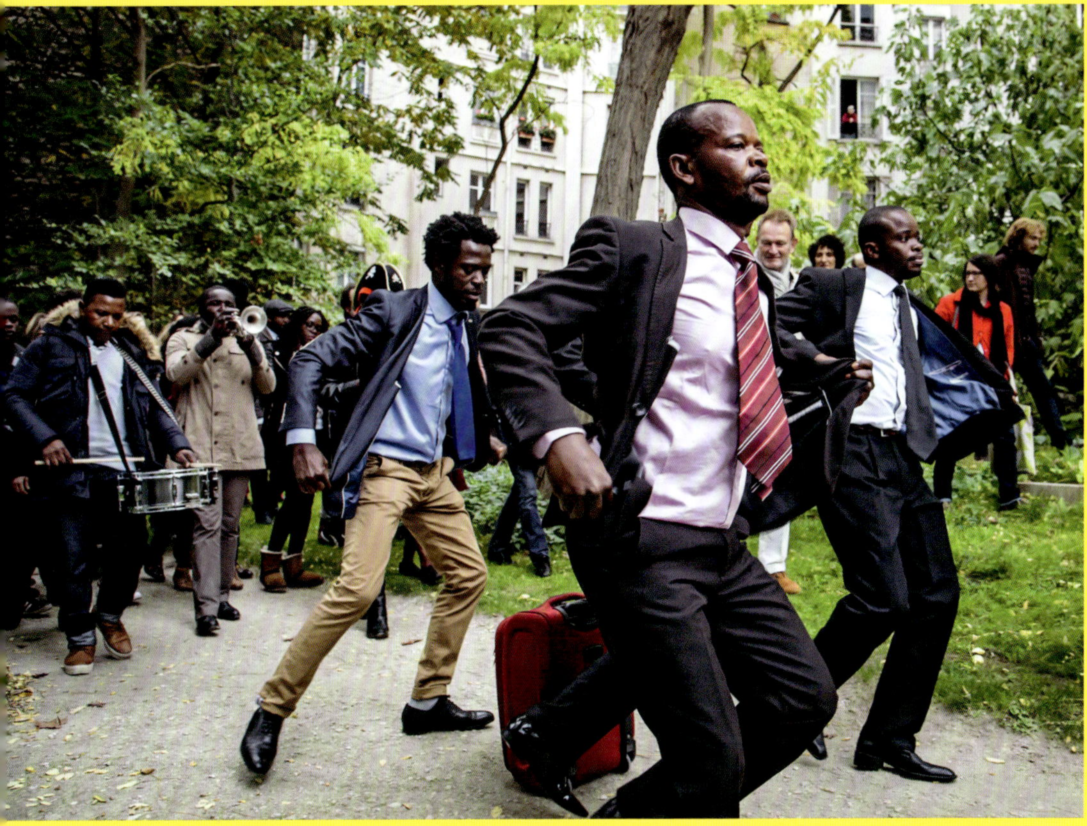

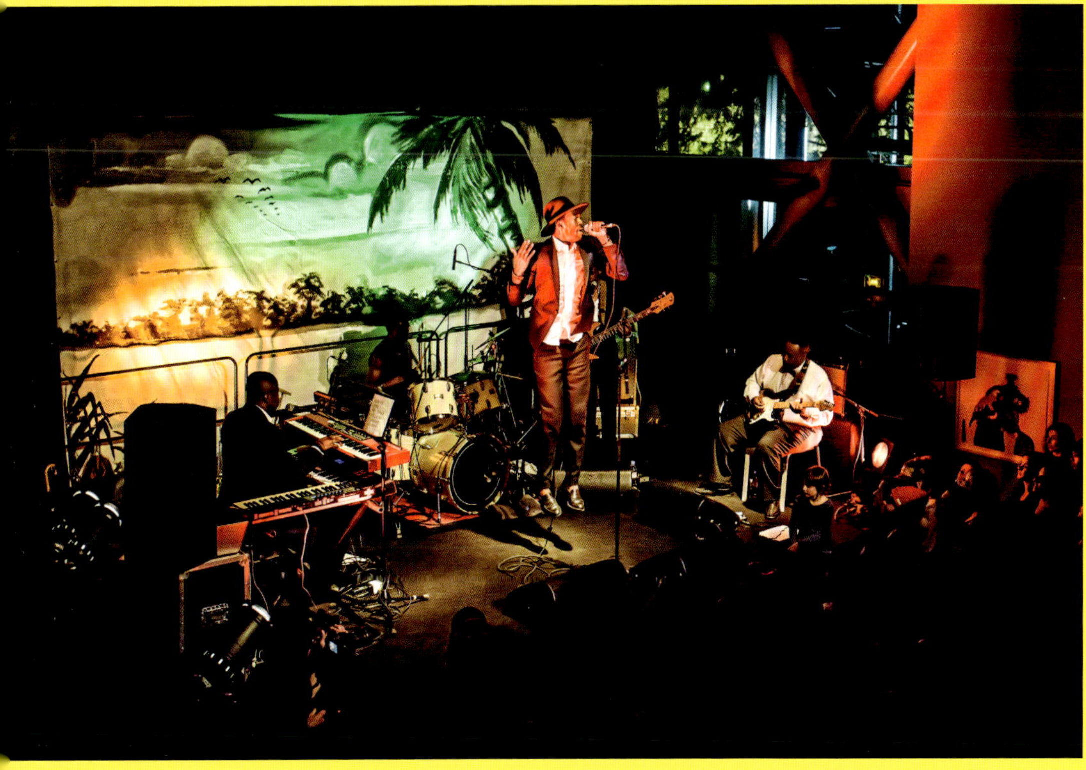

2015   On October 24, dancer and choreographer Faustin Linyekula presented the Nomadic Night *Fanfare Funérailles de Papy Ebotani*. On December 8, rapper Baloji and the Katuba Orchestra performed together for an electro-rap concert.

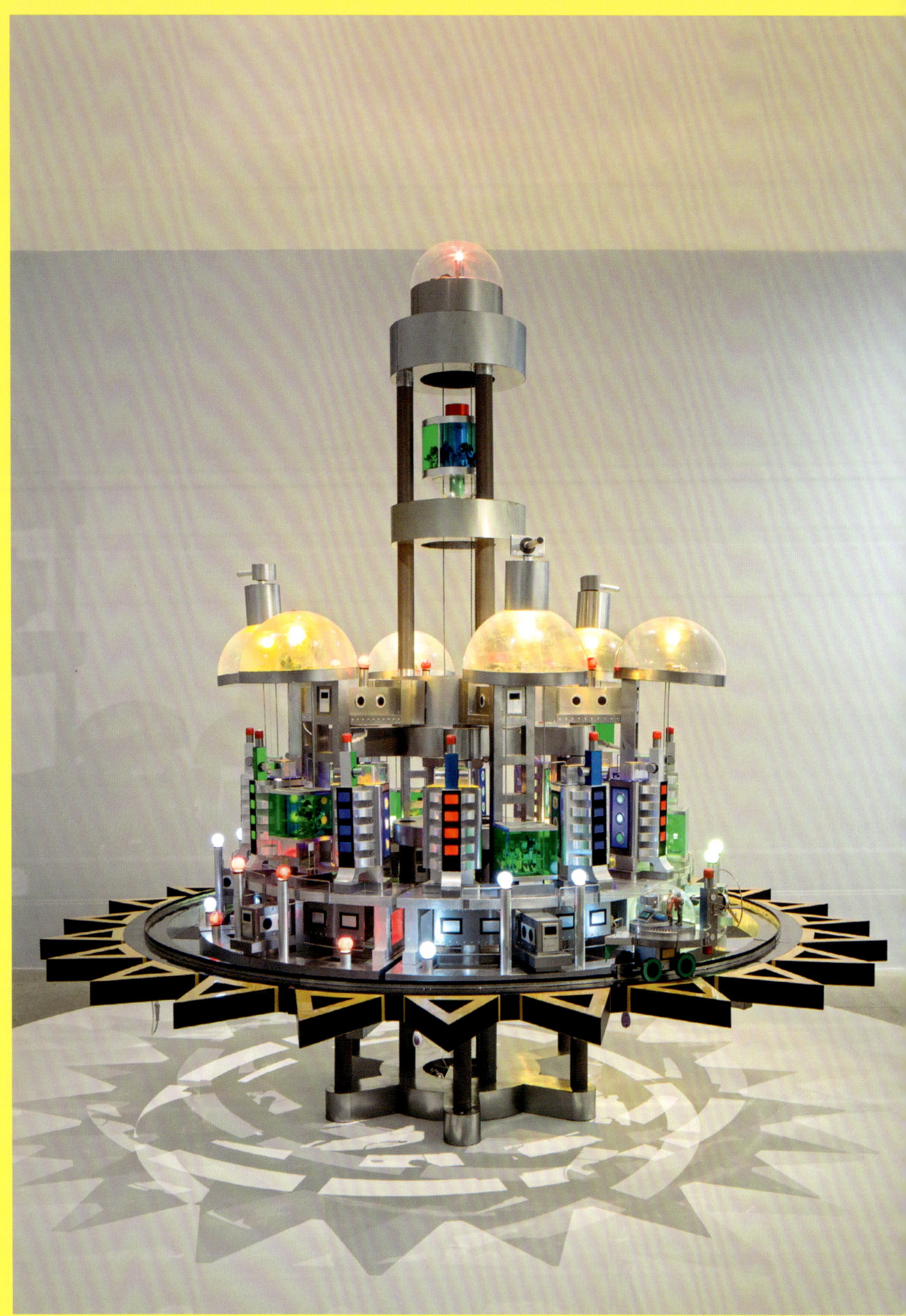

2015 Rigobert Nimi, *La Cité des étoiles*, 2006

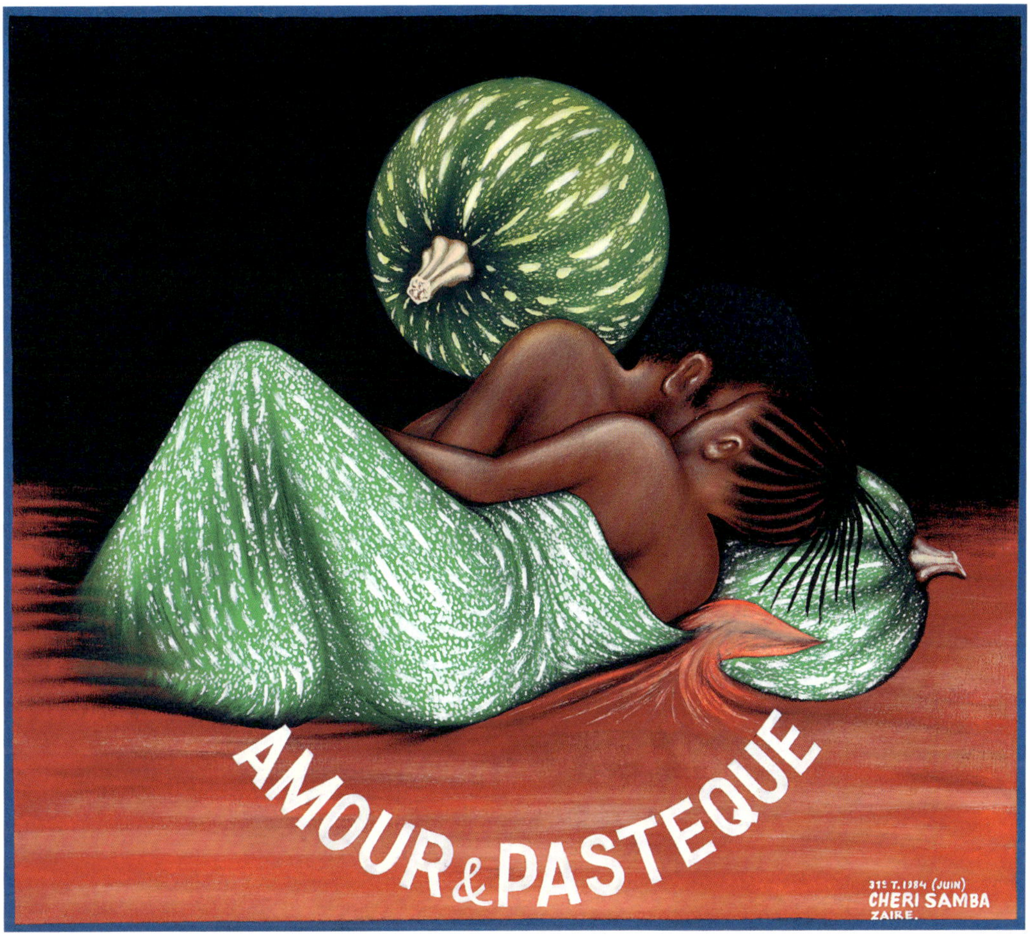

Chéri Samba, *Amour et Pastèque*, 1984

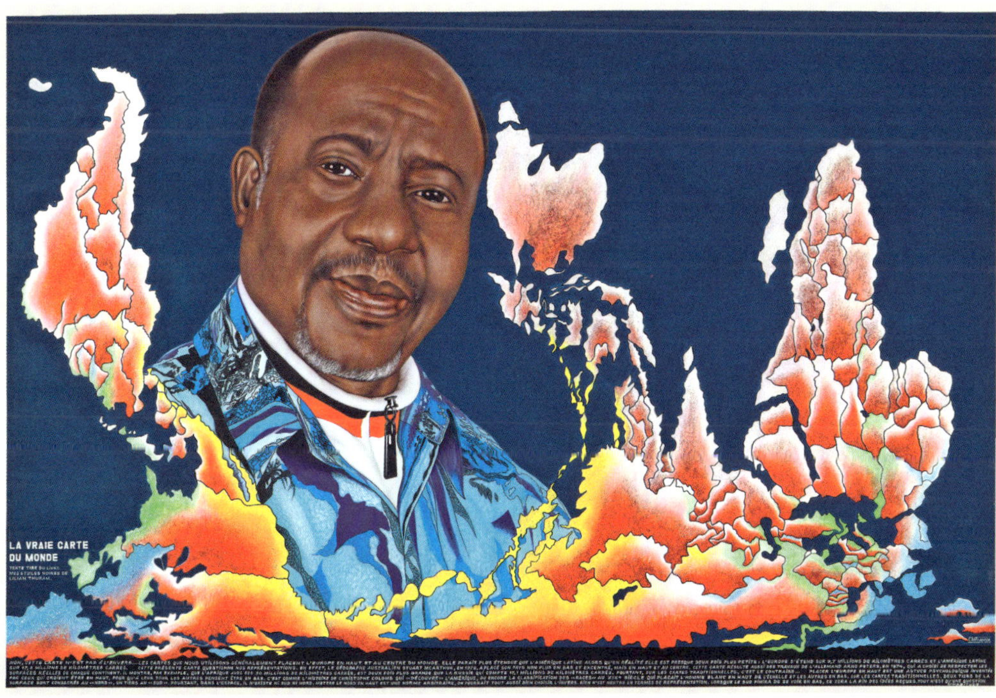

Chéri Samba, *La Vraie Carte du monde*, 2011. FC Collections (2012)

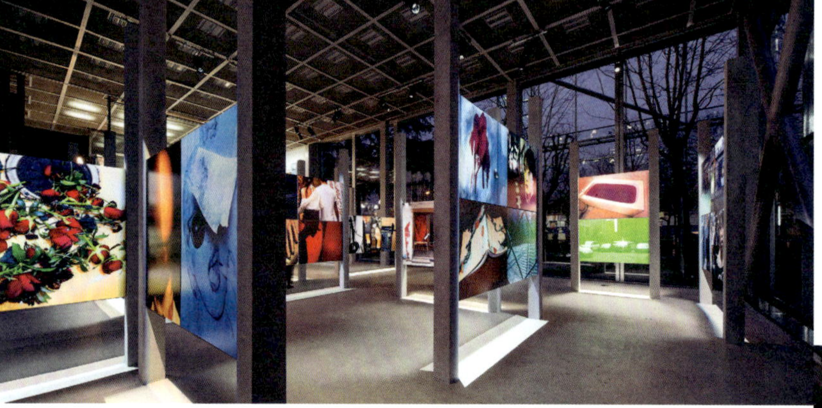

Daido Tokyo revealed a new series in color by Daido Moriyama.
Color is a little-known but essential part of his work.

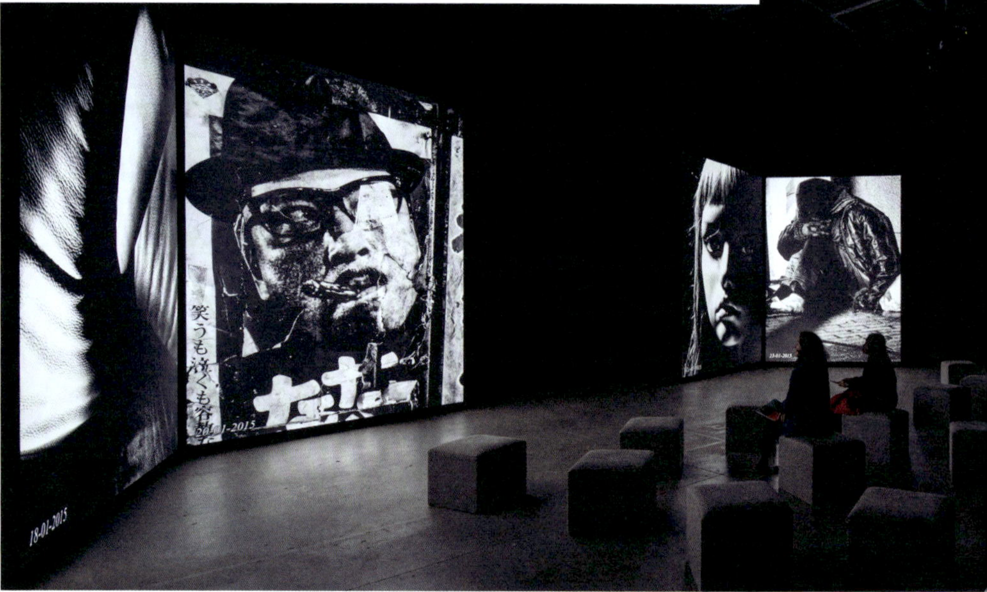

Daido Moriyama, *Dog and Mesh Tights*, 2014–2015. Creation for the exhibition
FC Collections (2016)

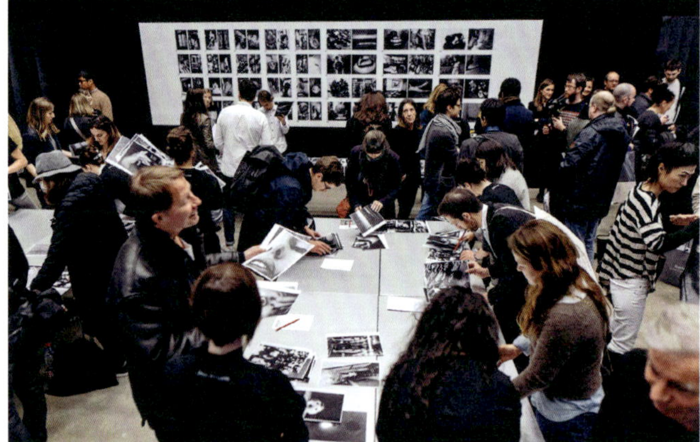

Nomadic Night *À la carte (Printing Show)*, February 5, 2016
For the Fondation Cartier, Daido Moriyama recreated
his famous *Printing Show* presented in Tokyo in 1974,
which involved the publishing, printing, and binding of
a photography book in a single day and in the same place.

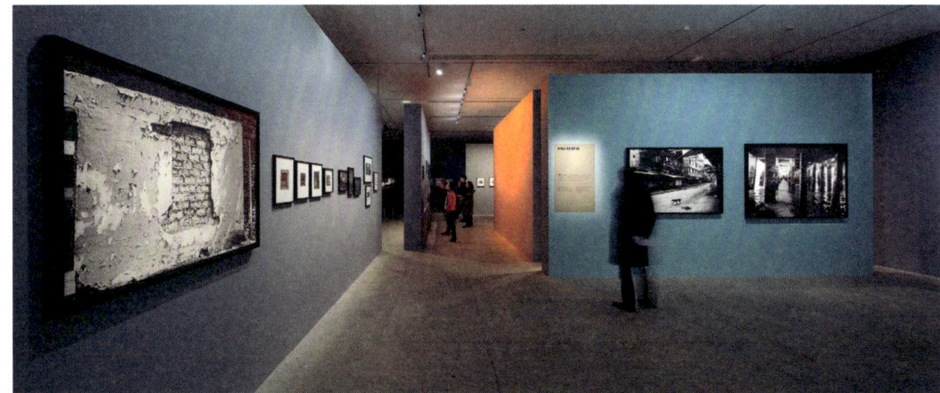

The first European retrospective devoted to Fernell Franco, *Cali clair-obscur* showcased over 140 photographs by the artist, coming from 10 different series produced between 1970 and 1996.

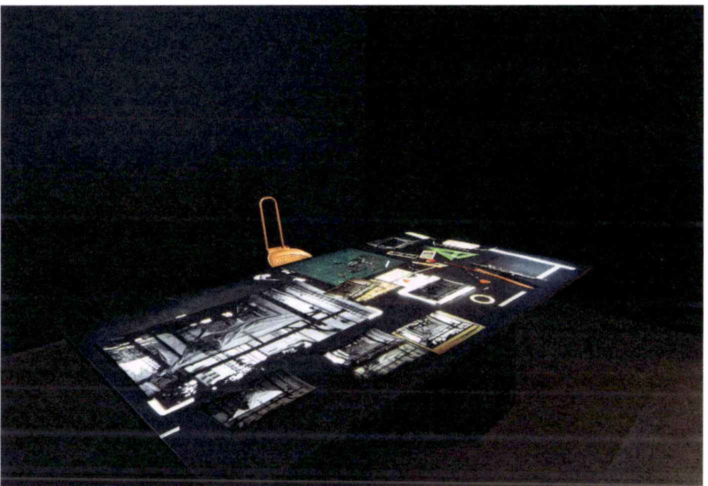

As a tribute to Fernell Franco, Colombian artist Oscar Muñoz produced a new work specially for the occasion.
Oscar Muñoz, *El Ejercicio de la Empatía*, 2016
FC Collections (2023)

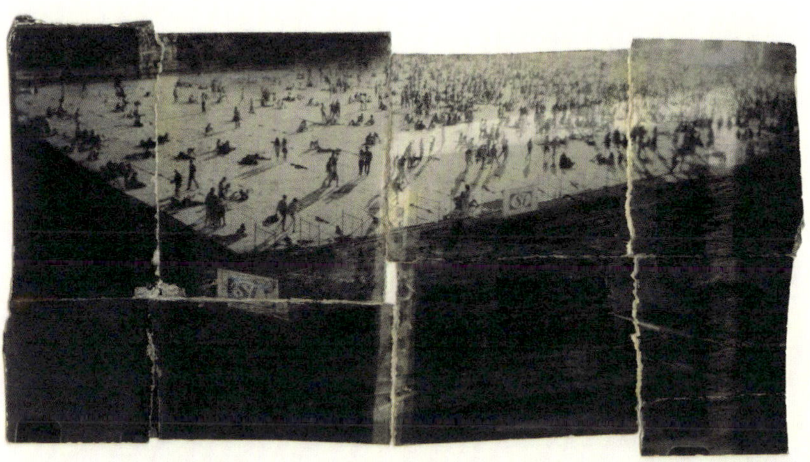

Fernell Franco, *Untitled, Retratos de Ciudad* series, 1994
FC Collections (2016)

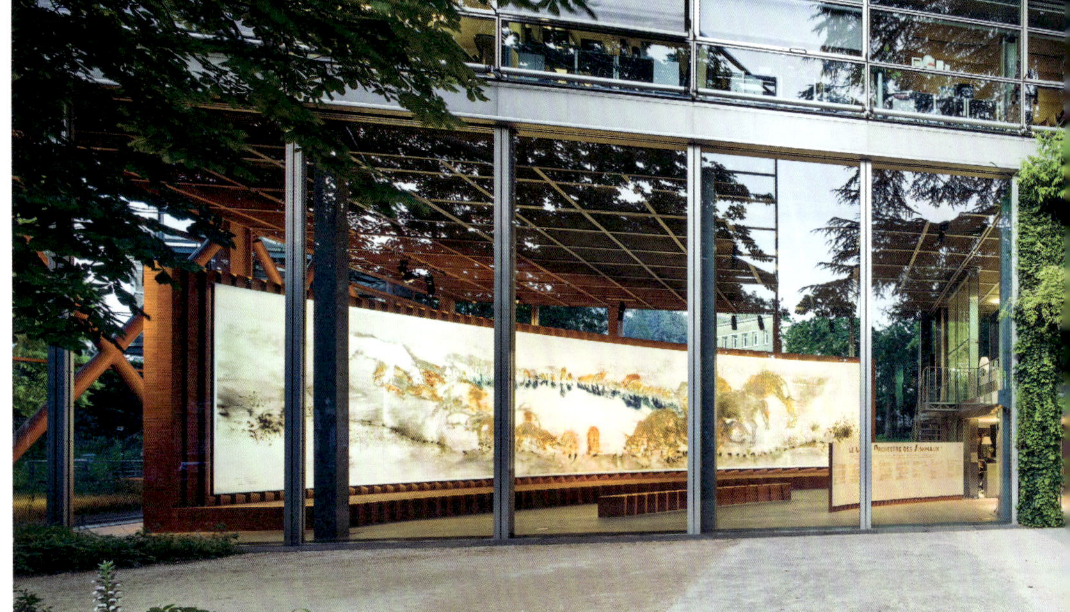

Inspired by the work of American bioacoustician Bernie Krause, this exhibition brought together artists from all over the world and invited them to engage in an aesthetic meditation, both visual and audio, on the animal world.
Cai Guo-Qiang, *White Tone*, 2016. FC Collections (2017)
Adriana Varejão, *Passarinhos*, 2012

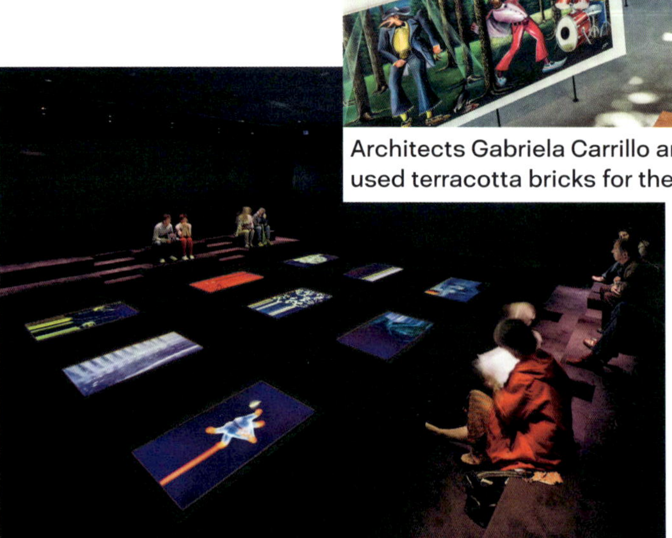

Architects Gabriela Carrillo and Mauricio Rocha used terracotta bricks for the exhibition design.

Plancton, Aux origines du vivant (2016), an installation by Shiro Takatani based on the videos and photographs of Christian Sardet and Les Macronautes, music by Ryuichi Sakamoto

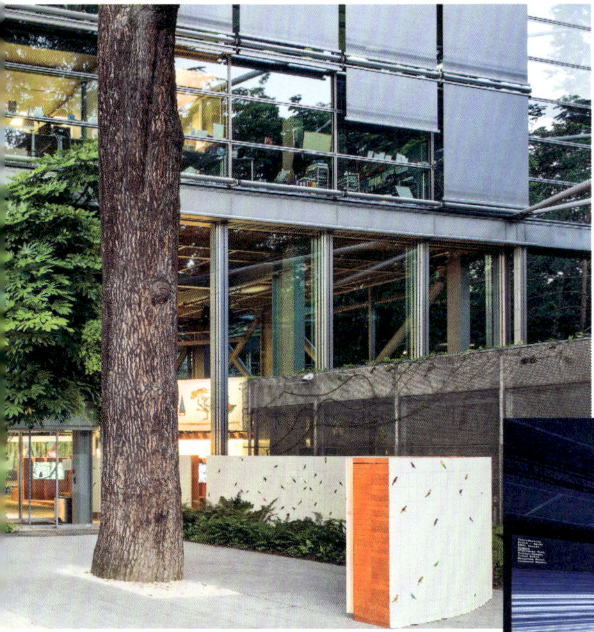

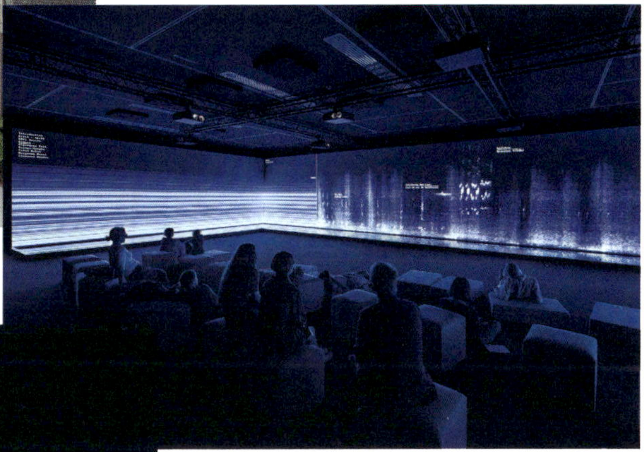

Bernie Krause and United Visual
Artists, *The Great Animal Orchestra*,
2016. Commission for the exhibition
FC Collections (2017)

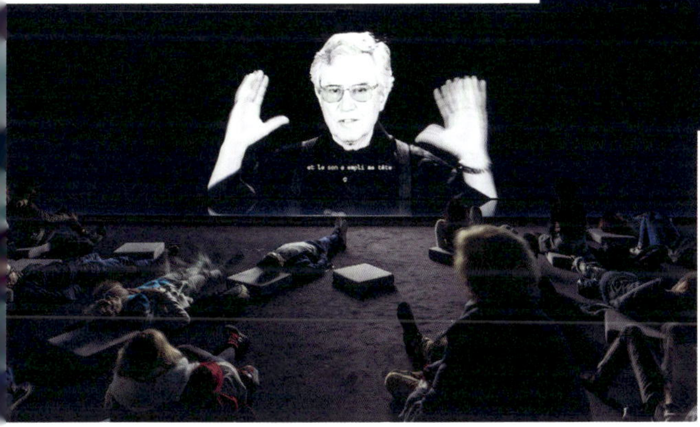

Bernie Krause filmed by Raymond Depardon and
Claudine Nougaret for *The Great Animal Orchestra*, 2016

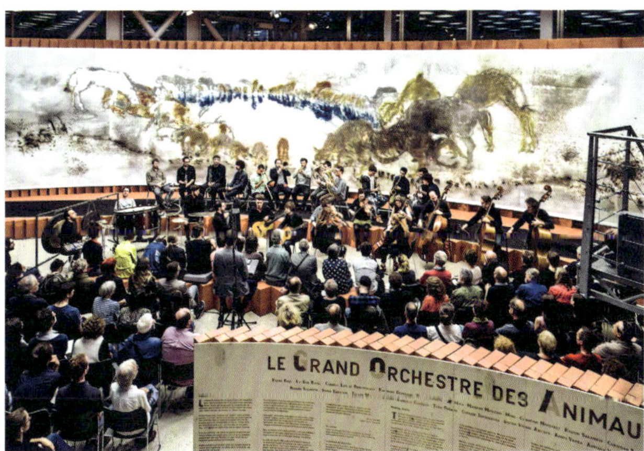

Nomadic Night with Éliane Radigue, *OCCAM OCÉAN*,
July 4, 2016

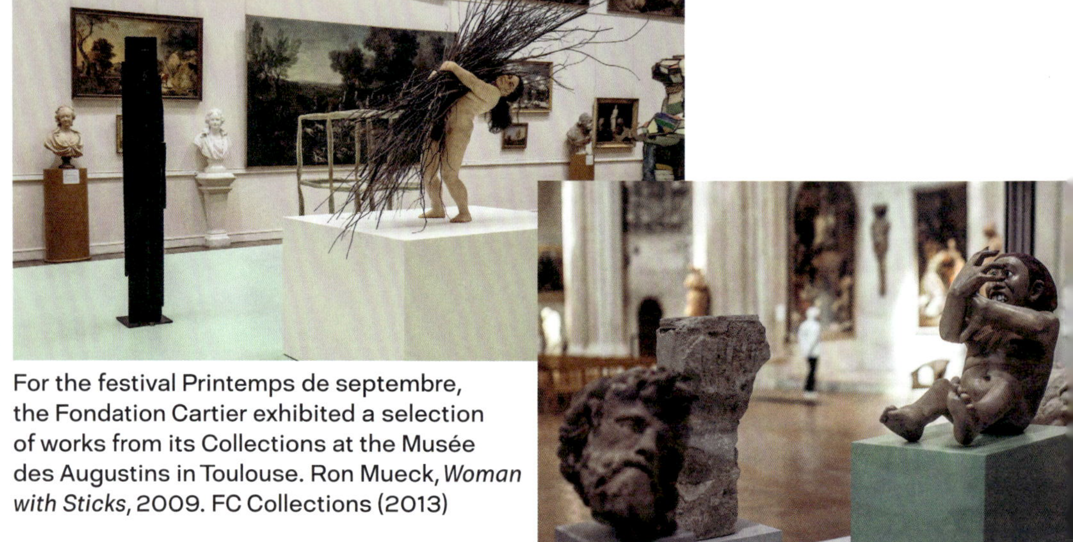

For the festival Printemps de septembre, the Fondation Cartier exhibited a selection of works from its Collections at the Musée des Augustins in Toulouse. Ron Mueck, *Woman with Sticks*, 2009. FC Collections (2013)

Roxanne Swentzell, *In Crises*, 2001
FC Collections (2001)

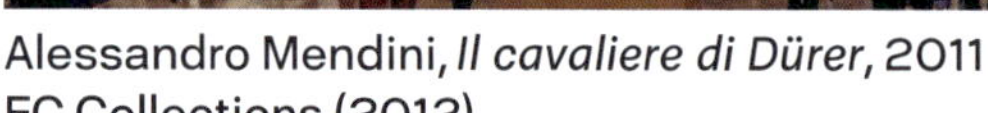

Alessandro Mendini, *Il cavaliere di Dürer*, 2011
FC Collections (2012)

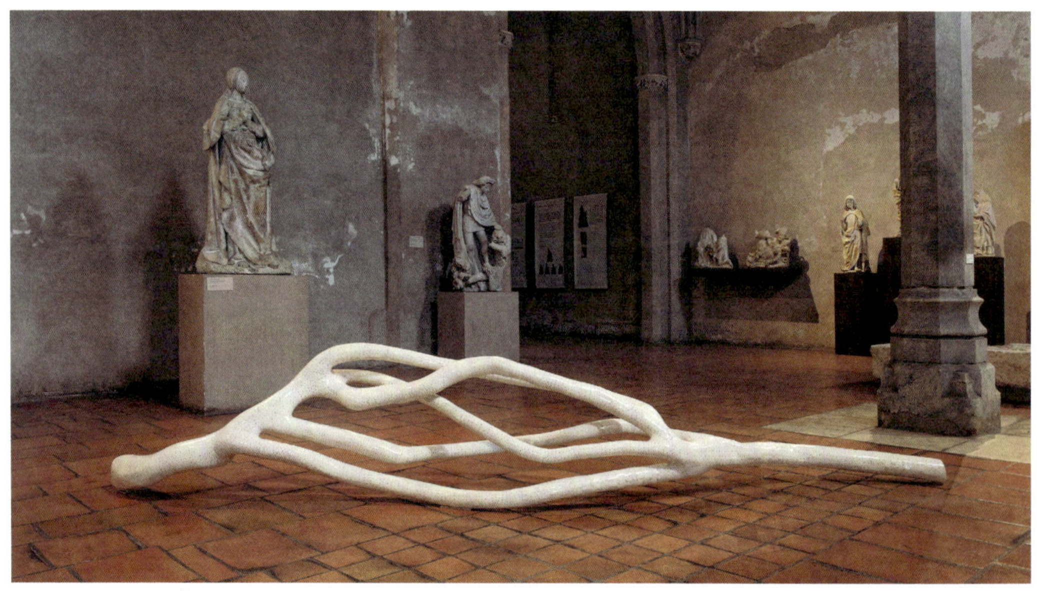

Hubert Duprat, *À la fois, la racine et le fruit*, 1997–1998. FC Collections (1998)

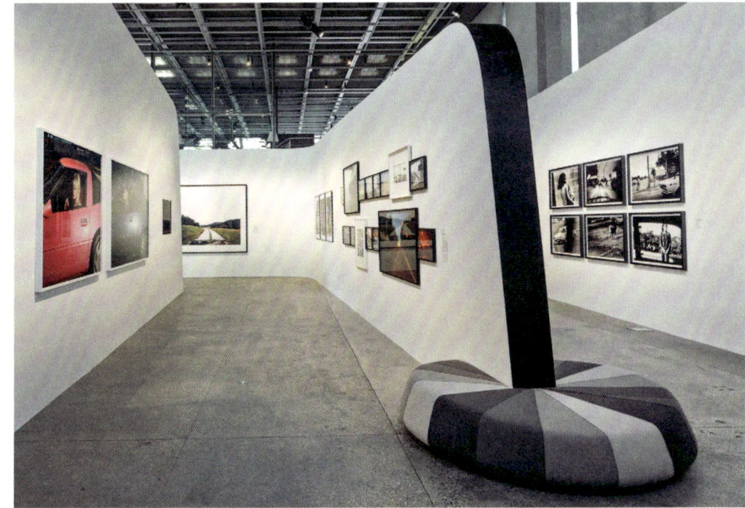

Through almost 500 works by 100 photographers, *Autophoto* explored photography's relationship to the automobile.

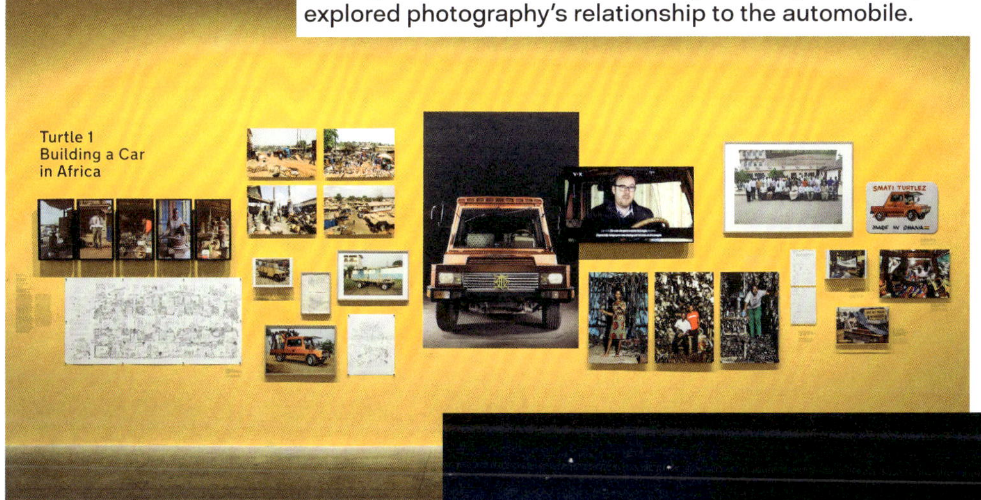

Melle Smets and Joost van Onna,
Turtle 1 – Building a Car in Africa, 2016

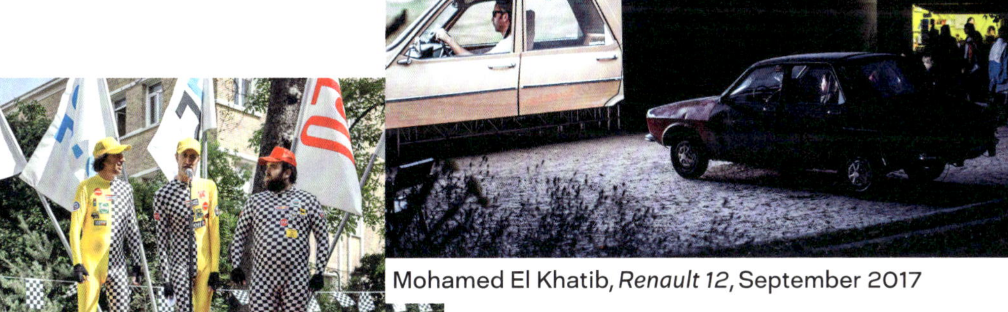

Mohamed El Khatib, *Renault 12*, September 2017

Nomadic Night with Clédat & Petitpierre,
Mille Bornes!, September 3, 2017

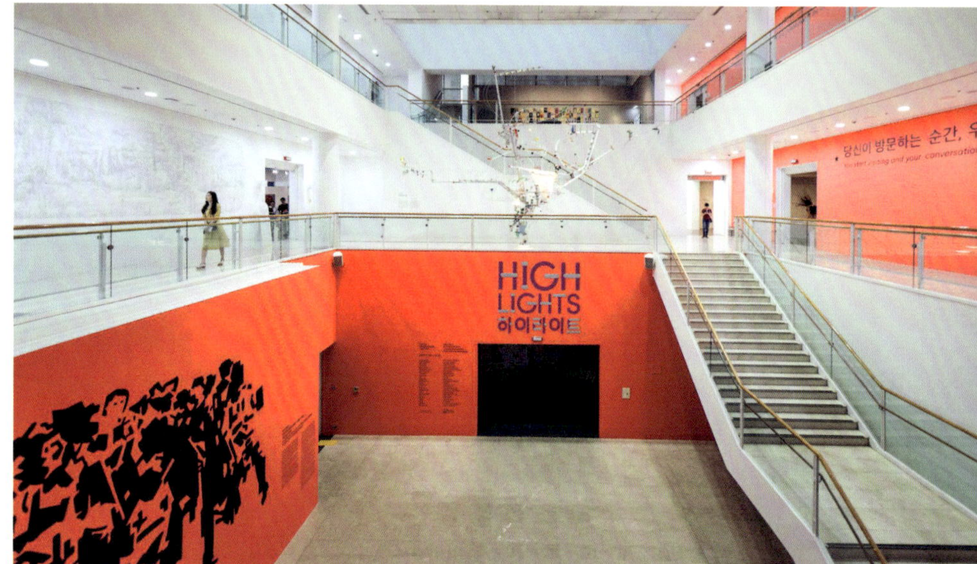

The exhibition *Highlights* at the Seoul Museum of Art brought together
over 250 works from the Collections of the Fondation Cartier. For the occasion,
Jean-Michel Alberola, Marc Couturier, and Sarah Sze produced monumental
installations specially created for the venue.

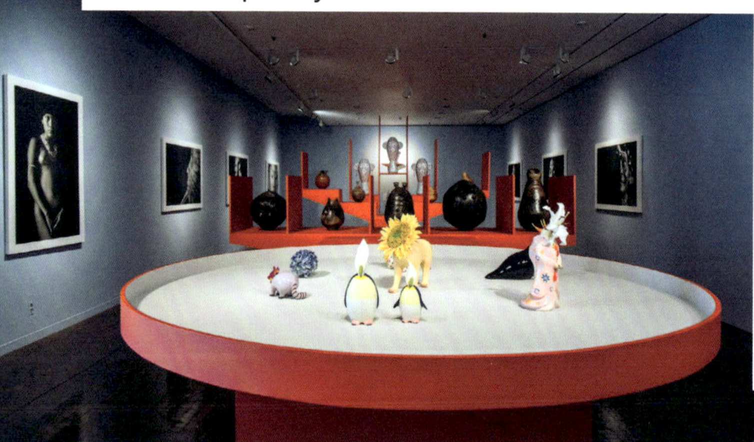

Photographs by Claudia Andujar, ceramics by
Takeshi Kitano, Julia Isidrez, and Alessandro Mendini
Exhibition design by Alessandro Mendini

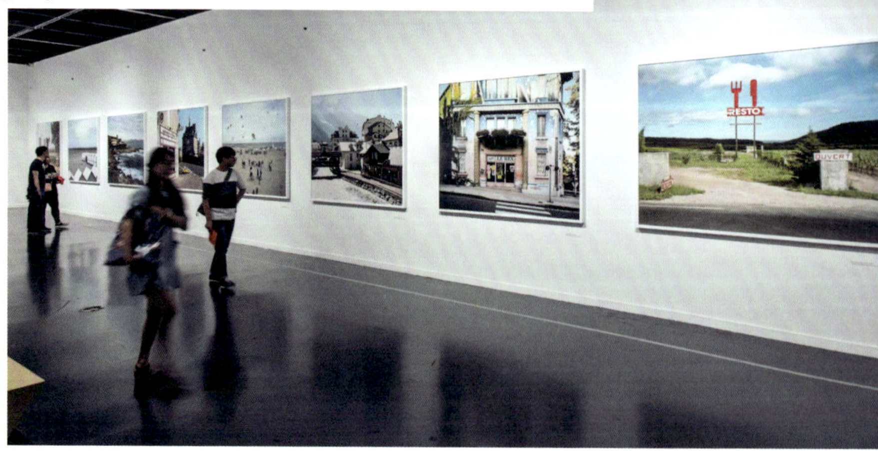

Raymond Depardon, *La France*, 2008. FC Collections (2013)

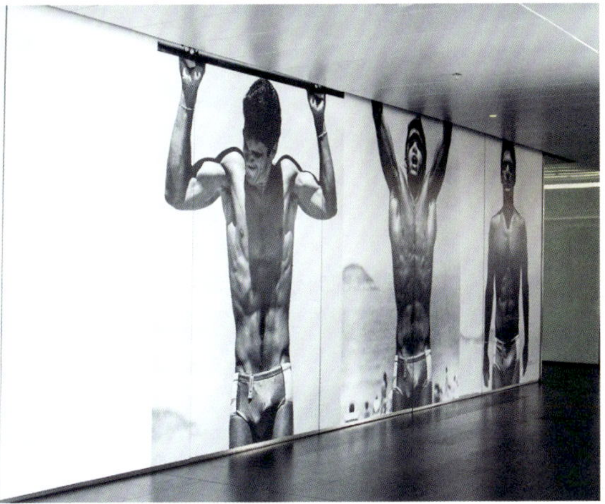

After *Les Habitants*, Guillermo Kuitca cast a new and highly personal gaze on the Collections of the Fondation Cartier in this exhibition featuring 23 artists at the CCK in Buenos Aires.
Alair Gomes, *Beach Triptych no.7*, c. 1980
FC Collections (1999)

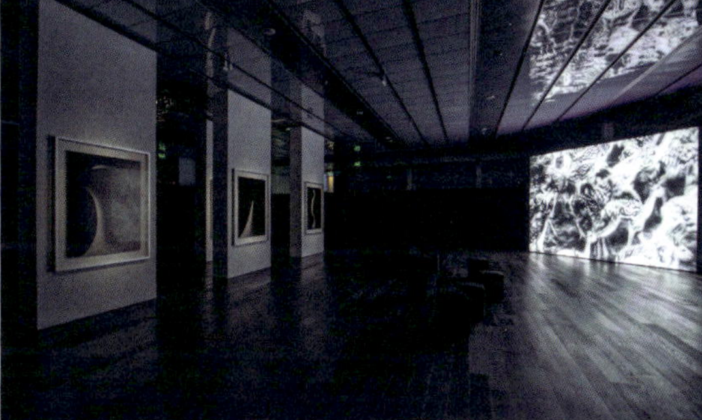

Hiroshi Sugimoto, *Mathematical Forms*, 2004, opposite Artavazd Pelechian's film *Les Habitants*, 1970. FC Collections (2005 and 2015)

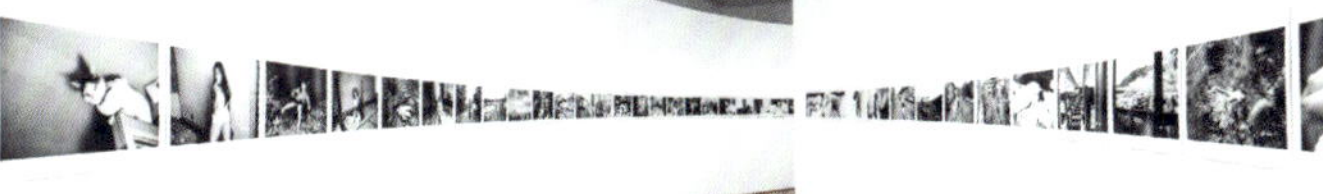

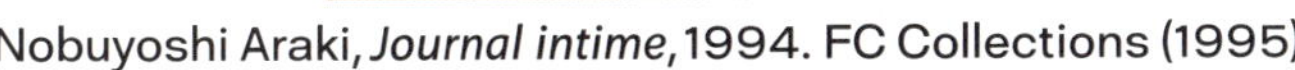

Nobuyoshi Araki, *Journal intime*, 1994. FC Collections (1995)

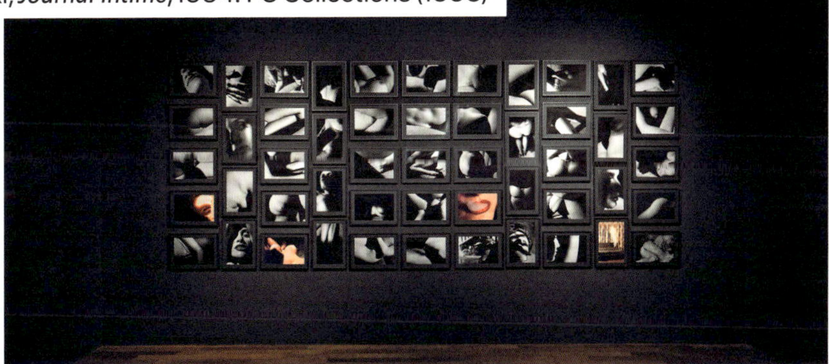

David Lynch, *Nudes*, 2017
FC Collections (2018)

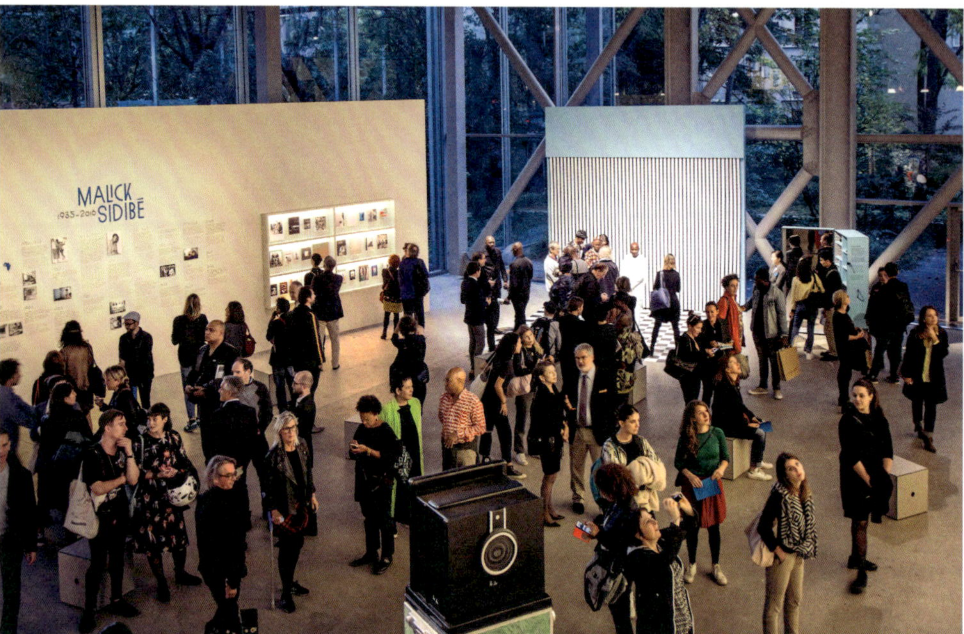

One year after Malick Sidibé's death, the Fondation Cartier paid him tribute
with this exhibition. Alongside his iconic works, a vast ensemble of vintage
photographs and rare portraits could be seen.

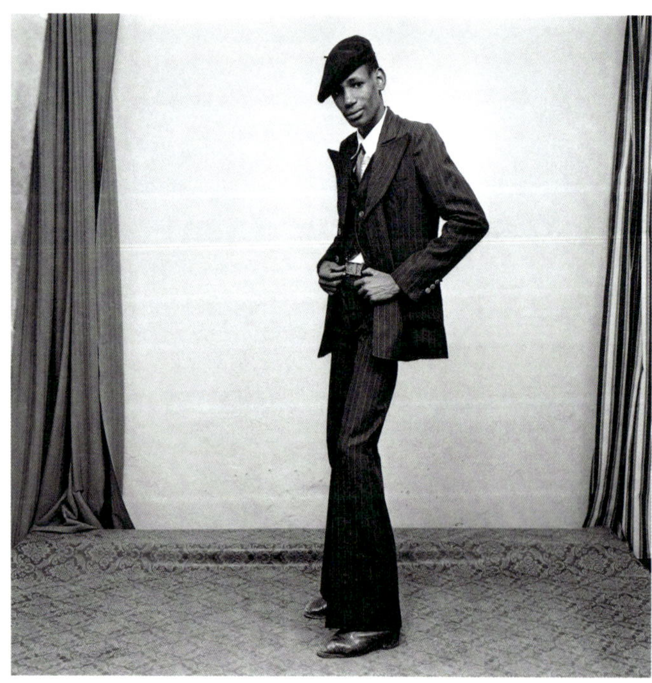

Malick Sidibé, *Un gentleman en position*, 1980
FC Collections (2018)

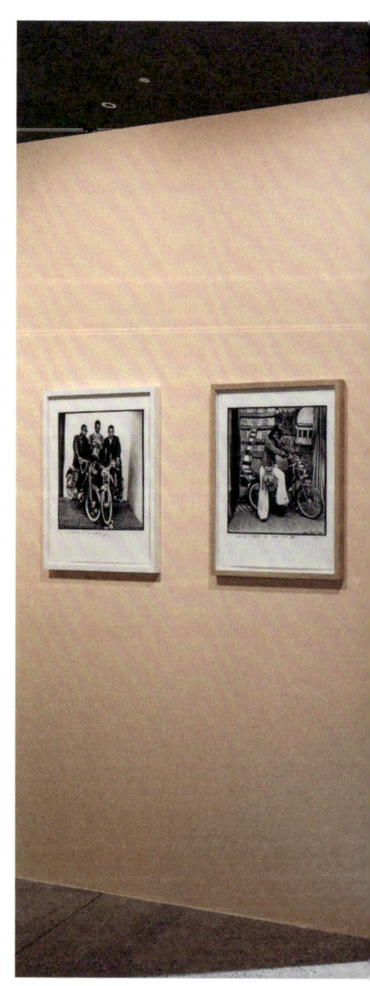

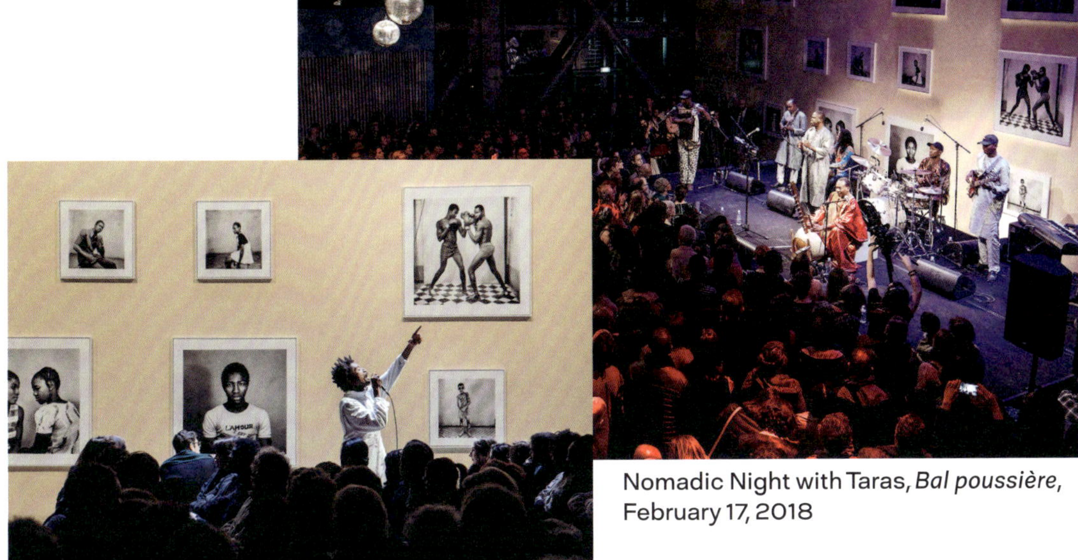

Nomadic Night with Taras, *Bal poussière*, February 17, 2018

Nomadic Night with Nástio Mosquito, *Respectable Thief*, February 12, 2018

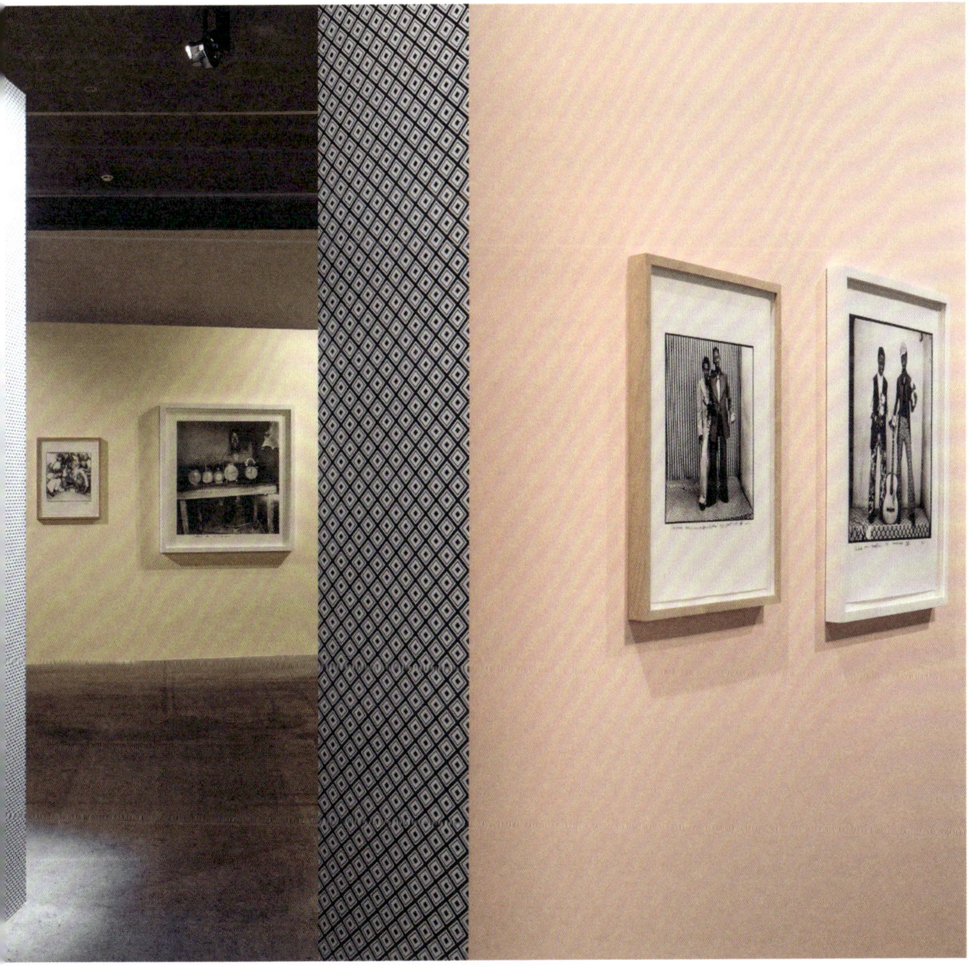

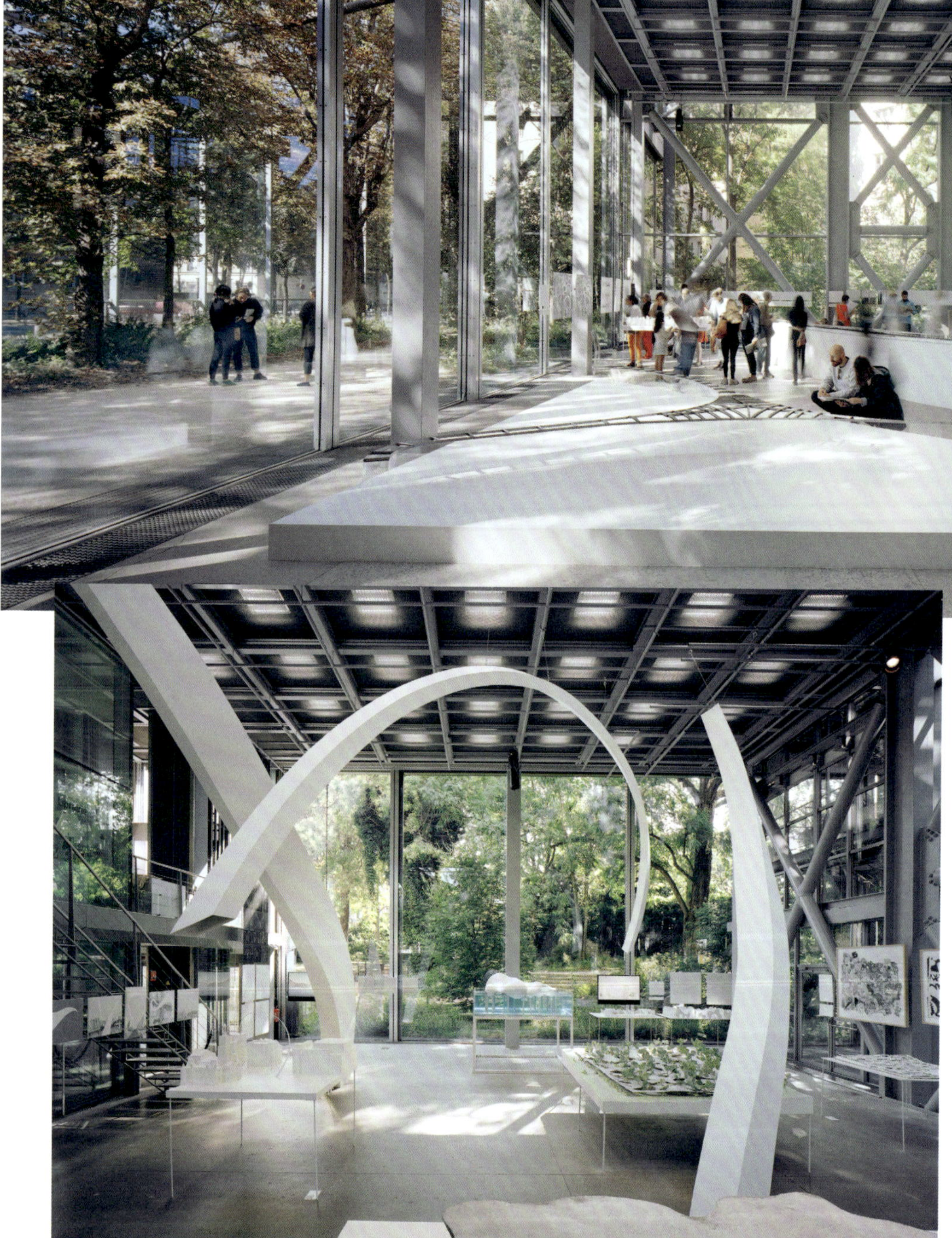

Specially designed for the Fondation Cartier, the exhibition *Freeing Architecture* revealed some 20 architectural projects by Junya Ishigami through large-scale maquettes. The following year, the exhibition traveled to the Power Station of Art, Shanghai.

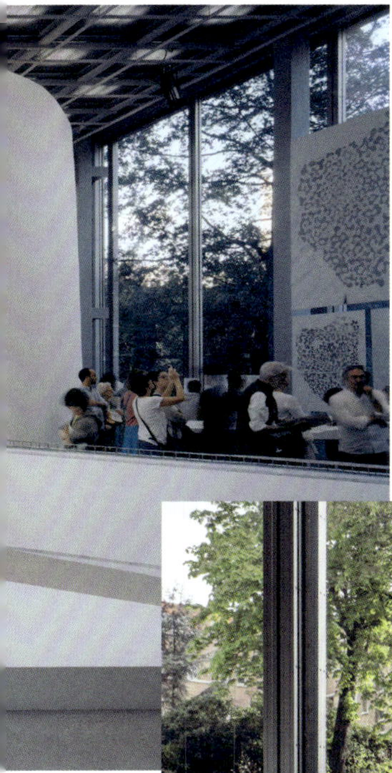

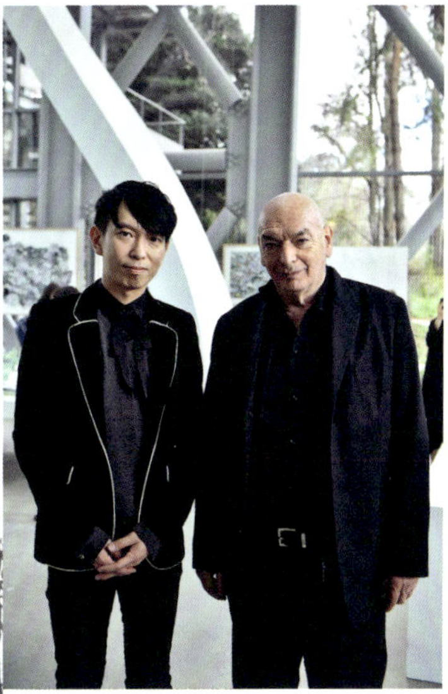

Junya Ishigami and Jean Nouvel

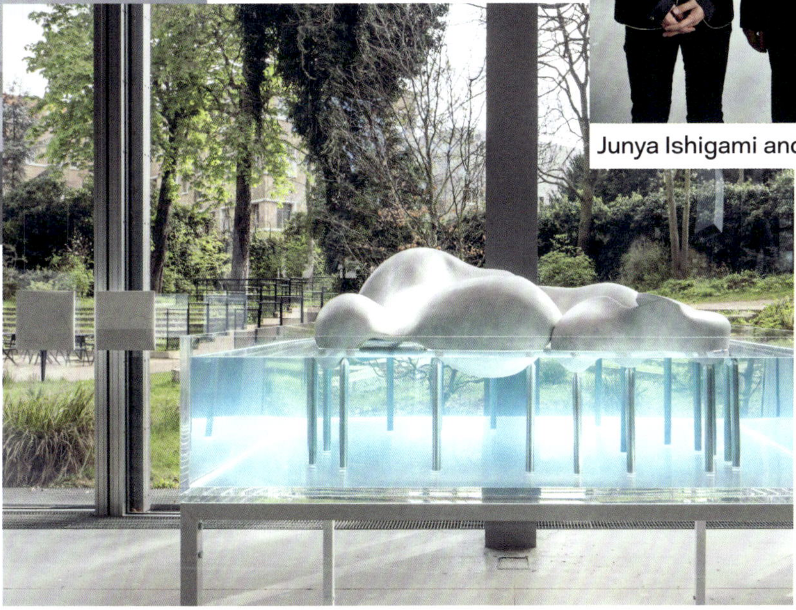

Junya Ishigami, *House of Peace*, 2018

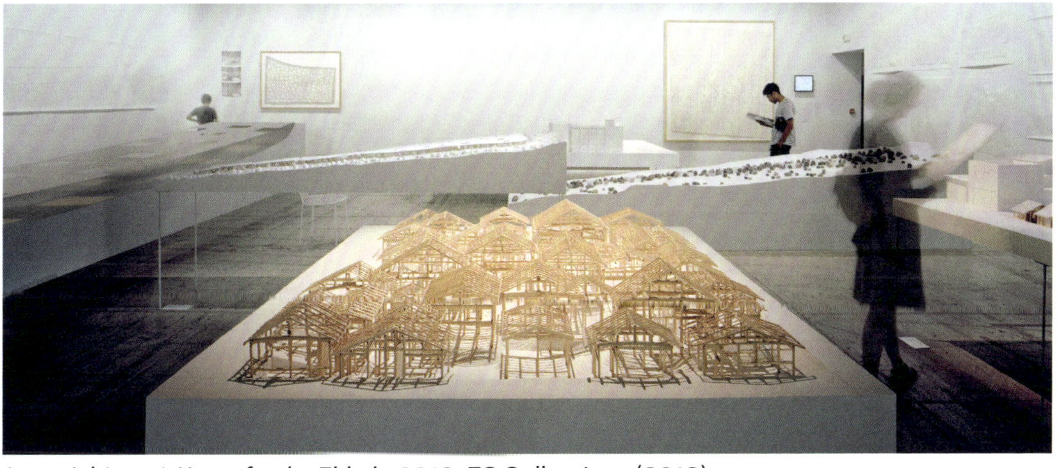

Junya Ishigami, *Home for the Elderly*, 2018. FC Collections (2018)

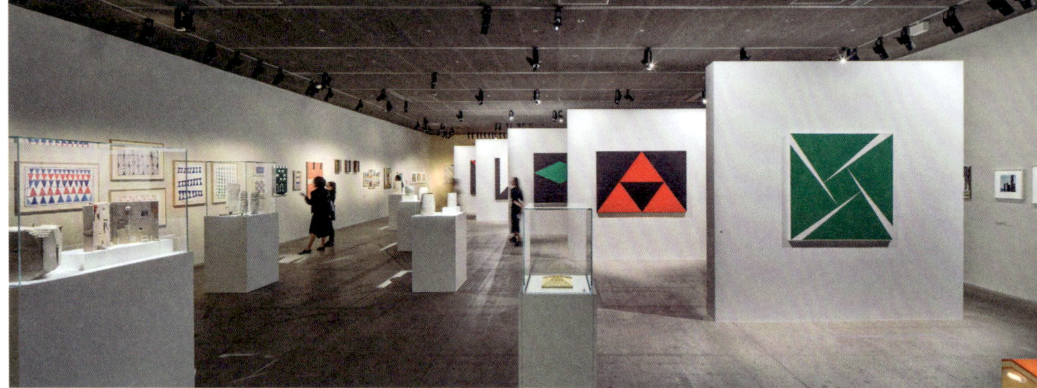

The exhibition *Southern Geometries* celebrated the wealth and variety of motifs, colors, and figures of Latin American art through nearly 250 works by almost 70 artists.

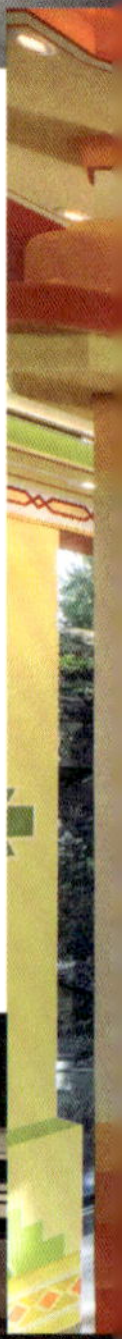

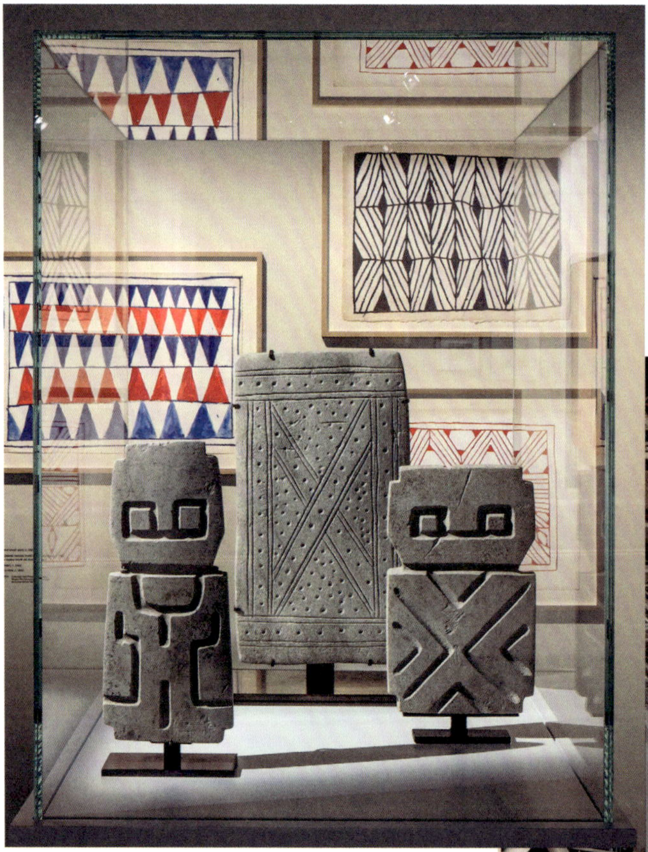

Valdivia sculptures, 3500–1500 BCE.
Drawings by Wauja artists, second half
of the 20th century

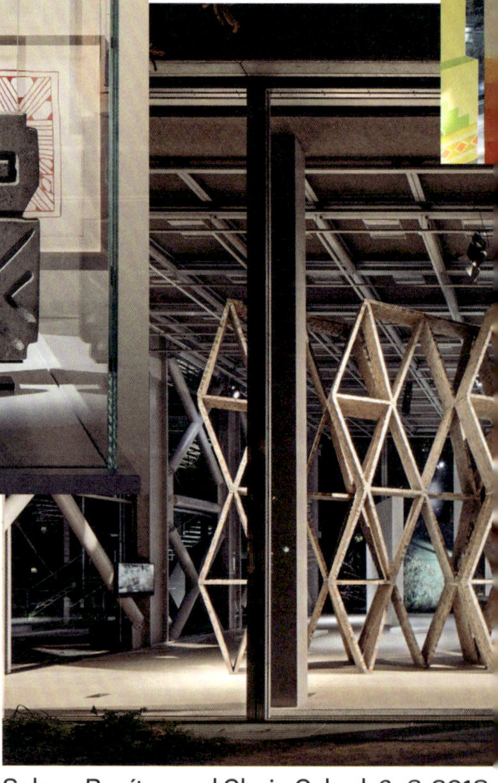

Solano Benítez and Gloria Cabral, *6×8*, 2018
Commission for the exhibition

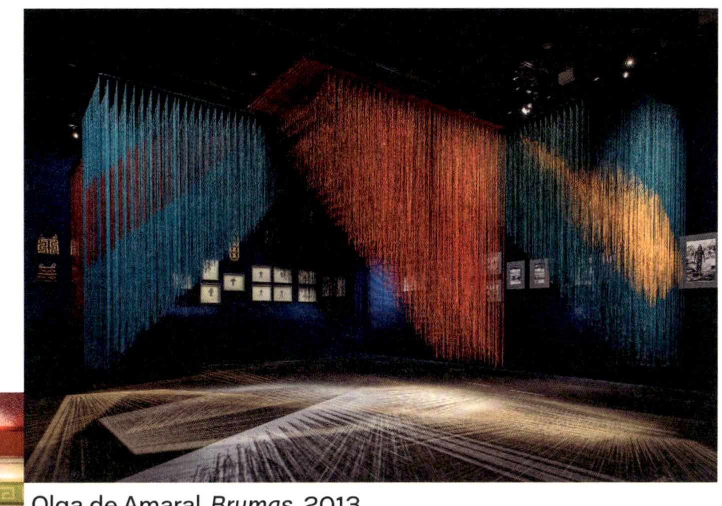

Olga de Amaral, *Brumas*, 2013

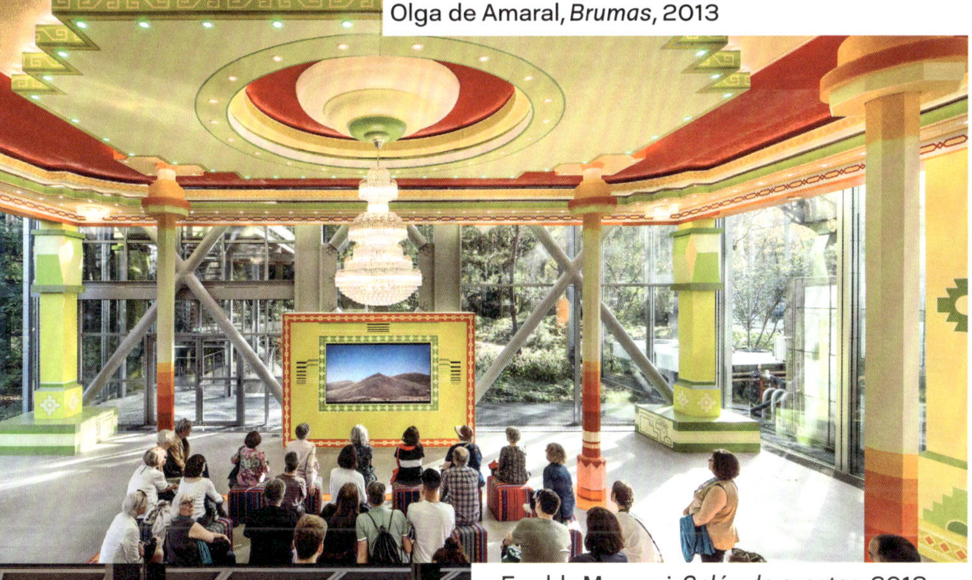

Freddy Mamani, *Salón de eventos*, 2018
Commission for the exhibition
FC Collections (2019)

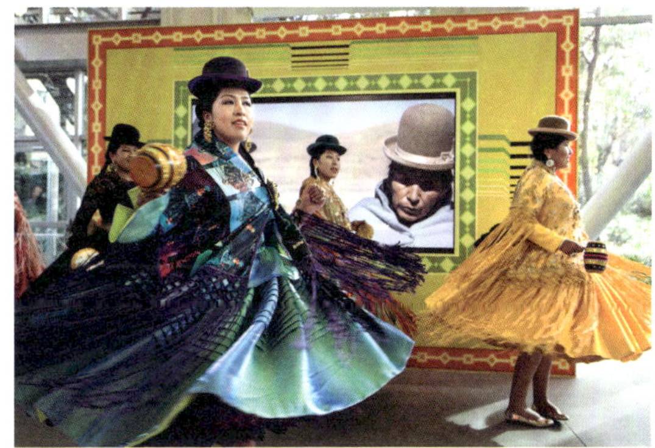

"Cholas" from Aymara communities
in La Paz and El Alto paraded during
the exhibition opening

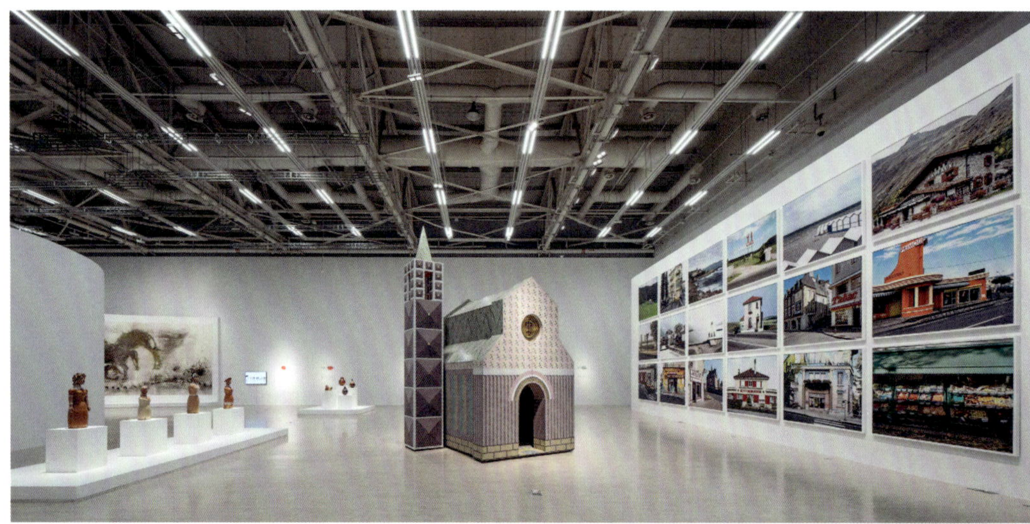

For the first time, the Fondation Cartier exhibited its Collections in Shanghai, inaugurating a long series of collaborations with the Power Station of Art.

Ron Mueck, *Woman with Shopping*, 2013, and David Lynch, lithograph series, 2007
FC Collections (2013 and 2011)

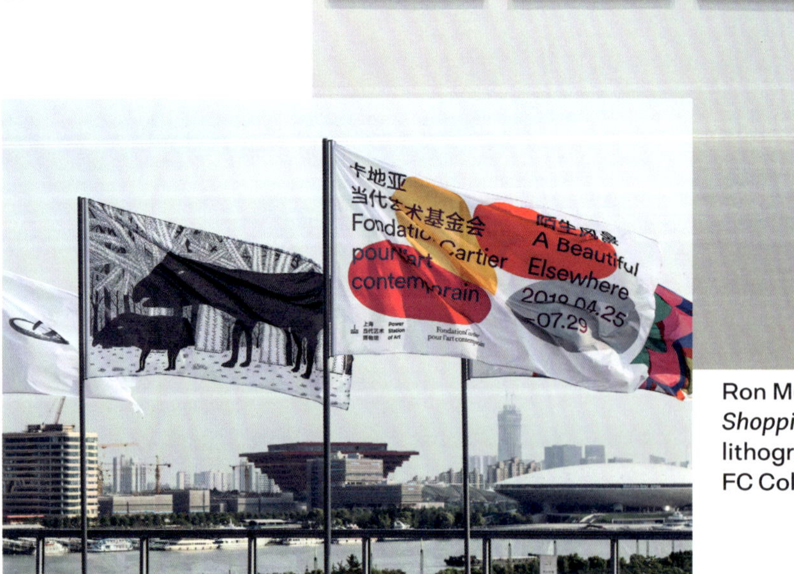

Based on an idea by Christian Boltanski, the Fondation Cartier commissioned flags from artists, scientists, and thinkers with whom it has close ties: *Dessine-moi un drapeau*, 2018.

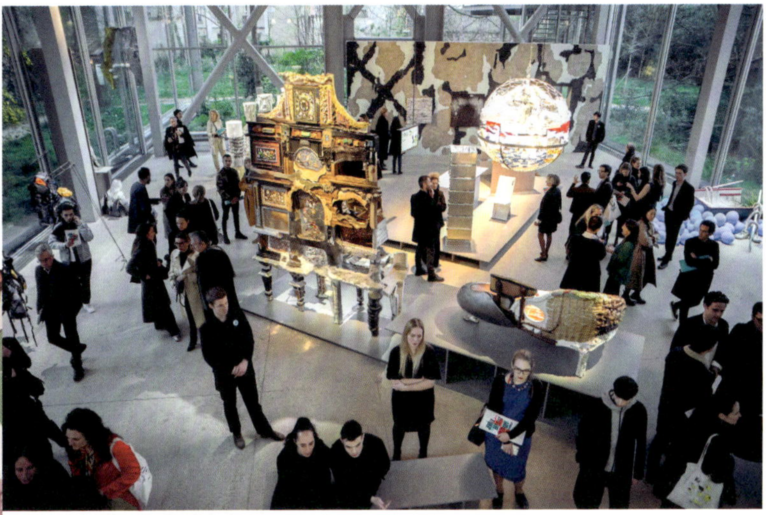

The Fondation Cartier shone a light on young European creation through the work of 21 artists from 16 different countries.

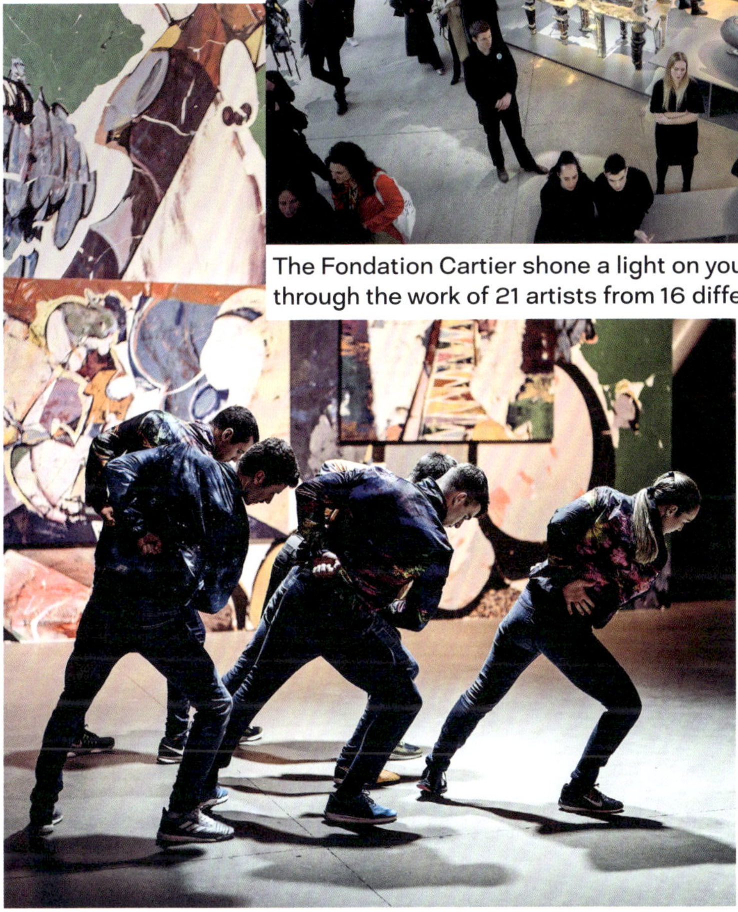

Nomadic Night with (La)Horde, *Keep Calm and Listen to Hardstyle*, April 25, 2019, in front of Alexandros Vasmoulakis's work *Tweak* (2019)

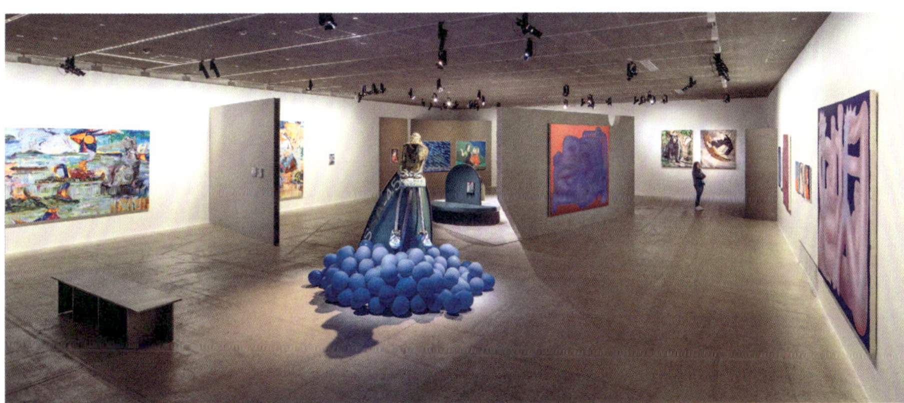

Works by Miryam Haddad, Kris Lemsalu, Klára Hosnedlová, Magnus Andersen, and George Rouy

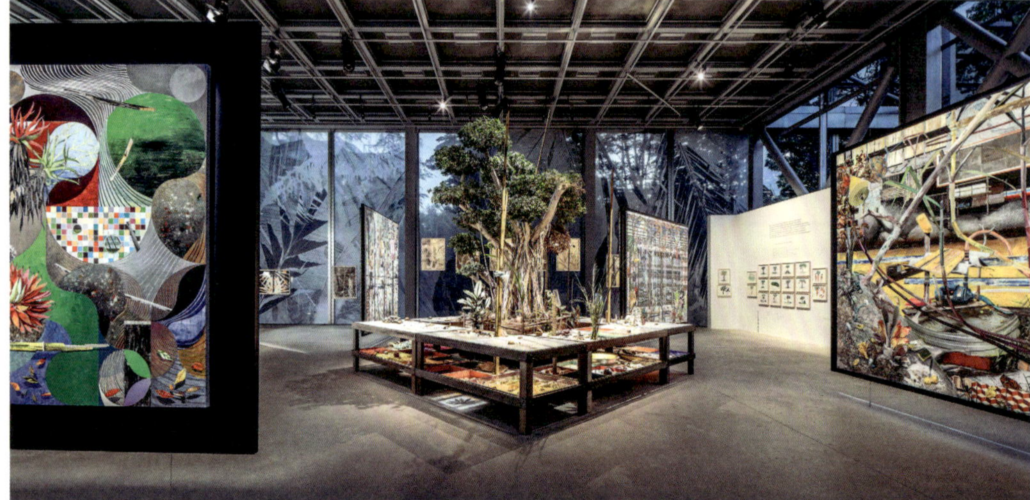

The exhibition *Trees* brought together a community of artists, botanists,
and philosophers, who have developed a strong and intimate connection with trees.
Luiz Zerbini, *Lago Quadrado*, 2010, *Natureza Espiritual da Realidade*, 2002–2019,
FC Collections (2019), and *Mamão Manilha*, 2012

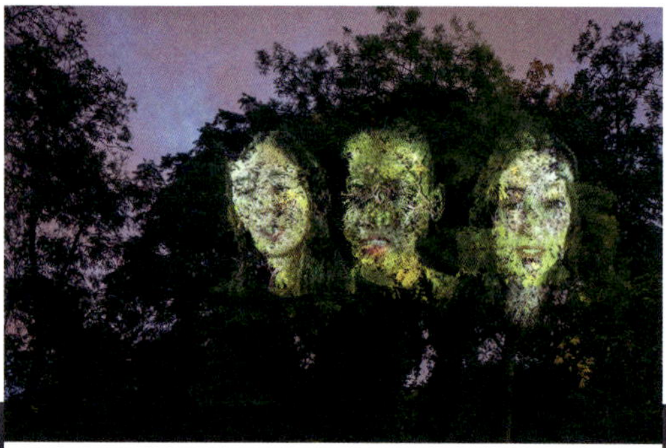

Tony Oursler produced the projection
Éclipse specially for the garden of
the Fondation Cartier, December 2019.

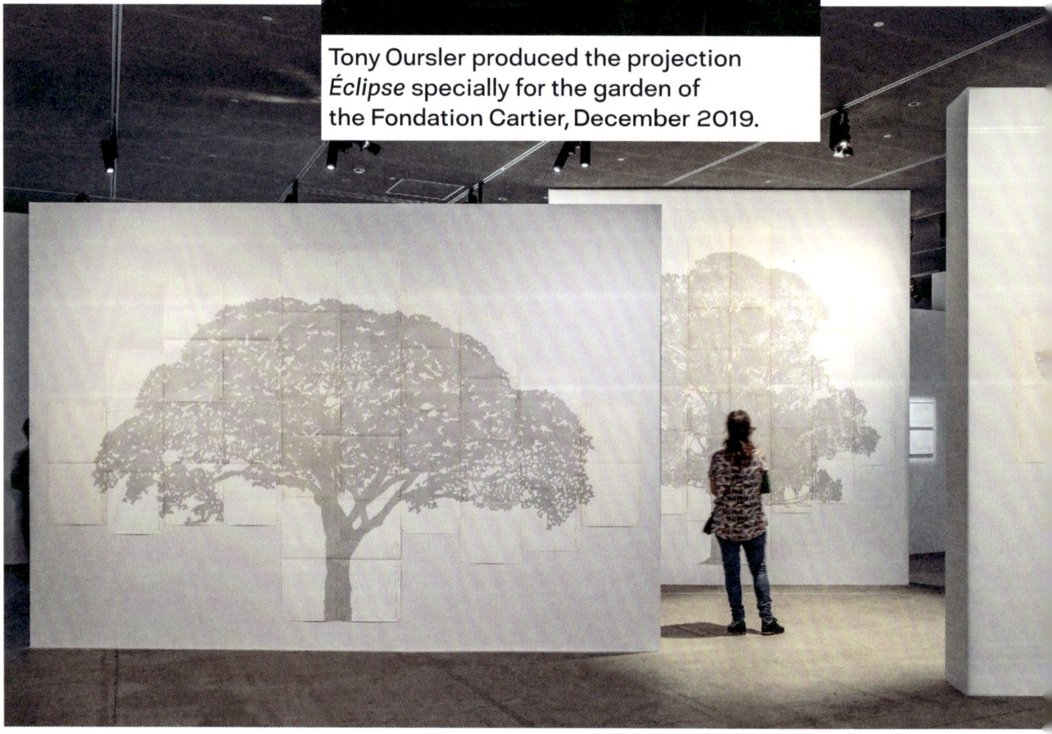

Johanna Calle, *Ceiba, Sangregado*, and *Nogal Andino*, 2014

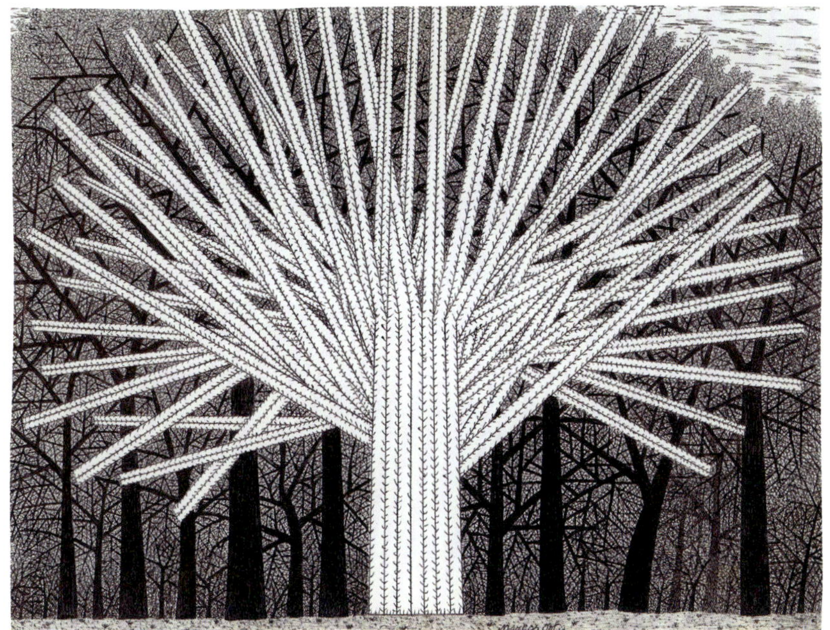

Marcos Ortiz, *Untitled*, 2018. FC Collections (2018)

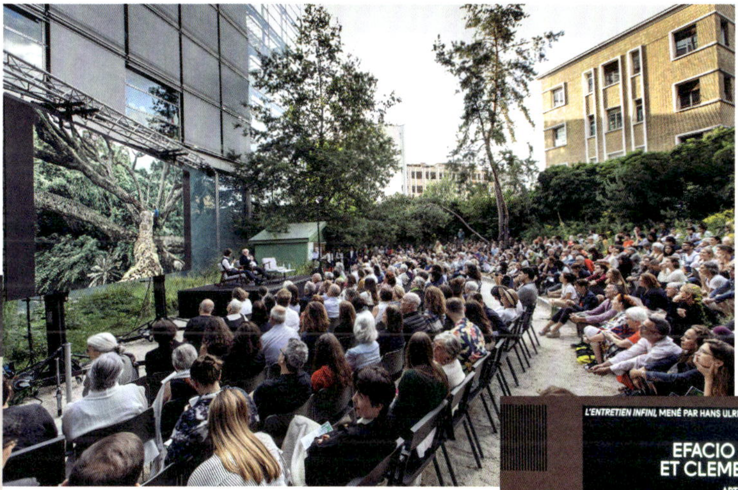

Cédric Villani and Francis Hallé
at the *Night of Trees*, July 13, 2019

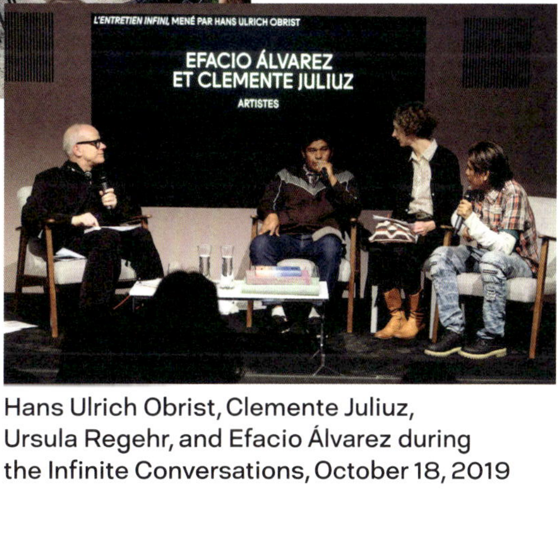

Hans Ulrich Obrist, Clemente Juliuz,
Ursula Regehr, and Efacio Álvarez during
the Infinite Conversations, October 18, 2019

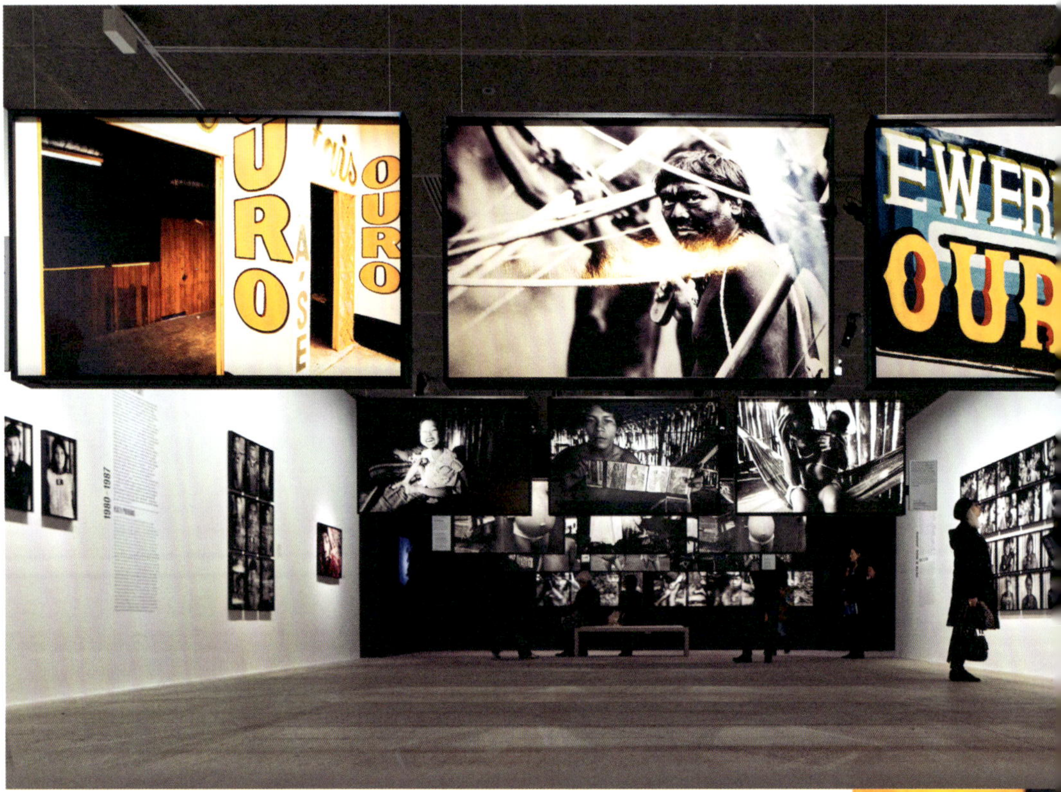

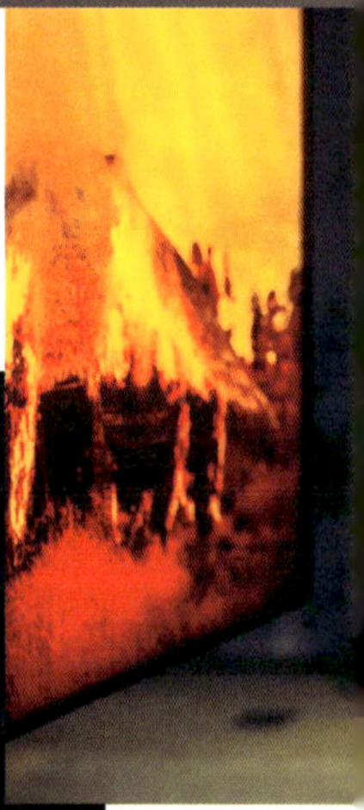

The Fondation Cartier presented the largest exhibition ever devoted to the work of Claudia Andujar, who since the 1970s, has dedicated her life to photographing the Yanomami and defending their territory. The Yanomami are one of the largest Amerindian groups living in the Brazilian Amazon.

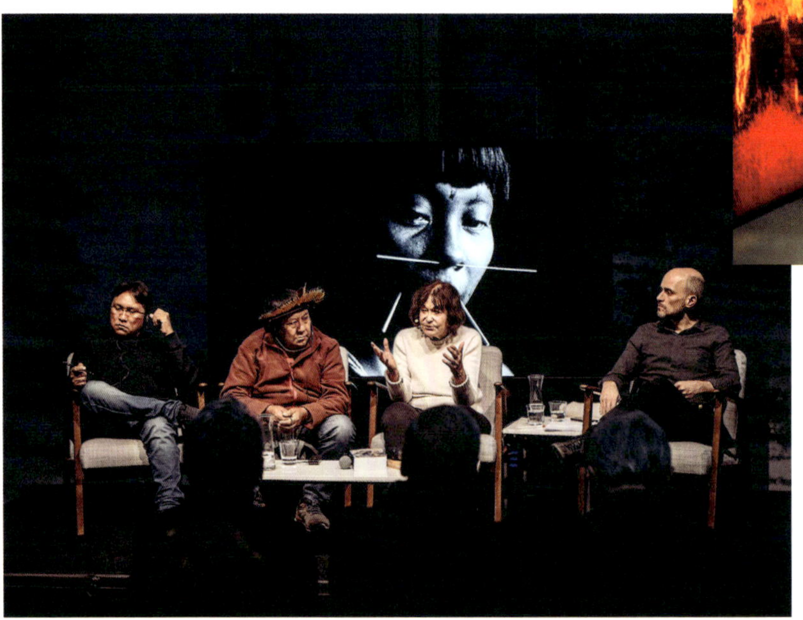

Dário and Davi Kopenawa, Claudia Andujar, and Thyago Nogueira, exhibition curator, during the Night of the Yanomami, January 30, 2020

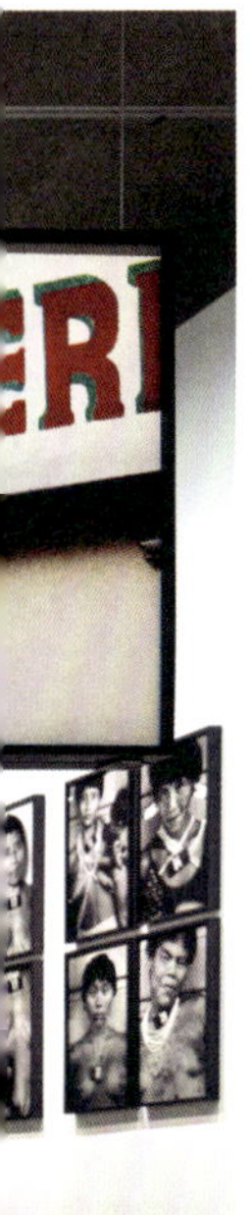

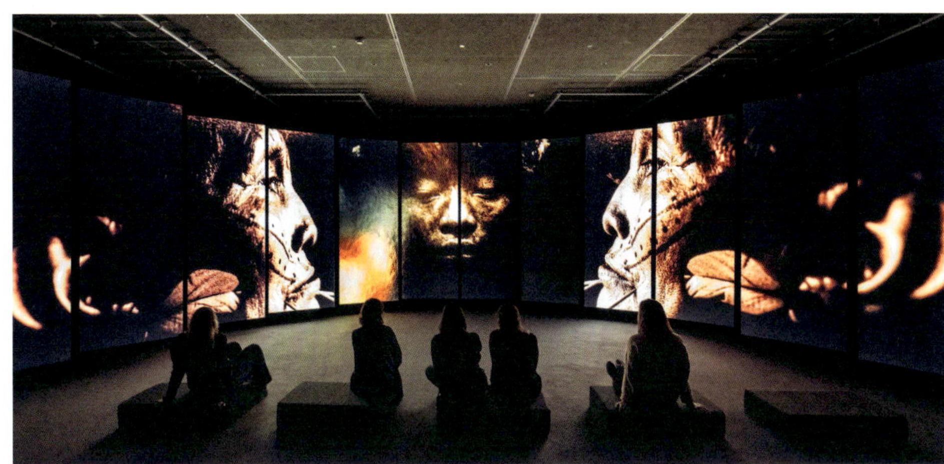

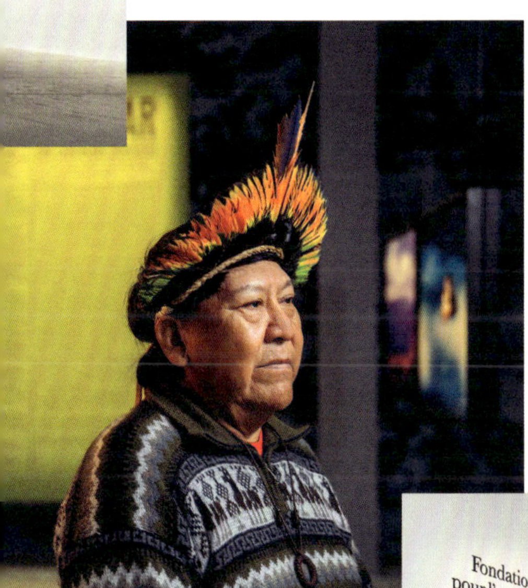

Yanomami shaman
Davi Kopenawa at
the exhibition opening

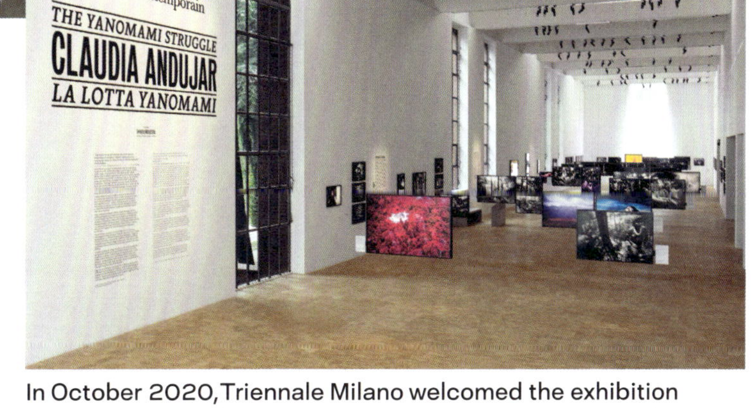

In October 2020, Triennale Milano welcomed the exhibition
La Lotta Yanomami, inaugurating a unique partnership with
the Fondation Cartier.

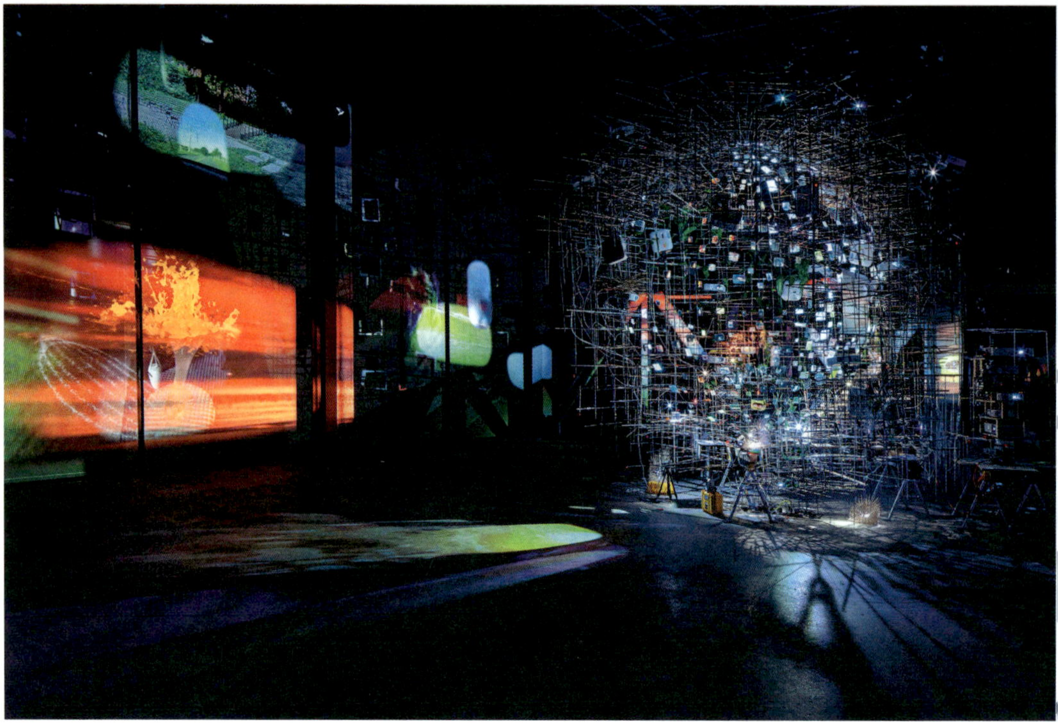

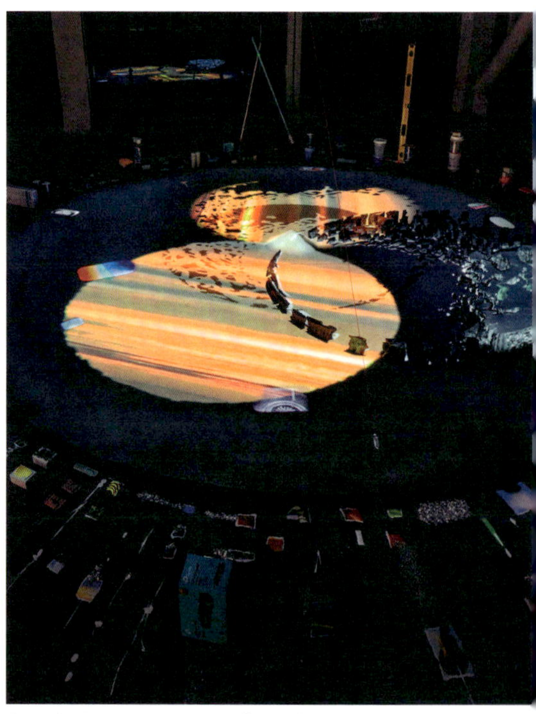

"Art and science history combined will record the fact that it was a sculptor from the US who gave Parisian visitors a chance to experience *the verifiable image of the world*, so perfectly adapted to the new spatial order they would have to learn to live in thereafter." Bruno Latour
Sarah Sze, *Twice Twilight*, 2020
Commission for the exhibition
FC Collections (2022)

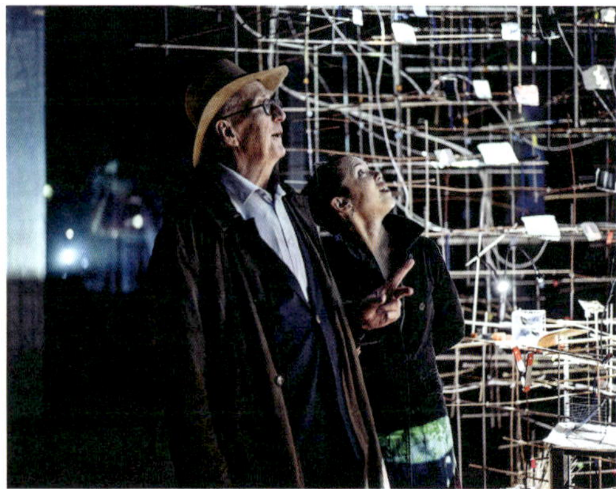

Bruno Latour and Sarah Sze in
the exhibition, October 19, 2020

Sarah Sze, *Tracing Fallen Sky*, 2020
Commission for the exhibition
FC Collections (2022)

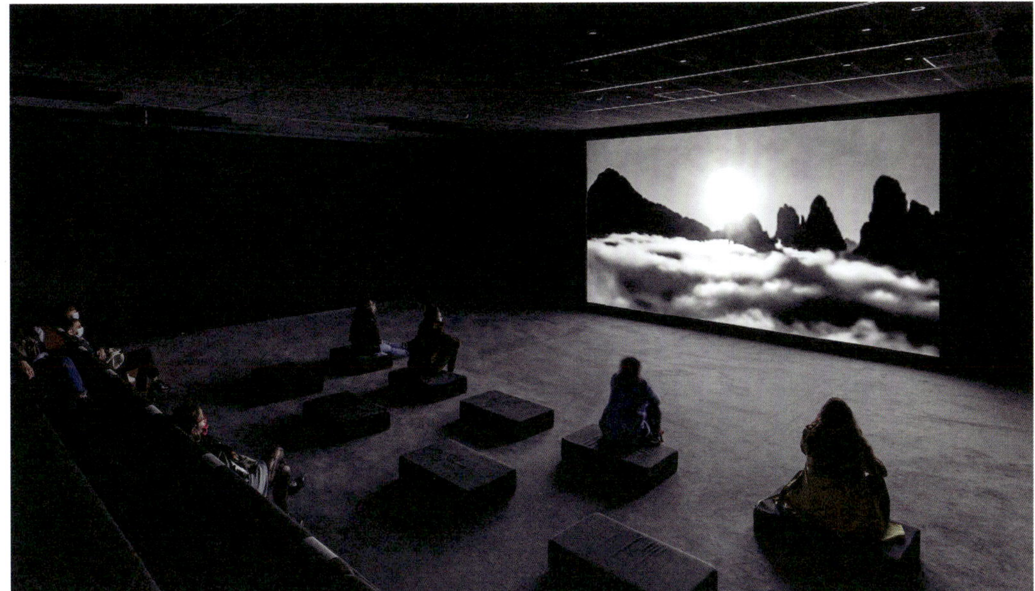

The result of a commission made in 2005 by the Fondation Cartier and the ZKM Filminstitut in Karlsruhe, Germany, *La Nature* is the culmination of fifteen years' work by filmmaker Artavazd Pelechian.

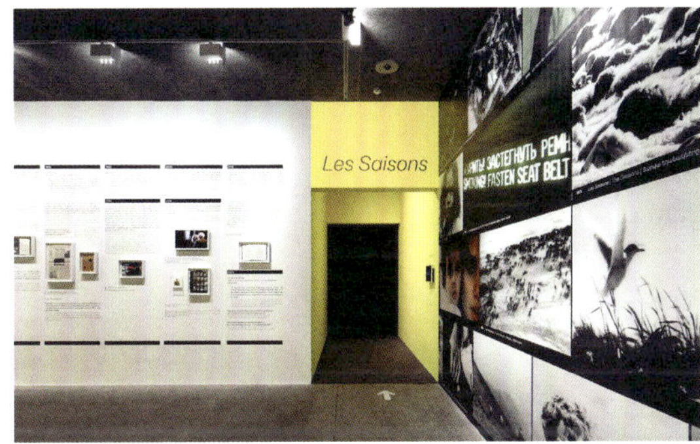

This first exhibition devoted to the filmmaker in France offered a unique dialogue between three of his works: *La Nature* (2020), *La Terre des hommes* (1966), and *Les Saisons* (1975).

Artavazd Pelechian

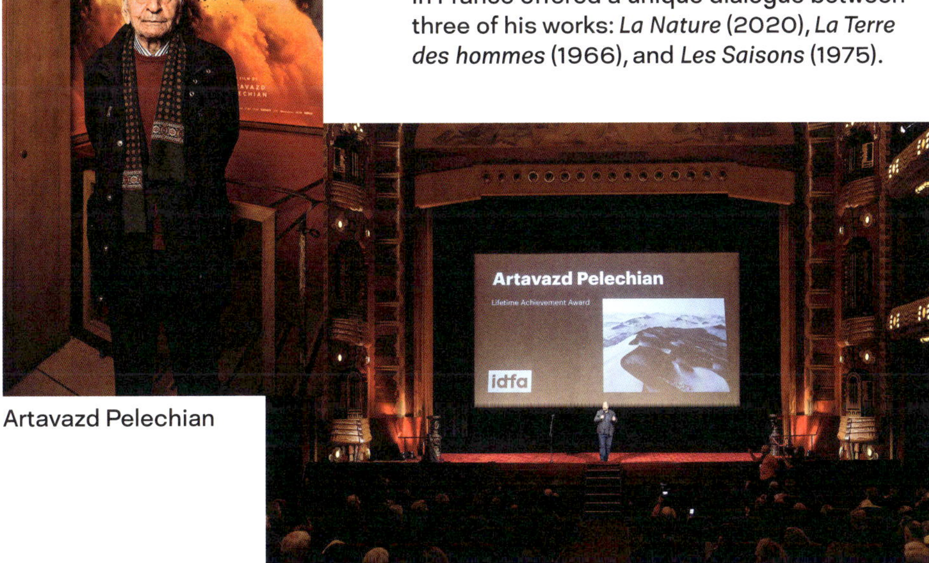

On November 19, 2021, Artavazd Pelechian received the Life Achievement Award from the IDFA (International Documentary Film Festival Amsterdam).

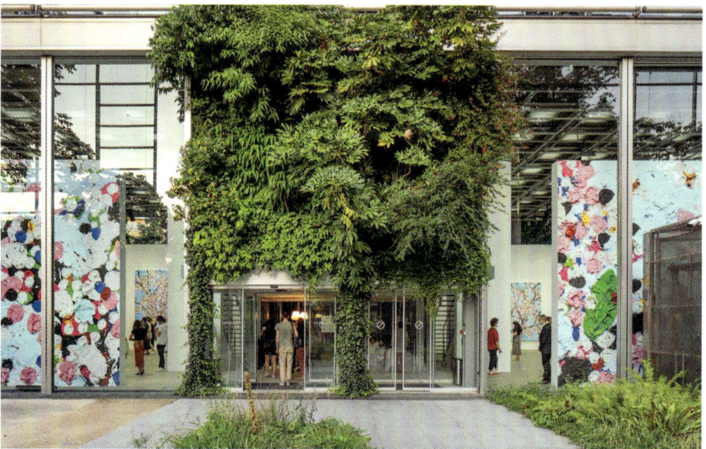

This exhibition presented 30 paintings chosen by Damien Hirst from the 107 canvases that make up his *Cherry Blossoms* series.

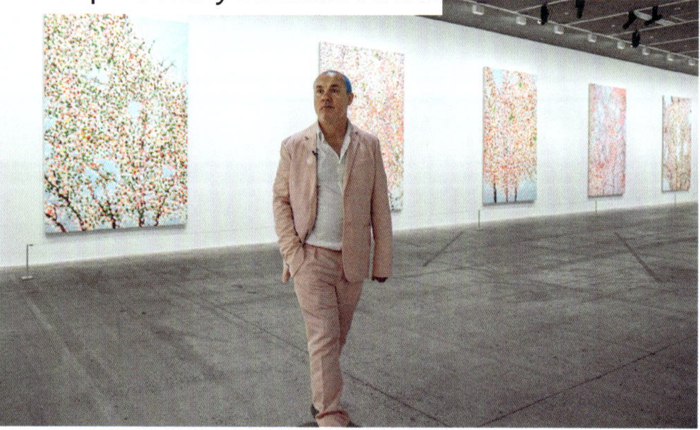

Damien Hirst at the exhibition opening

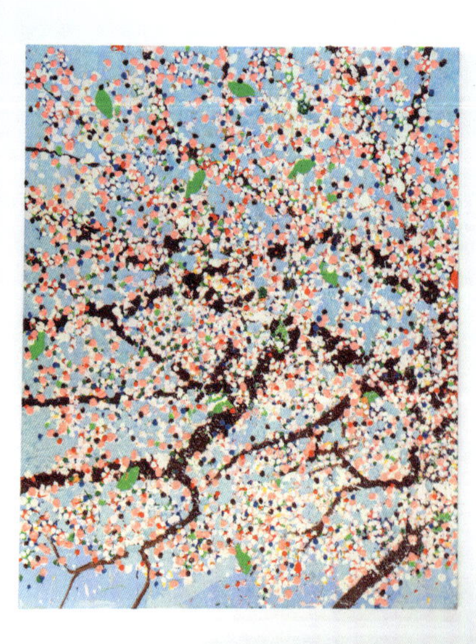

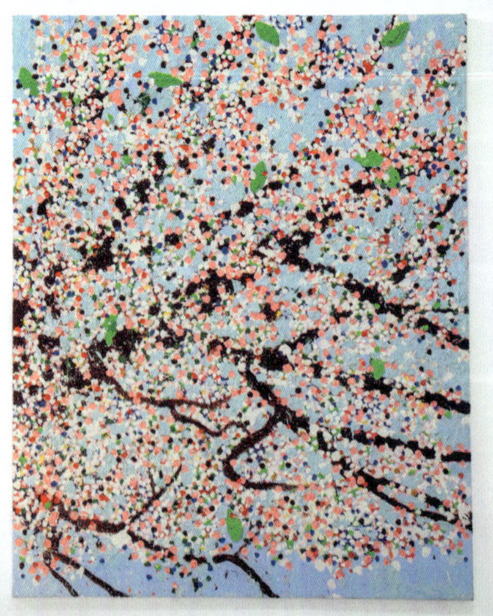

Damien Hirst, *Spiritual Day Blossom*, 2018. FC Collections (2021)

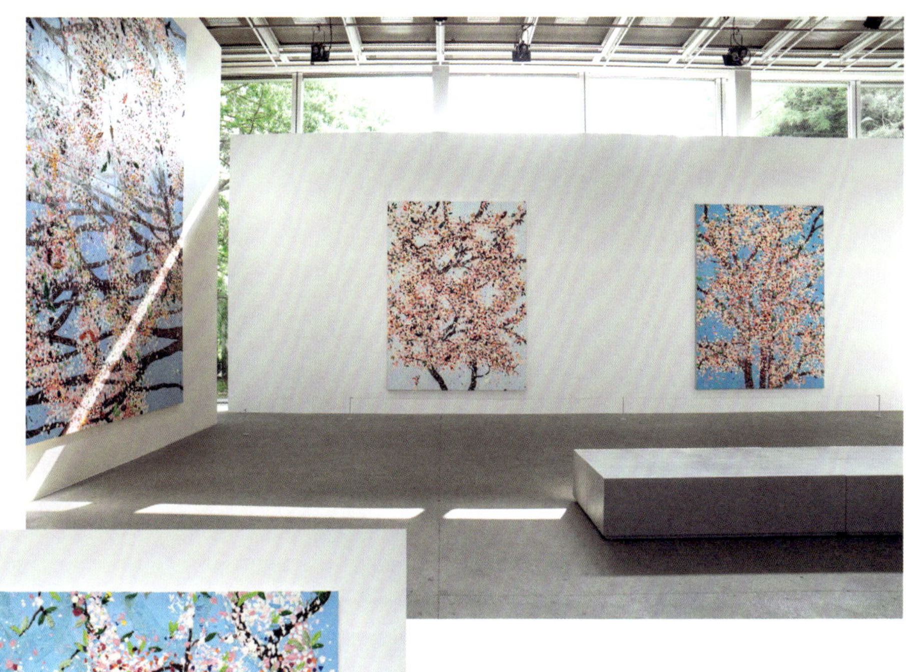

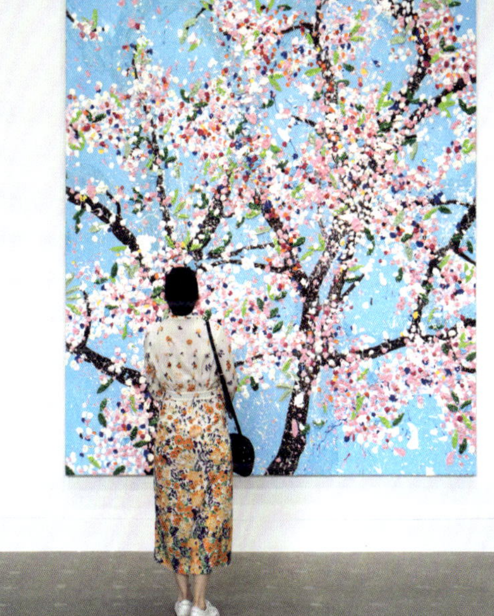

Damien Hirst, *Fragility Blossom*, 2018

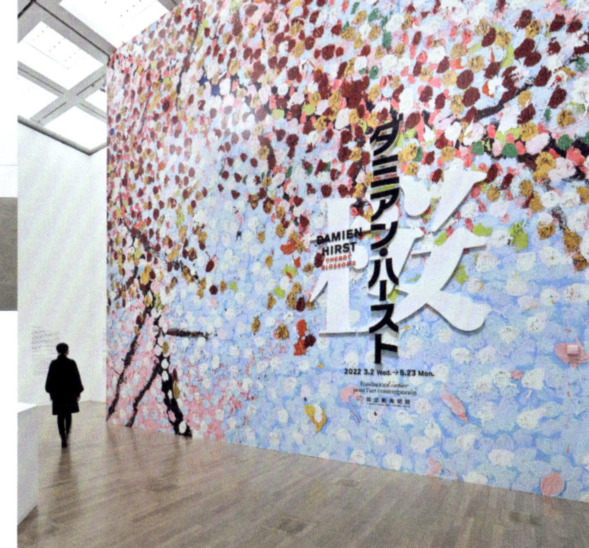

In 2022, *Cherry Blossoms* traveled to Tokyo's National Art Center for Damien Hirst's first major solo exhibition in Japan.

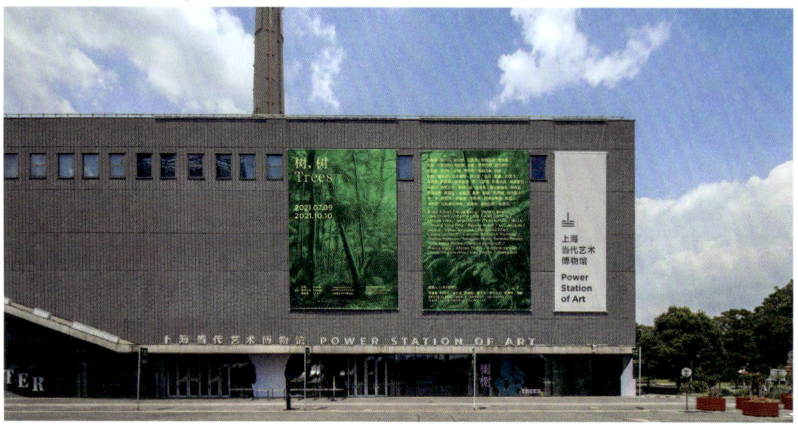

With the exhibition *Trees* at the Power Station of Art, the Fondation Cartier continued its exploration of the world of trees begun in Paris in 2019. In collaboration with curator Fei Dawei, works by Chinese artists including Huang Yong Ping, Hu Liu, and Zhang Enli, were added to the exhibition along with that of Milanese architect Stefano Boeri.

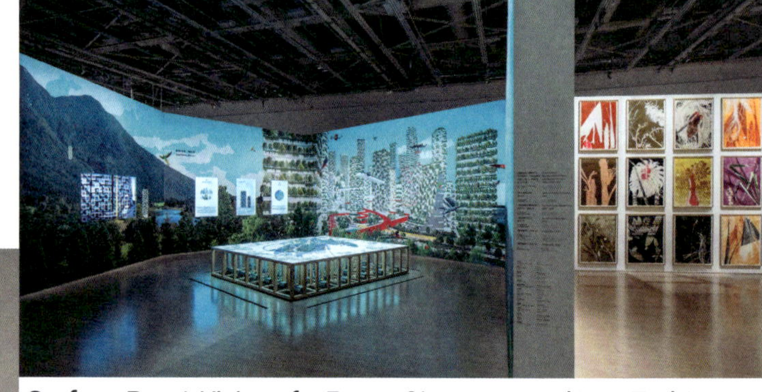

Stefano Boeri, *Vision of a Forest City*, 2021, and Luiz Zerbini, *Monotypes*, 2018-2021

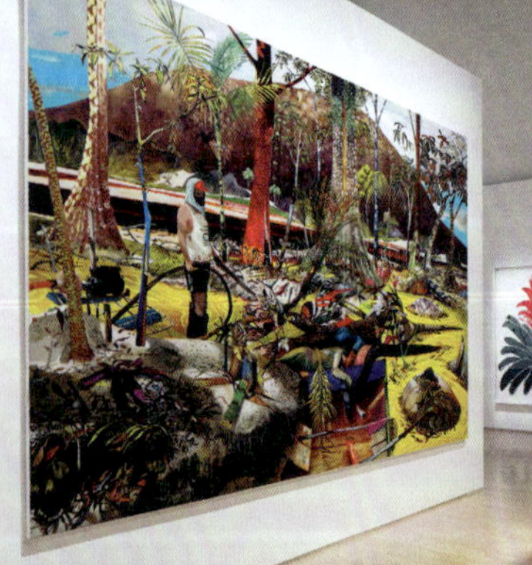

Luiz Zerbini, *Massacre de Haximu*, 2020, and Santídio Pereira, *Untitled*, 2017-2020

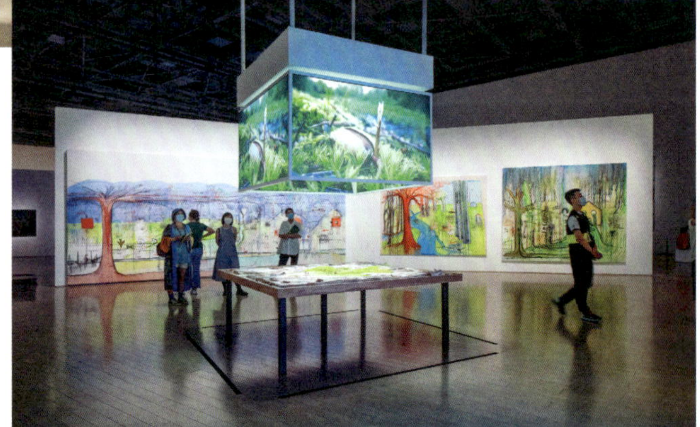

Fabrice Hyber, *Paysage biographique*, 2012, *L'Arbre rouge*, 2021, and *Born from Garbage*, 2010

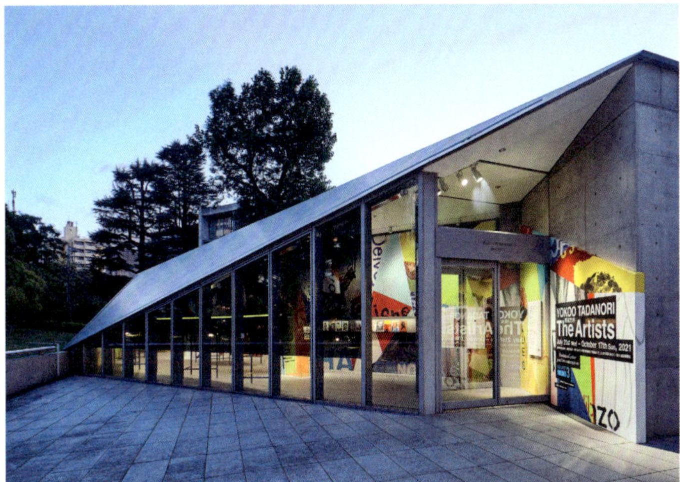

Between 2014 and 2021, Tadanori Yokoo produced a series of 139 portraits of artists, philosophers, critics, and scientists who have marked the history of the Fondation Cartier. These works, commissioned by the Fondation, were shown for the first time in Japan, at 21_21 Design Sight in Tokyo.

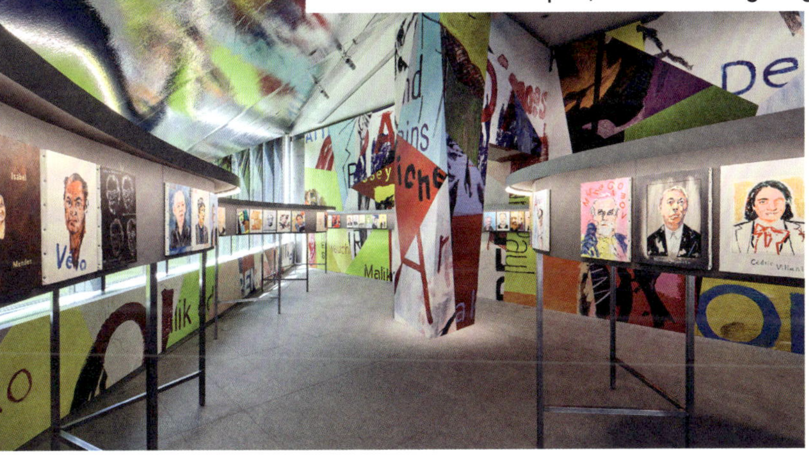

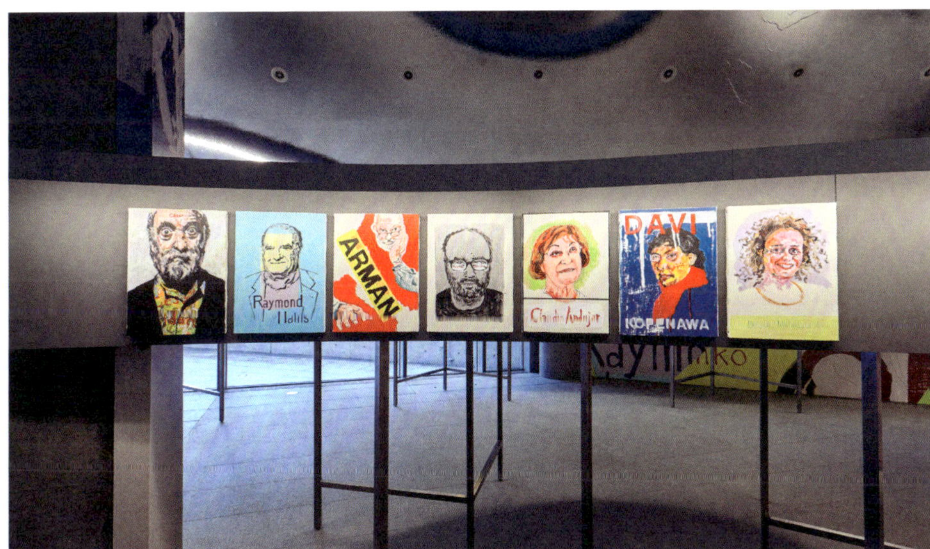

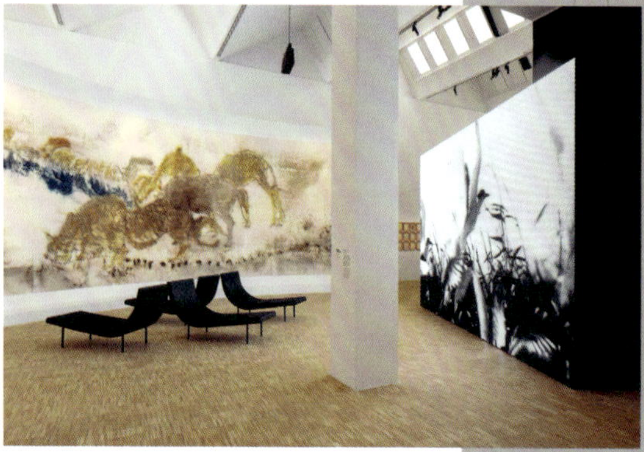

Presented at Triennale Milano, *Les Citoyens* was the third chapter in Argentinian artist Guillermo Kuitca's immersion in the Collections of the Fondation Cartier. This exhibition featured 120 works by 28 artists.
Cai Guo-Qiang, *White Tone*, 2016, and Artavazd Pelechian, *Les Habitants*, 1970. FC Collections (2017 and 2015)

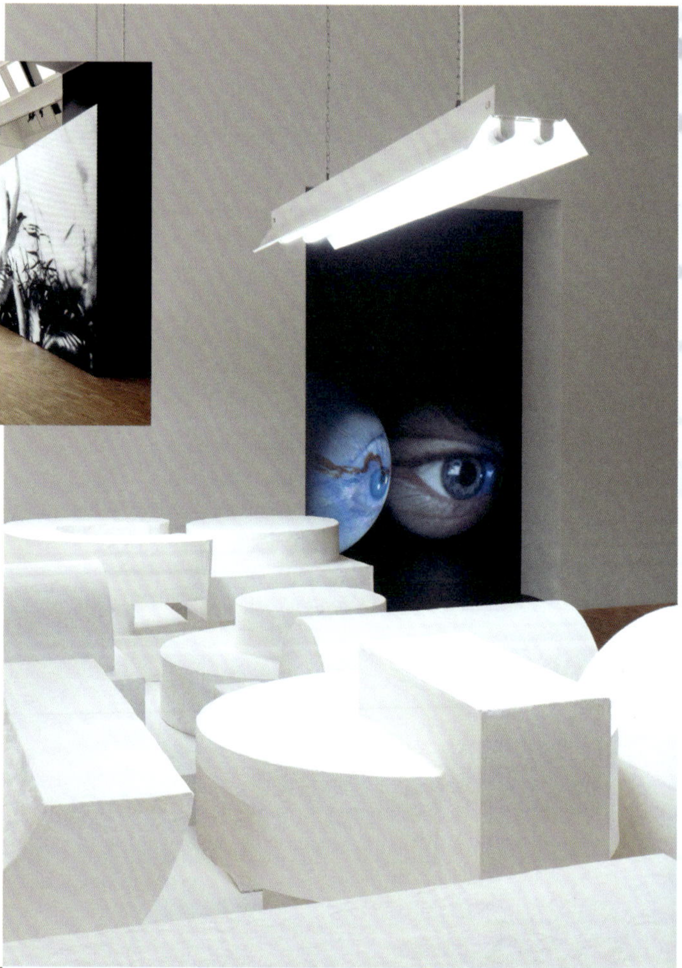

Absalon, *Propositions d'habitations*, 1990, and Tony Oursler, *Mirror Maze (Dead Eyes Live)*, 2003
FC Collections (1990 and 2003)

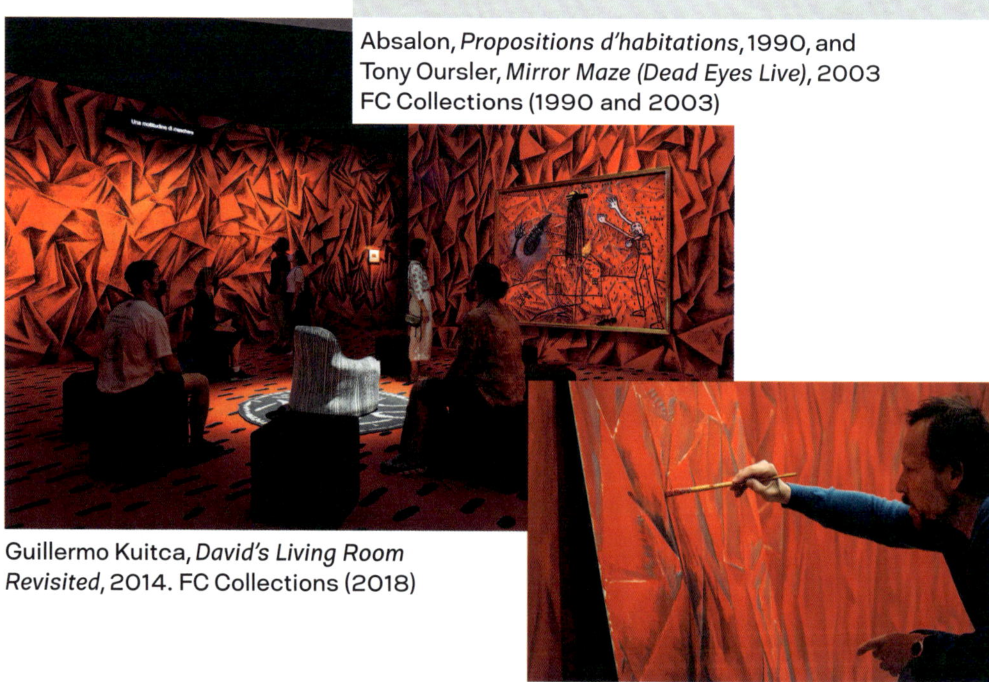

Guillermo Kuitca, *David's Living Room Revisited*, 2014. FC Collections (2018)

Guillermo Kuitca during the exhibition's installation

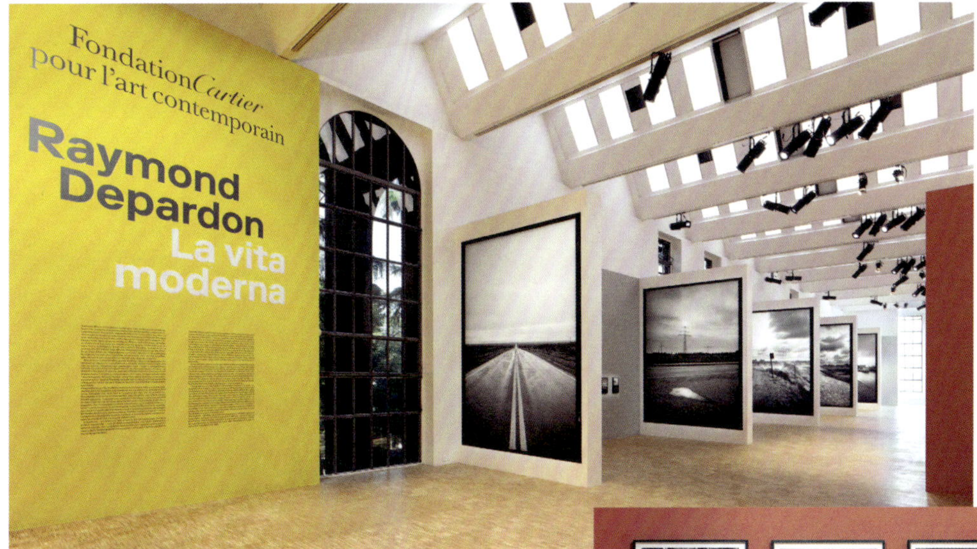

With eight series and two films,
La vita moderna was Raymond Depardon's
largest solo exhibition, produced
in collaboration with Jean-Michel Alberola.

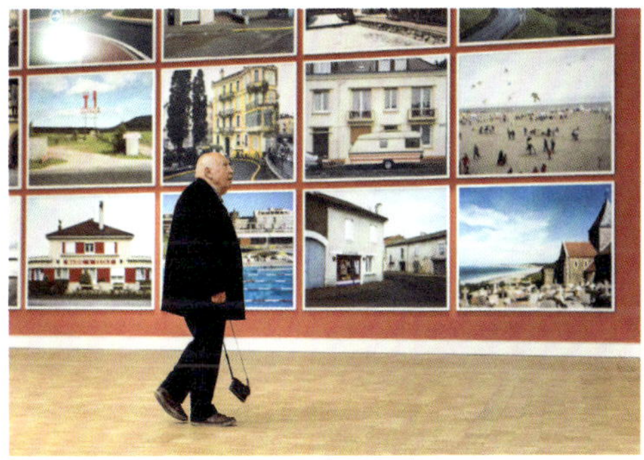

Raymond Depardon, *La France*, 2008
FC Collections (2013)

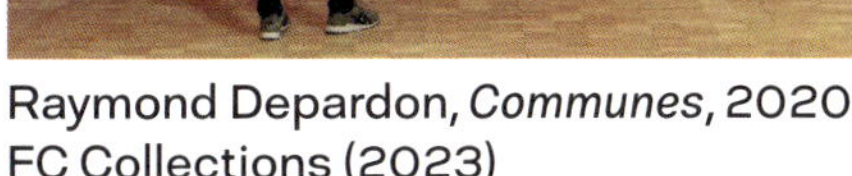

Raymond Depardon, *Communes*, 2020
FC Collections (2023)

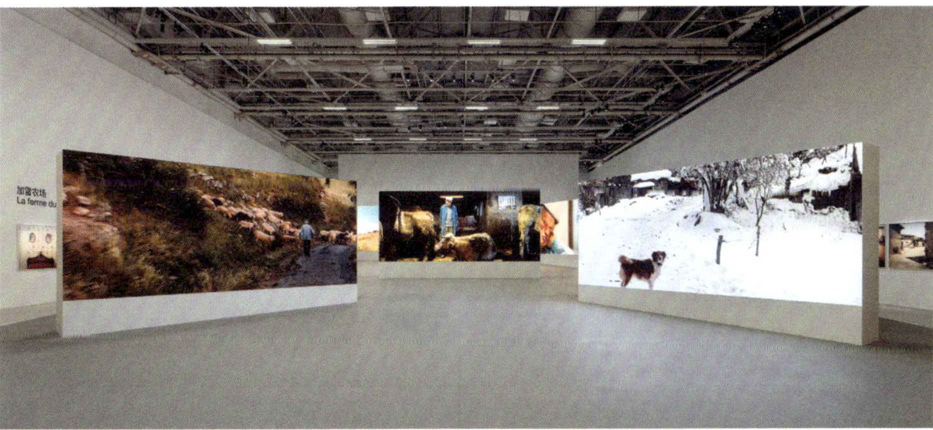

Two years later, the exhibition was presented at the Power Station of Art in Shanghai.

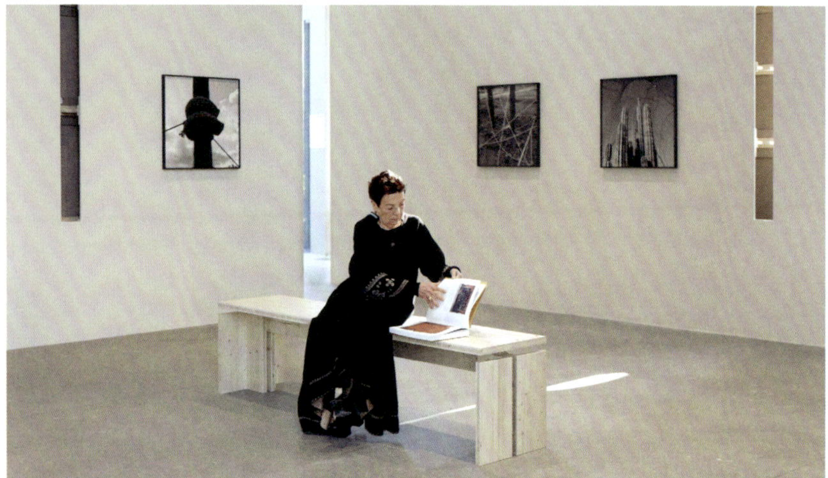

Heliotropo 37 featured over 200 photographs by Graciela Iturbide, from the most iconic to the most recent, including a color series specially taken for the exhibition. The photographer in the exhibition spaces, with the scenography designed by her son, architect Mauricio Rocha.

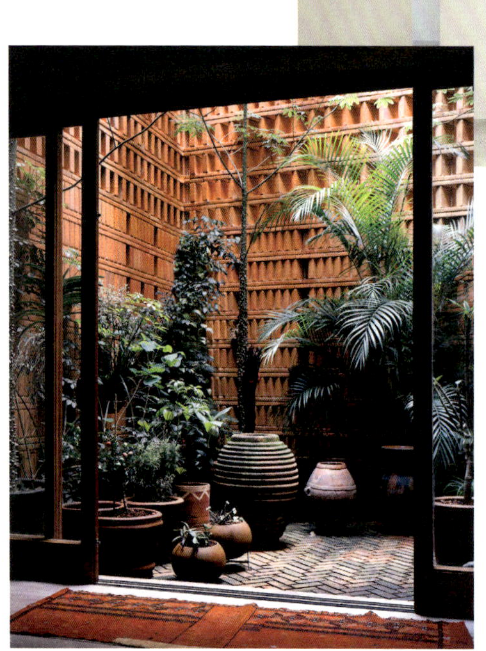

A series of photographs taken by Pablo López Luz reveal the house and studio of Graciela Iturbide.

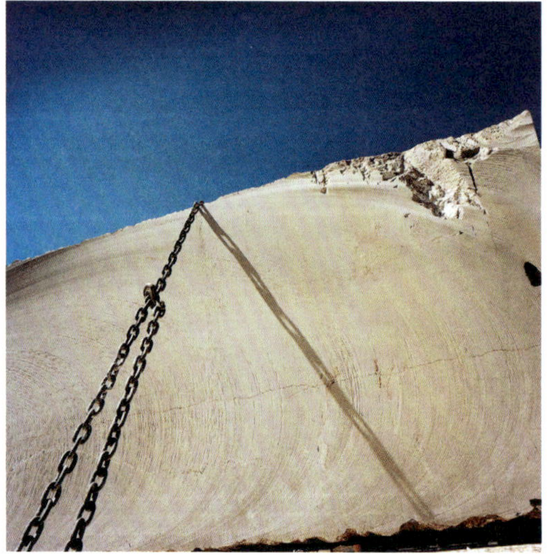

Graciela Iturbide, *Piedras, Tecali, Puebla*, 2021
FC Collections (2022)

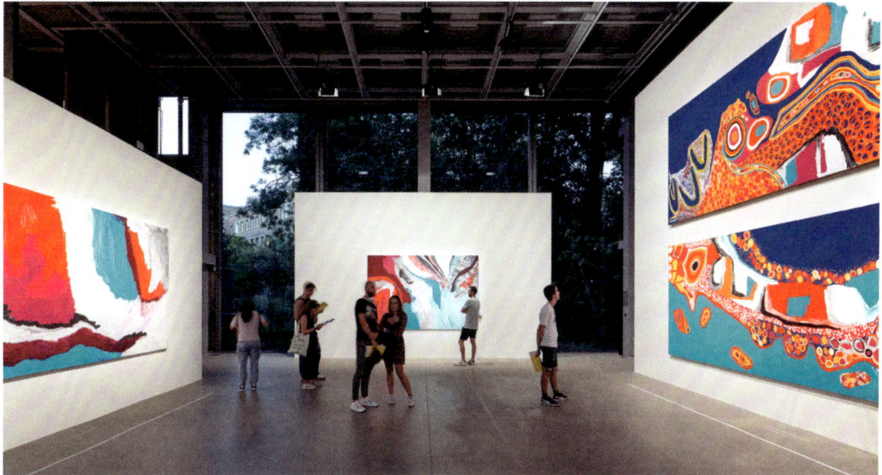

The Fondation Cartier hosted the first solo exhibition of indigenous artist Mirdidingkingathi Juwarnda Sally Gabori outside Australia, featuring some 30 monumental paintings.

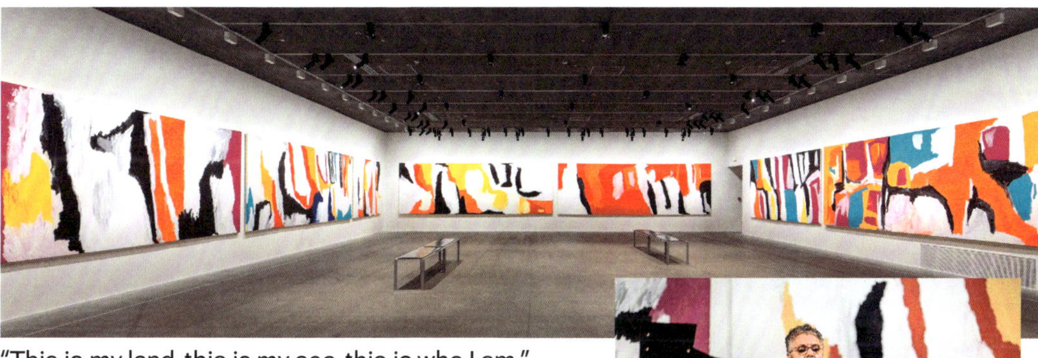

"This is my land, this is my sea, this is who I am."
Mirdidingkingathi Juwarnda Sally Gabori

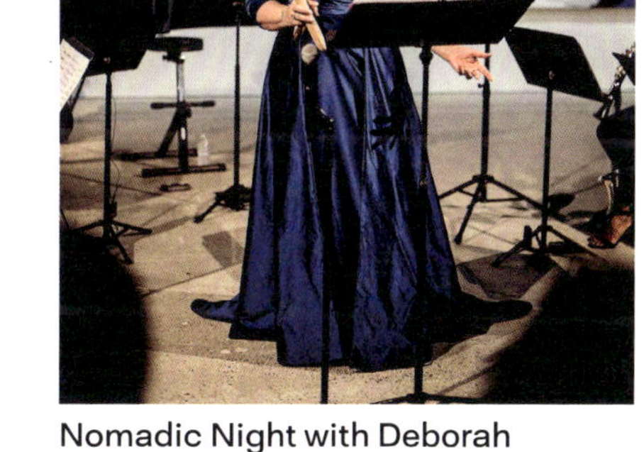

Nomadic Night with Deborah Cheetham, *Songs of Belonging*, July 4, 2022

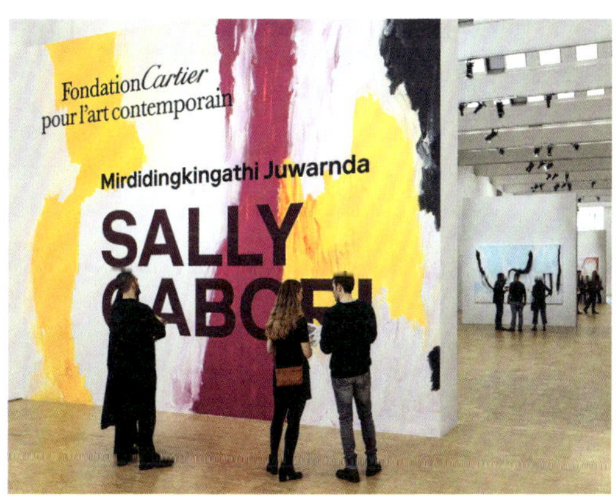

In 2023, Sally Gabori's works were exhibited at Triennale Milano.

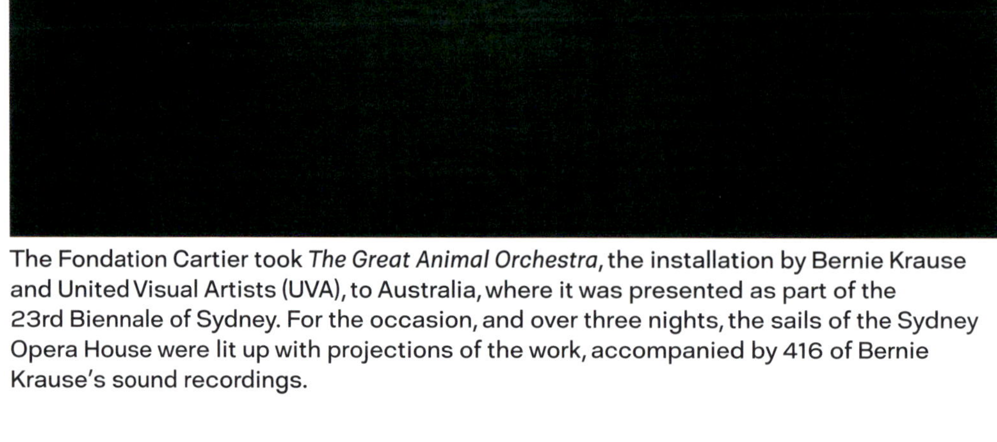

The Fondation Cartier took *The Great Animal Orchestra*, the installation by Bernie Krause and United Visual Artists (UVA), to Australia, where it was presented as part of the 23rd Biennale of Sydney. For the occasion, and over three nights, the sails of the Sydney Opera House were lit up with projections of the work, accompanied by 416 of Bernie Krause's sound recordings.

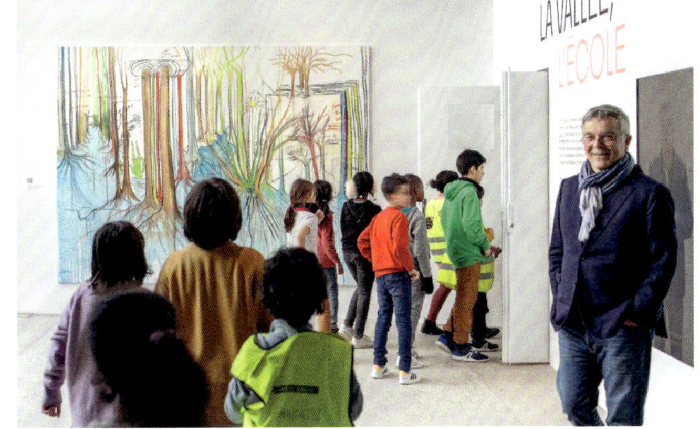

"I have always considered my canvases to be like classroom blackboards. Mine offer other worlds, whether possible or impossible. In this exhibition, I chose to install my works instead of blackboards in this ideal school setting." Fabrice Hyber
Fabrice Hyber, *Réinvention de la forêt*, 2022

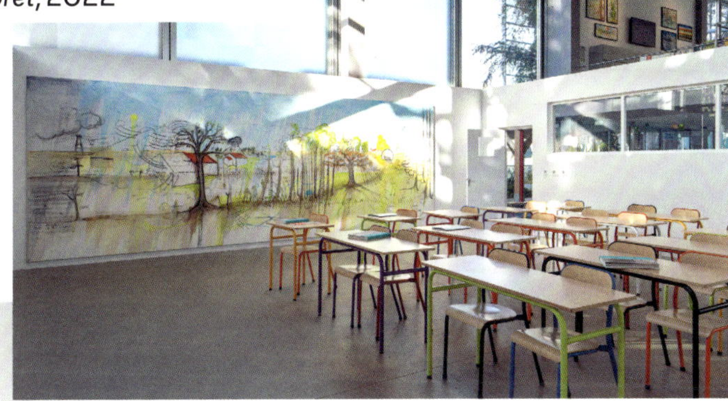

Fabrice Hyber, *La Serrie, paysage biographique de mes parents*, 2022

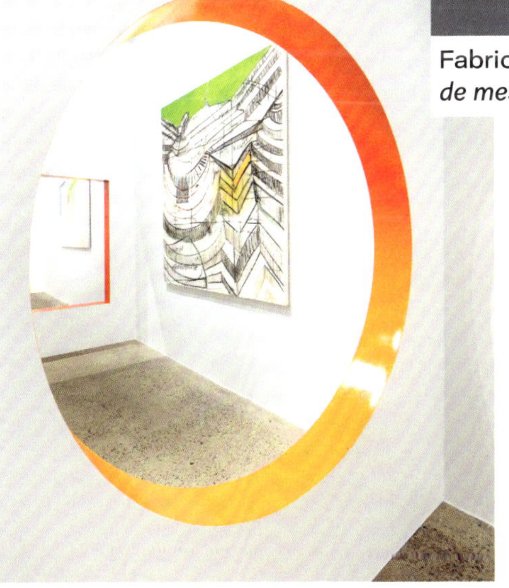

Fabrice Hyber, *Migration impossible*, 2006

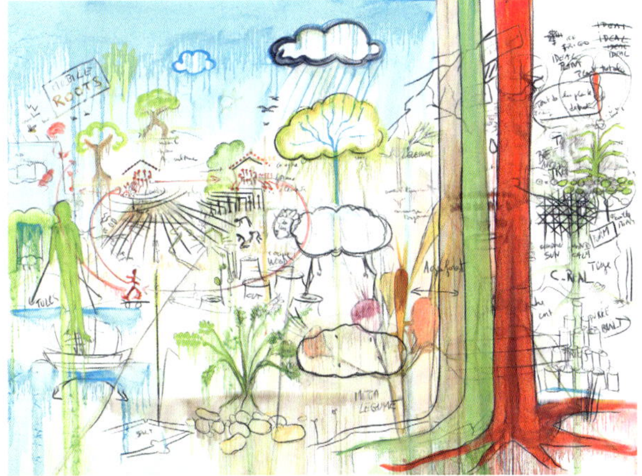

Fabrice Hyber, *L'Invention de l'agriculture*, 2022
FC Collections (2023)

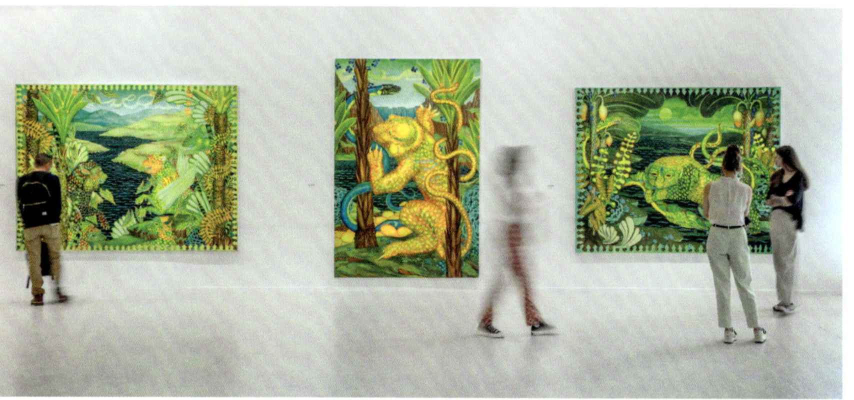

Presented at Le Tripostal in Lille, this exhibition brought together over 250 works and invited the public to look and to listen, and so to consider nonhuman life as our equals, part of the vast shared world of living beings.
Bruno Novelli, *Animalia*, *Colossal*, and *Leaõ verde*, 2021-2022

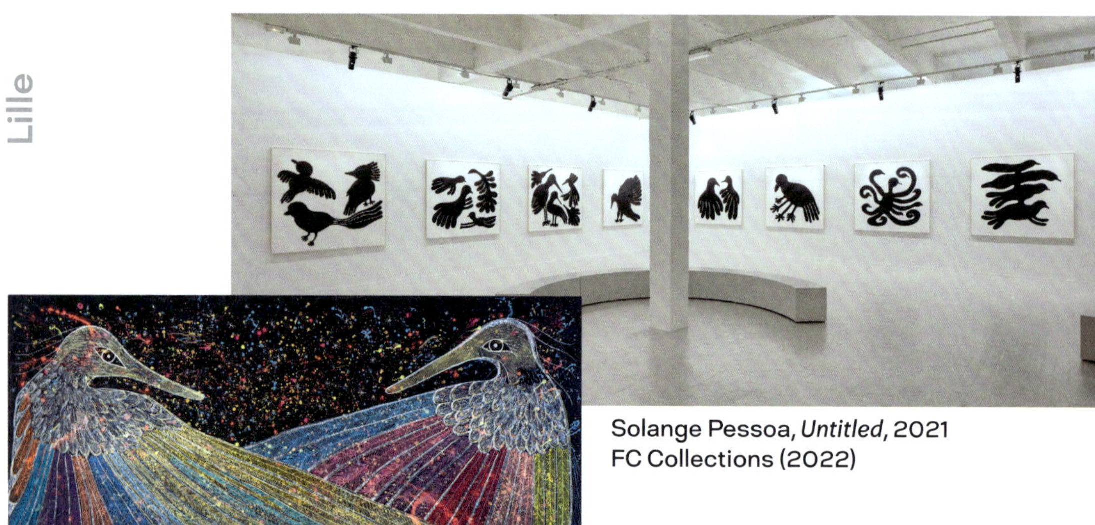

Solange Pessoa, *Untitled*, 2021
FC Collections (2022)

Jaider Esbell, *Makunaimî cria o espelho universal*, 2021. FC Collections (2023)

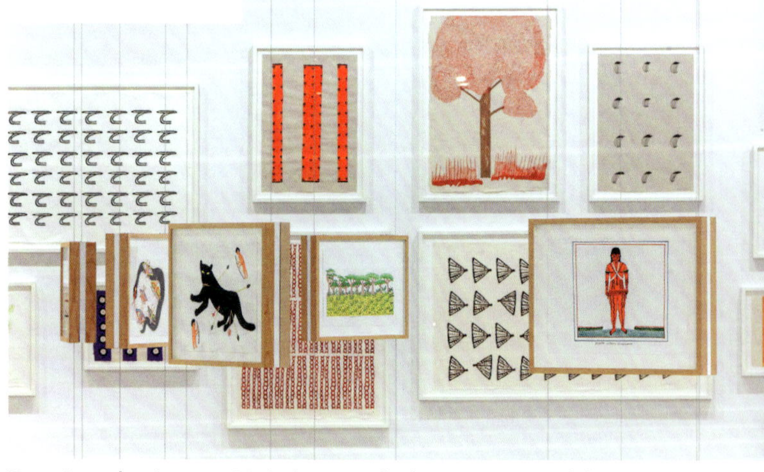

Drawings by Joseca Mokahesi and Sheroanawe Hakihiiwe, 2002-2021

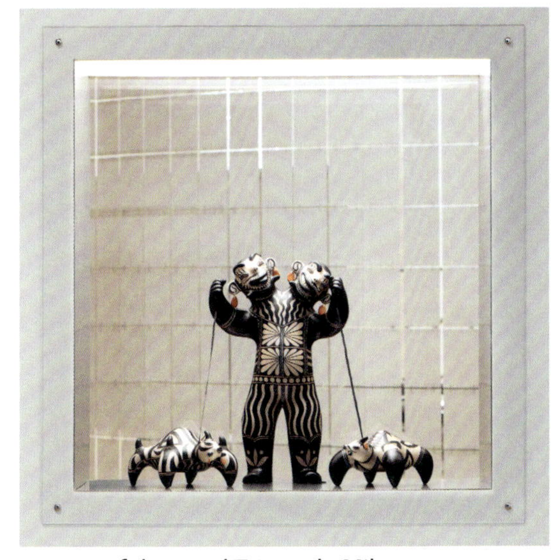

As part of the 23rd Triennale Milano International Exhibition, *Unknown Unknowns: An Introduction to Mysteries*, the exhibition *Mondo Reale* was designed as a return to the real world, a window open to the mysteries of the world that surrounds us. The scenography was entrusted to Italian designers Formafantasma.
Virgil Ortiz, *Ring Master and Tics*, 2022
FC Collections (2023)

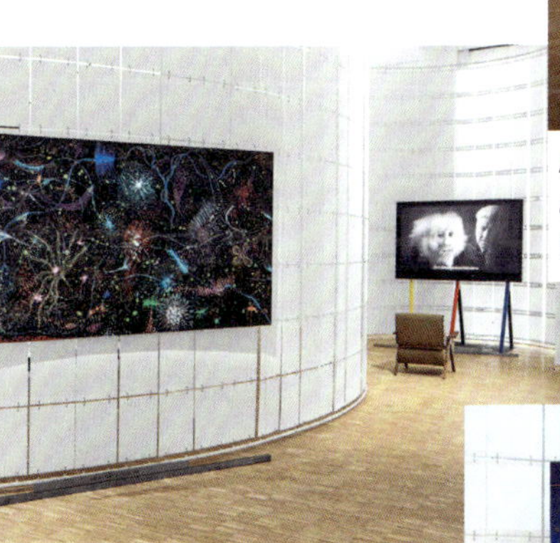

Alev Ebüzziya Siesbye, ceramics, 1997-2019, and Sho Shibuya, *Headlines*, 2020-2022
FC Collections (2023)

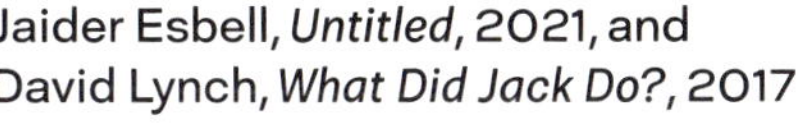

Jaider Esbell, *Untitled*, 2021, and
David Lynch, *What Did Jack Do?*, 2017

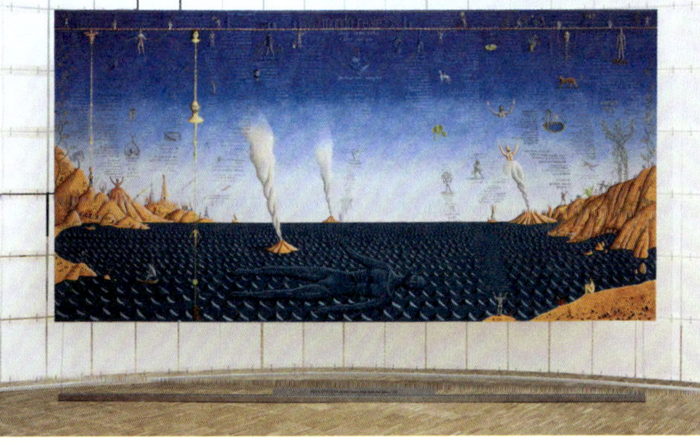

Alex Cerveny, *Mondo Reale: Stop, Look and Listen*, 2022
FC Collections (2023)

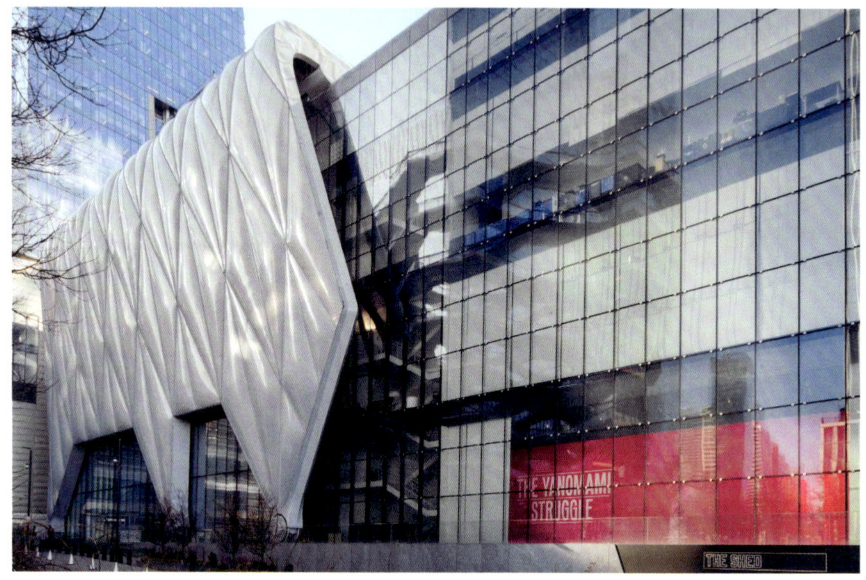

After Paris and Milan, the Fondation Cartier accompanied the Claudia Andujar exhibition *The Yanomami Struggle* to The Shed, in New York.

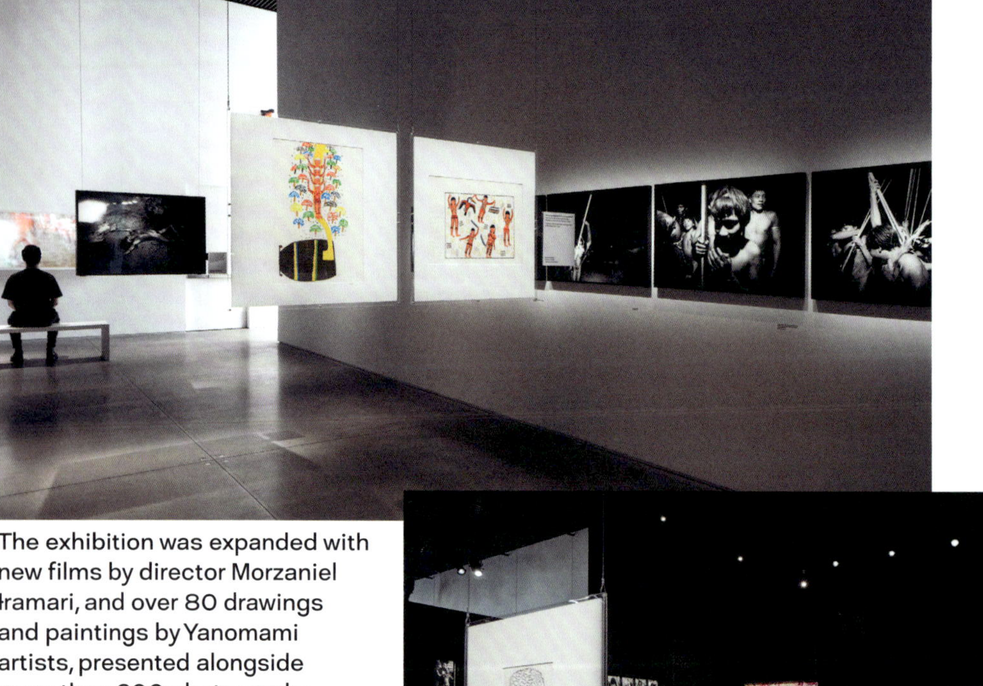

The exhibition was expanded with new films by director Morzaniel Ɨramari, and over 80 drawings and paintings by Yanomami artists, presented alongside more than 200 photographs by Claudia Andujar.

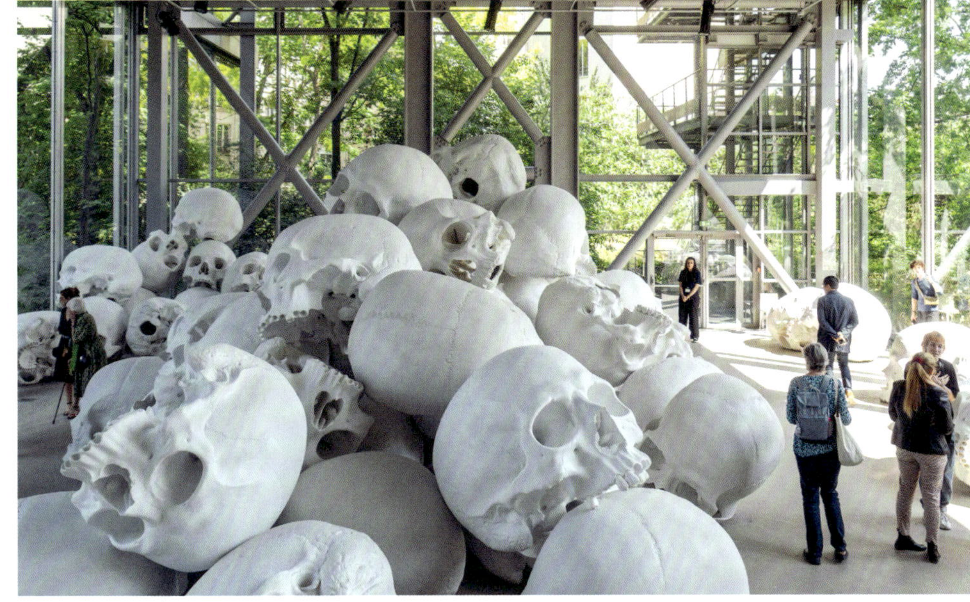

Ron Mueck, *Mass*, 2017

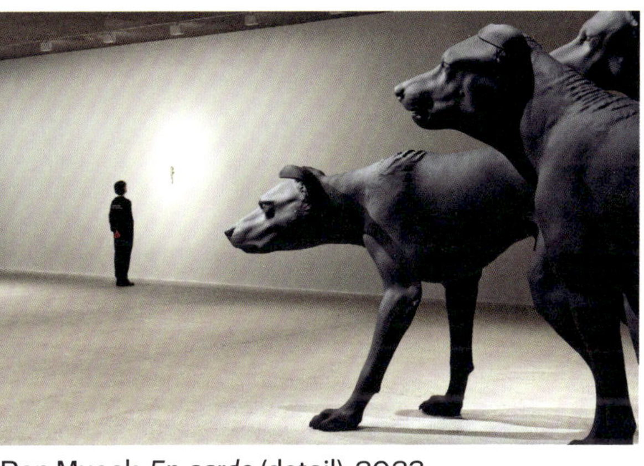

Ron Mueck, *En garde* (detail), 2023

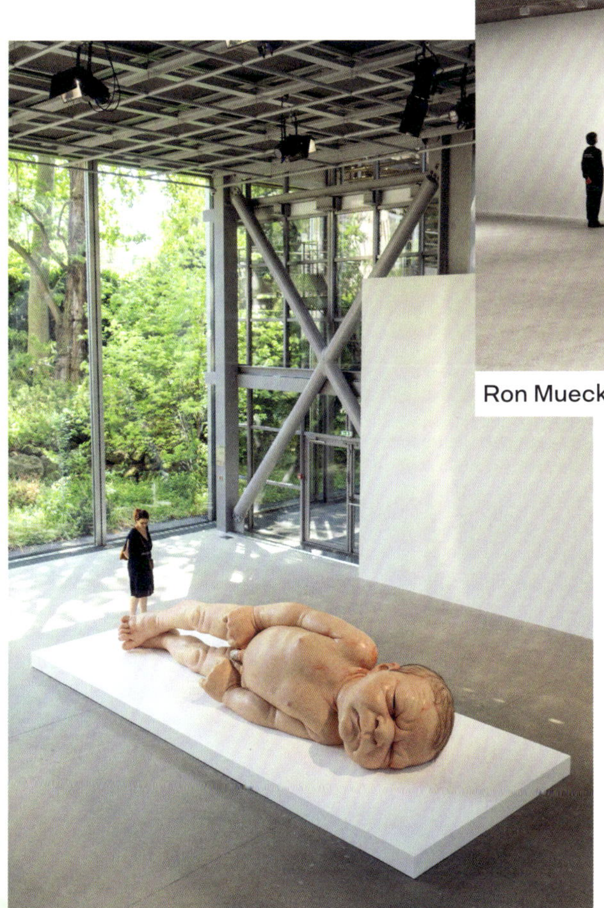

Ron Mucok, *A Girl*, 2006

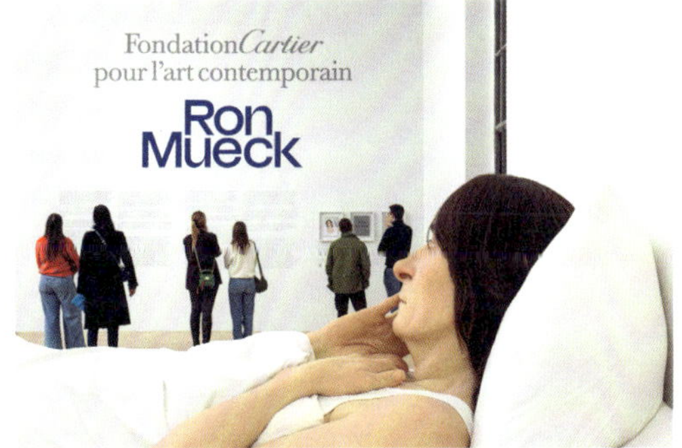

After Paris, Ron Mueck's exhibition
was presented at Triennale Milano
in December 2023. Ron Mueck, *In Bed*
(detail), 2005. FC Collections (2006)

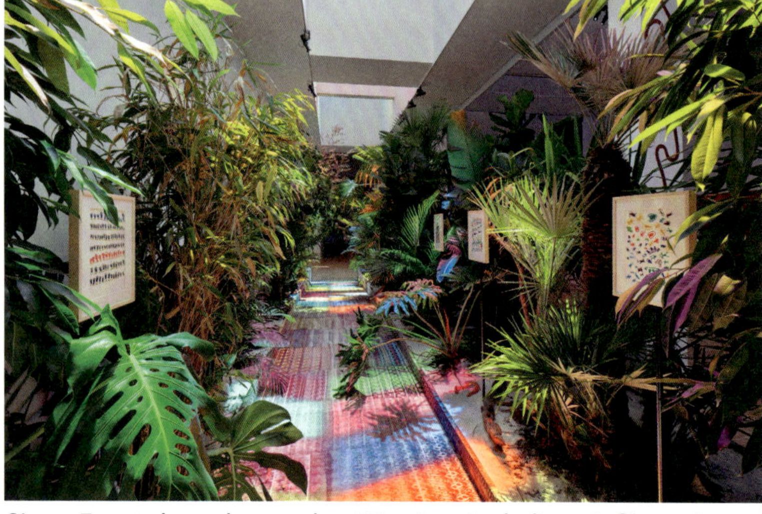

Siamo Foresta brought together 27 artists, including six filmmakers, with an original exhibition design by Brazilian artist Luiz Zerbini.

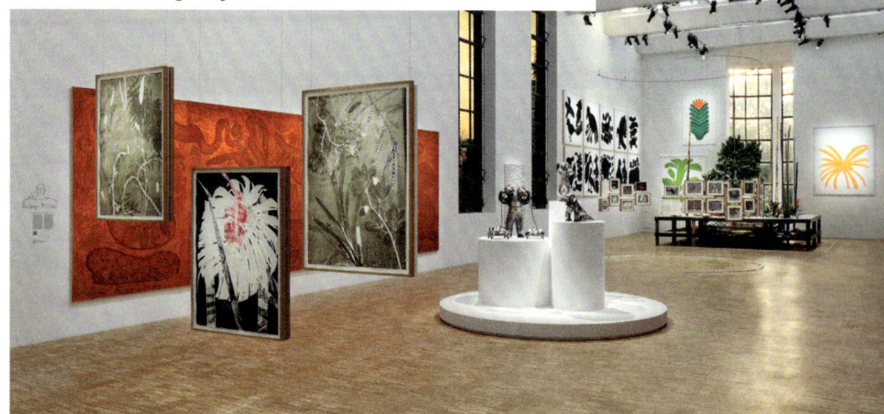

The exhibition was the result of a dialogue "from forest to forest" between indigenous artists from New Mexico to the Paraguayan Chaco to the Amazon, and also featured the works of nonindigenous artists from Brazil, China, Colombia, and France.

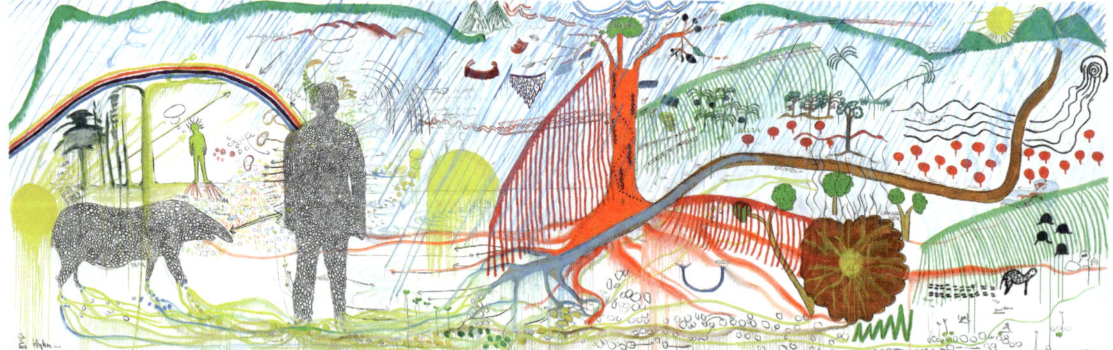

In April 2023, Fabrice Hyber invited the Yanomami artist Sheroanawe Hakihiiwe to his Valley in the Vendée for several days. Together, the two artists created several works, destined for the exhibition *Siamo Foresta*. Sheroanawe Hakihiiwe and Fabrice Hyber, *Untitled*, 2023

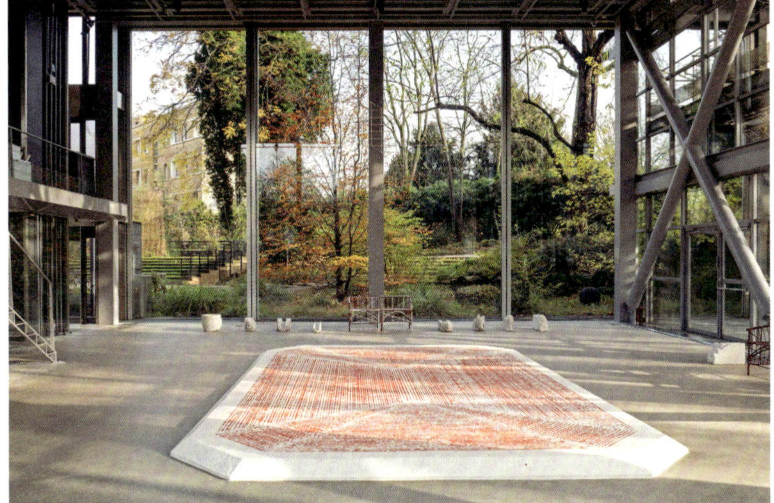

Founder of Studio Mumbai, Indian architect Bijoy Jain created
an exhibition specially for the Fondation Cartier that could be
lived as a physical and emotional experience, a space of dream
and contemplation in dialogue with Jean Nouvel's building.

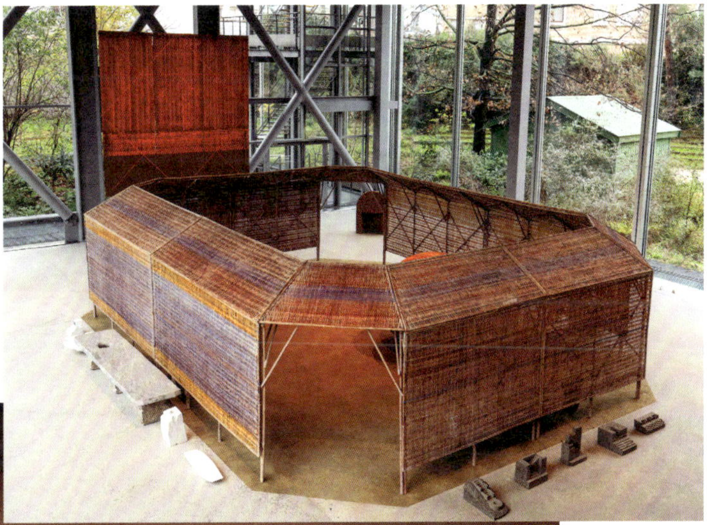

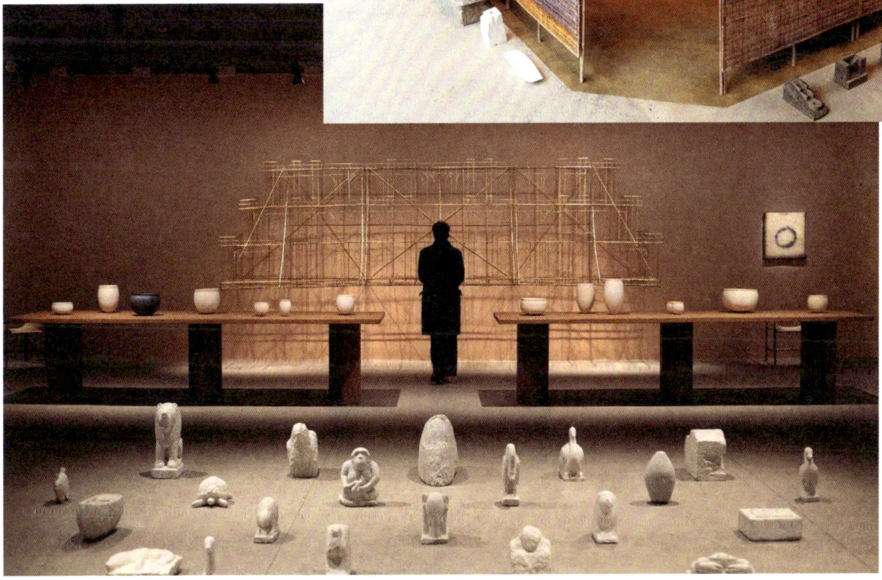

In the basement, Bijoy Jain's creations entered into a dialogue with
the ceramic works of Alev Ebüzziya Siesbye and drawings by Hu Liu.

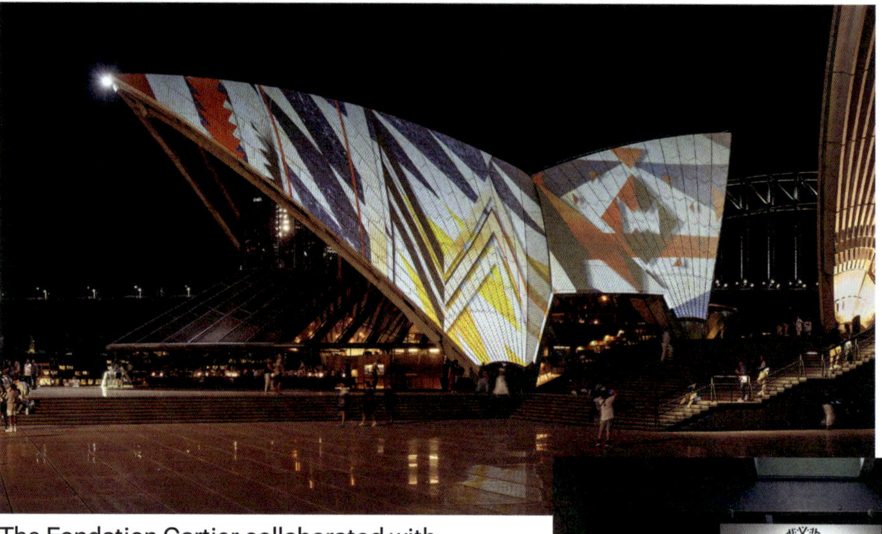

The Fondation Cartier collaborated with the Biennale of Sydney for its 24th edition and presented fourteen First Nations artists. Projection on the sails of the Sydney Opera House: Nikau Hindin, *Badu Gili: Celestial*, 2024

Mangala Bai Maravi, *Baiga Godna Indian Tribe*, 2024

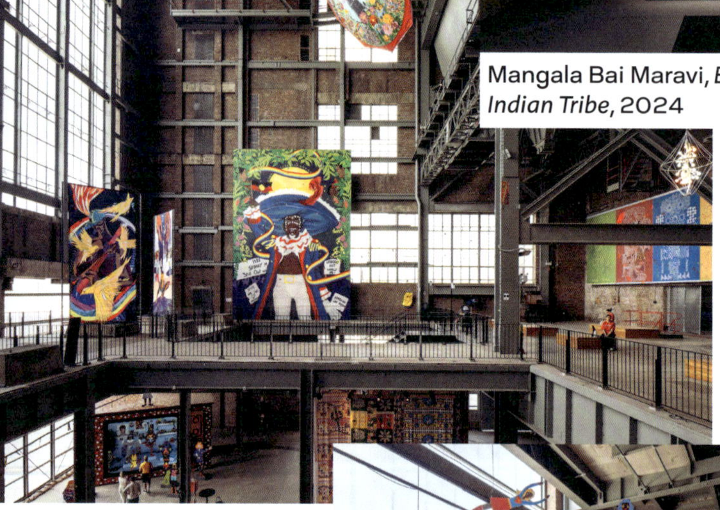

Dylan Mooney, *Malcolm Cole – Larger Than Life*, 2024

Kaylene Whiskey, *Kaylene TV*, 2023

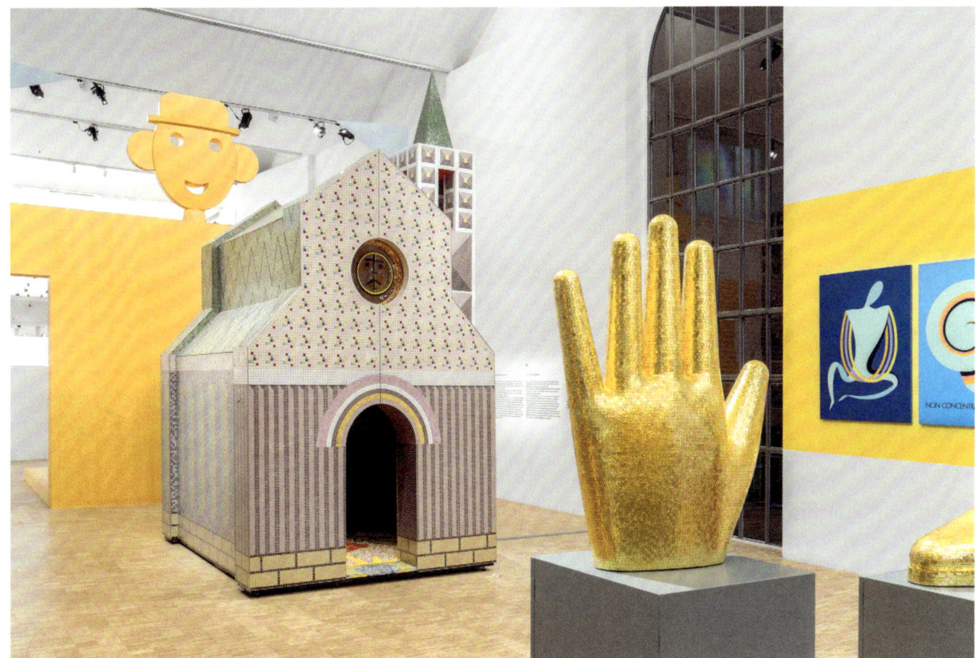

Alessandro Mendini, *Petite cathédrale*, 2002, FC Collections (2002) and
Collezione di mobili per uomo: Guanto, 1997

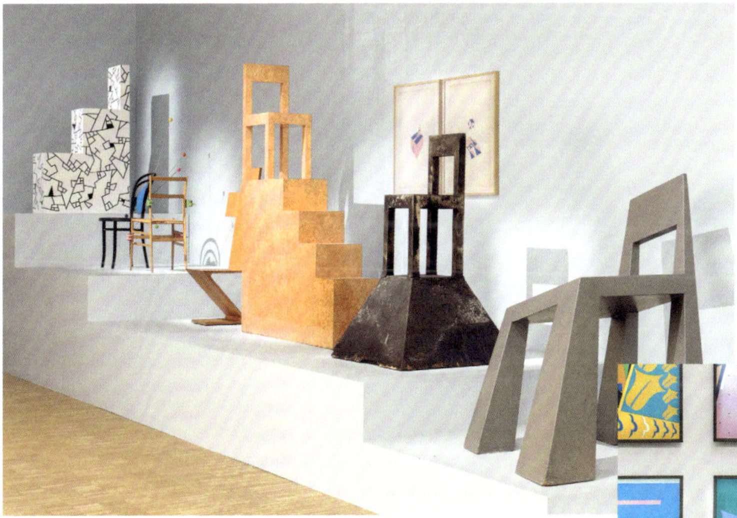

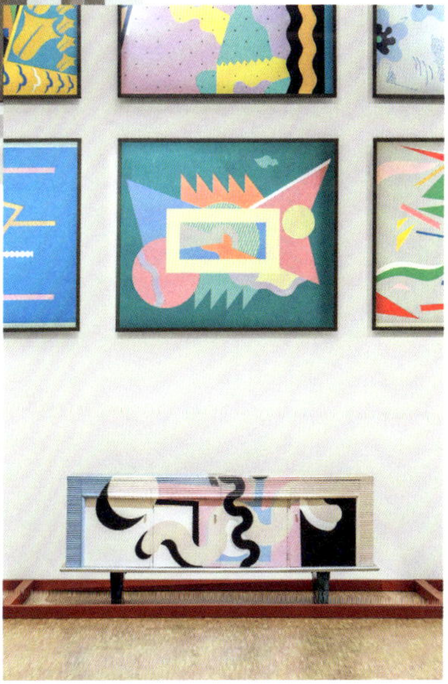

In 2024, Triennale Milano and Fondation Cartier
presented the exhibition *Io sono un drago. The True
Story of Alessandro Mendini*, a large retrospective
of the work of the Italian architect, designer,
artist, and theorist.

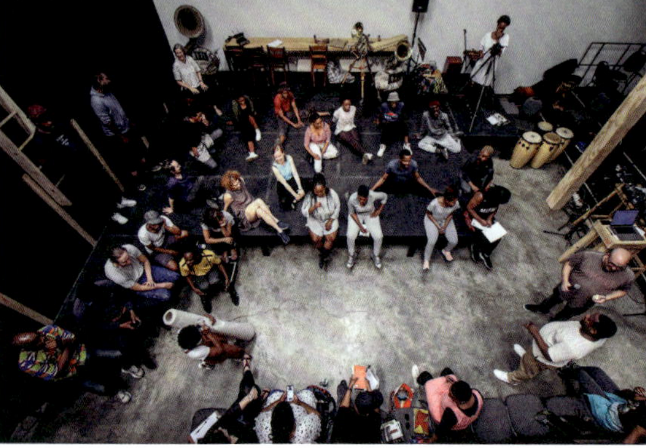

The Fondation Cartier invited The Centre for
the Less Good Idea, created by William Kentridge
and Bronwyn Lace, for a week of workshops,
performances, concerts, and encounters
with some 30 artists from South Africa,
Benin, Belgium, Holland, Austria, and France.

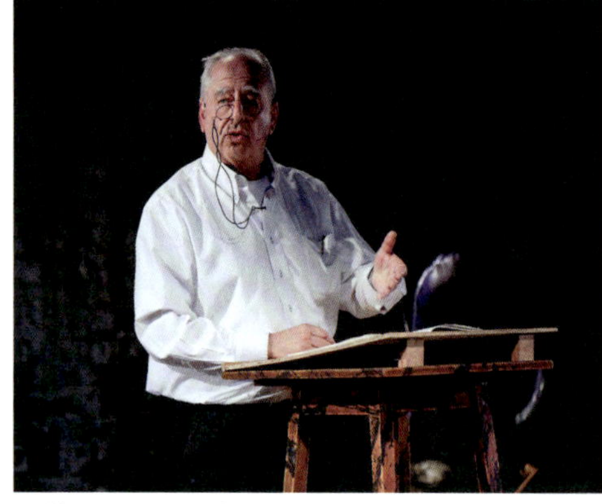

William Kentridge

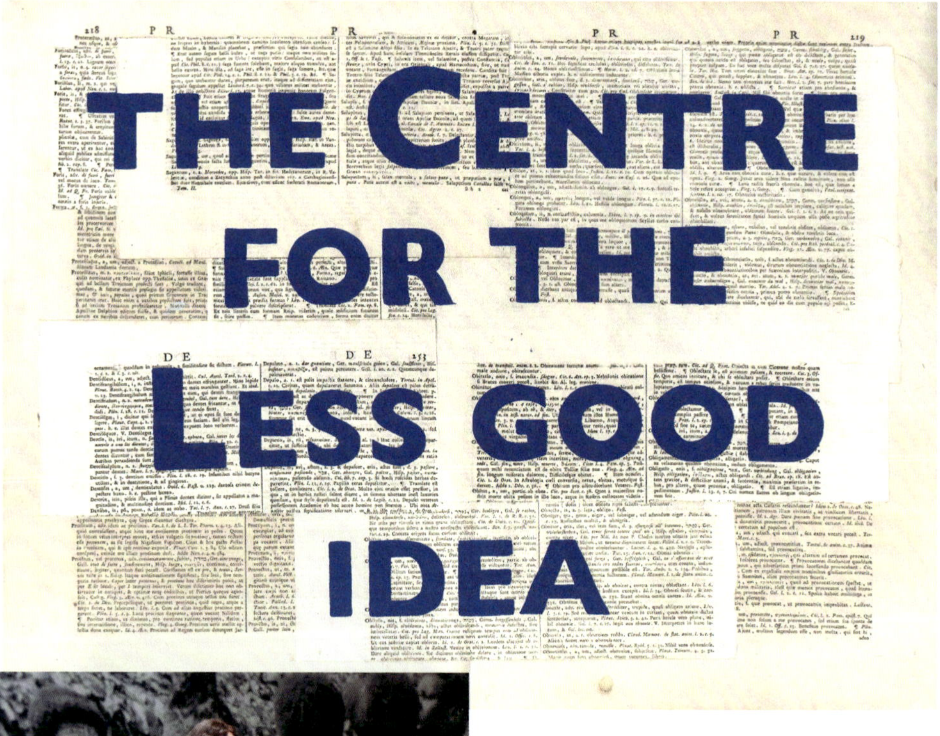

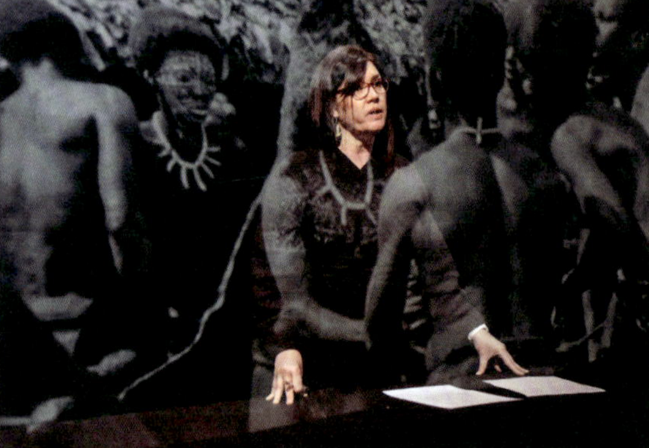

Bronwyn Lace

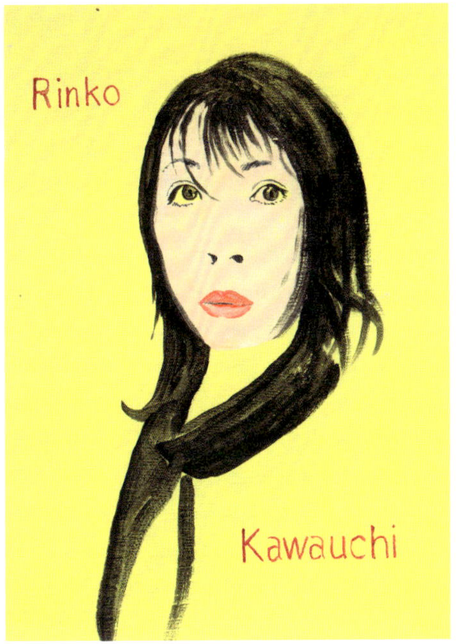

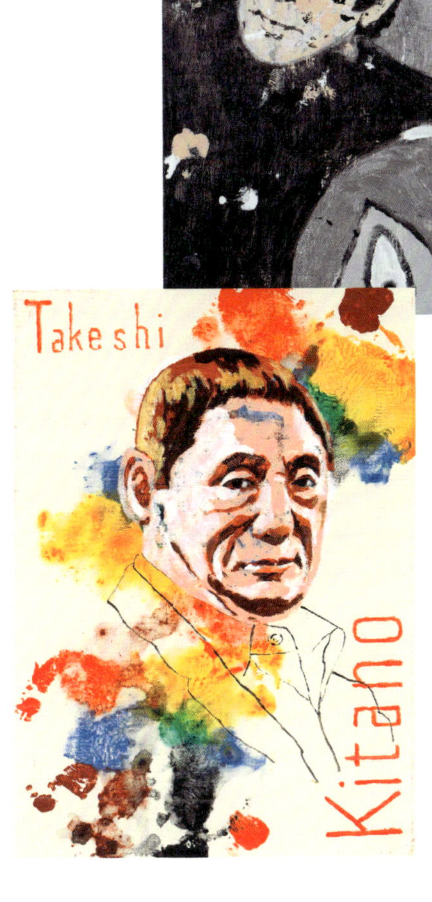

The Fondation Cartier presented
a selection of works at the Tokyo National
Museum by the Japanese artists it has
exhibited over the years. Tadanori Yokoo,
portraits of Rinko Kawauchi, Daido
Moriyama, Takeshi Kitano, Hiroshi Sugimoto,
Tatsuo Miyajima, and Issey Miyake,
2014–2018. FC Collections (2018)

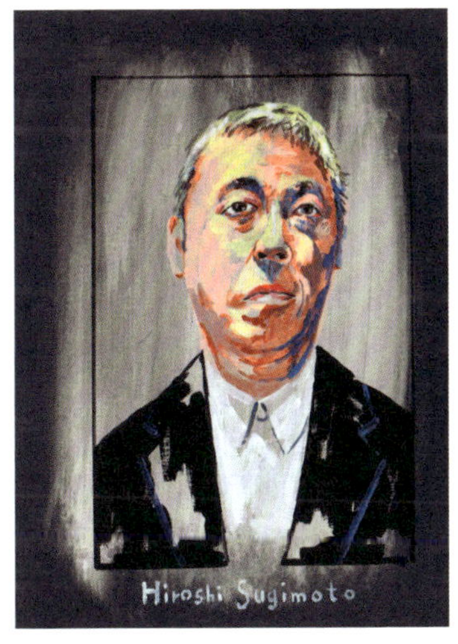

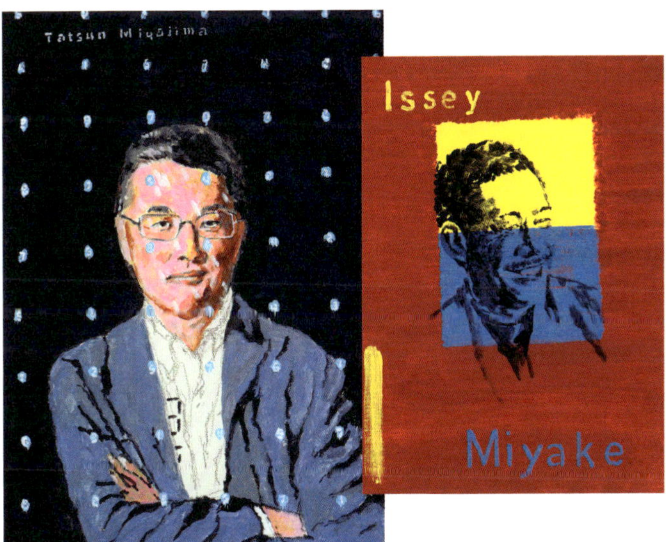

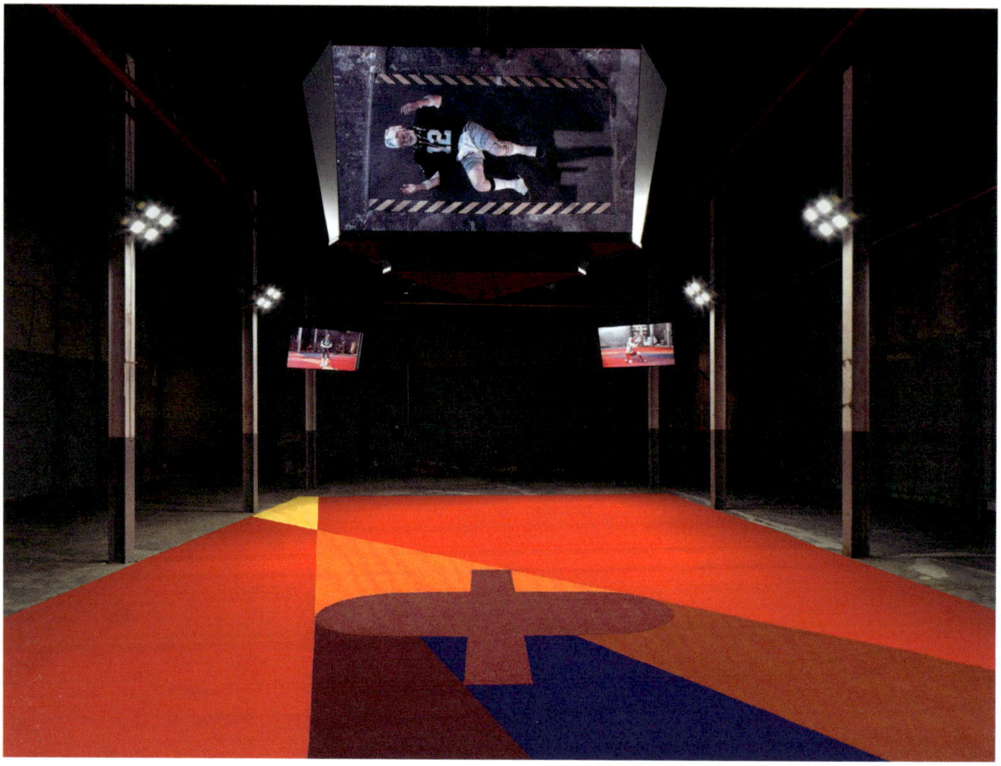

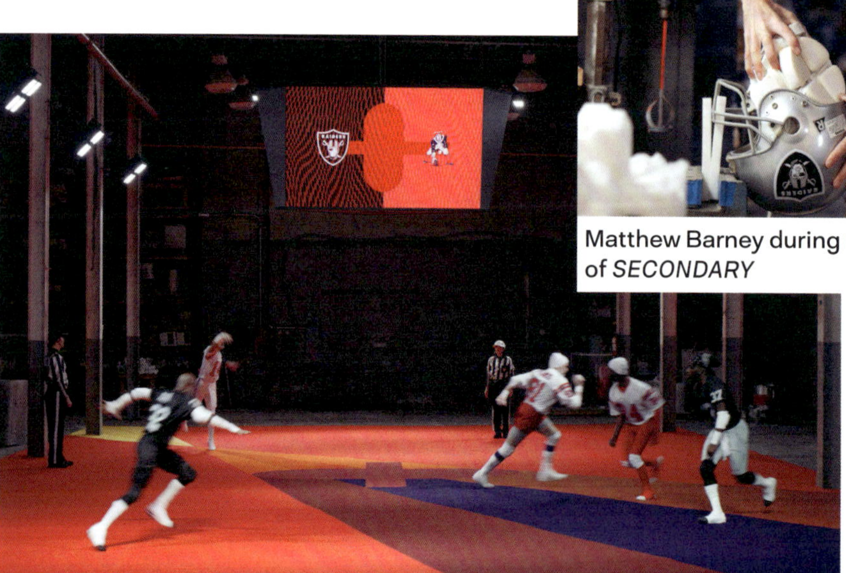

Thirty years after the presentation of Matthew Barney's first film, *CREMASTER 4* (1994), which it coproduced, the Fondation Cartier presented *SECONDARY* (2023), the artist's new video installation.

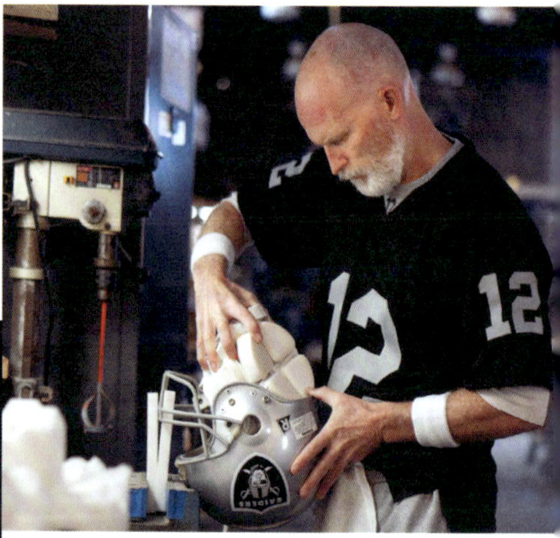

Matthew Barney during the filming of *SECONDARY*

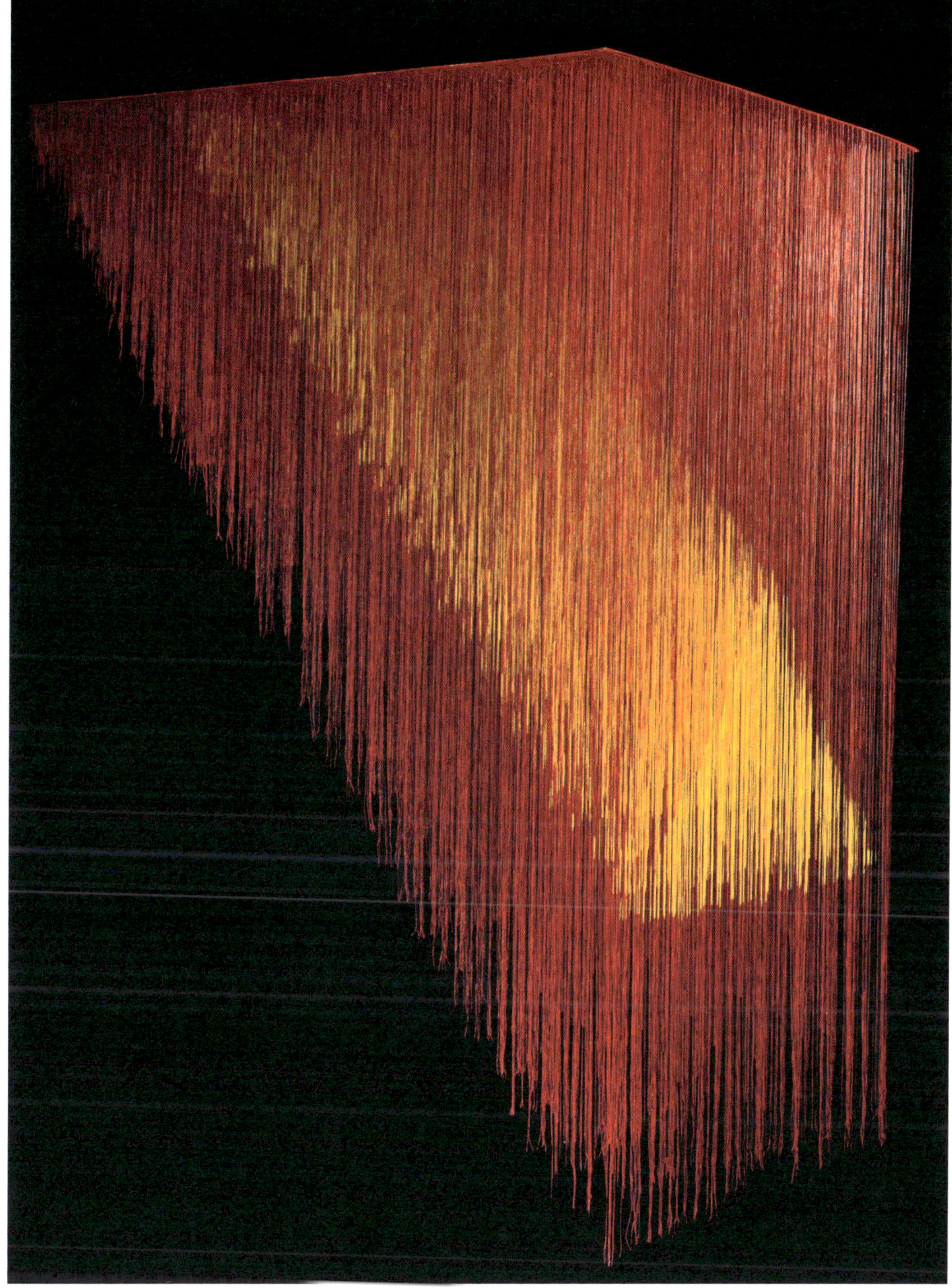

The first large retrospective in Europe of Olga de Amaral brought together
a large group of works by the Colombian artist, a major figure on the fiber art scene.
Olga de Amaral, *Bruma G,* 2013. FC Collections (2019)

*A Maison like ours, enduring
in its support of creation,
has a responsibility to art.
We want to fully assume that responsibility.*

*The past obliges us to do so.
The future compels us to do so.*

*Alain Dominique Perrin
Jouy-en-Josas, October 20, 1984*

Production Director
Lisa Seantier

Exhibitions Production Manager
Camille Chenet

Exhibitions Production Coordinators
Beatriz Forti
Mathilde Hervé

Exhibitions Technical Coordinator
Vincent Lecerf

Exhibitions Registrar Manager
Paola Sisterna

Exhibitions Registrars
Alexandre Bagnod
Élise Ventura

Gardener
Metin Sivri

Buildings Director
Philippe Lê

Communication and
Visitors Department Director
Naïa Sore

Deputy Director for Communication
Julie Auriol

Public Relations Manager
Pauline Duclos

Internal Communications
and VIP Treatment Manager
Johanne Legris

Media – Partnerships Manager
Christel Bortoli

File Management Coordinator
Eleonora Vitali

Digital Projects Coordinator
Tatiana Sanichanh

Digital Communications Coordinator
Valentin Guérin

Editorial communication Coordinator
Laure Alègre

Digital Producer
Solène Dupont-Delestraint

Press Manager
Matthieu Simonnet

Press Officer
Sophie Lawani-Wesley

Visitors Department Director
Tanguy Pelletier

Head of Ticketing and Booking
Élisa Pujol

Cultural Mediation Coordinator
Mariangela De Toni

Administrative and Financial Director
Caroline Valentin

Administrative and Financial Manager
Hélène Lornac

Administrative and Financial Controller
Éloïse Gineste

Financial Controller
Myriam Nguyen

Accounting and Payroll Manager
Alain Courteau

General Accountant
Jean-Paul Vantorre

Human Resources Director
Céline Riou

Human Resources and Workplace
Environment Coordinator
Aurore Guilbaud

Safety and Security Director
Sébastien Albertini

Bookshops Director
Vanja Merhar

Bookseller
Marha Jarton

Publication

The title *Voir venir, Venir voir* (Foreseeing, Seeing) comes from an expression used by Paul Virilio during the preparation of the exhibition *Native Land, Stop Eject* (2008). This publication is another opportunity for the Fondation Cartier to celebrate this great philosopher and friend, with whom it collaborated so closely.

Since 1984, the history of the Fondation Cartier pour l'art contemporain has been written by a community of artists, thinkers, scientists, close friends, and with all those who have worked to make this story so unique.

Thank you to all those, who through their help, advice, and support, have participated in creating this publication.

Alain Dominique Perrin and the Fondation Cartier pour l'art contemporain extend their warmest thanks to the members of the historical committee for their participation in the conception of this book:
Marie-Claude Beaud
Hervé Chandès
Michel Guten
Richard Lepeu
Jean de Loisy
Jean Nouvel
Pierre Rainero
Ute Schrader
and especially Christine Borgoltz Halff for her valuable input.

An immense thank you to Emanuele Coccia for his text *Voir venir*.

Graphic Design
deValence, Montreuil:
Alexandre Dimos and Ghislain Triboulet, with Alex Chavot and François Dézafit

Editorial team
Adeline Pelletier, Heritage Director

Pierre-Édouard Couton, Editorial Manager

Bérengère Gouttefarde, Writing and editing (French texts)

Flore Langlade and Raphaëlle Agimont, Editorial Assistants

Rights management and contracts
Canelle Axus, Nans Méger, and Lounès Senelet-Maïté

Translation
Juliet Powys (text by Emanuele Coccia)
Emma Lingwood (other texts)

Copyediting
Bronwyn Mahoney

Photoengraving
Clément Regard, Les artisans du Regard, Paris

Production
Camille Desproges, Actes Sud, Arles

Printing
Nava Press, Milan

Credits

Artworks that are part of the Collections of the Fondation Cartier pour l'art contemporain are indicated by "FC Collections," followed by the date of acquisition.

p. 10: photo © ministère de la Culture – Médiathèque du Patrimoine / Daniel Boudinet / dist. RMN • **pp. 11–12:** © SBJ / Adagp, Paris, 2024, photos: RR • **p. 13:** © SBJ / Adagp, Paris, 2024, photo © Dominique Faget / AFP • **p. 14:** © SBJ / Adagp, Paris, 2024, photo © François Willemin • **p. 15:** © Arman / Adagp, Paris, 2024, photo: RR (1); © Daniel Spoerri, photo: RR (2) • **p. 16:** photos: RR • **p. 19:** photo © Laurent Maous • **p. 20:** © José-Luis Pascual • **p. 21:** photo: RR (1); © Jean Pierre Raynaud / Adagp, Paris, 2024, photo: RR (2) • **p. 22:** photo: RR • **p. 23:** photo © Ling Fei (1, 4); photo © André Morain, Paris (2, 8); photo: RR (3, 6); photo © Jérôme Schlomoff (5); photo © Claude Gaspari (7) • **p. 24:** © Keiji Uematsu, photo: RR (1); © François Morellet / Adagp, Paris, 2024, photo: RR (2) • **p. 25:** © Jean Pierre Raynaud / Adagp, Paris, 2024, photo © ministère de la Culture – Médiathèque du Patrimoine / Daniel Boudinet / dist. RMN • **pp. 26–27:** © Giuseppe Penone / Adagp, Paris, 2024, photo © Florian Kleinefenn • **p. 27:** © The Estate of Joan Mitchell, photo © Jacqueline Hyde • **p. 28:** © Robert Combas / Adagp, Paris, 2024, photo © Patricia Canino (1); © Carlos Kusnir / Adagp, Paris, 2024, photo: RR (2) • **p. 29:** photo: RR (1); photo © Hugues Colson (2) • **p. 30:** © Présence Panchounette, photo: RR (1); photo © Jean-François Leroy (2) • **p. 31:** © Max Bill, photo: RR • **pp. 32–34:** photos: RR • **p. 37:** photos: RR (1, 2); photo © Luc Boegly (3); photo © Andrea Rossetti (4) • **p. 39:** © Jean Nouvel / Adagp, Paris, 2024, photo © Georges Fessy (1); © Jean Nouvel / Adagp, Paris, 2024, photo © Luc Boegly (2); photo Luc Boegly (3) • **p. 40:** photo © André Morain, Paris • **p. 42:** photo © Herb Ritts Foundation • **p. 44:** © SBJ / Adagp, Paris, 2024, photo: RR • **p. 45:** © SBJ / Adagp, Paris, 2024, photo Claude Gaspari • **p. 46:** © SBJ / Adagp, Paris, 2024, photo © Ling Fei • **p. 47:** photo © Chris Gelken / Marianne Kokkinis (1); © SBJ / Adagp, Paris, 2024, photo: RR (2) • **p. 48:** © SBJ / Adagp, Paris, 2024, photo © Luc Boegly • **p. 52:** © Estate of Lebbeus Woods, photos © Philippe Ruault • **p. 55:** © T.N.GON Co., Ltd., photo © Grégoire Eloy, Tendance Floue (1); photo © André Morin (2); © Jean Paul Gaultier, photo © Stefano Pandini (3); photo © ministère de la Culture – Médiathèque du Patrimoine / Daniel Boudinet / dist. RMN (4) • **p. 56:** © Cyprien Tokoudagba, © Pierre Bodo, photo © Luc Boegly • **p. 57:** photo © Olivier Ouadah (1); © Freddy Mamani, photo © Thomas Salva / Lumento (2); photo © Olivier Ouadah (3) • **p. 61:** © Nancy Rubins, photo © André Morin • **p. 63:** © Conner Family Trust, San Francisco / Adagp, Paris 2024, photo © André Morin • **p. 64:** © Artavazd Pelechian, photo © Luc Boegly • **p. 67:** © Diller Scofidio + Renfro, Mark Hansen, Laura Kurgan and Ben Rubin, in collaboration with Robert Gerard Pietrusko and Stewart Smith, photo © Luc Boegly • **p. 69:** © Cai Guo-Qiang, photos Courtesy Cai Studio • **p. 71:** photo © Marie Clérin • **p. 73:** © Diller Scofidio + Renfro, Mark Hansen, Laura Kurgan and Ben Rubin, in collaboration with Robert Gerard Pietrusko and Stewart Smith • **p. 74:** © Estate of Lebbeus Woods, photo © AFP / Daniel Janin • **pp. 76–77:** © Fondation Cartier pour l'art contemporain • **pp. 78–79:** © Diller Scofidio + Renfro, Mark Hansen, Laura Kurgan and Ben Rubin, in collaboration with Robert Gerard Pietrusko and Stewart Smith, photo © Luc Boegly • **p. 80:** © Estate of Lebbeus Woods, photo © Philippe Ruault • **p. 82:** © Jean Nouvel / Adagp, Paris, 2024, photo © Luc Boegly • **p. 83:** © Jean Nouvel / Adagp, Paris, 2024, photo © Eric Sander • **p. 84:** © Jean Nouvel / Adagp, Paris, 2024, photo © Luc Boegly (1); © Jean Nouvel / Adagp, Paris, 2024, photo © Eric Sander (2) • **p. 85:** photo © Ambroise Tézenas • **p. 86:** photo © Eric Sander • **p. 87:** © Giuseppe Penone / Adagp, Paris, 2024, photo © Luc Boegly (1); photo © Ambroise Tézenas (2) • **p. 89:** © Jean Nouvel / Adagp, Paris, 2024, photo © Eric Sander • **p. 90:** © Jean Nouvel / Adagp, Paris, 2024, © Ron Mueck, photo © Axel Dahl • **p. 93:** © Hiroshi Sugimoto, photo © Hiroshi Sugimoto • **p. 94:** © Jean Nouvel /

Adagp, Paris, 2024, photo © Georges Fessy (1), photo © Martin Argyroglo (2) • **p. 97:** © Jean Nouvel / Adagp, Paris, 2024 • **p. 98:** photo © Thomas Salva / Lumento • **p. 100:** © SBJ / Adagp, Paris, 2024, photo Gilbert Nencioli © Cartier • **p. 101:** © Jean Nouvel / Adagp, Paris, 2024, photo © Patrick Gries (1); photo © Alexis Duclos / Gamma Rapho (2) • **p. 102:** © SBJ / Adagp, Paris, 2024, photo © Olivier Benoit-Gonin • **p. 103:** © SBJ / Adagp, Paris, 2024, photo © Patrick Gries • **p. 104:** © Jean Nouvel / Adagp, Paris, 2024, photo © Martin Argyroglo • **p. 106:** © Joseca Mokahesi • **p. 108:** © Manabu Miyazaki • **p. 109:** photo © RR • **p. 110–111:** photos © Patrick Gries • **p. 113:** © Bernie Krause and United Visual Artists, photo © Luc Boegly • **p. 114:** © Thijs Biersteker and Stefano Mancuso, photo © Luc Boegly • **p. 116:** © Luiz Zerbini, photo © Thibaut Voisin • **p. 117:** © Palmeraie et désert, © Afonso Tostes, photo © Luc Boegly • **p. 119:** Archivio Architetto Cesare Leonardi, Modena © Cesare Leonardi and Franca Stagi • **p. 120:** © Damien Hirst and Science Ltd. All rights reserved, DACS 2024, photo © Calvin Courjon / Lumento • **pp. 122–123:** © Cai Guo-Qiang, photo © Luc Boegly • **p. 126:** © Jean Nouvel / Adagp, Paris, 2024, photo © Eric Sander • **p. 128:** © Fabrice Hyber / Adagp, Paris, 2024, photo © Luc Boegly • **p. 129:** © Francis Hallé, photo © Thibaut Voisin • **pp. 130–131:** © Fabrice Hyber / Adagp, Paris, 2024, photo © Luc Boegly (1); © Luiz Zerbini, photo © Luc Boegly (2) • **p. 132:** © Bruno Novelli, photo © Andrea Rossetti • **p. 134:** © Allan McCollum, photo © Andrea Rossetti • **p. 135:** © Jean-Michel Alberola / Adagp, Paris, 2024, photo © Florian Kleinefenn • **p. 137:** © Archives Simon Hantaï / Adagp, Paris, 2024, photo © Ling Fei (1); © Keita / SKPEAC, Courtesy CAAC – The Pigozzi Collection, photo © Jorge Miño (2); © Hu Liu / Adagp, Paris, 2024, © Jean-Michel Othoniel / Adagp, Paris, 2024, photo © Luc Boegly (3) • **p. 138:** © Nino, © Adriana Varejão, photo © Luc Boegly • **p. 139:** © Ron Mueck, © J.D. 'Okhai Ojeikere, © Keita / SKPEAC, Courtesy CAAC – The Pigozzi Collection, © Valérie Belin / Adagp, Paris, 2024, photo © Luc Boegly • **p. 140:** © Alessandro Mendini, photo © Lorenzo Ceretta • **p. 141:** © Richard Artschwager / Adagp, Paris, 2024, © Thomas Demand / Adagp, Paris, 2024, photo © Andrea Rossetti (1); © Huang Yong Ping / Adagp, Paris, 2024, photo © Luc Boegly (2) • **p. 142:** © Isaka • **p. 144:** © Chéri Samba, Courtesy Galerie Magnin-A, Paris, © Alessandro Mendini, © Peter Halley, photo © Luc Boegly • **p. 145:** © Marc Newson Ltd., © Sarah Sze, photo © Luc Boegly • **p. 146:** © Douglas Gordon, photo © Jorge Miño (1); © James Coleman (2) • **p. 147:** © Jeff Wall, photo © Patrick Goetelen (1); © Nan Goldin (2) • **p. 148:** © Véio, photo © Germana Monte-Mór • **p. 149:** © David Hammons / Adagp, Paris, 2024, photo © André Morin • **p. 150:** © Isabel Mendes da Cunha, photo © Olivier Ouadah • **p. 151:** © George Rouy, courtesy Hannah Barry Gallery, London, photo © Damian Griffiths • **pp. 152–153:** © Yann Kebbi • **p. 156:** photo © André Morain, Paris • **p. 158:** photo © AFP • **p. 159:** © SBJ / Adagp, Paris, 2024, photos: RR • **p. 160:** © SBJ / Adagp, Paris, 2024, photos © Peter Willi (Bridgeman Images) (1, 2, 4), photo Peter Willi (3) • **p. 161:** © SBJ / Adagp, Paris, 2024, photo: RR • **p. 162:** photo © P. Lenoir (1); © Julian Opie / Adagp, Paris, 2024, photo © André Morain, Paris (2); © Julian Opie / Adagp, Paris, 2024, photo © Peter Willi (Bridgeman Images) (3); © Lisa Milroy, photo © Peter Willi (Bridgeman Images) (4) • **p. 163:** © Arnaud Baumann • **p. 164:** © Jean Pierre Raynaud / Adagp, Paris, 2024, photo © Hugues Colson (1), photos: RR (2, 3) • **p. 165:** © Jean Pierre Raynaud / Adagp, Paris, 2024 • **p. 166:** © Jean Pierre Raynaud / Adagp, Paris, 2024, photo © Frédéric Gallier • **pp. 168–169:** © Jean Pierre Raynaud / Adagp, Paris, 2024, photo © Jean-François Leroy / Cartier • **p. 170:** © Jean Pierre Raynaud / Adagp, Paris, 2024, photo © Patrick Goetelen • **p. 171:** © Jean Pierre Raynaud / Adagp, Paris, 2024, photo © Archives Denyse Durand-Ruel • **p. 172:** Jean Pierre Raynaud / Adagp, Paris, 2024, photo © Elise Hardy / Gamma Rapho • **p. 173:** © Jean Pierre Raynaud / Adagp, Paris, 2024, photo © André Morain, Paris • **p. 174:** © Bernar Venet, photo © André Morain, Paris (1); © Richard Tuttle, photo: RR (2); © Keiji Uematsu, photo

This book was published by the
Fondation Cartier pour l'art contemporain
261, boulevard Raspail, 75014 Paris
fondationcartier.com

ISBN 978-2-86925-187-8

Distributed in the USA and Canada by
Artbook | D.A.P.
75 Broad Street, Suite 630
New York, NY 10004, USA
artbook.com

Distributed in all other countries by
Thames & Hudson Ltd.
181A High Holborn,
London WC1V 7QX, United Kingdom
thamesandhudson.com

Printed and bound in
July 2024 by Nava Press, Milan, Italy.

Legal Deposit: October 2024